THE FUNDAMENTAL TECHNIQUES OF CLASSIC CUISINE

Published in 2007 by Stewart, Tabori & Chang
An imprint of ABRAMS

Library of Congress Cataloging-in-Publication Data

Choate, Judith.
  The fundamental techniques of classic cuisine / The French Culinary
Institute with Judith Choate.
     p. cm.
  Includes bibliographical references and index.
  ISBN-13: 978-1-58479-478-3
  ISBN-10: 1-58479-478-X
  1. Cookery, French. I. French Culinary Institute (New York, N.Y.) II.
Title.

TX719.C4543 2007
641.5944--dc22

                              2007007530

Project Manager: Christine Gardner
Editor: Leslie Stoker
Designer: Debra Drodvillo/ Notion Studio
Art Director: Julie Hoffer
Production Manager: Jacquie Poirier

The text of this book was composed in Granjon and Trade Gothic.

Printed and bound in China
10 9 8 7 6 5 4

115 West 18th Street
New York, NY 10011
www.abramsbooks.com

THE FUNDAMENTAL TECHNIQUES OF
CLASSIC CUISINE

THE FRENCH CULINARY INSTITUTE

with Judith Choate

Photographs by Matthew Septimus

Stewart, Tabori & Chang
New York

Contents

A Note from Dorothy Cann Hamilton viii

Introduction x

Sessions

Acknowledgments

Running a school is a bit like producing a play. There are many moving parts and a huge team effort behind it. For a school, there are the teachers, administrators, and facilities staff who are the actors and stage crew. The voice and soul of a play, however, is found in the script. The same is true with a school; our voice and soul reside in the curriculum.

This book attempts to define the first part of The French Culinary Institute's classic culinary curriculum. It is an ever-evolving opus. Ours has evolved for over twenty years. Thus we have a lot of people to thank.

Our first thanks goes to Le Centre de Formation Technologique d'Alimentation, "Ferrandi," our sister school in Paris, from which the original curriculum was derived.

Updating and Americanizing the recipes and techniques has largely fallen to the teaching staff of The FCI. In the early days this was done by our imported Parisian chefs, Antoine Schaeffers and Christian Foucher. But in the last fifteen years, the curriculum has been honed to a fine edge by our executive dean, the incomparable Chef Alain Sailhac.

Along with Chef Sailhac, many of our teachers have had a defining role in the production of this book, most importantly Candy Argondizza, Marc Bauer, Dominick Cerrone, and Susan Lifrieri. Many thanks also have to be extended to Pascal Beric, Harold Begun, Greg Kearns, Rogers Powell, Martin Schaub, Michelle Spiegel, and Leah Stewart. We can't forget the chefs' assistants Victoria Jordan, Rita Kiser, Karen Shapiro, and Patricia Smith.

We also thank our contributing deans—Jacques Pépin, André Soltner, Jacques Torres, and Alice Waters—and graduates—Nino Antuzzi, Dan Barber, Wylie Dufresne, Bobby Flay, John Foster, Jenny Glasgow, Alan Hughes, Roy Ip, Daniele Kay, Matthew Kenney, Melissa Murphy, Laura Pensiero, Dan Silverman, and Cheryl Slocum—for not only their contributions to this book but their inspiration and knowledge, which they share so freely.

A special thanks to Sandy Antonelli and Joanne Watters, two of the best home cooks I know. Joanne and Sandy diligently read and tested this book to make sure that it was accessible for the serious amateur.

The smooth running of the school is the responsibility of the administration. There is no better school president than Gary Apito. As a leader and a manager, he is admired and loved. Without his oversight, the school and the curriculum would not perform at the world-class level that they do. His staff and the whole FCI team deserve our thanks for their support for this book.

Judie Choate, our coauthor, is an exceptionally talented and patient woman. Judie was able to take the universe of cooking and distill it into an accessible book. We are very appreciative of this extraordinary achievement and the vast amount of time she has put into this project.

We also would like to extend sincere thanks to the wonderful Leslie Stoker, our editor at Stewart, Tabori & Chang; Julie Stillman, our remarkable copy editor; Julie Hoffer, our inspired art director; Elizabeth Pilar, our artistic food and prop stylist; and Eric Wolfe, our wiz of a digital photo assistant.

I would like to give special recognition to the genius of Matthew Septimus, my favorite photographer, who truly captures The FCI spirit. In the same vein, a big *merci* to our project manager, Gwen Korbel, who did an exceptional job at picking up the pieces and coordinating many of the people and the minutiae to bring this book together.

There were products and vendors in the background who also lent their support. I would like to acknowledge Broadway Panhandler for their wonderful selection of equipment and dishes and D'Artagnan for their delicious products.

I cannot forget the people in my daily life who helped in their own way to bring this book to fruition. I want to thank my secretary, Robin Cohen, who tirelessly brings order to my chaotic schedule; my daughter, Olivia, who keeps me smiling, and last but not least, I would like to thank my husband and partner, Doug, who is my biggest cheerleader. It is easy to say that The FCI would not be where it is today without his wisdom and support.

Dorothy Cann Hamilton

A Note from Dorothy Cann Hamilton,
Founder and President, The French Culinary Institute

The French Culinary Institute has been teaching professional cooking for over twenty years. Acknowledged as one of the top cooking schools in the world, The FCI has been extremely successful in turning out some of the best chefs in the country. And the most startling fact is that the course is completed in a brief six to nine months!

Dean André Soltner, the fabled chef-owner of the restaurant Lutèce, once told me when I started the school in 1984 that The FCI couldn't possibly prepare a student for the professional kitchen in just six months. Now, Chef André teaches at the school and marvels at the results. Alain Ducasse has said that our six-month classical culinary course is equivalent to the knowledge that he acquired in a three-year apprenticeship in France.

How did all of this come about? Much like a great recipe: We started with a wonderful product, reinvented it with some ingenuity and efficiency, and maintained strict standards in turning out our "dish" with consistency.

The story began when I visited France on a professional educator's tour in 1980 and became enamored with "Ferrandi," the official cooking school for professional chefs in Paris. My father had founded a vocational school in New York City, and I dreamed of doing the same thing with a cooking school. With the support of my father and the wonderful collaboration of the chefs at Ferrandi, The French Culinary Institute was born.

Over the years, the course has been further enhanced. Alain Sailhac, the famed chef of Le Cirque and now our executive vice president and senior dean of studies, joined the school in 1990. Since that time, he has kept a careful watch, updating the curriculum to include the latest techniques and recipes that have been introduced to the industry.

Along with our other deans, Jacques Pépin, Jacques Torres, André Soltner, Alice Waters, Andrea Robinson (formerly Andrea Immer), Alan Richman, and Cesare Casella, the students and staff are challenged to perform at the highest levels. Our deans, all of whom hold demonstrations and lectures for our students, play an important role at the school. It is an FCI philosophy that rubbing shoulders with great chefs sets the standard for young chefs. I often reflect that our school is a bit like Florence during the Renaissance, with many masters working in their studios where aspiring artists can watch and work alongside.

A number of people have asked if this book replaces the value of studying at The FCI. Oh, it couldn't possibly! The school is a very exciting place. Our restaurant, L'Ecole, is one of the highest-rated restaurants in New York, serving a very serious clientele in SoHo. Our deans and more than one hundred visiting chefs keep our International Culinary Amphitheater alive with information and inspiration. Our master instructors, Marcella Hazan, Colette Peters, and Ron Ben Israel (to name just a few) teach, walk through the school, and hang out in the restaurant. The FCI actually feels like a culinary Hollywood.

With all of New York City at our door, our student clubs use the city as a gastronomic playpen. Through introductions given by the school, a student has the ability to meet and witness great chefs working in their own restaurants.

Another frequently asked question is, "Does this course teach only French cuisine?" The easy answer is "Look at our graduates!" From Bobby Flay (cuisine of the American Southwest) to Wylie Dufresne (cutting-edge modern), our graduates are recognized as great chefs in cuisines as diverse as Indian, Thai, and Italian as well as homegrown American. This is easy to understand, as the classical French cooking that we feature is all about technique. And to become a professional and eventually to excel as a master chef, you must master the basic techniques of fine cooking. That is the essence and the key to our program, and the key to our graduates' success. Bar none, The FCI deans and faculty are the absolute best in the country to teach these techniques and to guide an aspiring chef.

While it is ideal to attend The FCI to have the benefit of the full culinary course, this book will overwhelm you with knowledge. It captures the first 25 percent of our professional culinary program. You will learn the 250 basic techniques that are fundamental to classic French cooking. Rest assured, if you follow the book as directed, read it (and read it again and again), study it, and practice the techniques that it lays out, you, too, can start to feel the confidence of a trained chef.

We are excited that you have started on The FCI journey, whether here at the school or in your own kitchen. Please feel part of our family. Come to our restaurant. Introduce yourself and remember to enjoy every part of the experience.

Dorothy Cann Hamilton

Introduction

"I have so much respect for FCI that I hire their students the day they graduate."

David Bouley, Chef-Owner
Bouley Bakery, Danube

The Fundamental Techniques of Classic Cuisine distinguishes itself from other skill-directed teaching manuals in that it follows the first section of the basic culinary course, Classic French Cooking, Introduction to Basic Techniques, Segment 1, as taught at The French Culinary Institute in New York City. The course itself comprises the 250 competencies, first codified by the French, which are fundamental to mastering the classic French culinary repertoire. These rules and regulations of the traditional French kitchen are the foundation upon which most of our Western cuisine is built and are an integral part of understanding the development of most modern cuisines. The extraordinary example of The French Culinary Institute is that, within six to nine months, a student can learn the skills that have traditionally taken chefs three to five years to perfect. This short but profound course, adapted to the American kitchen, offers such total immersion into the classic French repertoire that graduates can be accepted immediately into the fast-paced and demanding world of the professional kitchen.

Working directly with the text, a home cook or a beginning professional cook will be submerged in the tenets of classic French cooking and can, through its direction and sequential lessons, accomplish the basic skills necessary to be a proficient cook. The succinct and workable course has had proven success over many years in the classroom, and we feel that it translates extremely well to the written word. In addition, the material in this expanded version of the course has been taken from both the basic book issued to incoming students and from the lectures and learning of the chef-instructors as presented in the classroom. Within this text are many of the classic French recipes. These are supported by contemporary recipes developed by a few of the many celebrated graduates of the school. Still other recipes have been culled from the files of our deans and visiting deans. Additionally, the book contains tips, techniques, and kitchen advice from our chefs and deans, as well as hundreds of photographs and illustrations highlighting the recipes and techniques taught. Through all of this, the reader and learning cook will be transported into the professional kitchen.

The broad experience and the depth of the professionalism of the masters of French cooking—renowned chefs Alain Sailhac, Jacques Pépin, André Soltner, and Jacques Torres, who direct the curriculum at The French Culinary Institute—are reflected throughout the text, which further enhances its proficiency. Building on the basic materials, this personal touch will help to create a very accessible learning experience for the reader.

In this beginning course, the chef-student is introduced to the basics of classic French cooking upon which all other curriculum segments will be built. This book should be used as a template for acquiring those skills. It is a succinct and workable course that can help you master the techniques necessary to delve into culinary exploration.

The implementation of our classroom agenda is best stated through a phrase commonly heard throughout the school: "the total immersion program of The French Culinary Institute." The daily lessons along with the text are fundamental to mastering the classic culinary repertoire. The curriculum has been adapted to the American kitchen from the Centre de Formations Technologiques des Mètiers de l'Alimentation (aka Ferrandi), the official Paris institution for training in the culinary arts. The schedule, whether through the six-month daily timetable or the nine-month evening plan, has been developed to move quickly and directly through the tenets, rules, terms, and recipes of the classic culinary repertoire. From the first day, the chef-student, led by the chef-instructor, is completely submerged in the classic French kitchen. Through this immediate baptism, the chef-student is able to exercise an instantaneous grasp of the requirements necessary to build on the remaining sessions. What is accomplished in the entire four-segment program of total immersion is the creation of a knowledgeable and able cook in months rather than the traditional years granted in the French apprentice system. This emphasis on the mastery of traditional French skills affords a cook the framework upon which to execute a full range of contemporary cuisines.

Since this book replaces the classroom kitchen's chef-instructor, we have expanded much of the basic material so that the home cook or learning professional cook will still benefit, through the written word, from the expertise offered by the professional chef-instructors at The French

Culinary Institute. In this book, acquired knowledge that is shared through conversation, demonstration, and hands-on teaching in the classroom has been compensated for with an expanded discussion of materials, history, and ingredients, as well as illustrations of techniques and methods.

"It is truly amazing what The FCI accomplishes with their students in as little as six months. It is the equivalent of years of a traditional apprenticeship."

Alain Ducasse, Chef-Owner,
Restaurant Plaza Athenée, Le Louis XV,
and Alain Ducasse at The Essex House

It is important to remember that, no matter how comprehensive this manual, working in the presence of a skilled chef and gaining practice under individual attention is an irreplaceable component of the total immersion program developed by The French Culinary Institute. To adhere to the classic method of measurement, all weights are given in metric amounts; however, we have also provided the equivalents in pounds, ounces, cups, and spoons, imperial measure and volumetric measure. To facilitate precise measurement, we urge you to purchase a fine-quality kitchen scale.

To further assist the reader and beginning cook, this manual provides the basic recipes, just as they are taught in the classroom, with accompanying illustrations and photographs to graphically assist in full comprehension of the techniques being taught. These recipes, along with those of our deans and graduates, will illustrate how the classic repertoire has an impact on the contemporary culinary scene. Notes and tips will further exploit the knowledge and skill of the classroom chef-instructor to bring the intensity of the learning experience alive.

As we focus on both theory and practice, the strong requisite base for a proficient culinary future is established. You will know how to work on a *brigade* with other cooks, how to correctly perform tasks (that you perhaps thought you had already mastered) as basic as washing and peeling vegetables and as complex as preparing classic and modern French desserts, how to properly command yourself in a kitchen environment (which applies to both the home and professional kitchen), and how to practice basic safety precautions. You will immediately become intimate with the classic culinary terminology, vocabulary, and equipment as well as become adept at the primary elements of the craft. This is a book for all cooks who wish to professionalize their technique.

In the classroom, as in this book, the lessons take you immediately into the kitchen, as we believe that the best way to learn is through experience. To help guide the reader, each session is divided into three sections: *Theory* provides the rationale behind the particular instruction, *Technique* provides the skill lesson, and *Demonstration* is the recipe itself. Each lesson differs in the program taught. Some might focus on both an ingredient and a technique, while others might focus totally on gaining a particular skill. For this reason, a poultry recipe may be found in both the poultry section and a section on a style of cooking. We might even say that by multitasking throughout the book, the novice cook will gain insight into the multitasking often necessary in a busy restaurant kitchen.

The Fundamental Techniques of Classic Cuisine is presented in the pattern of the curriculum course with each session sequentially interpreted for the reader. We advise the novice cook to read through it from beginning to end before embarking on the lessons to be learned. This is the first building block of a culinary education requiring diligence and practice. Using this book as the guideline, the reader can set the learning curve at a personally prescribed pace. However, in order to attain the proficiency desired, each session should be comfortably executed before moving on to the next sequence.

As a student once said, "I never imagined that I could learn so much in such a short time. FCI is a gold mine." We believe that all of this culinary knowledge has been carefully adapted to the written word and is comprehensible to both the interested home cook and the beginning professional cook, as well as effective and appropriate for other culinary institutions.

Dean's Tip on Using the Book

"Read the book twice to completely memorize it. Then, read each recipe twice and make the attempt to memorize it before you start cooking. Understand why you are doing it."

Dean André Soltner

The Basic Techniques of
Classic French Cooking

Theory

Understanding the Structure of the Professional Kitchen

It is important that the cook be familiar with all the basic principles and terminology used in the professional kitchen.

The Uniform

Worldwide, all professional cooks dress alike. Starting at the top with a **toque**, or chef's hat (a tall, often disposable, paper, pleated, or plain hat), down to the highly polished black leather shoes to protect from spills, the chef's dress code is standard. The complete uniform is always a double-breasted white jacket, a neckerchief tied neatly around the neck to absorb perspiration, a white apron tied to the front with a thick, absorbent towel (to grasp hot pans and dishes) tucked into the ties, and black-and-white houndstooth cotton or cotton-poly blend pants. Since kitchen chores allow the uniform to get increasingly soiled as the day progresses, the Head Chef or Chef-Owner will always have a fresh jacket to wear when appearing in the dining room or other public spaces. With the more relaxed climate of recent years, some chefs who work in their own kitchens will be found in brightly colored pants and extravagantly embroidered jackets as well as clogs or other utilitarian shoes. In an even more relaxed atmosphere, chefs' uniforms are also being worn by home cooks, probably as much for their convenience as for the feeling of professionalism that they impart. No matter how styles have changed, the entire *brigade* in a large hotel kitchen anywhere in the world still wears the standard-issue uniform. Tradition is important in the professional kitchen.

Organizational Structure

The professional kitchen is a highly organized and structured operation, in which each associate has a specific function with clearly defined responsibilities. Known as a *brigade*, this system of organization was instituted in the kitchens of London's famed Savoy Hotel in the late nineteenth century by the esteemed French chef Auguste Escoffier. It is assumed that the large number of kitchen personnel working in the vast hotel kitchen demanded that a new system of order be established to direct the flow of communication and to ensure the coordination of the multitudinous tasks required in this busy setting.

The *brigade* is a team of cooks and their **commis** (assistants) who are apportioned into different stations or **parties**. The entire *brigade* is headed by the **Executive** or **Head Chef** whose job is to orchestrate the overall food production and ensure the efficiency of each station. The Head Chef is assisted by the **Sous-Chef**, who works with individual station leaders called **chefs de parties**. Each *chef de partie* is assisted

Dean's Tip

"A clean kitchen and a clean, crisp uniform invite you to cook and put you in the proper state of mind."

Dean Jacques Pépin

"Stay in touch with other chefs in your field. Exchange ideas. Share discoveries. Go to work early and stay late."

Dean Jacques Torres

"Whether in a large or small brigade, *a cook must be very organized at all times."*

Dean André Soltner

by a *commis* or apprentice-assistant. The size and scope of the *brigade* will vary according to the size of the kitchen and the requirements of the establishment. There will be many more specific stations and specialized tasks in a large hotel kitchen than in a small restaurant or catering kitchen that may require just one person to cover many stations.

In a large hotel kitchen, a *brigade* would consist of:

Executive Chef: An administrator whose responsibilities include all kitchen-related operations, including menu planning, costing, and scheduling. This person is also responsible for maintaining communication with the department heads throughout the hotel system.

Working Chef or ***Chef de Cuisine*:** An active cook who works in the kitchen during preparation periods and during service. Also responsible for ordering and other designated administrative duties. Reports to the Executive Chef. In a very large hotel, the Executive Chef may have many more administrative duties than a *Chef de Cuisine*. In smaller establishments, the *Chef de Cuisine* may also be the Executive Chef.

Banquet Chef: A chef in charge of all banquets and parties, with the same responsibilities as a *Chef de Cuisine*. Reports to the Executive Chef.

Pastry Chef or ***Chef Pâtissier*:** A chef responsible for the preparation and plating of all desserts and pastries. Reports to the Executive Chef. In a very large kitchen, there may also be a ***Sous-Chef Pâtissier*.**

***Sous-Chef*:** Second in command under the *Chef de Cuisine*. Responsibilities include supervising all of the cooks in the *brigade.* In a large establishment, there will be a day *Sous-Chef* and an evening *Sous-Chef* as

well as a late-night *Sous-Chef* if room service is offered. Duties include overseeing the preparation and service of food and control of all stations and kitchen operations in the *Chef de Cuisine*'s absence.

Floor Chef or ***Chef de Partie*:** In charge of a specific station with an assistant, or ***commis*,** during preparation and service. Each *Chef de Partie* is assisted by a single (**premier**) *commis* or even by several *commis*. In Europe, the *commis* is assisted by **apprentices**.

Specific stations might be:

***Poissonnier*:** Responsible for the cleaning and preparation of all fish, along with their sauces and garnishes.
***Saucier*:** Responsible for the preparation of all stocks and sauces, as well as all meat and poultry. In a very large kitchen, there may also be a ***Rôtisseur*,** who would be responsible for roasted, grilled, and fried meats. In a small kitchen, the *saucier* and *poissonnier* may be the same person.
***Garde-Manger*:** Responsible for the preparation of all cold articles (*hors d'oeuvre, terrines, pâtés, galantines*) and sauces. This position is extremely important in a large hotel kitchen that is often responsible for large catered events, cocktail parties, and room service. In fact, this station may have up to twenty-five people working in it.
***Entremetier*:** Responsible for all vegetable and egg dishes, as well as for soups and side dishes.
***Potager*:** Responsible for all soups. This position is usually found only in a very large hotel where gallons and gallons of soups are made daily.

Technique
Setting Up the Standard Workstation (*Poste de Travail*)

The professional kitchen workstation is a universal setup that never changes. It can even carry over to the home kitchen, as working in this systematic fashion sets good organizational skills. The work area consists of an immaculate cutting board placed on a damp cloth or paper towel to prevent slipping. If the cook is right-handed, knives and other necessary equipment are placed to the right of the board. For those who are left-handed,

Chefs' Tips

"Keeping your workstation clean is one of the most important disciplines of a young cook."

Chef Candy Argondizza

"Always anchor your cutting board with wet paper towels to keep it from slipping."

Chef Henri Viain

materials are placed to the left. Bowls to hold ready-to-prepare and prepared vegetables or other products are placed at the top of the cutting board.

When peeling vegetables, place the unpeeled items in a container positioned on the left and transfer them, as finished, into a bowl placed on the right. Catch the peelings in a bowl placed in the center of the cutting board for easy cleanup. Keep the entire area clean and organized at all times.

It is on the workstation that a cook will prepare the necessary **mise en place** for a particular dish. This French term defines the organization of all the properly cut or otherwise prepared ingredients that will be required to put the dish together up to the point of its final cooking.

When moving from the home kitchen into the professional kitchen, it is necessary to rethink the habits of a lifetime. Cooking cannot make the leap from chore to art without many principles, rules, and terms becoming second nature. Before the basic cooking skills are taught, the fledgling cook must, without thinking, be able to step into the kitchen with a complete understanding of the classic culinary terms, the rules guiding personal and workspace hygiene, and the standards of food preparation, as well as the techniques practiced. When contemplating cooking as a profession, it is important to realize from the outset that a professional cook's life is a disciplined one guided by a set of unwavering standards. If you follow these standards and guidelines, the rewards will be greater efficiency and ease of preparation.

Principles for a Healthy Environment

Before any work can begin in a professional or culinary school kitchen, standards of cleanliness must be set and held. Excellent health and external cleanliness are prerequisites for the maintenance of a hygienic, disease-free environment. Not only is personal sanitation required, all materials and equipment, as well as the workspace itself, must also be antiseptic. To the novice, these rules may seem unnecessary or extreme; **however, any variance from these principles can result in extremely serious, even disastrous, results to the health of others**. Adherence to the following principles will help ensure that this does not occur.

○ General daily hygiene must be practiced; bathing, shaving, and tooth brushing are mandatory.

○ Hair must be clean, well groomed, and covered with an immaculate hat.

○ Nails should be well trimmed, clean, and polish-free.

○ All jewelry should be removed before entering the kitchen to avoid mishap through loss or entanglement with utensils or machinery.

○ Perfumes, colognes, and aftershave lotions are not permitted.

○ Hands must be washed upon entering the kitchen and after touching raw ingredients, telephones, money, soiled linens, meat, chicken, fish, eggs in and out of the shell, fresh produce, and soiled equipment and/or utensils, as well as after using chemicals or cleaners, picking up anything from the floor, performing personal actions such as using the lavatory, coughing, sneezing, smoking, eating, or drinking, or at any time necessary when working to ensure that the hands are always immaculately clean.

○ Proper hand-washing techniques include generously soaping; vigorously rubbing for at least 20 seconds to cover the backs of the hands, wrists, between the fingers, and under the nails; and rinsing under warm (38°C/100°F) running water. Dry with a paper towel and use the towel to turn off the water and open any doors necessary to exit the washroom.

- Do not enter the kitchen if you have a skin or respiratory infection, intestinal problem, or rash of unknown origin, as these may well cause the spread of disease.

- If working in a school or professional environment, clean uniforms should be issued and impeccably maintained. In a home kitchen, clothes should be clean and covered with a clean apron or smock. Street clothes should never be worn.

- Wear inexpensive and easily disposable rubber gloves when working with products that spoil easily or are known to readily transmit bacteria. These might include chicken, shellfish, sauces, stocks, meats, cream, and ice cream.

- Never use a kitchen towel, wipe cloth, or side towel for personal reasons.

- Never taste anything with your fingers. Use a fresh, clean spoon for each tasting.

- Never smoke, drink alcoholic beverages, or use controlled substances in any kitchen.

- Cover your face with an easily disposable paper towel or tissue when you sneeze or cough and discard it immediately. If you have to use a cloth, place it in a resealable plastic bag and remove it from the kitchen immediately. Wash your hands immediately. If the cough or sneeze seems to be an indication of the onset of an upper respiratory infection, ask to be excused from kitchen duties.

- Never sit on worktables or preparation areas.

- Wash and dry all knives after each use. Never leave knives in a sink.

- In the event of an accidental cut or burn, make immediate use of a first-aid kit or, if necessary, call for emergency assistance.

Dean's Tip

"Do not set up any raw vegetables on the cutting board; always place plastic film over the board to keep it from being infected by any bacteria or insects. Do not cut fish on the cutting board if you have cut chicken or meat, as the bacteria will rapidly multiply. After cutting chicken, fish, or meat, always sanitize your board by immersing it in hot, soapy water or with a disinfectant and rinsing well in very hot, running water. Once sanitized, rewrap your board in plastic film."

Dean Alain Sailhac

Theory
Principles of Sanitation

Preventing food-borne illness is the moral obligation of the food professional and is essential to the success of any food-related business. State and local boards of health set rigid standards for food service establishments, offer mandatory safety courses for food professionals, and routinely inspect food establishments to ensure that their standards are upheld; however, it ultimately remains the responsibility of the establishment to impose the most rigorous standards in the working environment. In the home kitchen, it remains the responsibility of the main cook to create impeccably clean conditions.

There are numerous principles that must be observed in the purchase, storage, preparation, and service of food to prevent contamination from the three most common contaminant sources, biological, chemical, and physical.

Biological Contamination

Bacterial contamination, the primary biological contaminant, is the cause of most food-borne illnesses. However, it is interesting to note that some bacteria are beneficial (such as those needed to produce some cheeses and cultured milk products, beer, and wine), and it is presently thought that most bacteria are benign. But those that are harmful can be deadly.

Bacteria are tiny, one-celled microscopic plants that are present everywhere and on everyone. They multiply by splitting in two, and under ideal circumstances, one single bacteria cell can multiply into 281 billion cells in three days.

Undesirable bacteria can cause spoilage in food that can usually be identified by the presence of odor(s), a sticky or slimy surface, discoloration, or

Conditions conducive to bacterial growth include:

Food: Almost all foods, except those that are dry or preserved by sugar or salt, can be used as a host for bacterial growth. High-protein foods such as meat, poultry, fish, game, eggs, or dairy products are very active supporters of speedy bacterial expansion.

Acidity or alkalinity: Acidity and alkalinity are measured by a pH factor that spans from 1 (strongly acidic) to 14 (strongly alkaline), with pure water measuring 7 (neutral) on the pH scale. Almost all bacteria thrive in a neutral or mid-level pH environment.

Time: All bacteria need time to adjust to their host environment before beginning to grow. For cooks, this allows a brief period to leave food at room temperature as preparation is commencing.

Temperature: Bacteria grow best in temperatures ranging from 4°C (40°F) to 60°C (140°F). This range is referred to as the **food danger zone,** as it is in this area that food finds a favorable climate for bacterial growth.

Oxygen: Most bacteria are aerobic, which means that they need oxygen to grow. However, some of the deadliest bacteria, such as those that cause botulism, are anaerobic, or able to grow without access to air.

Moisture: All bacteria require liquid to absorb nourishment; therefore, moist, damp foods such as cream-based salads make the perfect hosts.

PHF: This acronym stands for **potentially hazardous foods**. These are foods that particularly support the rapid growth of bacteria and include animal products such as raw or undercooked meat, poultry, fish, shellfish, or dairy products, and/or fully or partially cooked vegetables, raw seeds, or sprouts. A partial list of PHF items includes undercooked bacon, cooked beans, cut cheeses, fresh shelled eggs, shelled hard-cooked eggs or hard-cooked eggs cooled in liquid, unrefrigerated fresh garlic in oil, cooked pastas, meats, cheeses, pastry cream or cream-filled pastries, sour cream, soy protein and soy products, as well as any sauces containing PHF ingredients.

mold. Those bacteria that are also disease agents are known as pathogens. Pathogens may not be detectable through odor, taste, or appearance, and this makes them particularly noxious. They are the greatest concern in all kitchens. To lessen the risk of contamination, all food must be purchased from reliable sources and then protected from bacterial infection by the practice of good hygiene along with sanitary handling and proper storage to ensure that they remain free of pathogenic material.

There are two categories of diseases caused by pathogens: **intoxications** and **infections**.

Intoxications are the result of poisons or toxins that enter the system after they have been pro-duced in food as a result of bacterial growth rather than from the bacteria themselves. Infections are caused by bacteria or other organisms that enter and attack the human body.

Bacteria have no means of locomotion; they must be carried from one place to another. Travel may be instituted through hands, coughs, sneezes, other foods, unsanitary equipment or utensils, or environmental factors such as air, water, insects, and rodents. Only sterilization will eliminate bacteria, so it is extremely important to understand the simple rules governing bacteria's growth and travel to help prevent bacterial contamination in the kitchen.

Rule 1 **Keep bacteria from spreading.** Do not touch anything that may contain disease-producing bacteria. Protect food from bacteria in the air by keeping it covered at all times.

Rule 2 **Prevent bacterial growth**. Keep all food at temperatures that are out of the food danger zone.

Rule 3 **Kill bacteria.** Heat food to a temperature of 75°C (165°F) (or above) for 30 seconds through any heat source. Equipment used as a cooking vessel should be washed with hot water and detergent, then rinsed or sanitized.

Chemical Contamination

Chemical poisoning is the result of defective or improperly maintained equipment, or equipment that has been incorrectly used. Such poisons might include antimony from chipped gray enamelware, lead found in containers or soldering material, cadmium found in plating elements. All of the toxins found in these materials can cause illness in humans. Other chemical contamination can result from commercial cleaning compounds, silver polish, and insecticides.

To prevent chemical contamination,

° all food must be stored separately from cleaning or other chemically-based materials;

° all containers must be properly labeled and washed or otherwise cleaned; and

° all equipment must be thoroughly rinsed in extremely hot water.

Physical Contamination

Physical contamination is the result of the adulteration of food by a foreign object such as broken glass, hair, metal shavings, paint chips, insects, stones, and so forth. If you stringently follow safety guidelines, physical contamination should not occur. However, if it does, all raw and prepared foods affected should be discarded immediately.

Infectious Disease Chart

Disease: **Botulism (*Clostridium botulinum*)**
Category: **Intoxication**
Source: Contaminated soil on vegetables or other food
Food usually involved: Home-canned, low-acid vegetables; commercially packed tuna, smoked fish, or mushrooms; garlic packed in oil
Prevention: Use only commercially processed products that are properly dated and packed; never use anything packed in a damaged or bulging package or can.

Disease: **Staphylococcus (*Staphylococcus aureus*)**
Category: **Intoxication**
Source: Food handling: urine contamination by food handlers, open wounds and sores
Food usually involved: Custards, dairy-filled bakery products, hollandaise sauce, ham, poultry, protein-based salads, potato salads, other high-protein foods
Prevention: Maintenance of excellent hygiene and work habits. Keep kitchen workers away from all food when carrying any infection or disease.

Disease: **E. coli (*Escherichia coli*)**

Category: **Intoxication or infection**

Source: Intestinal tract of humans, some animals (especially cattle); contaminated water; fecal contamination/feces

Food usually involved: Raw or undercooked red meat, unpasteurized dairy products, fish from contaminated waters, some prepared food such as mashed potatoes and cream-based desserts

Prevention: Thoroughly cook all food, especially red meat; avoid cross-contamination with appropriate storage and handling; practice good hygiene.

Disease: **Salmonella (*Salmonella enteritides*)**

Category: **Infection**

Source: Contaminated poultry, poultry products, meat, eggs; fecal contamination by food handlers

Food usually involved: Poultry, meat, poultry stuffings, inadequately cooked or untreated egg products, gravies, raw food, shellfish from polluted waters

Prevention: Practice good personal hygiene. Properly store and handle all food. Control insect and rodent infestation. Properly wash hands and sanitize equipment and all surfaces after handling raw poultry and/or raw eggs. Use only certified shellfish.

Disease: ***Clostridium perfringens***

Category: **Infection**

Source: Soil; fresh meat; human carriers

Food usually involved: Meat and poultry, reheated or unrefrigerated gravies and sauces

Prevention: Cold foods kept at 4°C (40°F) or below. Hot foods kept at 60°C (140°F) or above.

Disease: **Strep (*Streptoccus*)**

Category: **Infection**

Source: Coughs and sneezes; infected food handler

Food usually involved: Any foodstuff contaminated by an infected handler and served without further cooking

Prevention: Quarantine infected kitchen workers to prevent them from handling food.

Disease: **Infectious hepatitis (A, B, C, D, and E viruses)**

Category: **Infection**

Source: Shellfish from polluted waters eaten raw; contaminated water used for drinking or washing either body or foodstuffs; fecal contamination by food handlers; sharing of contaminated materials such as toothbrushes; intravenous drug use; sexual contact or through skin breaks

Food usually involved: Raw shellfish, any food handled by an infected person

Prevention: Practice good hygiene. Maintain good personal health habits. Use only certified shellfish.

Disease: **Trichinosis (*Trichinella spiralis*) and tapeworm (*Taenia solium*)**

Category: **Infection**

Source: Infected pork or beef or their by-products

Food usually involved: Pork products, especially those that have been improperly or insufficiently cooked

Prevention: Cook all ground and injected pork products to an internal temperature of at least 68°C (155°F) or higher for 15 seconds. Cook all pork chops or roasts to 63°C (145°F) for 15 seconds and 4 minutes, respectively. The meat may also be frozen for a minimum of 8 days to prevent the development of trichinosis and taeniasis.

Temperature

Temperature control is critical to safe food handling. Bacteria grow best in warm temperatures, that is, those between 10°C (50°F) and 43°C (110°F). In this temperature range, disease and germs flourish, and most bacteria, including those that spoil meat and vegetables and cause milk to go sour, grow best. Pathogenic bacteria find their nourishment in the 21°C–52°C (70°F–125°F) range. Since the normal temperature of the human body is 37°C (98.6°F), one can see how germs, if unchecked, can readily multiply in this environment. Temperatures of 77°C (170°F) or over will kill most non-spore-forming bacteria and all pathogenic organisms. Although low temperatures (0°C/32°F) will not kill bacteria, they will hamper or slow down growth so food can be preserved through refrigeration or freezing.

A food thermometer should always be used to determine the exact temperature of foods. Never use the hands-on method to make this determination.

Partially processed or leftover food must be refrigerated at 4°C (40°F) or below. Refrigerated food should only be removed from the refrigerator just prior to serving or reheating. To reheat, food should be heated rapidly to serving temperature so that the internal temperature quickly reaches 74°C (165°F) and is held at that temperature for 15 seconds. *Never* reheat food in a steam table, as it does not provide adequate heat to rapidly bring the refrigerated food to the appropriate temperature.

The following temperature gauge lists kitchen temperatures with which all cooks should be comfortably familiar.

Storage

All food must be dated and labeled before storage. It should be stored in a manner that prevents contamination from exterior sources and from the growth of any existing bacteria already in the product. Once stored, all foodstuffs should be rotated according to **FIFO**—the first in, first out system. Following are the basic guidelines for safe storage.

Dry Storage

° Dry food storage refers to those foods that do not support bacterial growth because they are dry or dried. This includes flour, sugar, salt, cereal, rice and other grains, dried beans and peas, breads and crackers, oil and shortening, and canned and bottled foods.

° All dry food containers should be closed tightly to protect from insect and/or rodent infestation, as well as to prevent contamination from dust or other airborne materials.

° Dry food should be stored in a cool, dry place and raised off the floor, away from the wall, and not under a sewage line.

Freezer Storage

° All food items to be frozen must be tightly wrapped in plastic film followed by aluminum foil, packaged freezer bags, or sealed in Cryovac packaging to prevent freezer burn.

° All stored items should be labeled and dated.

° Frozen food must be kept completely frozen at -18°C (0°F) or lower until ready for use.

° All freezers must be equipped with an outside thermometer so that the freezer temperature can be read without opening the door or entering the holding box.

○ Frozen food must be stored to assure cold air circulation on all sides. This means that food should not be stored directly on the freezer floor.

○ Frozen food must be thawed under refrigeration or under cool, running water. Never thaw foods at room temperature because, at some point, this method will place the thawing product in the food danger zone.

Refrigerated Storage

○ Other than those foods listed for dry storage, all perishable foods should be refrigerated to protect them from contamination.

○ Refrigeration may be done with the use of a walk-in refrigerator, reach-in refrigerator, refrigerated show-case, refrigerated counter, or refrigerated table.

○ All refrigerators must be equipped with a calibrated thermometer.

○ Interior walls and shelves of the refrigerator should be kept immaculately clean.

○ All refrigerated foods should be properly labeled and wrapped or stored in a suitable container to avoid contamination.

○ Within the refrigerator, store raw and cooked foods separately.

○ Do not allow any unsanitary surface (such as the outside of a container) to touch any refrigerated food or food product.

○ Hot food to be refrigerated must be chilled as quickly as possible over ice or in a cold water bath before placing in the refrigerator to avoid compromising the refrigerator temperature. For instance, a gallon of hot stock placed in a refrigerator may take up to 10 hours to go below 4°C (40°F) and, while cooling, will raise the refrigerator temperature considerably.

○ Most perishable foods keep best at a lower refrigerator temperature.

○ Air must be able to circulate around all sides of refrigerated items; therefore, do not overcrowd a refrigerator. Keep all food off the refrigerator floor.

○ Always keep any refrigerator door closed except when placing food into or removing food from the interior.

Holding Food for Later Use

○ Bring food to holding temperatures as quickly as possible.

○ Food should be cooked and processed as close to the time of service as possible.

○ Prudent menu planning prevents excessive leftovers. Leftovers are not to be mixed with fresh food during storage.

○ Chilled food should be kept at 4°C (40°F) or below at all times.

○ When holding cold food, such as protein salads, over ice or in a refrigerated table for service, do not mound food above the level of the container, as this food would not be kept sufficiently chilled.

○ Food that is going to be served hot soon after cooking should not be allowed to drop below an internal temperature of 60°C (140°F).

○ Hot, perishable foods should not be kept below 60°C (140°F). Rare roast beef is the only exception to this rule. It may be held at 49°C (120°F).

○ If food is not be to served immediately, it may be kept at a temperature in excess of 60°C (140°F) by the use of warming cabinets, steam tables, or other devices suitable for this purpose. However, this should not be done for more than a couple of hours.

Equipment and Utensils Required for a Functional Kitchen

A well-stocked professional kitchen is built around a formal arrangement of restaurant ranges, stock kettles, refrigeration, ice-makers, dishwashers, workstations, and cleanup areas. The attendant cookware, knives, and other preparation materials can expect to see long and hard use and should be made of exceptionally strong elements that wear well. Any well-supplied home kitchen will have much of the same equipment, with less emphasis on quantity but the same insistence on quality. Affirming quality will ensure that equipment and utensils purchased for the kitchen will offer many years of valuable use.

Materials

The following materials are those that are typically used for professional cookware. These same elements are also found in most commercially available home cookware.

Professional cookware materials

Copper (a) is the most even heat conductor. It is often used for saucepans, sauté pans, sugar-boiling pots, and casseroles. Copper-made pans should be lined with nickel, tin, or stainless steel (except for the sugar-boiling pots used in candy making, as the lined copper pot heats and cools too quickly) and be extremely heavy. Unlined copper pans should *never* be used to prepare acidic substances (those having high content of vinegar, wine, citrus juice, tomato juice, or sour milk, among other acids), as the meeting of chemical compounds causes a toxic reaction that can lead to serious illness. Never cool any sauce or soup in an unlined copper pot, as it will affect the color and taste and can cause the product to become toxic.

Aluminum (b) is also an excellent heat conductor used for saucepans, sauté pans, and casseroles. Aluminum cookware is often coated with a layer of stainless steel or nickel to prevent a negative reaction (a metallic taste and color change) when used with acidic substances. Never cool any sauce or soup in an unlined aluminum pot, as it will affect the color and taste and can cause the product to become toxic.

Cast iron (c) is an extremely strong, heavy metal usually used for Dutch ovens, griddles, frying pans, and skillets. Relatively inexpensive, it is long-lasting and conducts and retains heat extremely well. It is available either uncoated or enameled (coated with a thin layer of borosilicate glass powder fused to the cast iron to prevent corrosion). Before use, uncoated cast iron must be seasoned by generously coating the inner surface with an unflavored cooking oil (such as peanut, canola, or grapeseed) and placing the pan in a preheated 121°C (250°F) oven for two hours. This keeps the metal from absorbing flavors and prevents food from sticking. Once seasoned, the pan should be gently cleaned and wiped dry before storing.

Black steel (d) is inexpensive, conducts heat quickly, and does not warp under high temperatures. Used for frying pans, omelette and crêpe pans, woks, and deep fryers, steel pans are often not washed, as washing causes rust. In this case, the pan is wiped clean and then rubbed with salt to remove any remaining particles. The pan is seasoned with a light coating of oil after each use to retain its nonstick capabilities.

Stainless steel (e) is an excellent nonreactive metal but an extremely poor heat conductor. It will not rust and does not require any seasoning. To be useful in a professional kitchen, stainless steel pots and pans must be quite thick, with a layer of copper or aluminum to help conduct heat.

Enamelware (f) is inexpensive, with a decorative layer of enamel over thin steel. It is a poor heat conductor and food tends to stick to the bottom, scorching and burning. It is impractical for the professional kitchen. **Nonstick (g)** cookware is often referred to by its various trade names such as Teflon or T-Fal. Nonstick pans are useful because they require minimal fat for browning, food does not stick to the bottom or edge, and they are easy to keep clean. However, with heavy use, the coating wears off quickly, rendering the pan useless for its designated purpose. Never heat a nonstick pan to a high temperature without any added fat, as the coating will be damaged and become toxic. Always use utensils made for cooking with nonstick pans or a wooden spoon.

Pots and Pans

As you work in the kitchen, always use the appropriate name for each pot or pan. It is extremely important that the correct names be learned, as often the chef or another cook will call out for a piece of equipment that must be delivered as quickly as possible. If the name is not at the tip of the tongue, time will be wasted while the desired piece of equipment is searched for. The assortment of pots and pans in a professional kitchen is referred to as the ***batterie de cuisine*** and will contain some or all of the following items:

Marmite: A stockpot of which there are two types: the tall ***marmite haute* (a)** and the shorter ***marmite basse* (b)**. Both can range in capacity from 2.5 to 40 gallons.

***Poêle:* (c)** A shallow pan used for cooking omelettes, crêpes, potatoes, or other items calling for a low, slanted-side pan. An American equivalent might be a cast-iron skillet. At FCI, nonstick *poêles* are used for omelette making. As with all nonstick cookware, metal or other abrasive tools should not be used.

***Rondeau* (d):** A large, round pan with handles, used for braising and stewing, usually no more than 5 to 6 inches deep. It should be of heavy construction and can range in capacity from 12 to 20 quarts.

Equipment in a typical batterie de cuisine

***Rôtissoire* (e):** A large, rectangular, heavy-bottomed pan with low to medium-high sides and two handles. It is used for oven-roasting meats as well as roasting bones for making brown stocks.

***Russe* (f):** A saucepan with a single, long handle that is used for making sauces.

***Sauteuse* (g):** A round, shallow pan with a single, long handle and sloping sides that is used to sauté.

***Sautoir or plat à sauter* (h):** A large, round, shallow pan with a single, long handle and straight sides that is used to sauté or to make sauces. It should be of heavy construction to prevent warping at high temperatures.

Sheet pan (i): A rectangular aluminum or stainless steel pan with very shallow sides that comes in various sizes; most typically a full-sheet pan (18 inches by 26 inches) and a half-sheet pan (18 inches by 13 inches). It is used for baking, roasting, and holding foods.

Hotel pan (j): A rectangular stainless steel pan with a lip designed to rest in a steam table or rack. It comes

Knife types

in various sizes, most typically a full hotel pan (12¾ inches by 20¾ inches by 2, 4, or 6 inches deep) and a half hotel pan. Also available at a third and a fourth of the basic size. It is used to cook, ice, store, or serve foods if solid, and to drain foods if perforated.

Square boys (k): Also known as steam table pans, these are almost square pans that are usually 6⅞ inches by 6¼ inches by 2½, 4, or 6 inches deep. Most often used to store items in the refrigerator or on the cooking line. Other sizes are also available.

Sizzle pans (i): Oval stainless steel or aluminum platters with raised edges used to cook or finish items in the oven or under a broiler or salamander. The raised edge keeps the juices from spilling out. Available in various sizes ranging from 9 to 13½ inches. When preheated, the platter is hot enough to cause the food applied to sizzle.

Knives

Knives are usually the personal property of each chef, and an individual's knife kit is guarded with great care. In the beginning of a professional culinary career, prudent investment in fine knives will be a lifelong one. Many kitchens also have an array of knives on hand for general use, but they are often not of the highest quality. Most knives are made either of high-carbon or forged stainless steel and, in fact, have often been referred to as simply that, a steel. This metal is generally resistant to rust and corrosion and does not stain easily. The knife handle can be made of wood, plastic, metal, or natural substances such as horn, shell, or plastic-wood. In fine knives, the end of the blade (called the tang) runs the length of the handle and is held in place by a number of rivets, creating a strong, well-balanced utensil. There are now very good knives of a one-piece construction (Global brand knives, Furi brand knives). Currently knives are being made from an extremely hard, durable material called *ceramic zirconia* that, reputedly, does not rust, corrode, interact with food, or lose its edge. There are a great number of styles of knives needed to properly cut and shape food. Each has a specific use that is often defined by its name.

One of the most important aspects to consider when purchasing knives is the material. Some of the desirable materials used to make knives are:

Carbon steel: An alloy of carbon and iron, its advantage is that it will hold a fine edge. Its disadvantage is that it requires a high degree of maintenance, as it corrodes very quickly and cannot be used in humid, salt-air climates or with highly acidic food.

Stainless steel: A combination of iron and chromium or nickel that is a very popular medium for chef's knives. It is resistant to abrasion and corrosion but it is also difficult to sharpen and does not maintain a fine edge.

High-carbon, no-stain steel: Contains many different materials, such as chromium, molybdenum, and vanadium. Most knives made for professional use are made of such compositions. Blades made from this material are less resistant to abrasion than pure stainless steel knives and are much easier to sharpen. They are also resistant to corrosion.

Every professional knife kit contains all of the following knives, along with auxiliary cutting and shaping utensils.

Chef's (or French) knife (a): The most versatile of all knives, this is used for chopping, slicing, dicing, and filleting. The blade can range from 6 to 14 inches in length.

Utility knife (b): Another versatile knife, used for coring vegetables and slicing tomatoes and other fruits and vegetables.

Boning knife (c): Used to bone various meats and poultry. This knife has a 6- to 7-inch curved blade, which may be firm or flexible.

Fillet knife (d): The most important feature of a fillet knife is a very sharp, flexible blade that is essential to complete the exacting process.

Slicing knife (e): Used for slicing large cuts of meat or fish such as roasts, ham, or smoked salmon. There are a number of types of slicing knives, with blades ranging from 12 to 16 inches. Some may be round-tipped, while others may have pointed tips. Pointed-tipped knives may also be used to make exact cuts such as those required when cutting large cakes.

Paring knife (f): A small-bladed knife used for peeling and/or turning vegetables.

Serrated knife (g): A bevel-edged blade that is used for slicing breads, rolls, and other soft items.

Steel (h): A hardened, finely ridged rod with a handle and guard and a round or slightly flat profile that is used to keep a knife edge aligned.

Sharpening stone (i): A natural stone, carborundum stone, or diamond-studded block that is available in a wide range of grits (degrees of coarseness) and is used to sharpen knives. The grit abrades the blade's edge, creating a very sharp cutting edge. A coating of water or mineral oil keeps the grit free of particles while being used.

Miscellaneous Tools of the Professional Kitchen

All kitchens, whether professional or home, are equipped with an assortment of tools that go beyond the essentials. As with pots and pans and knives, when used carefully, the highest-quality tools will last the longest.

Some of the small tools that might be found in a professional kitchen are:

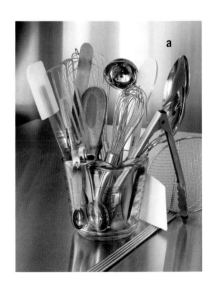

Channel knife (*canneleur*) (b): A small knife used to channel citrus fruit and various vegetables into decorative patterns for garnishes.

Chef's fork (c): A longer-handled, longer-tined fork that keeps the chef's hand slightly away from the heat when turning items during cooking.

***Chinois*:** A conical strainer with a handle. There are two types of *chinois*: **chinois etamine (d)** (also known as a bouillon strainer), constructed with fine metal mesh and used for fine straining; and a **perforated chinois (e),** which is used when fine straining is not required. Both types are often referred to as "china caps" because of their distinct conical hat shape. However, to give clarity to this nomenclature in the kitchen, it is useful to refer to the *chinois etamine* as a *chinois* and the perforated *chinois* as a "china cap."

Food mill (f): A metal basket-like utensil with interchangeable disks and a hand-turned crank used to separate solids from seeds, skin, and tough fibers.

Kitchen scissors (g): Sturdy shears used to cut butcher's twine or kitchen papers or for trimming fish and poultry.

Needle-nosed pliers or tweezers (h): Very useful for removing fine bones from fish.

***Parisienne* scoop (i):** Also known as a **melon baller**, this scoop is used to cut fruit or vegetables into small ball shapes.

Pastry spatula (a): A long, thin spatula that can have an offset handle. Used to assist in cake decorating and for spreading batters or icings.

Ricer (j): A basket- or cone-shaped utensil with small holes and a plunger that is used to force solid foods into small grains resembling rice. Also known as a potato ricer.

Scales (k): A variety of scales are available that can give an accurate measurement of all ingredients. Scales are essential in pastry making. Many chefs now prefer digital models.

Scrapers (a): There are a number of styles of scraping utensils. For example, a metal bench scraper is used to clean off a work surface, and a plastic bowl scraper is used to thoroughly remove doughs from mixing bowls.

Spatulas (a): Large, wide, metal spatulas are used in flipping or turning vegetables, meat, and/or poultry during cooking. Some of these also have offset handles. There are a variety of spatulas made of softer rubber or composite materials that are used for scraping bowls, folding ingredients, or spreading. High-heat silicone spatulas are used for stirring hot foods or making omelettes. Wooden spatulas are also used, particularly for making omelettes in nonstick, coated pans, stirring *pâte à choux*, stirring roasting bones for stock, deglazing pans, making *roux*, and stirring *crème anglaise*.

Deans' Tips

"Keep your eyes open for things that can be adapted to your needs in the kitchen. Some of my best desserts have been made with tools not found in a kitchen supply store."

Dean Jacques Torres

"I always use a scale to weigh everything. Whenever an ingredient is sifted, I weigh it before I sift it. I always measure ounces by weight not by volume."

Dean Jacques Torres

"I like to cook using all of my senses, and the mortar and pestle allows you to smell and feel and hear what you are preparing. When I cook in the fireplace, I use a Tuscan grill that has a lot of flexibility but is simply constructed."

Dean Alice Waters

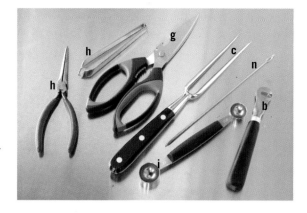

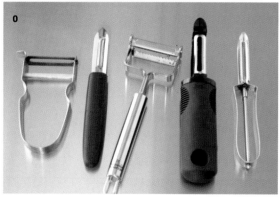

Spider (a): A long-handled device with a shallow, almost bowl-shaped disk at the end made of mesh or perforated wire.

Spoons (a): A wide variety of sizes and shapes of metal and wooden kitchen spoons are available with whole, slotted, or perforated bowls.

Stem thermometer (l): This common kitchen thermometer is provided to all students upon entering FCI. It measures degrees through a metal stem just past the dimple, which is located about 2 inches from the tip. The dimple must be placed in the middle of the food item to record an accurate temperature reading. To calibrate a stem thermometer, place it in heavily iced water for 3 minutes, stirring occasionally. Carefully adjust the nut under the reading dial if necessary. At this point, the thermometer should read 0°C (32°F). This type of thermometer should not be used for oven readings as it will melt.

***Tamis* (m):** A worsted cloth strainer often made from wool, used to do fine straining of liquids. Also known as a **tammycloth**. Also made in fine metal mesh.

Tongs (a): Tongs do not puncture food as forks do, so they are an essential and versatile tool in every kitchen. They are helpful in turning, lifting, and plating food. They are particularly useful when moving food items to be eaten raw or without further cooking so that contamination from hands or other contaminants can be avoided.

Trussing needle (n): A long, skewerlike needle used for trussing poultry or sewing stuffed cuts of meat closed.

Vegetable peeler (o): A small fixed or pivoting blade with a handle used to peel vegetables and fruit. A wide variety of types are now available.

Whisks (wire whips) (a): Thin, flexible wire whips used to incorporate mixtures that are not too dense. Balloon whisks have large, somewhat spherical centers and are used to incorporate air into foods such as egg whites.

Small Appliances

Some of the smaller appliances and equipment found in a professional kitchen are:

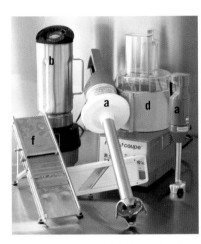

Ber mixer (a): An electric or battery-driven immersion blender, often handheld, that can be placed directly into a mixture for blending.

Electric blender (b): A machine that purées, emulsifies, and crushes, composed of a solid bottom housing the motor with a blender jar (often two different sizes) that fits over it. The jar is fitted with a removable lid. Never fill a blender jar to capacity, as the force of action will raise the lid with cold items, and a combination of force and steam will raise the lid when blending hot items. Even when filled the recommended two-thirds full, the lid, covered with a clean kitchen towel, should be held in place with both hands to prevent splattering or burning.

Electric food chopper or Buffalo chopper (c): A heavily built machine with a rotating bowl that passes under a hood where vertical blades chop the food. If all the parts are not properly aligned, the machine will not work.

Electric food processor (d): A machine with a heavy motor encased in a plastic or metal housing with a detachable bowl and cover and various blades with specific functions. The food processor can chop, blend, mix, purée, knead, grate, slice, and *julienne*. The machine processes best when the bowl is filled to half its capacity, and it will work only when all the pieces are properly aligned.

Electric meat grinder: A grinder consists of a freestanding motor housing or an electric mixer, as well as a feed tray, pusher, and blades and dies of varying sizes that are tightly screwed together by a ring. The attachment must be securely fastened before use. When used, the feed tray is filled with precut food that is then pushed through the selected die. *Never* put your hands in the feeding tube.

Electric meat slicer (e): A substantial piece of machinery with a large, stable, metal-encased motor as the foundation and a circular, cutting blade attached. The movable part is a carrier with a handle and a guard

that slides along the blade. The blade can be adjusted to the desired degree of thickness. Use only with the guard, as the blade is extremely sharp and dangerous.

Mandoline (f): Traditionally, a hand slicer made of a flat metal frame supported by folding legs that has a number of different-sized, extremely sharp blades used to cut vegetables into a variety of sizes, shapes, and thicknesses. Even if you feel that you are expert at its use, it is good practice to always use the protective guard when slicing with a mandoline. There is now an inexpensive Japanese-style mandoline available with a simplified design that is used for the same purpose.

Steam-jacketed kettle (electric or gas) (g): Used for making large quantities of stocks, soups, sauces, or pastas, these kettles are usually freestanding; some can be tilted and some may be fitted with spigots. The lid is usually attached, and they range in capacity from 2 quarts to over 100 gallons. The food is heated by steam that circulates through the kettle wall and provides even heat.

Tilting shallow kettle (electric or gas): A large, stainless steel unit with a hinged lid, used for making large quantities of sautés and braises.

Large Appliances

Both the professional kitchen and home kitchen require equipment for heating, refrigerating, and freezing food. Some of these appliances are:

Stoves, Ranges, and Ovens

There are many different types of stoves, ranges, and ovens available. Some of these have multiple uses, while others have a defined purpose.

Burners may be placed in a range top with an oven (or ovens) either below or above, or they may be placed alone into a stovetop that is fitted into a specific place. The burner types available are:

Open burner (gas) (a): Direct, adjustable heat.
Flat-top (gas or electric): A thick steel plate over the heat source that offers even, indirect heat. However, a flat-top burner requires flat-bottomed cookware and time to adjust to changes in temperature settings.
Ring-top (gas) (b): Concentric rings and plates that can be removed to expose the burner so that indirect heat can be converted to direct heat. Usually these burners have a higher BTU than a regular open burner. Ring-top burners are particularly well suited to stir-frying.

Some of the available ovens and other cooking or heating sources are:

Conventional oven (gas or electric): The indirect heat source is located on the bottom, underneath, or in the oven floor. An adjustable shelf is set at the desired level for proper cooking.
Deck oven (gas or electric) (c): A type of conventional oven that comes with single or multiple levels. The food is set directly on the oven floor. Allow a minimum of 20 minutes to preheat to temperature.
Convection oven (gas or electric) (d): In a convection oven, a fan blows hot air through the oven, allowing food to brown more efficiently than in a conventional oven. Often used for pastries and baked goods. Allow a minimum of 15 minutes to preheat to temperature. If a recipe is written with a temperature designated for a conventional oven, the temperature in a convection oven should be *lowered* by 10 percent.
Combi-oven (e): Temperature, moisture content, and air flow can be controlled with this type of oven. Its

design includes features from a conventional oven, a convection oven, and steamer. Used for both cooking and holding food, is ideal for use with catering and banquets.

Salamander (gas or electric) (f): An open boxlike apparatus that usually sits above a range top with the heat source located in its roof. It has adjustable racks to control cooking speed and is generally used for intense browning or *glaçages.*

Grill (gas, electric, wood, or charcoal) (g): The heating source is either built in (gas or electric) or added (wood or charcoal) and is located below a heavy-duty cooking rack. In many models the rack can be moved to allow for instant heat adjustment. Preheating usually takes about 20 minutes.

Refrigeration and Freezing Equipment

In addition to heating equipment, all kitchens require some type of refrigeration and freezing devices. Some of those available are:

Walk-in refrigeration: A large, box-shaped unit with a door large enough to allow a person to walk in without bending, walk-in refrigeration may be for cold storage or freezing. Generally it is outfitted with storage shelves. A compressor, often located outside the box, cools it.

Reach-in refrigeration (h): A single- or multiple-unit commercial refrigerator that is simply a larger version of a home refrigerator. Reach-ins come in various sizes and are equipped with adjustable shelving. Small freezers may also be reach-ins.

Under-counter refrigerator and refrigerated drawers (i): A small appliance used primarily around the work areas of professional kitchens to keep food cold until time of cooking or service. Some refrigerated drawers are designed to hold special products such as fish.

Freezers: Other than small ones used to hold frozen desserts, most professional kitchens do not use freezers. This is because food is bought in smaller amounts to ensure freshness and kept under refrigeration until prepared.

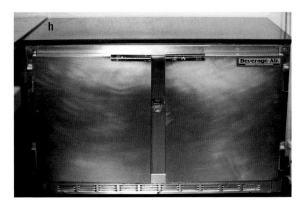

Principles of First Aid

Burns, abrasions, and cuts are part and parcel of work in the kitchen. These occupational hazards must be dealt with promptly and knowledgeably to ensure that additional damage is not done to the victim or to the workplace.

Follow these simple kitchen safety rules and many, many accidents will be avoided:

- A well-maintained fire extinguisher should be within arm's reach at all times.

- Immediately clean spills from floors and worktops. If a mop or other cleanup tool is not within reach, spread salt over floor spills to absorb moisture and prevent falls.

- Always use guards and other safety devices provided for small equipment.

- Never attempt to remove food from a machine that is in motion and always unplug electrical appliances before unloading, disassembling, or cleaning.

- Do not touch or handle electrical equipment, switches, or outlets with wet hands or if standing in water.

- Make certain that pilot lights are always lit and relight when necessary. Make sure that the kitchen is well ventilated.

- Do not attempt to lift very heavy objects without assistance and when obliged to lift heavy pots, bend your knees and lift up.

Burns

Burns are often the most serious kitchen accidents, so it is extremely important to know how to treat them.

Burns are classified in three categories:

First-degree burn: A burn caused by quick contact with a moderately hot surface or liquid, resulting in inflammation and reddening of the skin. Painful but not serious.

Cover the burn with a Band-Aid but **do not put any burn cream on the area**.

Second-degree burn: Most often associated with scalding, this is a very painful burn that forms a blister on a localized area. Do not pop or attempt to open the blister. Cover the burn with antiseptic or antibacterial cream and sterile gauze.

Third-degree burn: An extremely serious burn that destroys all layers of the skin. The damaged skin appears white but may well be charred. In the kitchen, these burns are most often the result of contact with hot (204°C/400°F) cooking oil or fat. Keep the victim warm to prevent shock. **Immediately call emergency medical assistance or, if necessary, transport the victim to the nearest medical facility.** Do not undress the victim unless the clothes are saturated with a liquid that is still burning. Do not touch the burn or attempt to treat it yourself beyond using cold water, as described. In an educational or professional setting, make certain that all necessary medical insurance and liability forms are complete and that all insurance and liability information is made available to the victim.

There are a number of steps to take that will greatly diminish the possibility of kitchen burns. Learn them early and you will save yourself and others from injury.

- Always warn your coworkers when you are moving hot pots, pans, and utensils, or when they are stationary but remain hot. It is particularly important to alert dishwashers and other cleanup personnel who handle soiled cookware and utensils. At home, these warnings should be directed to others present, especially young children and the elderly.

- Always use a dry side towel to handle hot cookware and utensils.

○ Keep pot handles on the stove turned in from the front and away from open flames. Remember that heat travels and consider that all areas of a pot are potentially hot.

○ Do not overfill pans.

○ Do not attempt to lift or move large containers of hot liquid or food without assistance.

○ To prevent steam burns when removing the lid from a pot, always lift the lid up from the back, forcing the steam away from your face.

○ To prevent oil or fat burns when frying, place the food into the pan from the front to the back, allowing the farthest edge to fall into the fat away from your hand.

○ Remember that **oil and water do not mix** and never attempt to put out a grease fire with water. If a small grease fire occurs, use salt or baking soda to extinguish it or cover it with a large lid to deprive the fire of oxygen.

○ Keep containers of liquid away from the deep-fat fryer.

○ To prevent hot grease splatters, dry all food well before placing it in hot fat.

Cuts

The seriousness of a cut is determined by its depth and place of occurrence. Obviously, a paper cut on the finger is treated quite differently from a knife slice that severs a vein or artery. When possible, cuts should be held under cold running water for at least one minute to cleanse the area. Then, using a clean towel, pressure should be applied to stop the flow of blood. If possible, elevate the cut area above the victim's heart to slow the flow. If the cut does not stop bleeding after a few minutes, is very deep, or bleeds profusely, it may require medical attention and/or stitches. **Immediately** call emergency medical assistance or transport the victim to the nearest medical facility while maintaining pressure to the cut area. Manageable hand cuts or those that have stopped

bleeding should be covered with an antibiotic ointment, a clean bandage, and a rubber glove or rubber finger cover. This is to protect the cut from infection as well as to prevent the spread of bacteria from the wound to any food being prepared, as uncovered wounds are a ready source of food contamination.

Kitchen cuts can be avoided if a few basic precautions are taken.

○ Learn good knife skills. Hold your knife properly, keeping the fingertips of the hand opposite your knife curled down when slicing and dicing.

○ Carry a knife properly at all times—at your side, point down, with the sharp edge to the back.

○ Warn coworkers when moving about the kitchen with an unsheathed knife.

○ Avoid cutting with the knife point moving toward you.

○ Pay keen attention when using a knife. Do not talk.

○ Keep all knives sharp. A dull knife has less control, as it takes more pressure to cut and affords more opportunity for slippage.

○ Keep cutting boards stationary by placing a damp kitchen towel or a layer of damp paper towel underneath.

○ Clean all knives carefully immediately after use, always keeping the sharp edge away from you.

○ Never place a knife in a sink of water or under dishes; this presents a safety hazard.

○ Never try to catch a falling knife. Jump backward to keep your feet out of range.

○ Never try to catch a falling roll of plastic film or aluminum foil, as the cutting edge is extremely sharp and dangerous.

○ Be extremely careful when using a mandoline, as the blades are razor-sharp. It is a good idea to always use the hand guard.

Session 2

Working with Vegetables

Technique

The Basic Rules for Washing, Peeling, and Cutting Vegetables

The basic rules for washing, peeling, and cutting vegetables have evolved with practical considerations. Careful washing ensures that all products are free of impurities when ready for preparation, while smooth peeling and uniform cutting ensure even cooking and enhanced presentation. Once learned, these rules are never forgotten and, without exception, offer a basic element that will move a dish from the everyday to the sublime. In the beginning of the learning process, it is extremely important to practice these rules over and over again.

The Washing Process (*Lavage*)

To wash (*laver*) is to eliminate impurities such as dirt, sand, insects, and insecticides from vegetables and herbs by submersion in cold water or by rinsing and scrubbing under cold, running water. Washing is important for aesthetic as well as sanitary reasons, especially when the vegetables and herbs are to be eaten raw, as these impurities are often unappetizing as well as unhealthy. Before washing, vegetables and herbs should be checked for freshness—any rotting leaves or vegetation will disintegrate in the washing process and contaminate the remaining product by clinging to it. It is suggested that you wash only the amount that you need.

Proper washing procedures are as follows:

○ Fill an appropriate large basin or sink with enough cold water to completely cover the vegetables to be washed.

○ For salad greens or other leafy green vegetables, as well as for cauliflower, a little vinegar may be added to the water to kill any insects.

○ Using your hands, agitate the items being washed in the water to loosen all impurities.

○ Using your hands, a skimmer, or a colander, lift the vegetables out of the water so that the impurities stay in the basin and are not lifted out with the vegetables.

○ Rinse the basin and repeat the washing process as many times as necessary until the water is clear and clean.

○ Some vegetables, particularly spinach and other leafy greens, are often very dirty and must be rinsed many times.

○ Mushrooms, particularly very clean, commercially grown button mushrooms, can often simply be wiped clean with a damp cloth or small brush made for this purpose. However, most mushrooms, especially wild mushrooms, require washing to rid them of the earth's impurities. Washing should be done just before use, or the mushrooms will hold the water and their flavor will be compromised.

○ Watercress (*cresson*) should be washed carefully and then soaked in cold water for 30 minutes to an hour to remove all grit. Discard any wilted or discolored branches.

○ Leeks (*poireaux*) should be cut in half lengthwise, and each half should be held upside-down under cold running water to dislodge any grit or dirt. Separate the leaves and rinse out the grit or dirt that is hidden under the layers. If the leeks are extremely dirty, it may be necessary to soak them in cool water to soften and dislodge the dirt.

The Peeling Process (*Épluchage*)

Related terms are ***éplucher, écosser,*** or ***éffiler.***
Épluchage literally defined means cleaning, peeling, and unwrapping—or dissection. The peeling process encompasses all of these activities. When peeling, it is important that only the peel or skin is removed, leaving as much flesh as possible. *Éplucher* means to peel by removing the skin or outer layer of a vegetable or fruit. *Écosser* means to shell or hull, as with peas. *Éffiler* means to pull off stringy side filaments, as with string beans. Memorize the proper name for each process and use it at all times.

○ The term *emonder* means to remove the skin of a tomato. Remove the core, score the opposite end in a crisscross, and dip in boiling water for a few seconds. Dip in ice water to chill; then push off the loose skin.

○ Pearl onions should be placed in warm water for a few minutes to rehydrate the skin for easy removal.

Proper peeling techniques are as follows:

○ All items to be peeled should be thoroughly clean and free of impurities before being placed on the cutting board.

○ When peeling vegetables, the workstation should be set up as described on page 3.

○ Peeling motions should be regular, consistent, and precise, removing as little of the flesh as possible. Most items can be peeled using a paring knife with a 3- to 4-inch blade or a functional vegetable peeler of which there are now many types available.

○ Peeling should proceed in an orderly and clean manner with the remains discarded as soon as the work is complete.

Methods of Cutting (*Taillage*)

Proper cutting results in vegetables of uniform size and shape and ensures that the items will cook evenly. It is particularly important to follow the guidelines for proper cutting because it allows more than one person to prepare items for a specific recipe. Appropriate cutting also is used to enhance the aesthetic of the finished presentation. These methods should be practiced over and over until the appropriate cut can be made almost with closed eyes. Just as the old joke says that the way to Carnegie Hall is through practice, practice, practice, so it is also that practice is the only way to master proper cutting techniques and sizes.

Again, it is extremely important to memorize the proper cut, as it is the only reference you will have to preparation of a properly peeled and cut vegetable. It is a good idea to practice these cuts outside the classroom using basic vegetables such as potatoes, carrots, and celery (which, once cut, can be tossed in a pot with a bit of water and stock, sea-

soned, and cooked to make a simple, healthy soup). When practicing on other vegetables, either put them all together for a soup, practice cooking methods, or make a raw or cooked vegetable salad, either tossed or composed.

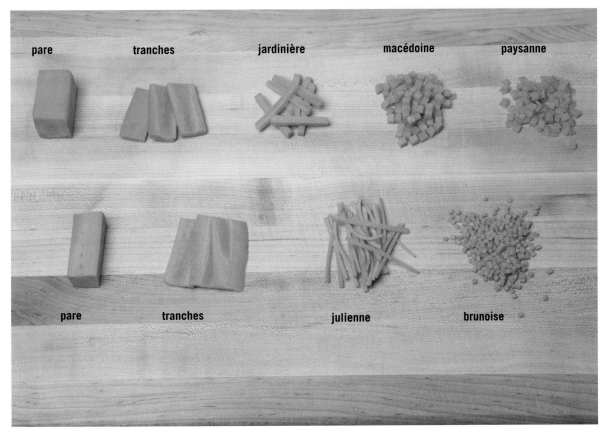

pare   tranches   jardinière   macédoine   paysanne

pare   tranches   julienne   brunoise

The traditional nomenclature for standard cutting procedures is as follows:

Émincer: To thinly slice.

Ciseler: To finely dice onions and shallots. This striation of cuts produces a fine, tiny dice that keeps the juices from being forced out, which is what happens with standard chopping.

Tronçonner: To cut into 4- to 7-centimeter (1½- to 2¾-inch) segments.

Parer: To trim round slices of washed, peeled, and *tronçonnéed* vegetables to obtain flat surfaces on every side so that even pieces can be uniformly cut.

at left: methods of cutting

opposite page: dicing shallots *ciselés*

25

Traditional *taillage* is as follows:

Pared items are first cut into slices that are called **tranches**; then into sticks or dice. Each cut size has a specific name.

Jardinière: Thin sticks, 5 millmeters (³⁄₁₆ inch) square and 4 to 5 centimeters (1½ to 2 inches) long.

Julienne: Very thin sticks, 1 to 2 millimeters (¹⁄₃₂ to ¹⁄₁₆ inch) square and 5 to 7 centimeters (2 to 2¾ inches) long.

Macédoine: Small cubes, 5 millmeters (³⁄₁₆ inch) square.

Brunoise: Minute cubes, 1 to 2 millimeters (¹⁄₃₂ to ¹⁄₁₆ inch) square.

Other traditional cuts are as follows:

Mirepoix: Unshaped large chunks, usually about 1 to 2 centimeters (³⁄₈ to ¾ inch) in size. These pieces are used as the aromatic elements to flavor the final product and are almost always strained out of the sauce at the end of cooking; therefore, a perfect symmetrical shape is not required. *Mirepoix* may be cut without first shaping the vegetable by any of the traditional cutting methods, but it is important that all pieces be of uniform size to ensure even cooking. This term is often applied to a mixture of equal parts onion and carrot; 50 percent onion,

25 percent carrot, and 25 percent celery; or equal parts onion, carrot, and celery (depending on the specific recipe) that is used to flavor stocks and sauces (see page 50). Onions are always a component of a *mirepoix,* though carrots and celery may not always be used.

Paysanne: This cut is tile-shaped or triangular, usually cut from *jardinière* sliced 1 to 2 millimeters (1/32 to 1/16 inch) thick, or it may also be cut without preshaping the item. Vegetables cut into *paysanne* are most often used for soups called **potages taillés.**

Chiffonade: This method of cutting produces thin strips or ribbons of herbs or leafy vegetables.

To cut into *chiffonade*:

1. Wash and thoroughly dry the leaves.

2. Lay the leaves in a flat stack of three or four.

3. Roll the stacked leaves into a cigar shape.

4. Cut the leaf roll, crosswise, to form very thin strips or ribbons (*julienne*).

at right: lettuce cut into *chiffonade*

opposite page: *mirepoix* vegetables

Concasser: To coarsely chop a vegetable, usually tomatoes.

Hacher: To finely mince small bunches of herb leaves, which are then used to flavor cooked dishes or to garnish finished dishes.

Traditionally, some vegetables require special cuts or preparation because of their unusual shape or structure. Among those requiring special attention:

- Watercress (*cresson*) requires that the leaves and approximately 5 centimeters (2 inches) of the stem be cut off.

at left: preparing tomatoes *concassé*

opposite page: parsley *haché*

○ Leeks (*poireaux*) must be well washed; to slice them, separate and flatten the leaves, stacking them to make a neat, even sur face, and then slice into desired size or shape.

○ Lemons (*citrons*) can be decorated with ridges using a channel knife or *canneleur*. After fluting (cutting into ridges as in photo) the whole lemon, cut it crosswise into slices or half slices. Lemons (or any other citrus fruit) can also be cut into baskets or cut in half with a paring knife in such a way as to leave a zigzag edge known as **dent de loup** (see photo), or wolf's tooth. Lemons cut in this manner are often used to decorate fried or poached fish.

Techniques of Shaping and Carving Vegetables (*Tournage*)

Dean's Tip

"The shaping of vegetables is a discipline and an important part of classic training."

Dean Jacques Pépin

Chefs' Tips

"Picking a vegetable with the right size and shape for the appropriate tournage *will help your cutting significantly."*

Chef Pascal Beric

"The best way to get good at knife skills, like tournage, *is practice, practice, practice."*

Chef Candy Argondizza

To **tourner** (literally, "to turn") is to cut or turn vegetables into traditional faceted-oval shapes. Like the traditional *taillage* cuts, these cuts are used to create a uniform shape that ensures even cooking and elevates the look of the finished presentation of a dish. It is one of the most difficult cutting techniques to master and requires patience and practice. In these beginning sessions in the classroom, *tournage* is practiced whenever there is an extra moment of time. It is also recommended that the student practice at home using the inexpensive potato. (Make sure that you have a use for the potatoes, as the foundation of classic cooking is the use of all ingredients, leaving no waste. Even the peels can be used to add to soups!) Once the technique is mastered, vegetables can be turned quickly to add a fine dimension to many simple dishes.

Turned vegetables have different names that are dependent upon the length of their cut.

Bouquetière: 3 centimeters (1¾6 inches) long.
Cocotte: 5 centimeters (2 inches) long.
Vapeur: 6 centimeters (2⅜ inches) long.
Château: 7.5 centimeters (3 inches) long.
Fondante: 8 to 9 centimeters (3⅛ to 3½ inches) long.

The standard technique for *tournage* is as follows:

1. Cut the vegetables to be *tournéed* into pieces of equal length (*tronçons*).
2. Cut each piece into the approximate finished shape.
3. Working with one piece at a time, firmly hold the piece with the fingertips of one hand. Holding a paring knife in the other hand, thinly slice off one side in a slightly curved stroke, making one stroke down. If you make more than one stroke, the piece will appear carved rather than have smooth edges. (It is a good idea to say "one stroke down" as you go, as it helps establish the cutting rhythm.) Turn the piece slightly and carefully remove another thin slice, making one stroke down.
4. Continue to work around the entire piece, slightly turning and making one stroke down, until the whole piece has been molded into the classic form: an even, seven-sided olive or barrel shape.

Two Classic Methods for Cooking Vegetables

When preparing vegetables for cooking, never leave the washed, peeled, and/or cut vegetables in water for an extended period of time, as this will leach out flavor and nutrients. The exception to this rule are those vegetables and fruits such as artichokes, apples, or pears, that will discolor if exposed to air. These can be placed in acidulated water (water with lemon juice or vinegar added) while being worked with. However, we feel that it is far better to rub the cut item with lemon (either a cut lemon half or the juice) to prevent discoloration than to compromise flavor and texture by an extended stay in water.

When cooking vegetables, each type should be cooked separately to retain its integrity of flavor and texture. In addition, since the cooking time required for each vegetable will often vary, combining different types can cause one vegetable to overcook, while another may need additional time.

These two basic methods for cooking vegetables—*à l'anglaise* and *à l'étuvé*—are at the core of all professional cooking. They are simple to learn and, with a little practice, easy to execute.

À l'anglaise

This useful method developed to add speed in the restaurant kitchen is equally well applied in a smaller kitchen. It allows vegetables to be cooked prior to use and then reheated at the time of service. This method is carried out as follows:

1. Fill a large pot with water. Add enough salt to give the water the taste of seawater: A good rule is 34 grams (1¼ ounces) of salt per liter (34 ounces) of water.

2. Place the water over high heat and bring it to a rolling boil (one that cannot be stirred down). Do not cover.

3. Add the vegetables to the boiling water and cook until just barely tender when pierced with the sharp point of a small knife. The vegetables should be slightly resistant so that reheating will not overcook them.

4. Drain well. Immediately immerse the vegetables in ice water for a minute to stop the cooking and set the color. This is generally referred to as **shocking** the vegetables.

5. Drain well.

6. Pat dry. Place in a clean container and cover with plastic film. Refrigerate until ready to use.

7. When ready to serve, reheat the required amount in a small pan with butter (or olive oil) and seasonings such as salt, pepper, and herbs. Serve immediately.

À l'étuvé

This method slowly cooks raw vegetables in a covered pan with their own juices, just a touch of fat (butter or olive oil), and salt. Just enough liquid (either water or stock) is added to allow the vegetables to exude their own moisture as they cook.

1. Place the properly cleaned and, if necessary, cut vegetables in a *sautoir* or *russe* large enough to hold them in a single layer.

2. Add the required water, which may be as little as a couple of tablespoons, to come halfway up the vegetables, depending on the moisture in the vegetable. Add the desired amount of fat and a pinch of salt.

3. Fold a piece of parchment paper into a cone shape by making 4 folds inwards. Using kitchen scissors, cut off a tiny piece of the tip of the cone and cut the cone shape to a size that will fit the top of the pan. Open up the cone and you should have a circle large enough to cover the top of the pan with a small hole in the center.

4. Place over high heat and bring to a boil.

5. Lower the heat to a simmer to maintain constant

steam. Watch carefully so that the liquid does not evaporate before the vegetables are cooked.

6. If water is evaporating too quickly, lower the heat. Ideally, the liquid should have completely evaporated just as the vegetables are fully cooked.

7. Cook until the vegetables are tender when pierced with the sharp point of a small knife.

8. Taste and, if necessary, adjust the salt and add pepper. Serve immediately.

Methods of Glazing Vegetables (*Glacer*)

Glazing (**glacer**) is similar to cooking *à l'étuvé*, but a small amount of sugar is added and the cooking liquid is reduced so that the butter and sugar form a shiny, slightly sweet coating on the cooking vegetables.

In this section, two different methods of cooking vegetables are introduced, **glacer à blanc** and **glacer à brun**. The technique is the same in both, but the degree to which the vegetable is cooked differs. The sugar is allowed to caramelize slightly in the *glacer à brun* method to achieve a darker, richer glaze on the vegetable. Since cooked vegetables are a component of most plated entrées, it is extremely important to master these methods early in the learning process.

Add water as for *à l'étuvé* (see page 32)

Cut a piece of parchment paper to fit the top of the pan and cut a small hole in the center of the parchment paper (see page 32).

The basic glazing method is as follows:

1. Cook only one type of vegetable at a time.

2. Place the cleaned, shaped vegetables in a *sautoir* or *russe* large enough to accommodate them in a single layer. Add water as for *à l'étuvé* (see page 32), butter, salt, and a pinch of sugar.

3. Cut a piece of parchment paper to fit the top of the pan and cut a small hole in the center of the parchment paper (see page 32). Cover the pan with the paper.

4. Place the pan over high heat and bring to a boil.

5. Immediately reduce the heat to a gentle simmer to maintain constant steam.

6. Simmer until all the liquid has evaporated and a thin syrupy liquid has coated each piece with a clear, shiny glaze.

7. If the vegetables are almost tender and excess liquid remains in the pan, remove the parchment paper cover to allow the liquid to evaporate more rapidly.

To *glacer à brun*, follow the preceding directions but allow the sugar syrup to cook until it caramelizes on the vegetables, turning them a golden brown. *Glacer à brun* is usually required for aromatics such as shallots or onions that will be served with or in brown sauces.

Methods of Cooking Potatoes

Potatoes are very often an important component of a plated entrée, so it is necessary to learn to cook them in a number of ways. (For further material on potatoes, see Session 7.)

Pommes Rissolés

A common classic method used to prepare shaped, cooked potatoes is called **pommes rissolés**, for which there is no equivalent term in English. Potatoes to be *rissoléed* are cooked in a three-step procedure. They are first blanched, then sautéed in hot fat to brown, and most often they are finished by roasting in a medium-hot oven.

The common shapes and sizes used for pommes rissolés are:

Tournéed: *Cocotte*, 5 centimeters by 1.5 centimeters (2 inches by ⅝ inch); and *château*, 7.5 centimeters by 3 centimeters (3 inches by 1³⁄₁₆ inches).

Diced: *Parmentier*, 1.5 centimeters to 1.8 centimeters square (⅝ inch to ¾ inch); and *vert prés*, 5 to 7 millimeters square (³⁄₁₆ inch to ¼ inch).

Balls (cut with a melon baller): *Olive* (elongated ball), *noisette* (round ball), and *Parisienne* (small ball).

The method for cooking and roasting *pommes rissolés* is as follows:

1. Place the peeled, shaped potatoes in a pan just large enough to hold them in a single layer with just enough cold water to cover. Do not use too much water or by the time the water boils, the potatoes will begin to overcook.

2. Bring to a boil.

3. Drain immediately. Do not shock.

4. Lay the potatoes out in a single layer on paper towels and allow to air dry.

5. Place the appropriate type and amount of fat in an ovenproof pan large enough to hold the potatoes in a single layer. Place the pan over medium heat.

6. When the fat is very hot but not smoking, add the potatoes.

7. Raise the heat and quickly sauté the potatoes, tossing to evenly brown. When the potatoes are lightly browned and almost cooked through, remove the pan from the heat and drain off all the fat. Set aside until needed.

8. When ready to serve, preheat the oven to 204°C (400°F).

9. Add the appropriate amount of butter to the pan and toss to coat the potatoes evenly with the butter.

10. Place the pan in the oven.

11. Roast, shaking the pan from time to time to toss the potatoes, until the sharp point of a small knife inserted into the center of a potato meets no resistance.

12. Remove from the oven and drain off the excess fat. Season with salt.

13. Serve immediately.

Dean's Tip

"When new potatoes have just come to the market, cook them, covered, in a touch of butter and oil, with very low heat. You will not need to blanch them, as potatoes contain much more moisture when new."

Dean Alain Sailhac

Chef's Tip

"When preparing to sauté, it is preferable to preheat the pan for a few minutes on low heat before adding any fat and then bring the pan and the fat to the proper temperature."

Chef Martin Schaub

Theory
About Artichokes

Globe artichokes were introduced into the French culinary repertoire in the mid-sixteenth century by Catherine de Medici, the Italian-born queen who was well known for her culinary interests as well as her prodigious appetite. Catherine de Medici's gluttony, although often debilitating for her, broadly expanded the French culinary repertoire, helping to establish its emphasis on rich sauces, exotic ingredients, and unusual preparations.

Artichokes, the sweet flesh of the dense petal-leaved flower bud of a thistle plant (*Cynara scolymus*, a member of the Asteraceae family) are eaten in both their raw and cooked states. The buds form on tall stalks with the primary globe developing at the top of each stalk and secondary buds appearing on the lower part. The very smallest buds that form on the lower part of the plant are most often sold as baby artichokes or processed for commercial use. The stalk may also be peeled and eaten.

Artichokes usually have a productive cycle of three to four years with two annual harvests, one in the spring and the other in the fall. The buds are harvested when young, as they grow increasingly woody, developing a large fuzzy choke as they mature. If left to mature, the buds will open and produce a purple thistlelike flower and be completely inedible. When purchasing tender young artichokes, you want buds that are tightly closed, blemish-free, firm-leaved, and dense, with clean, bright color (either green, greenish-purple, or purple). The cut stem, whether flat against the bud or long and slender, should be smooth and unwrinkled.

Whole globe artichokes are eaten raw only when very, very small, young, and tender. In France, these young buds are often eaten *à la croque au sel* (with but a grain of salt). The hearts of large artichokes are also eaten raw, thinly sliced, and served with a sprinkling of light vinaigrette or fine olive oil. Cooked artichokes may be served whole, halved, quartered, or as hearts or trimmed bottoms only. Each style has many applications in the classic French kitchen. From the hearty whole stuffed artichoke to the delicate *bouquetière garniture*, this vegetable lends itself to many preparations and garnishes.

Technique
Preparing Artichokes

Before cooking artichokes whole, you must trim them, taking care not to prick your fingers with the sharp thorns that are often on the tip of each leaf.

Artichokes are trimmed in the following manner:

1. Using a serrated knife, cut off the top third of the artichoke.

2. If leaving the stem on, cut about an inch off of the lower stem; then, using a vegetable peeler, peel off the tough outer covering to reveal the inner, tender, almost-white flesh.

Dean's Tip

"Violet or spring artichokes can be eaten raw. They are usually sliced and served with sea salt, butter or olive oil, and lemon."

Dean Alain Sailhac

3. If removing the stem, hold the trimmed artichoke in one hand and the stem in the other and, twisting in opposite directions, neatly pull off the stem. (On larger artichokes, the stem is often very fibrous, which makes for unpleasant eating.)

4. Using kitchen shears or a serrated knife, trim off the top bit of each leaf to eliminate any of the thornlike tips and to make a neat package.

5. Place in cold water to cover by at least 1 inch, swishing the water about with your hands to agitate and loosen any dirt or foreign matter.

6. Drain well.

7. Wash thoroughly under cold running water.

To trim artichokes for bottoms only:

1. Fill a large stainless steel bowl with very cold water and acidulate (*aciduler*) the water with the juice of one half lemon and add the juiced lemon half to the water.

2. Using a sharp chef's knife, cut off the top two-thirds of the artichoke, working quickly to prevent discoloration, and trim the artichokes down to the solid bottoms only.

3. If necessary, remove the stem by holding the trimmed artichoke in one hand and the stem in the other and, twisting in opposite directions, neatly pull off the stem.

4. If the stem has previously been removed, neatly trim the stem end to make a flat surface and rub the cut surface with a cut lemon.

5. Using a paring knife or your hands, neatly trim off all the tough bottom leaves, maintaining a neat, round shape.

6. Continuously rub the cut surfaces with the lemon to prevent discoloration.

7. Using the paring knife or a teaspoon, trim the top of the artichoke until a solid mass of fuzzy choke appears, continuing to rub the cut surface with lemon.

8. Using a soup spoon, scrape the fuzzy choke from the center of the artichoke, again rubbing the cut surface with the lemon.

9. Immediately drop the artichoke bottom into the acidulated water and leave it there until ready to cook.

Artichoke bottoms may be served hot, warm, or at room temperature as a component of a larger recipe, with vinaigrette or with a drizzle of extra virgin olive oil and fresh lemon juice.

Cooking Artichokes *à l'Anglaise*

Artichokes cooked *à l'anglaise* may be served hot, warm, or at room temperature with hollandaise sauce (see page 82), mousseline sauce (see page 81), mayonnaise (see page 87), or any vinaigrette (see page 240).

To cook artichokes:

If cooking whole artichokes *à l'anglaise*, place a fresh lemon slice on the stem cut and tie it in place with kitchen string. This will help keep the cut part from discoloring during the cooking process.

1. Place the artichokes in a saucepan large enough to allow plenty of room around each artichoke so that they can cook evenly on all sides. Place a plate or other heavy object directly on top of the artichokes to keep them submerged.

2. Place over high heat and bring to a boil.

3. Lower the heat to a simmer and cook for about 25 minutes, or until a small sharp knife can be easily inserted into the stem end. (This will be determined by the time of year picked as well as the age and size of the artichokes. In late spring, they will be very young and tender, while summer will yield firmer, tougher vegetables.)

4. Drain well.

5. Refresh under cold running water. Turn the artichokes upside down on a triple layer of paper towels and allow to drain well.

6. Remove the string and lemon slice.

7. Use as required in a specific recipe.

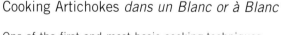

When cooking artichoke bottoms only, prepare them *dans un blanc* as follows:

○ Follow general directions on page 22 for washing and trimming.

○ Following the basic recipe, cook for about 12 minutes or until tender enough that the center is easily pierced with the point of a small, sharp knife.

○ Always allow the artichoke bottoms to cool in the *blanc* (where they will finish cooking).

Cooking Artichokes *dans un Blanc or à Blanc*

One of the first and most basic cooking techniques demonstrated in the classic French repertoire is the preparation of artichokes in a water/flour/oil/lemon/salt solution referred to as **cuisson dans un blanc** or **cuisson à blanc** (or cooking in a white). This cooking solution is used for any raw ingredient that easily discolors when freshly peeled or during the cooking process. Other such ingredients would be salsify, offal, and veal. The flour and lemon in the water solution bleach the ingredient and keep it white or pale in color while cooking, and the oil forms a layer on top of the liquid to prevent air from coming in contact with the artichoke bottoms.

The French term for the following cooking solution is *un blanc* (a white). Cooking foods in this solution, *cuisson dans un blanc* or *cuisson à blanc*, should not be confused with another French culinary term, *cuire à blanc*, which is used to describe the slow baking of an unfilled tart shell covered by pastry weights or dried beans.

Demonstration

Cooking *dans un Blanc*

Serves 4

Estimated time to complete: 1 hour 45 minutes

Note

The point of a small, sharp knife should meet just a tiny bit of pressure when inserted into the bottom center for barely tender artichokes.

The following solution is enough to prepare 4 whole artichokes (or 2 pounds of salsify, offal, or veal). When cooking artichokes, you should do so in a pot that will allow plenty of room between each one so that all sides cook evenly.

Ingredients

2 liters (2 quarts, 4 ounces) water
30 milliliters (2 tablespoons) canola oil
15 milliliters (1 tablespoon) fresh lemon juice
21 grams (¾ ounce) all-purpose flour
10 grams (⅓ ounce) coarse salt

Equipment

Russe
Whisk
Small, sharp knife

Prepare your *mise en place.*

Combine the water, oil, and lemon juice in the *russe* over medium heat.

Whisk in the flour and salt, beating until the mixture becomes opaque.

Add the ingredient to be cooked and raise the heat to high. Bring to a boil, then lower the heat slightly.

Cook at a low boil for about 30 minutes or until the item is just barely tender, as when a knife inserted into it meets just a bit of pressure (see note).

Remove from heat and allow the item to stand in the liquid for about 1 hour or until completely cool.

Demonstration

Bouquetière Garniture

Serves 4
Estimated time to complete: 1 hour, 45 minutes

A **bouquetière garniture**, composed of various cooked vegetables (usually three chosen from the following: potatoes, carrots, celery, turnips, and onions), is most often used as a garnish or accompaniment to meat or poultry entrées. It always contains carrots and turnips but all of the remaining vegetables can vary according to the season. Some elements might be **fleurettes** (tiny florets) of cauliflower or broccoli, **haricots verts** (tiny string beans), pearl onions, or peas. Potatoes that have been *tournéed* are also often a component. In the winter, carrots, turnips, celery root, potatoes, and other root vegetables are usually included, while the spring and summer will provide small tomatoes, small lettuces that have been quartered, string beans, peas, and a variety of baby vegetables such as zucchini, pattypan squash, and carrots.

In this recipe, the carrots, turnips, onions, and potatoes are cooked and kept warm for plating. The artichokes, string beans, and peas must be reheated. The classic method of reheating blanched vegetables was to place them in rapidly boiling water for 30 seconds. This, in effect, drew more nutrients from the vegetables and lessened their flavor so we no longer follow that tradition.

Please note that this recipe is for the final plating; the carrots, turnips, pearl onions, and potatoes must be prepared and incorporated, hot, into the recipe.

Dean's Tip

"When preparing artichokes, wash your knife, board, and hands often. Otherwise, the artichokes will have a bitter taste that will also linger on your hands for a long period."

Chef Alain Sailhac

Ingredients	Equipment
15 milliliters (1 tablespoon) water	Large *sautoir*
15 grams (1 tablespoon) unsalted butter	Slotted spoon
4 *tournéed* artichoke bottoms, slightly undercooked *dans un blanc*	Serving platter
100 grams (3½ ounces) string beans, cut into 5-centimeter (2-inch)-long pieces, cooked *à l'anglaise*	
100 grams (3½ ounces) fresh English peas, cooked *à l'anglaise*	
Coarse salt and freshly ground pepper to taste	
200 grams (7 ounces) carrots, cut *bouquetière*, cooked *glacer à blanc*	
200 grams (7 ounces) turnips, cut *bouquetière*, cooked *glacer à blanc*	
200 grams (7 ounces) pearl onions, peeled and trimmed, cooked *glacer à blanc*	
200 grams (7 ounces) russet potatoes, cut *cocotte*, cooked *rissolé*	

Prepare your *mise en place*.

Combine the water and butter in a large *sautoir* over medium heat.

Add the artichoke bottoms, string beans, and peas and cook for about 2 minutes or until hot.

Season with salt and pepper to taste. Remove from the heat and drain well.

Using a slotted spoon, transfer the artichoke bottoms to a serving platter.

Fill the artichoke bottoms with vegetables and surround the filled artichoke bottoms with any remaining vegetables.

Demonstration

Ratatouille

Serves 4
Estimated time to complete: About 90 minutes

Ingredients	Equipment

900 grams (2 pounds) ripe tomatoes, *émondées*

250 milliliters (1 cup plus 1 tablespoon) blended olive oil

2 medium onions, *ciselés*, 1.5 centimeter (⅝ inch) dice

1 green bell pepper, cored, seeded, and cut into
1.5 centimeter (⅝ inch) dice

1 red bell pepper, cored, seeded, and cut into
1.5 centimeter (⅝ inch) dice

Coarse salt and freshly ground pepper to taste

4 cloves garlic, peeled and crushed

Bouquet garni with fresh basil leaves added (see page 50)

675 grams (1½ pounds) eggplant, cut into
1.5 centimeter (⅝ inch) *macédoine*

550 grams (1 pound, 3 ounces) zucchini, cut into
1.5 centimeter (⅝ inch) *macédoine*

21 grams (about 4 tablespoons) fresh thyme leaves

Chef's knife
Chinois
Small bowl
Rubber spatula
Small *marmite* with lid
Colander
Wide *sauteuse*
Slotted spoon
Paper towels

Prepare your *mise en place.*

Cut the tomatoes in half, and squeeze out and reserve the seeds and their juices. Using a chef's knife, finely chop the tomatoes. Set aside.

Place the seeds into a *chinois* set over a small bowl and press on them with a spatula to extract all of their juice. Add any of the reserved juice along with enough water to yield 250 milliliters (1 cup plus 1 tablespoon) of liquid.

Heat about 100 milliliters (7 tablespoons) of the olive oil in a small *marmite* over medium heat. Add the onions and sauté for 5 minutes. Add the green and red bell peppers and cook for an additional 5 minutes. Add the chopped tomatoes and cook, stirring frequently, for 5 more minutes. Season the vegetables with salt and

pepper to taste as they are added to the pan.

Add the reserved tomato juice and water along with the garlic and *bouquet garni.* Cover and bring to a simmer. Lower the heat and cook at a bare simmer for 30 minutes or until the vegetables are very soft.

While the vegetables are cooking, place the eggplant in a colander and sprinkle with salt. Set aside and allow the eggplant to *degorger.*

Heat 50 milliliters (3½ tablespoons) of the remaining olive oil in a wide *sauteuse* over medium heat. When very hot but not smoking, add the zucchini and sauté for about 7 minutes or until golden. Using a slotted spoon, transfer the zucchini to a colander to drain. Season with salt and thyme and then add to the onion and tomato mixture.

Remove the eggplant from the colander and pat dry with paper towels.

Using the same *sauteuse*, add the remaining olive oil and heat until very hot but not smoking. Add the eggplant and sauté for about 10 minutes or until golden brown. Transfer the cooked eggplant to a colander to drain. Then, using a slotted spoon, transfer the eggplant to the vegetable mixture in the *marmite*.

Cook the vegetable *mélange* for an additional 15 minutes or until very tender and the flavors have melded. Remove and discard the *bouquet garni*. Taste and, if necessary, season with additional salt and pepper. Serve hot or at room temperature.

Alice Waters *Sustainable Agricultural Studies, The French Culinary Institute*

Green Garlic Pudding Soufflé

Serves 4 to 6

Green garlic, which resembles a scallion or very small leek, has a sweet pungency and a pure, clean flavor that is best highlighted by gentle simmering. Harvested just before the cloves have formed, it is available at farmer's markets in the early spring. This dish may be served as a simple first course or as a meatless entrée when paired with some lovely spring vegetables.

If green garlic is not available, you can substitute a mixture of leeks, scallions, and a few garlic cloves.

75 grams (5 tablespoons) unsalted butter
80 grams (¼ cup) all-purpose flour
350 milliliters (1½ cups) warm milk
3 grams (½ teaspoon) salt plus more to taste
2 sprigs fresh thyme
1 medium onion, chopped

230 grams (½ pound) green garlic, sliced
115 grams (4 ounces) grated Gruyère cheese
Pinch of cayenne pepper plus more to taste
Freshly ground pepper
3 large eggs, separated
75 milliliters (⅓ cup) heavy cream

Prepare your *mise en place.*

Make a *béchamel* by melting 45 grams (3 tablespoons) of the butter in a medium, heavy-bottomed saucepan over medium-low heat. Add the flour and cook, stirring constantly, for about 3 minutes or until the mixture is smooth but has not taken on any color. Whisking constantly, slowly add the warm milk, taking care that the mixture remains smooth. Add the 3 grams (½ teaspoon) salt along with the thyme sprigs. Cook, stirring frequently to keep the mixture from sticking to the bottom of the pan, for about 20 minutes or until the *béchamel* is of a medium thickness and lump-free. Remove from the heat and set aside to cool to room temperature. When cool, remove and discard the thyme.

Preheat the oven to 204°C (400°F).

Using 15 grams (1 tablespoon) of the remaining butter, lightly coat the interior of a 2-quart soufflé dish or six 8-ounce soufflé dishes or ceramic ramekins. Set aside.

Heat the remaining tablespoon of butter in a small saucepan. Add the onion and cook, stirring frequently, for about 5 minutes or until translucent but without any color. If necessary, add a tablespoon or two of water to keep the vegetables from taking on any color. Stir in the green garlic and salt to taste. Cook, stirring frequently, for about 7 minutes or until the vegetables are very soft and the moisture has evaporated. It is important that the vegetables do not take on any color, so add water as necessary to prevent this from occurring. Remove from the heat and set aside to cool.

When the garlic-onion mixture is cool, transfer it to the bowl of a food processor fitted with the metal blade. Process to a smooth purée. Stir the purée into the cooled *béchamel.*

Add the Gruyère, cayenne, and pepper to taste, stirring to blend well. Taste and, if necessary, adjust the seasoning with salt, pepper, and cayenne. The mixture should be highly seasoned. Whisk in the egg yolks. Set aside.

Place the egg whites in the bowl of an electric mixer fitted with the whip. Beat until soft peaks form. Fold the beaten egg whites into the garlic-onion mixture. When blended, spoon the mixture into the prepared dish. Place the dish in a baking pan with hot water to come halfway up the sides. Place in the oven and bake for about 30 minutes or until the soufflé is puffed and golden brown on top.

Carefully remove the pan from the oven and transfer the soufflé to a wire rack to cool for a couple of minutes. Using a paring knife, carefully run the knife around the edge of the soufflé, taking care not to puncture it. Invert the soufflé into the palm of your hand and then place it right side up in a baking dish. (The soufflé can now be held at room temperature for a couple of hours.)

When ready to serve, preheat the oven to 218°C (425°F).

Pour the cream over and around the soufflé. Place in the oven and bake for about 8 minutes or until the soufflé has puffed up again and the cream is bubbling hot. Remove from the oven and serve immediately with the hot cream spooned over the top.

Chef Dan Barber

*Chef/Co-Owner, Blue Hill Restaurant, New York City; Executive Chef/
Co-Owner, Blue Hill at Stone Barns, and Creative Director Stone Barns
Center for Food and Agriculture, Pocantico Hills, New York
The French Culinary Institute, Class of September 1994*

Pattypan Squash with Crabmeat and Soybean Vinaigrette

Serves 4

The basic techniques I learned at FCI have served me well as I have focused on cooking seasonally with local ingredients. Although I now grow the vegetables that I use in our kitchens, fresh pattypan squash and soybeans are available from specialty grocers, as are lemon *confit* and basil oil.

Four 5–7.5 centimeter (2- to 3-inch) round pattypan squash
115 grams (4 ounces) jumbo lump crabmeat, picked clean of
  all shell and cartilage
75 milliliters (¼ cup plus 1 tablespoon) white balsamic vinegar
5 grams (1 tablespoon) olive oil
5 grams (1 tablespoon) finely chopped fresh mint leaves
5 grams (1 tablespoon) finely chopped fresh tarragon
Coarse salt and freshly ground pepper

25 grams (1 tablepoon) puréed onion
120 milliliters (½ cup) basil oil
115 grams (4 ounces) fresh soybeans, blanched
50 grams (2 tablespoons) lemon *confit*
5 grams (1 tablespoon) finely chopped fresh
  flat-leaf parsley
5 grams (1 tablespoon) finely chopped fresh chives

45

Prepare your *mise en place*.

Using a *mandoline*, cut each squash into 6 very thin slices. Set aside.

In a small mixing bowl combine the crab, 15 milliliters (1 tablespoon) of the balsamic vinegar, the olive oil, mint, and tarragon. Season with salt and pepper to taste and toss to combine. Set aside.

Combine the remaining 60 milliliters (¼ cup) vinegar with the onion purée in a small mixing bowl. Using a whisk, slowly beat in the basil oil. When well com-

bined, fold in the soybeans, lemon *confit*, parsley, and chives. Season with salt and pepper to taste.

Place 3 slices of the squash in a small circle in the center of each of four luncheon plates. Spoon a heaping teaspoonful of the crab mixture on top of each slice and place a squash slice on top of each one. Spoon the soybean vinaigrette over the squash and around each plate. Serve immediately.

Previously published in Summer in New York, *by Alan Battman (Battman Studios, 2005).*

Chef Cheryl Slocum

Food Editor, Country Living *magazine*
The French Culinary Institute, Class of March 1995

Baked Acorn Squash Stuffed with Farro, Prunes, and Pears

Serves 4

This recipe is a classic use of seasonal ingredients paired in a way that balances the flavors of each one perfectly. It can be used as an entrée or a side dish.

2 small acorn squash
Coarse salt and freshly ground pepper to taste
8 dried plums (prunes), pitted and chopped
75 milliliters (5 tablespoons) Marsala wine
2 strips bacon
140 grams (⅓ pound) sweet Italian sausage meat
1 large onion, chopped
1 clove garlic, minced

115 grams (4 ounces) chopped celery
1 large crisp, sweet pear, peeled, cored, and chopped
3 grams (2 teaspoons) fresh thyme
Cayenne pepper to taste
340 grams (12 ounces) cooked farro or other hearty grain
Approximately 30 grams (2 tablespoons) unsalted
   butter, optional

Prepare your *mise en place*.

Using a sharp knife, carefully cut the squash in half crosswise. Scoop out and discard the seeds and stringy pulp. Season the flesh with salt and pepper to

taste. Place cut side down in a shallow baking dish. Add ½ cup water and cover the dish with aluminum foil. Place in the oven and bake for 35 minutes. Remove from the oven and invert the squash. Set aside. Do not turn the oven off.

While the squash is baking, prepare the prunes.

Combine the prunes with the wine in a small saucepan over medium-high heat. Bring to a boil and immediately remove from the heat. Set aside to steep for 20 minutes.

Place the bacon in a medium frying pan over medium-low heat. Fry, turning occasionally, for about 7 minutes or until crisp. Remove the bacon from the pan, pour the fat into a container, and set it aside. Drain the bacon on paper towels. Crumble the bacon into a small bowl and set aside.

Return the frying pan to medium heat. Add the sausage and fry for about 4 minutes or until just pink. Using a slotted spoon, remove the sausage from the pan and set aside on a small plate.

Drain any fat remaining in the frying pan. (If there are burned bits in the bottom of the pan, use a new pan.) Place 1 tablespoon of the reserved bacon fat in the pan and place over medium heat. Add the onion, garlic, and celery and sauté for about 5 minutes or until the onion is soft and translucent. Add the pear and thyme and season with cayenne, salt, and pepper to taste. If needed, add additional bacon fat to keep the mixture moist. Cook for another 3 minutes or just until the pear begins to soften.

Place the farro and prunes, along with their soaking liquid, in a mixing bowl. Add the vegetable mixture, along with the reserved bacon and sausage. Taste and, if necessary, add cayenne, salt, or pepper. Fill the center of each squash half with an equal portion of the farro mixture, heaping it into a mound. Dot the edges of the squash with butter, if using. Wrap the entire dish with aluminum foil and place it in the oven. Bake for about 30 minutes or until the squash is fork tender and the stuffing is hot.

Remove from the oven and serve.

Session 3

Stocks

Theory

About Stocks (*Fonds*)

Stocks (**fonds**) are the very core of classical French cooking. They are the indispensable ingredient in most of the classic sauces and soups, as well as the base for many refined culinary preparations. In his classic volume, *Le Répertoire de La Cuisine*, Louis Saulnier says that "it is impossible for the chef or cook to do excellent cooking if the '*fonds de cuisine*' are not made with the best ingredients. The better the ingredients employed, the better will be the final result. It is therefore false economy to neglect this very important part of the culinary arts."

Quite simply, a stock is an aromatic liquid made through a slow cooking process that melds the flavors of bones, trimmings, vegetables, and herbs into water until it has absorbed all of the nuances of these basic, inexpensive ingredients to make a flawless extract. Meat stocks are referred to as *fonds*, while fish and vegetable stocks are generally referred to as fumets. With the bones (or carcasses) of beef, veal, game, poultry, or fish as the base, the defining characteristics of a good stock are clarity and depth of flavor. To achieve this perfection, close attention must be paid to the quality and balance of the ingredients, the correct preparation of the individual ingredients, the ratio of liquid to solids, and the appropriate cooking time to ensure the proper balance of flavor required. You must remember that the quality of the stock will greatly affect the sauce or preparation of which it will be a component. Be well prepared when you make stock to ensure that you have the proper ingredients at hand and enough time to allow the liquid to achieve the desired depth of flavor. A stock cannot be hurried.

All stocks should be prepared in a large stockpot, a tall, heavy-bottomed pot made especially for this task. The pot is quite narrow so that the cooking surface is smaller than the depth, to allow for minimal evaporation during the long cooking process required for most stocks. An appropriately sized stockpot should have no less than a 10-quart volume. Whatever the size, the stockpot should be large enough to hold the required amount of solids and still allow for liquid to cover them by 2 inches, leaving at least another 2 to 3 inches at the top of the pot. If making a brown stock, you will also need a heavy roasting pan to brown the bones.

The most important aspect of any stock is its flavor. A strong, pure depth of flavor is best achieved through three elements: the quality of the basic ingredients, the ratio of solids to liquid, and the length of the cooking process.

> "Les fonds sont pour la cuisine, ce que les fondations sont pour la maison."
>
> *Auguste Escoffier*
>
> ("Stocks are to cooking what foundations are to a house.")

"When adding water to a cooking stock, add boiling water so the addition will not slow down the cooking process. The exception to this is when cooking stocks in huge stockpots overnight."

Chef Henri Viain

Quality of Ingredients

Bones and carcasses should be fresh and meaty; while the bones are the basis for the body of the stock, it is the meat that imparts the flavor required. The bones, particularly those from the joints with cartilage, add the gelatin that creates richness and density and lends a silken texture to the finished stock. The amount of bone should be greater than the meat. The vegetables and aromatics should be fresh and of the highest quality although for economy's sake, vegetable trimmings can also be used to add complexity to a finished stock. When making a white stock, the bones should be quickly blanched to remove excess blood that would result in a muddy color. Bones and vegetables should be cut to the size appropriate for the length of cooking—larger pieces for long-term cooking and smaller pieces for short-term cooking.

Ratio of Solids to Liquid

Just enough *cold* liquid should be added to the pot to cover the solids by no more than 2 inches. Additional liquid is required only when the amount falls below the top of the solids. Beginning with cold water and very slowly bringing it up to and maintaining a gentle simmer helps create a clean, clear, and tasty stock.

Cooking Time

The length of time a stock is to be cooked is determined by the base ingredient. Large, meaty raw beef or veal bones require a longer period of gentle simmering to extract all of the flavor contained in them than do smaller chicken bones. Brown stocks usually require longer cooking time (about 4 to 6 hours) than white stocks and vegetable stocks, which are generally fully flavored after about an hour. *Fumets* usually require no more than 30 minutes to maximize their flavor. It is a good idea to taste the stock regularly, as you want to stop the cooking process just when all the flavor has been extracted from the ingredients. If a stock is overcooked, it can turn bitter and saline and will not be salvageable; an undercooked stock will taste weak and watery. In the latter instance, if it has

already been strained and defatted, the stock may be returned to the heat, brought to a rapid boil, and reduced to intensify the flavor. However, when this rapid reduction is accomplished, the stock will almost always lose its fresh, clean flavor. (This is not to be confused with the reduction process used to achieve a highly reduced *demi-glace*.)

Although we talk about the depth of flavor of a quality stock, occasionally a light stock is called for that requires only clarity and the essence of the base ingredients. In this case, the base ingredients are never roasted and the cooking time is just enough to barely extract the required flavor. For instance, a whole chicken might be trussed and simmered in an aromatically flavored liquid just until the meat is cooked and a light broth has formed. *Tournéed* or baby vegetables may also be added to the pot. The chicken might then be cut into pieces and served, along with the vegetables, covered with broth.

Clarity of Stock

The clarity required to make a fine stock is dependent upon beginning with cold water, cooking at a slow, gentle simmer and continual, careful skimming of any fat, impurities, or scum that rise to the surface of the barely simmering liquid. This method not only assures that the base ingredients are cooked properly with every bit of flavor extracted, but also that any impurities in them will rise to the top to be removed during the cooking process. At about 82°C (180°F) the soluble proteins (albumins and globulins) in the bones begin to rise to the surface. At this point, if you allowed the liquid to come to a boil, these proteins would be incorporated back into the liquid. Following this slow cooking method precisely eliminates the possibility of a muddy stock. If a stock is allowed to boil or if it is stirred up from the bottom, the impurities in the meat and bones will dissolve into the liquid, making it cloudy, rather than rising to the surface so you can remove them.

Seasoning Stock

A stock is seasoned through the extraction of the flavors of the meat and bones as well as from the vegetables or aromatics used. Because stocks are used for so many culinary processes, they are almost never seasoned with salt and pepper. The long simmering process required for most stocks would cause these seasonings to become highly concentrated and mask the flavor of the base ingredients. The exception to this rule is vegetable stock, which is generally cooked for such a short period of time that the salt heightens the flavor of the vegetables rather than obscuring it.

Stock-Making Terminology

Bouquet garni: A mixture of herbs used to flavor stocks as well as various other culinary preparations. Unless otherwise stated, it consists of fresh thyme sprigs, parsley stems, bay leaf, and a few peppercorns that are tied together in leek greens or cheesecloth.

Deglaze (*déglacer*): To loosen *sucs* (see below) from the bottom of a roasting pan using a liquid such as water, stock, vinegar, wine, or juice.

Dégorger: To soak bones to remove blood to help produce a clearer, cleaner stock.

Degrease (*dégraisser*): To remove grease from the top of a stock or sauce with a ladle or metal spoon while it is still cooking or when it is cooling.

Mirepoix: Equal parts of uniformly cut pieces of onions and carrots or a mixture of 50 percent onions, 25 percent carrots, and 25 percent celery or equal portions of onions, carrots, and celery used to flavor stocks and sauces. (Also see page 26.)

Moisten (*mouiller*): To add water to bones and aromatics to produce a stock.

Mother sauces (*sauces mères*): The group of basic sauces of the classical French repertoire, many of which have a stock as their base.

Pass (*passer*): To strain or pass a stock through a *chinois* to remove the solids, which are then discarded.

Plug (*tamponner*): To dot the top of a sauce with butter to prevent the formation of a film (or skin) over the top.

Reduce (*réduir*): To boil a stock or sauce until the volume is reduced.

Remoisten (*remouillage*): To add water to cooked bones to extract their maximum flavor.

Roast (*rôtir*): To cook in direct, radiant heat in the dry atmosphere of a preheated oven. For stocks, this method is applied to bones and, sometimes, *mirepoix* cooked in a small amount of fat to keep it from drying out.

Simmer (*frémir*): To cook gently so that bubbles just break the surface.

Skim (*écumer*): To remove coagulated blood and impurities from a stock through skimming them off the top with a metal spoon or skimmer.

Sucs: Caramelized proteins that form on the bottom of a pan as ingredients are browned.

Sweat (*suer*): To cook ingredients, usually vegetables, in a small amount of fat, often covered by parchment paper or a lid, so that the ingredients cook in their own juices without taking on any color.

Winnow (*vanner*): To stir a stock or sauce, either while it is cooking or in an ice bath, to facilitate cooking or cooling.

Deans' Tips

"When soaking chicken bones to expel impurities, always use ice water to prevent multiplication of any bacteria."
Dean Alain Sailhac

"Always cool down a stock as quickly as possible. Even when I place the stock in an ice-water bath, I find that adding a tightly sealed bag of ice to the pot helps speed the cooling even more. Never put hot stock in the refrigerator to cool—not only will it immediately lower the refrigerator temperature, but cooling in this manner is ineffective, inefficient, and unsafe."
Dean Alain Sailhac

Guidelines for Stock Preparation

○ Use the highest quality ingredients.
○ Trim excess fat from meat and bones.
○ Always blanch beef and veal bones when making white stocks to remove albumins and eliminate strong flavors from the finished stock. This process is optional when making white chicken stock.

○ Never blanch fish bones when making a *fumet*; wash them only. Blanching will remove the gelatinous material that imparts rich flavor.
○ To better extract flavor and to preserve clarity, begin the cooking process with cold water.

- The higher the ratio of solids to liquid, the more intense the flavor.
- Simmer stocks slowly and uncovered. Never hurry a stock.
- Never allow a stock to come to a boil or it will become cloudy. Bubbles should barely break on the surface of the simmering stock.
- Do not stir up from the bottom of the pot during cooking as this process may also cloud the stock.
- To achieve the clearest stock possible, the surface should be skimmed carefully and degreased frequently during the cooking process. Always use a clean ladle so that you do not return fat or impurities to the pot.

- Taste throughout the cooking process.
- Stop the cooking process when the ingredients have released their maximum flavor.
- When cooking is complete, stocks should be poured out carefully and passed through a *chinois* into a clean container.
- *Fumets* should be ladled out and passed through a *chinois*.
- All stocks and *fumets* should be cooled quickly in an ice bath (see page 54) to halt bacteria growth and prevent spoilage.
- A properly prepared stock will be bright and clear.

Basic Stocks

White Stock (*Fonds blancs*)

Classically, a white stock is created when the principal elements (the bones) are placed in cold water, brought quickly to a boil, and immediately drained. This process of blanching eliminates excess blood and albumins so that a clearer, cleaner-tasting stock will result. The blanched bones are then combined with vegetables, a *bouquet garni*, and water. White stocks are made with either veal bones (*fond de veau blanc* or *fond blanc* or white veal stock), chicken bones (fond de volaille blanc or white chicken stock) or fish bones (*fumet de poisson* or fish stock). Carrots, onions, leeks, celery, and a *bouquet garni* are added to veal and chicken stocks; when making a fish *fumet*, the fish bones are not blanched nor are carrots and celery added as aromatic elements as they will add a defined flavor and color the stock slightly. In the contemporary kitchen, small chicken bones are often used to make a white stock without blanching.

   When making white sauces such as *béchamel*, milk, referred to as a natural stock, is used.

Dean's Tip

"The basic stocks and sauces are the tools with which you can create and interpret your own sauces."

Dean Jacques Pépin

Formulas for White Stocks
(*Fonds Blancs*) and *Fumets*

White Stock

CLEAN AND *DÉGORGE* BONES

BLANCH AND DRAIN BONES
(optional with small chicken bones)

COVER BONES WITH COLD WATER

BRING TO A SIMMER AND SKIM

ADD *MIREPOIX* AND *BOUQUET GARNI*

SIMMER AND SKIM FREQUENTLY
(Simmer white chicken stock for 2 hours)
(Simmer white veal stock for 4 to 6 hours)

DRAIN THROUGH FINE *CHINOIS*,
DISCARDING SOLIDS

Fumet

CLEAN AND *DÉGORGE* BONES

SWEAT VEGETABLES

ADD BONES AND CONTINUE TO SWEAT
WITHOUT ADDING COLORING

COVER WITH COLD WATER

ADD *BOUQUET GARNI*

SIMMER AND SKIM FREQUENTLY
(for 30 minutes only)

DRAIN THROUGH FINE *CHINOIS*,
DISCARDING SOLIDS

White veal stock (*fond de veau blanc*)
blanched veal bones, aromatics (carrots, onions,
leeks, celery, *bouquet garni*)

White chicken stock (*fond de volaille blanc*)
blanched chicken bones, aromatics (carrots, onions,
leeks, celery, *bouquet garni*)*

Fish stock (*fumet de poisson*)
Fish bones, onions, leeks, *bouquet garni*

Milk (natural stock)**
milk

* Classically, chicken bones are blanched but it is no
longer felt to be necessary to produce a clean,
clear stock.

**Milk, rather than a stock, is the base for white
sauces such as *béchamel*

Demonstration

Fond de Volaille Blanc (White Chicken Stock)
Fond de Veau Blanc (White Veal Stock)

Makes 5 liters (5⅓ quarts)
Estimated time to complete: About 4 hours

Chef's Tip

"Adding an onion pierced with a
whole clove (oignon clouté) *will add a*
very special flavor to white meat stocks."
Chef Sixto Alonso

Ingredients

3 kilograms (6½ pounds) chicken bones
  (or veal bones, see note)
6 liters (6 quarts, 11 ounces) cold water
250 grams (8¾ ounces) carrots, *mirepoix*
250 grams (8¾ ounces) onions, *mirepoix*
100 grams (3½ ounces) celery, *mirepoix*
2 cloves garlic, peeled and crushed
Bouquet garni

Equipment

Boning knife
Stockpot
Skimmer
Fine *chinois*
Storage container or saucepan
Ice-water bath

Note

The procedure for a white veal stock (*fond de veau blanc*) is the same as above except that the veal bones are first blanched and the cooking time is increased to 4 to 6 hours.

Prepare your *mise en place*.

Using a boning knife, trim the bones of all fat and skin. Place the bones under cold running water to rinse off any remaining fat particles.

Place the bones in a stockpot and cover them with cold water by 2 inches. Place the pot over medium heat and bring to just a simmer.

Skim off any foam that forms on top. Lower the heat and add the carrots, onions, celery, garlic, and *bouquet garni*.

Return to a simmer and cook for about 2 hours or until a rich, well-flavored liquid has formed.

Remove the pot from the heat and strain the stock through a fine *chinois* into a clean pan or storage container. Place the container in an ice-water bath and, skimming frequently, allow to cool for about 30 minutes or until the stock is well chilled. If not using immediately, cover and refrigerate or freeze.

Demonstration

Fumet de Poisson (Fish Stock or *Fumet*)

Makes 5 liters (5⅓ quarts)
Estimated time to complete: 1 hour

Ingredients	Equipment
2 kilograms (4½ pounds) fish bones from white-fleshed, nonoily fish such as sole, turbot, flounder, or whiting	*Rondeau*
	Skimmer
	Ladle
	Fine *chinois*
125 grams (½ cup plus 1 tablespoon) unsalted butter	Storage container or saucepan
250 grams (8¾ ounces) leeks, *émincé* white part with a bit of green	Ice-water bath
125 grams (4⅓ ounces) onions, *émincé*	
5 liters (5 quarts, 10 ounces) cold water	
300 milliliters (1¼ cups) dry white wine	
Bouquet garni	

Add the reserved fish bones and stir to allow the bones to begin to sweat some moisture. This allows the layer of protein on the bones to coagulate, which will keep the stock clear.

Add the water, wine, and *bouquet garni* and bring to a gentle simmer. Cook, skimming frequently, for about 30 minutes or until a clear, aromatic broth has formed.

Prepare your *mise en place*.

If the gills are still attached to the fish bones, remove them as they will muddy the *fumet*. Wash the bones in several rinsings of cold water to remove all traces of blood. Set aside.

Place the butter in a *rondeau* over medium heat. Add the leeks and onions and sauté, allowing the vegetables to sweat their liquid without browning, for about 4 minutes.

Remove the pot from the heat and carefully ladle the liquid through a fine *chinois* into a clean pot or container, discarding the solids.

Place the pot containing the hot, strained *fumet* in an ice-water bath and allow to cool rapidly, skimming off any fat or impurities that float to the surface.

If not using immediately, cover and refrigerate or freeze.

Brown Stocks (*Fonds Bruns*)

A brown stock is created when the principal elements have been evenly cooked to an all-over brown color in the oven or on the stovetop. Browning not only adds a deep color, hence the name, but also an intensely rich flavor to the finished stock. Brown stocks are made with either veal bones (veal stock or *fond de veau brun*), beef bones (beef stock or *braisière*), game bones (game stock or *fond de gibier*), or chicken bones (chicken stock or *fond de volaille brun*) with the addition of carrots, onions, celery, tomatoes, and garlic as well as a *bouquet garni*. The amount of vegetables used should be approximately 10 to 20 percent of the total weight of the meaty bones. The vegetables are added to the roasting pan shortly before the bones are completely browned so that they have just enough time to brown lightly without burning. When the bones to be used for stock are cut into the classically designated 5-centimeter (2-inch) pieces, the cooking time for a rich brown stock can be shortened to 3 to 5 hours.

Formulas for Brown Stocks
(*Fonds Bruns*)

Brown Stocks (*Fonds Bruns*)	Brown Stocks (*Fonds Bruns*)

Brown Stocks (*Fonds Bruns*)

PREHEAT OVEN

CLEAN AND, IF NECESSARY, BREAK BONES

BROWN BONES IN ROASTING PAN IN OVEN

ADD *MIREPOIX*

BROWN *MIREPOIX*

TRANSFER BONES AND *MIREPOIX* TO STOCKPOT

REMOVE ALL FAT FROM THE ROASTING PAN

DEGLAZE *SUCS*

COVER BROWNED INGREDIENTS WITH COLD WATER

SIMMER AND SKIM

ADD *BOUQUET GARNI* AND TOMATOES

SIMMER, SKIM, AND DEFAT FREQUENTLY
(Simmer brown chicken stock 4 hours)
(Simmer brown veal or game stock 6 to 8 hours)
(Simmer beef stock 8 to 12 hours)

DRAIN THROUGH FINE *CHINOIS*, DISCARDING SOLIDS

Brown Stocks (*Fonds Bruns*)

Brown veal stock (*fond de veau brun*)
Roasted veal bones, carrots, celery, onions, tomatoes, tomato paste, garlic, *bouquet garni*

Brown beef and veal stock (*braisière*)
Roasted beef or beef and veal bones, carrots, onions, tomatoes, celery, tomato paste, garlic, *bouquet garni*

Brown chicken stock (*fond de volaille brun*)
Roasted chicken bones, carrots, celery, onions, tomatoes, garlic, *bouquet garni*

Brown game stock (*fond de gibier*)
Roasted game bones, carrots, celery, onions, tomatoes, tomato paste, garlic, *bouquet garni*

Dean's Tip

"A chef who ignores stocks or who doesn't pay attention to the processes necessary to make them right will never be a great cook."

Dean André Soltner

Demonstration

Fond de Veau Brun (Brown Veal Stock)

Braisière (Beef Stock)

Makes 5 liters (5⅓ quarts)
Estimated time to complete: 10 to 13 hours

Ingredients

5 kilograms (11 pounds) veal or beef bones
Approximately 60 milliliters (¼ cup) vegetable oil
6 liters (6 quarts, 11 ounces) water
500 grams (1⅛ pounds) onions, *mirepoix*
250 grams (8¾ ounces) carrots, *mirepoix*
250 grams (8¾ ounces) celery, *mirepoix*
2 cloves garlic, peeled and crushed
250 grams (8¾ ounces) chopped tomatoes
30 grams (1 ounce) tomato paste
Bouquet garni

Equipment

Roasting pan
Wooden spoon
Stockpot
Skimmer
Storage container or saucepan
Ice-water bath

Dean's Tip

"Make sure that the bones are fresh and not smelly. If they have an unpleasant odor, place them in a large saucepan, cover with cold water and bring to a boil. Remove from the heat, drain, and rinse under cold, running water. Then proceed with the recipe."

Dean Jacques Pépin

Prepare your *mise en place.*

Preheat the oven to 204°C (400°F).

Using your hands, lightly coat the bones with vegetable oil. Place the bones in a roasting pan. Roast, turning and stirring occasionally, for about 30 minutes or until the bones begin to color and caramelize.

Add the onions, carrots, and celery and continue to roast, stirring occasionally, for an additional 15 minutes or until the bones and vegetables are nicely browned.

Remove the pan from the oven and transfer the bones and vegetables to a large stockpot. Add the water (6

Note

Beef stock (*braisière*) is prepared in this exact manner except that beef bones (with the addition of a few veal bones, if desired) are used as the base.

liters or enough to cover the solids by 2 inches), and place over medium-high heat.

Remove all the fat from the roasting pan and then place the pan on top of the stove over medium heat. Add just enough water to moisten the bottom and, stirring constantly with a wooden spoon, scrape all the *sucs* off the bottom of the pan. Transfer this mixture to the stockpot.

When the stock comes to a bare simmer, lower the heat to maintain a gentle simmer and begin skimming off any fat, foam, or impurities that rise to the surface.

Add the garlic, tomatoes, tomato paste, and *bouquet garni*. Continue to simmer, skimming often, for 8 to

12 hours, or until all the flavor has been extracted from the solids, and an intensely flavored stock is achieved. Add cold water as necessary to keep the solids covered with liquid throughout the long cooking process.

Remove from the heat and carefully strain through a fine *chinois* into a clean pot or container, discarding the solids.

Place the container of hot, strained stock in an ice-water bath and allow it to cool rapidly. Skim off any fat or impurities that float to the surface.

If not using immediately, cover and refrigerate or freeze.

General Information on Glazes

Glazes (*glaces*) are strained stocks that have been reduced to about one-tenth their original volume to reach a syrupy consistency and an extreme depth of flavor. This savory concentration is achieved by slowly simmering a finished stock over a prolonged period of time, resulting in substantial evaporation. The purity of the glaze is ensured by careful skimming throughout the cooking process. Since the flavor is deeply intensified by this reduction, it is absolutely imperative that you begin with a carefully prepared and delicately flavored stock. Any error in the balance of the base flavor will become even more evident in the finished glaze.

Glazes are used to:

○ Reinforce the character of a sauce if the stock used to make it was weak.

○ Add nuance to a sauce.

○ Serve as a sauce with added butter and cream, most particularly with a fish glaze.

When reduced, these stocks produce the corresponding glazes:

○ Brown stock
meat glaze (*glace de viande*)

○ Poultry stock
poultry glaze (*glace de volaille*)

○ Game stock
game glaze (*glace de gibier*)

○ Fish *fumet*
fish glaze (*glace de poisson*)

A ***demi-glace*** is a basic sauce made from brown stock that is used in the preparation of derivative sauces. Classically, it is a **basic brown sauce (*sauce espagnole*)** refined and reinforced with a meat glaze. In fact, Escoffier defined it as "*sauce espagnole* taken to the limit of perfection." However, since the mid-twentieth century, the term *demi-glace* most often refers to a veal stock that has been reduced by approximately half or until quite thick, shiny, and full-flavored.

Session 4

Sauces

Theory

General Information on Sauces

Well-prepared sauces, a crucial component of French cuisine, are the primary reason for its renown. In the classical repertoire, sauces are defined as any liquid that intensifies, adds moisture to, and/or enriches the dish for which it is a component. A sauce is generally begun with a flavor base such as a *mirepoix* or other aromatic vegetables, herbs, spices, or other highly flavored ingredients sautéed in fat such as butter or bacon. These aromatics are then cooked with the designated stock, as well as any additional flavoring enhancements, for a prescribed period of time, skimmed frequently, and strained. Almost all of the classic sauces are based on stocks that have been thickened with some kind of *liaison* (binding agent) and finished with wine, liqueur, herbs, spices, or other aromatic elements used to enhance the base flavor.

Creating perfectly seasoned and well-balanced sauces is often considered to be the most difficult task in the kitchen. A *saucier* must have a strong culinary background and a well-developed palate to fully realize the task at hand. In addition, it is necessary to be conscious of the ultimate role of the sauce so that it will complement and harmonize with, but never overwhelm, the dish it accompanies. The sheen, texture, and color of a sauce are equally important elements to its success.

Antonin Carême, the esteemed and innovative French chef, codified all the sauces in the nineteenth century. The primary codified sauces of the French repertoire are referred to as **mother sauces (*sauce mères*)** because they are the foundation from which all other sauces rise. These sauces are **sauce béchamel** (white sauce, milk or cream based), **velouté** (white sauce, veal stock based), **sauce espagnole** (basic brown sauce), and **sauce hollandaise** (*sabayon* based, see page 82). Once mastered, all other sauces in French cooking can be made with the addition of the components necessary to offer the seasoning, flavor, or accent required to define the sauce.

Some very specific tools are helpful in creating well-balanced sauces. A two- to three-quart heavy-bottomed saucepan is essential; one with sloping sides will speed the process of reducing the base liquid. In addition, a skimmer, a whisk, and a wooden spoon will all facilitate sauce making. A *chinois* (see page 15) is necessary when straining a sauce and either a double boiler or *bain-marie* is useful for holding sauces for service.

Liaisons — The Binding Agents

The purpose of a *liaison* is to thicken a liquid in order to add body and thickness to the finished product. It is also often referred to as a binder or binding agent and a sauce thus thickened is described as "bound." There

Dean's Tip

"A sauce is a complement to a dish and should not dominate it."

Dean Jacques Pépin

Chef's Tip

"When thickening a sauce, always remember to bring it to a boil to activate the starch."

Chef Candy Argondizza

are several different binding agents used in classical cooking, as well as a number of methods employed to incorporate them into the liquid. A good rule to keep in mind is:

Basic Stock + Binding Agent = Basic Sauce

Among the binding agents used to create a liaison are flour and other starches, cream, mustard, egg yolk, vegetable purée, tapioca, and butter.

White Flour

Flour is used as a binder in *roux, beurre maniés,* and as a dry ingredient to *singer.*

A **roux** is made by cooking together flour and fat, usually butter, usually equal portions by weight. The fat is first melted and then the sifted flour is stirred into it and heated until the flour loses its raw taste and the mixture thickens. The cooking time is dependent on the color desired for the final product: a *roux blanc* (white roux) is cooked for the shortest period of time, about 3 to 5 minutes, and will yield a pale sauce; *roux blond* (light roux) is cooked somewhat longer, about 6 to 7 minutes, and will produce a golden sauce; and *roux brun* (brown roux) is cooked until the mixture has taken on a rich brown color, about 8 to 12 minutes, so that the resulting sauce is also deeply colored.

Beurre manié is simply softened butter that has been kneaded into flour until well incorporated. The mixture, usually composed of equal amounts of butter and flour, is then formed into small pieces or pea-size balls that can be whisked into a simmering sauce or liquid just before the end of the cooking period to thicken it slightly. When adding *beurre manié* to a sauce, the mixture is never brought to a boil, as boiling can cause the sauce to separate. Since the sauce will not be cooked for any length of time, it is suggested that only a small amount of the thickener be used or the finished sauce will taste of uncooked flour.

A dry flour-based *liaison* is made by a process known as **singer.** The liquid to be thickened is sprinkled with sifted flour and then either sautéed or placed in the oven for 1 to 2 minutes. It is then mois-tened further and cooked for the time specified in the recipe.

Flour-based *liaisons* can also made by roasting flour in a preheated oven until lightly colored and then using it to *singer* or as a base for a *roux brun.*

Other Starches: Potato Starch, Cornstarch, Arrowroot, Rice Flour

A **slurry** is created by whisking any of these starches into a cold liquid such as stock, water, or Madeira wine until dissolved. The slurry is poured into the boiling liquid in a slow, thin stream, whisking constantly to keep lumps from forming. The liquid is then cooked, whisking constantly, until thickened and the raw starch taste has been cooked out.

Double Cream

Heavy (or whipping) cream is simmered and reduced by half. A wide pan is useful when reducing cream, as it heats faster and keeps the cream from scorching around the edges, which would discolor it. Whisking about every 5 minutes also helps to keep the cream homogenous and will prevent scorching. It cannot be reduced further or it will break and be rendered useless. The reduced cream is then whisked into a hot liquid.

Mustard

French Dijon mustard has a slight thickening effect. It should always be vigorously beaten into a sauce after the sauce has been removed from the heat. The sauce must not be boiled again or it will break and be rendered unusable.

Egg Yolk

To use egg yolk as a binding agent, first temper it (warm and blend slightly by whisking a small amount of hot liquid into the yolks to prevent them from scrambling when added to hot liquid or sauce) with a bit of the hot sauce to which it will be added; then, whisking vigorously, incorporate the tempered egg yolk into the hot sauce. Do not return the sauce to a boil or the yolk will curdle.

Vegetable Purées

Any cooked vegetable or combination of vegetables that is a component of a sauce (or whose flavor would make a nice addition to a sauce), may be puréed and added to a sauce as a thickener.

Tapioca

Pearl tapioca can be used to add consistency to a sauce, but if the sauce is left to sit for any period of time, the thickening will continue and, perhaps, render the sauce unusable.

Butter

Butter is often used to finish a sauce by adding a silky, velvetlike thickness. It is infrequently used as a primary thickener.

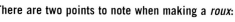

Technique
General Principles of the *Roux*

When making a *roux*, it is important that the flour and fat be whisked constantly and cooked slowly over very low heat to ensure even texture. If the *roux* is cooked too fast, the starch in the flour will become grainy and render the *roux* unusable. When adding the liquid to the *roux*, it is best to whisk warm liquid into the warm *roux* to avoid the formation of lumps. If lumps are formed, strain the sauce through a fine *chinois* before completing the recipe.

There are two points to note when making a *roux*:

○ The flour particles contain starch that will swell and absorb the fat evenly at low heat. However, if the heat is too high, the starch will shrink and its activity will be inhibited, destroying the effectiveness of the *liaison*.

○ A darker *roux* will add the deepest flavor to a sauce, but the longer cooking period required to achieve the desired color yields less thickening strength due to the breakdown of the starch, and renders the fat less digestible.

The basic method for making a *roux* is as follows:

1. Melt the butter or other fat over medium heat. (The pan used will depend on the amount of liquid to be thickened.)

2. Add the flour.

3. Lower the heat and cook, stirring constantly, for the prescribed amount of time for the desired *roux*: 3 to 5 minutes for a *roux blanc*; 6 to 7 minutes for a *roux blond*; and 8 to 12 minutes for a *roux brun*.

4. Add the liquid to be thickened and cook until the appropriate degree of thickness and fully realized taste have been achieved.

Chemical Composition of a *Roux*

Butter	Flour
Minimum fatty material: 80%	Starch: 60–72%
Maximum water: 18%	Water: 11–12%
Soluble elements: 2%	Gluten: 8–12%
Sugar: 1–2%	Fatty materials: 1.2–1.4%
	Minerals: .45–.6%
	Vitamin B

Demonstration

Sauce Espagnole (Basic Brown Sauce)

Makes 2 liters (2¼ quarts)
Estimated time to complete: 1 hour, 30 minutes

Dean's Tip

"When I was an apprentice, Chef taught us how to toast flour before making the roux. The color of the sauce was then very intense but sometimes the burned flour gave a bitter taste to the final sauce. Plus, it was necessary not to forget the flour in the oven."

Dean Alain Sailhac

Chef's Tip

"The old kitchen adage of combining cold stock with hot roux or hot stock with cold roux will improve the dispersion of the flour granules through the liquid. Always remember to allow your sauce plenty of time to cook out any raw flour taste in the roux."

Chef Dominick Cerrone

Ingredients

3 liters (3 quarts, 6 ounces) Beef Stock
  or Veal Stock (see page 57)
35 grams (2 tablespoons plus 1 teaspoon) unsalted butter
75 grams (2¾ ounces) bacon, cut into *lardons* (see note)
150 grams (5¼ ounces) carrots, *mirepoix*
150 grams (5¼ ounces) onions, *mirepoix*
40 grams (1½ ounces) all-purpose flour
250 grams (8¾ ounces) tomatoes *concassé*
50 grams (1¼ ounces) tomato paste
1 clove garlic, peeled and crushed
1 sprig fresh tarragon
Mushroom stems and trimmings, optional

Equipment

Russe
Skimmer
Rondeau
Wooden spoon
Whisk
Chinois
Bain-marie
Ice-water bath, optional
Storage container, optional

Prepare your *mise en place.*

Place the beef or veal stock in a heavy *russe* over medium-high heat. Bring to a boil and skim off any particles or foam that rises to the top. Remove from the heat and set aside to cool.

Place about 5 grams (1 teaspoon) of the butter in a *rondeau* over medium heat. Add the bacon and sauté for about 5 minutes or until the bacon has rendered all of its fat and is lightly browned.

Add the carrots and onions and continue to sauté for about 4 minutes or until the vegetables begin to take on some color.

Add the remaining butter and sauté until melted.

Sprinkle the mixture with the flour (*singer*) and stir vigorously with a wooden spoon for about 3 minutes or until the flour begins to brown.

Add the reserved stock and whisk vigorously to keep lumps from forming. Bring to a simmer and then add the tomatoes and tomato paste, whisking to combine.

Add the garlic and tarragon along with any mushroom trimmings you have available and again bring to a simmer. Lower the heat and cook at a low simmer, skimming frequently, for 1 hour.

Remove from the heat and strain the sauce through a *chinois* into a *bain-marie* to keep warm until ready for service. If not serving immediately, place in an ice-water bath to chill quickly.

When cool, transfer to a storage container, cover, and refrigerate until ready to use.

Note

Lardons are slab bacon cut into cubes 1 centimeter (⅜ inch) thick and then into pieces about 1 centimeter (⅜ inch) wide and then fried until browned.

Dean's Tip

"A well-made sauce espagnole *should be as clear as a* fond lié. *If the sauce is cooled long enough after it has been combined with the* roux, *only the protein element of the flour will remain."*
Dean Jacques Pépin

Demonstration

Sauce Tomate (Tomato Sauce)

Makes 1.5 liters (1¼ quarts)

Estimated time to complete: 1 hour, 30 minutes

Ingredients	Equipment
1 liter (1 quart, 2 ounces) White Veal Stock	*Russe*
or White Chicken Stock (see page 53)	Skimmer
20 grams (1 tablespoon plus 1teaspoon)	*Rondeau*
unsalted butter	Wooden spoon
50 grams (1¾ounces) bacon, cut into *lardons*	Whisk
60 grams (2 ounces) onions, *mirepoix*	Food mill
60 grams (2 ounces) carrots, *mirepoix*	*Bain-marie*
30 grams (1 ounce) celery *mirepoix*	Ice-water bath, optional
20 grams (¾ounce) all-purpose flour	Storage container, optional
230 grams (8 ounces) fresh or canned	
Italian plum tomatoes, *concassé*	
60 grams (2 ounces) tomato paste	
2 cloves garlic, peeled and crushed	
Bouquet garni	
Coarse salt to taste	
Sugar, optional (see note)	

Prepare your *mise en place.*

Place the stock in a heavy *russe* over medium-high heat. Bring to a boil and skim off any particles or foam that rises to the top. Remove from the heat and set aside to cool.

Place about 5 grams (1 teaspoon) of the butter in a *rondeau* over low heat. Add the bacon and sauté for about 5 minutes or until it has rendered all its fat and is lightly browned.

Add the remaining butter along with the onions, carrots, and celery and sauté for about 4 minutes or until the vegetables are soft.

Sprinkle the mixture with the flour (*singer*) and cook, stirring constantly with a whisk, for 2 minutes without allowing the flour to color.

Immediately add the reserved stock and bring to a simmer, whisking constantly. Add the tomatoes and tomato paste and whisk to combine. Then, add the garlic and *bouquet garni* along with salt and sugar to taste. Bring to a simmer. Lower the heat and cook at a low simmer, skimming frequently, for 1 hour.

Remove from the heat and pass the sauce through a food mill into a *bain-marie* to keep warm until ready for service. Taste and, if necessary, adjust the seasoning with additional salt and sugar.

If not using immediately, place in an ice-water bath to chill quickly. When cool, transfer to a storage container, cover, and refrigerate until ready to use.

Note

When the flavor of tomatoes is not fresh and bright, a bit of sugar is often added to liven up the taste in cooked sauces.

Demonstration

Fond de Veau Lié (Thickened Veal Stock)

Makes 2 liters (2 quarts, 4 ounces)
Estimated time to complete: 30 minutes

Ingredients	Equipment
2.5 liters (2 quarts, 21 ounces) Brown Veal Stock (see page 57)	*Russe*
	Skimmer
7 grams (2 tablespoons) mushroom trimmings	Whisk
1 gram (1 scant teaspoon) chopped fresh chervil	Small bowl
30 to 60 grams (1 to 2 ounces) cornstarch or arrowroot, as needed	*Chinois*
	Bain-marie
100 milliliters (7 tablespoons) Madeira wine	Ice-water bath, optional
	Storage container, optional

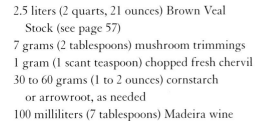

Prepare your *mise en place.*

Place the stock in a heavy *russe* over medium-high heat.

Add the mushroom trimmings and chervil and bring to a boil.

Lower the heat and cook at a gentle simmer, skimming frequently, for about 20 minutes or until reduced by one quarter.

Whisk the wine into the cornstarch the in a small bowl, beating to form a slurry.

Pour half of the slurry in a thin stream into the simmering stock, whisking constantly. Because the starch will not thicken until it comes to a boil, immediately raise the heat and bring to a boil, whisking constantly. Test for consistency. If the mixture has not reached a smooth sauce consistency, whisk in a bit more of the slurry. Add the slurry slowly to avoid overthickening the sauce.

When the desired consistency has been reached, boil the sauce for 5 minutes, stirring and skimming frequently.

Remove from the heat and strain through a *chinois* into a *bain-marie* to keep warm until ready for service.

If not using immediately, place in an ice-water bath to chill quickly. When cool, transfer to a storage container, cover, and refrigerate until ready to use.

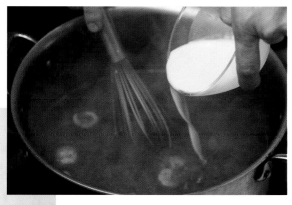

Demonstration

Sauce Béchamel (Béchamel Sauce)

Makes about 700 milliliters (3 cups)
Estimated time to complete: 30 minutes

Ingredients	Equipment
60 grams (4 tablepoons) unsalted butter	*2 russes*
50 grams (1¾ ounces) all-purpose flour	Wooden spoon
750 milliliters (3¼ cups) whole milk	Whisk
Coarse salt to taste	*Chinois*
Cayenne pepper to taste	*Bain-marie*
Freshly ground nutmeg to taste	Ice-water bath, optional
	Storage container, optional

Prepare your *mise en place*.

Place 50 grams (3 tablespoons plus 1 teaspoon) of the butter in a medium *russe* over low heat. When melted, slowly add the flour, stirring constantly with a wooden spoon. Cook, stirring constantly, for about 2 minutes or until the *roux* becomes frothy and a mass of bubbles. Immediately remove from the heat and set aside.

Place the milk in another *russe* over medium heat and bring to just a boil. Immediately remove the milk from the heat and slowly add it to the *roux*, whisking constantly.

Return the pan to medium heat and bring the sauce to a boil so that the starch achieves full thickening power.

Lower the heat, season with salt, cayenne, and nutmeg to taste, and simmer, whisking constantly, for 10 to 15 minutes or until the sauce has thickened and no raw flour taste remains.

Remove from the heat and strain through a *chinois* into a *bain-marie* to keep warm until ready for service.

Using the remaining 10 grams (2 teaspoons) of butter, dot the surface of the sauce to prevent a skin from forming over the top (*tamponner*).

If not using immediately, place in an ice-water bath to chill quickly. When cool, transfer to a storage container, cover, and refrigerate until ready to use.

Demonstration

Sauce Bordelaise (Bordelaise Sauce)

Makes about 240 milliliters (1 cup)
Estimated time to complete: 30 minutes

Ingredients	Equipment
40 grams (1½ ounces) bone marrow	2 medium saucepans
270 milliliters (1 cup plus 2 tablespoons) red wine	Sieve
40 grams (1½ ounces) shallots, *ciselé*	Ice-water bath
3 grams (2 teaspoons) cracked peppercorns	Chef's knife
1 sprig fresh thyme	*Russe*
1 bay leaf	*Chinois*
270 milliliters (1 cup plus 2 tablespoons) Basic Brown Sauce (see page 65)	
Coarse salt and freshly ground pepper to taste	
Few drops fresh lemon juice	
10 grams (2 teaspoons) unsalted butter	

Prepare your *mise en place.*

Bring a medium saucepan of water to boil over high heat. Add the marrow and poach for about 15 seconds or just until set.

Immediately remove from the heat, drain, and refresh the marrow in an ice-water bath. Pat dry and, using a chef's knife, cut into *macédoine* (see page 26). Set aside.

Combine the wine, shallots, peppercorns, thyme, and bay leaf in a heavy *russe* over medium heat. Cook without stirring for about 15 minutes or until reduced to about 60 milliliters (¼ cup).

Add the brown sauce and bring to a boil. Lower the heat and simmer for 10 minutes. Remove from the heat and pass through a *chinois* into a clean saucepan. Season the sauce with salt, pepper, and lemon juice (note that the lemon is being used to *accentuate* the flavor, not dominate it).

Place the sauce over medium heat and bring to a simmer.

Immediately remove from the heat and gently swirl in the butter (*monter au beurre*, see note), a bit at a time. Stir in the reserved marrow, mixing until well blended. Remove from the heat and use immediately.

Note

Monter au beurre means to swirl small lumps of cold butter into a warm sauce just at the end of the cooking process. When incorporated properly, the butter thickens as it becomes suspended in the sauce.

Dean's Tip

"A robust, fruity red wine that is fairly young is best for red wine sauces. An old wine loses its color and flavor when exposed to high heat."

Dean Jacques Pépin

Demonstration

Sauce Chasseur (Hunter Sauce)

Makes about 350 milliliters (1½ cups)
Estimated time to complete: 30 minutes

Ingredients	Equipment
15 grams (1 tablespoon) unsalted butter	*Poêle* or *sautoir*
150 grams (5¼ ounces) button mushrooms, cleaned and *émincer*	Wooden spoon
25 grams (¾ ounce) shallots, *ciselé*	*Bain-marie*
25 milliliters (1½ tablespoons) cognac	Ice-water bath, optional
50 milliliters (3 tablespoons) white wine	Storage container, optional
270 milliliters (1 cup plus 2 tablespoons) Thickened Veal Stock (see page 69)	
50 milliliters (3 tablespoons) Tomato Sauce (see page 67)	
Coarse salt and freshly ground pepper to taste	
3 grams (2 teaspoons) fresh chervil, *haché*	
3 grams (2 teaspoons) fresh tarragon, *haché*	

Prepare your *mise en place*.

Place 10 grams (2 teaspoons) of the butter in a *poêle* or *sautoir* over medium heat. Add the mushrooms and sauté for about 6 minutes or until the mushrooms begin to brown.

Add the shallots, lower the heat, and sauté for 1 minute.

Drain off any excess butter. Return the pan to medium heat and *flambé* (see note) with the cognac. As soon as the flames quiet, add the wine and, using a wooden spoon, stir to deglaze the pan. Cook without stirring for about 4 minutes or until just about 15 milliliters (1 tablespoon) of liquid remains.

Add the veal stock along with the tomato sauce and bring to a simmer. Simmer, stirring occasionally, for 5 minutes.

Taste and, if necessary, season with salt and pepper. Return the sauce to a simmer.

Gently swirl in the remaining 5 grams (1 teaspoon) butter (*monter au beurre*, see page 73), a bit at a time. Add the chervil and tarragon and transfer to a *bain-marie* to keep warm until ready to serve.

If not using immediately, place in an ice-water bath to chill quickly. When cool, transfer to a storage container, cover, and refrigerate until ready to use.

Note

To *flambé* food, it is necessary to add alcohol to the pan (or dish) and then ignite the alcohol by carefully tipping the pan slightly to catch a bit of the flame from the burner. The pan remains stationary while the alcohol burns off; if it is moved around on the burner, the alcohol can splash out of the pan and cause a stovetop fire. This method infuses the food with the flavor of the alcohol without leaving a strong taste. It is often used for a dramatic, tableside presentation.

Derivatives of the Basic Sauces

The basic stock- and *liaison*-based sauces (thickened stocks, basic brown sauce, *béchamel*) are the bedrock for a wide range of derivatives. Many of the resulting sauces are finished by the process *monter au beurre*. This adds a glossy sheen and richness to the finished sauce. Once the butter is added, the sauce cannot be boiled or it will break.

Basic Brown Stocks and Their Derivatives

Basic Stock	Binding Agent	Basic Sauce	Derivatives
Brown veal stock (*fond de veau brun*)	Arrowroot, potato starch, cornstarch	Thickened veal stock (*fond de veau lié*)	*Bordelaise, Bercy, Robert*
Beef stock (*braisière*)	*Roux brun* (*singer*)	Basic brown sauce (*sauce espagnole*) *Demi-glace* (classic)	*Charcutière, Madère Chasseur*
Brown chicken stock (*fond de volaille brun*)	*Roux*, starch	Thickened poultry stock (*fond de volaille lié*)	
Game stock (*fond de gibier*)	*Roux*	Thickened game stock (*fond de gibier lié*)	*Poivrade, Grand Veneur, Diane*

Derivatives of Basic Sauces Made from Brown Stocks

Sauce	Ingredients	Uses
Bordelaise	Reduction of shallots, peppercorns, thyme, bay leaf, and red wine combined with a basic brown stock (*fond brun*) sauce	Steaks and other meat
Moëlle	*Sauce bordelaise* made with white wine rather than red; finished with parsley	Meats, vegetables, poached eggs
Robert	Reduction of *cisélé* onions and white wine combined with thickened veal stock and tomato paste; mounted (see note, page 76) with Dijon mustard	Pork, especially chops
Charcutière	*Sauce robert* with cornichon julienne	Pork/charcuterie

Sauce	Ingredients	Uses
Chasseur	Sautéed mushrooms and shallots flambéed with cognac, deglazed with white wine, and combined with thickened veal stock or *demi-glace*; finished with a bit of tomato, tarragon, and chervil	Veal and chicken
Diable	Reduction of *ciselé* shallots, peppercorns, white wine, and white wine vinegar added to a brown stock basic sauce; finished with chervil and tarragon	Grilled poultry
Bercy	Reduction of shallots, peppercorns, bay leaf, thyme, and white wine with thickened veal stock or *demi-glace*; finished with parsley or tarragon	Grilled fish, red and white meats
Madère	Reduced Madeira wine combined with *demi-glace*, mounted with butter, and seasoned	Beef and veal
Financière	*Sauce madère* with truffle juice	Beef
Perigueux	*Sauce madère* with truffle juice and chopped truffles	First courses, hot *pâtés*, *timbales*
Piquante	Reduction of shallots, white wine, and white vinegar combined with *demi-glace* or thickened veal stock; finished with sliced cornichons, parsley, chervil, and tarragon	Roasted and boiled beef, pork, and tongue
Milanese	Sautéed mushroom julienne, ham, and tongue, deglazed with Madeira; reduced and combined with thickened veal stock	Veal

Derivatives of Basic Sauces Made from Game Stock

Sauce	Ingredients	Uses
Poivrade	*Mirepoix* of carrots, onions, thyme, parsley, and bay leaves, sautéed and deglazed with vinegar; reduced to a	Game (venison, wild boar, hare, or rabbit)

Note

To mount — *monter* — a sauce is to swirl in butter or other emulsifying agent to enrich the flavor and texture and to give a glossy finish.

	glaze, *singer*; combined with brown game stock; cooked for 1 hour with peppercorns and then strained		
Chevreuil	*Sauce poivrade* combined with red wine and reduced; finished with cayenne pepper		Game (venison)
Diane	Strongly flavored *poivrade* combined with whipped cream		Game (venison)
Grand Veneur	Five parts *poivrade* to one part currant jelly and one part heavy cream		Game (venison)

Sauces Based on White Stocks

Basic Stock	Binding Agent	Basic Sauce	Derivatives
White veal stock (*fond de veau blanc*)	White *roux* (*roux blanc*)	Veal *velouté* (*velouté de veau*)	*Allemande, Poulette*
White chicken stock (*fond de volaille blanc*)	White *roux* (*roux blanc*)	Chicken *velouté* (*velouté de volaille*)	*Suprême, Ivoire, Albufera*
Fumet	White *roux*	Fish *velouté* (*velouté de poisson*)	*Aurore, Bretonne*
Milk	White *roux*	*Béchamel*	*Mornay, Soubise, Smitane*

Derivatives of Basic Sauces Made from White Stocks

Sauce	Ingredients	Uses
Suprême	Chicken *velouté* combined with cream and seasoned	Eggs, *fricassées*, poultry
Ivoire	*Sauce suprême* combined with meat glaze	Poached or pan-fried poultry
Albufera	*Sauce ivoire* mounted with pimento butter	Braised poultry
Chaud-Froid	Chicken *velouté* combined with cream and gelatin	Cold poultry dishes

Derivatives of Bound Fish *Fumet* (*Velouté de Poisson*)

Sauce	Ingredients	Uses
Bercy	Shallots combined with white wine and reduced with *fumet*; added to a fish *velouté*; finished with chopped parsley	Grilled fish and seafood
Aurore	Fish *velouté* combined with tomato coulis	Fish, seafood, eggs
Bretonne	*Julienned* leeks, celery, onions, and mushrooms cooked *à l'étuvé*, deglazed with white wine, and reduced; added to fish *velouté*; finished with heavy cream or *crème fraîche*	Braised or baked fish or seafood
Chaud-Froid	Bound fish *velouté* combined with heavy cream and gelatin	Cold fish dishes

Derivatives of *Sauce Béchamel*

Sauce	Ingredients	Uses
Mornay	*Béchamel* combined with Gruyère cheese and egg yolks	Egg and vegetable dishes
Crème	*Béchamel* with heavy cream and lemon juice	Vegetable *gratins*
Soubise	Onions sweated in butter; added to *béchamel*	Poached eggs
Smitane	Classically but no longer made from *béchamel*. Now made with chopped onions sweated in butter, moistened with white wine, and reduced; sour cream added	Veal Pojarski

Emulsified Sauces

Emulsified sauces are made by combining two normally incompatible liquids through the incorporation of a binding or emulsifying agent. The resulting union created by the emulsifying agent is the stable, or permanent, dispersal of microscopic droplets of two nonmixable liquids (such as oil and vinegar). It is important to note that a stable, lasting, emulsified sauce cannot be created without a binding or emulsifying agent. To illustrate this point, vigorously beat oil and vinegar together with a wire whisk or an electric mixer. The two liquids will separate into microscopic droplets and temporarily bind together but, as the beating ceases, they will begin to separate and will eventually resume their original form, with the heavier liquid falling to the bottom of the container.

In the classic kitchen, the egg yolk is the most common emulsifying agent. This is because egg yolks have two properties: They are lipophilic, with an affinity for fat, and hydrophilic, with an affinity for water. These properties enable yolks to bind oil and water (or other water-based liquids such as vinegar) together in a stable, emulsified mixture. One large egg yolk is generally capable of binding up to 200 milliliters (about 14 tablespoons) of oil. An egg yolk emulsion will create a rich, satiny, smooth sauce.

Warm Emulsified Sauces

These sauces are prepared by whisking egg yolks and flavoring components into a foamy mixture over a hot water bath until they are thick and airy and have formed an emulsion. This emulsion is referred to as a *sabayon,* and it serves as the base for many warm emulsified sauces. Clarified butter is then added in a steady stream and the sauce is whisked until smooth. Different flavorings can be added, either directly, as with the addition of lemon juice to *hollandaise* sauce, or in the form of a reduction, as with the shallots, tarragon, and peppercorns in *béarnaise* sauce.

Clarified butter is an essential ingredient for warm emulsified sauces. It is simply butter that has been very slowly melted, allowing most of the water to evaporate and the milk solids to separate and settle in the bottom of the pan. The liquid is then carefully poured off the solids. The resultant clear, yellow liquid has a lighter flavor and much higher smoke point than pure butter, and can be used for frying and sautéing. Without the milk solids, clarified butter does not become rancid as quickly as other butter and can be stored for longer periods of time.

Warm emulsified sauces are quite delicate and will break or curdle if not prepared or held properly. The ideal temperature for making warm emulsified sauces is 49°C (120°F); heat above this temperature will always cause a problem in the finished sauce.

Possible reasons for failure are:

○ The *sabayon* was insufficiently cooked.

○ The *sabayon* was overcooked.

○ The clarified butter was incorporated too quickly.

○ Excess heat made the butter separate from the yolks.

In the past, when a sauce curdled, it was impossible to restore it. However, modern kitchen conveniences have changed that, and a quick turn in a blender or with an immersion blender will immediately reconstitute the sauce. If a warm emulsified sauce breaks or separates, it is possible to restabilize it using one of the following methods:

○ Beat a few drops of water into the sauce by working it in from the bottom inner edge of the bowl and, using a small wire whisk, gradually bringing the whole sauce into the process.

○ If the sauce broke because it was too hot, add a few drops of **cold** water.

○ If the sauce broke because it was too cold, add a few drops of **warm** water.

○ If the sauce appears about to break, dip the bottom of the bowl into an ice-water bath and whisk constantly until the sauce smooths.

Chefs' Tips

"When adding the butter to the sabayon, *do not whisk too fast, as you will incorporate cold air and cool down the sauce. When making large amounts of* sabayon *for an emulsified sauce, it is recommended to let the bowl touch the warm water underneath for increased heat transfer."*

Chef Sixto Alonso

"Always make sure that your emulsified sauces are kept at a consistent temperature so that you don't have to whip up a sabayon *during service."*

Chef Marc Bauer

"Never throw away a broken emulsified sauce, because it can usually be saved."

Chef Candy Argondizza

The two basic warm emulsified sauces are **sauce hollandaise** and **sauce béarnaise**. The same technique is employed for the preparation of each; however, the flavoring for *béarnaise* is achieved through the addition of a reduction of highly flavorful ingredients (in this case, shallots, tarragon, and peppercorns) cooked in white wine and/or white wine-vinegar until only a tiny amount of intensely flavored liquid remains. The sauce is strained through a fine *chinois* before service. Each of these sauces serves as the base for many other classic sauces.

Formula for Warm Emulsified Sauces

CLARIFY BUTTER

COOK *SABAYON* OVER HOT WATER BATH, WHISKING CONSTANTLY

WHISKING CONSTANTLY, SLOWLY ADD WARM CLARIFIED BUTTER

IF TOO THICK, ADD DROPS OF WARM WATER, WHISKING CONSTANTLY

SEASON WITH SALT, CAYENNE, AND LEMON JUICE

HOLD AT 49°C (120°F)

Chef's Tip

"Try to have the sabayon *and the butter at the same temperature when creating a warm emulsified sauce."*

Chef Henri Viain

Warm Emulsified Sauces

Sauce	Ingredients	Uses
Hollandaise	Egg yolks, clarified butter, lemon juice, salt, cayenne pepper	Warm vegetables, artichoke hearts, fish, eggs
Mousseline	Three parts *hollandaise* and one part whipped cream	Same as *hollandaise*
Moutarde	*Hollandaise* and mustard	Same as *hollandaise*
Maltaise	*Hollandaise*, blood orange juice, blanched orange zest	Fish *mousses* or turbot
Mikado	*Hollandaise*, mandarin orange juice, blanched mandarin orange zest	Corn or poached fish
Béarnaise	Egg yolks, clarified butter, salt, tarragon, chervil, reduction of white wine, vinegar, shallots, tarragon, peppercorns	Grilled meats or fish

Sauce	Ingredients	Uses
Foyot or *Valois*	*Béarnaise* and meat glaze	Grilled fish
Choron	*Béarnaise* and tomato *concassé* (see note)	Grilled meat or fish
Paloise	*Béarnaise* with mint instead of tarragon	Lamb or shrimp brochettes
Tyrolienne	*Béarnaise* with a neutral oil instead of clarified butter	Grilled meat

Note

A *concassé* is any mixture that is coarsely chopped or ground.

Demonstration

Sauce Hollandaise

Makes about 350 milliliters (1½ cups)
Estimated time to complete: 15 minutes

Ingredients	Equipment
2 large egg yolks, at room temperature 30 milliters (2 tablespoons) water 200 milliters (14 tablespoons) warm clarified butter 10 milliliters (2 teaspoons) fresh lemon juice Salt to taste Cayenne pepper to taste	Heatproof bowl Whisk Saucepan with a rim large enough to hold the heatproof bowl

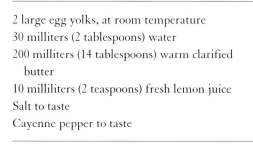

Prepare your *mise en place.*

Place the egg yolks and water in a heatproof bowl and whisk them together.

Fill a saucepan large enough to hold the bowl with water and place over medium-high heat. Bring to a low simmer.

Place the bowl over the simmering water, taking care that the bottom of the bowl does not touch the simmering water. (This system is called a *bain-marie* or double-boiler system.)

Immediately begin whisking the egg yolk mixture and continue whisking for about 3 minutes or until it thickens and becomes quite thick and airy. This light, frothy mixture is known as a *sabayon.* Great care must be taken when whisking the *sabayon* over the simmering water, as if it gets too hot, the eggs will scramble and the sauce will not be salvageable.

Remove the mixture from the heat and add the warm clarified butter in a slow, steady stream, whisking constantly. Start this process slowly so that an emul-

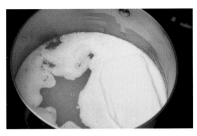

sion begins to form; the sauce will break if the butter is added too quickly. If the sauce gets too thick, carefully thin it with a few drops warm water to achieve the proper consistency.

Season the sauce with the lemon juice and salt and cayenne to taste, stirring to combine.

If not serving immediately, keep warm, uncovered, over 49°C (120°F) water, taking care that the sauce does not overheat, or it will break. If keeping for a few hours, place a piece of plastic film directly on the surface of the sauce to keep a "skin" from forming. If you cover the sauce with a tight lid, moisture can form on the lid and drip down into the sauce, thereby thinning it.

If the clarified butter has not been prepared, clarify approximately 300 grams (2 sticks plus 5 tablespoons) unsalted whole butter by placing it in a small saucepan over very low heat without allowing it to simmer.

Remove the melted butter from the heat and set it aside for 5 minutes, skimming the foam off the top.

Pour off the clear yellow butter, leaving the water and milk solids that have settled on the bottom of the pan. Use warm as directed in the recipe or store, covered and refrigerated, until ready to use. Reheat before using.

Demonstration

Sauce Béarnaise

Makes about 240 milliliters (1 cup)
Estimated time to complete: 20 minutes

Ingredients	Equipment
95 milliliters (¼ cup plus 2½ tablespoons) water (see note)	Small saucepan
40 milliliters (2 tablespoons plus 2 teaspoons) white wine vinegar	Heatproof bowl
40 grams (1½ ounces) shallots, *cisclé*	Whisk
5 grams (1 tablespoon) crushed peppercorns	Saucepan
3 grams (2 teaspoons) minced fresh tarragon	Fine *chinois*
2 large egg yolks, at room temperature	Storage container, optional
200 milliliters (14 tablespoons) warm clarified butter	
10 milliliters (2 teaspoons) fresh lemon juice	
Coarse salt and freshly ground pepper to taste	
3 grams (2 teaspoons) fresh tarragon, *haché*	
3 grams (2 teaspoons) fresh chervil, *haché*	

Prepare your *mise en place.*

To make the reduction, combine 75 milliliters (¼ cup plus 1 tablespoon) of the water, the vinegar, shallots, peppercorns, and tarragon in a small saucepan over medium heat.

Bring to a simmer and simmer for about 5 minutes or until the liquid has been reduced by 80 percent. Remove the reduction from the heat and combine it with the egg yolks and remaining water in a heatproof bowl. Rapidly whisk them together.

Fill a saucepan with a rim large enough to hold the heatproof bowl with water and place over medium-high heat. Bring to a low simmer.

Place the bowl over the simmering water, taking care that the bottom of the bowl does not touch the water.

Immediately begin whisking the egg yolk mixture, and continue whisking for about 3 minutes or until it thickens and becomes quite thick yet airy. This light, frothy mixture is known as a *sabayon.* Great care must be taken when whisking the *sabayon* over the simmering water because if the mixture gets too hot, the eggs will scramble and the sauce will not be salvageable.

Remove the mixture from the heat and add the warm clarified butter in a slow, steady stream, whisking constantly. Start this process slowly so that an emulsion begins to form; the sauce will break if the butter is added too quickly. If the sauce gets too thick, carefully thin it with a few drops of warm water to achieve the proper consistency.

Season the sauce with the lemon juice, salt, and pepper to taste, stirring to combine.

Strain the sauce through a fine *chinois* into a clean container.

Deans' Tips

"Hollandaise or béarnaise *sauce may not be refrigerated and reused. However, either one of these sauces may be kept warm in a* bain-marie *over warm water or in a warm spot for up to 2 hours."*
Dean André Soltner

"Adding a little acid such as lemon juice or white wine to the sabayon *will freshen the flavor and help hold the emulsion. If you do not have a double boiler or* bain-marie *to hold your sauce at the perfect temperature, place it in a china or ceramic bowl close to a warm spot and cover."*
Dean Alain Sailhac

Whisk in the tarragon and chervil. Taste and, if necessary, adjust the seasoning with additional salt and pepper.

If not serving immediately, keep warm, uncovered, over very hot water, taking care that the sauce does not overheat, or it will break. If keeping for a few hours, place a piece of plastic film directly on the surface of the sauce to keep a "skin" from forming and hold at a temperature approved by the Department of Health. If you cover the sauce with a tight lid, moisture can form on the lid and drip down into the sauce, thereby thinning it.

Cold Emulsified Sauces

Mayonnaise (sauce mayonnaise) is the basic as well as the basis for all cold emulsified sauces. It is made by first combining egg yolks with mustard, salt, and white pepper, and then slowly whisking in oil until the mixture emulsifies into a smooth, thick sauce. Once thickened, vinegar or lemon juice is whisked in. It is important that all the ingredients be at the same temperature to ensure that the egg yolks will absorb the oil. Mayonnaise should be used immediately upon preparation or chilled rapidly and stored, covered and refrigerated, for a short period of time, to prevent contamination from the uncooked egg yolks.

Although we have come to know mayonnaise as nothing more than a slightly sweet, thick condiment for dressing sandwiches or salads, true classic mayonnaise is a fresh-tasting, tangy sauce. Its flavor is dependent upon the freshness of the egg yolks, the clarity of the oil, and the addition of just the right amount of acid to add zest to the rich egg and oil. Traditionally, mayonnaise is made with a fine quality, unflavored vegetable oil (such as peanut, grape seed, or safflower) but it can also be made with olive or nut oils; however, these strongly-flavored oils have a great impact on the final taste of the mayonnaise.

When making fresh mayonnaise it is particularly important to have all the ingredients at room

"When making a mayonnaise *that starts to turn shiny and begins to break, add a few drops of vinegar or hot water and it will stabilize immediately."*

Chef Marc Bauer

Dean's Tip

"Any sauce with eggs must be held in a stainless steel, glass, or ceramic container to prevent oxidation."

Dean Alain Sailhac

temperature to assist in the emulsification process— cold ingredients simply do not meld together as easily. An egg can be quickly brought to room temperature by holding it under hot water for about 30 seconds.

When adding the oil to the egg yolk emulsion, remember that one egg yolk can emulsify a maximum of 200 milliliters (14 tablespoons) of oil. If the emulsion begins to separate, you can repair it by whisking an additional egg yolk in a separate small stainless steel bowl and then begin slowly whisking in the broken mayonnaise. Additional oil may be required to balance the extra yolk. If the sauce is too thick, whisk in room-temperature water, a drop at a time, until the appropriate consistency is reached.

Formula for *Sauce Mayonnaise*

COMBINE ROOM TEMPERATURE EGG YOLKS, MUSTARD, AND SALT

WHISK FOR 20 SECONDS

ADD THE OIL, DROP BY DROP, WHISKING CONSTANTLY, UNTIL EMULSIFIED

SEASON WITH SALT AND WHITE PEPPER

ONCE EMULSIFIED, WHISK IN REMAINING OIL IN A SLOW, STEADY STREAM

WHISK IN VINEGAR OR LEMON JUICE

USE IMMEDIATELY OR CHILL RAPIDLY

Cold Emulsified Sauces

Sauce	Ingredients	Uses
Mayonnaise	Egg yolks, mustard, oil, acid	Salads, cold fresh shellfish, and meats
Verte	*Mayonnaise* and green herbs	Cold fish, shellfish, and meats
Rémoulade	*Mayonnaise*, capers, cornichons, chervil, tarragon, parsley, chives; chopped onion and hard-cooked egg are optional	Fried fish, cold meats, and poultry
Gribiche	*Mayonnaise*, hard-cooked eggs, mustard, cornichons, parsley, chervil, tarragon	Cold fish and deep-fried foods
Chantilly	Two parts *mayonnaise* and one part whipped cream	Cold asparagus or artichokes

Aïoli	Mayonnaise, garlic, sometimes saffron	Vegetables and fish
Rouille	Mayonnaise, white bread, garlic paprika, saffron	Traditional accompaniment to Provençal fish soups or stews, especially *bouillabaisse*
Andalouse	Mayonnaise, tomato coulis, diced peppers	Hard-cooked eggs and vegetables

Demonstration

Sauce Mayonnaise

Makes about 240 milliliters (1 cup)
Estimated time to complete: 10 minutes

Ingredients	Equipment
1 large egg yolk, at room temperature 10 grams (1 teaspoon) Dijon mustard Salt to taste 150 milliliters (⅔ cup) vegetable oil 15 milliliters (1 tablespoon) white wine vinegar or fresh lemon juice Freshly ground white pepper to taste	Stainless steel bowl Whisk Storage container, optional

Prepare your *mise en place.*

Combine the yolk, mustard, and salt in a small stainless steel bowl and whisk together for 20 seconds.

Begin adding the oil, drop by drop, whisking continuously until an emulsion forms; then add the remaining oil in a thin, steady stream, whisking to emulsify.

Whisk in the vinegar and pepper to taste, adding additional salt if needed. If not using immediately, place in a clean container, cover, and refrigerate.

Session 5

Preserving Food

Theory

A Brief History of Food Preservation

Food preservation can be defined as the keeping of perishable foods in a consumable form for a long period of time. This can be accomplished in a number of ways, each dependent upon the type of food being preserved. Refrigeration, freezing, pickling, salting, fermenting, drying, freeze-drying, smoking, salting, canning, and dehydrating are the most common methods used to prepare food for long-term storage.

As one can imagine, the preservation of food has been a major preoccupation of mankind for centuries. People have been preserving food since the beginning of recorded time and, surely, even before then to ensure that a supply of nourishment was available when fresh food was unobtainable as a result of climatic changes or natural disaster. In ancient times there were four fundamental methods of preserving: drying, salting, pickling, and fermenting. However, it has also been shown that in Paleolithic times, some food was kept in natural caves or cellars, underwater, or buried in holes dug deep in the earth, where the constant cold would serve to keep perishable food intact, a practice still held in many primitive societies today.

Early in the development of preservative methods, it was understood that it was the practice of coating food with impenetrable materials such as clay or honey (and later with fat, vinegar or wine, or oil) that kept them free of contact with air, moisture, and light that would ensure their preservation. Then came the addition of antiseptic and dehydrating elements such as salt and ashes, which not only preserved but modified the taste and appearance of the food. Smoking and drying were the most commonly used methods to preserve meat and fish. Both of these methods reshaped the chemical and biological actions that would normally affect decomposition. Simple meat dehydration was practiced primarily in areas where salt was either unavailable or a costly commodity.

Throughout the centuries, the preservation of meat, fish, and breadstuffs was the primary aim, as these were the most constant sources of dependable nourishment. However, at the end of the Middle Ages, when sugar became more available, sweets were preserved through the application of high heat to sugar. This method was also used for preserving meats, with a modicum of success. The success of preserving sweets was ultimately the beginning of ventures in commercial food preservation.

With the dawn of the nineteenth century, there was a reformation in food preservation that, in hindsight, has been as important in the history of man's sustenance as was the discovery of fire's ability to cook raw food. This technological revolution was seen in Nicolas Appert's discovery that sterilization is a means of preservation. Appert was a small-town French brewer who became an innovative confectioner. His quest for a method

to keep fresh, extremely perishable food such as milk, meat, and green vegetables led to his discovery that heating sealed glass jars of fresh vegetables and cream for a sustained period of time killed off the microorganisms naturally carried in these foods that caused them to deteriorate under normal conditions. Appert's method of preserving peas and beans through sterilization, once known as "appertization" in his honor, is the basis of all modern sterilization methods.

Appert's discoveries and scientific examinations were the foundation of the major advances brought forth by the brilliant calculations of Louis Pasteur in the mid-nineteenth century. Pasteur's discovery of anaerobic organisms (organisms that can exist and ferment without oxygen) led to the invention of a method of sterilization called "pasteurization" that revolutionized the food and dairy industries. His method of sterilization enabled fresh milk to be stored in a refrigerated environment for several days while still retaining its fresh-tasting goodness. Pasteurization was later applied to the preservation of almost all dairy products as well as beer, fruit products, and wine, along with many other products.

Until the end of the nineteenth century, refrigeration was accomplished by cutting natural ice from mountains and lakes and storing it in huge icehouses for commercial and home use. A technique for the assured freezing of food was not perfected for another fifty years. In 1929, Clarence Birdseye developed a freezing method that preserved the basic molecular structure of meat, based on his observations of the practices of the Inuit of Labrador. In the bitter northern climate, meat and fish were exposed to sudden intense cold that caused them to freeze instantly. When subsequently thawed, these products retained their organic structure because they had been frozen before the water in the cells had a chance to expand, thus leaving them intact. Birdseye went on to develop a super-powerful freezer that accomplished this job reliably. By the 1950s, almost every home had a refrigerator, a freezer, or a combination of both, and the commercial frozen food industry was born.

Methods of Preserving Food

The breakdown and spoilage of all food is caused by the actions of mold, yeast, and bacteria that exist throughout the universe in air, water, and, in fact, all matter. Mold feeds on sugar and mainly attacks fruits and vegetables that convert their starch into sugar as they ripen, beginning the process that leads to ultimate deterioration. Yeast also feeds on sugars but causes fermentation as it consumes its host food. All three types of microorganisms require food, warmth, oxygen, and moisture along with a degree of alkalinity and time to survive and flourish. Preservation methods, therefore, are intended either to deprive the microbes of a hospitable environment in which to grow or to encourage the development of different microorganisms that will preserve the food and render it safe (as is the case with fermentation).

Dehydration

This process draws moisture from the product and thus eliminates any medium in which bacteria can grow. It is used most frequently for fruit, herbs, beans, and other vegetables.

Alcohol

Preserving with alcohol is primarily used for fruit. The alcoholic content of the preserving liquid kills active microorganisms.

Sugar

Preserving with sugar is almost always used with fruit. The density of the sugar in the cooking process retards the growth of enzymes because there is a lower ratio of water. Fruit preserves normally contain a minimum of 60 percent sugar and are usually pasteurized; otherwise, once the jar is sealed, the sugar can break down into alcohol over time. In the case of fruit preserves, a metal seal or a protective layer of wax prevents the development of surface mold during a long storage period.

Liquid Cure/Brine

Liquid cures are accomplished through the submersion of the food in brine, an intense solution of water combined with salt and sometimes a sweetener and some spice. The product to be cured is submerged for a time that can range from an hour to several months, depending on the size of the product and the desired result.

Pickling/Fermentation

Pickling preserves food by impregnating it with acid. Food can be pickled by submersion in vinegar or another acidic liquid or by creating some type of environment that encourages **fermentation**.

When preserving food in vinegar or other acidic liquid, the item is generally precooked or soaked in a brine for a short time to draw out excess moisture before the pickling process proceeds. The food is then placed in vinegar or other acidic liquid to cover. Cucumbers (in the form of sweet and sour pickles and *cornichons*, or tiny French pickles), onions, and other vegetables are some of the foods typically preserved in acidic liquids.

When using fermentation to preserve food, the item is submerged in a brine that enters the cell membranes and draws out moisture. The brine eliminates the undesirable bacteria while promoting the growth of lactic acid bacteria that, in turn, cause fermentation. Sauerkraut and dill pickles are examples of foods preserved by fermentation. Fermentation also plays a part in the production of wine and cheese.

Dry Cure/Salt

In a dry cure, all surfaces of the food are rubbed with salt and the item is left to cure for the time designated in the recipe. Dry curing can be applied to various fish and meat products but is generally not an effective method for safely preserving large pieces, with the exception of country hams such as prosciutto, Smithfield, or Westphalian hams. Both dry and liquid curing are usually done as a preliminary step to smoking. The product is then rinsed of excess curing agents before the smoking process begins.

Smoking

This is one of the most ancient methods of preservation. Many different types of woods can be used to successfully smoke (and consequently flavor) food. Hardwoods, such as hickory, ash, mesquite, and all fruitwoods, are best, as their smoke is clean tasting and often adds a slightly sweet flavor. Woods with high resin content such as pine should be avoided, as they will impart an unpleasant taste to the food.

Smoking is separated into two categories, cold smoking and hot smoking.

Cold smoking is achieved through two phases. The product must first be cured, usually brined, and then the smoke is applied at temperatures below 38°C (100°F). This cold smoke prevents the coagulation of the protein in meat and fish, which means that the product remains uncooked. When using cold smoke to cure, it must be done in a controlled atmosphere and the heat source must be separate from the unit holding the product to be smoked to avoid cooking. An example of a cold-smoked product would be Scottish smoked salmon.

Hot smoking actually cooks the product with the heat of the smoke. This changes both the taste and the texture of the smoked item. As with cold smoking, the food to be smoked is usually cured before smoking to remove excess moisture that would allow bacteria to grow. Smoke contributes certain antioxidant qualities to the product by forming a protective layer on the food. Types of meat and fish that are frequently cured by hot smoke are chicken, turkey, pork, and trout.

Pasteurization

With this method, preservation is accomplished by rapidly cooling liquid that has first been heated to 80°C (180°F) to destroy disease-causing bacteria. This is a commercial process primarily used for milk and cream. Ultra High Temperature (UHT) is a variation on pasteurization in which milk (or another liquid) is brought to an extremely high temperature in less than one second by the injection of pressurized steam. UHT kills almost all microbes, so it allows for very long storage even without refrigeration, but it generally leaves a slight aftertaste when the liquid is consumed.

Sterilization

Microbes are destroyed through the sterilization of the container before it is filled with the product. The filled container is then brought to a high temperature through the application of steam, dry heat, or boiling hot water. This process seals the container against air and humidity, rendering it safe for long-term storage. This method is primarily used in canning fruits and vegetables.

Refrigeration

Enzyme activity is slowed but not completely stopped at 0°C–3°C (32°F–38°F). Adequate refrigeration is met when cool air is allowed to circulate freely around the stored product and the humidity level is controlled. The length of safe storage is dependent upon the item stored.

Freezing

To safely freeze a product, the holding temperature must be below -18°C (0°F). Freezing is most effective when the item to be stored is tightly packed so that air does not circulate around it. Most food products can be frozen for long periods, but freezing does cause water to expand and rupture cell walls which, in turn, will change the texture of the thawed product.

Quick Freezing

Products are immediately cooled to -5°C (-40°F) and held at -15°C (-4°F). This method lowers the risk of cell breakage, which makes it the preferable method for freezing fresh fish, meats, fruit, and cooked preparations. Quick-frozen products can be safely frozen for up to one year.

Freeze Drying

This method involves the total elimination of all moisture, which is accomplished through a combination of repeated freezing and dehydrating of the product. Once the humidity is removed, the freeze-dried product does not need to be refrigerated. This method is generally applied to coffee, potatoes, and industrial products.

Sealing and Coating

When a food is sealed or coated, a barrier to outside microorganisms and bacteria is formed. Meat *confit*, an ancient method of preserving duck, goose, or pork by salting and slow cooking in the product's own fat then storing the cooked meat covered in this cooking fat, is a classic example of preserving through coating. The *confit* is cooled so long that any liquid or gelatin (which could cause bacterial growth) no longer remains. Today, *confit* is made more for its rich taste than for the actual benefit of preservation.

Dean's Tip

"The preservation of food through salting, curing, and canning has saved the world from famine through the centuries, and these processes are still very useful to the contemporary chef."

Dean Jacques Pépin

Vacuum-Pack (*Sous Vide*)

Also known by the brand name Cryovac, the method of preserving by vacuum-packing is accomplished by eliminating all air from a plastic bag or container in which cooked food is stored. Food stored in this manner is said to retain its fresh flavor for longer periods. This system is also used to wet-age beef (see page 166). *Sous vide* preservation has become quite controversial, with many state health departments in the process of establishing guidelines for standardization.

Dried Beans, Peas, and Legumes

Although many types of vegetables can be preserved through dehydration, beans, peas, and legumes are the most frequent benefactors of this method of preservation. Dehydrated vegetables generally require cooking before they can be eaten, and with most beans, a period of presoaking is also mandatory. For best results, dehydrated products should be used within one year of drying. With beans, cooking times depend on the age of the product, as the longer the period of dehydration, the longer the cooking time required to tenderize them.

Presoaking

Beans, peas, and legumes that are more than a couple of months old or are of inferior quality always require soaking before cooking. It was once thought that these dried products required a presoaking of at least eight hours, but it is now felt that a three-hour soaking period is sufficient to soften them for cooking; a longer period allows the lime and iron content of the soaking water to harden the outer casing of the product, which would require even longer cooking. Prolonged soaking can also cause fermentation to begin. Most beans, peas, and legumes can be tenderized for cooking by covering them with cold water, bringing them to a quick boil, and then draining. Split peas do not require soaking prior to cooking.

Cooking Beans, Peas, and Legumes

First, any broken pieces or foreign matter should be removed from the product. This is accomplished by carefully sorting through by hand. Then, a thorough rinsing should be done, either by placing the beans in a bowl of cold water and swishing them around or by placing the beans in a strainer and holding the strainer under rapidly flowing cold water. This is followed by either presoaking or blanching and then draining off the liquid.

To cook the product, cover with two to three times its volume of fresh, cold water. Place over high heat and bring to a boil. Add any flavoring ingredients, with the exception of salt, lower the heat, and slowly simmer. Because it tends to toughen dried products when added early in the cooking process, salt should be added only toward the end. The liquid in the pot should always cover the product being cooked, so add water or broth, if necessary. For a more intense flavor, the liquid can be allowed to just barely cover the product as the cooking time comes to an end. The product is perfectly cooked when it breaks open easily when pinched between the thumb and index finger.

Salted and Dried Fish

Salt cod, the best-known dried fish, is simply cod that has been preserved by salting and drying. It is sold as fillets, either with or without skin. The fillets should appear white with a slight silvery sheen. Salt cod often has a rather intense odor, but with proper preparation it can be transformed into a very delicate dish.

"One of the first things I learned to make when I was an apprentice was brandade de morue. *And the one thing I know is that without garlic it is not a true* brandade—*the garlic is like a smile on a happy person."*

Dean Alain Sailhac

Salt cod must first be soaked in several changes of cold water to soften and desalinate it. The soaking period can range from 24 to 48 hours; 36 hours is usually sufficient for skinless cod. Cod with skin may take up to 48 hours of soaking before the skin can easily be peeled off. The cod should be refrigerated during the soaking process, as once the salt has been expelled, it returns to a perishable state.

Salt cod is a familiar source of protein throughout the Mediterranean, where one of its most famous incarnations is in French cuisine with a preparation known as *brandade de morue.* A specialty of the Languedoc and Provence regions, this is a rich purée of skinless salt cod, olive oil, and milk. In some versions, garlic and/or puréed potatoes may be added.

Demonstration

Potage Saint-Germain aux Croutons (Split Pea Soup with Croutons)

Serves 4

Estimated time to complete: 1 hour, 15 minutes

Ingredients

350 grams (12¼ ounces) split green peas
40 grams (1½ ounces) slab bacon, cut into *lardons*
20 grams (1⅓ tablespoons) unsalted butter
80 grams (2¾ ounces) onions, *mirepoix*
40 grams (1½ ounces) leeks, *émincé*
40 grams (1½ ounces) carrots, *mirepoix*
1.5 liters (1½ quarts) water or White Veal Stock (see page 53)
Bouquet garni
1 clove garlic, peeled
60 milliliters (¼ cup) heavy cream
Coarse salt and freshly ground pepper to taste

For the garnish

50 grams (1¾ ounces) clarified butter
80 grams (2¾ ounces) white bread, cut into 1-centimeter (⅓-inch) cubes
Parsley leaves, optional

Equipment

Strainer
Small saucepan
Paper towels
2 large saucepans, one with lid
Food mill, blender, or food processor
Chinois
Bain-marie
Ice-water bath, optional
Storage container, optional
Small sauté pan
Slotted spoon
Ladle

Prepare your *mise en place.*

Pick through the peas, checking for damaged peas or stones. Place the peas in a strainer under cold running water to eliminate any dust or dirt.

Place water in small saucepan and bring to a boil over high heat. Add the *lardons* and again bring the water

to a boil. Blanch the *lardons* for 3 minutes, then remove from the heat and drain. Transfer to a double layer of paper towels and pat dry.

Heat 10 grams (2 teaspoons) of the butter in large saucepan over medium heat. Add the *lardons* to the saucepan and sauté for about 5 minutes or until all the fat has been rendered.

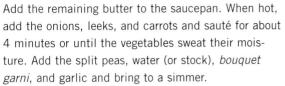

Add the remaining butter to the saucepan. When hot, add the onions, leeks, and carrots and sauté for about 4 minutes or until the vegetables sweat their moisture. Add the split peas, water (or stock), *bouquet garni*, and garlic and bring to a simmer.

Continue to simmer for 45 minutes or until the peas are mushy and the flavors have blended. (If the soup begins to reduce too quickly, cover with a lid and lower the heat.)

Remove the soup from the heat and process it through a food mill, blender, or food processor to make a smooth purée. Pass the purée through a *chinois* into a clean saucepan.

Add the cream and season with salt and pepper to taste. Place over low heat and bring to a bare simmer. Taste and, if necessary, adjust the thickness with

additional water or stock and the seasoning with salt and pepper. Transfer to a *bain-marie* to keep warm for service. (If not serving immediately, place in an ice-water bath to quickly chill. When cool, transfer to a storage container, cover, and refrigerate until ready to serve.)

Prepare the garnish. Heat the clarified butter in a small sauté pan over low heat. Add the bread cubes and sauté for about 5 minutes or until golden. Using a slotted spoon, transfer the croutons to a double layer of paper towels to drain.

When ready to serve, ladle the soup into warm, shallow soup bowls and garnish with a few croutons and, if desired, parsley leaves.

Demonstration

Salade Niçoise

Serves 4

Estimated time to complete: 1 hour

Ingredients	Equipment
	5 small bowls
For the vinaigrette	Whisk
40 milliliters (2 tablespoons plus 2 teaspoons) wine vinegar	Medium saucepan
2 cloves garlic, peeled and lightly crushed	Small knife
Coarse salt and freshly ground pepper to taste	Colander
100 milliliters (7 tablespoons) olive oil	Vegetable peeler
	Large bowl
For the salad	Platter or salad bowl
300 grams (10½ ounces) waxy potatoes, such as small red potatoes	
4 medium tomatoes, *émondé*	
Coarse salt	
100 grams (3½ ounces) green bell pepper	
100 grams (½ cup) canned tuna	
½ head Boston lettuce, pulled into leaves, washed, and dried	
200 grams (7 ounces) *haricots verts* or very thin string beans,	
cut into 5-centimeter (2-inch) pieces and cooked, crisp-tender, *à l'anglaise*	
2 hard-cooked eggs	
4 anchovy fillets (see note)	
5 grams (1 tablespoon) chopped fresh parsley or chervil	
20 pitted Niçoise olives	

Prepare your *mise en place.*

Make the vinaigrette by combining the vinegar, garlic, and salt and pepper to taste in a small bowl and whisking vigorously. Let stand for about 2 minutes, then gently whisk in the oil. Taste and, if necessary, adjust the seasoning.

Scrub the potatoes under cold running water to remove any dirt. Place the potatoes in a medium saucepan, cover with cold water, and place over high heat. Bring to a boil. Lower the heat and simmer for 20 minutes or until the potatoes are tender when pierced with the point of a small knife (see note). Remove from the heat and drain well. Set aside for about 10 minutes until cooled slightly.

While still warm, peel the potatoes. Slice the warm potatoes, crosswise, into 3-millimeter (⅛-inch)-thick slices. Place the warm potato slices in a small bowl and add enough vinaigrette to just lightly coat. Toss to combine.

Cut the tomatoes into 4 to 6 wedges each and remove the seeds. Place the tomatoes in a colander and salt lightly. Place the colander over a bowl and allow the tomatoes to drain for about 5 minutes to remove excess liquid.

Using a vegetable peeler, peel the green pepper. Cut the peeled pepper in half lengthwise and remove the core, membrane, and seeds. Cut the pepper into

Note

If the anchovies contain excess salt or oil, soak them for about 5 minutes in cold water and then drain well on paper towels. Any small bones can be removed by scraping lightly with a paring knife.

Do not overcook the potatoes or they will crack open and be mushy. You want tender but firm potatoes that slice easily.

2-x-50-millimeter (1⁄16-x-2-inch) strips. Set aside.

Place the tuna in a colander for about 2 minutes to drain off excess oil. Break the tuna into chunks.

Place the lettuce in a large bowl, add enough vinaigrette to coat, and toss to combine. Line a platter or salad bowl with the seasoned lettuce.

Place the tomatoes, *haricots verts*, and peppers in separate small bowls. Add just enough vinaigrette

to each bowl to lightly coat the vegetables. Toss to combine.

Place the tuna in the center of the seasoned lettuce on the platter. Arrange the potatoes, tomatoes, *haricots verts*, peppers, and hard-cooked eggs around the tuna. Crisscross the anchovy fillets on top of the tuna. Sprinkle the salad with the chopped herbs and place the olives around the edge. Serve immediately.

Demonstration

Brandade de Morue (Purée of Salt Cod and Garlic)

Serves 4

Estimated time to complete: 48 hours soaking, 30 minutes preparation

Ingredients	Equipment
230 grams (8 ounces) salt cod	Medium bowl
60 milliliters (1⁄4 cup) milk or half-and-half	Colander
150 milliliters (2⁄3 cup) extra-virgin olive oil, plus more if necessary	Small saucepan
120 grams (1⁄4 pound) boiled Idaho potatoes, mashed with a fork	Fine sieve
2 cloves garlic, *haché*	Flat-bottomed saucepan
	Wooden spoon

Prepare your *mise en place.*

Place the cod in a medium bowl covered with 3 inches cold water. Allow to soak for 24 to 48 hours, changing the water periodically, until excess salt has been removed and the dried cod has softened. Drain well.

Cut the cod into pieces and place in a small saucepan covered with about an inch of cold water. Place over medium-high heat and bring to a simmer. Lower the heat and simmer for about 8 minutes or until the fish flakes easily when pierced with a fork. Remove from the heat and place in a fine sieve to drain well.

When the cod is cool enough to handle, remove and discard any skin and bones that remain. Set aside.

Place the milk in the small saucepan over medium heat and bring to a boil. Remove from the heat and set aside.

Place the olive oil in a flat-bottomed saucepan over high heat. When it is smoking, reduce the heat and add the reserved cod. Using a wooden spoon, work the cod into the hot oil for about 5 minutes or until a pastelike mixture has formed.

Remove the pan from the heat. Add the potatoes and garlic and continue to work the mixture with a wooden spoon, adding the warm milk and, if necessary, more olive oil (see note) until a smooth, thick mixture has formed. Remove from the heat and serve.

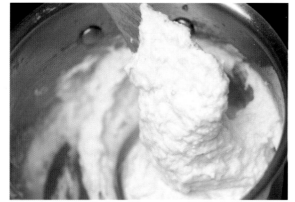

Note

The amount of oil required depends upon the dryness of the cod.

Dean's Tip

"A bit of the skin of the fish added to the mixture gives a velvety texture to the finished brandade."

Dean Jacques Pépin

Session 6

Working with Eggs

Chefs' Tips

"Eggs are extremely temperature sensitive so, in most cases, cook them with gentle heat."

Chef Candy Argondizza

"In sweet and savory preparations, the temperature of the raw egg can influence the outcome of the recipe."

Chef Dominick Cerrone

Theory

Understanding the Egg

An egg is composed of a brown or white outer shell, consisting primarily of calcium carbonate, that contains seven interior elements. The shell color does not affect the thickness of the shell nor the quality, flavor, nutritive value, or cooking characteristics of the egg but is determined by the breed of chicken that produced it. Eggs stand alone as the most versatile and nutritious food given to mankind. One large egg contributes approximately 6.5 grams of protein (or about 13 percent of the average adult's minimum daily requirement), as well as substantial amounts of iron, choline, thiamin, phosphorus, and the vitamins A, D, and E. The yolk contains most of the fat, cholesterol, vitamins, and half of the protein while the white, also known as the albumen, is composed almost entirely of water and proteins called albumins. It also contains niacin, riboflavin, and minerals. The most common eggs used today are those of chickens, although turkey, goose, duck, and quail eggs are also sold.

The outer shell accounts for about 9 to 12 percent of the total weight of an egg. It is the egg's first line of defense against bacterial contamination. A protective coating called the cuticle, or bloom, covers the surface and serves to preserve freshness and prevent microbial contamination of the contents by blocking the pores in the shell. The strength of the shell is greatly influenced by the vitamins and minerals in the hen's diet: The higher the content of calcium, phosphorus, manganese, and vitamin D, the stronger the shell. There are anywhere from seven to seventeen thousand almost infinitesimal pores distributed throughout the shell that permit moisture and carbon dioxide to escape and air to move in and form the air cell.

Brown eggs come from reddish-brown hens such as Rhode Island reds, Plymouth Rocks, and New Hampshires (obviously all New England favorites). White eggs are produced by white hens such as white leghorns (America's most common chicken). Rare breeds such as Araucana will produce eggs in an array of pastel blue and green colors. No matter the color, if the eggs are handled in the same manner, the taste and nutrition will be equal.

The Internal Composition of an Egg

Air cell: The pocket of air found at the larger end of the egg. It is easily observed at the flattened end of a peeled, hard-boiled egg. When laid, the egg is quite warm. As it cools, the contents contract and the air cell is formed as the inner shell membrane separates from the outer membrane. The air cell increases in size as the egg ages and air enters, replacing the original moisture and carbon dioxide that has leaked through the pores of the shell as time passes. The size of the air cell is one means used for determining the grade of an egg.

Shell membranes: Immediately inside the shell, two membranes—inner and outer—surround the albumen (white) to provide a protective barrier against bacterial penetration. The air cell forms between these two membranes.

Albumen: The albumen, the white part of the egg surrounding the yolk, is made up of four alternating layers of thin and thick consistencies. Listing from the yolk outward, the layers consist of the inner thick chalaziferous white; the inner thin white; the outer thick white; and finally, the outer thin white. The outer thin layer, located nearest to the shell, encloses the thicker layers of albumen in a high-quality egg. In these same eggs, the thicker layers stand higher and spread less than thin albumen, while in lower-grade eggs they thin and become indistinguishable from the thinnest layer. As the egg ages, the albumen tends to thin, as the egg protein changes in character over time. Together, the two albumens account for about 67 percent of an egg's liquid weight as well as half of the protein and a good portion of niacin, riboflavin, chlorine, magnesium, potassium, sodium, and sulfur. Albumen is actually more opalescent than pure white, with its cloudy appearance linked to the carbon dioxide contained in the white. Since, as the egg ages, carbon dioxide escapes, the albumen of older eggs is clearer and more transparent than that of fresh eggs. When vigorously beaten by hand or machine, albumen foams and increases in volume by six to eight times. Beaten egg whites are essential for the creation of successful soufflés, meringues, angel food and sponge cakes, and light, fluffy omelettes.

Chalazae: Thick, twisted, ropelike strands of egg white attached to two sides of the yolk, which serve to hold it in place at the center of the thick egg albumen. If readily observed upon cracking the raw egg open, they are a sign of freshness. Although sometimes rather strange looking, chalazae are neither imperfections nor beginning embryos and do not interfere with any cooking or beating process;

however, most chefs strain them out when making a stirred custard.

Vitelline membrane: A transparent, paper-thin seal that covers and keeps the egg yolk intact. It is weakest at the germinal disc and tends to become more fragile as the egg ages.

Germinal disc: This is the entrance of the latebra, the channel leading to the center of the yolk. It is a barely noticeable slight depression on the surface of the yolk through which the sperm enter and travel to the center when an egg is fertilized and the embryo begins to form.

Yolk (vitelline): The interior yellow globe that accounts for about 33 percent of the egg's total liquid weight and includes all the fat and half the protein, as well as the higher proportion of vitamins and minerals (except niacin and riboflavin) such as phosphorus, manganese, iron, copper, iodine, and calcium. One of the few foods with vitamin D, the yolk contains all the egg's vitamins A, D, and E. The color will vary, depending upon the type of feed given, but pale or deep, it is not indicative of the nutritive value contained therein. The yolk is responsible for the emulsifying and enrichment properties of the egg. The yolk carries 59 calories, which is 90 percent of the calories in a whole egg.

Egg Terms

Candling: Years ago, inspectors checked egg quality by holding a candle up against the egg to view the interior. This process is now mechanized, with eggs moving along on rollers over high-intensity lights, but it is still referred to as "candling."

Breakout: In commercial production, eggs are randomly selected to be broken on a clean, flat surface where, for quality assurance, the height and thickness of the albumen and the shape, color, and density of the yolk are measured.

Washing: The law requires that eggs be washed and sanitized before being packed for shipping. The natural protective layer, the bloom that coats the shell and seals the pores to prevent moisture loss and interior bacterial contamination is thus removed. Some producers then coat the eggs with a very thin layer of mineral oil to replace it for consumer assurance of safety.

Determining the Freshness of an Egg

Is a farm-fresh, just-laid egg the freshest you can buy? There is some debate on this issue, as so many other factors help determine the freshness of an egg: the temperature at which it has been held, the storage humidity, and the handling process to name three. Proper handling translates to prompt gathering, washing, and oiling within a few hours after being laid. Most commercially produced eggs are handled with extreme care from laying to market and reach the marketplace within a few days of leaving the laying house. So, if handled properly by the producer, the market, and the buyer, an egg should be "farm-fresh" when it reaches the table.

An egg deteriorates very rapidly at room temperature, as the warmth allows moisture and carbon dioxide to escape through the pores in the shell. This, in turn, causes the air cell to expand and the albumen to thin. The ideal storage temperature is one that does not go above 4°C (40°F) with a relative humidity of 70 to 80 percent. Consequently, a freshly laid egg held at room temperature for one day will age as much as a properly refrigerated egg will age in a week.

As an egg ages, the albumen becomes thinner and the yolk becomes flatter. These changes do not have any significant effect on the nutritional quality or the functional cooking properties of the egg. However, age will affect the appearance of a cooked egg; fresher eggs hold a tall, firm shape in a pan, while older eggs spread out. This is particularly important when poaching, frying, or coddling. On the other hand, when boiled, older eggs are generally easier to peel than very fresh eggs.

As a general rule of thumb when purchasing and storing eggs, choose a reputable market with high volume and rapid turnover, where eggs are kept in cartons in a refrigerated case. Before buying, open the carton and check for dirt and cracked shells and, of course, do not purchase eggs in anything less than pristine condition. If an egg is damaged after purchasing and leaks into the carton, discard it and wash and dry the remaining eggs before refrigerating. Do not remove eggs from the storage carton, as it helps preserve their freshness and prevent moisture loss as well as the absorption of odors from other foods stored alongside them.

Do not rely on old wives' tales to determine the freshness of an egg. For instance, freshness cannot be judged by placing an egg in salt water to determine if it sinks or floats. A carefully controlled brine test is sometimes used in the commercial marketplace to judge shell thickness of eggs for hatching purposes, but it has no application to the freshness of table eggs.

Grading, Sizing, and Packaging of Eggs

In the grading process, eggs are judged on both their interior and exterior quality and are sorted according to weight. Grade and size are not related to each other. In descending order of quality, standard grades are AA, A, and B. There is no difference in nutritive value among the different grades.

Deans' Tips

"When you separate eggs, crack them on the work surface. If you crack them on the edge of the bowl, the broken shell may pierce the yolk, which can cause a bit of the yolk to go into the egg whites. If this happens, a meringue will not reach its full volume because of the fat in the egg yolks."

Dean Jacques Torres

"The egg is the perfect food, the perfect shape, and one of the most versatile ingredients for the cook."

Dean Jacques Pépin

	Grade AA	Grade A	Grade B
Breakout appearance	Covers a small area.	Covers a moderate area.	Covers a wide area.
Albumen appearance	Thick and stands high; chalazae prominent.	Reasonably thick, stands fairly high; chalazae prominent.	Small amount of thick white; chalazae small or absent; appears weak.
Yolk appearance	Firm, round, high.	Firm and fairly high.	Somewhat flattened and enlarged.
Shell appearance	Approximates usual shape; generally clean; ridges or rough spots that do not affect strength are permitted.	Same as for AA.	Abnormal shape; some slight stained areas permitted; unbroken; ridges and thin spots permitted.
Usage	Ideal for any use but especially desirable for poaching, frying, and cooking in shell.	Same as for AA.	Good for scrambling and baking, and in recipes.

Several factors influence the size of an egg, including the breed of chicken, the age and weight of the laying bird, and the environmental conditions in which the hen was raised. Obviously, a healthy, drug-free, well-adjusted bird raised in a natural setting will produce more and better eggs than one raised in less-than-desirable conditions. And, in general, the older the hen, the larger the egg.

Eggs are sized based on their minimum weight per dozen, as follows: jumbo, extra large, large, medium, small, and peewee, with the most commonly available sizes being extra large, large, and medium.

Jumbo: 30 ounces per dozen, 56 pounds per standard 30-dozen case

Extra Large: 27 ounces per dozen, 50½ pounds per standard 30-dozen case

Large: 24 ounces per dozen, 45 pounds per standard 30-dozen case

Medium: 21 ounces per dozen, 39½ pounds per standard 30-dozen case

Small: 18 ounces per dozen, 34 pounds per standard 30-dozen case

Peewee: 15 ounces per dozen, 28 pounds per standard 30-dozen case

For commercial distribution, eggs are packed in flats. There are 30 eggs in one flat; 12 flats in one case to equal 30 dozen eggs; and 6 flats in a half-case to equal 15 dozen eggs. Sizes vary according to weight and are classified according to the minimum net weight expressed in ounces per dozen.

Egg Safety

Although very, very few eggs carry internal bacterial infection at the beginning of their cycle, through improper handling or cooking eggs can become contaminated. Most often, the *Salmonella enteritidis* bacteria that can cause severe gastrointestinal illness are found to be the culprit. As well as being contracted through improper handling or cooking, these virulent bacteria can survive and grow in hens and subsequently be transmitted to the egg. This is a very rare happenstance—about 1 in 20,000 eggs—but it indicates that all eggs should be

"Occasionally, I cook an egg in a beautiful, long metal fireplace spoon that a friend made for me, but in general I don't like equipment to get in the way of handling the food."

Dean Alice Waters

"If the whipping bowl is not thoroughly clean, any fat clinging to it will keep the egg whites from beating properly by preventing the albumen from coagulating."

Dean Jacques Pépin

Chef's Tip

"Always cover egg yolks if you are not using them immediately, as they quickly form a skin on top."

Chef Susan Lifrieri

treated with respect. The yolk of the egg is generally the point of infection, with the white almost never infected. The bacteria rarely causes fatalities in healthy adults but can be extremely serious to infants and small children, pregnant women, the infirm, those with compromised immune systems, or the elderly.

Because of the virulence of the *Salmonella* bacteria, kitchen sanitation is of the utmost importance when using eggs.

° Eggs, raw or cooked, should always be refrigerated as quickly as possible and left unrefrigerated for as short a period as is sensible.

° Hands, utensils, work surfaces, and pots and pans should be washed in very hot, soapy water after coming into contact with eggs.

° Raw eggs should not be served to infants and small children, pregnant women, the infirm, those with compromised immune systems, or the elderly.

° Before adding eggs to other ingredients, they should be checked for purity by breaking them, one at a time, into a small bowl.

° If concerned about egg safety, bring poached, fried, coddled, baked, or soft-boiled eggs to 60°C (140°F) for 3½ minutes to ensure that enough heat has penetrated to kill any existing bacteria. This amount of heat and cooking time will cause the white to be solid and the yolk to firm slightly, but the yolk will not be hard.

Technique
Methods of Cooking Eggs

Eggs Separated for Preparation

Either the white or the yolk may be used separately. Egg whites can be beaten until stiff for *soufflés* or meringues, or to lighten cakes and mousses. Yolks are used as a *liaison* to thicken and enrich sauces, and as an emulsifying agent in sauces such as *hollandaise* and *mayonnaise*. Yolks can also be folded or stirred into beaten egg whites to create dishes with a lighter, fluffier texture, as in baked Alaska (*omelette norvégienne*).

Eggs Cooked in the Shell

Eggs cooked in the shell should be placed in a saucepan without a lid over medium-high heat, covered by 1 inch of cold water and timed from the point at which the water comes to a boil. Adding 45 milliliters (about 3 tablespoons) white vinegar for every quart of water helps prevent the albumen from leaking into the water if any shells crack. The hot water should be drained when the cooking time is complete. If the eggs will not be used immediately, it is necessary to chill them. Cover the drained, hot eggs with ice water to cool them as quickly as possible. Cooking times are as follows:

° Soft-boiled (*oeuf coque*): 3 minutes

° Medium-soft-boiled (*oeuf mollet*): 5 minutes

° Hard-boiled (*oeuf dur*): 10 to 11 minutes

Cooked Whole and Out of the Shell

In this process, whites and yolks are not mixed together but are cooked so that the yolk remains intact. Generally, these preparations are cooked until the white has set and the yolk is soft and runny.

- Baked in a dish with cream (*oeuf cocotte*)

- Deep-fried (not usually done in America) (*oeuf frit*)

- Poached (*oeuf poché*)

- Fried (actually sautéed) (*oeuf poêlé*)

- Sunny-side up (*oeuf au plat*)

Cooked with Whites and Yolks Mixed

In this process, the white and yolk are beaten and cooked together for uniform consistency and taste.

- Scrambled (*oeuf brouillé*)

- Flat omelette (*omelette plate*)

- Rolled omelette (may be filled) (*omelette roulée*)

Theory
The Omelette

In both classical and traditional French cooking, an omelette is made in a specialized pan called a **poêle à omelette**. This pan, usually 9 to 10 inches round, with low, slightly sloping sides, is an integral element in the execution of a properly made omelette. The best possible pan is one that is nonstick with a heavy bottom and comfortable handle. If it is not nonstick, it should be carefully seasoned (see page 12) so that the eggs do not stick. A well-seasoned *poêle* should never be washed but it must be kept scrupulously clean to avoid bacterial contamination or imparting unpleasant tastes to the finished omelette. When necessary, clean the *poêle* with coarse salt and a clean towel.

Important guidelines to remember when preparing omelettes:

- Omelettes must be prepared to order; they cannot be held successfully.

- It is not necessary to add much fat (butter or oil) to the pan when using a well-seasoned *poêle*.

- The *poêle* should be thoroughly heated but not so hot that the fat burns or decomposes.

- The eggs should be at room temperature and moderately beaten. The goal is to combine them thoroughly without incorporating excess air.

- Adding water, milk, or cream to the beaten eggs will dilute the egg protein and create an omelette that is more tender.

- There is no hard-and-fast rule about the degree to which an omelette should be cooked. Some cooks prefer them lightly browned, while others prefer no coloration at all. The French generally prefer no coloration, particularly on rolled omelettes.

- Flat omelettes can be cooked until fairly firm and lightly browned, while rolled omelettes generally should be served as the French prefer — loose and slightly runny in the center (*baveuse*).

- Just before serving, lightly brush the finished omelette with melted butter (*lustrer*).

Technique

General Procedure for Making Flat (*Plate*) or Rolled (*Roulée*) Omelettes

1. Clean and season a *poêle* well or use a nonstick omelette pan with a nonabrasive utensil to keep from damaging the nonstick coating as you stir.

2. Use two large eggs for an appetizer omelette and three large eggs for a breakfast or entrée omelette.

3. For quality assurance, break the eggs, one at a

time, into a ramekin or small bowl. If the eggs are perfect, with unbroken yolks, transfer them one at a time to a mixing bowl.

4. Add 10 milliliters (2 teaspoons) of cream per egg to the mixing bowl.

5. Season the egg-cream mixture with salt and pepper and gently beat with a fork.

6. Heat the *poêle* over medium heat; when hot, add 5 grams (1 teaspoon) unsalted butter.

7. When the butter foam subsides, proceed as described below, according to the kind of omelette you are making.

To make a flat omelette:
Add the eggs to the *poêle* without stirring. Do not stir for 5 seconds. Pull in the sides with a fork, lightly

scramble the eggs, and tap the bottom of the pan against the stove to help spread the eggs evenly over the bottom. When the omelette is lightly colored on the bottom, loosen the edges with a spatula, flip it, and cook the other side until it is lightly browned. (Alternatively, instead of flipping, place the omelette under the salamander or broiler.) The omelette should be soft but not runny in the center. *Lustrer* (lightly brush the top with melted butter), garnish according to the requirements of the recipe, and serve.

To make a rolled omelette:

Add the eggs to the foaming butter, stirring continuously with a fork. When the omelette has set slightly, stop stirring. Cook, without turning, until the omelette is soft but not runny in the center. Carefully roll the omelette onto a warm plate, seam side down. If necessary, adjust the shape into a neat roll using a clean kitchen towel. (The point at which the stirring stops is the key to creating a smooth, even omelette.) A runny (*baveuse*) omelette will require less stirring than a firm one. A rolled omelette should have an even, smooth, uncolored surface.

To make a filled rolled omelette:

Place the desired filling in the center of the omelette as soon as it has reached the desired degree of doneness. Fold one edge of the omelette over onto the other to cover the filling. If necessary, lift the pan by the handle, tilt and lightly tap the handle so that the omelette will move up from the pan to completely enclose the filling. You can also use a fork to help fold the omelette over. Carefully roll the filled omelette onto a warm plate, seam side down. If necessary, adjust the shape into a neat roll using a clean kitchen towel.

Chef's Tip

"When making an omelet, salt the eggs after beating them so that they won't break down and get watery."

Chef Henri Viain

Rolled Omelettes	Ingredients
Omelette au fromage	Omelette with cheese, usually Gruyère
Omelette aux fines herbes	Omelette with parsley, chervil, tarragon, and chives
Omelette aux champignons	Omelette with sliced, sautéed mushrooms
Omelette Richemonde	Omelette with morels, lightly coated with Mornay sauce and glazed under a salamander
Omelette à la confiture	Omelette with jelly, usually currant, sprinkled with confectioners' sugar and *quadrilléed* with an iron (see page 168)

Flat Omelettes	Ingredients
Omelette fermière	Omelette with vegetables *paysanne*, ham, and *fines herbes*
Omelette Gasconne	Omelette cooked in goose fat with ham, onions, parsley, and garlic
Omelette paysanne	Omelette with sorrel, potatoes, and *fines herbes*
Omelette Basquaise	Omelette with a mixture of tomato, bell pepper, and onion

General Procedure for Making Poached Eggs (*Oeufs Pochés*)

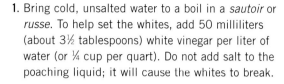
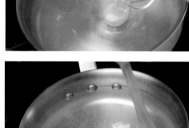

1. Bring cold, unsalted water to a boil in a *sautoir* or *russe*. To help set the whites, add 50 milliliters (about 3½ tablespoons) white vinegar per liter of water (or ¼ cup per quart). Do not add salt to the poaching liquid; it will cause the whites to break.

2. Set aside a bowl filled with clean, cold water.

3. When the water comes to a boil, lower the temperature to 82°C (180°F) for poaching.

4. For quality assurance, break the eggs, one at a time, into a ramekin or small dish. If the eggs are perfect, with unbroken yolks, one at a time, carefully slip the whole eggs into the poaching liquid.

5. Cook for 3 minutes or until the whites are firm and the yolks are covered with a thin, almost transparent film and remain soft and runny.

6. Using a slotted spoon, lift the eggs one at a time from the poaching liquid and place them in the reserved bowl of cold water to stop the cooking and remove any trace of the vinegar flavor.

7. Using a slotted spoon, transfer the eggs to a double layer of paper towels or a clean kitchen towel to drain.

8. Using a small, sharp knife or kitchen scissors, trim off any ragged edges.

9. If holding poached eggs for more than a few minutes, refrigerate. Poached eggs may be chilled and held for up to 2 hours. When ready to serve, quickly reheat the poached eggs in simmering, salted water for about two minutes and serve hot as directed in a specific recipe.

General Procedure for Making Sunny-side Up Eggs *(Oeufs au Plat)*

1. Place 5 grams (1 teaspoon) unsalted butter in a small frying pan or round, heatproof dish (*plat rond*).

2. Lightly season the butter with salt and pepper.

3. Place the pan over medium heat until just hot.

4. For quality assurance, break the eggs, one at a time, into separate ramekins or small dishes.

5. If the eggs are perfect, with unbroken yolks, gently slide the eggs into the hot pan or *plat* and cook over medium heat just until the white firms without blistering around the edges.

6. Slip the eggs out of the pan onto a warm plate and serve hot.

Variations:

Oeufs miroir: Preheat the oven to 177°C (350°F). Place the eggs into the oven in a *plat rond* and bake for about 2 minutes or just until set.

Oeufs poêlé: Cook the eggs in a well-seasoned *poêle*. When the eggs are just set as for *oeufs au plat*, flip them and cook for 10 seconds on the other side. In English this preparation is known as eggs over easy.

General Procedure for Making Scrambled Eggs (*Oeufs Brouillés*)

1. For quality assurance, break the eggs, one at a time, into a ramekin or small dish. If the eggs are perfect, with unbroken yolks, transfer them one at a time to a mixing bowl.

2. Season the eggs with salt and pepper. If desired, add 10 milliliters (2 teaspoons) cream per egg.

3. Heat 10 grams (2 teaspoons) unsalted butter per egg in a *sautoir* or *russe* over medium heat.

4. Pour the eggs into the hot, buttered pan. Immediately lower the heat and cook, stirring constantly, for about 4 minutes or until the eggs are soft and slightly runny but thick.

5. Remove the eggs from the heat. If desired, add additional butter and, if necessary, adjust the seasoning. Serve hot.

General Procedure for Making Boiled Eggs (*Oeufs à la Coque*)

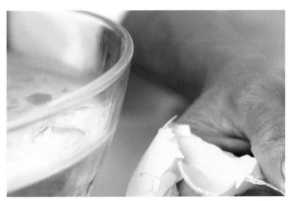

1. Eggs to be boiled should be at room temperature.

2. Place the eggs in a saucepan with cold water to cover by 1 inch over medium-high heat.

3. Add 50 milliliters (about 3½ tablespoons) white vinegar per liter of water (or ¼ cup per quart), if using.

4. Bring to a boil; then immediately reduce the heat to a gentle simmer.

5. Cook as desired (see time chart).

6. Soft-boiled (*oeufs coques*) and medium-soft-boiled eggs (*oeufs mollets*) should be served immediately.

7. Hard-boiled eggs (*oeufs durs*) should be transferred immediately to ice water to set until completely cool and to prevent a gray-green ring from forming around the firm yolk. Chill until completely cold.

8. To facilitate peeling for hard-boiled eggs, you can lift the warm eggs from the chilling water, crack the shells slightly, and return them to the cold water until completely cold. When chilled, the shell should peel right off.

Demonstration

Oeufs Cocottes à la Crème (Eggs Baked in Cream)

Serves 4

Estimated time to complete: 40 minutes

Ingredients	Equipment
200 milliliters (14 tablespoons) heavy cream	One 8-inch square baking dish at least 2½ inches deep
20 grams (1½ tablepoons) unsalted butter, at	Parchment paper
room temperature	Medium saucepan
Coarse salt	Four 4-ounce *cocottes* (ramekins)
4 large eggs, at room temperature	Ramekin or small dish
14 grams (2 tablespoons plus 2 teaspoons) minced fresh	Ladle
flat-leaf parsley	4 small plates
4 slices white toast, crusts removed, cut into triangles	

Prepare your *mise en place*.

Preheat the oven to 177°C (350°F).

Line a baking dish large enough to hold four *cocottes* or small ramekins with parchment paper. Set aside.

Place the cream in a medium saucepan over medium heat. Bring to a gentle simmer and cook, stirring occasionally, for about 10 minutes or until the cream has reduced by two thirds. Take care that it does not boil or it will quickly bubble up and over the sides of the pan. Remove the pan from the heat and set aside.

Butter and lightly salt the inside of each *cocotte*.

One at a time, break each egg into a ramekin or small bowl. If the egg is perfect, with an unbroken yolk, transfer it to a seasoned *cocotte*. (This method also ensures that no bacteria is transmitted from the egg shell to the finished dish.)

Ladle an equal portion of warm cream into each *cocotte*. The cream should come halfway up the egg. Place the filled *cocottes* into the lined baking dish. Add boiling water to come halfway up the sides of the

cocottes. The parchment paper will anchor the dishes in place, and the water will help keep the mixture moist.

Bake for 8 to 10 minutes or until the whites are firm and the yolks are covered with a light film but still runny.

Remove the dish from the oven and place a *cocotte* on each of four small plates. Sprinkle with parsley and place with two toast points on each plate.

Session 7

Working with Potatoes

Theory

General Information About the Potato

Potatoes (*Solanum tuberosum*) are tubers that form on underground vines developed from seed potatoes, small pieces of the previous year's crop. Composed mostly of water but rich in carbohydrates, potassium, and nitrogen, potatoes are an important cultivar throughout the world. They thrive in moist, volcanic soil where temperatures range in the sunny 60s during the day and drop precipitously during the night. Now quite blight resistant, potatoes come in a wide variety of shapes, colors, and sizes. Their flesh can be white, ivory, yellow, pink, red, purple, or blue; their skin (which holds the primary nutritional components) can be smooth, rough, pebbly, or even slightly scratchy; their shape can be elongated, oval, or round; they can be as tiny as a marble or weighty as a pound.

Potatoes were introduced into Europe in the 1500s as explorers of the New World returned bringing exotic specimens from the countries of the Andes Mountains. As a member of the deadly nightshade family (like tomatoes, another New World discovery), Andean potatoes were first thought to be poisonous and, as such, were greeted with much suspicion. The fact that they can develop toxins when not stored properly did not help broaden their appeal. However, the ease with which they can be grown, harvested, and transported; their acceptance of long storage periods; their versatility in the kitchen; and their nutritious makeup all helped make potatoes become the fourth most cultivated crop worldwide after corn, wheat, and rice.

Because of the initial suspicion that greeted potatoes in Europe, they were at first designated as food for the poor. However, even facing starvation, many peasants refused to eat them because of the stigma that surrounded them. The fact that some religions thought potatoes "ungodly" because they grew so deep in the ground and were therefore close to the devil, combined with the fact that the cooking water of potatoes darkened as the vegetable cooked, only served to attach further sinister qualities to this most nutritious food.

In France, potatoes had a very difficult start, as priests claimed that they caused leprosy and, in some areas, even banned their production. In addition, bread was so ingrained in the diet of the poor that many refused to replace their daily ration with a cooked potato. However, in the 1600s, when peasants in the mountainous region of eastern France discovered that potatoes would thrive in their inhospitable growing climate, they began making inroads into the culinary fare of the country.

In 1771, Antonin-Auguste Parmentier, a French agronomist who was fed potatoes when he was a German prisoner during the Seven Years War, wrote a thesis saluting the potato as a vegetable that could stave off starvation during famines and shortages. Parmentier's enthusiastic support and proof that the tuber could be

easily and successfully cultivated and harvested in France engaged the attention of King Louis XVI. The king granted Parmentier twenty hectares of impoverished land in the Gironde on which he was to attempt an experimental potato production. Parmentier was so successful that potato flowers became a much-desired decoration in the court, and within twenty years, the potato was a respected ingredient on the tables of the upper classes. It is interesting to note that potatoes have come to be known by a number of names in France—from the simple *patate* to the proper *pommes de terre* to the elegant *truffes* (designating potatoes as truffles for the poor). Through the evolution of classic French cooking, we now have many potato dishes that honor Parmentier by using his name in their title (for example *potage Parmentier*, or potato soup).

Potatoes are grown all over the world, but some of the most desirable varieties thrive in France. The Loire region produces the much-respected *fine de ratte de Loire*; the *Bintje*, *Roseval*, and *Picardine* are grown in northern France; Brittany grows the *Noirmoutier*; and Île de Ré gives us the *Charlotte* and *Amandine*, among others. Many of these potatoes are now also being grown as heirloom or heritage potatoes in the United States.

Essentially there are two categories of potatoes, mealy and waxy. Mealy potatoes have low moisture, high starch, and a dry flesh that, when cooked, can be fluffed with ease. Waxy potatoes are denser and tend to hold their shape when cooked. Mealy potatoes are used for baking, mashing, and frying; waxy potatoes are used primarily for boiling and roasting, although they can also be fried. In the United States, the most popular potatoes are the russet (also known as Idaho or baking potatoes), Irish cobbler, Katahdin, Kennebec, Yukon gold, creamer, and red bliss. When buying potatoes, look for those that are of a uniform size with clean, unblemished skins and no sign of a green blush (which may signify that they contain toxic alkaloids), sprouting, or shriveling. It is not always important to check the grading size, as "U.S. No. 1" designates only the largest, most uniform potatoes. Heirloom potatoes that are often bumpy and odd shaped or small potatoes would, therefore, not qualify for this grade but are nonetheless delicious.

Only potatoes that are straight from the vine, extremely thin-skinned, slightly immature, and hard should be called new potatoes. However, you will often find older, small potatoes labeled "new" in the supermarket. Mature potatoes are harvested after the vines have begun to bloom or turn color, when the skins are tougher and the flesh drier. Since the fragile skins are susceptible to damage when being harvested by machine, mature potatoes are cured in cool, dry storage for a few weeks to allow the skins to heal before being moved to long-term storage at a much lower temperature. In the kitchen, potatoes should be stored in a cool, dry spot and used as soon as possible after purchased.

Technique
Classic Cuts for Potatoes (*Taillage*)

Proper cutting results in potatoes of uniform size and shape and ensures that the potatoes will cook evenly. It is particularly important to follow the guidelines for proper cutting because it allows more than one person to prepare the items required for a specific recipe. Appropriate cutting also is used to enhance the aesthetic of the finished presentation.

The traditional nomenclature for standard cutting procedures for potatoes is as follows:

Hairs (*cheveux*): 7 centimeters by .5 millimeter square (2¾ inches by ¹⁄₆₄ inch)

Straws (*pailles*): 7 centimeters by 1.5 millimeters square (2¾ inches by ¹⁄₁₆ inch)

Matchsticks (*allumettes*): 7 centimeters by 5 millimeters square (2¾ inches by ³⁄₁₆ inch)

Thin fries (*mignonettes*): 7 centimeters by 6 millimeters square (2¾ inches by ¼ inch)

Regular fries (*frites*): 7 centimeters by 8 millimeters square (2¾ inches by ⁵⁄₁₆ inch)

Thick fries (*pont-neuf*): 7 centimeters by 9 millimeters square (2¾ inches by ⅜ inch)

Hazelnut shape (*noisettes*)

Small ball (*Parisienne*)

Olive-shaped (*olives*)

Parmentier: 1.2-centimeter (½-inch) squares

Vert pres: 7-millimeter (¼-inch) squares

Potato chips (*pommes chips*): Mandoline-cut paper-thin slices

Puffed potato chips (*pommes soufflées*): 7 centimeters by 3 millimeters (2¾ inches by ⅛ inch)

Waffle chips (*gaufrettes*): Mandoline-cut round or oval double waffle chips 1.5 millimeters (¹⁄₁₆ inch) thick

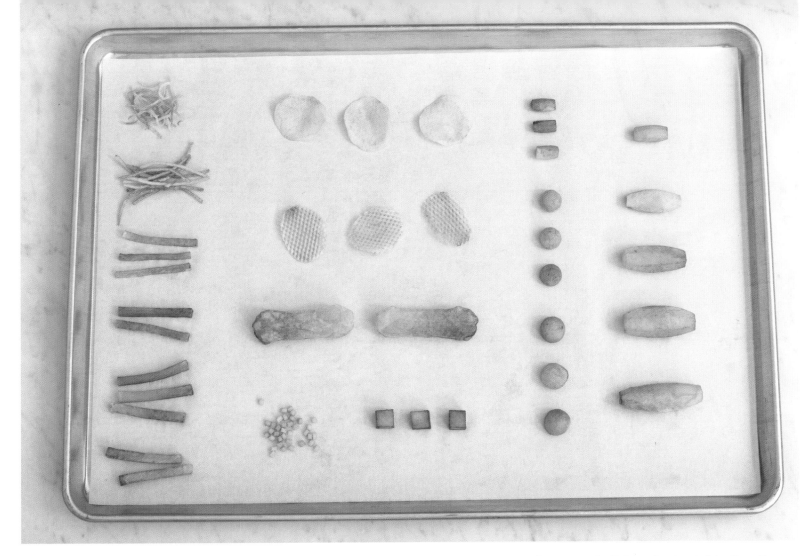

Rounds (*liards*): 4 centimeters diameter by 1.5 millimeters (1½ inches by ⅙ inch) thick, evenly shaped with a biscuit cutter and then mandoline-cut into slices

Tournée

Gousse d'ail, tournée: The size of a garlic clove

Cocotte, tournée: 4 centimeters tall by 2 centimeters wide (1½ inches by ¾ inch)

Château, tournée: 7.5 centimeters tall by 3 centimeters wide (3 by 1³⁄₁₆ inches)

Steamed potatoes (*vapeur*), tournée: 6 centimeters tall by 3 centimeters wide (2⅜ by 1³⁄₁₆ inches)

Melted potatoes (*fondante*), tournée: 8 centimeters tall by 4 centimeters wide (3⅛ by 1½ inches)

Methods of Cooking Potatoes

There are a great many methods of cooking the versatile potato. They range from the simple—boiled—to the elaborate—rich *gratin Dauphinois* (see page 132). A few of those methods are explained in the following pages.

Deep-Frying

Deep-fried potatoes are probably the most popular vegetable in the world, particularly with the proliferation of fast-food restaurants featuring French fries. To deep-fry is to submerge an item entirely in hot fat (oil or other fats) until completely cooked and crisp. When deep-frying, the goal is to obtain a golden-brown, crisp crust, which occurs when the external protein coagulates. The interior should be moist and tender. This method of cooking is applied to many other vegetables, as well as to meat, poultry, and seafood.

Guidelines for Deep-frying

When the item to be fried is very dry on the surface, the caramelization of the natural juices and sugars transforms starch into a substance known as dextrin, giving it color and texture. The item should be rinsed and very thoroughly dried unless directed otherwise in a specific recipe. With the exception of *pommes souf-flées*, potatoes are always rinsed to remove excess starch and then well-dried and deep-fried raw with no external coating. Other moister vegetables should also be rinsed and well dried; in addition they will require a surface coating of flour, breadcrumbs, or batter when being deep-fried. When properly deep-fried, this outer crust forms immediately, preventing the fried item from absorbing the hot fat. For this reason, deep-frying is considered a dry-heat method of cooking. (Dry-heat cooking is achieved through broiling, baking, grilling over coals, or through cooking directly on an ungreased pan. This method usually results in deep color, crisp texture, and refined flavor.) Salt is never added before deep-frying.

Deep-frying is most often done in a deep-fat fryer, which can be either a permanent installation in the kitchen or a special stovetop pot with a wire basket insert made especially for this purpose. Deep-frying can also be done on the stovetop in a deep, heavy saucepan, with a wire basket or sieve used to hold the food. A basket should always be used so that the food can be easily lifted from the fat when done.

The fat used for deep-frying can be either a vegetable oil with a high smoke point and mild flavor (such as peanut oil), or a solid vegetable shortening designed especially for frying. Never combine different types of fats, as this may cause foaming that may result in a fire. Oil can be reused for some period of time, but if it is reused it must be strained after each use, covered, and stored in a cool, dry place. However, oil should *not* be reused when it foams up, has an odor, darkens in color, or its smoke point lowers to the point that it begins smoking as it gains heat. Note that various strong-flavored foods such as fish can impart an undesirable flavor to the frying fat that will transfer to other foods, so it is suggested that these fats not be reused. Never combine fresh oil with used.

When deep-frying, the pot should be no more than half full of fat or it will overflow when the food is added. The fat should be brought to the desired temperature before the food is added or the item will absorb too much fat before being thoroughly cooked. The correct temperature is determined by the item being cooked, but it should never exceed 218°C (425°F). Avoid preheating the fat too far in advance or overheating it, as both can cause it to decompose more quickly. Always test temperature with one piece of the item being deep-fried before adding the entire quantity. When the fat is ready, add the food in small quantities so that the temperature does not drop significantly and the fat can circulate freely around the frying food for even coloration.

If the fat catches fire, *never pour water on it in an attempt to put out the fire*. Turn off the heat and cover the fryer with a metal tray or lid to smother the flames. If it continues to burn, immediately call the fire department and use a fire extinguisher (which must always be at hand in a kitchen) intended for grease fires. Evacuate the area, if necessary.

Deep-frying Techniques

There are three basic deep-frying techniques used for potatoes: one-step, two-step, and three-step. Whatever method is used, after frying, potatoes should always be drained well on paper towels to absorb excess grease, salted when hot, and served immediately.

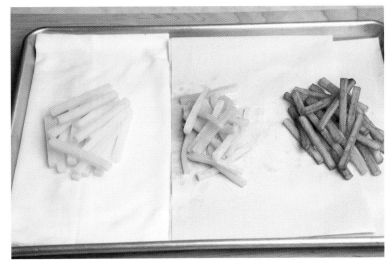

Chef's Tip

"Essential details for frying are the temperature of the oil and the amount of oil corresponding to the amount of food being fried. Overheated oil breaks down over time, darkens, and loses viscosity, changing the flavor of the oil."

Chef Henri Viain

One-step method: The potatoes are fried completely at one temperature, usually 177°C–191°C (350°F–375°F). **Two-step method:** The potatoes are first partially cooked or poached, without taking on any color, at 149°C–160°C (300°F–320°F) for about 5 or 6 minutes, depending upon thickness. They are then finished at 177°C–191°C (350°F–375°F) to quickly color and crisp the outside. The two-step method is usually applied to thicker cuts to allow the interior to be fully cooked before the outside becomes too brown. **Three-step method:** *Pommes soufflées* are the only deep-fried potato cooked using the three-step method. These puffed chips are very dramatic and make a definite statement on the plate. They are first cut into 3-millimeter (⅛-inch) slices. Without rinsing, they are cooked very slowly in fat heated to a minimum temperature of 138°C (280°F), or 160°C (320°F) at the maximum, or until just softened. The poached potatoes are then transferred to fat in a different pot that is 177°C (350°F). This second frying causes the rounds to inflate, but they are removed from the fat before they take on any color. They are then drained on paper towels and covered with a clean kitchen towel until ready to serve. Don't panic, they deflate almost immediately. Just before serving, return the potatoes to the 177°C (350°F) fat and cook until golden brown, puffed (*souffléed*), and

crisp. Using a slotted spatula or spider, carefully lift the potatoes from the fat and drain well. Salt and serve immediately.

There are a number of possible causes of deep-fried potato failure:

○ The potato slices were not properly rinsed and excess starch remained.

○ The potato slices were wet when added to the oil.

○ The oil was too cold, allowing the potatoes to absorb too much fat before cooking.

○ The oil was too hot, causing the potato exterior to burn before the interior was cooked.

○ The oil was too old or of a poor quality.

Cooking Process (*Cuisson*) for Deep-Fried Potatoes

The following chart gives the appropriate deep-frying temperatures and methods for individual cuts, which should, when properly applied, yield the perfect texture and color.

Type	Method / Temperature
Potato hairs (*pommes cheveux*)	Cooked once at 177°C–191°C (350°F–375°F)
Potato straws (*pommes pailles*)	Cooked once at 177°C–191°C (350°F–375°F)
Potato chips (*pommes chips*)	Cooked once at 177°C–191°C (350°F–375°F)
Waffle chips (*pommes gaufrettes*)	Cooked once at 177°C–191°C (350°F–375°F)
Potato matchsticks (*pommes allumettes*)	Cooked twice: first at 149°C–160°C (300°F–320°F), then at 177°C–191°C (350°F–375°F)
Thick-fried potatoes (*pommes pont-neuf*)	Cooked twice: first at 149°C–160°C (300°F–320°F), then at 177°C–191°C (350°F–375°F)
Puffed potato chips (*pommes soufflées*) (280°F–320°F),	Cooked three times: first at 138°C–160°C then twice at 177°C–191°C (350°F–375°F)

Dean's Tip

"Potatoes sautéed in duck or goose fat have a crisp outside and a moist inside and the most wonderful flavor imaginable."

Dean Jacques Pépin

Sautéed Potatoes

Pommes sautées à cru are raw, neatly trimmed, 3-millimeter (⅛-inch)–thick potato rounds that have been rinsed in cold water and thoroughly dried, sautéed in a single layer in hot oil, and finished with a bit of butter. The oil provides the higher heat necessary to give the potatoes a rich, brown color; the butter adds rich, nutty flavor. If there is too much oil in the pan, it is drained off before the butter is added. The potatoes should have a crisp exterior and a moist, tender interior.

Pommes lyonnaise are peeled, whole potatoes that are cooked until tender in salted water, then cut crosswise into rounds and sautéed in hot fat with sliced onions.

Boiled and Steamed Potatoes

Potatoes to be boiled or steamed should be 6 x 3 centimeters wide (2⅜ x 1³⁄₁₆ inches). The exceptions are *pommes de terre en chemise*, small whole potatoes boiled in their skins, and *pommes fondants*, which are cut into somewhat larger pieces.

Defining characteristics:

° Boiled potatoes (*pommes nature*) are *tournéed* to the 6-x-3-centimeter (2⅜-x-1³⁄₁₆-inch) size.

° English-style potatoes (*pommes à l'anglaise*) are simply boiled whole potatoes.

° Parsley potatoes (*pommes persillées*) are boiled potatoes garnished with chopped parsley.

° Steamed potatoes (*pommes vapeur*) are simply steamed potatoes.

° Melted potatoes (*pommes fondantes*) are boiled in consommé (chicken or beef broth).

Puréed Potatoes

The basic potato purée is made from peeled potatoes that have been cut into large pieces, boiled until tender in salted water, and then puréed. The method by which the potatoes are puréed is important to their quality. The hot potatoes are first passed through a sieve or food mill, and the crushed potatoes are then beaten with milk (or cream), salt, pepper, and sometimes freshly ground nutmeg. The beaten mixture is mounted with butter to lighten and enrich the purée. Because of the butter's richness, the amount added will often be the signature flavor of the purée. Potatoes are *never* puréed in a food processor or other electric appliance, as the speed and heat develop the gluten in the potatoes and turn them gluelike and starchy. Puréed potatoes can be served alone or used as the basis for a number of other dishes.

Pommes gratinées: Puréed potatoes sprinkled with shredded cheese and melted butter, placed in a gratin dish in a hot oven or under the salamander, and cooked until the cheese has melted and the top is golden brown.

Pommes mont d'or: Puréed potatoes with a *liaison* of egg yolk incorporated and then prepared as for *pommes gratinées*.

Pommes mousseline: Puréed potatoes with heavy cream substituted for the milk and a substantial amount of butter added.

Duchess potatoes (*pommes duchesse*): Peeled, boiled potatoes or baked potato flesh that has been dried out in the oven, puréed, seasoned, and combined with egg yolk and butter. The purée is either piped into small shapes through a pastry bag or formed into *croquettes* (small rounds, cylinders, or other neat shapes), coated with breadcrumbs, and baked or fried.

Potato croquettes (*pommes croquette*): Duchess potatoes piped into 5-x-3-centimeter (2-x-1¾₆-inch) logs, coated in breadcrumbs and deep-fried.

Potatoes dauphine (*pommes dauphine*): Equal parts cooked, dried, puréed potatoes and *pâte à choux* (see page 373), seasoned, formed into *quenelles* (small oval shapes), and deep-fried.

Potato Dishes That Are Baked

For the following molded potato dishes, the potatoes are not rinsed after being cut, as the starch is needed to help the preparations hold their shape.

Potatoes darphin (*pommes darphin*): Peeled potatoes are placed in cold water, then *julienned* without rinsing after being cut. The potato *julienne* is seasoned and placed in a 2½-centimeter (1-inch) layer in a well-oiled, heated *poêle* and cooked on the stovetop over medium heat until the bottom is golden brown. The potato cake is then flipped and the pan is transferred to a preheated 177°C (350°F) oven. The potato cake is baked for about 40 minutes or until golden brown and the potatoes are cooked through. To serve, the hot, crisp cake is cut into wedges.

Potatoes Anna (*pommes Anna*): Peeled potatoes are cut, usually on a mandoline, into 3-millimeter (⅛-inch)–thick slices and tossed in clarified butter. The potato slices are then arranged in a layer of concentric circles in a slightly heated and buttered *poêle*. Clarified butter, salt, and pepper are sprinkled over the layer. The layering and seasoning is repeated until the potatoes are 3 centimeters (1¾₆ inches) deep. The pan is placed on the stovetop to brown the bottom of the potatoes (which will prevent sticking), then placed in a preheated 177°C (350°F) oven to bake. The entire cake is flipped over halfway through the baking process to ensure even browning.

Potato gratin (*gratin Dauphinois*): Peeled potatoes are sliced 2 millimeters (¹⁄₁₆ inch) thick, simmered in heavy cream for 3 minutes, and transferred to a casserole that has been rubbed with a peeled garlic clove. Additional cream is added to the casserole to cover about half of the depth of the potatoes. Grated Gruyère cheese is sprinkled over the top and the potatoes are placed in a preheated 177°C (350°F) oven to bake for about 30 minutes or until the potatoes are tender when pierced with the point of a small, sharp knife.

Pommes campagnarde: Similar to *gratin dauphinois*, but the sliced potatoes are baked in white veal stock instead of cream, and onion and bacon are added for a richer flavor.

Demonstration

Pommes Pont-Neuf (Thick-Cut French Fries)

Serves 4

Estimated time to complete: 30 minutes

Ingredients	Equipment
600 grams (1 pound, 5 ounces) russet potatoes	Vegetable peeler
Approximately 1.9 liters (2 quarts)	Chef's knife
vegetable oil	Deep-fat fryer with basket
Coarse salt to taste	Instant-read thermometer
	Paper towels

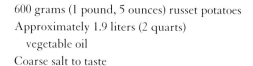

Prepare your *mise en place.*

Using the vegetable peeler, peel the potatoes and, using the chef's knife, cut them into sticks 7 centimeters (2¾ inches) long by 9 millimeters (⅜ inch) thick. Rinse under cold running water and pat very dry.

Heat the oil in the fryer over high heat to 149°C–160°C (300°F–320°F) on an instant-read thermometer.

Add the potato sticks a few at a time and poach for about 2 minutes or until the potatoes are limp and pale. Lift the basket from the fryer, gently shake off excess oil, and transfer the potatoes to paper towels to drain.

Repeat with the remaining potatoes. Set aside until you are almost ready to serve.

When ready to serve, turn the oil to high heat and bring it to 177°C–191°C (350°F–375°F) on the instant-read thermometer. Add the poached potatoes a few at a time and fry for about 3 minutes or until the potatoes are golden brown and crisp. Lift the basket from the fryer, gently shake off excess oil, and transfer the potatoes to paper towels to drain.

Season with salt while still hot and serve immediately.

Demonstration

Pommes Frites (French-Fried or Deep-Fried Potatoes)

Serves 4

Estimated time to complete: 30 minutes

Ingredients	Equipment
500 grams (1 pound, 1½ ounces) russet potatoes	Vegetable peeler
1 liter (1 quart) peanut oil	Medium bowl
Coarse salt to taste	Chef's knife or mandoline
	Deep-fat fryer with basket
	Instant-read thermometer
	Paper towels

Prepare your *mise en place*.

Using a vegetable peeler, peel the potatoes. Rinse them and place them in a bowl with cold water to cover.

Using a chef's knife or a mandoline, cut the potatoes into sticks 7 x 8 millimeters square (2¾ x ⁵⁄₁₆ inches).

Rinse the cut potatoes in cold running water and pat dry.

Heat the oil in a deep-fat fryer over medium-high heat to 149°C–160°C (300°F–320°F) on an instant-read thermometer.

Follow the two-step method for deep-frying potatoes as described on page 116: Poach the potatoes in the preheated oil for about 5 minutes or until just tender—they should not have taken on any color. Place them on paper towels to drain until you are almost ready to serve.

Raise the temperature of the oil to 177°C–191°C (350°F–375°F). Add the poached potatoes and fry for a couple of minutes or until crisp and golden brown.

Transfer the potatoes to paper towels to drain. Season with salt to taste and serve piping hot.

Demonstration

Pommes Sautées à Cru (Sautéed Potatoes)

Serves 4

Estimated time to complete: 30 minutes

Ingredients	Equipment
500 grams (1 pound, 1½ ounces) russet, Yukon gold, or other heirloom potatoes	Vegetable peeler
	Large bowl
60 milliliters (¼ cup) vegetable oil	Paring knife
20 grams (1½ tablespoons) unsalted butter	Mandoline
5 grams (1 tablespoon) fresh flat-leaf parsley, *haché*	Colander
Coarse salt and freshly ground pepper to taste	Paper towels
	Poêle
	Slotted spoon
	Plate

Prepare your *mise en place.*

Using the vegetable peeler, peel the potatoes and place them in the bowl with cold water to cover.

Working with one potato at a time and using the paring knife, shape the potatoes into neat cylinders of equal size. Return the cut potatoes to the cold water to keep them from oxidizing.

When all the potatoes are shaped, using the mandoline, cut them crosswise into 3-millimeter (⅛-inch)–thick slices.

Place the potatoes in a colander under cold running water and rinse well.

Fill the bowl with fresh cold water and place the potatoes in it, making sure that the water covers the potatoes.

When ready to cook, drain the potatoes and again rinse them in the colander under cold running water. Using paper towels, pat the slices completely dry.

Heat the oil in a *poêle* over medium-high heat. Add enough potatoes to make a single layer and sauté for about 6 minutes or until the potatoes are lightly browned. Using a slotted spoon, transfer the potatoes to a plate. Continue sautéing until all the potatoes are lightly browned. Set aside until ready to serve. Clean the *poêle.*

When ready to serve, melt the butter in the *poêle* over medium heat. Add the potatoes and toss to coat. Fry, tossing frequently, for about 5 minutes or until the potatoes are crisp yet tender and moist in the interior.

Season with the parsley and salt and pepper to taste and serve immediately.

Demonstration

Pommes Purées (Mashed Potatoes)

Serves 4

Estimated time to complete: 35 minutes

Ingredients	Equipment
1 kilogram (2¼ pounds) russet, Yukon gold, or other heirloom potatoes	Vegetable peeler
250 milliliters (1 cup plus 1 tablespoon) hot milk	Chef's knife
100 grams (7 tablespoons) unsalted butter	Large bowl
Coarse salt and freshly ground pepper to taste	Medium saucepan
	Colander
	Food mill
	Heatproof bowl
	Wooden spoon
	Bain-marie, optional

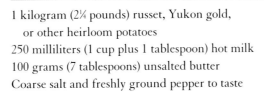

Prepare your *mise en place.*

Peel, rinse, and cut the potatoes into large, even pieces and place them in the bowl with cold water to cover.

Place the potatoes in a medium saucepan over medium-high heat and bring to a boil. Lower the heat and simmer for about 20 minutes or until the potatoes are completely tender. Remove from the heat and, using the colander, drain well.

Transfer the potatoes to the food mill and pass them into the heatproof bowl.

Using the wooden spoon, beat in the hot milk and butter. When well blended, season with salt and pepper to taste.

Serve immediately or place in a *bain-marie* and keep warm until ready to serve.

123

Demonstration

Pommes Duchesse (Duchess Potatoes)

Serves 4
Estimated time to complete: If baking, 1 hour, 30 minutes; if boiling, 1 hour

The potatoes may be baked or boiled for this recipe. Baked potatoes will produce a somewhat drier mixture.

Ingredients		Equipment
	If baking	*If boiling*
500 grams (1 pound, 1½ ounces) russet potatoes, washed and dried		
Vegetable oil for the pan	Baking pan	Vegetable peeler
2 large egg yolks, at room temperature	Rock salt	Chef's knife
25 grams (2 tablespoons plus 1 teaspoon) unsalted butter	Small, sharp knife	Medium saucepan
Freshly ground nutmeg to taste	Chef's knife	Colander
Coarse salt and freshly ground pepper to taste	Tablespoon	Baking pan

For the egg wash

For both methods

1 large egg
7 milliliters (1½ teaspoons) milk

Half-sheet pan
Food mill
Stainless steel bowl
Wooden spoon
Whisk
Small bowl
Rubber spatula
Pastry bag fitted with a star tip
Pastry brush

Prepare your *mise en place.*

If baking the potatoes, preheat the oven to 191°C (375°F).

Cover the bottom of the baking pan with a 2.5-centimeter (1-inch) layer of rock salt. Nestle the potatoes in the salt. Place the pan in the oven and bake for about 1 hour or until the point of a small, sharp knife can be easily inserted into the center. Do not turn off the oven.

Remove the potatoes from the oven and, using the chef's knife, cut them in half lengthwise. Using a

tablespoon, scoop the pulp from the skins, reserving the pulp and discarding the skins.

If boiling the potatoes, preheat the oven to 149°C (300°F).

Using a vegetable peeler, peel the potatoes and rinse well. Using the chef's knife, cut the potatoes into large, even pieces. Place in a medium saucepan with cold water to cover over medium-high heat and bring to a boil. Lower the heat and simmer for about 20 minutes or until tender. Remove from the heat and drain well in the colander.

Transfer the potatoes to the baking pan. Bake, tossing occasionally, for about 5 minutes or until the potatoes are quite dry.

Raise the oven temperature to 191°C (375°F) and lightly oil a half-sheet pan.

Whether using baked or boiled potatoes, from this point on the procedure is identical:

Transfer the hot potato pulp or hot, dried potatoes to the food mill and pass into the stainless steel bowl. Add the egg yolks and butter and, using the wooden spoon, immediately beat to incorporate. Season with nutmeg, salt, and pepper to taste.

Make the egg wash by whisking the egg and milk together in a small bowl. Set aside.

Using a rubber spatula, transfer the potato mixture to a pastry bag fitted with a star tip. Pipe the potatoes out into small mounds onto the prepared half-sheet pan, leaving at least an inch between each one.

Using a pastry brush, lightly coat each potato mound with egg wash.

Place the potatoes in the oven and bake for 12 minutes or until cooked through, slightly crisp, and golden brown. Remove from the oven and serve immediately.

Variation

Pommes croquettes are made by piping out logs about 3 centimeters (1¾₆ inches) in diameter onto a sheet pan lined with plastic film or parchment paper. The entire pan is then covered with plastic film and refrigerated until very cold.

The logs are then cut into cylinders 4 to 5 centimeters (1½ to 2 inches) long and dredged in all-purpose flour. Any excess flour is brushed off and then the logs are dipped in beaten eggs and rolled in breadcrumbs (this procedure is known as *paner à l'anglaise*).

The coated *croquettes* are deep-fat fried at 177°C (350°F) until golden brown, drained well, and served hot.

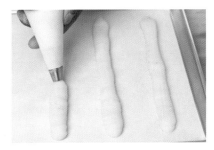

Demonstration

Pommes Dauphine (Potato Croquettes)

Serves 4
Estimated time to complete: 1 hour

Ingredients	Equipment
250 grams (8¾ ounces) russet potatoes	Vegetable peeler
250 grams (8¾ ounces) *Pâte à Choux* (see page 373)	Chef's knife
Coarse salt and freshly ground pepper to taste	Medium saucepan
2 liters (2 quarts, 4 ounces) vegetable oil	Colander
	Baking pan
	Food mill
	Stainless steel bowl
	Wooden spoon
	2 tablespoons
	Deep-fat fryer fitted with a basket
	Instant-read thermometer
	Paper towels

Prepare your *mise en place.*

Preheat the oven to 149°C (300°F).

Using a vegetable peeler, peel the potatoes and rinse well. Using the chef's knife, cut the potatoes into large, even pieces. Place in a medium saucepan with cold water to cover over medium-high heat and bring to a boil. Lower the heat and simmer for about 20 minutes or until tender. Remove from the heat and drain well in the colander.

Transfer the potatoes to the baking pan. Bake, tossing occasionally, for about 5 minutes or until the potatoes are quite dry.

Transfer the potatoes to the food mill and pass them into the stainless steel bowl.

Add the *choux* paste and, using the wooden spoon, beat to combine well. Season with salt and pepper to taste.

Using 2 tablespoons, form the potatoes into *quenelles*, or small ovals.

Place the oil in the deep-fat fryer over medium-high heat and bring to 177°C (350°F) on an instant-read thermometer.

Add the *quenelles*, a few at a time, and fry for about 3 minutes or until cooked through and golden brown. Lift the basket from the pan, gently shake off excess oil, and transfer the *quenelles* to paper towels to drain. Season with salt and serve hot.

Variation

Pommes Lorette are made with the same recipe, but the mixture is piped through the pastry bag in small cigar-shaped pieces directly into the deep-fat fryer and cooked until golden brown.

Demonstration

Pommes Anna (Potatoes Anna)

Serves 4

Estimated time to complete: 1 hour, 15 minutes

Ingredients

500 grams (1 pound, 1½ ounces) russet potatoes
80 grams (2¾ ounces) clarified butter
Coarse salt and freshly ground pepper to taste

Equipment

Vegetable peeler
Medium bowl
Chef's knife
Mandoline
Stainless steel bowl
Ovenproof sauté pan with lid
Pastry brush

Prepare your *mise en place.*

Using the vegetable peeler, peel the potatoes. Rinse under cold running water and then place in a bowl filled with cold water to cover.

Working with one potato at a time and using the chef's knife, shape the potatoes into even cylinders. Then, using the mandoline, cut each potato crosswise into 2-millimeter (⅟₁₆-inch)–thick slices. Place the slices in the stainless steel bowl, add half of the clarified butter, and toss to coat.

Preheat the oven to 204°C (400°F).

Heat a medium, ovenproof sauté pan over very low heat. Using a pastry brush, lightly coat the bottom of the pan with clarified butter.

Arrange a layer of potatoes in slightly overlapping concentric circles over the bottom of the pan.

Drizzle with clarified butter and season with salt and pepper to taste. Continue making and seasoning layers until you have a cake about 4 centimeters (1½ inches) deep.

Raise the heat to medium to briefly sear the bottom. This will prevent the potatoes from sticking to the pan while baking.

Cover the pan and transfer it to the oven. Bake for 20 minutes.

Uncover, drain, and flip the cake. Pat it down into the pan and continue to bake, uncovered, for about 20 minutes or until cooked through, crisp, and golden brown.

Remove the potato cake from the oven and carefully drain off excess butter.

Cut into wedges and serve hot.

Demonstration

Pommes Darphin (Potatoes Darphin)

Serves 4

Estimated time to complete: 45 minutes

Ingredients	Equipment
500 grams (1 pound, 1½ ounces) russet potatoes	Vegetable peeler
Coarse salt and freshly ground pepper to taste	2 medium bowls
25 milliliters (1½ tablespoons) vegetable oil	Mandoline
75 grams (6 tablespoons) unsalted butter, softened	Kitchen towel
	Medium ovenproof sauté pan
	Spatula
	Wooden spoon
	Paper towels

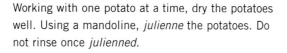

Prepare your *mise en place.*

Preheat the oven to 232°C (450°F) (see note).

Using a vegetable peeler, peel the potatoes and wash them under cold running water. Place in a bowl with cold water to cover.

Working with one potato at a time, dry the potatoes well. Using a mandoline, *julienne* the potatoes. Do not rinse once *julienned.*

Place the *julienned* potatoes in a clean kitchen towel, tightly pull the edges up and together to make a bag, and then firmly twist the towel to drain off any liquid remaining in the potatoes.

Place the potatoes in a bowl and season with salt and pepper to taste.

Place enough oil in a medium ovenproof sauté pan to just coat the bottom. Place over medium-high heat and, when hot but not smoking, add the potatoes to make a 2.5-centimeter (1-inch)–thick layer. Using a spatula, lightly press on the potatoes to make a neat, even layer. The heat should be strong enough to keep the potatoes from sticking.

Cook, without turning, for about 7 minutes or just until the bottom is nicely brown, without any signs of burning. Carefully pour off excess fat and flip the potato cake back into the hot pan. Using a wooden spoon, swirl soft butter around the edge of the pan.

Place in the oven and bake for about 15 minutes or until the top is golden brown and crisp and the potatoes are cooked through.

Remove from the oven and carefully slide out onto paper towels to drain. (*Pommes darphin* may be cooked up to this point and held for service. When ready to serve, place on a small sheet pan in a preheated hot oven to warm.)

Cut into wedges and serve hot.

Note

If your oven runs slightly cool, raise the heat to 260°C (500°F).

Demonstration

Gratin Dauphinois (Cream and Garlic Scalloped Potatoes)

Serves 4
Estimated time to complete: 1 hour

Ingredients	Equipment
500 grams (1 pound, 1½ ounces) russet potatoes	Vegetable peeler
250 milliliters (1 cup plus 1 tablespoon) heavy cream	Medium bowl
Freshly ground nutmeg to taste	Mandoline
Coarse salt and freshly ground pepper to taste	*Russe*
1 clove garlic, peeled	Wooden spoon
25 grams (1 ounce) Gruyère cheese, grated	*Gratin* dish

Prepare your *mise en place*.

Preheat the oven to 191°C (375°F).

Using a vegetable peeler, peel the potatoes. Place in a bowl with cold water to cover.

Using a mandoline, cut the potatoes into 2-to-3-millimeter (⅟₁₆-to-⅛-inch)–thick slices. Do not rinse the slices.

In a *russe* combine the potatoes with the cream and the nutmeg, salt, and pepper to taste over medium heat, stirring carefully with a wooden spoon so that the potatoes don't break apart and the mixture does not stick to the bottom of the pan.

Rub the gratin dish with the garlic clove. Pour the potato mixture into the dish, spreading it into even layers.

Sprinkle the cheese over the top.

Place the gratin in the oven and bake for about 30 minutes or until it is cooked through and the top is nicely browned and bubbling.

Remove from the oven and serve hot.

Session 8

Working with Poultry

Theory

General Information About Poultry

It is said that a great chef is measured by the ability to roast a perfect chicken — a seemingly easy task that is just the opposite. The structure of a chicken and the different densities of its meat serve to challenge even the best cook. A dressed bird has a large hollow cavity with dense, tender, white breast meat that takes a short blast of heat to keep it moist and delicate while the legs and thighs have compact, sinewy dark meat that requires longer cooking to reach the proper degree of tenderness. Each chef has a favorite method of roasting — breast up, breast down, frequent rotating, on a rack or not, and so forth. And all chefs will attest that their chosen method is the best!

From the origins of the 1600 dictate from King Henri of France that all French citizens should have *la poule au pot* (a chicken in the pot) every Sunday to the urging of President Herbert Hoover that there should "be a chicken in every pot" for Americans, chicken has been the holy bird. Although mass-marketed in the millions by multinational companies, the most desirable birds are those that are from small farms and hand-raised. Many of these chickens are called "free-range," but all this terminology means is that the birds have some access to the outdoors; it does not mean that they have the freedom to roam the barnyard at will. Many free-range chickens are also labeled "organic" or "all-natural" but, again, there is some ambiguity about this terminology. It is best to purchase freshly killed birds directly from the farm on which they were raised under organic conditions that are guaranteed.

In France, all chickens are classified according to their weight, diet, age at slaughter, and method of breeding. The most famous chickens are those from Bresse, where they are grown under very strict provisions that result in a richly flavored, delicate, white-meat bird (with blue feet!), which has not been duplicated anywhere else in the world. The corn-fed, yellow-fleshed chickens of Landes are also prized. Some of the small-farm birds on the American market now closely resemble these birds in flavor.

Mass-market birds tend to be bland and their flesh rather spongy. This is because they are sped to market about forty days after hatching, with little or no exercise. This does not give them time to mature into deep flavor. In addition, all mass-market birds are fed antibiotics to keep them healthy in less than desirable growing conditions.

For the most part, turkeys fall under the same terms as chickens. In recent years, the demand for turkey year-round has changed that marketplace, with frozen turkeys, turkey parts, and processed meat now commercially available all through the year. Fresh turkeys are generally available only at holiday times, such as

Thanksgiving and Christmas. It is recommended that only small-farm-raised turkeys be used.

Ducks and geese are generally commercially available only in frozen form, but they can sometimes be bought fresh locally from small farmers. Both of these birds are composed entirely of dark meat. Duck is similar to chicken, but the breast meat is richer and more tender and the legs and thighs are tough and dense. Although a whole roasted duck with a well-done breast is delicious, many chefs prefer to cook the breasts separately to a rare, slightly gamy juiciness, and use the legs in other preparations such as *confit* (cooked and preserved in duck fat).

Goose, though dark red in color, does not have a gamy flavor. In fact, its taste is often likened to well-done roast beef. The goose is extremely deceiving, as it looks quite large and plump but the ratio of meat to skin, fat, and bone is small. Goose meat is quite lean, even though the bird itself is very fatty—a roasting goose often releases a quart of fat while cooking. Rarely served on the contemporary American table, roast goose is, nonetheless, a classic culinary treat.

All game birds are now available year-round through such companies as D'Artagnan, a pioneer in the development and marketing of *foie gras* and exotic meats. Most of them are no longer from the wild but are farm-raised. Almost all game birds are very high in nutrition and low in calories and fat. Due to breeding conditions, reliable feed, and care, farm-raised birds are obviously quite different in flavor and texture than those taken in the wild that must forage on their own. The flesh of farm-raised birds can be moist and juicy, while that of wild birds is often so lean that barding (adding fat) is required to make it palatable. Farm-raised birds can take many different types of preparation, while wild birds, because they are so lean and muscular, particularly if older, need braising. Only the breasts of young wild birds are suitable for quick cooking.

All poultry should be handled with great care due to the possibility of salmonella contamination (see page 9). It should be purchased only from the most reliable sources, stored in the coldest part of the refrigerator (4°C/39°F) to achieve an internal temperature for the bird of 5°C (41°F) for no more than a day or two after purchase, and refrigerated up to the moment it is to be prepared for cooking. When handling, your hands as well as all utensils and cutting boards must be well washed, sanitized, and dried according to the proper sanitary requirements (see page 6) both before and after the poultry has been processed.

Poultry Classifications

The classification of poultry available in the United States is as follows:

Type	Age	Weight	Sex
White-Flesh Poultry			
Chicken			
Broiler/fryer	9–12 weeks	900 grams–1.1 kilograms *(2–2 ½ pounds)*	M/F
Roaster	5 months	1.25–2.25 kilograms *(2 ¾–5 pounds)*	M/F
Capon	Less than 8 months	1.75–2 kilograms *(4–4 ½ pounds)*	M (Castrated)
Fowl/stewing hen	More than 10 months	1.4–2.75 kilograms *(3–6 pounds)*	F
Cock	More than 10 months	1.75–3.25 kilograms *(4–7 pounds)*	M
Poussin (chick)	3–4 weeks	450 grams *(1 pound)*	M/F
Rock Cornish hen	5–7 weeks	450 grams–1 kilogram *(1–2 ¼ pounds)*	M/F
Turkey			
Fryer/roaster	Less than 16 weeks	1.75–3.5 kilograms *(4–8 pounds)*	M/F
Young hen	5–7 months	3.5–6 kilograms *(8–13 pounds)*	F
Young tom	5–7 months	3.5–6 kilograms *(8–13 pounds)*	M
Yearling	Less than 15 months		M/F
Mature	More than 15 months		M/F
Dark-Flesh Poultry			
Duck			
Duckling	Less than 1 year	1.25–3.25 kilograms *(2 ¼–7 pounds)*	M/F
Goose			
Young goose	10–22 weeks	3.5–6 kilograms *(8–13 pounds)*	M/F
Game birds			
Young squab	28–30 days	350–450 grams *(12¼ ounces–1 pound)*	M/F

Type	Age	Weight	Sex
Young guinea fowl	3 months	900 grams–1.4 kilograms *(2–3 pounds)*	M/F
Baby pheasant	15–30 days	400–560 grams *(14 ounces–20 ounces)*	M/F
Pheasant	2–3 months	800 grams–1.75 kilograms *(1¼ pounds–4 pounds)*	M/F
Red Leg Partridge (Wild)	2–3 months	450 grams *(1 pound)*	M/F
Quail	6 weeks	100 grams *(4 ounces)*	M/F
Grouse (Wild)	2–3 months	300–340 grams *(10–12 ounces)*	M/F

Dean's Tip

"When roasting a chicken, put a quart of water in a pan in the oven. The moisture will ensure juicy meat and will also keep the chicken fat from splattering on the oven walls."

Dean Alain Sailhac

Poultry Characteristics

Chicken: Plump with full, round breasts and short, meaty legs. The skin color varies from creamy white to almost yellow, depending on the diet and breed of chicken. Skin should be soft and smooth with some flexibility. In younger birds, the breastbone is flexible, the spur is barely formed on the foot, and the neck is meaty.

Turkey: Today bred to maximize breast size, yielding a greater amount of white meat. The female turkey is generally preferred to male because of its larger breasts and fattier meat. Females are identified by an extra piece of meat under the throat and spurred, black feet. The desired texture and skin color are similar to the chicken. Turkeys over 25 pounds are not recommended because it is difficult to evenly cook the delicate breast meat and tough legs.

Duck: Should have a flexible breastbone and beak, both of which indicate a young bird. Ducks have a heavy skeleton, a plump breast, very short, plump legs, and a dense fatty layer under the skin. The color of the meat and fat content vary with the type of duck.

Goose: Despite its size, a fairly small amount of meat in proportion to bone structure. It is a very fatty bird with a large, elongated breast and dark red, very rich meat throughout.

Squab/Pigeon: Young, small birds that have never flown and are firm-fleshed and very tender.

Guinea Fowl: A small, dark-fleshed, gamy-flavored bird that is a relative of the chicken and partridge. The flesh is quite dry and is often barded (wrapped or studded with fat) before cooking to ensure moist meat. The guinea hen is preferable to a male bird.

Pheasant and baby pheasant: Baby pheasant are favored for their delicate flesh. The female is preferable to the male because her flesh is juicier and plumper and stays moist during roasting. More mature birds that have drier, leaner flesh require barding and/or slow, moist heat to keep their meat juicy.

Partridge: A game bird with plump breasts and white, tender flesh, having a slightly gamy flavor. Depending upon the region of the United States, other birds, such as quail and ruffed grouse, are often erroneously called partridge.

Quail: Today mostly farm-raised, very small, light-fleshed birds that can be cooked in almost any way.

Deans' Tips

"Roasted wild pheasant is often a challenge to cook well, as the thighs are quite tough and the breast quite tender. Therefore, it is a good idea to braise the thighs until very well done and serve the savory meat with a piece of the breast. The same principle can also be applied to turkey, goose, and duck."

Dean Alain Sailhac

"The chickens that we use in the restaurant are allowed to forage outdoors for grasses and bugs, and are fed a mixture of organic corn and soybeans. This wholesome and organic diet gives the chickens an extraordinary flavor. We brine our chickens a day in advance, and I like to spit-roast them. I always let them rest for a few minutes before serving."

Dean Alice Waters

Technique
Working with Chicken

With chicken a mainstay of French and American kitchens, it is important to master the techniques needed to prepare it for cooking.

Preparing Chicken for Cooking

Most chickens are now purchased already cleaned (RTC, or ready-to-cook), but it remains important for a cook to know how to clean them. With the rise in free-range and hand-raised chickens, it is now possible to buy a freshly killed chicken that has not been processed commercially. In this case, the cook must be prepared to fully clean the bird.

1. If the chicken still has pinfeathers or follicles — tiny under-feathers or the feather base — that have not been cleaned off, hold the chicken high over a flame to singe off the pinfeathers and use a paring knife or a kitchen tweezer to pull out the follicles.

2. Using a chef's knife, cut off the feet and wing tips.

3. Using a chef's knife, slit the skin on the back of the neck lengthwise, and pull it away. Cut off the

neck at the body, then cut off the head. Reserve the neck for stock or sauce making.

4. Wearing latex gloves, insert one finger into the neck opening and detach and discard the two red lungs from the thorax.

5. In a neat, clean motion, cut off and slightly enlarge the circular anal opening.

Trussing a Chicken

Trussing (**bridage**) is a method of tying a whole bird (or a large piece of meat) into a compact bundle to facilitate handling when cooking. It is also used to hold the legs, wings, and any stuffing in place for neater presentation. With poultry, trussing is classically done after the bird has been cleaned using one or two pieces of trussing twine threaded through a trussing needle. When a bird is properly trussed, it will sit neatly on a rack or spit or in a pan, which allows it to cook evenly and makes it easier for the cook to baste or turn. When untied, a cooked trussed bird will hold its shape for service.

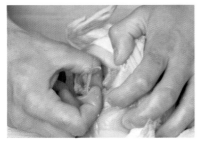

6. Using your fingers, clean out the interior cavity, removing the liver, heart, windpipe, and other organs, but keeping them intact. Separate the organs on a cutting board. Trim the gizzard, cut it open horizontally, and rinse out the contents. Carefully separate the liver from the bitter gallbladder.

7. Rinse the chicken under cold running water and pat dry.

There are several methods used to truss poultry, but we will address only two: using a trussing needle and twine, and using twine alone. Today the most common practice is to use twine alone.

Preparation for All Methods of Trussing

1. Trim off any excess fat from the cleaned chicken.

2. Remove the wishbone: Push the skin back on the breast and either cut an incision on each side of the wishbone or scrape it clean. Slide your fingers through the incision, gently forcing the meat away from the bone. Pull out the wishbone.

3. Cut the wings at the second joint.

4. Rinse the chicken under cold running water.

5. Pat dry.

6. Season the cavity according to the recipe.

7. Cut a piece of trussing twine to a length of approximately 75 centimeters (29½ inches).

Trussing with Twine Only

After preparing the bird for trussing as directed:

1. Push the legs toward the breast. If you keep the legs tucked tightly to the sides of the bird, they will force the breast up and make it plump.

2. Slide the twine under the back next to the tail.

3. Lift the twine up on both sides, bring it up and over the drumsticks, and cross.

4. Slide the twine under the ends of the drumsticks and pull it tight.

5. Bring the twine along both sides of the chicken between the leg and the breast.

6. While holding the twine tightly, turn the chicken on its breast. Bring one end of the string above the wing and under the bone of the neck, securing the loose neck skin as you go.

7. Tightly secure the twine with a knot and cut off excess twine.

Trussing with a Needle

After preparing the bird for trussing as directed:

1. Thread the needle with the twine.

2. Push the legs toward the breast. If you keep the legs tucked tightly to the sides of the bird they will force the breast up and make it plump.

3. Lift the drumstick and insert the needle in the soft spot in the lower part of the backbone. Be sure the needle is anchored into the bone rather than the skin.

4. Push the needle out on the opposite side into the middle joint of the leg, where the thigh and drumstick meet.

5. Turn the chicken on its breast and push the needle through the wing section, the loose neck skin, the skin of the back, and the other wing.

6. Place the chicken on its back and push the needle into the middle joint of the leg, where the thigh and drumstick meet, through the lower back.

7. Lift the skin of the tail end and push the needle

through. It is important that the needle goes through the lower part of the skin because it makes a small, tight loop that holds the drumstick in place.

8. Tightly pull both ends of the twine and secure with a knot.

Quartering Chicken

There are several methods used to cut a chicken into four pieces (two breast-wing pieces and two leg-thigh pieces). Differences may occur based on how the chicken is going to be cooked or served, as well as the preference of a particular chef.

There is not one prescribed method but the following is a suggested approach:

1. Remove the wishbone as described on page 139.

2. Cut the wing off at the second joint.

3. Place the chicken on its back.

4. Using a chef's knife, cut off the skin between the leg and the breast, leaving a substantial part of the skin covering the breast to protect it during cooking.

5. Cut around the thigh and disjoint it to completely separate it from the carcass. Be sure to include the oyster, the tender oval of meat that sits in a hollow along the backbone.

6. Expose the thigh bone.

 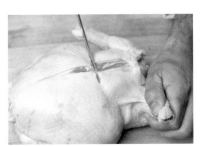

 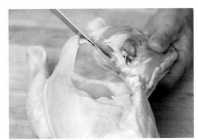

7. Make an incision through the skin and tendons near the knuckle of the thigh, chop off the cartilage, and scrape the skin back. This procedure, which fashions a more attractive presentation, is referred to as *manchonner*.

8. Repeat the above procedure on the remaining leg.

9. By making cuts on both sides between the spine and the shoulder blades, remove the whole breast section, including the bones, from the backbone.

10. Cut the breast section in half lengthwise along the breastbone, separating the whole breast into two equal pieces. Trim off any remaining cartilage.

11. *Manchonner* the wing tips.

12. Remember to save all bones, hearts, and gizzards for making stock.

Theory
About Duck

In the United States, almost all commercially available duck is produced from strains of the white Pekin duck domesticated in China about two thousand years ago. Pekin ducks were first imported in the late 1800s and used primarily by ethnic groups in the preparation of traditional dishes. Wild duck was generally the only duck used in restaurant kitchens. Over time, duck-breeding techniques improved, and relatives of the original Pekins found their way onto the restaurant (and home) table.

The commercial breeding of ducks began in earnest about a hundred years ago in California. Significant production of Pekin duck also took place on Long Island, New York, early in the development of the industry. It was from these producers that the name Long Island duck (or duckling) originated. The duck industry was so productive on Long Island that, at one time, this small stretch of land was producing over 60 percent of the nation's farm-raised duck.

Today, due to land lost to housing development, Long Island produces only about 10 percent of all farm-raised ducks. Most American ducks are now raised in the western and midwestern United States; although they are often called Long Island duck, only ducks produced on Long Island may legally be so labeled. For the most part, any duck referred to as Long Island duck is actually a Pekin duck.

There are ducks other than the Pekin raised in the United States, but in limited numbers. With revitalized interest in small farms, many people are attempting to reintroduce other breeds to the market. Domesticated muscovy, mullard, and mallard ducks can now be purchased through mail order or at specialty grocers.

In France, the most common breeds are the Nantes and Barbary ducks. A particularly succulent bird is also raised in the area of Rouen, but it is usually available only locally. The moulard duck, a cross between the Pekin and muscovy ducks, is raised in southwestern France, primarily for the production of *foie gras*. In French, a young duck is referred to as a **caneton**, a young female as a **canette**, and a bird two to four months old as a **canard**.

In the United States, the terms duck and duckling are used interchangeably, as most ducks are slaughtered at less than sixteen weeks old. Broilers and fryers are less than eight weeks old, while roasters are no more than sixteen weeks old, with weight ranging from 1.4 to 2.5 kilograms (3 to 5½ pounds). Male ducks are called drakes. The meat of a duck is entirely dark red; there is no white meat. Most ducks are sold cleaned and ready to cook (RTC).

Farm-Raised Ducks Available in the United States

Besides the Pekin (or Long Island) duck, the following ducks are commercially available in the United States:

Muscovy: Originating in South America, the muscovy duck is leaner and gamier in taste than the Pekin. The meat is deep red, and the breasts are full-fleshed and plump, perfect for a quick sauté. Small females may be roasted. Male breast meat is used in sautéed preparations, but the legs tend to be tough and are better used in braises and *confits*. Muscovy ducks are used for the production of *foie gras* both in the United States and France.

Mullard (*moulard*): A cross between a male muscovy and a female Pekin duck, mullard ducks are very large birds. In France, their primary use is as a producer of *foie gras*. The French term, **magret**, refers to the breast of this duck. Weighing about 1 kilogram (almost 2 pounds), the breast can easily feed four people. The meat is quite gamy, with a chewy texture. Only the breasts of small birds are used for sautéeing or grilling. The legs are often used for *confits*. Once slaughtered, the carcass of the mullard duck is often hung under controlled temperature for a week to tenderize it (**faisander**). Larger, older birds are used whole for braises and *confits*.

Mallard (Barbary): Mallard duck has a limited, seasonal availability, as they are not commonly bred. In fact, they are more often available from the wild through specialty producers or mail-order sources. They are very lean with silky, juicy, almost beeflike meat. The breasts are generally sautéed and served along with the braised legs.

The classification of ducks available in the United States is as follows:

Duck	Age	Sex	Weight*	Cooking Method
Pekin	5–6 weeks	M/F	1.75–2.75 kilograms (4–6 pounds)	Whole: roast Breast: sauté Legs: braise
Muscovy	9 weeks	F M	Up to 1.75 kilograms (4 pounds) Up to 3.5 kilograms (8 pounds)	Breast: sauté Legs: braise and *confit* *Foie gras*
Mullard	12–14 weeks	F/M	Double breast: 700–900 grams (1½–2 pounds) Each leg: 350–450 grams (¾–1 pound)	Legs/breast sold separately *Magrets*: sauté, grill Legs: braise and *confit* *Foie gras*
Mallard	15–25 weeks	F/M	1.1–1.4 kilograms (2½–3 pounds)	Whole: roast Breast: sauté Legs: braise

*All weights are for RTC birds.

Dean's Tip

"Reserve any duck fat to help preserve other items such as stews and black truffles."

Dean Alain Sailhac

Methods of Cooking Duck

The French are considered masters at cooking duck. Only the very young, plump female is considered appropriate for roasting to a juicy pale-pink color. Older, less tender duck may also be roasted, but it will usually be cooked until well-done. Often, when roasting, the breast might be removed while still slightly rare and served, sliced on the bias, as a separate course, while the remainder of the duck continues to cook to well-done to be served in a later course. Also, in classic French cooking, the breast and the leg are often handled in separate preparations. Because duck lends itself to such a wide array of preparations, it is an extremely valuable ingredient in the restaurant kitchen. It may be roasted whole, or the breast may be removed and sautéed or grilled, while the leg meat can be braised separately. Although the breast is quite tasty cooked to well-done, contemporary cooks often prefer to cook it until, at the most, medium-rare. Legs, on the other hand, are always cooked to well-done. Traditional garnishes for duck include turnips, English peas, olives, and fruits such as oranges, pineapples, and cherries.

Duck meat may also be used in sausages, *galantines, terrines*, and *confits*. Duck gizzards may be cooked as *confit* or cooked and thinly sliced for use in salads. Duck skins can be fried to a rich crispness to be used as "cracklings" for garnish for other dishes or in salads. Duck fat is often used to fry potatoes or in the preparation of many traditional French dishes. Duck carcass is used to make stocks and *consommés*.

Some ducks are raised solely for their livers. In this case, particular feeding techniques are used so that the liver becomes quite enlarged. The resultant liver is referred to as *foie gras*, and it is most commonly served on its own, sautéed and presented with some type of acidic garnish to balance its richness or used in the preparation of *terrines* or *pâtés*.

Roasting

Roasting is the most traditional cooking method for duck. It has a certain advantage over other methods, as it is relatively simple to complete, and the meat, roasted on the bone, tends to be more flavorful and tender. The roasted bird may also be prepared for cooking in advance. However, when working with the economical, fatty Pekin duck, roasting may also pose problems. Since the Pekin duck has a very thick layer of fat just below the skin, if roasted to the point where the breast meat is still pink, the fat under the skin will remain unrendered and the legs will be underdone. One contemporary solution to this problem is to quarter the duck and cook it by a combination of sautéing and braising.

Sautéing or Grilling

These methods are used *only* for the breast portion of the duck. In French, technically only the breast of the mullard duck can legitimately be called *magret*, and the breasts of other ducks should be called *suprêmes*, although in casual use the terms are sometimes applied interchangeably. Sautéing the breast offers the advantage of allowing the cook to quickly render the fat, leaving a crisp outer skin with juicy, moist pink breast meat. It also allows the thighs to be removed and separately braised to the correct level of doneness. The braising liquid is also useful, adding richness and savor to any sauce made to accompany the duck meat. Sautéed, grilled, or roasted duck breasts are sliced into **aiguillettes** (thin strips cut lengthwise from any poultry or game bird breast) for serving.

Technique
Working with Duck

The following instructions will ensure a well-roasted duck with minimal fat.

Preparing Duck for Roasting

Almost all farm-raised duck has been dressed and is ready to cook (RTC). If the duck is not completely RTC:

1. Singe off any remaining down and feathers over an open flame. Using a kitchen tweezer, pull out and discard any pin feathers.

2. Place the duck on its breast, feet facing you.

3. Cut off and discard the two olive-shaped glands on top of the tail in a V-cut. These are oil glands that will impart an unpleasant taste.

Trussing a Duck with a Needle

1. Trim off and discard (or render) any excess fat.

2. If desired, for easy slicing at service, remove the wishbone in the following manner: Push the skin back on the breast and cut an incision on each side of the wishbone. Slide your fingers through the incision, gently forcing the meat away from the bone. Pull out and discard the wishbone.

3. Using a chef's knife, cut off the wings at the second joint.

4. Season the interior cavity of the duck with salt and pepper to taste.

5. Cut a piece of kitchen string about 75 centimeters (28 inches) long. Thread the larding needle with the string.

6. Push the duck legs up toward the breast. Tuck them tightly against the breast to plump it up.

7. Lift the drumstick and insert the needle in the soft spot in the lower part of the backbone, making certain that the needle is anchored in the bone rather than just the skin.

8. Push the needle out on the opposite side where the thigh and drumstick join.

9. Turn the duck on its breast, push the needle through the wing section, the loose neck skin, the skin of the back, and the other wing.

10. Turn the duck on its back and push the needle into the middle joint of the leg, through the lower back, and reverse the preceding step.

11. Lift the skin of the tail end and push the needle through. It is important that the needle go through the lower part of the skin so that it makes a tight loop that will hold the drumstick in place.

12. Tightly pull up both ends of the string and secure with a knot.

13. Push the tail into the anal opening and the duck is ready to roast.

The Technique of Roasting

Roasting (*rôtir*) is often employed to cook all types of poultry, as well as the first category of large cuts of meat and game. All items to be roasted must contain either an inherent degree of fattiness or be basted with a fat throughout the cooking process or they will dry out. Generally, small pieces are roasted for a shorter period of time at a higher degree of heat, while larger pieces are cooked for a longer period of time at a lower temperature so that the heat can penetrate the interior before the exterior becomes overcooked and unpalatable.

With roasting, the coagulation of the surface protein seals in the nutritive elements and juices. This is a perfect example of cooking by concentration (which is discussed in Session 9, page 168), whereby the coagulation of albumins on the surface of the product being cooked nicely caramelizes and browns the skin. Never prick or puncture roasting poultry or meat; the flavorful juices will be released and escape from the interior.

When young, whole chickens are roasted, the birds are cleaned, seasoned, and trussed, then placed in a roasting pan (sometimes on a wire rack) in an oven preheated to between 204°C (400°F) and 246°C (475°F). The bird may or may not be brushed with butter or oil before being placed in the oven. The cooking time depends upon the shape, size, and quantity, as well as the oven temperature. Since breasts tend to cook more quickly than thighs, exposing the thighbone and leaving the breastbone and ribs attached during cooking ensures that the two are done at the same time.

A roast chicken is done when the breast has swelled slightly, the skin has bloomed away from the flesh, and the leg meat is tender when pressed and can be easily moved in the socket. When pricked, the meatiest part of the thigh should emit clear, yellow juice. To be completely sure the chicken is done, carefully lift it from the pan and drain the juices from the interior. If the last bits are clear yellow, the chicken is done. Of course, the easiest method of all is to insert an instant-read thermometer into the thickest part of the bird. It should read 71°C (160°F)—remember that the chicken will continue to cook to the desired 79°C (175°F) as it rests before carving.

Roasted poultry or meat is removed from the oven and allowed to rest for 10 to 15 minutes on a wire rack in a warm spot before being carved. This permits the hot juices, forced to the center of the item by the intense heat of roasting, to redisperse evenly throughout the bird or meat. This creates moist meat that holds together and makes carving easier.

"A great way to enhance the savor of a roast chicken is to stuff the cavity with sprigs of fresh thyme and rosemary, some cloves of garlic, and two lemons cut into quarters. The meat is infused with the wonderful flavors of the herbs and garlic and scented with aromatic lemon. Délicieux!"*

Dean Alain Sailhac

The Technique of Sautéing

To sauté (from ***sauter***, or literally, "to jump") is to quick-sear a food in some type of fat in a shallow, uncovered pan over high heat. This seals in the juices by coagulating the surface proteins and begins the caramelization process. The cooking is then completed over lower heat. Since this is a relatively quick method of cooking, it is often applied to small, uniformly sized pieces of poultry such as bone-in quarters or boneless breasts. It is also used for most meats and for many vegetables. Sautéing is not generally used for thick pieces of food, as the process tends to burn the exterior before the interior is cooked.

It is important that the item to be sautéed is quite dry, as moisture will cause it to steam rather than brown. To this end, items to be sautéed are often lightly coated with seasoned flour or breaded to ensure that the exterior is dry. In addition, the sauté pan should not be crowded; this causes the temperature of the pan to drop and steam to form. One of the greatest benefits of sautéing is the formation of *sucs*, small bits of caramelized protein that accumulate on the bottom of the pan and add depth of flavor to a finishing sauce. It is important to watch the degree of heat so that the *sucs* do not burn—once burned they are rendered unusable.

Guidelines for sautéing:

○ The ingredient to be sautéed should, ideally, be at room temperature and quite dry.

○ The pan must be very hot. If you feel the heat rising when you hold your hand over the pan, it is hot enough. You can also tell it is hot when the oil shimmers but does not move.

○ The surface of the pan should be covered with just a film of fat.

○ The pan must not be crowded. If necessary, cook the food in batches.

○ Do not cover the pan.

○ Do not shake the pan immediately after adding the food; allow it to sear and detach itself from the pan first.

The Technique of Grilling

Grilling is a method of cooking food by concentration under very high heat. The grilling process, which usually begins with a hot grill and a tender food item, sears the item and locks in the juices by forming a dry surface crust (with meat, it is the coagulation of the proteins on the surface). With the exception of grilled vegetables, which can be served at room temperature, grilled items are cooked to order and served immediately.

The relationship between the surface sear and the interior doneness is the key to great grilling. It is, therefore, extremely important to learn how to judge the heat of the grill, its hottest and coolest areas, as well as to understand the degree of grilling necessary in relationship to the size, shape, and texture of the food. Like many kitchen skills, this is best done over time through trial and error and lots of practice.

To prevent food from sticking, the grill must be cleaned, preheated, and lightly oiled before the food is placed on it. Cleaning the grill is particularly important. It should not be moistened or washed, but scrubbed with a metal brush and then wiped with a clean kitchen towel while still hot to eliminate any particles stuck to it that would burn and impart a bitter flavor to the food. Often these particles are not evident, and it seems okay to forego cleaning, but it is a good idea to remember that cooking on a dirty grill is just like cooking in a dirty pan.

The presentation side of grilled foods should be grilled first. This side should be carefully marked in *quadrillage* (see page 168). It is also important to use tongs when turning meat on the grill; if the meat is pierced with a fork, it will release some of its flavorful juices. Before serving, *lustrer* grilled meat with melted butter to add an appetizing sheen and flavor.

Grilling Chicken

Chicken that is to be grilled (or broiled), such as in the recipe for *Poulet Grillé à l'Américaine* (see page 154), should be cut in a way that provides maximum surface contact with the heat source.

To prepare a chicken for grilling:

1. Using a chef's knife, remove the backbone by cutting through each side of the cavity of the chicken.

2. Flatten the chicken out by pushing on the breast area. At this point, the breastbone can also be removed to facilitate carving as well as eating.

3. Leave enough bone structure so that the chicken will hold its shape while cooking.

Variation: A similar presentation is referred to as **en crapaudine**. In this method, the chicken is split horizontally from the tip of the breast up to the wings, but not in half. It is opened up, flattened, and then secured by means of a skewer. The resulting presentation resembles a toad (*crapaud*) from which the classic dish of grilled, breaded chicken, *poulet en crapaudine*, gets its name.

(see page 154)

Chefs' Tips

"Keep your grill clean and hot."
Chef Pascal Beric

"Before you start grilling, pass your hand about 12 inches above the preheated grill in order to sense the variation in temperature."
Chef Martin Schaub

Demonstration

Poulet Rôti Grand-mère (Grandmother's Roast Chicken)

Serves 4

Estimated time to complete: 1 hour 30 minutes

Ingredients	Equipment
One 1.5-kilogram (3-pound, 5-ounce) roasting chicken, including gizzard, neck, and heart, prepared for cooking (see page 138)	Chef's knife
	Trussing twine
	Trussing needle, optional
Coarse salt and freshly ground pepper to taste	Heavy-bottomed roasting pan
30 grams (2 tablespoons) unsalted butter	or *poêle*
30 milliliters (2 tablespoons) vegetable oil	Instant-read thermometer, if necessary
100 grams (3½ ounces) carrots, *mirepoix*	Paring knife
100 grams (3½ ounces) onions, *mirepoix*	

For the garnish

400 grams (14 ounces) russet potatoes, peeled
100 grams (3½ ounces) slab bacon
125 grams (4⅓ ounces) button mushrooms, cleaned
Coarse salt and freshly ground pepper to taste
70 grams (2½ ounces) pearl onions
40 grams (3 tablespoons) unsalted butter
7 grams (1 teaspoon) sugar
30 milliliters (2 tablespoons) vegetable oil
10 grams (2 tablespoons) finely chopped fresh flat-leaf parsley

For the gravy

50 milliliters (3½ tablespoons) dry white wine
500 milliliters (2 cups plus 2 tablespoons)
   Brown Veal Stock (see page 57)
Coarse salt and freshly ground pepper to taste, optional

Large shallow saucepan
Strainer
Small, sharp knife
Sauté pan
Slotted spoon
Paper towels
Stainless steel bowl
Sautoir or *russe*
Parchment paper
Ovenproof *poêle*
Heatproof bowl
Wire rack
Baking pan
Wooden spoon
Boning knife
Large metal spoon
4 warm dinner plates

Prepare your *mise en place.*

Preheat the oven to 232°C (450°F).

Remove and reserve the gizzard, neck, and heart from the chicken; set the liver aside for another use (such as a *terrine* or simple sauté). Using a chef's knife, carefully trim the chicken of excess fat. Season and truss the chicken, with or without a needle (see page 139).

Heat the butter and oil in a heavy-bottomed roasting pan or *poêle* over medium-high heat. Add the chicken and sear, turning frequently without pricking the skin, for about 10 minutes or until the thighs and legs are well browned and the breast is just lightly browned.

When all sides have browned, turn the chicken on its back and add the gizzard, neck, and heart to the pan. Place the pan in the oven and roast for 10 minutes.

Add the *mirepoix* vegetables and toss to coat with a bit of the fat.

Continue to roast, basting frequently, for about 40 minutes or until the skin is golden brown and the juices run clear from a hole poked in the thigh or when the internal temperature measured between breast and thigh registers 60°C (140°F) to 66°C (150°F).

While the chicken is roasting, prepare the garnish.

Using a paring knife, turn the potatoes into 5-centimeter (2-inch) *cocottes*. Place the potatoes in a single layer in a large shallow saucepan with cold water to just barely cover over high heat. Bring to a simmer. Immediately remove from the heat, drain well without refreshing, and set aside to air dry.

Cut the bacon into 1.3-centimeter (½-inch)–thick slices and then into strips about 1.3 centimeters (½ inch) wide to form *lardons*.

Place the bacon in a sauté pan over medium-high heat and sauté for about 5 minutes or until the bacon has rendered its fat but has not browned. Using a slotted spoon, transfer the *lardons* to paper towels to drain, leaving the rendered fat in the sauté pan.

If the mushrooms are small, leave them whole; if large, cut them into quarters. Add the mushrooms to the rendered bacon fat. Place the pan over medium heat, season the mushrooms with salt and pepper to taste, and sauté for about 5 minutes or until just lightly browned on the edges. Set aside.

Place the onions in a stainless steel bowl with hot water to cover. Soak for about 3 minutes or until the skins have loosened. Drain well and, using your fingertips, push off the skins.

Place the onions in a single layer in a *sautoir* or *russe* just large enough to accommodate them over medium heat. Add 15 grams (1 tablespoon) of the butter, the sugar, and just enough water to barely cover the bottom of the pan. Salt to taste. Cover with a piece of parchment cut to the exact size of the pan opening to make a loose lid and *glacer à brun*. (Take care not to use too much water, as the onions will steam and overcook rather than brown. They should begin to brown in the remaining butter after the water has evaporated.) Taste, and if necessary, add seasoning. Set aside to keep warm until ready to serve.

About 10 minutes before the chicken is ready to come out of the oven, heat an ovenproof *poêle* over medium heat. When hot but not smoking, add the oil. Add the potatoes, keeping them in a single layer. Sauté for about 5 minutes or until all of the potatoes are evenly browned. Add the remaining 25 grams (about 2 tablespoons) butter and season with salt and pepper to taste. Place the potatoes in the oven and roast for 10 to 12 minutes or until golden brown and tender when pierced with the point of a small, sharp knife.

When all the garnish items have been cooked, combine them in a heatproof bowl. Toss to blend, then sprinkle with parsley. Set aside and keep warm for service.

When the chicken is done, remove it from the oven, drain off and reserve the fat, and transfer the bird to a wire rack placed over a baking pan to rest. While the chicken is resting, make the gravy (*jus de rôti*).

If the pan drippings have not caramelized during roasting, place the pan on the stovetop over high heat and bring to a boil. Boil just until the drippings caramelize; take care that they do not burn. Carefully drain off the fat. Lower the heat and add the white wine to the pan, stirring constantly with a wooden spoon to lift up the *sucs* and deglaze the pan. Add the stock and stir to combine. Bring to a boil, then

lower the heat and cook at a bare simmer, stirring frequently, for about 10 minutes or until the mixture is slightly reduced and full-flavored. Taste, and if necessary, season with salt and pepper. Strain. Keep warm until ready for service.

Using a boning knife, remove the breasts and the thighs from the chicken. *Manchonner* the ends of the drumsticks and the wings. Cut each breast half into two pieces on the bias. Cut the legs in half at the joint. Remove the thigh bones and any cartilage. You should now have 8 pieces.

Assemble one leg piece with one breast piece on each of four warm dinner plates, taking care that only one of the pieces on each plate has a bone.

Garnish each plate with an equal portion of the warm vegetables. Spoon the gravy around the chicken pieces. Any remaining gravy can be served on the side.

Demonstration

Poulet Sauté Chasseur (Chicken Chasseur)

Serves 4

Estimated time to complete: 1 hour

Ingredients	Equipment
One 1.5-kilogram (3-pound, 5-ounce) chicken, including gizzard, neck, and heart, prepared for cooking (see page 138)	Chef's knife
	Russe
15 milliliters (1 tablespoon) vegetable oil	Wooden spoon
60 grams (2 ounces) carrots, *mirepoix*	Metal spoon
60 grams (2 ounces) onions, *mirepoix*	*Chinois*
500 milliliters (2 cups plus 2 tablespoons) Brown Chicken	Medium saucepan
Stock or Brown Veal Stock (see page 57)	Ovenproof *sautoir*

Bouquet garni

Up to 5 grams (1 teaspoon) cornstarch, if necessary

Coarse salt and freshly ground pepper to taste

45 milliliters (3 tablespoons) clarified butter

For the sauce

125 grams (4⅓ ounces) mushrooms, *émincé*

25 grams (1 ounce) shallots, *ciselé*

40 milliliters (2 tablespoons plus 2 teaspoons) cognac

50 milliliters (3½ tablespoons) dry white wine

250 milliliters (1 cup plus 2 tablespoons) enriched stock from
   chicken preparation

15 grams (1 tablespoon) tomatoes *concassé*

25 grams (1 tablespoon plus 2 teaspoons) unsalted butter

5 grams (1 tablespoon) finely chopped fresh chervil

5 grams (1 tablespoon) finely chopped fresh tarragon

Coarse salt and freshly ground pepper to taste, optional

Tongs

Sizzle pan

Instant-read thermometer

Cutting board

Boning knife

4 warm dinner plates

Prepare your *mise en place*.

Using a chef's knife, cut the chicken into quarters, keeping the breast skin intact and leaving the oyster attached to the leg. Expose the thighbone and *manchonner* the ends of the drumsticks and wings. Reserve all bones and trimmings as well as the gizzard, neck, and heart.

Using a chef's knife, chop the reserved chicken bones and trimmings.

To make the enriched stock, heat the oil in a *russe* over medium heat. Add the chopped bones, trimmings, gizzard, neck, and heart and, stirring with a wooden spoon, sauté for about 5 minutes or until lightly browned. Add the *mirepoix* vegetables and continue to sauté for another 5 minutes or until the vegetables are beginning to brown and *sucs* have formed on the bottom of the pan.

Add the stock and *bouquet garni* and bring to a simmer, stirring occasionally. Lower the heat and cook at a bare simmer for about 40 minutes or until reduced to a saucelike consistency.

Remove from the heat. Using a metal spoon, remove any fat from the top of the stock, then pour the stock through a *chinois* into a clean saucepan, discarding the solids. Remove any fat that remains on top of the stock.

If the enriched stock is not as thick as you like, return it to medium heat and simmer until reduced to the desired consistency. If necessary, bind the sauce with the cornstarch dissolved in a bit of cold water. Season with salt and pepper to taste. Remove from the heat and set aside until you prepare the sauce.

Thirty minutes before serving, preheat the oven to 191°C (375°F).

Season the chicken on all sides with salt and pepper.

Heat the clarified butter in an ovenproof *sautoir* over medium-high heat. Add the chicken pieces, skin side down, and cook for about 5 minutes or until golden brown. Using tongs, transfer the chicken to a sizzle pan. Place the sizzle pan in the oven and roast the chicken for about 30 minutes or until the skin is crisp and brown, the juices run clear from a hole poked in the thigh, and the internal temperature when measured at the thickest part registers 60°C–66°C (140°F–150°F).

Dean's Tip

"Chicken is the perfect canvas for a chef. It adapts itself to all types of cooking techniques and to all seasonings."

Dean Jacques Pépin

until the sauce is **nappant** (coats the back of a spoon). Immediately swirl in the butter (*monter au beurre*). Remember that once the butter has been added, the sauce cannot be further reduced or it will break. It is better if the sauce gets slightly overreduced before adding the butter, as it can easily be thinned to the proper consistency.

Add the chervil and tarragon. Taste, and if necessary, adjust the seasoning with salt and pepper. Set aside in a warm spot until ready to serve.

When the chicken is done, remove it from the oven and place on a cutting board. Using a boning knife, carefully remove the breastbone from the chicken breast. (Removing the breastbone after the chicken has been cooked helps to retain the meat's shape, flavor, and moisture.) Cut each breast half into two pieces on the bias. Cut the legs into two pieces at the joint and remove the thighbones. You should now have 8 pieces of chicken.

Assemble one leg piece with one breast piece on each of four warm dinner plates, taking care that only one of the pieces on each plate has a bone. Using a spoon, nap the chicken pieces with the warm sauce and serve immediately.

While the chicken is roasting, prepare the sauce.

Drain the excess fat from the *sautoir* you cooked the chicken in, leaving just enough to sauté the mushrooms. Place the *sautoir* over medium heat. Add the mushrooms and sauté for 2 minutes. Add the shallots and continue to sauté for an additional minute.

Remove the pan from the heat and drain off any fat. Add the cognac and return the pan to medium heat. Ignite the cognac and *flamber*. When the flames have died down, add the white wine and bring to a simmer. Simmer until reduced by half.

Add 250 milliliters (1 cup plus 1 tablespoon) of the reserved enriched stock and again bring to a simmer. Simmer for 3 minutes and then add the tomato *concassé* and continue to simmer for about 3 minutes or

Demonstration

Poulet Grillé à l'Américaine, Sauce Diable

(Mustard-Crusted Grilled Chicken with Devil Sauce)

Serves 4

Estimated time to complete: 2 hours

Ingredients	Equipment
One or two 1.5-kilogram (3-pound, 5-ounce) chickens (see note)	Chef's knife
200 grams (about 7 slices) white bread	Boning knife
	Plate
For the sauce	Plastic film
250 milliliters (1 cup plus 1 tablespoon) Brown Chicken Stock or Brown Veal Stock (see page 57)	

40 grams (1½ ounces) shallots, *cisclé*
10 grams (2 tablespoons) peppercorns, crushed
80 milliliters (¼ cup plus 1 tablespoon) white wine
80 milliliters (¼ cup plus 1 tablespoon) water (see note)
60 milliliters (¼ cup) white wine vinegar
10 grams (2 tablespoons) chervil, *haché*
1 sprig fresh tarragon, *haché*
Coarse salt and freshly ground pepper to taste, optional

For the garnish
2 large, ripe tomatoes, washed and dried
4 large mushroom caps, cleaned
20 milliliters (1 tablespoons plus 1 teaspoon) olive oil
Fresh herbs to taste, *haché* (see note)
Four 3-millimeter (⅛-inch)–thick slices bacon

To finish the dish
20 milliliters (1½ tablespoons) vegetable oil
Leaves from 4 sprigs fresh thyme
Coarse salt and freshly ground pepper to taste
25 grams (1 tablespoon) Dijon mustard
40 grams (3 tablespoons) unsalted butter, optional
Few sprigs fresh watercress

Drum sieve or food processor
Small saucepan
Small, nonreactive saucepan
Chinois
Bain-marie
Skewers, if necessary
Pastry brush
Tongs
2 baking pans
Baking sheet
4 warm dinner plates

Prepare your *mise en place.*

Using a chef's knife, remove the wishbone from the chicken. Do not trim the wing tips. Remove the backbone by cutting through each side of the cavity of the chicken. Flatten the chicken out by pushing on the breast area. Remove the breastbone, and using a boning knife, remove the hipbone and expose the thigh bone.

Make a small incision in the skin between each leg and breast tip and insert the end of each drumstick into each incision. Place on a plate, cover with plastic film, and refrigerate until ready to cook.

Remove the crusts from the bread and then break the bread up into small pieces. Sift the bread pieces through a drum sieve or process them in a food processor fitted with the metal blade to make fine crumbs. Set aside.

To prepare the sauce, place the stock in a small saucepan over medium heat and bring to a simmer. Simmer for about 30 minutes or until reduced by half. Remove from the heat.

155

  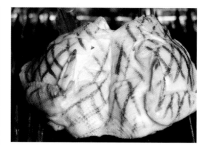 

Notes

Use two chickens if you want to serve a half chicken per person.

Water is often added to reductions of a small amount of liquid in order to lengthen the infusion time, as small amounts will frequently evaporate before the desired flavor is achieved.

To season the garnish, use either one herb or a mixture of any herbs that please your palate. Parsley, chives, basil, and thyme are a few that work well with tomatoes and mushrooms.

While the stock is reducing, combine the shallots and peppercorns with the wine, water, and vinegar in a small, nonreactive saucepan over medium heat. Bring to a simmer and cook for about 20 minutes or until reduced by half.

Combine the reduced stock and wine mixture and place over medium heat. Bring to a simmer and cook for 5 minutes. Remove from the heat and pass through a *chinois* into a *bain-marie*. Stir in the chopped chervil and tarragon. Taste, and if necessary, adjust the seasoning with salt and pepper. Keep warm for service.

To prepare the garnish, using a chef's knife, cut the tomatoes in half crosswise. Squeeze lightly to push out the seeds and pulp. (If you have very small tomatoes or cherry tomatoes, leave them whole and skewer them for grilling.)

Using a pastry brush, lightly coat the tomatoes and mushrooms with olive oil. Sprinkle with a mixture of chopped fresh herbs to taste. Set aside. Remove the bacon from the refrigerator in preparation for grilling.

Preheat and oil the grill and preheat the oven to 204°C (400°F).

Using a pastry brush, lightly coat the chicken skin with the remaining vegetable oil and fresh thyme. Season with salt and pepper to taste.

Place the chicken, skin side down, on the hot grill and *quadriller* (see page 168). Using tongs, turn the chicken and *quadriller* the other side. Transfer the chicken to a baking pan and place in the oven for 15 minutes. Do not turn off the grill.

Place the tomatoes and mushroom caps on the hot grill and *quadriller*. Season with salt and pepper to taste, remove from the grill, and set aside.

Place the bacon on the hot grill and *quadriller*. Remove from the grill and set aside.

Remove the chicken from the oven. Using a boning knife, remove the rib bones from the breast, leaving the wing bones intact. Quarter the chicken and remove the thighbones. Separately reserve the bones and any fat that is left in the baking pan.

Raise the oven temperature to 260°C (500°F). Using a pastry brush, generously coat the chicken with the mustard.

Sprinkle a thin coating of the reserved breadcrumbs over the skin side of each chicken piece and drizzle with any cooking fat that remains in the baking pan. If desired, the breadcrumbs can first be mixed with the cooking fat and some olive oil and then placed on the chicken. This method will actually make the breadcrumbs adhere to the chicken and will produce a more evenly browned dish.

Place the reserved bones on a baking sheet and then place the chicken pieces, breaded side up, on top of the bones. Place in the oven and bake for about 10 minutes or until a golden brown crust has formed.

Place the tomatoes, mushrooms, and bacon on a baking pan and bake along with the chicken to finish cooking.

If desired, using the butter, *monter au beurre* the sauce. (This is always done in the classic recipe.)

Remove the chicken and garnish from the oven. Place one piece of chicken in the center of each of four warm dinner plates. Surround with potato straws (*pommes pailles*) (page 114), if desired, along with the tomatoes, mushrooms, and bacon. Garnish with a few sprigs of watercress and serve with the sauce on the side.

Demonstration

Canard Rôti à l'Orange (Duck with Orange Sauce)

Serves 4

Estimated time to complete: 2 hours

Ingredients	Equipment
One 2.5-kilogram (about 5-pound) Pekin duck	Chef's knife
Coarse salt and freshly ground pepper to taste	Trussing needle
30 milliliters (2 tablespoons) vegetable oil	Trussing twine
50 grams (1¾ ounces) carrots, *mirepoix*	Kitchen fork
50 grams (1¾ ounces) onions, *mirepoix*	Roasting pan
500 milliliters (2 cups plus 2 tablespoons) Brown	Instant-read thermometer, if necessary
Chicken Stock or Brown Veal Stock	*Sautoir*
(see page 57, see note)	Wooden spoon
2 oranges	*Chinois*
15 milliliters (1 tablespoon) orange liqueur	2 small saucepans
	Metal spoon
For the *gastrique*	Zester
80 grams (¼ cup) sugar	Slotted spoon
120 milliliters (½ cup) white vinegar	Paper towels
	2 small bowls
To finish the dish	Small nonstick saucepan
15 grams (1 tablespoon) unsalted butter, optional	*Bain-marie*
Few sprigs fresh watercress, optional	Boning knife
	4 warm dinner plates

Prepare your *mise en place*.

Preheat the oven to 260°C (500°F).

Using a chef's knife, remove the wishbone and trim the wings from the duck. Season the interior cavity with salt and pepper to taste, and using a needle, truss the duck as directed on page 145. Reserve the trimmings. Using a kitchen fork, prick the skin all over the duck to help render the fat during the roasting process. Using about 5 milliliters (1 teaspoon) of the vegetable oil, rub the entire exterior of the duck and then season with salt and pepper to taste.

Place the duck in the roasting pan and roast for 20 minutes. Lower the oven temperature to 204°C (400°F) and continue to roast, basting with the pan drippings every 10 minutes for about 1 hour or until an instant-read thermometer inserted into the thickest part of the thigh reads 82°C (180°F). Regularly remove excess fat that accumulates in the pan as the duck roasts.

While the duck is roasting, prepare the sauce.

Chop all the duck trimmings, except for the liver. Heat the remaining vegetable oil in a *sautoir* over medium heat. Add the duck trimmings and sauté for about 7 minutes or until nicely browned. Add the carrots and onions and continue to cook, stirring frequently with a wooden spoon, for about 5 minutes or until the vegetables begin to soften and color.

When *sucs* have formed on the bottom of the pan, pour off and discard the excess fat.

Add the stock to the pan and bring to a simmer, stirring constantly to deglaze the pan. Simmer for at least 15 minutes or until nicely flavored. Remove from the heat and strain through a *chinois* into a clean saucepan, discarding the solids.

Using a metal spoon, skim off and discard any fat that floats to the surface of the liquid. Return the liquid to medium heat and bring to a simmer. Lower the heat and simmer for about 20 minutes or until slightly reduced and well balanced. This will be the reinforced stock used to make the *sauce à l'orange*.

Place one of the oranges under very hot water and then pat dry. Zest the orange.

Bring a small saucepan of water to a boil. Add the orange zest and blanch for 4 minutes. Using a slotted spoon, transfer the zest to a double layer of paper towels to drain. When well drained, place in a small bowl and add the orange liqueur. Set aside.

Remove the white pith from the zested orange. This process is known as **peler à vif**. Working over a small bowl, cut the orange between the membranes into *suprêmes* (sections), saving the juice that falls into the bowl. You will need 8 nice *suprêmes* for garnish. Set the *suprêmes* aside.

Juice the remaining orange and combine it with the juice from the sectioned orange. Set aside.

To prepare the *gastrique*, place the sugar in a small nonstick saucepan over medium heat. Cook, without stirring, for about 6 minutes or until it begins to caramelize. Stir in the vinegar and cook for about 5 minutes or until syrupy. Remove from the heat and add an ice cube or two to stop the cooking. Remove and discard the ice as soon as the temperature drops. Set the *gastrique* aside.

When the duck is done, remove it from the oven and allow it to rest for 15 minutes.

Combine the reinforced stock with the reserved orange zest, liqueur, and orange juice. Add the *gastrique* a bit at a time, until a well-balanced, tart-sweet sauce is achieved. Place the pan over medium heat and bring to a simmer. Simmer, stirring frequently, for about 3 minutes or just until well blended. Taste, and if necessary, adjust the seasoning. Transfer to a *bain-marie* to keep warm for service.

Using a boning knife, carve off the leg quarter portions from the duck, saving any juices to add to the sauce. Separate the thighs from the drumsticks and remove the thighbones from the thigh portions.

Remove half-breast portions from the carcass. Cut the breast meat into long, thin slices (*aiguillettes*).

If desired, using the butter, *monter au beurre* the sauce. (This is always done in the classic recipe.)

Place one piece of leg meat (either the leg or the thigh) in the center of each of four warm dinner plates. Arrange an equal portion of sliced breast meat halfway over the top of the leg. Nap with the sauce and garnish with two orange *suprêmes* and, if desired, a few sprigs of watercress. Serve immediately.

Demonstration
Suprêmes de Caneton Sautée et Cuisse Braisée à l'Orange
(Breast of Duckling with Braised Leg, Orange Sauce)

Serves 4

Estimated time to complete: 2 hours

Note

If you have duck stock on hand, it may be used in place of the veal stock.

Chef's Tip

"When making gastrique, *especially with dark-colored vinegar, dry cook the sugar to the dark caramel stage first and then deglaze with the vinegar and cook down until syrupy."*

Chef Sixto Alonso

Ingredients

One 2.5-kilogram (about 5-pound) Pekin duck
20 milliliters (1 tablespoon plus 1 teaspoon) vegetable oil
Coarse salt and freshly ground pepper to taste
50 grams (1¾ ounces) carrots, *mirepoix*
50 grams (1¾ ounces) onions, *mirepoix*
500 milliliters (2 cups plus 2 tablespoons) Brown Chicken Stock or Brown Veal Stock (see page 57)
Bouquet garni
2 oranges
15 milliliters (1 tablespoon) orange liqueur

For the *gastrique*
80 grams (¼ cup) granulated sugar
120 milliliters (½ cup) white vinegar

To finish the dish
15 grams (1 tablespoon) unsalted butter, optional
Few sprigs fresh watercress, optional

Equipment

Chef's knife
Boning knife
Sautoir with a tight-fitting lid
Wooden spoon
Poêle
Parchment paper
Zester
2 small saucepans
Slotted spoon
Paper towels
2 small bowls
Small nonstick saucepan
Plate
Chinois
Metal spoon
Bain-marie
Tongs
Instant-read thermometer, if necessary
4 warm dinner plates

Prepare your *mise en place.*

Preheat the oven to 163°C (325°F).

Using a chef's knife, remove the excess fat and the wishbone from the duck. Trim the wings at the second joint. Remove the leg quarters using the same technique as for chicken. Separately reserve all of the pieces.

Using a boning knife, cut along the breastbone from the neck to the tail. Following the rib cage and working with one half at a time, remove the breast pieces to create *suprêmes* (boneless breasts). Set the pieces aside.

Chop the carcass and the reserved trimmings (except the liver) into small pieces.

Heat half of the oil in a *sautoir* over medium heat. Add the chopped duck pieces, season with salt and pepper to taste, and sauté for about 7 minutes or until nicely browned. Add the carrots and onions and continue to cook, stirring frequently with a wooden spoon, for about 5 minutes or until the vegetables begin to soften and color.

While the *mirepoix* is browning, heat the remaining oil in a *poêle* over medium heat. Add the duck legs and sear, turning frequently, until all sides are nicely browned.

Place the browned legs on top of the browned duck pieces in the *sautoir.* Add the stock and *bouquet garni* and season lightly with salt and pepper. Cover with a piece of parchment paper cut to fit the top of the

sautoir perfectly (see page 32), then cover with a tight-fitting lid. Place in the oven and braise for 40 minutes or until very tender.

Score the breast skin and the underlying layer of fat in a crisscross pattern, taking care not to penetrate the meat. Set aside.

Place one of the oranges under very hot water and then pat dry. Zest the orange.

Bring a small saucepan of water to a boil. Add the orange zest and blanch for 4 minutes. Using a slotted spoon, transfer the zest to a double layer of paper towels to drain. When well drained, add about one quarter of the zest to the braising liquid in the oven and place the remainder in a small bowl with the orange liqueur. Set aside.

Remove the white pith from the zested orange (*peler à vif*). Working over a small bowl, cut the orange between the membranes into *suprêmes* (sections), saving the juice that falls into the bowl. You will need 8 nice *suprêmes* for garnish. Set the *suprêmes* aside.

Juice the remaining orange and combine it with the juice from the sectioned orange. Set aside.

To prepare the *gastrique*, place the sugar in a small nonstick saucepan over medium heat. Cook, without stirring, for about 6 minutes or until it begins to caramelize. Stir in the vinegar and cook for about 5 minutes or until syrupy. Add an ice cube or two to stop the cooking. Remove and discard the ice as soon as the temperature drops.

Remove the *sautoir* from the oven. Using a slotted spoon, transfer the duck legs to a plate. Separate the thighs from the drumsticks and remove the thigh-bones from the thighs. Set aside.

Strain the braising liquid through a *chinois* into a clean saucepan. Using a metal spoon, skim off and discard any fat that floats to the surface of the liquid. Place over medium heat and bring to a simmer. Cook, skimming off any fat that rises to the surface, for about 20 minutes or until slightly reduced and well-balanced in flavor. Stir in the reserved orange zest and liqueur, along with the orange juice. Add the *gastrique* a bit at a time, until a well-balanced sweet-tart sauce is achieved. Return to a simmer over medium heat and cook, stirring frequently, for about 3 minutes or just until well blended. Taste, and if necessary, adjust the seasoning. Transfer to a *bain-marie* to keep warm for service.

Season the reserved breast meat with salt and pepper to taste.

Wipe the *poêle* clean and place it over medium-high heat; add the seasoned breasts, skin side down. Lower the heat and cook slowly for about 15 minutes or until the skin is crisp and the fat has rendered out.

Using tongs, turn the breasts, increase the heat to medium-high, and sear for 1 minute or until the breast meat is cooked to medium (60°C/140°F on an instant-read thermometer).

Remove the breasts from the pan and set aside to rest for a couple of minutes.

If desired, using the butter, *monter au beurre* the sauce. (This is always done in the classic recipe.)

When ready to serve, cut the breast meat into long, thin slices (*aiguillettes*). Place one piece of leg meat (either the drumstick or the thigh) in the center of each of four warm dinner plates. Arrange an equal portion of sliced breast meat halfway over the top of the leg. Nap with the sauce and garnish with two orange *suprêmes* and, if desired, a few sprigs of watercress. Serve immediately.

Theory
General Information About Meat

Meat is one of the most regulated food products in America, with national regulations and laws governing many aspects of it, including butchering, processing, grading, and distribution. By United States Department of Agriculture (USDA) standards, the term "meat" specifies the muscle of cattle, pigs, sheep, and goats, and it is the role of this agency to ensure that all meat from these animals processed for human consumption be safe to eat. However, errors do occur, which makes it important for the consumer and the cook to be vigilant with kitchen sanitation.

Meat and meat products are still the major source of protein in the United States. The fact that they are now leaner than in years past make them even more in demand. Unfortunately, this leanness also means that most meats are not as juicy and savory as they once were. Since the meat dishes of the classic French repertoire were based on meat that was fattier, more intensely flavored, and free of additives and growth enhancers, this newly lean meat presents a particular challenge to the cook who must create dishes that highlight the lack of fat but mimic the flavor that fat provides.

It is important to remember that as meat cooks it loses some of its moisture and becomes denser. These two effects can make the meat juicy and beautifully textured, but they also can, when taken to the extreme, make the meat unpalatable. Muscle is made up primarily of proteins and water, and once the protein rises above 68°C (155°F), it loses its ability to retain moisture. In well-marbled meat, the fat melts as the heat increases, resulting in the desired juiciness. Although marbling helps eliminate some shrinkage because the fat enrobes the muscle fibers, overcooking can dry out even a piece of well-marbled prime beef.

Because so few skilled butchers exist today, it is important for the cook to be very knowledgeable about the processing of meats. Neighborhood butchers once broke down whole carcasses, using every piece in some capacity. Today, most meat is fabricated in processing plants and shipped to market in prepackaged individual cuts known as "boxed meat." Most of us will never see a whole carcass and, in fact, it is rare to even see a whole side (half a carcass) in the marketplace.

In general, the cook must learn the cuts that are available and used most often, the appropriate method of cooking for each cut, and how to distinguish the type of meat necessary for a specific recipe. The quality of the meat — or the muscle — is determined by the quality of the animal; how, where, and on what it was raised; and how it was processed. Prime meat is handled in one fashion, select in another. The muscle receiving less wear and tear (such as the tenderloin) will be tenderer and juicier than the well-worn neck or leg muscle. The tender muscles need very little cooking to reach the height of their succulence, while the tougher muscles, made up of gristle, sinew, and connective tissue, need long, slow, moist heat to be delicious; each type can be equally inviting in the hands of a skilled chef.

About Beef

Beef, America's favorite meat, is defined as the meat from all large domesticated adult cattle including cow, heifer, steer, or bull. However, most modern beef comes from castrated bulls up to eighteen months old. Through advanced scientific developments in animal husbandry and crossbreeding, there are now over ninety breeds of beef cattle in the United States, where as recently as the 1950s there were less than thirty.

Beef cattle are raised for the quantity of meat that they will ultimately produce; the quality and yield also depend on the breed. They have a much higher ratio of muscle to fat than other breeds. In addition, contemporary butchering techniques tend to eliminate much of the fat, so that beef has become a very lean meat. When butchering for the marketplace, beef is cut between the twelfth and thirteenth rib to produce the fore- and hindquarters.

Today beef is brought to market much more quickly than in the past. This is partly because of the enormous expense of raising cattle, as well as consumer demand for tender but lean meat. Mature animals usually have tougher meat that requires longer periods of cooking to tenderize it. Unfortunately, lean beef does not have the internal tenderizer that fat marbling creates, so it easily becomes tough and dry when improperly cooked.

The most delicious beef, in both texture and taste, comes from an animal between the ages of eighteen and twenty-four months and is bright red, firm-grained, and well-marbled with fat. Meat from more mature animals has very good flavor, but it is usually tougher, with a deeper purplish-red color, and requires longer cooking methods. In the best beef, yellowish-white fat indicates that the animal was corn-fed, one of the most desirable diets for cattle. The fat should be plentiful around the organs and throughout the muscle to keep the meat moist during cooking.

For the most part, cattle raised in the United States are grass- and hay-fed for three to six months before being sent to market. Then they are fed a high-energy diet of grain that results in enormous weight gain and an increase in the development of fat in the muscle. Most cattle from other parts of the world, such as Australia and South America, are kept on a grass-based diet and, therefore, possess less water and are leaner and gamier in flavor than American beef cattle.

The USDA is responsible for inspecting beef, but quality grading of beef is voluntary. Quality grading indicates the palatability of the meat, which translates to the eventual tenderness, juiciness, and depth of flavor. Beef has been assigned many grades, but only three of them have any importance to the general consumer—Prime, Choice, and Select. Prime beef, the highest grade, is now very difficult to obtain and consequently is extremely expensive. Most of it—which is only about 2 percent of all marketable beef—is used by fine dining establishments and steakhouses. It is beautifully marbled with almost alabaster-colored fat, which is one of the signs of a well-fed animal. Choice, with less marbling and little aging, is the highest grade carried by most supermarkets and specialty stores, even by the few remaining small butchers. Select is the lesser grade marketed for general consumption. It has very little marbling and lends itself to long, intense cooking methods.

The remaining grades—Standard, Commercial, Utility, Cutter, and Canner—are mainly used commercially in manufactured food products such as canned soups or stews. These grades are from more mature animals; they have an unrefined texture and almost no marbling or external fat.

Chef's Tip

"For proper results, it is important to pair the right category of meat with the particular cooking method."

Chef Pascal Beric

In addition, there is another type of grade, yield grade, which refers to the "cuttability" of the meat. Yield grades, ranging from 1 to 5, are classified by the amount of exterior and interior fat in the piece of meat. A yield grade of 1 would have the least fat; a yield grade of 5 would have the most. This grade is not directed to the consumer but to the wholesale market.

In French cooking, beef cuts are classified by category and use, which refers to the tenderness of the cut. First-category cuts can be cooked using dry-heat methods (concentration, see page 168) because they are very tender. Second and third category cuts require cooking methods that tenderize such as stewing and braising (extraction, see page 168).

French category classifications are as follows:

Category	Cut	Cooking Method
First	Rib	Roast, grill, sauté
	Short loin	Roast, grill, sauté
	Sirloin	Roast, grill, sauté
	Rump	Roast, sauté
Second	Short ribs	Braise, poach
	Chuck	Braise or use for ground beef
Third	Brisket	Braise
	Shank	Braise

The Aging of Beef

Beef is often aged under special conditions to tenderize the meat and enhance the flavor. Originally, beef was dry-aged, whereby the entire carcass (or a large piece of meat) was hung in a controlled environment with a temperature ranging from 1°C–3°C (34°F–38°F) for at least three weeks. This method, which is infrequently used today due to its cost, causes the beef to lose moisture and to develop, through enzymatic activity, a deep, rich flavor. The aged exterior must be trimmed from the carcass, and the loss of moisture causes the carcass to drop a considerable amount of weight, which means a major reduction in yield. This translates to a much higher cost to the consumer. However, it also results in exceptionally tender, firm-fleshed meat having a great depth of flavor.

Today's beef is aged primarily through a system of vacuum-packing or wet-aging. With this method, fresh cuts of meat are sealed in Cryovac packaging (see page 93) and then aged in the same controlled temperature used for dry-aging for seven to twenty-eight days. This is an effective and more cost-efficient method than dry-aging, but it does not result in the same texture and depth of flavor. Fast-aging is also done at 21°C (70°F) for a period of two days, with ultraviolet light used to control bacterial growth.

About Veal

Veal is the meat of young calves, between eight and twelve weeks old ideally, from animals that have not yet been weaned from mother's milk. High-quality veal is white to slightly rose in color, with an almost iridescent shine. Most veal in today's market comes from animals that have been fed a rich formula that is comparable to mother's milk, which also helps produce very light-colored meat. Using a method called the Danish Process, unweaned veal calves are usually raised in confined situations that limit their movement, which further ensures that their meat remains very tender and pale in color.

Veal is usually not graded; by definition it is supposed to be pale and tender. Much of the veal sold today is sold under a specific brand name that guarantees its quality. When buying veal, purchase only meat that is very pale and uniform in color, with no marbling. The exception to this is veal breast or chuck meat, which should have layered fat to ensure that the tougher meat stays tender throughout the longer cooking processes generally used for these cuts. Exterior fat, if any, should be creamy white, and the fat around the kidneys very white. The flesh of fine-quality veal should be dense and slightly elastic but still firm to the touch, and the bones should be cleanly white with a bright red interior.

Inferior veal comes from calves that were weaned too early, grazed in a pasture, or slaughtered too young or too old. Pasture grazing and maturity produces meat that is deep rosy-red in color with gray-white fat and almost striated flesh. When cooked, this meat is stringy, dry, and chewy. Calves that were slaughtered too early produce meat that is virtually fat-free and very soft, flaccid, and lacking in flavor.

As with beef, in French cooking, veal cuts are classified by category and use:

Category	Cut	Cooking Method
First	Rib	Roast, grill, sauté
	Loin	Roast, grill, sauté
	Sirloin	Roast, grill, sauté
	Round (leg)	Roast, sauté
Second	Shoulder	Roast, braise
Third	Shank	Braise
	Breast	Braise, poach

Methods of Cooking Meat

There are two basic methods of cooking meat (as well as other foods): cooking by **extraction** and cooking by **concentration**. These names refer to whether the cooking process draws out the juices from the item being cooked — extraction — or locks the moisture in the item — concentration.

Chef's Tip

"When grilling steaks, it is important to quadriller *properly, not only for looks but to increase the amount of caramelization. After you* quadrillage *the steak, cook it for 1 minute on each edge to help caramelize and baste it with the wonderful flavor of its fat."*

Chef Pascal Beric

Extraction

With this method, the ingredient and the liquid medium in which it is going to be cooked are started at a cold temperature. This enables the natural juices to be extracted and dissolve into the cooking liquid, flavoring it. Poaching, simmering, and boiling are all methods of cooking by extraction. Poaching and simmering entail cooking at lower temperatures than does boiling; poaching is usually done at just a bare simmer, while simmering is accomplished when the liquid is bubbling gently. For the most part, poaching and simmering are the most desirable methods because the violent movement caused by hard boiling often damages the ingredient being cooked or causes it to disintegrate. When making a stew, meat or poultry is blanched in boiling liquid and removed and refreshed as soon as the liquid has come to a boil. It is then returned to a pot of cold water (or other liquid) and again brought to a boil. The cooking temperature is then lowered to a simmer, the liquid is skimmed, and aromatic elements are added, usually a *bouquet garni*, leeks or onions, carrots, celery, an onion stuck with a whole clove (*oignon clouté*), and seasonings. The pot is covered, and the mixture slowly cooks, infusing the liquid with the flavors of the meat, vegetables, and seasonings. Creamy stews like *blanquettes*, *marmites*, and poached chicken are all examples of cooking by extraction.

Concentration

When meat cooks by concentration, the juices are sealed inside. Roasting, sautéing, and grilling (covered in Session 8) are all methods of cooking by concentration. The meat must never be pricked or punctured when cooking or the essential juices will be released and the flavor and texture will be compromised.

When grilling, the grill must be absolutely clean, very hot, and lightly oiled. The item to be grilled should also be oiled to prevent sticking. Grilled items are usually marked with crisscross grill marks (*quadrillage*). This is accomplished by placing the item on the hot grill at a 30 degree angle, toward the right. The item is grilled without moving for a few minutes, or just until the grill marks are seared into the meat (or other item). The item is then turned at a 30 degree angle to the left and grilled without moving, just until the grill marks are seared into it. The process is then repeated on the opposite side of the item. Meat to be grilled should be brought to room temperature before being placed on the grill to ensure that it is does not remain cold in the center when cooked to rare and that the intense heat does not cook the exterior before the interior reaches the desired degree of doneness.

"Beef cooking and carving is a noble occupation. In the Iliad *Agamemnon carved the beef for his guests."*

Chef Jacques Pépin

Checking the Temperature of Meat

Except when cooking by extraction, where the meat is cooked for fairly long periods of time to reach extreme tenderness, meat usually has to be checked for the desired degree of doneness with an instant-read thermometer or by the touch test. The touch test is extremely important to learn, as it is an expedient way to determine doneness in the speed of a restaurant kitchen. The touch test is best practiced on the fleshy part of the palm of your hand. When the hand is relaxed, the softness of the fleshy part is equal to the elasticity of rare meat; as you open your hand and the fleshy part gets firmer, it will gradually equal medium and then well-done meat. However, touch-test accuracy is also a function of the type of meat, cut, age, thickness, and so on; each type has to be learned. For instance, a filet does not feel like a strip steak. Again, time and practice are necessary to gain confidence at this age-old cook's skill. Until you master it, check yourself with a thermometer.

The degrees of doneness for all cuts of meat are categorized as:

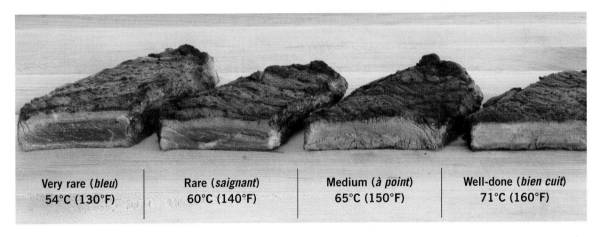

| Very rare (*bleu*) 54°C (130°F) | Rare (*saignant*) 60°C (140°F) | Medium (*à point*) 65°C (150°F) | Well-done (*bien cuit*) 71°C (160°F) |

Demonstration

Faux Filets Grillés avec Sauce Choron
(Grilled Beef Steak with Choron Sauce)

Serves 4

Estimated time to complete: 45 minutes

Note

Choron is a *béarnaise* sauce reduction that has a tomato *fondue* added for color and flavor.

Ingredients

For the *fondue*

10 grams (2 teaspoons) unsalted butter

10 grams (⅓ ounce) shallots, *ciselé*

½ clove garlic, crushed

100 grams (3½ ounces) tomatoes *concassé*

Coarse salt and freshly ground pepper to taste

Equipment

Sautoir or *russe*

Wooden spoon

Small nonreactive saucepan

Chinois

Small stainless steel bowl

For the *béarnaise* sauce reduction

90 milliliters (6 tablespoons) water

40 milliliters (2 tablespoons plus 2 teaspoons) white vinegar

20 grams (¾ ounce) shallots, *cisclé*

3 grams (2 teaspoons) dried tarragon

3 grams (2 teaspoons) cracked black pepper, *mignonette*

2 large egg yolks, at room temperature

200 milliliters (14 tablespoons) warm
   clarified butter

3 grams (2 teaspoons) fresh tarragon, *haché*

3 grams (2 teaspoons) fresh chervil (or flat-
   leaf parsley), *haché*

Coarse salt and freshly ground pepper to taste

For the steak

40 milliliters (2 tablespoons plus 2 teaspoons) vegetable oil

Four 150-gram (5¼-ounce) pieces well-trimmed strip loin of beef

Coarse salt and freshly ground pepper to taste

10 grams (2 teaspoons) unsalted butter for *lustrer*

¼ bunch watercress, washed, tough stems removed

Whisk
Small saucepan
Grill
Pastry brush
4 warm dinner plates

Prepare your *mise en place.*

Before preparing the steaks, make the sauce. Start with the tomato *fondue*, which is a component of Choron sauce. Heat a *sautoir* or *russe* over medium heat. When just hot, add the butter. When melted, add the shallots and garlic and sauté for about 4 minutes or just until they have sweated their liquid, are soft, and have not taken on any color.

Add the tomatoes and lower the heat. Cook, stirring occasionally with a wooden spoon, for about 10 minutes or until almost all the moisture has evaporated. Season with salt and pepper to taste and remove from the heat. Set the *fondue* aside and keep warm.

Prepare the *béarnaise* sauce reduction. Combine 75 milliliters (5 tablespoons) of the water with the vinegar, shallots, dried tarragon, and cracked pepper in a small nonreactive saucepan over medium heat. Bring to a simmer and cook for about 10 minutes or until reduced to one fifth its original volume. Remove from the heat and set aside to cool.

When the vinegar reduction is cool, strain through a *chinois* into a small stainless steel bowl. Add the egg yolks and the remaining 15 milliliters (1 tablespoon) water and whisk together to combine.

Place the bowl over a small saucepan of boiling water, taking care that the bottom of the bowl does not touch the boiling water. Heat, whisking constantly, for about 5 minutes or until the *sabayon* is thick and light.

Remove the bowl from the heat and, whisking constantly, add the clarified butter in a slow, steady stream. When all the butter has been incorporated, whisk in the reserved tomato *fondue*, the fresh tarragon, chervil, and salt and pepper to taste. Set aside and keep warm for service.

Preheat and oil the grill.

Trim and discard the excess fat from the steaks. Lightly oil and then season both sides of the steaks with salt and pepper.

Place the steaks on the grill and *quadriller*, then grill both sides to the desired degree of doneness. Remove from the grill and set aside to rest for 2 minutes. Using a pastry brush, *lustrer* each steak with the butter.

Place each steak on a warm dinner plate and garnish with watercress. Serve it with the sauce and, if desired, French fries (*pommes frites*, page 121).

Dean Jacques Pépin | *Dean of Special Programs, The French Culinary Institute*

Wine Merchant Steak

Serves 4

The steaks in this classic bistro dish are relatively small compared to those served in restaurants a few years ago. In addition, the meat is trimmed of all fat, leaving each portion with a weight of about 7 ounces, an ample serving.

Although these steaks can be grilled and served plain, I extend the dish with a sauce made of shallots, mushrooms, garlic, and a good, earthy wine, which I thicken with Dijon mustard and then garnish with some fresh chives.

Four 250-gram (9-ounce), 2-centimeter (¾-inch)–thick New York strip steaks,
    trimmed of all visible surface fat and sinew
Coarse salt and freshly ground pepper to taste
30 milliliters (2 tablespoons) extra virgin olive oil
2 shallots, finely chopped
4 large button mushrooms, trimmed and *julienned*
2 large cloves garlic, crushed and minced
237 milliliters (1 cup) red Beaujolais style wine
237 milliliters (1 cup) defatted chicken stock or fat-free, low-sodium
    canned chicken broth
15 milliliters (1 tablespoon) Worcestershire sauce
25 grams (1 tablespoon) Dijon mustard
1.5 grams (1 teaspoon) potato starch dissolved in 2 teaspoons cold water
5 grams (1 tablespoon) finely chopped fresh chives

Prepare your *mise en place.*

Generously sprinkle the steaks with salt and pepper.

Place the oil in a large skillet over high heat. When hot, add the steaks and sear for 2½ minutes per side for medium-rare.

Transfer the steaks to a serving platter and set aside in a warm spot.

Return the skillet to medium heat. Add the shallots and sauté for 10 seconds. Add the mushrooms and garlic and sauté for a minute. Stir in the wine, raise the heat, and boil for about 7 minutes or until only

30 milliliters (2 tablespoons) of liquid remain. Add the stock and again bring to a boil. Lower the heat and simmer for about 5 minutes or until the sauce has reduced by a quarter. Stir in the Worcestershire sauce and mustard along with salt to taste. Stir in the potato starch mixture and bring to a boil, stirring constantly.

Transfer each steak to a serving plate. Spoon an equal portion of the sauce over and around each steak. Sprinkle chives over the top and serve immediately.

Previously published in *Today's Gourmet*. Published by KQED-TV in conjunction with the show of the same name.

Chef Bobby Flay

Chef/Co-Owner, Mesa Grill, Bolo, and Bar Americain, New York City
Chef/Co-Owner, Mesa Grill, Las Vegas
The French Culinary Institute, Class of August 1984

Black Pepper–Crusted Filet Mignon with Goat Cheese and Roasted Red Pepper–Ancho Chile Vinaigrette

Serves 4

I was in the first graduating class at FCI. It seems so long ago, and yet so much of what I learned there is still with me. My style of cooking has veered far away from classic French, but the techniques that I absorbed during my classroom time have served me well through the years.

Four 284-gram (10-ounce) filet mignon steaks
Olive oil for brushing
Coarse salt to taste
5 grams (1 tablespoon) freshly ground pepper
One 227-gram (8-ounce) log goat cheese, cut crosswise into 4 equal pieces
Roasted Red Pepper–Ancho Chile Vinaigrette (recipe follows)

Prepare your *mise en place*.

Oil a grill and preheat it to high.

Using a pastry brush, lightly coat each side of the steaks with olive oil. Season both sides with salt to taste and then season one side of each steak with ¼ teaspoon of the pepper.

Place the steaks, peppered side down, on the grill. Grill for 2 to 3 minutes or until slightly charred and a crust has formed. Turn and grill the remaining side for 3 to 4 minutes for medium-rare. During the last minute of grilling, place a piece of cheese on top of each steak. Close the cover (or tent with aluminum foil) and cook just until the cheese has melted.

Remove the steaks from the grill and place on a serving platter. Drizzle the vinaigrette over the steaks and around the platter. Serve immediately.

Roasted Red Pepper–Ancho Chile Vinaigrette

2 ancho chiles

2 red bell peppers, roasted, peeled, stems, seeds, and membranes removed

3 cloves garlic, crushed

45 milliliters (3 tablespoons) red wine vinegar

14 grams (1 tablespoon) honey

Coarse salt and freshly ground pepper to taste

60 milliliters (¼ cup) canola oil

15 grams (3 tablespoons) chopped fresh cilantro

Prepare your *mise en place*.

Place the ancho chiles in a heatproof bowl. Cover with boiling water and set aside to soften for 1 hour.

Remove the softened chiles from the water but reserve the water. Remove and discard the stems. Coarsely chop the chiles and place them in a blender. Coarsely chop the bell peppers and place them in the blender. Add the garlic along with 60 milliliters (¼ cup) of the chile soaking liquid. Process until smooth. Add the vinegar, honey, and salt and pepper to taste and blend for 2 seconds. With the motor running, slowly add the oil, blending to emulsify. Pour into a nonreactive container and stir in the cilantro. Serve as directed.

Demonstration

Blanquette de Veau à l'Ancienne avec Riz Pilaf
(Old-Fashioned Veal Stew with Rice Pilaf)

Serves 4

Estimated time to complete: 1 hour, 30 minutes

Ingredients	Equipment
700 grams (1½ pounds) veal breast or shoulder, bones removed	Boning knife
One 100-gram (3½-ounce) white onion, peeled	*Rondeau*
1 bay leaf	Large metal spoon
1 whole clove	Colander
100 grams (3½ ounces) carrots, peeled and halved lengthwise	Paring knife
	Kitchen twine
100 grams (3½ ounces) leeks, white part with some green, well washed and halved lengthwise	Cheesecloth, if necessary
	Small stainless steel bowl
50 grams (1¾ ounces) celery, washed, trimmed, and halved lengthwise	2 *sauteuses*
	3 small bowls
About 10 parsley stems	Parchment paper
1 sprig fresh thyme	*Chinois*
7 peppercorns	Medium saucepan
2 cloves garlic	Wooden spoon
	Whisk

"If you simply skim the surface of the poaching liquid and strain and reuse it to continue cooking the rinsed veal, you will preserve all of that flavor for your blanquette de veau. *After cooking and straining the veal, keep the meat covered with a damp towel to avoid darkening."*

Chef Sixto Alonso

"A little lemon juice can be added to the cooking liquid of a blanquette *to ensure that it remains white."*

Chef Martin Schaub

1 liter (1 quart) White Veal Stock (page 53)
Coarse salt to taste

For the garnish

125 grams (4⅓ ounces) or 16 pearl onions
20 grams (1 tablespoon plus 1 teaspoon) unsalted butter
7 grams (1 teaspoon) sugar
Coarse salt to taste
125 grams (4⅓ ounces) button mushrooms, washed and dried
Juice of ¼ lemon
Freshly ground pepper to taste

For the sauce

30 grams (2 tablespoons) unsalted butter
30 grams (2 tablespoons) all-purpose flour
100 milliliters (7 tablespoons) heavy cream
1 large egg yolk
Coarse salt and freshly ground pepper to taste, optional
Rice Pilaf (recipe follows)
5 grams (1 tablespoon) chopped fresh flat-leaf parsley

Ring-shaped mold
Warm plate
Ladle

Prepare your *mise en place*.

Using a boning knife, trim all excess fat from the veal. Cut the meat into cubes. Rinse the cubes under cold running water.

Place the veal in a *rondeau* with cold water to cover by 2.5 centimeters (1 inch). Place over medium heat and bring to a gentle boil. Using a large metal spoon, skim off and discard any scum that rises to the top as the liquid comes to a boil. Then remove the pan from the heat and drain the meat well.

Rinse both the meat and the *rondeau*. Set aside.

Using a paring knife, make an incision in the onion and insert the bay leaf into the incision, securing it in place with the clove. (In classical cooking, this is known as an *oignon clouté*.)

Using kitchen twine, tie the carrots, leeks, celery, parsley stems, and thyme sprig into large bundles. Tie the peppercorns and garlic into a cheesecloth *sachet* or into the leftover leek greens.

175

Return the veal to the *rondeau*. Add the veal stock to cover the meat by at least 2.5 centimeters (1 inch). Add coarse salt to taste and place over high heat. Bring to a simmer, skimming off any fat and scum that float on the surface. Add the *oignon clouté*, vegetable bundles, and *sachet* and return to a simmer.

Lower the heat and simmer, uncovered, for about 1 hour or until the veal is very tender. Check for tenderness by pinching a piece of the meat between your fingertips; it should easily crush rather than spring back. Do not allow the liquid to boil during the cooking process, as this causes the meat to disintegrate.

While the veal is cooking, prepare the garnish and the rice pilaf as directed in the recipe.

Place the pearl onions in a small stainless steel bowl with hot water to cover for 5 minutes. Drain well and peel off the skins.

Heat 10 grams (2 teaspoons) of the butter in a *sauteuse*. Add the pearl onions along with the sugar and just enough water to cover the onions by half. Season with coarse salt to taste and cook *glacer à blanc*. Do not add too much water or the flavor of the onions will be leached out. There should be no water left in the pan at the end of the cooking process and the onions should be glazed but still almost white in color. Remove from the heat.

Leave the mushrooms whole, or halve or quarter them, depending on their size. Place the mushrooms in a small bowl, add the lemon juice, and toss to coat.

Heat the remaining 10 grams (2 teaspoons) of butter in a *sauteuse* over medium heat. Add the mushrooms and season with salt and pepper to taste. Cover with a parchment paper circle with a small hole cut in the center to make a perfect lid (see page 32), and cook

for about 4 minutes or until just tender. Remove from the heat.

When the veal is tender, remove it from the heat and drain it in a colander, setting aside the poaching liquid. Remove and discard the *oignon clouté*, vegetable bundles, and *sachet*. Transfer the meat to a small bowl, cover, and set aside.

Strain the poaching liquid through a fine *chinois* and set aside. Clean the *rondeau*.

Prepare the sauce. First, make a *velouté* by heating the butter in a medium saucepan over medium heat. Add the flour and, using a wooden spoon, stir to make a white roux (see page 62). Cook for 1 minute, then whisk in the reserved poaching liquid and bring to a simmer. Cook, whisking constantly, for about 3 minutes or until thickened. Lower the heat under the *velouté* and cook, whisking frequently, for an additional 10 minutes.

To finish the sauce, whisk 50 milliliters (3½ tablespoons) of the cream into the *velouté* and, whisking constantly, cook for 5 minutes.

Combine the egg yolk with the remaining 50 milliliters (3½ tablespoons) cream in a small bowl. Remove the hot *velouté* from the heat and, whisking constantly, add a small amount of the hot sauce to the egg and cream mixture to temper it. Whisk the tempered egg yolk mixture into the hot *velouté* and return it to medium heat. Cook, stirring constantly with a wooden spoon, for a couple of minutes or just until the sauce almost returns to a simmer. Immediately remove it from the heat and strain through a *chinois* into the clean *rondeau*. Taste, and if necessary, adjust the seasoning with salt and pepper.

To finish the stew, add the reserved veal along with the reserved onions and mushrooms to the sauce. Place over medium heat and bring to a bare simmer. Check for consistency, flavor, and seasoning, and make any necessary adjustments.

Fit the warm rice pilaf into a small *timbale* mold, if available, and then unmold it into the center of a warm plate. Ladle the hot stew around the rice, sprinkle chopped parsley over all, and serve.

Demonstration

Riz Pilaf (Rice Pilaf)

Serves 4

Estimated time to complete: 30 minutes

Ingredients	Equipment
190 milliliters (13 tablespoons) White Chicken Stock, plus more if needed (page 53)	Medium saucepan
	Russe with lid
40 grams (2 tablespoons plus 2 teaspoons) unsalted butter, at room temperature, plus more for the parchment	Wooden spoon
	Parchment paper
60 grams (2 ounces) onions, *ciselé*	Medium bowl
125 milliliters (½ cup plus 1 teaspoon) white rice	Kitchen fork
Bouquet garni	
Coarse salt and freshly ground pepper to taste	

Prepare your *mise en place.*

Preheat the oven to 177°C (350°F).

Place the stock in a medium saucepan over medium heat and bring to a boil. Immediately remove from the heat and cover to keep hot.

Heat 20 grams (1½ tablespoons) of the butter in a *russe* over medium heat. Add the onions and lower the heat. Cook, stirring frequently with a wooden spoon, for about 3 minutes or until the onions have softened and sweated their liquid but have not taken on any color.

Stir in the rice and cook, stirring constantly, for about 4 minutes or until the rice is opaque. Do not allow the rice to brown.

Add the hot stock and *bouquet garni.* Season with salt and pepper to taste and return to a simmer. Cover with a circle of buttered parchment paper cut to make a neat lid (see page 32). Then cover with the *russe* lid.

Transfer to the oven and bake for 17 minutes or until all the liquid has been absorbed by the rice. If the rice is not tender by the time all the liquid has been absorbed, add additional stock and continue baking until the rice is tender.

Remove from the oven and spoon into a bowl. Cut the remaining butter into cubes. Using a fork, toss the rice while adding the butter. This process is known as **engrainer**. Cover and keep warm until ready to mold or serve.

Executive Chef Jenny Glasgow

Olivier Cheng Catering and Events, New York City
The French Culinary Institute, Class of October 1993

Veal and Tarragon Meatballs with Puttanesca Dipping Sauce

Serves 4 to 6

All the techniques that I learned while at FCI have made it possible for me to expand my own style of cooking to include flavors and ingredients from all over the world. These Italian-accented meatballs make an elegant *hors d'oeuvre* when each one is skewered with a 3.8-centimeter (1½-inch) rosemary branch. They are also a boon to the kitchen in that they can be made in advance and frozen. Thaw and reheat in a 177°C (350°F) oven before serving.

21 grams (1½ tablespoons) unsalted butter
73 grams (2½ ounces) finely chopped onion
14 grams (⅓ ounce) minced garlic
450 grams (1 pound) ground veal
1 large egg
70 grams (2½ ounces) freshly grated Parmesan cheese
26.5 grams (¾ ounce) chopped fresh flat-leaf parsley

12 grams (⅓ ounce) fresh white breadcrumbs
45 milliliters (3 tablespoons) heavy cream
1.5 grams (1 teaspoon) finely chopped fresh tarragon
Coarse salt and freshly ground pepper to taste
45 milliliters (3 tablespoons) canola oil
Puttanesca Dipping Sauce (recipe follows)

Prepare your *mise en place.*

Heat the butter in a small sauté pan over medium heat. Add the onions and garlic and cook, stirring frequently, for about 4 minutes or until the vegetables have sweated their liquid but not taken on any color. Remove from the heat.

Place the veal in a medium mixing bowl. Add the egg, Parmesan, parsley, breadcrumbs, cream, and tarragon. Stir in the onion mixture and season with salt and pepper to taste. Blend well.

Preheat the oven to 177°C (350°F).

To test the seasoning, make a very small patty from the meat mixture. Heat a bit of oil in a small frying pan over medium heat. When hot, add the patty and

fry, turning once, for about 3 minutes or until cooked through. Taste and add salt and pepper as needed.

Form the remaining veal mixture into balls about 2.5 centimeters (1 inch) in diameter.

Heat the remaining oil in a large, ovenproof frying pan over medium-high heat. Add the meatballs and sear, turning frequently, for about 3 minutes or until all sides are well colored. Transfer the pan to the oven and bake for an additional 4 minutes or until cooked through.

Remove from the oven and arrange the meatballs on a serving platter. Place a bowl of the dipping sauce in the center of the platter and a small container of toothpicks on the side. Pass as an *hors d'oeuvre.*

Puttanesca Dipping Sauce

One 794-gram (28-ounce) can San Marzano tomatoes,
  drained
30 milliliters (2 tablespoons) olive oil, plus more as
  needed
1 clove garlic, sliced
11 grams (⅓ ounce) black olive paste
7 grams (¼ ounce) capers, drained
Pinch of dried red pepper flakes
Coarse salt and freshly ground pepper to taste, optional

Prepare your *mise en place.*

Preheat the oven to 149°C (300°F).

Carefully remove the seeds and as much of the juice as possible from the tomatoes. Place the tomatoes in a baking pan large enough to hold them in a single layer. Add 15 milliliters (1 tablespoon) of the olive oil and toss to coat. Spread out to a single layer. Place in the oven and roast for 1 hour or until the flavor has concentrated and the tomatoes are slightly shriveled. Remove from the oven and set aside.

Heat the remaining 15 milliliters (1 tablespoon) of olive oil in a large sauté pan over medium heat. Add the garlic and sauté for about 2 minutes or until golden. Add the tomatoes and cook for 2 minutes. Stir in the olive paste, capers, and red pepper flakes.

Transfer the mixture to a blender and process to a smooth purée, adding additional olive oil as necessary to achieve dipping consistency.

Taste and, if necessary, season with salt and pepper to taste.

Serve at room temperature.

Session 10

Methods of Cooking Meat: *Mixte* Cooking and Cooking Lamb

Theory

The *Mixte* Method of Cooking

Mixte cooking combines — mixes — elements of cooking both by extraction and concentration. The term "mixte" simply means that two or more items are being referred to. It is used for small cuts of second- and third-category meats (see page 166) and for poultry. The item to be cooked is first sautéed (concentration) and then moistened with stock or other liquid (extraction). The liquid used varies with the dish being prepared. Because a successful result depends on the tenderness of the meat and the development of a rich flavor, every element of proper *mixte* cooking is important. There are two types of *mixte* cooking: *mixte à brun* and *mixte à blanc*.

For a *mixte à brun* such as lamb stew (*navarin d'agneau*), the meat is first sautéed until well-colored, and a brown stock is used to complete the cooking. For a *mixte à blanc* such as a chicken stew in a white sauce (*fricassée de volaille*), the meat is first sautéed without allowing any coloring, and a white stock is used to complete the cooking.

Mixte à brun cooking is essential to the preparation of a properly made stew or braise and should result in fork-tender meat and a rich, deeply flavored sauce. The differences between a stew and a braise are in the size of the meat pieces to be cooked and in the amount of liquid used to prepare them. A stew is generally prepared with very small cuts of meat, with the addition (either during the cooking period or as a garnish) of vegetables that are cooked in enough liquid to generously cover. A braise is most often accomplished using larger cuts of meat, such as pot roasts, which are cooked, covered, with aromatics in just enough liquid to cover the meat. Stews often cook for a shorter time than do braises. Both of them are usually prepared in a heavy-bottomed casserole-type dish such as a Dutch oven. (Note: Braising is covered in detail in Session 17.)

In the first phase of a *mixte à brun*, the meat is cut into pieces and quickly sautéed over high heat. Rapid coagulation of the surface protein seals the exterior and traps the nutritive elements inside the meat. Depending upon the particular recipe, the meat may or may not take on coloration. If coloration is desired, it is important that the meat be carefully browned to achieve a rich caramelized flavor in the end.

In the second phase of a *mixte à brun* extraction, the sautéed meat is moistened with liquid (stock, water, or other juices). The meat flavors the cooking liquid while the liquid ensures that the meat remains moist during a somewhat extended period of cooking that will tenderize the meat. It is important that the liquid used also be a good balance for the other ingredients as well as flavorful on its own. Water can be used, but the final dish will not be as complex in taste.

Consider the following guidelines when using the *mixte* technique:

○ If the pan in which the meat is sautéed is not hot enough, the meat will boil or steam rather than sauté.

○ When preparing a *mixte à brun*, if the meat boils or steams, it will not be able to caramelize, nor will *sucs* form on the bottom of the pan.

○ *Sucs* are necessary during the sauté phase to add color and flavor to the brown sauce.

○ If the pan in which the meat is sautéed is too hot, the meat will caramelize too much and the juices and *sucs* will burn and render the sauce bitter and too dark in color.

○ Do not rush the extraction phase of *mixte* cooking. Patience will reward you with a final dish of complexity and depth of flavor.

○ During the extraction phase, if the pan is too wide, the cooking liquid will evaporate too quickly, the meat will not have enough time to cook properly, and the sauce will reduce too much.

About Lamb

Lamb is the meat of sheep of either sex, usually younger than fourteen months old (younger than six months in Europe) with a dressed weight of about 65 pounds. Most lamb is brought to the market between the ages of five and seven months old, though baby lamb less than six weeks old is sometimes available. Spring lamb is from smaller lambs, usually under 50 pounds, that have been milk-fed.

Mutton comes from animals fourteen months to two years of age and is rarely available in America unless through a Middle Eastern market. Mutton is very strongly flavored, quite dark red in color, and fatty. Mutton can be used in any lamb recipe that calls for a long period of cooking, as time is required to tenderize this mature meat.

In the contemporary American marketplace, much lamb comes from New Zealand and Australia, although lamb is grown and processed throughout the United States. New Zealand lamb has become quite desirable due to the fact that the lambs are younger and smaller when butchered, and it is available year-round, usually frozen.

In France, lamb falls into three categories: milk lamb (*agnelet*), butchered about thirty days before being weaned; white lamb (*agneau blanc* or *laiton*), the most common type, marketed from two and one half to five months of age and available from late December through June; and grazing lamb (*broutart*), which is six-to-nine-month-old pasture-grazed lamb that is also known as *agneau gris* because its diet causes its fat to color. Milk lamb is extremely tender, with a very faint and delicate flavor. White lamb has dense, deep pink meat and very white fat, which, when heated, helps to tenderize the meat. Grazing lamb has the most defined flavor and is often the choice of the discerning diner.

Lamb, like beef, is graded by the United States Department of Agriculture. The grades that reach the general marketplace are Prime and Choice, with Good, Utility, and Cull (mutton) being used for other purposes. Less than 10 percent of all lamb is graded Prime, with Choice being the most readily available. Lamb is graded by the quality of the muscles in the loin and rib cuts rather than by marbling, as beef is.

The best-quality lamb is pinkish-red with fat that is deeply white and almost like wax. Dark red meat and grayish-white fat signals an older, more strongly flavored animal. The texture of the meat should be quite dense, with no marbling, and the flavor should be delicate, with a hint of grassiness. Its subtleness and elegance makes lamb a perfect foil for fresh herbs and aromatics as well as exotic flavors.

Lamb cuts are often covered with a substantial amount of fat, which should be trimmed before cooking, as it tends to have an acute woolly or musty taste when heated. Lamb fat also has a high water content that causes it to melt quickly during cooking. The larger cuts of lamb may be covered by a paper-thin membrane called a **fell**, which must be removed before the meat is cooked. This is generally done by the processor or butcher, but occasionally it must be done by the cook. The fell is not only unattractive, it is indigestible and prevents the meat from cooking properly.

Category	Cut	Cooking Method
First	Rib	Grill, sauté, roast
	Loin	Grill, sauté, roast
	Sirloin	Grill, sauté, roast
	Leg	Roast, grill (butterflied)
Second	Shoulder	Braise, roast
Third	Breast	Braise
	Neck	Braise
	Shank	Braise

Demonstration

Navarin Printanier (Lamb Stew with Spring Vegetables)

Serves 4

Estimated time to complete: 1 hour, 30 minutes

Dean's Tip

"A lamb chop is one of the most delicate cuts of meat. It benefits from leaving a thin layer of fat on the edge, not close to the bone."

Dean Alain Sailhac

Ingredients

20 milliliters (1 tablespoon plus 1 teaspoon) vegetable oil

750 grams (1 pound, 10 ounces) lamb shoulder, trimmed and cut into 25-gram (1-ounce) cubes

Coarse salt and freshly ground pepper to taste

100 grams (3½ ounces) carrots, *mirepoix*

100 grams (3½ ounces) onions, *mirepoix*

1½ cloves garlic, peeled and crushed

20 grams (¾ ounce) all-purpose flour

20 grams (¾ ounce) tomato paste

1 teaspoon *beurre manié* (see page 62), if necessary

10 grams (2 tablespoons) fresh flat-leaf parsley, *hacher*

For the vegetable garnish:

250 grams (8¾ ounces) boiling potatoes, *cocotte*, blanched

125 grams (4⅓ ounces) carrots, *cocotte, glacer à brun*

125 grams (4⅓ ounces) pearl onions, *glacer à brun*

125 grams (4⅓ ounces) turnips, *cocotte, glacer à blond*

50 grams (1¾ ounces) string beans, cut into 5-centimeter (2-inch) pieces, *à l'anglaise*

50 grams (1¾ ounces) English peas, *à l'anglaise*

Equipment

Rondeau with lid

Tongs

Slotted spoon

2 small bowls

Wooden spoon

Metal spoon

Chinois

Narrow *russe*

Sautoir

Small saucepan

Small, sharp knife

Paper towels

4 warm shallow soup bowls

Dean's Tip

"Remember that the strong, woolly taste of lamb or mutton is always in the fat. Proper trimming is essential for good results."

Dean Jacques Pépin

Prepare your *mise en place* for the meat.

Preheat the oven to 177°C (350°F).

Place the *rondeau* over medium heat and add the oil. When very hot but not smoking, add the meat, in batches if necessary to keep from crowding the pan, and sear, turning frequently with tongs, for about 4 minutes or until the meat is nicely browned and a generous number of *sucs* have formed on the bottom of the pan. Take care that the *sucs* do not burn. Season the meat with salt and pepper to taste.

Using a slotted spoon, transfer the meat to a small bowl and set aside.

Remove the *rondeau* from the heat and drain off all but about 15 milliliters (1 tablespoon) of the oil. Add the carrots, onions, and garlic, and sauté for 1 minute.

Return the browned meat to the *rondeau*. Sprinkle with the flour and stir with a wooden spoon. Sauté for 5 minutes or until the raw flour taste has been eliminated and some caramelization has begun.

Add the tomato paste and stir to combine.

Add water to cover and season with salt to taste. Stir to combine, raise the heat, and bring to a boil. Using a metal spoon, skim off any fat or scum that rises to the top.

Cover and place in the oven. Braise for 60 minutes, uncovering and stirring every 15 minutes, taking care that the liquid does not come to a boil.

While the meat is braising, prepare the vegetable garnish as described in the ingredient list.

When the meat is done and the garnish *mise en place* is complete, remove the meat from the oven. Strain the liquid through a *chinois*, reserving the meat and the cooking liquid separately. Discard the vegetables and aromatics that have flavored the cooking liquid.

Place the meat in a small bowl, cover lightly, and keep warm.

Place the strained cooking liquid in a narrow *russe* and, using a metal spoon, remove any fat that is floating on the surface. Place over medium heat and cook, stirring occasionally, for about 10 minutes or until the liquid is slightly thick but viscous enough to lightly coat the back of a spoon (*nappant*). If necessary, add about 1 teaspoon of *beurre manie* to thicken and create the necessary *nappant*. Taste, and if necessary, adjust the seasonings with salt and pepper.

Bring a small saucepan of water to a boil. Lower the heat to a simmer.

Return the meat to the sauce, add the blanched potatoes, and bring to a bare simmer. Simmer for about 5 minutes or just until the potatoes are tender when pierced with the point of a small, sharp knife. Stir in the carrots, pearl onions, and turnips.

Place the string beans and peas in the simmering water and cook for about 30 seconds or just until heated through. Using a slotted spoon, lift the beans and peas from the water and allow to drain on paper towels.

Ladle the stew into the center of each of four warm shallow soup bowls. Garnish each plate with an equal amount of string beans and peas. Sprinkle parsley over the top and serve.

Note

Chicken fricassee is a classic example of *mixte* cooking.

Chef's Tip

"Because of the very fatty skin on stewing chickens, I prefer to discard all of the fat after cooking and before plating this dish."

Chef Sixto Alonso

Demonstration

Fricassée de Volaille Printaniére
(Chicken Fricassee with Spring Vegetables)

Serves 4

Estimated time to complete: 1 hour

Ingredients	Equipment
One 1.5-kilogram (3 pounds, 5 ounces) chicken	Chef's knife
Coarse salt and freshly ground pepper to taste	2 *sautoirs*
30 grams (2 tablespoons) unsalted butter	Tongs
60 grams (2 ounces) onions, *mirepoix*	Plate
30 grams (1 ounce) all-purpose flour	Wooden spoon
500 milliliters (2 cups plus 2 tablespoons)	Whisk
White Chicken Stock (see page 53)	Metal spoon
100 milliliters (7 tablespoons) heavy cream	*Chinois*
125 grams (4⅓ ounces) warm pearl onions, *glacer à blond*	*Sauteuse*, optional
10 grams (2 tablespoons) fresh flat-leaf parsley, finely chopped	4 warm dinner plates

For the vegetable garnish

125 grams (4⅓ ounces) carrots, *cocotte, à l'anglaise*

125 grams (4⅓ ounces) turnips, *cocotte, à l'anglaise*

50 grams (1¾ ounce) string beans, cut into 5-centimeter (2-inch) pieces, *à l'anglaise*

50 grams (1¾ ounces) English peas, *à l'anglaise*

Pat of butter, if necessary

Coarse salt and freshly ground pepper to taste, if necessary

Prepare your *mise en place* for the chicken.

Using a chef's knife, cut the chicken into quarters as directed on page 141. Rinse well and pat dry. Season with salt and pepper to taste.

Heat the butter in a *sautoir* over medium heat. Add the chicken and cook, skin side down, for about 3 minutes or just long enough to seal the skin without adding any color. Using tongs, turn the chicken. Lightly sear the remaining sides. Do not allow the chicken to take on any color. Remove the seared chicken from the pan and set aside on a plate.

Add the chopped onions to the hot pan and sauté for about 3 minutes or just until the onions are translucent. Using a wooden spoon, stir in the flour and continue to sauté for another 3 minutes or until the raw flour taste has been eliminated but no coloration has occurred.

Whisk in the stock and cook, whisking constantly, for about 4 minutes or until the liquid has thickened to a *velouté*.

Place the chicken pieces in the *velouté*. Cover and bring to a simmer. Lower the heat and cook at a bare

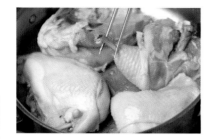

simmer for 20 minutes or until the chicken is cooked through, occasionally skimming off any fat that rises to the top with a metal spoon.

While the chicken is cooking, prepare the garnish.

When the chicken is cooked and the garnish *mise en place* is complete, remove the chicken from the sauce. Cut each piece in half, then remove and discard the thigh and breast bones. Set the chicken aside, cover lightly, and keep warm.

Using a metal spoon, skim off any fat that has risen to the surface of the sauce. Strain the sauce through a *chinois* into a clean *sautoir* and add the cream. Place the pan over medium heat and bring to a simmer. Taste for consistency and seasoning. If necessary, cook for a few additional minutes to reduce the liquid to a saucelike consistency and add salt and pepper to taste.

When the sauce has reached the desired consistency, return the chicken to the sauce.

When ready to serve, add the pearl onions to the *fricassée*. If necessary, reheat the carrots, turnips, string beans, and peas in a small *sauteuse* with a pat of butter and 15 milliliters (1 tablespoon) water and season with salt and pepper to taste.

Place half of a leg and half of a breast piece in the center of each of four warm dinner plates. Nap the chicken with the sauce and garnish each plate with an equal amount of the vegetables. Sprinkle the parsley over all and serve.

Chef Matthew Kenney

Chef/Founder, Organic Umbrella, New York City
The French Culinary Institute, Class of March 1990

Roasted Lamb Loin Stuffed with Almonds, Dates, Goat Cheese, and Mint

Serves 4

These thin lamb loins with flavorful stuffing cook quickly, and the finished dish is colorful and delicious. It is rustic rather than fancy, drizzled with a simple orange and honey vinaigrette and garnished with chewy chopped dates and toasted almonds. The meat and stuffing are tied together, not rolled, so slice carefully. But don't worry if the package falls apart a little—it will still be beautiful, especially when arranged on a large serving platter.

Two 285-gram (10-ounce) lamb loins, trimmed to leave a thin layer of fat
Coarse salt and freshly ground pepper to taste
55 grams (2 ounces) soft goat cheese
7 grams (1½ tablespoons) coarsely chopped fresh mint leaves
85 grams (3 ounces) chopped, toasted almonds
100 grams (3½ ounces) chopped pitted dates
30 milliliters (2 tablespoons) extra virgin olive oil
Orange Vinaigrette (recipe follows)

Prepare your *mise en place.*

Preheat the oven to 204°C (400°F).

Place each lamb loin between 2 pieces of plastic film and, using a meat mallet, pound until about 19 millimeters (¾ inch) thick.

Remove the film. Lay one of the loins out on a flat surface. Season with salt and pepper to taste. Spread the goat cheese on top, leaving a 1.3-centimeter (½ inch) border all around. Top with the mint and about half of the almonds and dates. Season the remaining loin with salt and pepper to taste and carefully place the seasoned side down on top of the cheese-topped loin, overlapping the edges as much as possible to prevent the filling from oozing out. Using kitchen twine, tightly tie the loins together crosswise at about 1.9-centimeter (¾-inch) intervals. Season the tied loins with salt and pepper to taste.

Place the oil in a large, ovenproof skillet over medium-high heat. When very hot but not smoking, add the loins and sear, turning frequently, until brown on all sides. Transfer to the preheated oven and roast for about 7 minutes or until the interior is hot and the meat is cooked to medium-rare.

Remove from the oven and let rest for a minute or two. Using a sharp knife, cut off the twine and then cut the lamb, crosswise, into 1.9-centimeter (¾-inch) thick slices. Cut straight up and down so that the filling remains intact.

Place the slices on a serving platter, drizzle with the vinaigrette, and sprinkle the remaining almonds and dates over all. Serve immediately.

Orange Vinaigrette

120 milliliters (½ cup) fresh orange juice
30 grams (2 tablespoons) honey
20 grams (¼ cup) loosely packed cilantro leaves
30 milliliters (2 tablespoons) extra virgin olive oil
Coarse salt and freshly ground pepper to taste

Prepare your *mise en place.*

Combine the orange juice and honey in a small nonreactive bowl. Add the cilantro and stir to blend. Slowly whisk in the oil. When emulsified, season with salt and pepper to taste. Set aside at room temperature until ready to serve. Whisk to re-emulsify before serving.

Previously published in *Matthew Kenney's Big City Cooking: Recipes for a Fast-Paced World* (Chronicle Books, 2003).

Session 11

Methods of Cooking Meat: *Poêle*, Breading and Sautéing, Cooking Pork

Theory
The *Poêle* Method of Cooking

According to Auguste Escoffier:

> *Poêles* are, practically speaking, roasts, for the cooking periods of each are the same, except that the former are cooked entirely or almost entirely with butter. They represent a simplified process of old cookery, which consisted in enveloping the object to be treated, after frying it, in a thick coating of *matignon* (vegetables stewed in butter). It was then wrapped with a thin slice of pork fat, covered with buttered paper, placed in the oven or on a spit, and basted with melted butter while it cooked. This done, the vegetables of the *matignon* were put in the braising pan wherein the piece had cooked, or in a saucepan, and were moistened with excellent Madeira or highly seasoned stock. Then, when the liquor had thoroughly absorbed the aroma of the vegetables, it was strained, and its grease was removed just before serving.

Certainly, this method of cooking is not for the calorie-conscious! It is used primarily for cooking large-size roasts of pork or veal, but it can also be used for large birds such as turkey.

Technique

The procedure for the *poêle* method of cooking:

1. Preheat the oven to 177°C (350°F).

2. Season the meat well.

3. Sear the meat on the stovetop in hot fat to brown all sides.

4. Place the bones, trimmings, *mirepoix*, and a *bouquet garni* in a *rondeau*.

5. Place the browned meat over the bones and flavorings.

6. Top the meat with a generous knob of butter.

7. Cover the *rondeau* with a tight-fitting lid and place in the oven.

8. Cook, basting frequently, until the desired degree of doneness is reached. The meat is cooked when the juices run clear with no trace of blood or when the internal temperature reaches between 60°C (140°F) and 66°C (150°F) on an instant-read thermometer.

9. Remove the pan from the oven. Transfer the meat to a warm platter, tent lightly with aluminum foil, and keep warm.

10. Place the *rondeau* on the stovetop over medium heat, leaving the flavoring elements in the pan.

11. Add white wine and a well-flavored thickened veal stock (see *fond de veau lié*, page 69).

12. Bring to a simmer and cook for 15 minutes.

13. Remove from the heat and pass the liquid through a *chinois*, discarding the solids.

14. Transfer the liquid to a clean saucepan and, using a metal spoon, remove any fat that rises to the surface.

15. Place over medium heat and bring to a simmer.

16. Simmer until the liquid reaches a saucelike consistency.

17. Taste and adjust the seasoning with salt and pepper.

18. If the roast is to be presented as a whole piece on a platter, using a pastry brush, lightly coat the meat with the sauce and return the meat to a pre-heated oven to glaze, adding as many coats of the sauce as necessary to achieve a shiny glaze.

Theory

The Breading and Sautéing Method of Cooking

Breading or the coating of meat (or other items) with a thin layer of breadcrumbs, flour, or other sealants, not only adds texture and flavor to the meat, it helps seal in moisture. A thick cut of meat should never be prepared in this fashion, as the exterior will burn before the interior is fully cooked. It is most useful with very thin pieces of meat, which can dry out quickly during even a short period of cooking. The breading should result in a thin, delicate crust that just enfolds the meat but does not create a cloying cover.

There are many different methods of breading. One of the most common is the three-step method known as ***paner à l'anglaise***, where an item is dipped first in flour, then egg, and finally in breadcrumbs. This should not be confused with the vegetable-cooking method known as *à l'anglaise* (see page 32).

When meat is breaded, it is almost always then sautéed. This takes a great deal of care and attention,

"When breading an item, try to use one hand for the wet ingredients and the other hand for the dry ingredients to create less of a mess."

Chef Candy Argondizza

as you want the breading to be crisp, even, and golden brown, while the meat should be well cooked but moist and flavorful. It is essential that the meat be sliced as thin as possible as well as pounded lightly to produce an even thickness. (This thin, flat piece of meat is known as a **suprême** or **paillard**.) The meat of choice can be veal, chicken, or turkey (*escalopes de veau, volaille*, or *dinde*) or very thin lamb or pork chops (*côtes d'agneau* or *côtes de porc*). It is cooked very quickly in clarified butter over high heat until just cooked through, with a golden brown exterior.

Technique

The procedure for correct breading and sautéing:

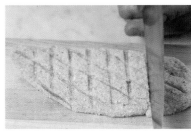

1. Arrange three shallow containers in a row.

2. Place sifted flour in one container.

3. Place eggs whisked together with a bit of oil and salt in the second container.

4. Place finely sifted breadcrumbs made from the crusts of white bread that have been dried out in the oven and blended in a food processor in the third.

5. Trim the meat of all excess fat.

6. Place each piece of meat between two pieces of plastic film or parchment paper.

7. Using a meat mallet or the flat side of a cleaver or chef's knife, pound each piece of meat flat. Uncover the meat and season both sides with salt and pepper to taste.

8. Working with one piece at a time, lightly dip each piece in the flour, shaking off the excess.

9. Dip both sides of each piece in the egg mixture. Remove any excess with your fingertips or tap it on the edge of the bowl to release.

10. Place each piece in the breadcrumbs to lightly but completely coat both sides.

11. With the dull side of a knife, make a crisscross design (*quadrillage*) into the breadcrumbs, taking care not to dislodge them.

12. Heat the clarified butter (or vegetable oil) in a *sautoir* over medium heat.

13. Add the breaded meat and cook for the recommended amount of time to achieve a golden exterior and a just-cooked, moist interior.

14. Using a slotted spatula, remove the meat from the pan and place it on paper towels to drain for a few seconds before serving.

Theory
About Pork

Pork is the meat of the domesticated pig and can come from either the male (boar) or female (sow). Young pigs, called piglets or suckling pigs, are also eaten. In the past, pork was considered a food of the "common folk" because the animals were raised on a diet of kitchen leftovers. It was a rich, fatty meat that was cooked for long periods of time to eliminate the possibility of trichinosis contamination. Today, due to changes in breeding, pork has become the "other white meat" and is used in many exquisite dishes that once featured the more expensive veal or white poultry meat.

In France, pork is one of the most widely consumed meats and, in recent years, its popularity has rapidly grown in the United States. In northern and eastern France, very white pork is considered the most desirable. But in the United States and the rest of France, pink-flesh pork is preferable. To this end, fine quality pork has very firm, finely grained, deep-pink flesh with almost no marbling. The fat should be tight, very smooth, and milky white with absolutely no discoloration. In general, meat that is flat in color or very red, limp, or fatty should be avoided.

In French cooking, pork cuts are not classified by categories as are beef, veal, and lamb. In the United States, the USDA is responsible for inspecting and grading pork. The cuts of pork are standardized throughout the country. The grades are, in descending order of quality: U.S. No. 1, U.S. No. 2, U.S. No. 3, and U.S. No. 4.

Most of the pork marketed today has been bred under highly controlled conditions. Although the parasite responsible for trichinosis has not been eradicated, occurrences of trichinosis-related illnesses are rare. Since trichinosis is destroyed at 58°C (137°F) — substantially less than the recommended internal temperature of cooked pork — this problem is generally no longer an issue in the commercial kitchen. At this time, it can be safely stated that pork no longer requires long periods of cooking in the interest of safety, which is a very good thing because pork is now so lean that the slightest overcooking dries it out very quickly.

In the United States most pork is used for processed products such as ham, bacon, sausage, and luncheon meat. Only about one-third is sold as fresh meat. In France, there is a tradition that all parts of the pig can come to the table and it is a fact that every part — from the tail to the ears — has a use in the kitchen, either fresh or in *charcuterie* (cured or salted meats, pâtés, and other delicatessen-style products).

The most popular of the fresh cuts in America are from the loin — the muscle that runs along the backbone starting at the shoulder and continuing to the leg. Because of its desirability, breeders have developed pigs with abnormally long loins and more ribs. There are two loins, one on each side of the backbone, weighing about 20 pounds, and they each contain ribs, a center loin, a tenderloin, and a sirloin. The loin also provides roasts, chops, and the tenderloin, as well as back and country-style ribs. Much meat from the loin is labeled "center-cut," which simply means that the meat has been cut from the largest part of the loin, the center.

Other cuts of pork come from the shoulder, leg, and underbelly. The shoulder may be cut into two pieces: the arm or picnic shoulder, and the butt or Boston-style shoulder. The arm section is often also cut into two pieces, the shoulder end and the shank, both usually of equal weight. The leg, when available fresh, is also called a fresh ham. Spareribs, one of the most popular pork items, come from the underside of the pig.

Pork can be cooked in a variety of ways, each depending upon the thickness and fattiness of the meat. It is cooked by the *poêle* method as discussed in this session, roasted, sautéed, fried, grilled, stewed, barbecued, and braised. Lean pork should, obviously, be cooked by the quickest, simplest methods until just pink and large; tough pieces lend themselves to slow roasting or braising.

Demonstration

Carré de Porc Rôti Choisy (Roast Loin of Pork Choisy)

Serves 4

Estimated time to complete: 1 hour, 30 minutes

Ingredients	Equipment
	Cleaver or kitchen saw
¼ pork loin, about 1 kilogram (2¼ pounds)	Kitchen twine
30 milliliters (2 tablespoons) vegetable oil	*Rondeau* with lid
55 grams (about 4 tablespoons) unsalted butter	Tongs
Coarse salt and freshly ground pepper to taste	Plate
120 grams (4¼ ounces) carrots, *mirepoix*	Wooden spoon
120 grams (4¼ ounces) onions, *mirepoix*	Instant-read thermometer
Bouquet garni	Small, sharp knife
	Warm platter
For the *choisy* garnish	Aluminum foil
2 full heads Boston lettuce	2 medium saucepans
30 grams (2 tablespoons) unsalted butter	Ice water bath
40 grams (1½ ounces) carrots, *brunoise*	*Sautoir*
40 grams (1½ ounces) onions, *ciselé*	Parchment paper
40 grams (1½ ounces) lean bacon, rind removed and finely diced	Cutting board
350 milliliters (1½ cups) White Chicken Stock (see page 53)	Chef's knife
Coarse salt and freshly ground pepper to taste	Small *sautoir*
400 grams (14 ounces) cooked russet or other floury	*Chinois*
potatoes, cut *château*	Metal spoon
	4 warm dinner plates

For the sauce

250 milliliters (1 cup plus 1 tablespoon) full-flavored Thickened
    Veal Stock (see page 69)

50 milliliters (3½ tablespoons) white wine

Coarse salt and freshly ground pepper to taste, optional

5 grams (1 tablespoon) minced fresh flat-leaf parsley

5 grams (1 tablespoon) minced chervil

To finish the dish

5 grams (1 tablespoon) finely chopped fresh flat-leaf parsley

¼ bunch fresh watercress, tough stems removed, washed and dried

Prepare your *mise en place*.

Preheat the oven to 177°C (350°F).

Using a cleaver or kitchen saw, carefully remove the chine bone (the backbone) from the ribs. *Manchonner* the ribs (see page 142) and, using kitchen twine, tie the rack in place. Chop the bones into 2.5-centimeter (1-inch) pieces; set aside the bones and the trimmings.

Combine the oil and 15 grams (1 tablespoon) of the butter in the *rondeau* over medium-high heat. When the fat is very hot but not smoking, season the meat with salt and pepper to taste and place it in the hot fat. Sear the meat, turning it frequently, for about 5 minutes or until all sides have browned nicely. Using tongs, remove the meat from the pan and set it aside on a plate.

Lower the heat to medium and add the reserved bones and trimmings along with the *mirepoix* vegetables and *bouquet garni*. Using a wooden spoon, stir to combine, then place the meat on top of the vegetables and meat trimmings. Place the remaining 40 grams (about 3 tablespoons) of butter on top.

Cover with a tight-fitting lid and place in the oven. Roast, basting with pan drippings every 10 minutes, for 1 hour or until the meat registers 63°C–68°C (145°F–155°F) on an instant-read thermometer for 4 minutes and the juices run clear with no trace of blood when the meat is pricked with the point of a small, sharp knife.

Remove the meat from the pan, place on a warm platter, tent lightly with aluminum foil, and keep warm.

30 minutes before the meat is ready, prepare the garnish.

Remove any wilted leaves from the lettuce. Trim, stem, and wash the lettuce heads at least three times in cold water.

Bring a medium saucepan of salted water to a boil over high heat. Add the lettuce heads and blanch for 2 minutes or just until wilted. Drain well and refresh the lettuce in an ice-water bath. Shake off excess water and then gently press to exude additional moisture.

Place the butter in a *sautoir* over medium heat. Add the carrots, onions, and bacon — the *matignon* — and stir to blend. Add the lettuce along with just enough stock to cover the lettuce by half. Season with salt and pepper to taste.

Cover the vegetables with a circle of parchment paper cut to make a perfectly fitting lid (see page 32) and place in the oven along with the roasting meat. Cook for about 30 minutes or until the lettuce core offers no resistance when pricked with the point of a knife.

Remove the pan from the oven and, using tongs, lift the lettuce from the pan. Place the lettuce on a cutting board and, using a chef's knife, cut each head in half lengthwise. Slice off the stem end and carefully fold each half into a neat 7.5-centimeter (3-inch) packet.

When ready to serve, place the lettuce in a small *sautoir* along with the potatoes and just enough stock to moisten slightly. Place over medium heat and cook just long enough to heat through. Taste, and if necessary, season with salt and pepper.

To make the sauce, return the *rondeau* with the pan drippings to the stovetop over medium heat. Add the stock and white wine and bring to a simmer. Simmer for 15 minutes or just until the liquid has taken on the flavors of the cooked *mirepoix* and trimmings. Taste, and if necessary, season with salt and pepper.

Remove the pan from the heat and pass the liquid through a *chinois* into a clean saucepan. Using a metal spoon, skim off any fat that rises to the surface. Taste, and if necessary, season with additional salt and pepper. Return to medium heat to reduce to a more saucelike consistency, if desired.

When ready to serve, stir in the minced parsley and chervil.

Carve the roast into 8 pieces, 4 with bone and 4 without. Place a piece of each type on each of four warm dinner plates. Nestle equal portions of the lettuce and potato duo next to the meat. Sprinkle with chopped parsley and garnish each plate with watercress. Serve the sauce on the side.

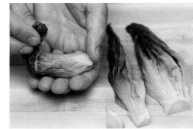

Demonstration

Escalopes de Volaille Viennoise (Viennese-Style Chicken Scallops)

Serves 4

Estimated time to complete: 30 minutes

Ingredients	Equipment
For the *Viennoise* garnish	Small bowl
4 anchovy fillets	Paper towels
2 large hard-cooked eggs, peeled	Small knife
1 lemon, washed and dried	Drum sieve
4 green olives, pitted	2 small bowls
4 sprigs fresh flat-leaf parsley, washed and dried	Paring knife
	Boning knife
For the chicken	Plastic film or parchment paper
2 whole small chicken breasts (see note)	Meat mallet or cleaver
2 large eggs	3 shallow bowls
40 milliliters (2 tablespoons plus 2 teaspoons) vegetable oil	Whisk
Coarse salt and freshly ground pepper to taste	Chef's knife
200 grams (7 ounces) fine breadcrumbs (see note)	*Poêle*
150 grams (5¼ ounces) all-purpose flour, sifted	Slotted spatula
100 milliliters (7 tablespoons) clarified butter	Paper towels
100 milliliters (7 tablespoons) warm thickened	4 warm dinner plates
Veal Stock (see page 69) or *demi-glace*	
To finish the dish	
20 grams (¼ cup) chopped fresh flat-leaf parsley	
40 grams (1½ ounces) capers, drained	

Prepare your *mise en place.*

As the garnish can easily be prepared in advance, prepare it first and hold it, covered and refrigerated, until ready to serve.

Place the anchovy fillets in a small bowl with cold water to cover and let soak for 5 minutes. Drain well, pat dry with paper towels, and, using a small knife, scrape off and discard any bones that remain in the fillets.

Cut the eggs in half lengthwise and carefully remove the yolks, separately reserving the whites and the yolks. Separately pass the yolks and whites through a drum sieve into small bowls.

Using a paring knife, carefully remove the lemon peel, taking care not to leave any of the white pith attached (*peler à vif*), and slice, crosswise, into 3-millimeter (⅛-inch) slices. Carefully remove any seeds, keeping the lemon slices whole.

Note

It is best to use breasts from small chickens, those weighing no more than 1 kilogram (about 2 to 2½ pounds).

If it is necessary to make the bread-crumbs, trim the crusts from a loaf or slices of fine-quality white bread. Use only the crusts, alone, or combine them with the bread that has been cut into croutons. Place the pieces on a baking pan in a very low oven to dry for about 30 minutes. Do not allow the bread to take on any color. When dry, place the pieces in a food processor fitted with the metal blade and process to a fine crumb.

Wrap an anchovy fillet around each olive, then place a small parsley sprig into the hole in each olive. Place each finished olive on a lemon slice. (At this point, the garnish items can be covered and refrigerated until ready for service.)

Next, prepare the chicken. Using a boning knife, remove the skin from and debone the chicken breasts. You should have two pieces from each breast.

Remove the tenderloin from each piece and reserve it for another use.

Place each breast piece between two sheets of plastic film or parchment paper and, using a meat mallet or the flat side of a cleaver or chef's knife, pound the chicken into even 6-millimeter (¼-inch)–thick flat *suprêmes*. (If the *suprêmes* are very large, you should cut them in half crosswise and make two scallops instead of one from each piece.)

Proceed with the breading. Combine the eggs, vegetable oil, and salt and pepper to taste in a shallow bowl and whisk to blend.

Place the breadcrumbs and flour in two separate shallow bowls. Line up the breading elements in a row, first the flour, then the egg, and finally the breadcrumbs.

Working with one piece at a time, dip both sides of each piece of chicken into the flour. Lift the chicken

up and, holding it over the bowl, gently pat off any excess flour. (Too much flour will make the surface of the chicken gluey.)

Again, working with one piece at a time, dip the floured chicken into the egg mixture, removing any excess with your fingers. (You can also gently tap the chicken on the edge of the bowl to eliminate excess egg.)

Finally, press both sides of each piece of chicken into the breadcrumbs, making sure that each side is evenly and smoothly covered.

Select the presentation side of each piece and, using a chef's knife, lightly mark each piece in a *quadrillage* pattern, taking care to not damage the breading.

Heat the clarified butter in a *poêle* over medium heat, taking care that the butter does not get too hot and begin to burn. Place the breaded chicken scallops, presentation side down, into the hot butter. Fry for 1 minute or until just golden brown. Turn and cook for an additional minute or so, depending upon the thickness of the meat, or until the meat is just cooked through and the breading is golden brown on both sides.

Using a slotted spatula, transfer the chicken to paper towels to drain.

Place one piece of chicken on each of four warm dinner plates. Place an olive-topped lemon slice in the center of each piece of chicken. To garnish the dish, spoon a small semicircle of egg yolk to the side of the chicken. Follow it with a semicircle of chopped parsley nestled into it, then one of egg white, and lastly one of capers.

Spoon a ring of the veal stock around the chicken on each plate and serve immediately.

Dean Jacques Pépin | *Dean of Special Programs, The French Culinary Institute*

Fillet of Pork *Charcutière*

Serves 4

For this classic pork recipe, pork fillets are trimmed of all fat, so they have no more cholesterol than chicken breasts and are also relatively low in calories. The acidic sauce served with the pork is particularly complementary. It consists of dried tomatoes and the liquid used to reconstitute them, onions, garlic, scallions, white wine, and *cornichons*.

237 milliliters (1 cup) water
30 grams (1 ounce) sun-dried tomatoes
14 grams (1 tablespoon) unsalted butter
15 milliliters (1 tablespoon) extra virgin olive oil
Two 285-gram (10-ounce) pork fillets, trimmed of fat and sinew, cut crosswise into 4 equal pieces
60 grams red onion, cut into ¼ inch dice (2 ounces)
40 grams (1½ ounces) minced scallions
4 grams (1 teaspoon) chopped garlic
60 milliliters (¼ cup) dry white wine
30 grams (1 ounce) sliced *cornichons*
8 grams (1 teaspoon) Dijon mustard
1.5 grams (¼ teaspoon) coarse salt
1 milliliter (¼ teaspoon) hot pepper sauce

Previously published in *Today's Gourmet*, and published by KQED-TV in conjunction with the show of the same name.

Prepare your *mise en place*.

Place the water in a small saucepan over high heat and bring to a boil. Add the tomatoes and immediately remove from the heat. Set aside for 30 minutes to reconstitute. When softened, drain well, setting aside the soaking liquid. Cut the tomatoes into 13-millimeter (½-inch) pieces and set aside.

Place the butter and oil in a large, heavy skillet over medium-high heat. When hot, add the pork and sear for 4 to 5 minutes or until well colored. Turn the pork and cover the pan. Reduce the heat to medium-low and cook the pork for another 5 minutes.

Uncover and transfer the meat to a serving plate. Tent lightly with aluminum foil and set aside to allow it to continue cooking in its own heat.

Place the skillet over medium-high heat and add the onion, scallions, and garlic. Sauté for 1 minute. Add the wine and cook for 30 seconds. Stir in the reserved tomatoes and soaking liquid and bring to a boil. Boil for 2 minutes or until the liquid has reduced slightly. Stir in the *cornichons*, mustard, salt, and hot pepper sauce. Cook for a minute to heat through.

Uncover the pork and pour the sauce over and around the meat. Serve immediately.

Chef John Foster

Chef/Co-Owner, Harvest Restaurant, Lexington, Kentucky
The French Culinary Institute, Class of November 1989

Roasted Boneless Pork Loin with Coffee and Cream, Fried Apples, and White Cheddar Mashed Potatoes

Serves 4

Looking back to the lessons I learned at FCI, I realize how very important it is that all of the ingredients in the dish be pristine. In this dish, everything must be of the highest quality as it is quite honest and direct in its preparation. I make it often at Harvest, using locally raised ingredients.

Four 230-gram (8-ounce) pieces boneless pork loin, trimmed of all fat
Coarse salt to taste
Coffee Rub (recipe follows)
60 milliliters (¼ cup) clarified butter
470 milliliters (2 cups) heavy cream
White Cheddar Mashed Potatoes (recipe follows)
Fried Apples (recipe follows)

Prepare your *mise en place*.

Preheat the oven to 204°C (400°F).

Season the pork with salt to taste and then rub it generously with the coffee rub.

Heat a large, ovenproof sauté pan over medium-high heat. Add the clarified butter and when very hot but not yet smoking, add the pork and sear, turning once, for about 4 minutes or until each side is nicely browned. Transfer the pork to the oven and roast for about 10 minutes or until an instant-read thermometer inserted into the thickest part reads 71°F (160°F).

Remove the pan from the oven and transfer the pork to a platter. Tent lightly with aluminum foil to keep warm.

Place the sauté pan over medium heat. Add the cream, stirring to deglaze the pan. Add coffee rub to taste and cook, stirring frequently, for about 4 minutes or until the cream has reduced slightly and coats the back of a metal spoon (*nappant*, as I learned in the classic French lingo). Remove from the heat and keep warm.

To serve, mound about ¾ cup of the potatoes in the center of each of four dinner plates. Place a piece of the pork to one side and spoon the sauce over the top. Place an equal portion of the apples on each plate and serve.

Coffee Rub

150 grams (5¼ ounces) finely ground dark roast coffee
beans
100 grams (3½ ounces) light brown sugar
5 grams (1 tablespoon) cracked black pepper
6 grams (1 tablespoon) freshly grated orange zest
500 milligrams (½ teaspoon) ground mace

Prepare your *mise en place.*

Combine the coffee, brown sugar, pepper, orange zest,
and mace in a small bowl, stirring to blend well.
Store, covered and refrigerated, until ready to use.

White Cheddar Mashed Potatoes

6 russet potatoes, peeled and cut in half crosswise
40 grams (3 tablespoons) unsalted butter, softened
28 grams (1 ounce) sour cream, at room
temperature
340 grams (12 ounces) shredded medium-sharp white
Cheddar cheese
Coarse salt and freshly ground pepper to taste

Prepare your *mise en place.*

Place the potatoes in a large saucepan with cold water
to cover by 2.5 centimeters (1 inch) over medium-
high heat. Bring to a boil; then lower the heat and
simmer for about 20 minutes or until the potatoes
crumble when pierced with the point of a small, sharp
knife. Remove from the heat and drain well.

Transfer the potatoes to a mixing bowl. Add the butter
and sour cream and, using a whisk, beat until well
incorporated. Add the cheese and beat until blended.
Season with salt and pepper to taste.

If not serving immediately, place in a *bain marie* and
keep warm until ready to serve.

Fried Apples

14 grams (2 teaspoons) sugar
7 grams (1 tablespoon) ground cinnamon
55 grams (4 tablespoons) unsalted butter
4 large McIntosh, Black Twig, or other tart, firm
apples, peeled, cored, and cut into wedges
Apple cider or juice, if necessary

Prepare your *mise en place.*

Combine the sugar and cinnamon in a small bowl.
Set aside.

Heat the butter in a large sauté pan over medium
heat. Add the apples, followed by the sugar and cinnamon mixture. Lower the heat and sauté for about 7
minutes or until the apples are nicely browned. If the
apples brown too quickly or if the pan seems dry, add
a bit of apple cider or juice to help the caramelization. However, don't add too much, as you don't want
the apples to poach; they need to have some texture
and color.

Remove from the heat and serve warm or at
room temperature.

Session 12

Pot au Feu

Theory

Introducing *Pot au Feu*

Pot au feu, literally "pot on the fire," is a meal unto itself. It is more traditional French home cooking than what we consider *haute cuisine*, but it is, nonetheless, part of the classic culinary repertoire. This quintessentially French dish provides all of the elements of a complete meal — the soup (from the broth), boiled meat, and vegetables (usually root but leafy greens can also be added). A very ancient dish, some version of this boiled dinner has been seen throughout the history of French cuisine.

The "*pot*" in the dish refers to the large pot that was used to cook the dinner, originally, over an open fire. All the elements of the dish are cooked together in this large, deep pot with flavorings added to complete the depth of flavor in the broth. The dish is at its best when prepared the day before being served, with all the fat removed to make a more refined soup.

The most accomplished *pot au feu* is composed of a number of textures and flavors. Lean cuts of meat such as the shin bone, fatty, flavorful cuts of meat such as the belly, gelatinous cuts such as oxtail, as well as meaty pieces (preferably with some marrow) can all be used. The marrow can be cooked separately and served as a garnish on the finished dish. Root vegetables such as carrots, parsnips, leeks, turnips, and onions along with celery and celeriac are among the classic additions. If potatoes and cabbage are used, they are usually cooked separately and added to the broth at the end. This is to keep the potatoes from overcooking and the cabbage flavor from overpowering the dish. As you can see, although there are traditional ingredients, there can also be many, many variations on the theme, a number of them reflecting the region of France where that version of the dish originated.

Because they require long cooking to extract the maximum flavor and to ensure tenderness, beef cuts such as the shin, chuck, or short ribs are the most suitable for a *pot au feu*. To add depth to the broth, the meat is usually started in cold water. However, some cooks maintain that the best meat flavor is achieved by adding the meat to boiling water, which results in a nicer finish to the meat. Again, as with many traditional dishes, variations are many.

The slow simmering of the meat, bones, and vegetables produces a full-flavored broth called a **marmite.** The characteristic warm amber color of the broth comes from the addition of **oignons brûlées,** burnt onion halves. The judicious use of burnt onion is essential to the perfect broth — one pound of onions per gallon of liquid is a good guideline. Too many onions added and the broth will turn unpleasantly dark and bitter. The *marmite*, often used as the base for a consommé, is such an important part of the presentation of the dish that it is necessary to treat it with great respect.

While the long, slow-cooking method makes the meat in a *pot au feu* very tender, it also has a tendency to extract all of the flavor from the meat into the broth, leaving the meat extremely bland. For this reason, strongly flavored condiments are traditionally served alongside a *pot au feu*; among them coarse sea salt, strong mustards, pickled onions, and *cornichons*. Sauces with well-defined flavors are also often served as a garnish to the delicately flavored meat and vegetables. In our classic version, we have added a *sauce raifort*, a horseradish-based, roux-thickened sauce.

The leftover meat from a *pot au feu* is often as welcome as the original dish. It can be eaten hot or cold along with the traditional garnishes. Many a home cook transforms it into a salad with boiled potatoes, shallots, and *cornichons*. It can also be used as the base of *boeuf mironton* (sliced, boiled beef reheated with vinegar, onions, and bacon) or for a shepherd's pie, *croquettes*, or hash, often incorporating some of the leftover vegetables as well.

Some regional variations of *pot au feu* are:

- **Hochepot:** This is a traditional mixture from Flanders in northern France. From it, we get the English word "hodgepodge." Almost any type of meat is used, along with sausages. It differs from the classic *pot au feu* in that the meat is browned before any liquid is added.
- **Potée:** Technically, any dish cooked in a large earthenware pot, but it generally applies to a dish made with a mixture of meats but mainly pork, both fresh and cured, along with vegetables, most particularly potatoes and cabbage. It is found throughout rural France with many regional differences: in Berry, red kidney beans and red wine are added; in Auvergne, cabbage is always included; and in Lorraine, potatoes and/or beans are favored.
- **Poule au pot:** This classic home-style dish originated in Béarn. Made with a whole chicken poached with aromatics and garnished with root vegetables, it often features rice as an accompaniment.
- **Garbure:** A type of stew or thick soup that also originated in Béarn, it is based on vegetable stock flavored with salted meats and *confit d'oie* (preserved goose). A *garbure* almost always contains white beans, often whatever type is indigenous to the region.

Demonstration

Pot au Feu (Boiled Beef Dinner)

Serves 4

Estimated time to complete: 4 hours

50 grams (1¾ ounces) celery, *mirepoix*
1 clove garlic
Bouquet garni
Coarse salt and freshly ground pepper to taste

For the garnish
200 grams (7 ounces) carrots, *cocotte*
100 grams (3½ ounces) leeks, white part only, washed and
    cut into 5-centimeter (2-inch) pieces
100 grams (3½ ounces) celery, washed, peeled, and
    cut into 5-centimeter (2-inch) pieces
200 grams (7 ounces) potatoes, *cocotte*
200 grams (7 ounces) turnips, *cocotte*

For the condiments
Sauce Raifort (Horseradish Sauce) (recipe follows)
Coarse sea salt
Strong-flavored mustard such as Dijon
Cornichons

3 small saucepans
4 large, shallow soup bowls
Ladle

Prepare your *mise en place.*

Place the onion halves, cut side down, on a preheated flat top or in a cast iron skillet placed over medium-high heat. Sear for about 3 minutes or just until the onion flesh is nicely browned but not blackened.

Remove the onion from the heat and stick a clove into each half. Set aside.

Using a chef's knife, trim the excess fat from the short ribs. Tie the meat together with kitchen twine. Set aside.

If using marrow in the finished dish, use a cleaver to carefully break the bones open. Remove the marrow and reserve it in very cold water (*dégorger*) until needed.

Place the meat and bones in a stockpot of boiling water for a few minutes to just blanch. Drain well in a colander.

Return the meat and bones to the stockpot along with the cold water. Place over high heat and bring to a boil. Immediately lower the heat to a simmer and, using a metal spoon, skim off any foam, fat, or particles that rise to the top.

Add the *mirepoix* carrots, leeks, and celery along with the browned onion halves, garlic, and *bouquet garni* and again bring to a simmer. Season with salt and pepper to taste and simmer, skimming frequently, for about 3 hours or until the meat is very tender and the

Dean's Tip

"If you simmer pot au feu *instead of boiling it, you will produce a clear broth."*
Dean Alain Sailhac

Notes

If you can't find a large, one-pound onion, use two or three smaller onions.

If it is convenient, the *pot au feu* can be made at least a day in advance and chilled. Any remaining fat can then easily be removed and the broth will be the richer for the extra resting time.

marmite is a clear, light-amber color. Remember to skim constantly so that the broth is as near fat-free as possible.

About 30 minutes before the meat is done, organize the garnish.

Place the carrots in a piece of cheesecloth large enough to enclose them, pull the sides up, and using kitchen twine, tie the cheesecloth into a bag. Using another piece of cheesecloth, tie the leeks and celery together in a bag.

About 20 minutes before the meat is done (it will be very tender and the bones will fall out easily), add both bags to the simmering pot. Cook for 10 to 20 minutes or just until the vegetables are tender. Using a slotted spoon, lift the cheesecloth bags from the pot and set aside until ready for service.

While the carrots, leeks, and celery are cooking, place the potatoes in one small saucepan and the turnips in another, both with just enough of the *marmite* to cover. Bring to a simmer over medium-high heat. Lower the heat and simmer for about 10 minutes or just until tender. Remove from the heat and set aside until ready for service.

If using marrow, either cut it into small cubes or into 3-millimeter (⅛-inch)–thick slices. Place it in a small saucepan with just enough *marmite* to cover the bottom of the pan over medium heat. Bring to a simmer and poach for about 30 seconds or just until warm. Immediately remove from the heat and set aside.

If serving the dish immediately (see note), use a slotted spoon to transfer equal portions of the meat to each of four large, shallow soup bowls. Remove the carrots, leeks, and celery from their cheesecloth bags. Arrange an equal portion of the vegetables around the meat. Place the marrow, if using, on top of the meat, then ladle the hot *marmite* into each bowl.

Serve with the horseradish sauce, sea salt, mustard, and *cornichons*.

Demonstration

Sauce Raifort (Horseradish Sauce)

Makes about 710 milliliters (24 ounces)
Estimated time to complete: 20 minutes

Ingredients	Equipment
15 grams (1 tablespoon) unsalted butter	Small saucepan
15 grams (½ ounce) all-purpose flour	Wooden spoon
250 milliliters (1 cup plus 1 tablespoon)	Whisk
marmite (cooking broth from *pot au feu*) (see page 207)	*Bain-marie* or storage
100 milliliters (7 tablespoons) heavy cream	container with lid,
Freshly grated horseradish to taste	optional
Coarse salt and freshly ground pepper to taste	

Prepare your *mise en place.*

Melt the butter in the small saucepan over medium heat. Using a wooden spoon, stir in the flour and cook for 1 minute.

Whisk in the *marmite* and bring to a simmer, whisking constantly. Lower the heat and cook, stirring frequently with a wooden spoon, for about 15 minutes or until a smooth *velouté* has formed.

Stir in the cream and continue to cook, stirring constantly, for a minute or two, or just until the cream is well incorporated.

Stir in the horseradish and season with salt and pepper to taste. Serve hot.

Alternatively, transfer the sauce to a *bain-marie* to keep warm until service, or place it in a covered container and refrigerate for up to 2 days. Reheat before serving.

Session 13

Soups

Theory
General Information About Soup

Whether called *potages* or **soupes**, soups are technically any blend of meat or fish and vegetables cooked in seasoned liquid. They can be served hot or cold, as a first course or snack or one-dish meal, puréed or chunky. In fact, soup can be served any time or in any way or style that pleases the cook or the diner. However, it is said that classic French cuisine, with its system of ordained recipes, is the only one where such basic dishes as soups are categorized according to a number of different classifications, each having its own subgroup.

Potage and *soupe* technically mean the same thing: soup. The words are sometimes used interchangeably, but there are differences in meaning. *Potage* has roots in the Latin word *potare*—to drink—because in ancient times liquid foods such as soups were slurped up rather eaten with a spoon. In early France, *soupe* was a very basic dish of a piece of bread (or sop) over which the contents of the cooking pot (*potage*) was poured. Nowadays, *soupe* usually refers to mixtures composed of pieces of meat or fish and vegetables garnished with bread, rice, or pasta, or to regional or classic mixtures with bread as a component or garnish, such as gratinéed onion soup (*soupe à l'oignon gratinée*). *Potage* generally signifies a puréed vegetable mixture that has been thickened with cream or egg yolks.

It is interesting to note that the word *restaurant* is derived from the fact that the first commercial eating establishments in eighteenth-century France were spots serving rich, hearty, and nourishing soups to *restaurer* (restore) the Parisian diner. Over the years, the importance of *potages* and *soupes* to the French menu grew, until, during the nineteenth century, it was not unusual to find as many as fifteen soups listed on a restaurant menu. The original soup was more porridgelike, with the "sop" the most important part of the eating experience. But as French cuisine became more refined and the broth was elevated to grander heights, the roles reversed and the liquid became the "soup." In contemporary cooking, we have seen a return to the "sop" in a far more elegant fashion, with exquisite morsels such as delicate raviolis or *quenelles* of shellfish mousse or *foie gras* in the center of the soup plate.

There are two basic categories of *potages* in classic French cuisine: **clear soups (*les potages clairs*)** and **bound soups (*les potages liès*)**. The following chart summarizes these categories.

Dean's Tip

"A soup, consommé, or potage starts the meal, so it should impress the guest with a lightness and delicacy so as not to overpower the rest of the menu."

Dean Jacques Pépin

Clear Soups (*Potages Clairs*)

Classification	Ingredients	Example
Beef *consommé*	Beef meat and bones, carrots, onions, leeks, celery, garlic, *bouquet garni*, tomatoes, egg whites, seasoning	*Consommé brunoise* or *madrilène*
Chicken *consommé*	Same as above but chicken meat and bones replace beef	*Ambassadeur*

Bound Soups (*Potages Liés*)

Classification	Ingredients	Example
Puréed vegetable soups (*les purées*)	Leeks, potatoes, butter, cream, chervil	*Parmentier*
	Split peas, leeks, carrots, onions, *bouquet garni*, bacon, butter	*Saint-Germain*
	White beans, *consommé* or water, cream, butter	Soissonnais
	Leeks, carrots, onions, rice, cream, butter	*Crécy*
	Lentils, white stock, cream, butter	*Esaü*
Shaped-vegetable soups (*potage taillés*)	Leeks and potatoes cut in *paysanne*	*Parisien*
	Leeks, potatoes, turnips, carrots, cabbage cut in *paysanne*, string beans, peas, bacon	*Cultivateur*
Cream soups and *veloutés* (*crèmes*)	Asparagus, white stock, *liaison* of *roux*, cream, and egg yolks	*Argenteuils*
Bound *consommés*	*Consommé* bound with egg yolk and cream, sorrel	*Germiny*

Classification	Ingredients	Example
Bisques	Lobster, *fumet*, white wine, *mirepoix*, cognac, tomatoes, cream	*Bisque de homard*
Soupes	Fish, oyster, mussel, and onion soup; French *soupes* (as opposed to *potages*) by definition, have a particular regional character and an individual recipe rather than a single base formula	*Gratinée à l'oignon Lyonnaise*

Consommés

A *consommé* is a meat, game, poultry, or fish stock from which all impurities have been removed, leaving an almost-transparent broth. The most common *consommés* are made from beef broth (see *marmite*, page 207), white stock (see *fond blanc*, page 52) with the addition of tomatoes, game stock (see *fond de gibier*, page 56), or white poultry stock (see *fond de volaille blanc*, page 53). Whatever the variety, it always begins with an intensely flavored and richly colored broth made with lean meat, highly gelatinous bones such as knuckle, feet, and shin, and blackened onions (*oignons brûlées*). The purity and flavor are achieved through a two-step operation by which the broth is clarified. This occurs when a broth is enriched through the addition of lean chopped meat, egg whites, finely chopped vegetables, herbs, and, sometimes, spices, and then gently simmered. As the mixture simmers, particles that might otherwise cloud the broth are entrapped by the eggs' albumen and blood in the added ingredients.

Learning About Clarification

Through clarification, a *consommé* becomes flavorful, perfectly clear, and fat-free. The three essential ingredients necessary to the process are

° lean ground meat,

° egg whites (generally 2 large egg whites per liter or quart of liquid), and

° aromatics such as carrots, celery, leeks, tomatoes, herbs, and spices.

The meat and the aromatics are put through a meat grinder to achieve a medium-grind texture. The mixture should not be puréed.

The broth is then blended with the clarification mixture, placed over medium heat, stirred frequently, and brought to a simmer. Just before the boiling point is reached, the stirring is stopped, and the minute impurities that cloud the broth adhere to the clarification ingredients and are carried to the surface by the albumen in the egg white and by the blood. The particulate matter will form a solid raft that will float.

At this point, it is critical that the raft not be broken by stirring or boiling, as the *consommé* continues to clarify as it cooks, and it is essential that the raft remain intact to hold on to any floating particles. When the *consommé* is finished, it is ladled out through a hole made in the raft.

Once the *consommé* has finished simmering, it should be chilled. Any remaining fat will rise to the surface and congeal so that it may be easily removed. If time does not permit chilling, strips of parchment paper may be pulled across the surface of the hot *consommé*, causing any remaining fat to cling to the paper.

All clarified broths, regardless of the basic ingredients, are classified as *consommés*. A *consommé* that has been further enriched and reduced to one half its volume is called a **consommé double**.

Consommés may be served hot, cold, or iced, as well as plain or garnished. When served iced, the gelatin from the meat and bones that has dissolved in the *consommé* causes it to set to a jellied consistency. This is known as an aspic jelly (or *gelée*). Some traditional *consommés* and their garnishes are as follows:

○ *Consommé brunoise*: *brunoise* of vegetables.

○ *Consommé célestine*: *crêpe* flavored with *fines herbes* and cut into *chiffonade*.

○ *Consommé aux profiteroles*: tiny *choux*.

○ *Consommé aux diablotins*: toasted bread with grated cheese.

○ *Consommé aux paillettes*: baked strips of pastry dough (*pâte feuilleté*).

○ *Consommé germiny*: liaison of egg and cream, finished with sorrel *chiffonade*.

Technique
General Procedure for Making *Consommés*

Making a *consommé* is a two-step operation:

1. Begin with a *marmite* of beef, game, chicken, or fish. Do not use veal, as it does not carry enough flavor.

2. Clarify the *marmite*. This is the process that creates a more flavorful *marmite* that is perfectly clear and fat-free.

The general cooking procedure to make a perfect *consommé* is as follows:

1. Place the *marmite* in a stockpot over high heat and bring to a boil. Immediately turn off the heat and allow the *marmite* to cool to 71°C (160°F).

2. Combine the ground meat, egg white, and aromatics in a large, heatproof mixing bowl.

3. Pour the warm *marmite* over the meat mixture and stir together. The stock should not be hot or it will cook the egg whites and destroy their capacity to clarify.

4. Pour the mixture back into the stockpot. Place over medium-high heat and, stirring frequently, bring to a simmer.

5. Once the mixture comes to a gentle simmer, immediately lower the heat. Do *not* stir and do *not* boil or the mixture will not clarify.

6. The albumins in the egg whites and the blood in the meat will attract the impurities in the *marmite* and bring them to the surface. A solid raft will form that should not be broken.

7. Gently simmer for 40 minutes to 1 hour or until the mixture has a deep flavor and is quite clear.

8. Periodically during the cooking process, carefully make a small hole in the center of the raft with a small ladle and moisten the raft with stock, ladling it over the raft so that the raft does not dry out.

9. When the cooking is complete, let the *consommé* rest for 15 minutes, then, using a ladle, lift it through the hole in the center of the raft and remove the liquid from the pot.

10. Pass the *consommé* through a *chinois* lined with cheesecloth or a damp napkin.

11. If using immediately, remove any fat with strips of parchment paper as directed on page 32.

12. Season the strained *consommé* with salt to taste.

13. If not using the *consommé* immediately, cool it in an ice-water bath, cover, and refrigerate.

14. When cool, remove any congealed fat that has risen to the top.

Theory

Puréed Vegetable Soups (*Les Purées*)

Puréed vegetable soups are *potages*, created by cooking liquid and fresh or dried vegetables together and then puréeing the mixture to thicken it to a smooth, viscous consistency. Occasionally, the soup is bound with the puréed vegetables, as well as a starchy element such as rice. Classically, however, no puréed soup would be bound with flour. Just before serving, unsalted butter or egg yolks can be added to enrich the soup.

Some of the more common soups in the classic repertoire and their binders are as follows:

° *Potage parmentier*: bound by potatoes.

° *Potage Saint-Germain*: bound either by dried split peas or fresh peas.

° *Potage Soissonnais*: bound by dried white beans.

° *Potage Esaü*: bound by lentils.

° *Potage Crécy*: bound by fresh carrots and rice.

Many classical *potages* serve as the base soup to which a specific garnish is added, creating a derivative soup that is then given a definitive name. For instance, *potage parmentier* has many such derivatives. It is made from leeks that have been sweated in unsalted butter and then cooked in water or stock with potatoes and seasonings. The potatoes serve as the binding ingredient. After cooking, the soup is puréed and finished with heavy cream and more butter.

When different garnishes are added to the *potage parmentier* base, the following derivatives result:

° *Julienne Darblay*: garnish of *julienne* of leek, carrot, turnip, celery, and chervil.

° *Santé*: *chiffonade* of sorrel and chopped chervil.

° *Sport*: *chiffonade* of sorrel, chopped vermicelli, and chervil.

A number of other puréed vegetable soups are made using the same technique as that employed for *potage parmentier*, with other vegetables being the dominant flavor. Some of them are as follows:

° *Potage freneuse*: turnips with a garnish of croutons and chervil.

° *Potage Bonvalet*: turnips with a garnish of white beans, peas, string beans, white leek *julienne*.

° *Potage champenois*: celeriac (celery root) with a garnish of celery and carrot *brunoise*.

○ *Potage Malakoff*: tomatoes with a garnish of spinach *julienne*.

Potage Saint-Germain, which was prepared in Session 5 (see page 94), is another classic puréed vegetable soup; however, its thickening agent is dried split peas. Other potages may be made using other types of dried vegetables. For instance, *potage Soissonnais* and *potage Esaü* are essentially the same soups as *potage Saint-Germain*, but dried white beans are used as the base for the former and lentils for the latter.

The following chart illustrates *potages* that are made with dried vegetables and the derivative soups created by a change of garnish to the base soup.

Some potages made from dried vegetables:

Potage Base	Derivative	Garnish
Saint-Germain	Ambassadeur	Sorrel and lettuce *chiffonade* with rice and chervil garnish
Soissonnais	Compiégne	Sorrel and chervil
Soissonnais	Dartois	*Brunoise* of vegetables sweated in butter
Soissonnais	Faubonne	*Julienne* of vegetables sweated in butter
Esaü	Choiseul	*Julienne* of vegetables and chervil
Esaü	Conti	Bacon, croutons, chervil
Esaü	Chantilly	Addition of cream with garnish of chicken *quenelles* (see page 127)

When a puréed soup is bound with vegetables plus rice, the rice is cooked along with the vegetables and then the mixture is puréed. The most common rice-bound soup is *Potage Crécy*, which is based on carrots plus rice. The carrots and onions are sweated in unsalted butter, then a white chicken stock (see page 53) and rice are added. The mixture is then cooked, and, when done, puréed. The puréed soup may be finished with a bit of heavy cream and garnished with croutons.

Some derivatives of *Potage Crécy* are:

○ *Potage velours*: bound with tapioca in place of the rice.

○ *Potage Crécy aux herbes*: chopped herbs are added to the base.

○ *Potage Crécy à la briarde*: bound with rice and potatoes; garnished with croutons and chervil.

Shaped-Vegetable Soups (*Potages Taillés*)

The vegetables for **potages taillés** must be uniformly cut, since they are not puréed nor passed through a *chinois*. They are usually cut into a *paysanne*, but other uniform cuts can be used. Most of these soups are not bound by anything but the starch contained in the vegetables, although there are a few variations that do include cream. The two principal examples of a *potage taillé* are *potage Parisien*, garnished with chervil leaves, and *potage cultivateur*, garnished with oven-dried croutons and grated Gruyère cheese.

Some classic shaped-vegetable soups are:

° *Cultivateur*: a base of bacon, leeks, potatoes, turnips, celery, carrots, string beans, peas, and cabbage with a garnish of chervil sprigs; served with *baguette* slices and grated Gruyère cheese on the side.

° *Parisien*: a base of leeks and potatoes finished with unsalted butter and a garnish of chervil leaves.

° *Bonne femme*: a base of leeks and potatoes finished with butter and heavy cream; served with *baguette* slices on the side.

° *Ardennaise*: a base of leeks, potatoes, Belgian endive, and milk, finished with butter; served with *baguette* slices on the side.

° *Jeannette*: a base similar to *cultivateur*, finished with heavy cream and served with a garnish of sorrel and watercress.

° *Normande*: a base similar to *cultivateur*, finished with unsalted butter and heavy cream and served

with a garnish of *flageolets* (very small, pale green to white French kidney beans).

Guidelines for Preparing Vegetable Soups

Three important points should be kept in mind when preparing *potages taillés*:

° The vegetables should be completely sweated in butter to extract the utmost flavor.

° Green vegetables, such as string beans or peas, should be first cooked *à l'anglaise* and then added to the soup at the very end of the cooking process after it has reached a full, rolling boil. This helps retain both color and texture.

° Since small pieces of potatoes cook relatively quickly, add them toward the end of the cooking process so that they don't overcook, disintegrate, and thicken the soup, unless you have used starchy potatoes (such as russet) with the intent to have them break up and bind the soup.

Technique
General Procedure for Shaped Vegetable Soups

With the exception of *cultivateur*, the technique for making *potages taillés* does not vary much from soup to soup. It is as follows:

1. Keeping all the vegetables separate, *émincer* the leeks and celery; dice the string beans; cut the carrots, potatoes, and turnips into *paysanne*; and *chiffonade* the cabbage.

2. Cook the peas and string beans *à l'anglaise*, refresh, and set aside.

3. Remove the rind from the bacon or salt pork, cut the remaining meat into strips and then into *macédoine*-size *lardons*.

4. Blanch any meat used.

5. Gently sweat the meat in butter — do *not* brown it.

6. To develop their flavor, sweat the leeks, celery, carrots, and turnips in the same pan.

7. Add the liquid and bring to a simmer.

8. Add the cabbage and simmer for 10 minutes.

9. Add the potatoes and cook for an additional 10 minutes or until the potatoes begin to soften.

10. Adjust the seasoning to taste.

11. When ready to serve, garnish with chervil or other designated garnish.

Theory

Cream Soups (*Crèmes*) and *Veloutés*

Classically, cream soups and *veloutés* are bound with a white roux (*roux blanc*) (see page 62) and a mixture of heavy cream and egg yolks (*liaison*) or cream alone, added at the end of the cooking process. Cream soups are always made with milk, since the soup will be finished with heavy cream. The classic preparation of a *velouté* is similar, except that stock is used as the liquid in place of milk, and a *liaison* of egg yolks and heavy cream is added just before serving; it cannot then be reheated or it will curdle. Both cream soups and *veloutés* should have a velvety-smooth consistency. The stock or liquid used to make the soup or its dominant ingredient determine its name. Unfortunately, the classic distinctions between these two soups are now less clear, as modern kitchen appliances such as the blender and food processor have replaced the traditional techniques of emulsification required to obtain a thick, creamy soup.

Some classic cream soups and *veloutés* are:

° *Crème Dubarry:* a base of cauliflower and milk (see page 230) with a garnish of blanched cauliflower florets and chervil. Finished with cream.

° *Crème Choisy:* a base of lettuce and milk with a garnish of lettuce *chiffonade* and chervil. Finished with cream.

° *Velouté Argenteuil:* a base of asparagus and white veal stock (see page 53) with a garnish of blanched asparagus tips and chervil.

° *Velouté Agnes-Sorel:* a base of mushrooms and chicken stock (see page 53) with a garnish of mushroom *julienne*.

Technique

Binding Cream Soups

The classic techniques for binding cream soups make use of a *roux*, rice, or a *liaison*.

To bind a soup with a white roux (*roux blanc*):

1. Heat the butter in a saucepan over medium heat.

2. Add the vegetables. Cook, stirring occasionally, for about 5 minutes or until the vegetables have sweated their liquid but not taken on any color.

3. Sprinkle the flour over the vegetables and lower the heat. Cook, stirring frequently, for about 1 minute or until the flour coats the vegetables.

4. Add the liquid. Raise the heat to medium-high and bring to a simmer, whisking constantly.

5. Simmer, whisking occasionally, until the vegetables are tender and the mixture has thickened. Remove from the heat.

6. Purée in a blender, and, if a smoother texture is required, strain it through a *chinois*.

7. Finish the soup with heavy cream. Taste, and if necessary, adjust the seasoning.

To bind a soup with cream of rice (white rice that has been pulverized in a grinder or blender) or rice starch:

1. Dilute the cream of rice in a little cold stock to make a slurry.

2. Stirring constantly, add the slurry to the boiling soup liquid.

3. Add the dominant flavoring ingredient.

4. Finish as for a soup made with a white *roux*.

To bind a soup with a *liaison* (see page 60):

1. Whisk the egg yolks and heavy cream together in a saucepan.

2. Remove the hot soup from the heat.

3. Whisking constantly to avoid cooking the egg yolks, whisk the hot soup into the egg and cream mixture. If the soup does not bind, return the saucepan to medium heat and, whisking constantly, bring just to the point of a simmer. Do *not* boil or the mixture will curdle.

4. If necessary, adjust the consistency with additional cream. Taste, and if necessary, adjust the seasoning.

Theory
Bisques

A ***bisque*** is a well-seasoned puréed shellfish soup. The shells are used to make the initial broth and then the shellfish base is fortified with white wine, cognac, and heavy cream. Many *bisques* are also thickened with rice or breadcrumbs. The cooking method employed to prepare a *bisque* is *l'américaine* or *l'armoricaine* (fully discussed in Session 16). The finished soup is garnished with tiny diced pieces of the dominant shellfish.

Originally, *bisques* were strong-flavored dishes of game or meat that had been boiled in a spiced broth. From this early dish evolved soups made with quail and pigeon that were garnished with crayfish or cheese croutons. In the early seventeenth century, a *bisque* became a more elegant soup with crayfish as the main ingredient and then moved on to embrace all types of shellfish as the primary flavor. Today, lobster or shrimp is most often the dominant component of this rich, thick soup.

Aspics (Jellied Stocks)

An aspic or *gelée* results when a clarified stock that has a high content of gelatinous material solidify. Aspics can be made from any type of clarified stock and flavored with wines such as port, sherry, Madeira, Sauternes, or champagne. The finished color of the jelly will depend on the type of stock used. Aspics are used to glaze cold dishes, to make terrines and pâtés, in the preparation of sauces such as *chaud-froid* (a cooked dish served cold, coated with a gelatin film or gelatinous sauce), or as a simple jelly cut into decorative shapes and used to garnish cold dishes.

When making a broth to be jellied, the best pieces of meat to use are veal knuckles, calves' or pigs' feet, pork rind, or any other piece having a high percentage of cartilage and tendons. If the broth does not contain enough animal gelatin, culinary gelatin must be added. Culinary gelatin, obtained by a partial hydrolysis of the collagen in animal bones or extracted from algae, has no taste, color, or smell. It is sold in sheets (or leaves) or as a granulated powder. Gelatin swells in cold water, dissolves in warm water, and gels when cool. Sheet (or leaf) gelatin must first be soaked in cold water, then drained thoroughly before being plunged into hot liquid. Granulated gelatin may be added directly to hot liquid.

Aspic is quite difficult to make and requires great care and attention to detail. The clarification process must be carefully executed so that a perfectly clear broth is obtained; when it gels it will then be absolutely transparent. It takes great patience, but the reward of a pristine aspic is well worth the effort.

Some of the classic _gelées_ and their uses are as follows:

- *Gelée ordinaire*: made from beef and veal bones, pork rinds, calves' feet, aromatics, and clarification elements; used for *oeufs en gelée* (poached or hard-cooked eggs in a gelatin mold), various aspics, cold meat plates, and *pâté en croute* (dense meatloaf covered in pastry and served sliced).

- *Gelée de volaille*: made with the same ingredients as *gelée ordinaire* plus poultry carcasses, offal, and trimmings; used for gelatin *terrines*, cold chicken *à la gelée, chaud-froid* sauce.

- *Gelée de gibier*: made with the same ingredients as *gelée ordinaire* plus game bones, offal, and trimmings; used for cold plates and *chaud-froid* sauce.

- *Gelée de poisson*: made from clarified fish *fumet* that was made with fish bones and trimmings; used for cold fish plates and cold shellfish dishes.

Demonstration

Consommé Brunoise (Beef Consommé with Vegetable Garnish)

Serves 4

Estimated time to complete: 2 hours

Ingredients	Equipment
For the _consommé_	Stockpot
1½ liters (1 quart, 19 ounces) Beef Broth (*marmite*) (see page 207)	Meat grinder or buffalo chopper
200 grams (7 ounces) lean beef or turkey	Large heatproof bowl
40 grams (1½ ounces) carrots, *julienne*	Wooden spoon
40 grams (1½ ounces) leeks, *julienne*	Ladle
20 grams (¾ ounces) celery, *julienne*	*Chinois*
3 large egg whites	Cheesecloth or damp kitchen
100 grams (about 1 large) chopped fresh peeled and cored tomato	towel or napkin
20 grams (¾ ounce) tomato paste	Large container
Coarse salt, optional	Metal spoon
	Bain-marie, optional
For the garnish	Ice-water bath, optional
40 grams (1½ ounces) carrot *brunoise, à l'anglaise*	Medium saucepan
40 grams (1½ ounces) turnip *brunoise, à l'anglaise*	4 warm, shallow soup bowls
20 grams (¾ ounce) diced string beans, *à l'anglaise*	
20 grams (¾ ounce) English peas, *à l'anglaise*	

Prepare your *mise en place.*

Place the *marmite* in a stockpot over medium-high heat and bring to a boil. Immediately remove from the heat and set aside to cool for about 10 minutes or until warm. The stock should not be hot or it will cook the egg whites and destroy their capacity to clarify.

Trim the meat of all fat and then run it through a meat grinder or buffalo chopper. Place the ground meat in a large heatproof bowl and add the carrots, leeks, and celery along with the egg whites, tomato, and tomato paste. Using a wooden spoon, stir to combine.

Pour the warm *marmite* over the meat mixture and stir to combine.

Pour the mixture into the stockpot. Place over medium-high heat and, stirring frequently, bring to a gentle simmer. A raft will form. Immediately stop stirring so that you do not break up the raft.

As soon as the mixture comes to a simmer, reduce the heat to maintain just a bare simmer. Continue to cook, undisturbed, for about 1 hour or until the meat and vegetables are well cooked and have enriched the stock with a depth of flavor. Do *not* stir and do *not* boil or you will break the raft and the mixture will not clarify.

Immediately remove the *marmite* from the heat and, using a ladle, carefully break a hole in the center of the raft. Ladle out the *consommé* and pass it through a *chinois* that has been lined with cheesecloth or a damp kitchen towel or napkin into a clean container.

Using a metal spoon, remove any remaining fat or impurities that rise to the surface. Taste, and if necessary, adjust the seasoning with salt.

If not serving immediately, transfer to a *bain-marie* to keep warm for service or place in an ice-water bath, cover, and refrigerate.

When ready to serve, place the *consommé* in a medium saucepan over medium heat. Add the carrot, turnip, string bean, and pea garnish and cook for just a minute or two to heat through.

Place equal portions of the hot *consommé* and its garnish in each of four warm, shallow soup bowls and serve immediately.

Dean Alain Sailhac

Executive Vice President and Senior Dean of Studies, The French Culinary Institute

Lobster Consommé with Tarragon Essence

Makes about 3 liters (3 quarts, 5 ounces)

The classic French technique for clarifying stock to make *consommé* can be applied when working with stocks other than the typical beef or chicken. For instance, in this recipe, which I often prepared when I was executive chef at Le Cirque restaurant in New York City, I use lobster stock. The flavoring ingredients can also be altered. The herbs used in the raft can be varied; vegetables, such as celery or tomato, can be introduced. The *consommé* will acquire the fragrance and taste of the specific herbs or vegetables used in the clarification process.

For the stock

30 milliliters (2 tablespoons) olive oil

4 lobster bodies, cleaned and chopped into 3.8-to-5-centimeter (1½-to-2-inch) pieces

200 grams (7 ounces) yellow onions, *mirepoix*

200 grams (7 ounces) carrots, peeled and trimmed, *mirepoix*

200 grams (7 ounces) celery, washed, *mirepoix*

200 grams (7 ounces) leek greens, washed, *mirepoix*

200 grams (7 ounces) fennel bulb, washed, *mirepoix*

4 cloves garlic, chopped

1¼ liters (5¼ cups) cold water

200 grams (7 ounces) tomatoes, peeled and cored, *mirepoix*

Bouquet garni

40 grams (2 tablespoons) coarse salt or to taste

For the clarification

200 grams (7 ounces) tomatoes, peeled and cored, *mirepoix*

100 grams (3½ ounces) celery, *mirepoix*

100 grams (3½ ounces) leek greens, washed, *mirepoix*

100 grams (3½ ounces) carrots, peeled and trimmed, *mirepoix*

42.5 grams (1½ ounces) tomato paste

10 black peppercorns

1 bunch fresh tarragon, well-washed and chopped

12 large egg whites

Prepare your *mise en place.*

Preheat the oven to 400°F (204°C).

Place the olive oil in a large ovenproof saucepan over medium heat. When very hot but not yet smoking, add the lobster bodies. Sear, stirring occasionally, for about 5 minutes or until the shells are bright red. Immediately transfer the saucepan to the oven and roast the lobster for 5 minutes.

Add the onions, carrots, celery, leek greens, fennel, and garlic to the lobster, stirring to mix. Roast for an additional 30 minutes or until the lobster is deep, deep red and the vegetables are nicely colored.

Remove the pan from the oven and place on the stovetop over medium heat. Add the water, followed by the tomatoes and *bouquet garni.* Season lightly with salt and bring to a simmer. Simmer for about 1½ hours or until a well-flavored stock has been achieved.

Remove from the heat and strain through a *chinois* into a clean container. Place in an ice-water bath to chill quickly. You should have about 3.3 liters (3½ quarts.) When cool, cover and refrigerate overnight.

The next day, clarify the stock.

Place the clarification vegetables (tomatoes, celery, leek greens, and carrots) in the bowl of a food processor fitted with the metal blade. Process, using quick on and off turns, until the vegetables are finely chopped but not puréed and watery. Using a spatula, scrape the vegetables into a clean work bowl. Fold in the tomato paste along with the peppercorns and tarragon, mixing to combine. Add the egg whites, stirring to make a mixture that holds together.

Place the cold stock in a stockpot or other large, deep, narrow pan. Whisk the clarification vegetables into the cold stock and place the pan over medium-high heat. Cook, stirring slowly and constantly, until a raft begins to form. As soon as the raft forms, lower the heat and continue to cook, without stirring, at a bare simmer.

Using a ladle, gently scoop a small hole into the center of the raft. Gently deposit the contents of the ladle on top of and around the raft. Continue to cook at a bare simmer for another hour, occasionally ladling out some of the broth and pouring it over the raft.

Remove the *consommé* from the heat and let it rest for 15 minutes.

Double a large piece of cheesecloth and place it under cold running water until very wet. Remove from the water and squeeze until almost dry.

Arrange the damp cheesecloth inside a *chinois* or other fine-mesh sieve placed over a clean, china container. (Do not use a metal storage container, as the metal may alter the taste and color of the *consommé*). Carefully ladle the *consommé* through it, taking care to work slowly, allowing the broth to strain at its own pace. Do not push it through the sieve, as particulate matter can penetrate and cloud the *consommé*. When all the *consommé* has been strained, cover tightly and refrigerate until needed.

When ready to use, reheat gently and serve hot, plain or garnished with chopped herbs, lobster medallions, or a *croûton.*

Demonstration

Potage Cultivateur (Vegetable Soup)

Serves 4
Estimated time to complete: 1 hour

Ingredients	Equipment
40 grams (1½ ounces) slab bacon or salt pork	Saucepan
30 grams (2 tablespoons) unsalted butter	Paper towels
80 grams (2¾ ounces) leeks, with 2.5-centimeter (1-inch) green part, *émincer*	Stockpot
80 grams (2¾ ounces) carrots, cut *paysanne*	Wooden spoon
40 grams (1½ ounces) celery, *émincé*	Baking sheet
40 grams (1½ ounces) turnips, cut *paysanne*	Serving plate
1.25 liters (1¼ quarts) water (or Vegetable Stock, see note)	Doily
Coarse salt and freshly ground pepper to taste	Ladle
40 grams (1½ ounces) cabbage leaves, washed and dried, cut into *chiffonade*	4 warm, shallow soup bowls
150 grams (5¼ ounces) potatoes, cut *paysanne*	
20 grams (¾ ounce) string beans, diced, cooked *à l'anglaise*	
20 grams (¾ ounce) English peas, cooked *à l'anglaise*	

For the garnish

Twelve 1.25-centimeter (½-inch)–thick slices *baguette*
40 grams (1½ ounces) grated Gruyère cheese
Approximately 12 leaves chervil, washed and dried

Prepare your *mise en place*.

Remove and discard the rind from the bacon. Cut the bacon into strips and then into *macédoine*-size *lardons*.

Bring a saucepan of water to a simmer over high heat. Place the *lardons* in the simmering water and blanch for 2 minutes. Drain well and pat dry with paper towels.

Heat the butter in a stockpot over medium heat. Add the bacon and cook, stirring occasionally with a wooden spoon, for about 5 minutes or until the bacon has sweated its moisture but not taken on any color.

Add the leeks, carrots, celery, and turnips and sweat, stirring occasionally, for 10 minutes or until the flavors are well developed and the vegetables are tender.

Add the water, season with salt and pepper, and bring to a simmer. Immediately add the cabbage and simmer for 10 minutes. Add the potatoes and simmer for an additional 10 minutes or until the potatoes are tender. Add the beans and peas and simmer for an additional 5 minutes. Taste, and if necessary, season with additional salt and pepper.

While the soup is cooking, prepare the garnish.

Preheat the oven to its lowest setting.

Place the bread on a baking sheet and bake for about

Note

Since you want the fresh vegetable flavor to shine in this soup, the liquid used is most often water. However, you can also use a light vegetable stock. When making a light vegetable stock, make sure that the flavors are well balanced and that one vegetable flavor does not predominate. Do not use strong-flavored vegetables such as broccoli. The general procedure is to sweat an equal portion of leeks, carrots, and celery (about 80 grams/2¾ ounces each) in unsalted butter, then add 1½ liters (1 quart, 19 ounces) water and any herb stems you have on hand as well as a bay leaf. Season with salt and pepper to taste and simmer for 30 minutes. Strain well before using.

Chef's Tip

"An impromptu vegetable stock can be made for this recipe by sweating all of the vegetable trimmings in butter and then moistening them with the required amount of water. The resulting lightly flavored stock can be used to cook the soup's vegetables."

Chef Dominick Cerrone

15 minutes or until the bread is quite dry but has not taken on any color. You do not want toast!

Line a serving plate with a paper doily. Place the cheese in the center of the plate. Surround the cheese with the dried bread slices. Set aside.

Ladle equal portions of the soup into each of four warm, shallow soup bowls. Place a few chervil leaves in the center of each bowl and serve with the cheese and dried bread on the side.

Demonstration

Gratinée à l'Oignon (Onion Soup)

Serves 4

Estimated time to complete: 90 minutes

Ingredients	Equipment
Eight 6-millimeter-thick (¼-inch) *baguette* slices	Baking sheet
25 milliliters (1½ tablespoons) vegetable oil	*Rondeau*
15 grams (1 tablespoon) unsalted butter	Wooden spoon
600 grams (1 pound, 5 ounces) white onions, *émincé*	4 small, ovenproof earthenware soup crocks
1 clove garlic, chopped	Ladle
100 milliliters (7 tablespoons) port wine	
1 liter (1 quart) White Chicken Stock or Beef Stock (see pages 53, 57) or water or a combination thereof, hot	
Coarse salt to taste	
Freshly ground pepper to taste	
240 grams (8½ ounces) grated Emmenthaler or Gruyère cheese	

Prepare your *mise en place.*

Preheat the oven to 191°C (375°F).

Place the baguette slices on a baking sheet and bake for about 6 minutes or until nicely browned. Remove from the oven and set aside.

Heat the oil and butter in a *rondeau* over medium heat. Add the onions and cook, stirring occasionally with a wooden spoon, for about 20 minutes or until the onions are soft and just beginning to take on color.

Raise the heat and continue to cook, stirring occasionally, for about 20 minutes or until the onions have caramelized. It is extremely important that the onions be thoroughly cooked and well browned or the soup will lack richness and color.

Stir in the garlic and cook for an additional 2 minutes. Then add the port and cook for about 10 minutes or until the liquid is reduced by half.

Add the hot stock and bring to a simmer. Season with salt to taste and lower the heat to a bare simmer. Cook at a low simmer for 20 minutes. Taste, and if necessary, adjust the seasoning with salt and pepper.

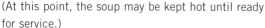

(At this point, the soup may be kept hot until ready for service.)

When ready to serve, preheat the oven again to 191°C (375°F).

Place 2 slices of the toasted baguette in the bottom of each of four small, ovenproof earthenware soup crocks. Ladle an equal portion of soup into each crock, making sure that the crock is filled to the rim. Sprinkle about 60 grams (2 ounces) of grated cheese on top, taking care that the cheese covers the entire surface and adheres to the edge of the crock.

Place the filled crocks on a baking sheet and bake for about 10 minutes or until the cheese is bubbling and melted.

Transfer the soups to a salamander or place under the broiler and cook for an additional minute or two or until the cheese is golden brown.

Remove from the heat and serve immediately.

Demonstration

Crème ou Velouté Dubarry (Cream of Cauliflower Soup)

Serves 4

Estimated time to complete: 1 hour

Ingredients	Equipment
1 head cauliflower	Chef's knife
40 grams (3 tablespoons) unsalted butter	Stockpot
75 grams (2½ ounces) leek, white	Wooden spoon
part only, well-washed, *émincé*	2 saucepans
40 grams (1½ ounces) all-purpose flour	Metal spoon
1.25 liters (1 quart, 10 ounces) White Veal Stock	Whisk
or White Chicken Stock	Wooden spatula
(see page 53), or water or milk	Food mill or blender
100 milliliters (7 tablespoons) heavy cream	*Chinois*
Milk, if needed	

1 large egg yolk
Coarse salt and freshly ground pepper to taste, optional
Chervil leaves, washed and dried

Bain-marie, optional
4 warm, shallow soup bowls

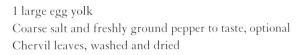

Prepare your *mise en place*.

Wash and core the cauliflower. Pull off and reserve about 12 tiny florets. Using a chef's knife, chop the remaining cauliflower and set aside.

Cook the florets *à l'anglaise*, refresh, and set aside.

Heat the butter in a stockpot over medium heat. When hot, add the leek and cook, stirring occasionally with a wooden spoon, for about 3 minutes or until the leek has sweated its liquid but not taken on any color.

When well blended, return the stockpot to medium heat and bring to a simmer. Immediately add the reserved cauliflower and return to a bare simmer. Simmer, stirring occasionally with a wooden spatula to ensure that the bottom does not stick or burn, for about 20 minutes or until the cauliflower is tender. If at any point the bottom sticks or scalds, remove the pot from the heat, transfer the soup to a clean pot without scraping the burned portion into the new pot, and return it to the stove. Do not allow the soup to continue cooking once it begins to stick or burn.

Remove the pot from the heat and either pass the soup through a food mill or purée it in a blender. Once processed, pass the purée through a *chinois* into a clean saucepan.

Place the saucepan over medium heat. Add 75 milliliters (¼ cup plus 1 tablespoon) of the cream and bring to a simmer. Immediately check the consistency. If too thick, add milk, 15 milliliters (1 tablespoon) at a time.

Make a liaison with the remaining 25 milliliters (1½ tablespoons) cream and the egg yolk. Whisk in a bit of the hot soup to temper the mixture before whisking it into the simmering soup. Taste and, if necessary, season with salt and pepper.

Serve immediately or transfer the soup to a *bain-marie* and keep warm for service. When ready to serve, pour an equal portion into each of four warm, shallow soup bowls. Place 3 of the reserved cauliflower florets in the center of each bowl and garnish with chervil leaves.

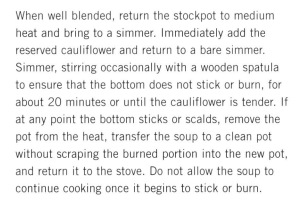

Add the flour and *singer*. Remove from the heat and set aside for about 10 minutes or until cooled slightly.

Place the stock in a saucepan over medium-high heat. Bring to a simmer, skimming off any foam or particles that float to the surface with a metal spoon. Remove from the heat and, whisking constantly, add the hot stock to the leek mixture.

Chef Alan Hughes   *Executive Chef/Co-Owner, One Ninety Catering, Miami, Florida*
The French Culinary Institute, Class of October 1989

Fennel Bisque with Aged Goat Cheese Toast

Serves 4

I am a firm believer in the idea that with good caramelization you can extract incredible flavor from very simple ingredients. I believe that this recipe illustrates that point perfectly.

---

57 grams (4 tablespoons) unsalted butter
680 grams (1½ pounds) fennel bulb, well-washed, trimmed, and thinly sliced
115 grams (¼ pound) yellow onion, thinly sliced
78 milliliters (¼ cup plus 1 tablespoon) sherry wine
2.8 liters (3 quarts) vegetable stock or broth
Coarse salt and cracked white pepper to taste
237 milliliters (1 cup) heavy cream
Aged Goat Cheese Toast (recipe follows)

Prepare your *mise en place.*

Place the butter in a heavy-bottomed saucepan over medium heat. Cook, stirring occasionally, for about 5 minutes or until it reaches the nut brown (*noisette*) stage. Add the fennel and onion and cook, stirring frequently with a wooden spoon, for about 10 minutes or until the vegetables are golden and caramelized. Do not let them get too dark.

Add the sherry and stir with a wooden spoon to deglaze the pan, scraping up all of the browned bits. Cook, stirring frequently, for about 4 minutes or until the sherry has evaporated. Add the stock, raise the heat, and bring to a boil. Season with salt and cracked white pepper, lower the heat, and simmer for 25 minutes.

Remove the soup from the heat and transfer to a blender. Process, in batches if necessary, to a smooth purée. Strain through a fine-mesh sieve or *chinois* into a clean saucepan.

Stir in the cream and place over medium heat. Bring to a gentle simmer. Immediately remove from the heat. Taste and, if necessary, adjust the seasoning with salt and pepper.

To serve, pour an equal portion of the soup into each of four warm, shallow soup bowls. Place a piece of goat cheese toast in the center of each bowl and serve.

Aged Goat Cheese Toast

4 slices bias-cut *ficelle* or *baguette*
59 milliliters (¼ cup) extra virgin olive oil
Fleur de sel and cracked black pepper to taste
57 grams (2 ounces) Boucherondin or other aged
  goat cheese

Prepare your *mise en place.*

Preheat the oven to 204°C (400°F).

Using a pastry brush, generously coat each piece of bread with olive oil. Season with *fleur de sel* and cracked pepper and place on a baking sheet. Transfer to the oven and bake for about 5 minutes or until lightly browned.

Remove from the oven and generously spread the cheese over one end of each toast, to cover about half. Return to the oven and bake for another minute or just until the cheese begins to melt. Remove from the oven and serve.

Demonstration

Gelée Ordinaire (Plain Aspic)

Serves 4
Estimated time to complete: 10 hours

Ingredients	Equipment
For the stock	Roasting pan
1.5 kilograms (3¼ pounds) veal and beef bones	Wooden spoon
2 kilograms (4½ pounds) lean beef, trimmed of all fat	2 stockpots
2 calves' feet	Metal spoon
1.5 kilograms (3¼ pounds) veal knuckle	Wooden spatula
250 grams (8¾ ounces) pork rind	*Chinois*
250 grams (8¾ ounces) carrots, *mirepoix*	Large, heatproof bowl
250 grams (8¾ ounces) onions, *mirepoix*	Ladle
90 grams (3¼ ounces) leeks, white and some green part, *mirepoix*	Cheesecloth or a damp kitchen towel or napkin
90 grams (3¼ ounces) celery, *mirepoix*	Storage container
Bouquet garni	Shaped cutters, optional
8 liters (8½ quarts) cold water, or more as needed	
Coarse salt and freshly ground pepper to taste	
For the clarification	
250 grams (8¾ ounces) well-washed leek greens	
150 grams (5¼ ounces) carrots, *mirepoix*	
120 grams (4¼ ounces) peeled and cored tomatoes, *mirepoix*	
60 grams (2 ounces) celery, *mirepoix*	
6 large egg whites	
750 grams (1½ pounds) very lean ground red meat	
30 milliliters (2 tablespoons) Madeira, port, or sherry, optional	
Commercial gelatin, if needed	

Prepare your *mise en place.*

First, prepare the stock.

Preheat the oven to 191°C (375°F).

Place the bones in the roasting pan and roast, stirring occasionally with a wooden spoon, for about 30 minutes or until lightly browned.

Transfer the bones to a stockpot. Add the meat, feet, knuckle, pork rind, carrots, onions, leeks, celery, and *bouquet garni.* Add the water, making sure there is enough to cover by 2 inches.

Using a metal spoon, skim any fat from the bones left in the roasting pan. Place the roasting pan over medium-high heat, add a bit of water, and, using a wooden spatula, stir to deglaze the pan, dissolving the *sucs.*

Scrape the dissolved sucs into the stockpot, season with salt and pepper to taste, and place the stockpot over high heat.

Bring the stock to a boil, using a metal spoon to frequently skim off any fat or impurities that rise to the surface. Lower the heat and cook at a gentle simmer for about 8 hours or until an intensely flavored stock has been achieved.

Remove from the heat and strain through a *chinois* into a clean stockpot. Keep warm.

Prepare the clarification mixture.

Combine the leek leaves, carrots, tomatoes, and celery with the egg whites and ground meat in a large, heat-proof bowl.

Stirring constantly, pour the warm stock over the meat mixture and mix until well blended.

Pour the mixture into the stockpot. Place over medium-high heat and, stirring frequently, bring to a gentle simmer. A raft will form. Immediately stop stirring so that you do not break up the raft.

As soon as the mixture comes to a simmer, reduce the heat to maintain a bare simmer. Continue to cook, undisturbed, for about 1 hour or until the meat and vegetables are well cooked and have enriched the stock with a depth of flavor. Do *not* stir and do *not* boil or you will break the raft and the mixture will not clarify.

Immediately remove the *consommé* from the heat and, using a ladle, carefully break a hole in the center of the raft. Ladle out the *consommé* and pass it through a *chinois* that has been lined with cheese-cloth or a damp kitchen towel or napkin into a clean saucepan or container.

Using a metal spoon, remove any remaining fat or impurities that rise to the surface. Taste, and if necessary, adjust the seasoning with salt.

While still warm, add Madeira, port, or sherry, if desired.

The natural gelatin in the meat and bones should allow the *consommé* to begin to set as it cools. If necessary to add commercial gelatin, you will need about 12 to 15 grams (½ ounce) of sheet gelatin softened in cool water for every liter (33 ounces) of hot *consommé.*

Any type of container may be used to store the gelatin, as it will most often be reheated before being used as a coating aspic in a specific cold dish. However, if using the gelatin as a garnishing aspic, the liquid should be poured into shallow pans and refrigerated until set. Once gelled, the aspic can be cut into attractive shapes (either by hand or with shaped cutters made specifically for this purpose) or used as a base for a cold platter.

Demonstration

Oeufs Moulés au Madère (Eggs in Aspic with Madeira)

Serves 4

Estimated time to complete: 1 hour 45 minutes

Ingredients	Equipment
40 milliliters (3 tablespoons) Madeira wine	Four 6-ounce ramekins
455 milliliters (2 cups) hot Plain Aspic (see page 220)	Wooden spoon
Coarse salt and freshly ground pepper to taste	Chef's knife
1 large tomato	Medium shallow bowl
1 thin slice lean ham	*Russe* or *sautoir*
1 large leek green, blanched	Small dish
1 liter (1 quart) cold water	Slotted spoon or skimmer
40 milliliters (3 tablespoons) white vinegar	Paper towels
Ice	Small knife or kitchen scissors
4 large eggs	Baking pan
About 12 tarragon leaves, blanched	Ladle

Prepare your *mise en place*.

Place the ramekins in the refrigerator to chill thoroughly.

Using a wooden spoon, stir the Madeira into the hot aspic. Taste, and if necessary, adjust the seasoning with salt and pepper. Set aside to cool (see note).

Peel, core, and seed the tomato and remove all membranes. Cut the remaining flesh into a decorative shape. Trim the ham and the blanched leek into complementary decorative shapes. You will need enough to decorate the bottom of the four ramekins. Set aside.

Fill a medium shallow bowl with cold water. Set aside.

Pour the 1 liter of cold water into a *russe* or *sautoir*. Add the vinegar and place over medium-high heat. Bring to a simmer.

Working one at a time, break each egg into a small dish, check for quality and that the yolk is not broken, and gently drop it into the simmering water. Cook the eggs for about 4 minutes or until the whites are firm but the yolks are still soft and creamy.

As soon as each egg is cooked, using a slotted spoon or skimmer, gently lift it from the simmering water. Lightly touch the center to ensure that the yolk is still soft. Transfer the egg to the bowl of cold water to stop the cooking and to remove the vinegar taste.

Once cool, using a slotted spoon or skimmer, transfer the eggs to a double layer of paper towels to drain. Using a small knife or kitchen scissors, carefully trim off any ragged edges from the eggs.

Place a layer of ice in a small baking pan.

Ladle a small amount of the aspic into the bottom of each chilled ramekin. You should have about a 2-millimeter (1⁄16-inch) layer of gelatin. Place the ramekins into the ice-lined baking pan to chill.

Arrange the tomato, ham, and leek pieces along with the tarragon leaves in a decorative pattern over the set jelly in each ramekin. Ladle in just a bit more of the aspic to set the pattern. Return the ramekins to the ice to set the gelatin.

When set, place an egg into each ramekin and ladle in enough of the aspic to fill the mold.

Transfer the ramekins to the refrigerator for about 1 hour or until completely set.

Keep refrigerated until ready to serve with a simple salad, cold vegetables such as asparagus, or with any sauce suitable for cold eggs (see page 85).

Note

When working with an aspic, it should be fairly cold so it will set quickly but still in a liquid stage.

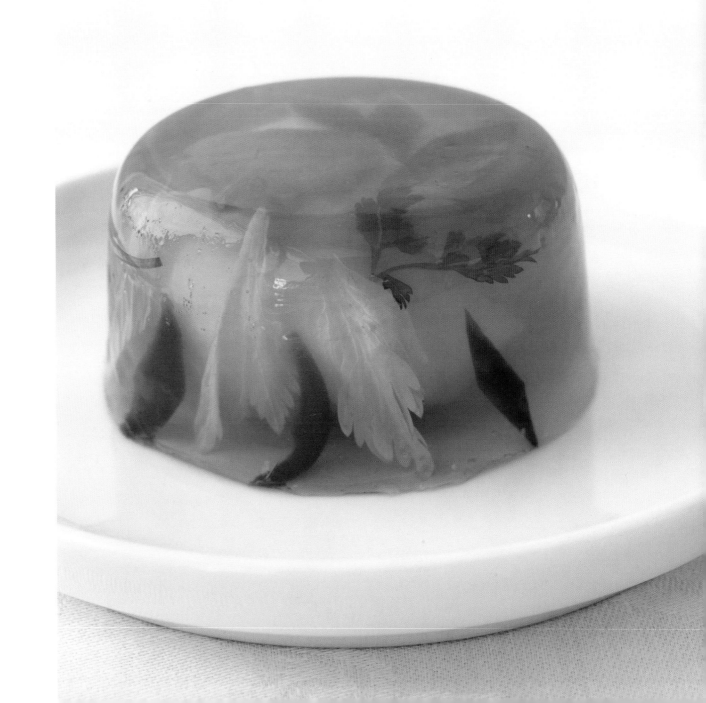

Theory

General Information About Salads

"Any variety of herb in existence may go by the name of salad," said Prosper Montagne, one of the great chefs of twentieth-century France. A salad may, in fact, be composed of an almost infinite variety of herbs or meat, poultry, game or fish, grains, pastas, legumes, and vegetables in an almost infinite variety of combinations. *Larousse Gastronomique* defines it as "any dish of raw or cold, cooked or uncooked foods that are usually dressed and seasoned." In addition, many contemporary menus now also offer warm or room-temperature salads.

Salads can be as diverse as a simple green side dish composed of one or more lettuces or a composed salad of meat, poultry, or fish combined with vegetables and grains or pasta that serves as an entrée. The making of a salad gives the cook a great opportunity to express personal creativity. It is important, however, to use restraint, as the flavors, colors, and textures must be well-balanced and harmonious or the salad will not be enjoyable for the diner.

In the classic French culinary repertoire, salads are most often served as an appetizer at the beginning of the meal. The primary exception to this is the **salade digestive**, which marks the end of the savory portion of the meal and cleanses the palate in preparation for dessert. It is always a combination of lettuces, seasoned and tossed with a simple *vinaigrette*.

Classic French salads can be classified into three categories:

- **Simple salads (*salades simples*):** Salads made with one main ingredient, usually some type of lettuce, and seasoned with an appropriate dressing. An example is *salade digestive*.

- **Mixed salads (*salades mixtes*):** Salads that are a mixture of several ingredients that have been combined and then seasoned. An example is *macédoine de légumes*.

- **Composed salads (*salades composées*):** Salads that feature several ingredients that have been separately seasoned and then presented together on a plate. An example is the classic *salade niçoise* (see page 96).

Preparing Greens for a Salad

Lettuces or other leafy greens are most often the main ingredients in salads. There are many, many varieties of salad greens available year-round, each with its own unique character, flavor, and texture. They range from delicate, tender lettuces such as *mâche* (also known as lamb's lettuce), Boston, and Bibb, to hearty, rather tough greens from the chicory family such as radicchio and escarole. Currently, one of the most popular salad ingredients is *mesclun* (mix), which was originally a French mixture of wild baby field greens, but has come to mean a mixture of the leaves of different types of cultivated lettuces and greens, some baby and some mature.

No matter the type of green, preparing it for salad is a tedious and delicate process. Proper handling is crucial to the success of a salad. Do not let the apparent simplicity of the salad undermine the care needed to bring out its best.

You must begin with the freshest greens possible, crisp, brightly colored, and free of any wilt, damage, or decay. Obviously, those just picked are the best, and, when available, those with their roots still attached are very desirable and generally have deeper flavor.

Once purchased or picked, greens should be handled carefully to ensure fresh flavor and damage-free leaves. It is best to use them as soon as they are purchased or picked. However, if it is necessary to store them, they are best stored unwashed. Before storing, remove and discard any rubber band or wire used to hold the head or stems together and remove and discard any damaged parts. Place the greens in a resealable plastic bag with a few holes poked in it, then place the bag in the vegetable storage bin of the refrigerator. They should stay relatively fresh for about three days.

If too much time has elapsed between purchase and storage, greens will sometimes begin to wilt. If this is the case, it is best to revive them with a thorough washing in ice water and then a careful drying before storing as described above. Prewashed greens may be stored for a day or two. Never cut or tear greens into pieces before storing, as this will only expedite decay.

There is nothing more unappetizing than biting into a salad only to have your teeth meet grit, sand, pebbles, or, even worse, an insect. To prevent this, lettuce heads should be carefully pulled apart and, if necessary, cored. Greens with stems (such as arugula or spinach) should have the tough stems removed. All damaged parts must be removed and discarded. The greens should then be plunged into a sinkful of ice-cold water and gently agitated to loosen any dirt or debris so that it falls to the bottom of the sink. If the greens are very dirty, this process should be done multiple times until the bottom of the sink is perfectly

clean. If each leaf is covered with dirt, it is sometimes necessary to wash them one at a time under cold, running water — a tedious but essential chore to ensure clean greens.

Once the greens are clean, using wide-open hands, lift them gently from the water. Dry them either by spreading the leaves or stems out on clean kitchen towels or paper towels or by using a salad spinner. Spinners work extremely well, but they should be used with a gentle hand so that the greens are not damaged. Fill the spinner no more than two-thirds full and gently spin until no more water drops through the basket holes. If the basket is crowded, the greens push together and do not adequately dry. It is essential that the greens be very dry, as water causes rot and prevents the dressing from adhering when the greens are seasoned.

The dried greens should be well chilled before making a salad. This can be done either by placing them in a resealable plastic bag with a few holes poked into it and placing the bag in the vegetable storage bin of the refrigerator for up to a day, or by wrapping them in damp kitchen or paper towels and refrigerating for up to a day. If you are using the greens within a couple of hours, you can line the salad bowl or serving platter with damp paper towels, lay the greens on it, cover with plastic film, and refrigerate until ready for the final preparation or service. Remove the towels before serving.

When ready to finish the salad, make a final check of the greens for any damage or decay, as it can happen quickly. If any stems remain, remove them. Gently tear or, when required, cut or shred the greens into bite-size pieces small enough to be easily picked up with a fork.

The *Vinaigrette*

The classic French *vinaigrette* is composed of three to four parts oil slowly whisked into one part acid (usually wine vinegar) seasoned with salt and freshly ground pepper. Because the addition of oil slows down the infusion of flavor, any seasoning, even the basic salt and pepper, should be added before the oil. Using fine quality oils and vinegars allows such a simple combination to be sublime. A *vinaigrette* can also contain prepared mustard, which not only adds zest but helps create emulsification. Chopped shallots or garlic and fresh herbs can also be incorporated for added flavor. Any additions should be made before the oil is integrated.

Although the ingredients are quite simple, their mixing requires a practiced hand. Left to their own devices, oil and vinegar do not mix. Oil always rises to the top, leaving the vinegar at the bottom. To make a well-emulsified mixture, the oil must either be whisked or shaken into the vinegar so that the two ordinarily immiscible liquids will blend, dispersing the oil as tiny droplets in the vinegar. Once emulsified, the oil and acid stay together for only a short period of time, usually less than 10 minutes. Remixing will reincorporate them.

To ensure a proper emulsification, first add all the seasonings to the acid. Using a wire whisk, blend well. Add the oil in a slow, steady stream, whisking constantly, until the mixture thickens and takes on a slightly thick, satiny sheen.

A straight *vinaigrette* can be stored in a nonreactive container, covered, and refrigerated for up to two weeks. If fresh herbs or other fresh ingredients are added, the shelf life will be somewhat reduced. The *vinaigrette* should be brought to room temperature and whisked before adding it to a salad to ensure that it is emulsified. It is important that all the components of the dressing be well distributed before pouring it over a salad.

Never pour a *vinaigrette* directly onto a salad, as this risks overdressing, leaving drenched leaves sitting in a puddle of dressing on the bottom of the plate. Begin to dress a salad by placing a small amount of the *vinaigrette* in a stainless steel bowl large enough to easily hold the amount of salad greens being used. Just before serving, add the greens and toss to coat lightly, using tongs or clean, gloved hands. Alternatively, you can pour the dressing around the salad along the edge of the bowl and then toss the greens into it. There should be no *vinaigrette* left in

the bowl after the greens have been removed. If *vinaigrette* remains, you have used too much. Serve immediately, as the greens begin to wilt as soon as they have been dressed.

Ingredients for *Vinaigrettes*

The most important factors in making a successful *vinaigrette* are choosing the appropriate oil and acid, and the proportion of each. Since there are now so many different types of oils and acids available, these two relatively simple ingredients, when chosen with care, offer almost limitless opportunity for variation.

Oils range from the neutral oils such as canola, peanut, and rice bran, to the intensely flavored oils such as extra virgin olive oil and fragrant walnut oil. If you prefer a mild flavor, a neutral oil is the best choice; when defined character and rich flavor are the requisite, extra virgin olive oil or a nut oil might be the choice. Whichever oil is chosen, it must also balance the acid, as well as the basic ingredients of the dish in which it is going to be used. All oils must be handled with care, as they tend to turn rancid (musty, bitter flavored) quickly. Oils that have a higher level of monounsaturates (such as olive and peanut) are the most perishable. Unrefined oils should always be refrigerated to ensure freshness.

Although red wine vinegar is the acid used most often in a classic *vinaigrette*, other vinegars, as well as citrus juices, can also be used. Whichever acid is used, the flavor should be pleasant, not sour or harsh tasting. All vinegars vary enormously in quality, and should be tasted to determine their level of acidity and balance of flavor before being used. Citrus juices should be strained.

When making a highly flavored *vinaigrette*, use only one dominant ingredient, such as a vinegar with very defined character or a pungent mustard. If you combine two or more elements with bold flavoring, you will either create a salad dressing that overpowers the basic salad ingredients, or the flavors will cancel each other out, creating a dressing without defined integrity. The ingredients for a *vinaigrette* should complement each other, as well as the ingredients on which the *vinaigrette* will be used. The end result should be a perfect marriage, with the main ingredient the dominant flavor and the dressing offering gentle enhancement.

Olive Oils

Olive trees are indigenous to the Mediterranean areas of southern France, Italy, Greece, and Spain. Both the trees and the oil of their fruit are mentioned throughout the Bible, and again and again in the history of classic Greece. Oil has been extracted from olives for over 5,000 years, used as a fuel source, an unguent, and an integral part of the diet, as well as a major trading commodity. It has often been said that "the Mediterranean ends where olive trees cease to grow."

The word *oil* is derived from the Latin *oleum*, which is the oil of *olivae* (olives). In modern commerce, olive oil remains one of the most important exports of the Mediterranean area, with over 98 percent of all olive oil coming from this ancient source. The types of olive oil now available range from artisanal, family-produced oils to commercially-produced oils that might be a mixture of olive oils from two or three different countries. In America, a variety of olive oils from California are most frequently made in small batches on family-run farms.

Although France produces only about 0.02 percent of all Mediterranean olive oil, its oils are very desirable for their light fruitiness. By law, French olive oils are rated by their acid content, with extra virgin olive oil (*huile vierge extra*) having 1 percent, the smallest amount. The acidity rises with the decrease in quality. Some artisanal oils are labeled extra virgin nonfiltered olive oil (*huile d'olive vierge extra nonfiltrée*), which yields a cloudy, slightly thick oil that is purported to be healthier than filtered oils. There are two olive oils labeled AOC (*Appellation d'Origine Contrôlée*, a guarantee of the provenance of an agricultural product): *Les Beaux-de-Provence* and *Nyons*, both from Provence. These oils are first cold-pressed to ensure the purity of flavor, and are used more for garnish than for *vinaigrettes* or general frying or cooking.

The production of olive oil begins with the harvest. In most instances, the olives are handpicked or shaken from the trees in a time-consuming process. They are harvested at different stages of maturity to yield oil with specific characteristics. Each olive tree may be harvested several times during picking season, either to produce a few oils of differing characteristics or one oil with complexity.

To reduce their moisture content, olives are allowed to rest before the production of oil begins. After resting, they are crushed into a paste or formed into cakes that are then pressed to extract the oil. The simplest method for crushing, still used in many areas of the Mediterranean, is a very ancient, primitive one that employs a large granite stone. Screw or hydraulic presses are then used for the actual pressing. The best producers accomplish this task without the aid of water or heat, which would affect on the purity of the finished oil. Smaller producers allow the fresh oil to settle and then either filter it or leave it unfiltered, depending upon the final product desired. The resulting oil is called "cold-pressed" and, if made with fine-quality olives, it is graded extra virgin. These unrefined oils retain their essential nutrients and have distinctive rich, delicate flavors and aromas. They have a low smoke point and should not be subjected to high heat, which will destroy their inherent fine qualities. Cold-pressed olive oils are the oil of choice for dressing salads, steamed or grilled vegetables, and, in fact, any dish requiring the hint of green acidity that they offer.

Most commercial olive oils go through additional processing, and some of them are made from second pressings. Larger producers use other methods of extraction, which may involve the use of heat, solvents, and chemicals that greatly affect the integrity of the oil. Several different oils from different countries may also be combined to arrive at a balanced oil. These oils constitute much of the inexpensive olive oil available in the commercial marketplace.

Commercially, as in France, olive oil is graded according to its acidity. The level of oleic acid in an olive oil indicates the degree to which the fat has broken down into fatty acids. The percentage of fatty acids determines the smoke point of the oil.

The grades are as follows:

◦ **Extra virgin olive oil:** produced by the first, cold press of high-quality olives and has an acidity level of less than 1 percent. Used in dressings, emulsions, and sauces, and as a condiment, garnish, or flavoring. Its smoke point is 121°C (250°F).

◦ **Virgin olive oil:** the next highest quality oil, also the result of a first pressing, with an acidity level no greater than 3 percent. It is used for frying, sautéing, and baking. Its smoke point is 121°C (250°F).

◦ **Pure olive oil:** the result of the second or third pressing of olive cakes, with up to 10 percent virgin olive oil added, having an acidity level of no more than 4 percent. The process used to produce pure olive oil, whether heat or chemical, permits a longer shelf life than that of extra virgin or virgin oil but also yields an oil that has little flavor or color. It is a good cooking oil when a delicate flavor is unimportant or when the oil will be subjected to high heat, as its smoke point is 210°C (410°F).

◦ **Light olive oil:** A recent introduction to the American market, light olive oil has the same properties and caloric count as pure olive oil, but through an exceptionally fine filtration process, it is lighter in color with almost no flavor or aroma. It is used for cooking with high heat and for any dish calling for no additional oil flavor. Its smoke point is 210°C (410°F).

Fine-quality olive oil should be anywhere from golden yellow to almost bright green in color and have a definite aroma. The latter is determined by the type of olive and process used, the growing conditions, weather, and locale. Flavor and aroma can range from slightly sweet, delicate, and nutty to almost grassy. Some artisanal oils even have the flavor and aroma of fruits such as bananas or cherries.

It is a good idea to test many different oils before zeroing in on the ones you prefer. You will want to have oils to use as condiments and oils to cook with—both types will be quite different. Buy only a small amount at one time as olive oils, particularly those of the highest quality, become rancid very quickly.

Other Oils

In addition to olive oil, there are a number of other oils that can be used in *vinaigrettes* and other salad dressings.

◦ **Nut oils** (hazelnut, walnut, almond, etc.): Most nut oils, obviously, carry the flavor of the nut from which they have been taken and impart a very defined character to a salad dressing or *vinaigrette*. Since they are unstable oils that are very perishable, nut oils should be purchased in small amounts from reputable vendors and refrigerated once open. They make a defining statement and should be used with great care, as you want them to accent the other elements of the salad, not overpower them. They can be used in *vinaigrettes*, dressings, and sauces; for light sautéing; or as a flavoring garnish.

◦ **Peanut oil:** One of the heavier oils, peanut oil is not really suitable for *vinaigrettes*, although it is now used for those having Asian seasonings. In French cooking, it is generally reserved for frying, deep-frying, and emulsions.

◦ **Sesame oil:** Light sesame oil, made from raw sesame seeds, is very light and almost milky in texture. Dark brown sesame oil is made from toasted sesame seeds and is most often used in Asian cooking or for salads using Asian ingredients. It has a very assertive, easily recognized flavor which, when a lighter touch is desired, can be diluted with other nonflavored oil. It is used for accenting strong-flavored or bitter greens, for stir-frying or sautéing, or as a flavoring garnish. Sesame oil has a smoke point of 210°C (410°F).

◦ **Corn oil:** One of the most common refined vegetable oils, corn oil is extremely bland. It is infrequently used for making *vinaigrettes*. It is an excellent multipurpose cooking oil with a high smoke point of 210°C (410°F) and is used for frying, deep-frying, sautéing, and searing. Unrefined corn oil is also available; with a low smoke point of 121°C (250°F), it is used mainly in emulsions and dressings.

○ **Canola oil:** Also known as Canadian rapeseed oil, canola oil lacks any flavor and is very low in saturated fats. With a high smoke point of 224°C (435°F), it is used for light *vinaigrettes* and for frying, deep-frying, and sautéing.

○ **Sunflower oil:** A neutral, pale oil, sunflower oil is high in polyunsaturated fats. With a smoke point of 199°C (390°F), it is used for light *vinaigrettes* or for frying and sautéing.

○ **Infused oils:** A recent innovation, infused oils are made by infusing fine-quality oils, even highly fragrant extra virgin olive oil, with herbs, spices, aromatics such as garlic or shallots, ginger, fruits, and fruit peels. These oils can be used in *vinaigrettes* but are used mainly as a flavored garnish or plate accent.

Vinegars and Other Acids

Vinegar has been used for centuries for the preservation of foods, as a component of light and often healing beverages, as a deodorizer and cleanser, and even as a health aid. Vinegar is the result of the natural acid fermentation that occurs in wine or other alcoholic liquids. It literally means sour wine (*vin aigre*) in French. The first fermentation converts sugars in liquids such as grape juice or malt wort into alcohol; the second, which is known as acetous fermentation, converts the resulting alcoholic liquid into vinegar. This acetous fermentation comes about from the action of the bacterium *Acetobacter xylinum*. This bacterium occurs naturally in wine-growing areas and the first vinegar was probably made accidentally when wine was left in the hot sun. Today, most vinegar is produced with the addition of a cultivated bacteria starter. The bacteria reacts with the alcohol in the wine and turns it into acetic acid. Vinegar is produced all over the world, with wine vinegars generally made in wine-producing areas and grain or other fruit vinegars made in regions producing grain or a particular fruit.

Although red wine vinegar is the acid used in the basic, classic French *vinaigrette*, many other acids can be used, including a variety of different styles of vinegar as well as citrus or highly-acidic vegetable juices. Again, the choice depends upon the elements of the salad or dish to be dressed as well as the oil used.

The basic vinegar types are those made from wine or champagne, distilled alcohol, sherry, and cider, with champagne and sherry producing some of the most appealing options. The quality of the vinegar depends on the quality of the base ingredient used to make it. It also must contain between 4 and 7.5 percent acetic acid to be labeled vinegar. Vinegar is occasionally marked in terms of "grains," with every 10 grains equaling 1 percent acidity. Therefore, a vinegar labeled "50 grain" would contain 5 percent acidity.

Some of the most commonly used vinegars are:

○ **Red wine vinegar:** Red wine vinegar is sharp, slightly sweet, and full-bodied, and complements intensely flavored foods such as bitter greens. One of the best red wine vinegars comes from Orléans in France where, at one time, half of all the vinegars consumed in that country were produced. Now, only one producer, Martin Pouret, makes this ***vinaigre à l'ancienne*** (old-style vinegar) using the Orléans method. In this time-honored tradition, oaken barrels are filled three-quarters full with wine and turned on their sides with small holes drilled into the top. They are kept at a steady 21°C (95°F) temperature, and over time a thick, tacky skin called the "vinegar mother" forms over the surface, turning the wine into acetic acid. The vinegar settles in and is subsequently drawn off the bottom of the barrel and more wine is added (without disturbing the mother skin) to continue making vinegar. Only vinegar produced in this fashion can be labeled *vinaigre à l'ancienne*.

○ **White wine vinegar:** White wine vinegars tend to be sweeter and cleaner tasting than red wine vinegars. They go particularly well with mild greens and are used in *vinaigrettes*, dressings, and emulsions, as well as to make herb- and fruit-infused vinegars.

- **Champagne vinegar:** Made from fermented champagne grapes, this vinegar is usually mellow and delicately flavored, although it can be sharp. It tends to not compete with other flavors. It is used in fruit vinegars and light *vinaigrettes* and dressings.

- **Cider vinegar:** Cider vinegar is produced from naturally sweet apple juice with yeast added to convert the sugar to alcohol. The resulting hard cider is converted into vinegar following the usual process. Cider vinegar has a low percentage of alcohol and acidity and is used in *vinaigrettes*, dressings, and pickling solutions.

- **Traditional balsamic vinegar:** A traditional vinegar produced from the white Trebbiano grape in Modena, Italy, through a years-long aging process in wooden barrels of changing types of wood (chestnut, followed by cherry, ash, and mulberry) and graduating sizes. The vinegar is moved from one barrel to the next after a one-year aging, with the complete aging process taking at least five years. Traditional balsamic vinegar, labeled *aceto balsamico tradizionale*, is extremely expensive and thicker than ordinary vinegars. It should be almost molasseslike in consistency, with a mildly acidic aroma and a smooth, yin-yang taste of sweet-sour. Like fine-quality olive oils, it is often used as a condiment or a flavored garnish on the plate.

- **Balsamic vinegar:** Commonly available and more affordable than the traditional balsamic vinegar, *aceto balsamico di Modena* (or *aceto balsamico industriale*) is a red wine vinegar fortified with caramelized sugar, herbs, and other flavorings. It is now widely used in America in *vinaigrettes*, dressings, and marinades.

- **Sherry wine vinegar:** The most acclaimed sherry vinegars are made from the sweet, deeply colored and richly flavored Oloroso cream sherry from Spain. They are barrel-aged with a smooth, mellow, full-bodied taste. Sherry vinegars marry particularly well with delicate nut oils. They are used in *vinaigrettes*, dressings, and sauces.

- **Malt vinegar:** Malt vinegar is produced from malted barley and is a favorite of the British Isles. This grain vinegar is dark gold in color, with a strong, sharp flavor and an acidity level from 4 to 6 percent.

- **Rice wine vinegar:** Most commonly produced in Asia, rice wine vinegar is a by-product of rice production. Chinese rice wine vinegar is sharp and tangy, while its Japanese counterpart is smooth and mellow. Rice wine vinegar is a perfect partner for sesame oil, and is most often used in Asian cuisine.

- **Infused/flavored vinegars:** Vinegar can be flavored with a wide variety of ingredients. The most common are infusions of herbs (particularly tarragon and basil) or fruits (raspberry, pear, and so forth), as well as garlic and shallots.

Using Cooked Vegetables in Salads

For use in salads, different vegetables require particular preparations and seasonings. Because they are going to be served cold or at room temperature, each vegetable must have its flavor reinforced with more seasoning than is used for general cooking. Following are some of the most common salad vegetable preparations:

- **Artichokes (*artichauts*):** Artichokes may be served whole, or the trimmed bottoms may be served alone. If preparing whole, trim the artichoke and cook it *à l'anglaise*. Artichoke bottoms or hearts are usually cooked *dans un blanc*. They are usually served with a mustard *vinaigrette* or mayonnaise-based sauce.

- **Asparagus or leeks (*asperges* or *poireaux*):** Using kitchen twine, tie the asparagus or leeks in small bunches, taking care not to break the asparagus heads, and cook the vegetables *à l'anglaise*. The vegetables are tied to maintain their shape and form. Drain well and carefully refresh under cold running water. Dry well on clean kitchen towels. Either vegetable can be served with a *vinaigrette*,

mustard, mayonnaise, or *mousseline* (see page 81) sauces.

○ **Beets** (*betteraves*): In France, beets are often found precooked and vacuum packed for use in salads. In America, they are usually found either fresh, frozen, or canned. To prepare fresh beets for use in a salad, place them, skin on, in cold salted water and simmer for about 45 minutes or so, depending upon their size, or coat them lightly with olive oil, wrap tightly in aluminum foil, and roast in a preheated 177°C (350°F). Once cooked, slip off the skins and cut the roots into the desired shape. Season with a *vinaigrette*, dressing, or with fresh herbs.

○ **Cauliflower** (*chou-fleur*): Cauliflower should be cooked *à l'anglaise* just until it is slightly crunchy. It should not retain any cooking water. Drain well, refresh, and, if desired, pull apart into small florets. Season with a mustard and herb *vinaigrette*, or a mustard or mayonnaise sauce.

○ **Celery hearts** (*coeurs de céleris*): Celery hearts should also be cooked *à l'anglaise*, with lemon juice added to the water. They are served whole, seasoned with a mustard or herb *vinaigrette*.

○ **Hearts of palm** (*coeurs de palmier*): Hearts of palm are usually purchased cooked and canned. They may be minced, sliced, or served whole with a mustard *vinaigrette* or flavored mayonnaise.

○ **Red and green bell peppers** (*poivrons rouges et verts*): Bell peppers may be served raw or cooked. To serve peppers raw, peel them using a vegetable peeler, cut them in half lengthwise, then remove and discard the seeds and white membrane. Cut the pepper halves into *julienne* and marinate in a mild *vinaigrette*. To cook peppers, roast the whole pepper under a broiler or over an open flame until the skin is completely charred. Immediately place the charred peppers in a bowl, tightly cover with plastic film, and allow to steam for at least 10 minutes. Remove the plastic film and, working with one pepper at a time, push the skin off by scraping with the back of a paring knife or rubbing with a paper towel. The peppers may then be cut in half lengthwise, and the stem, seeds, and white membrane removed and discarded. The peppers may be left in halves, or cut into *julienne* or pieces and marinated in a *vinaigrette*, or simply seasoned with fresh herbs, salt, and pepper.

○ **White beans and lentils** (*haricots blancs* and *lentilles*): Prepare dried beans and lentils seasoned with *mirepoix* vegetables, bacon, and a *bouquet garni* with garlic and extra peppercorns for use in salads.

Preparing Vegetables *à la Grecque*

À la grecque simply means to cook vegetables in the style of the Greeks. The basic preparation is a mixture of olive oil, onions, dry white wine, coriander, peppercorns, lemon, salt, and *bouquet garni*. The method is used to cook a variety of vegetables, and they can be served hot or cold.

Traditionally, only olive oil is used as the fat partly because butter or other solid fats will solidify once the mixture cools. The coriander seeds should be toasted and then tied, along with the peppercorns, in a cheesecloth bag (*sachet*) before being added to the simmering wine and oil mixture. After cooking, the sachet remains in the liquid until it has cooled thoroughly so that the flavor of the spices fully infuse the liquid. The lemon juice and wine add a pleasantly acidic edge and prevent the vegetables from oxidizing during cooking. The acid component also helps give the vegetables the desired crunchiness.

In a classic *à la grecque* presentation, three or four different vegetables are served together. Each is cooked separately, as the cooking times will vary, and it is important that each maintain its integrity. Different ingredients are often used with each vegetable to give them interesting character and contrasting flavor. For instance:

*"I like to introduce people to the foods
that are grown right where they live. If I
can make the connection between the
local farmer and the taste of something
that is truly fresh and truly in season, it is
easy to seduce people into trying something new. It is all a matter of education
that can come through the menu word-
ing or the waiter at the table."*

Dean Alice Waters

Celeriac may be prepared with curry powder, cauliflower with saffron, fennel with paprika, artichokes with anise seeds, zucchini with fresh tomatoes and garlic, pearl onions with dried currants, bell peppers with toasted almonds, and mushrooms with tarragon.

Demonstration
Assiette de Crudités (Raw Vegetable Plate)

The word *assiette* literally means plate, and an **assiette de crudités** refers to a plate of separately prepared raw, simple salads. In the recipes that follow, it may not be possible to present all of the salads at once, but there should be at least five on a plate. It is particularly important that a pristine workstation be set up and that a complete *mise en place* be organized before beginning to cook.

Carottes à la Citronette (Carrots in Lemon *Vinaigrette*)

Serves 4
Estimated time to complete: 20 minutes

Ingredients	Equipment
200 grams (7 ounces) carrots, washed and peeled	Chef's knife
15 milliliters (1 tablespoon) fresh lemon juice, strained	2 small mixing bowls
Coarse salt and freshly ground pepper to taste	Whisk
30 milliliters (2 tablespoons) vegetable oil	
5 grams (1 tablespoon) finely chopped fresh flat-leaf parsley	

Prepare your *mise en place*.

Cut the carrots crosswise into even lengths and neatly trim three sides to make a triangle shape. Using a chef's knife, thinly slice the carrot pieces lengthwise and then cut the slices into a fine *julienne*. Place the carrots into a small mixing bowl.

Combine the lemon juice with salt and pepper to taste in a small bowl. Whisking constantly, add the oil in a slow, steady stream. When well emulsified, pour the *vinaigrette* over the carrots and toss to combine.

When ready to serve, sprinkle the salad with the parsley.

Céleri Rémoulade (Celery Root in *Rémoulade* Sauce)

Serves 4

Estimated time to complete: 20 minutes

Ingredients	Equipment
For the *rémoulade*	2 small mixing bowls
1 large egg yolk, at room temperature	Whisk
30 grams (1 ounce) Dijon mustard, or to taste	Paring knife
Coarse salt and freshly ground pepper, optional	Chef's knife
150 milliliters (⅔ cup) vegetable oil	
White wine vinegar to taste	
For the celery root	
200 grams (7 ounces) celery root	
½ lemon	

Note

In classic French cooking, *sauce rémoulade* gets its zest from capers and *cornichons*. An exception to the recipe is in the preparation of *céleri rémoulade,* in which the strong flavor required is obtained through the addition of Dijon mustard.

Prepare your *mise en place.*

To make the *rémoulade*, combine the egg yolk with 10 grams (about 2 teaspoons) of the mustard and salt and pepper to taste in a small mixing bowl. Add the oil in a slow, steady stream, whisking constantly, until the mixture thickens. Add vinegar to taste and adjust the seasoning, if necessary.

Whisk up to 20 grams (4½ teaspoons) of mustard, to taste, into the mayonnaise mixture (see note). Taste and, again, adjust the seasoning, if necessary.

Using a paring knife, peel the celery root, constantly rubbing the peeled part with the cut side of a lemon half to keep it from oxidizing.

Using a chef's knife, cut the celery root into thin slices and then into fine *julienne*. (Alternatively, you can use a mandoline.) Place the cut celery root in a small mixing bowl. As you cut the celery root, moisten the *julienne* with a bit of the sauce to keep it from oxidizing.

Add enough of the *rémoulade* to generously coat the celery root. Taste and, if necessary, adjust the seasoning with salt and pepper. If not serving immediately, cover and refrigerate.

Concombres à la Crème (Cucumbers in Cream)

Serves 4

Estimated time to complete: 45 minutes

Ingredients	Equipment
For the cucumbers	Chef's knife
200 grams (7 ounces) cucumbers, peeled	Teaspoon or melon baller
Coarse salt	Colander
	Large bowl, optional

For the sauce

50 milliliters (3½ tablespoons) heavy cream

Juice of 1 lime

5 grams (1 tablespoon) fresh mint leaves, washed and dried

Freshly ground pepper to taste

Coarse salt to taste, optional

Mixing bowl
Ice-water bath
Whisk

Prepare your *mise en place*.

Using the chef's knife, cut the cucumbers in half lengthwise. Using a teaspoon or melon baller, carefully scrape out and discard the seeds.

Émincer the cucumbers into 3-milliimeter (⅛-inch) pieces and place them in a colander. Sprinkle coarse salt over the top and then toss to coat lightly. If the colander does not have legs, place it over a large bowl. Set aside for 30 minutes to allow excess liquid to drain (*dégorger*) from the cucumbers.

After 30 minutes, rinse the cucumbers under cold running water to eliminate the saltiness. Pat dry.

Make the sauce: Place the heavy cream and lime juice in a bowl set over an ice-water bath and, using a whisk, beat until soft peaks form.

Using a chef's knife, finely chop the mint and fold it into the cream along with pepper to taste. Taste and, if necessary, adjust the seasoning with additional salt and pepper.

Place the cucumbers on a serving plate and lightly nap with the sauce.

Choux Rouge à la Vinaigrette (Red Cabbage in Vinaigrette)

Serves 4

Estimated time to complete: 45 minutes

Ingredients	Equipment
200 grams (7 ounces) red cabbage, cut into fine *chiffonade*	2 medium mixing bowls
65 milliliters (4½ tablespoons) red wine vinegar	Colander
3.5 grams (½ teaspoon) coarse salt, plus more to taste	Small mixing bowl
Freshly ground pepper to taste	Whisk
40 milliliters (2 tablespoons plus 2 teaspoons) vegetable oil	

Prepare your *mise en place*.

Place the cabbage *chiffonade* in a medium mixing bowl. Add 50 milliliters (3½ tablespoons) of the vinegar and salt. Add cold water to cover by 1 inch. Set aside to soak for about 30 minutes or just until the cabbage is slightly soft and the flavor has mellowed somewhat.

Transfer the cabbage to a colander. Drain well and pat dry.

To make the *vinaigrette*, combine the remaining vinegar with salt and pepper to taste in a small mixing bowl. Add the oil in a slow, steady stream, whisking constantly, until the mixture has emulsified.

Place the cabbage in a clean bowl and add just enough *vinaigrette* to lightly cover. Toss to coat. Taste and, if necessary, adjust the seasoning with salt and pepper.

Tomates à la Vinaigrette (Tomatoes in *Vinaigrette*)

Serves 4

Estimated time to complete: 20 minutes

Ingredients	Equipment
200 grams (7 ounces) tomatoes, peeled	Chef's knife
Coarse salt, optional	Colander, optional
15 milliliters (1 tablespoon) red wine vinegar	Medium mixing bowl
Coarse salt and freshly ground pepper to taste	Small bowl
40 milliliters (2 tablespoons plus 2 teaspoons) vegetable oil	Whisk
5 grams (1 tablespoon) chopped fresh chives	

Prepare your *mise en place*.

Using a chef's knife, cut the tomatoes into wedges and carefully remove the seeds. (If they are underripe or lacking in flavor, place them in a colander, sprinkle lightly with coarse salt, toss, and set aside for about 30 minutes to *dégorger*. Rinse lightly and pat dry. This will help enhance the flavor.)

Place the tomatoes in a medium mixing bowl.

To make the *vinaigrette*, combine the red wine vinegar with salt and pepper to taste in a small mixing bowl. Add the oil in a slow, steady stream, whisking constantly, until the mixture has emulsified.

Add just enough *vinaigrette* to the tomatoes to lightly cover. Toss to coat and sprinkle with chives.

Serve immediately.

Champignons à l'Estragon (Mushrooms in Tarragon *Vinaigrette*)

Serves 4

Estimated time to complete: 1 hour, 15 minutes

Ingredients	Equipment
15 milliliters (1 tablespoon) white wine vinegar	Small bowl
Coarse salt and freshly ground pepper to taste	Whisk
40 milliliters (2 tablespoons plus 2 teaspoons) vegetable oil	Paring knife, optional
200 grams (7 ounces) button mushrooms, wiped clean	Medium mixing bowl
5 grams (1 tablespoon) chopped fresh tarragon	

Prepare your *mise en place.*

To make the *vinaigrette*, combine the vinegar with salt and pepper to taste in a small bowl. Add the oil in a slow, steady stream, whisking constantly, until the mixture has emulsified.

If the mushrooms are discolored, using a paring knife, peel off any discoloration.

Émincer thinly and, if large, cut in half.

Place the mushrooms in a medium mixing bowl. Add the *vinaigrette* and toss to coat. Set aside to marinate for at least 1 hour at room temperature.

Just before serving, stir in the tarragon and toss to incorporate.

Demonstration
Assortiment de Légumes à la Grecque
(Assortment of Greek-Style Vegetables)

Champignons à la Grecque (Greek-Style Mushrooms)

Serves 4

Estimated time to complete: 30 minutes

Ingredients	Equipment
400 grams (14 ounces) button mushrooms, washed and trimmed	Medium saucepan
50 milliliters (3½ tablespoons) olive oil	Parchment paper
75 grams (2½ ounces) chopped white onion	
150 milliliters (⅔ cup) white wine	
25 milliliters (1½ tablespoons) water	
Juice of ½ lemon	
5 grams (¾ teaspoon) toasted coriander seeds (see note)	
Bouquet garni	
Coarse salt and freshly ground pepper to taste	

Prepare your *mise en place.*

If the mushrooms are large, quarter or slice them vertically. Set aside.

Heat the olive oil in a medium saucepan over medium heat. Add the onions and sweat for 4 minutes. Do not allow them to take on any color.

Add the mushrooms, wine, water, lemon juice, coriander seeds, and *bouquet garni* to the saucepan.

Season with salt and pepper to taste and place a parchment paper lid with a hole in the center (see page 32) over the saucepan. Bring to a simmer, then lower the heat and cook at a bare simmer for about 15 minutes or until the mushrooms are just cooked.

Remove from the heat, uncover, and taste. If necessary, adjust the seasoning with salt and pepper.

Set aside to cool to room temperature before serving.

Chou-fleur à la Grecque (Greek-Style Cauliflower)

Serves 4

Estimated time to complete: 30 minutes

Ingredients	Equipment
50 milliliters (3½ tablespoons) olive oil	Medium saucepan
75 grams (2½ ounces) chopped white onion	Parchment paper
2 cloves garlic, peeled	
400 grams (14 ounces) cauliflower florets, washed	
150 milliliters (⅔ cup) white wine	
25 milliliters (1½ tablespoons) water	
Juice of ½ lemon	
5 grams (¾ teaspoon) toasted coriander seeds (see note, page 252)	
Pinch of saffron threads, optional	
Coarse salt and freshly ground pepper to taste	

Prepare your *mise en place*.

Heat the olive oil in a medium saucepan over medium heat. Add the onion and garlic and sweat for 4 minutes. Do not allow them to take on any color.

Add the cauliflower, wine, water, lemon juice, coriander seeds and, if using, the saffron to the saucepan. Season with salt and pepper to taste and place a parchment paper lid with a hole in the center (see page 32) over the saucepan. Bring to a simmer, then lower the heat and cook at a bare simmer for about 15 minutes or until the cauliflower is just cooked.

Remove from the heat, uncover, and taste. If necessary, adjust the seasoning with salt and pepper.

Set aside to cool to room temperature before serving.

Courgettes à la Grecque (Greek-Style Zucchini)

Serves 4

Estimated time to complete: 30 minutes

Ingredients	Equipment
5 grams (¾ teaspoon) toasted coriander seeds (see note, page 252)	Cheesecloth
3.5 grams (½ teaspoon) black peppercorns	Chef's knife
400 grams (14 ounces) zucchini, washed	Medium saucepan
50 milliliters (3½ tablespoons) olive oil	Parchment paper
75 grams (2½ ounces) chopped white onion	
2 cloves garlic, peeled	
150 grams (5¼ ounces) peeled, seeded, and coarsely chopped ripe tomatoes	
150 milliliters (⅔ cups) white wine	
25 milliliters (1½ tablespoons) water	

Juice of ½ lemon
Bouquet garni
Coarse salt to taste

Note

After covering with parchment, this dish may also be covered with a lid and baked, in a preheated 176°C (350°F) oven for about 20 minutes.

Prepare your *mise en place*.

Wrap the coriander seeds and peppercorns in cheese-cloth and tie as for *bouquet garni*. Set aside.

Leaving the zucchini skin on, trim both ends and, using a chef's knife, either slice crosswise into 2.5-centimeter (1-inch) lengths and *tournée*, or cut the zucchini lengthwise into equal pieces. Set aside.

Heat the olive oil in a medium saucepan over medium heat. Add the onions and garlic and sweat for 4 minutes. Do not allow them to take on any color.

Add the tomatoes and stir to combine.

Add the zucchini, wine, water, lemon juice, *bouquet garni*, and coriander-peppercorn *sachet* to the saucepan. Season with salt to taste and place a parchment paper lid with a hole poked in the center (see page 32) over the saucepan. Bring to a simmer, then lower the heat and cook at a bare simmer for about 12 minutes or until the zucchini is just cooked.

Set aside to cool to room temperature before serving.

Demonstration

Macédoine de Légumes (Diced Vegetable Salad)

Macédoine de légumes, one of the most popular Parisian bistro salads of the late nineteenth century, can still be found on contemporary bistro menus. This is in no small measure due to its combination of familiar tastes and textures that, somehow, always seem fresh. Similar to a *salade russe* (mixed, diced vegetables in a mayon-naise dressing), the elements in this salad can be bound together with a variety of dressings—*vinaigrette*, cream and vinegar sauce, mayonnaise, or hard-cooked egg sauces. The recipe that follows uses a simple may-onnaise, but flavored mayonnaises, such as tomato, tarragon, or basil could also be used. For presentation, you can use any of the suggestions given or your own imagination to create an inviting plate.

Serves 4
Estimated time to complete: 30 minutes

Ingredients	Equipment
For the mayonnaise	Small stainless steel bowl
1 large egg yolk, at room temperature	Whisk
10 grams (⅓ ounce) Dijon mustard, at room temperature	Chef's knife
Coarse salt to taste	Medium saucepan
150 milliliters (⅔ cup) vegetable oil	Strainer
Vinegar to taste	Medium mixing bowl
Freshly ground pepper to taste	

For the vegetables
300 grams (10½ ounces) carrots, peeled and trimmed
200 grams (7 ounces) white turnips, peeled and trimmed
100 grams (3½ ounces) string beans, washed
100 grams (3½ ounces) frozen petite peas, thawed
Coarse salt and freshly ground pepper to taste

Prepare your *mise en place*.

First, make the mayonnaise. Combine the egg yolk, mustard, and salt to taste in a small stainless steel bowl, whisking for 20 seconds. Begin adding the oil, drop by drop, whisking constantly, until the mixture has emulsified and thickened. Whisk in the remaining oil in a thin, steady stream. Add vinegar and salt and pepper to taste. The dressing should be slightly more acidic than normal for this salad. Cover and refrigerate until ready to use.

Using a chef's knife, cut the carrots and turnips into *jardinière* and then into *macédoine*. Set aside.

Break the ends off the beans and then cut the beans into pieces the same size as the carrots and turnips. Set aside.

Bring a medium saucepan of salted water to a boil over high heat. Place a strainer in the water and add the carrots. Cook for about 3 minutes or just until tender. Remove the strainer from the water and place it under cold running water to refresh the carrots. Drain well and pat dry. Set the carrots aside and continue cooking and refreshing the remaining vegetables in the same fashion until all the vegetables have been cooked, refreshed, drained, and patted dry. The turnips and beans will take approximately the same amount of time as the carrots. The peas will take about 30 seconds.

Combine the vegetables in a medium mixing bowl. Season with salt and pepper to taste. Begin adding the mayonnaise, a bit at a time, until the vegetables are bound together but not overdressed. Taste and, if necessary, adjust the seasoning with salt and pepper.

There are a number of possibilities for presentation:

° Mounded on lettuce leaves or in lettuce cups, garnished with hard-cooked eggs or with anchovy fillets crisscrossed over the top.
° Mounded on a plate with chopped herbs sprinkled over the top.
° Mounded on thin tomato or cucumber slices that have been formed in a circle of overlapping slices.
° With additional mayonnaise or a *sauce verte* (see page 86) thinned with vinegar or *court bouillon* (see page 269).
° Or—Escoffier's suggestion—with a decoration of diced cooked beets and caviar.

Chef Roy Ip

Chef/Owner, Le Petit Café, Branford, Connecticut
The French Culinary Institute, Class of January 1996

Vine-Ripened Tomato Filled with Crabmeat and California Pluots with Light Curry-Lemon Vinaigrette

Serves 4

This dish only achieves its maximum deliciousness when the fruits are at their ripest. I still use the technique for preparing tomatoes for stuffing that I learned at FCI when I make this salad. It is one of the favorite summer lunch entrées at Le Petit Café. The vinaigrette makes more than you will need for this recipe, but it can be stored, covered, and refrigerated for a few days and it is an excellent dressing for grilled vegetables, seafood, pork, or poultry.

4 large vine-ripened tomatoes, *émondé*
Coarse salt to taste
227 grams (8 ounces) lump crabmeat, picked clean of all shell and cartilage
Light Curry-Lemon Vinaigrette (recipe follows)
1 large California pluot, peeled and cut into *brunoise*
28 grams (1 cup) upland cress, well-washed and dried

Prepare your *mise en place*.

Bring a medium saucepan of water to a boil over high heat.

Using a chef's knife, make a neat cut crosswise, about 6 millimeters (¼ inch) from the stem end of each tomato. Set the slices aside. Carefully scoop out the interior of each tomato, discarding the seeds and pulp, leaving a tomato shell. Lightly salt the interior of each tomato, then turn the salted tomato shells upside down on a double layer of paper towels to drain for 10 minutes. Then quickly rinse out the interiors, shaking off any excess water. Set aside.

Place the crabmeat in a mixing bowl. Add 30 milliliters (2 tablespoons) of the vinaigrette and, using a fork, toss to coat lightly. Let marinate for 5 minutes before proceeding.

Place an equal portion of the seasoned crabmeat in each tomato shell. Spoon an equal portion of the pluot on top of the crab in each tomato.

Place the upland cress in a small bowl and season lightly with a bit of the vinaigrette.

Place the reserved tomato caps in the center of each of four luncheon plates. Place a filled tomato on top of each cap. Garnish with a few sprigs of the seasoned cress and drizzle some of the vinaigrette around each plate. Serve immediately.

Light Curry-Lemon Vinaigrette

118 milliliters (½ cup) fresh lemon juice
57 grams (¼ cup) sugar
7 grams (1 teaspoon) sea salt
14 grams (½ ounce) minced shallot
7 grams (¼ ounce) minced garlic
4 grams (scant 1 tablespoon) dried *herbes de Provence*
Scant 2 grams (1 teaspoon) fine quality curry powder
Scant 2 grams (1 teaspoon) freshly ground pepper
355 milliliters (1½ cups) olive oil

Place the lemon juice in a nonreactive mixing bowl. Add the sugar and salt, mixing to dissolve. Add the shallot, garlic, *herbes de Provence*, curry powder, and pepper, stirring to combine. Slowly add the olive oil, whisking briskly until the mixture is emulsified. Use immediately or store, covered, in the refrigerator.

Theory

General Information About Fish

The French are experts at fish and seafood cookery and have, over centuries, perfected the art of turning a simple piece of fish into a masterpiece at the table. In the following pages you will find information about the multitude of methods of cooking fish, including recipes for *Filet de Sole de Bonne Femme* and *Filet de Truite Grenobloise*, two of the most famous classic French fish dishes.

Found in both salt and fresh water, fish (*poissons*) are composed of four main sections: the head (*la tête*), the trunk (*le tronc*) or body, the tail (*la queue*), and the fins (*les negeoires*). If the fish is not served whole, the trunk and tail are generally the parts brought to the table, while the head and fins are most frequently used as flavoring agents for fish stocks (*fumets*, see page 52). There are thousands of species of fish to be found swimming in the world's waters, and many of them are individually known by a battery of names, so it is necessary for the cook to become familiar with the nomenclature used locally.

It is important to note that there is, increasingly, a shortage of all types of fish worldwide. This is due in part to the globalization of cuisines and air transportation, both of which have caused chefs to experiment more broadly with once-uncommon varieties of fish and consumers all over the world to demand the fish of the moment. In addition, many of the waters in which they swim suffer from contamination. Even with the advent of fish farming and instant processing — or perhaps because of these developments — many types of fish are on the endangered list, and the catch of many fish is limited by law. This makes it even more important for a cook to learn as much as possible about the marketplace.

Fish Classifications

Almost all fish is very low in cholesterol and fat. The fat is usually only about 1 percent, and of that small amount, only about 10 percent is saturated. Most fish are composed of 70 percent water and 10 to 20 percent protein, plus traces of minerals; vitamins A, B, and D; glucides; and lipids. Calorie content is approximately 160 per 100 grams (about 4 ounces) for fatty fish and 70 calories per 100 grams (about 4 ounces) for lean fish.

Some fish may even promote good health. In fact, it has been known for some time that diets high in fish oils, such as those of Scandinavians, Japanese, and Inuit, seem to be coupled with low rates of heart disease and many cancers. Studies suggest that it is the omega-3 fatty acids in fish that are the source of this benefit. Fatty fish such as salmon, mackerel, and tuna, seem to be the most beneficial.

Fat Content of Fish

Saltwater	Fresh Water	Degree of Fattiness
Sole, lemon sole, brill, turbot, whiting	Trout, perch, pike, carp	Lean (less than 5%)
Sardine, herring, hake, mackerel, hog-fish		Medium (5% to 10% fat)
Salmon, tuna	Eel	Fatty (more than 10%)

There are two types of fish — roundfish and flatfish. Roundfish are generally served whole or cut into boneless sides called **filets** in French (fillet in English), vertical slices or steaks (**darnes**), or sections (**tronçons**). Flatfish are served in the same cuts, with the exception of vertical slices, which are impossible to cut because of the structure of the fish.

Roundfish Anatomy

A typical roundfish, such as bass or pollock, is shaped rather like an oval tube, with the backbone running down the top center between two thick strips of flesh. A line of bones extends upward from the spine. Along the bottom of the spine, a double line of bones fans out vertically to enclose the entrails. Other bones support the dorsal and anal fins.

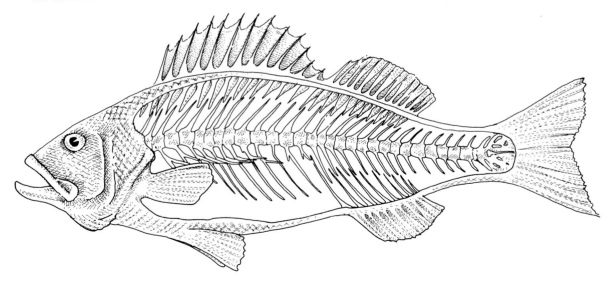

Flatfish Anatomy

A flatfish, such as sole, is composed of two thin layers of flesh separated by small bones that fan out from the backbone. Along the outer edges of the flesh small bones attach the dorsal and anal fins. Flatfish swim horizontally along the sea bottom with both eyes facing upward.

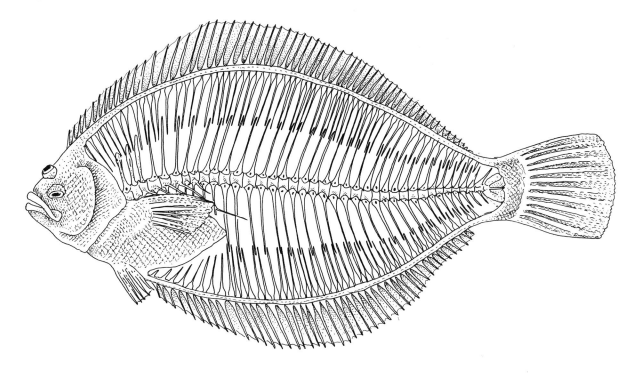

Buying Fish

With the increased speed and safety of shipping, fresh fish from all over the world is now quickly transported and readily available almost everywhere in the United States, and American fish and seafood can be found in the major cities outside the country. For instance, it is now not uncommon to find Maine lobster on the table in Paris, or Dover sole on a Chicago menu. Since fish found in the market may no longer be a "local" or "regional" catch, it is extremely important to learn how to identify freshly caught and properly stored fish.

In general, if the fish looks like it was just pulled from the water and if it smells fresh, it is fresh. The smell is the foremost indicator of freshness, and it is always good practice to smell before buying, rejecting any fish with the slightest hint of odor. Any fish that is dull colored, mushy fleshed, or discolored should be passed on.

Other than adhering the basic rules of kitchen cleanliness and safety (see Session 1), there are a few basic rules to follow to ensure fish safety. These are particularly important in the contemporary kitchen, where much fish is eaten rare. Some of the rules are based on common sense and a few on government regulations.

Saltwater

Type	Pound Weight	Type	Pound Weight
Barracuda, Pacific	3 to 5	Mullet, American	.5 to 4
Bass, sea and striped	3 to 50	Perch, ocean	.5 to 2
Blackfish	2 to 5	Pollock	1.5 to 8
Blowfish	.33 to .75	Pompano	.5 to 2
Bluefish	1 to 20	Porgy, scup	.5 to 5
Butterfish	.25 to 1.25	Red snapper	2 to 40
Cod, Atlantic	3 to 25	Rockfish	1 to 25
Croaker	1 to 3	Sablefish	3 to 40
Cusk	1.5 to 20	Salmon, Atlantic	5 to 10
Drum, redfish	1 to 30	Salmon, Pacific	3 to 30
Drum, black	5 to 100	Sardines	.12
Flounder (lemon, gray, Dover or English sole, blackback)	1 to 7	Scrod (small cod)	1.5 to 10
		Sea trout (weakfish)	1 to 40
Fluke	1 to 5	Shad	1.5 to 5
Grouper	5 to 1,000	Skate	1 to 20
Haddock	1.5 to 7	Smelt	.12
Hake	1 to 30	Swordfish	50 to 800
Halibut	5 to 75	Tilefish	4 to 60
Herring	.025 to .12	Tuna, albacore	15 to 40
John Dory	2	Tuna, bluefin	75 to 1,000+
Lingcod	3 to 50	Tuna, bonito	1 to 8
Mackerel, Atlantic and Pacific	1 to 2	Tuna, yellowfin	20 to 375
Mackerel, king	5 to 15	Turbot	2.5 to 30
Mackerel, Spanish	2 to 3	Whiting	4 to 18
Mahi-mahi	5 to 50	Wolf fish	8 to 40
Monkfish	1 to 50		

Freshwater

Type	Pound Weight	Type	Pound Weight
Arctic char	4 to 25	Pike	1.5 to 20
Bass, freshwater	1 to 15	Shad	3 to 8
Buffalofish	3 to 50	Smelt	1.5 to 5
Burbot	2.5 to 3	Sturgeon	10 to 30
Carp	2 to 10	Tilapia	1.5 to 3
Catfish	1 to 5	Trout, brook	1 to 6
Eel	1 to 5	Trout, lake	10 to 100
Lake herring	.33 to 1	Trout, rainbow	.12 to 6
Perch, walleye	1 to 2	Trout, steelhead	Up to 12
Perch, yellow	.5 to 1	Whitefish	3 to 20
Pickerel	2 to 10		

○ Become familiar with the source of your fish. Many fishmongers have a preference for certain wholesalers, which will help ensure the ability to track the trail of the fish served.

○ Work with and support programs to clean the world's waters and develop sustainable harvesting and sensible inspection systems.

○ Use many different types of fish. This is both for variety in the kitchen and on the table, as well as to ensure that, should one type contain high levels of any environmental pollutant, you and those you cook for will not accumulate dangerous doses in your system.

○ Buy fish caught in tropical waters through reputable dealers only, as these fish often have concentrated levels of ciguatoxin, brought about by a marine microalgae, gambierdiscus toxicus, that occurs naturally in tropical waters. this toxin can be life-threatening and, at best, causes a severe flulike illness that can be recurring.

○ If serving or eating raw fish, first freeze it as directed by health regulations.

The primary characteristics of fresh fish are:

○ Shiny, almost slick appearance.

○ Clean, almost sweet smell.

○ Flesh that is firm and resistant to the touch.

○ Flesh of a consistent color for the type of fish.

○ Bright, moist red gills.

○ Clear, bright eyes that fill the socket and are shiny and convex.

○ Tidy, unblemished scales or skin.

○ Tightly closed anus.

○ Firm, intact stomach.

○ Absolutely no discoloration of the flesh.

Storing and Preserving Fish

Fresh fish must be properly stored from the moment it is caught to the moment that it is served. This storage can be either short term or long term. Short-term storage entails keeping fish fresh under extremely cold conditions; long-term storage can be achieved through freezing, salting, smoking, pickling in brine, or canning.

Short-term Storage

While still whole and intact, most fish (with the exception of very delicately fleshed fish such as wild trout, which should be eaten as soon as it is caught) should be stored under refrigeration, packed in crushed ice in a container with drain holes so that the water from the melting ice can be expelled. Fish fillets or steaks should be packed on top of crushed ice with a layer of plastic film separating the flesh from the ice so that there is no direct contact. For every degree over 0°C (32°F) that a fresh fish is allowed to go, its wholesomeness decreases rapidly. For instance, a fish held at 10°C (50°F) will deteriorate four times faster than one held at 0°C (32°F).

Since enzymes in fresh fish break down quickly, fish must be gutted and cleaned as soon as possible once taken from ice storage. Immediately upon delivery to the kitchen, it is the responsibility of the *poissonier* to clean, trim, and store the fish. Once cleaned or trimmed into fillets or steaks, the fish must be stored again on clean, crushed ice, separated from the ice by a layer of plastic film. Fresh ice should be added to the storage unit frequently and, if storing for longer than one day, all the ice must be changed daily. Under no circumstances should the fish be allowed to rest in water of any temperature.

Even if stored at the optimum temperature, any fish that is held for too long in ice will lose its flavor as well as the natural elasticity of its flesh. Certain saltwater fish such as brill, sole, and turbot can be held for several days, while others such as whiting, red mullet, sardines, skate, and most freshwater fish are too fragile to withstand long periods of storage in ice. However, it is a good idea to use all fish as quickly as possible.

Long-term Storage

At this point, we will only address long-term storage through freezing. Although fresh fish is much preferable to frozen, freezing is sometimes necessary. Eating a piece of properly frozen fish is far more satisfying than eating fish that has been refrigerated for a few days. In fact, many fish are now processed and frozen at sea when caught to ensure fresh flavor and safe handling.

Fish that is going to be frozen should be pristine. It should be gutted and cleaned and then wrapped immediately in plastic film. A further wrapping in freezer paper will protect it from freezer burn. The package should be firmly closed, labeled, and quickly placed in the coldest part of the freezer with at least an inch around all sides — the bottom is a recommended spot — so that it freezes in a flash. Fish should never be frozen, thawed, and refrozen.

Technique
Preparing Fish for Cooking

Although much fish is purchased already portioned into fillets or steaks, the economy of the kitchen often requires that whole fish be "butchered" on site. There is considerable loss when cleaning and portioning fish, as the edible portion may be only about 40 percent of the original weight. Typically, gutting a fish removes about 30 percent of its overall weight and removing the head, skin, and bones may account for another 20 to 30 percent. Generally, a 180- to 240-gram (6½- to 8½-ounce) portion is considered an appropriate *entrée* serving.

The gills must always be removed from fish that is to be served whole or from a head that will be used for a fish stock (*fumet*). This is because they can impart a bitter, sharp taste to the fish or the stock. They can be cut off using either a knife or scissors. When serving fish whole, the head and tail are often left on, both for an appealing presentation and for ease of turning during cooking. The head also offers tasty eating, particularly from the cheeks.

Guidelines for Preparing Fish

1. Using fish scissors or kitchen shears, carefully cut off the fins.

2. Holding the fish by the tail as tightly as you can and using a fish scaler, the edge of a spoon, or the back of a knife, remove the scales. Scrape up from the tail to the head, using short, firm strokes. Remove the scales from the entire fish. If the fish is very slippery, wrap a clean kitchen towel around your hand to help with the grip. This tends to be a very messy operation, so make sure that the work surface is covered for easy disposal of the slippery scales. The whole process can also be done in a kitchen sink to facilitate cleanup.

3. Using the scissors or a very sharp chef's knife, open the belly from the anus to the gills.

4. Using a sharp knife or scissors, cut off and discard the gills.

5. Using your fingertips, carefully pull out the entire intestinal track. If a roe sack (fish eggs) is evident, carefully remove it and set aside for cooking with the fish.

6. Using a spoon, carefully scrape out any viscera that remain in the cavity.

7. Thoroughly rinse the cavity under cold running water. If serving whole, the fish is ready to be cooked. If cutting into fillets, further butchering is required.

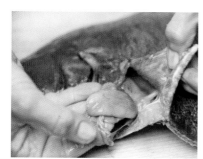

To cut fillets from flatfish:

1. Lay the fish on a clean cutting board.

2. Using a fillet knife, make a cut along the central backbone from the head to the tail.

3. Insert the blade of the knife at a shallow angle at either end of the backbone.

4. Using smooth, even strokes and keeping the blade side of the knife as close to the rib bones as possible, begin to cut away the fillet, lifting the flesh up and away as you cut the entire length of the fish.

5. Turn the fish over and repeat the process to remove the remaining fillet.

6. If a skinless fillet is preferred, lay the fillet skin side down on a clean work surface. Using a sharp knife and starting at the tail end, cut away about 2.5 centimeters (1 inch) of flesh from the skin. Using your fingertips, grasp the skin and pull it up and out as you cut away from yourself, using short strokes to separate the fillet from the skin.

 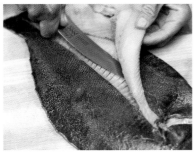  

To cut fillets from roundfish:

1. Lay the fish on a clean cutting board.

2. Using a fillet knife, make a 5-millimeter (3/16-inch)–deep cut along the backbone under the dorsal fin running from the head to the tail.

3. Insert the tip of the knife at a shallow angle into one end of the incision.

4. Using smooth strokes and keeping the blade side of the knife as close to the skeletal structure as possible, separate the fillet from the bones, lifting the flesh up and away as you cut along the entire length of the fish.

5. Turn the fish over and repeat the process to remove the remaining fillet.

6. If a skinless fillet is preferred, lay the fillet skin side down on a clean work surface. Using a sharp knife and starting at the tail end, cut away about 2.5 centimeters (1 inch) of flesh from the skin. Using your fingertips, grasp the skin and pull it up and out as you cut away from yourself, using short strokes to separate the fillet from the skin.

Methods of Cooking Fish

Although there are a multitude of methods to cook fish in classic French cuisine, the most typical is poaching in white wine and finishing the dish with a rich wine sauce. Among the classic methods for cooking fish, the following simple techniques are most commonly used.

À l'anglaise

This technique, which involves both breading and frying, is used for fish that have been cleaned and boned, usually whiting, sole, and brill.

1. Prepare the fish for cooking and pat dry.

2. Prepare three shallow containers; one with all-purpose flour, one with a mixture of an egg beaten with coarse salt to taste and about ¼ teaspoon vegetable oil (increase this amount as necessary, depending upon how much fish you are cooking; one egg will coat about 2 fillets), and one with fine white breadcrumbs. Line the filled bowls up — first the flour, then the egg, and finally the bread crumbs.

3. Season the fish with salt and pepper to taste.

4. Place the fish in the flour, turning to coat all sides and then lifting up and shaking off any excess.

5. Dip the floured fish into the egg mixture, turning to coat. Using your fingertips, skim off any excess egg from the fish.

6. Lay the fish in the breadcrumbs, pressing firmly to make sure that it is evenly coated. Turn and coat the remaining side.

7. Using the dull edge of a knife blade, make a quadrillage (see page 168) design on the top of the fish.

8. Heat a mixture of vegetable oil and butter in a poêle over medium heat.

9. Carefully place the fish, quadrilléed side down, into the hot fat.

10. When nicely browned, using a fish spatula, turn the fish over. Lower the heat and cook slowly until golden brown.

11. Remove from the pan and place on a double layer of paper towels to drain before serving.

Alternatively, the coated, seasoned fish can be deep-fried in 177°C (350°F) oil until golden brown.

À la française

This technique is used to grill fish fillets.

1. Prepare the fish for cooking and pat dry.

2. Clean, preheat, and oil a grill.

3. Using a cleaver or heavy spatula, flatten the fillets to an even thickness.

4. Using a sharp knife, trim off the uneven edges.

5. Using a pastry brush, lightly coat all sides of the fillet with clarified butter.

6. Coat one side of the fillet with a thin layer of fine white breadcrumbs.

7. Place on a platter, cover loosely with plastic film, and refrigerate for at least 30 minutes to allow the breadcrumbs to adhere.

8. Season the fillets with coarse salt and freshly ground pepper to taste.

9. Using the dull edge of a knife blade, make a quadrillage design on the breaded side of the fish.

10. Carefully place the fish, quadrilléed side down, onto the hot grill.

11. When the first side is nicely marked and light brown, turn and grill the remaining side.

Alternatively, the quadrilléed fish may be finished in a preheated oven.

Grilling

This method is used for small and medium whole fish as well as breaded fillets, *darnes* and *tronçons* (see page 261). A whole fish can also be *quadrilléed* on the grill, with the cooking finished in a preheated oven.

1. Prepare the fish for cooking and pat dry.

2. Clean, preheat, and oil a grill.

3. *Quadrillér* the fish by placing it presentation side first on the hot grill at a 30-degree angle toward the right.

4. After 1 to 2 minutes, slide a fork under the fish, taking care not to pierce it. Turn the fish at a 30-degree angle toward the left to finish the marking.

5. Cook for 1 to 2 minutes, then turn the fish and repeat the *quadrillage* process on the remaining side.

6. If desired or necessary, finish cooking in a preheated oven.

7. To serve, *lustrer* the fish with clarified butter, if desired, and garnish with parsley sprigs and lemon slices or wedges.

8. If serving a single serving whole fish, the head should be presented facing the left with the side that was first *quadrilléed* facing up.

Poaching in *Court Bouillon*

This method is used when the fish is to be briefly cooked and lightly flavored. *Court bouillon* literally means "short broth" and refers to the fact that it has been cooked for only a short time. Its purpose is to lightly flavor the flesh of a fish. The *court bouillon* is always cold when the fish is placed in it because if it is hot, the fish will contract and curl up and will not be presentable.

The liquid is then brought to 82°C (180°F), a temperature that should remain constant during the poaching process. The length of time that a fish cooks in a *court bouillon* depends on the size of the fish. If the fish is to be served cold, it should be allowed to cool in the *court bouillon*. This must be taken into consideration when determining the total cooking time, since the fish will continue to cook while the liquid remains hot.

The composition of a *court bouillon* may vary in the following ways:

À blanc: Water, milk, lemon slices, salt, black peppercorns, bay leaves, and thyme are combined and the fish is added before any cooking begins. Used for turbot and large brill.

Au vinaigre: Water, carrots, onions, salt, parsley sprigs, bay leaves, and thyme are simmered together for 30 minutes. White wine vinegar and black peppercorns are then added and the liquid is simmered for an additional 10 minutes. The finished *court bouillon* is strained and cooled thoroughly before being used to poach fish. Used for pike and hake.

Au vin blanc: The same ingredients and cooking process as for *au vinaigre*, except that the vinegar is replaced by dry white wine. This *bouillon* is used for fish with pink-colored flesh such as salmon and lake trout.

Au vin rouge: The same ingredients and cooking process as for *au vinaigre* except that the vinegar is replaced by red wine. Usually for a hearty piece of meat, usually beef.

À la nage: A fish that is served *à la nage* (swimming) is presented in the *court bouillon* in which it was cooked. The vegetables in this preparation must be cut evenly so that they make an attractive presentation. Water, white wine, or a combination of white wine and white wine vinegar, fluted and thinly sliced carrots, thinly sliced onion rings, parsley sprigs, salt, peppercorns, and a *bouquet garni* are combined and simmered for 40 minutes. Then the mixture is set aside until needed for service. When ready to serve, the fish is placed in the liquid and simmered for the appropriate amount of time. The *bouquet garni* is removed and the fish is served in a shallow bowl along with the *bouillon*. This variation is used for trout and other white-fleshed fish.

Au bleu: This technique is used exclusively for poaching live trout. However today it's not often we have the opportunity to work with live fish. To authentically prepare *truite au bleu*, you must begin with a live trout and first stun it with a wooden club or mallet before proceeding to gut and cook it. The best definition of this classic dish comes from Auguste Escoffier in his book *Ma Cuisine*: "Start with a live trout in a tank. Keep a shallow pan of salted and vinegared boiling water at the ready. Ten minutes before they are to be served, take the trout from the tank and stun them by hitting them on the head. Rapidly gut and clean them. Place them on a plate and sprinkle with vinegar. Slip them into the boiling water where they will immediately curl up and their flesh will flake. It only takes a few minutes to complete the cooking."

We follow this procedure to prepare a trout *au bleu* with whole, uncleaned fish available from the fishmonger:

1. Prepare a *court bouillon* of white wine, white wine vinegar, sliced carrots, sliced onions, parsley sprigs, salt, peppercorns, and a *bouquet garni*. Cook at a bare simmer for 25 minutes.

2. Do *not* wash the trout.

3. Hold the trout by the gill openings and remove the guts through the openings. Or make a small incision in the center of the trout's belly and carefully remove the guts.

4. Pour white wine vinegar over the trout. The protective mucous substance on the trout's surface will become iridescent and bluish.

5. Bring the *court bouillon* to a boil and add the trout. The nerves will immediately contract when the fish hits the boiling liquid and the fish will curl into a semicircle. This is a sign of freshness.

6. Simmer for about 3 minutes.

7. Using a skimmer, gently lift the fish from the hot liquid and place on a serving plate.

8. Decorate the plate with parsley sprigs and, if desired, serve with melted butter (*beurre fondue*) or white butter sauce softened with heavy cream (*beurre nantais*) and boiled potatoes (*pommes anglaise*, see page 118). *Truite au bleu* is traditionally presented tableside on a platter covered with white napkins to accentuate the blue color of the fish.

Braising (*Braiser*) Fish

This is a relatively simple cooking method that enhances the natural flavor of fish. It is extremely important in classic French cooking. In a **braiser**, a fish is placed on a bed of aromatic garnish, moistened with an aromatic liquid, and cooked in the oven. It is frequently basted with the aromatic juices. This method is often used for whole or large cuts of fish, as well as for meats.

The bed of garnish on which the fish is cooked (*fond de braisage*) provides the aromatic element of the dish and often determines the name: **bonne femme** contains shallots, mushrooms, and parsley; **dugléré** has shallots, onions, chopped fresh tomatoes, and parsley; **foyot** has shallots, meat glaze, and parsley.

The moistening liquid is generally made with fish *fumet* (see page 54) to which white wine (or other aromatic liquid such as red wine, champagne, or cider) has been added.

After the fish is cooked, the garnish and cooking liquid are reduced to make the sauce. Once cooked together, they are often bound with *beurre manié* (see page 62) or a cream reduction.

Some preparations are glazed under a salamander (or broiler). In that case, it is advisable to add a *sabayon* (see page 79) to the finished sauce to highlight the color and to stabilize the sauce so that it is less likely to break when glazed.

Poisson au Plat

This method is applied to fish that have been cut into fillets, *darnes*, or *tronçons*.

1. Butter the bottom of a shallow, oval ovenproof serving dish (preferably a decorative one that can come to the table) that can also be placed on the stovetop.

2. Preheat the oven to 177°C (350°F).

3. Add the garnish, which will be determined by the dish. Often, the garnish consists of shallot *ciselée*, minced mushrooms, chopped fresh tomatoes, and chopped parsley.

4. Place the fish on top of the garnish, and season with salt and pepper to taste. Moisten with just enough fish stock and white wine to come halfway up the sides of the fish.

5. Cover and bring to a boil over high heat.

6. Immediately transfer the dish to the oven, and bake, basting frequently, for half the time required for the specific recipe (or fish).

7. Uncover and continue cooking until the fish is cooked through and the pan juices are fully flavored.

8. Remove the fish from the oven, leaving the oven on. Using a fish spatula, carefully lift the fish from the pan and place on a platter.

9. *Monter au beurre* (see page 73) and then return the fish to the baking dish.

10. Return the fish to the hot oven and bake, basting several times, just until it is perfectly glazed.

11. Remove the baking dish from the oven and serve.

Poisson en Sauce

This method is also used for fish that have been cut into fillets, *darnes*, or *tronçons*.

1. Prepare the designated style of fish.

2. Butter a *sautoir*.

3. Preheat the oven to 177°C (350°F).

4. Evenly distribute the required garnish across the bottom of the pan.

5. Add the fish and season with salt and pepper to taste. Add enough fish stock and white wine to come halfway up the sides of the fish.

6. Cover the fish with parchment paper cut into a circle to fit the pot with a small hole cut in the center and place over high heat. Bring to a boil. Immediately transfer the pan to the oven and bake until fish is cooked through.

7. Remove from the oven and keep hot. Carefully pour the cooking liquid into a *russe* or *sauteuse* and place over high heat. Cook, without stirring, until reduced by four fifths. When the color deepens and the liquid thickens, add heavy cream and again bring to a boil.

8. Lower the heat and simmer until the sauce is thick enough to coat the back of a spoon (*nappant*). If desired, the sauce may also be thickened with a *velouté* (see page 60) or a *beurre manié*.

9. Remove the sauce from the heat and *monter au beurre*. Taste, and if necessary, adjust the seasoning with salt and pepper.

Poisson à la Meunière or à la Grenobloise

Meunière literally means "miller's wife" in French, so the name presumably acknowledges the skill of these women at this preparation. The technique may be used to cook several types of fish, either whole or cut into fillets, *darnes*, or *tronçons*. Sole *meunière* is probably the most famous of all classic dishes prepared in this manner.

When cooked *à la meunière*, fish is always seasoned, lightly floured, and then fried in clarified butter. Once the fish is removed from the pan, whole butter is added and browned to the nut-brown (*noisette*) stage. In French, this is referred to as *beurre noisette*. Fresh lemon juice and chopped parsley are added to the browned butter and then the hot butter mixture is spooned over the hot fish just before serving. Frogs' legs, scallops, and brains can also be prepared *à la meunière*. It is important that this dish be served extremely hot so that the butter does not begin to pool or solidify.

Poisson à la Grenobloise is a variation on the classic *meunière* preparation. The basic recipe is followed, but capers, finely diced lemon pulp, and croutons are added to the *beurre noisette* before serving.

1. Clean and portion the fish. Pat dry.

2. Season both sides with coarse salt and freshly ground pepper to taste.

3. Lightly coat each side with all-purpose flour, shaking off any excess. (Certain delicate types of fish, such as lemon sole, are often dipped in milk before being floured.)

4. Heat a combination of butter and vegetable oil in an oval fish *poêle* over medium heat.

5. Carefully place the floured fish in the hot fat, presentation side down.

6. Cook slowly, the time to be determined by the type and thickness of the fish. When the presentation side is nicely browned, using a fish spatula, turn the fish.

7. When cooked, transfer the fish to a serving dish.

8. Prepare the *beurre noisette*, adding the *Grenobloise* garnish if required.

9. Serve very hot.

Deep-frying

This technique may be used to cook a variety of fish that have been cut into fillets, *darnes*, or *tronçons*. It is also the preferred method of preparation for miniature whole fish, such as *goujon*, a French fish that is similar to the American smelt. When larger fish fillets are cut into strips about the same size as a *goujon*, they are called *goujonettes* and, they too, are always fried. Deep-frying is a superb medium for cooking fish because it cooks so quickly it does not allow the fish to dry out or toughen. When done properly, it creates a beautiful, crisp crust that surrounds moist meat. Fried fish is traditionally served with fried parsley sprigs.

The following preparation is used for deep-frying all types of fish:

1. The fish is either dipped in milk and then all-purpose flour or breaded *à l'anglaise*.

2. The oil is heated to 177°C (350°F) on an instant-read thermometer in a deep-fat fryer.

3. The floured or breaded fish is placed in the hot fat and fried until golden brown, the time determined by the type and thickness of the fish. Oil that has been used to fry fish must *never* be used for any other purpose as it will impart a fishy taste to any other food.

Theory

General Information About Fish *Mousseline*

A fish *mousseline* is a savory dish that is extremely light in texture (the word *mousse* means "foam" or "froth"). A fish *mousseline* is made from a forcemeat consisting of puréed raw fish, egg white, and heavy cream. A white fish *mousseline* may be tinted green with chlorophyll extracted from green plants (such as spinach or parsley) or tinted red with lobster or scallop roe. Pike, sole, flounder, whiting, scallops, or perch are fish commonly used to create a white *mousseline*. It can also be made with raw salmon to create a pink mousseline. Meat *mousselines* are made from poultry or veal using the same methods as for fish.

The most common stuffing for fish is made from a *mousseline* forcemeat mixture. It is used to stuff large fish or **paupiettes** (thin slices of fish that are stuffed, rolled, and tied) that are then braised, poached, or baked. The forcemeat mixture can also be used in hot fish *mousses* or *soufflés* or molded into *quenelles*.

The fish used to make a *mousseline* must be very cold and fresh, and the remaining ingredients must also be kept very cold throughout the preparation period. It is a good idea to chill the equipment to be used to help ensure that everything remains cold.

The puréed raw fish is passed through a fine sieve or *tamis* to give it a very smooth texture. It is then seasoned and bound with egg white and enriched with heavy cream. The *mousseline* is then placed in a mold or formed into a shape suitable for presentation and cooked either by baking or steaming.

Preparing Compound Butters (*Beurres Composée*s)

Compound butters are created by incorporating one or more aromatic ingredients into unsalted butter. It is appropriate that we discuss these butters here, as one of the most common classic presentations for fish is a slice of cold compound butter placed on top of a hot piece of fish so that it melts over the top at service. However, meat and poultry are also finished in this way.

Composed butters are generally prepared by whipping butter **en pommade** (to a thick, creamy consistency) and then blending in raw or cooked flavoring ingredients—the variety is almost endless. The mixture is then formed into a neat log shape, wrapped in plastic film, and refrigerated until firm. At service, a thick slice is cut from the log and placed on the hot fish so that the melting begins as the item is being served. Uncooked compound butters are used as a garnish that will melt into a sauce. Cooked compound butters are used to finish sauces.

Some compound butters are made from the shells of crustaceans. In this case, the shells and an equal amount of butter by weight are ground with a mortar and pestle. The mixture is then melted in a *bain-marie* to extract the maximum flavor from the shells and is strained through a fine sieve into a bowl placed in an ice bath so that the compound butter hardens almost immediately. The shell remains are discarded.

Chef's Tip

"To properly form a goujonette, *the fish should be rolled between your palms on a 45-degree angle to create a pointed tip."*
Chef Dominick Cerrone

Some Classic Compound Butters

	Compound Butter	Flavoring Element	Use
Uncooked Butters	Anchovy butter (*beurre d'anchois*)	Anchovy fillets or sauce	Grilled meat or fish
	Shallot butter (*beurre d'echalote*)	Shallots	Grilled meat or fish
	Snail butter (*beurre d'escargots*)	Garlic, shallots	Snails
	Tarragon butter (*beurre d'estragon*)	Tarragon	Fish
	Maître d' butter (*beurre maître d'hotel*)	Lemon juice, parsley	Grilled meat or fish
	Mustard butter (*beurre moutarde*)	Dijon mustard	Meat and fish

Some Classic Compound Butters (continued)

Compound Butter	Flavoring Element	Use
Horseradish butter (*beurre raifort*)	Horseradish	Meat
Bercy butter (*beurre Bercy*)	Shallots, white wine, marrow, parsley	Meat and fish
Hotel-style butter (*beurre hôtelier*)	Lemon juice, parsley, *duxelles*	Meat and fish
Wine-flavored butter (*marchand de vin*)	Lemon juice, parsley, shallots, red wine, meat glaze	Grilled meat

Cooked Butters

Compound Butter	Flavoring Element	Use
Lobster butter (*beurre homard*)	Lobster shells	*Sauce cardinale, sauce homard*
Crayfish butter (*beurre d'ecrévisses*)	Crayfish shells	*Sauce Nantua*
Red butter (*beurre rouge*)	Various crustacean shells	To finish *sauce poisson*

Demonstration

Filet de Sole Bonne Femme (Fillet of Sole with Vegetables)
Serves 4
Estimated time to complete: 90 minutes

Ingredients	Equipment
1-kilogram (2¼ pounds) whole sole or flounder, cleaned and filleted into 4 pieces (save the bones)	Chef's knife
	Russe
25 grams (1 tablespoon plus 2 teaspoons) unsalted butter	*Chinois*
75 grams (2½ ounces) button mushrooms	Medium bowl
30 grams (1 ounce) shallots, *ciselé*	Pastry brush
40 grams (1½ ounces) onion, *émincé*	*Sautoir*
40 grams (1½ ounces) leek, green part only, chopped	Parchment paper
Bouquet garni	Small *sautoir* or *russe*
Coarse salt and freshly ground pepper to taste	Fish spatula
45 milliliters (3 tablespoons) dry white wine	Platter
250 milliliters (1 cup plus 1 tablespoon) heavy cream	Aluminum foil
10 grams (2 tablespoons) chopped fresh flat-leaf parsley	Heatproof bowl
5 milliliters (1 teaspoon) fresh lemon juice	Electric mixer and whisk attachment or bowl and whisk
	5 heatproof dinner plates

Prepare your *mise en place*.

Fillet the fish into 4 pieces, reserving the bone; you will use them to make stock. Store the fish in the refrigerator until ready to cook. To prepare the garnish, remove the stems and any brown parts from the mushrooms and set the trimmings aside for the stock. Slice the mushroom caps vertically and combine them with the shallots. Set aside.

To make the fish stock, rinse the fish bones under cold running water to remove all traces of blood. Using a chef's knife, chop the bones into small pieces. Set aside.

Heat 10 grams (2 teaspoons) of the butter in a *russe* over medium heat. Add the onion and leek and sauté for 5 minutes or just until the vegetables have sweated their liquid but not taken on any color. Add the reserved fish bones and sweat for an additional 3 minutes. Add just enough cold water to cover along with the reserved mushroom trimmings and the *bouquet garni*. Bring to a simmer and cook gently for 30 minutes.

Remove from the heat, strain through a *chinois* into a medium bowl, and set aside.

Using a pastry brush, lightly coat the bottom of a *sautoir* large enough to comfortably hold the fish fillets with the remaining 15 grams (1 tablespoon) butter. Sprinkle the mushroom mixture over the bottom and then place the fish on top. (The fillets may be left flat or folded, as desired.) Season with salt and pepper to taste.

Add the white wine and enough of the reserved *fumet* to come halfway up the sides of the fillets. Cover with a piece of parchment paper cut to fit the top and place over medium-high heat.

Bring to a simmer, then immediately lower the heat and cook at a bare simmer for about 3 minutes or until slightly underdone. (It is best, especially if using flounder, to leave the fish a little bit underdone, as it will cook further during the glazing process.

To make the sauce, place 200 milliliters (14 tablespoons) of the cream in a small *sautoir* or *russe* over medium heat and bring to a simmer. Lower the heat and cook, watching carefully to prevent the liquid from boiling over, for about 10 minutes or until reduced by about a third and thickened. Remove from the heat.

Using a fish spatula, remove the fillets from the pan and set aside on a platter to drain. Tent lightly with aluminum foil to keep warm.

Return the pan to the stovetop over medium-high heat and bring to a boil. Boil for about 10 minutes or until reduced by half. Stir in the reduced cream and return to a simmer. Simmer for about 5 minutes or until the sauce is thick enough to coat the back of a spoon (*nappant*).

Remove from the heat and transfer to a heatproof bowl. Set aside to cool slightly.

Using an electric mixer or a bowl and a whisk, beat the remaining 50 milliliters (3½ tablespoons) cream until it holds a medium peak.

Fold about 25 milliliters (1½ tablespoons) of the whipped cream into the sauce along with the parsley and lemon juice. Taste, and if necessary, adjust the seasoning with salt and pepper.

Place a spoonful of the sauce on a heatproof plate and place under the salamander (or broiler) to test for consistency and color of the glaze. It should be the consistency and color of thick cream. If necessary, add additional whipped cream to thin the sauce.

Place one fillet on each of four heatproof serving plates. Nap each one with some of the sauce, allowing the mushrooms to fall naturally over the fish.

Place the plates under the salamander (or broiler) and heat just until the fillets are nicely glazed. Serve immediately.

Demonstration

Poisson en Papillote (Fish Cooked in Parchment)

Serves 4

Estimated time to complete: 90 minutes

Ingredients	Equipment
	Chef's knife
	2 pastry brushes

For the fish

2 large (about 900 grams or 2 pounds) bass
30 milliliters (2 tablespoons) vegetable oil
3 grams (2 teaspoons) chopped fresh thyme

For the *fondue*

10 grams (2 teaspoons) unsalted butter or olive oil
15 grams (½ ounce) onion, *ciselé*
15 grams (½ ounce) shallots, *ciselé*
1 clove garlic, peeled and crushed
200 grams (7 ounces) ripe tomatoes, *émondé* and *concassée*
5 grams (¼ teaspoon) sugar, optional
Coarse salt and freshly ground pepper to taste, optional

For the *duxelles*

200 grams (7 ounces) button mushrooms
2½ milliliters (½ teaspoon) fresh lemon juice
25 grams (1 tablespoon plus 2 teaspoons) unsalted butter
30 grams (1 ounce) shallots, *ciseler*
Coarse salt and freshly ground pepper to taste

For the garnish

10 grams (2 teaspoons) unsalted butter
Coarse salt and freshly ground pepper to taste
50 grams (1¼ ounces) carrots, *julienne*
50 grams (1¼ ounces) leeks, *julienne*
50 grams (1¼ ounces) celery, *julienne*
To finish the dish:
4 sprigs fresh thyme
30 milliliters (2 tablespoons) dry white wine
1 egg white
30 milliliters (2 tablespoons) vegetable oil

Equipment

Chef's knife
2 pastry brushes
Plate
Plastic film
2 *sautoirs* or *russes*
Parchment paper
Bowl
Colander
Small bowl
Whisk
Baking tray
4 warm dinner plates

Prepare your *mise en place.*

To prepare the fish: Clean and portion the fish into four 150-gram (5¼-ounce) skin-on fillets. Using a chef's knife, lightly score the skin side of the fillets, making two perpendicular lines. This will prevent the skin from contracting (which causes the fish to curl during cooking).

Using a pastry brush and the vegetable oil, lightly coat each fillet and then sprinkle with chopped thyme. Place on a plate, cover with plastic film, and refrigerate.

To make the *fondue*, heat the butter or oil in a *sautoir* or *russe* over medium heat. Add the onion, shallots, and garlic and sauté for about 5 minutes or until the vegetables have sweated their liquid and are soft but have not taken on any color. Stir in the tomatoes and, if they are underripe and lacking in flavor, the sugar. Cover with a piece of parchment paper that has been cut to fit the pan and has a small hole cut in the center.

Lower the heat and cook for about 12 minutes or until the excess liquid has evaporated. Taste and, if necessary, adjust the seasoning with salt and pepper. Remove from the heat and set aside.

For the *duxelles*, trim the mushrooms of any tough stems or discoloration. If they are not very white, place them in a bowl of cold water, add a dash of the lemon juice, and swish to rinse. Drain the mushrooms and then chop them very fine. Set aside.

Heat the butter in a *sautoir* or *russe* over medium heat. Add the shallots and sauté for about 5 minutes or until the shallots have sweated their liquid but not taken on any color. Stir in the mushrooms and the remaining lemon juice. Cover with a piece of parchment paper that has been cut to fit the pan and has a small hole cut in the center. Cook, without disturbing, for about 7 minutes or until there is no liquid left in the pan. Remove from the heat and adjust the seasoning with salt and pepper to taste.

To prepare the garnish: Using the butter and salt and pepper to taste, cook the carrots, leeks, and celery *julienne à l'étuvé*. Set aside.

Cut two large sheets of parchment paper in half crosswise. Cut each half into a heart shape about 30.5 centimeters (12 inches) tall and 45.75 centimeters (18 inches) wide.

To assemble: Place 30 milliliters (2 tablespoons) each of the mushroom *duxelles* and the tomato *fondue* next to each other in the center of each parchment heart. Place a fillet on top, skin side up. Place an equal portion of the garnish on top of each fillet. Top with a sprig of thyme and a drizzle of white wine.

Place the egg white in a small bowl and lightly beat it with a whisk.

Using a pastry brush, lightly coat the edges of the parchment hearts with beaten egg white. Fold the heart shape in half to cover the fish and press the edges together to seal. Using the pastry brush, lightly coat the sealed edges with the egg white. Make a series of short folds along the edge to reinforce the packet. If space allows, you can again brush the sealed edges with beaten egg white and again make a series of short folds along the edge to make an even tighter seal.

Using a pastry brush, lightly coat the top of the packet with the vegetable oil. If not cooking immediately, refrigerate until ready to cook.

When ready to serve, preheat the oven to 233°C (450°F).

Place the packets (*papillotes*) on a baking tray in the oven. Bake for about 8 minutes or until the packets puff up and the fish is cooked through. Remove from the oven and place one *papillote* on each of four warm dinner plates. Serve immediately, cutting open the packet at the table so that each diner can enjoy both the presentation and the delicious aroma when the steam puffs out of the packet.

Demonstration

Basic Fish *Mousseline*

Makes approximately 1 pound

Estimated time to complete: 30 minutes

Ingredients	Equipment
450 grams (1 pound) fish fillets (see note)	Food processor fitted with metal blade
1 large egg white, chilled	*Tamis*
240 milliliters (1 cup) heavy cream, or as needed	Bowl scraper
Flavoring ingredients as required for the specific *mousseline* recipe	Medium chilled bowl
Coarse salt and freshly ground pepper to taste	Plastic film
	Ice bath
	Wooden spoon
	Small saucepan
	Slotted spoon

Prepare your *mise en place*, remembering that all ingredients and equipment should be kept cold at all times.

Place the fish in a food processor fitted with the metal blade and process to a smooth purée.

Scrape the puréed fish from the processor bowl to a *tamis* and, using a bowl scraper, press the purée through the *tamis* into a chilled bowl. The texture should be extremely smooth. Cover with plastic film and refrigerate for about 1 hour or until very cold.

Place the bowl with fish purée in a bowl of ice and, using a wooden spoon, beat in the egg white.

When the egg white is incorporated, begin beating in the cream. Begin with about half of the cream and continue to add it as needed until the mixture is very light and creamy. If the mixture does not stay cold, return it to the refrigerator until well chilled.

Season with whatever seasonings and flavorings are required for your recipe.

Bring a small saucepan of water to a boil over high heat. Lower the heat to a gentle simmer. To check for quality, shape a small amount of the mixture into a *quenelle* and carefully drop it into the simmering water. Poach for about 3 minutes or until cooked through. Using a slotted spoon, lift the *quenelle* from the water. Taste, and if necessary, adjust the seasoning, flavoring, and texture; then proceed with your recipe.

Demonstration

Filet de Truite Grenobloise
(Trout Fillet with Lemon, Butter, and Parsley Sauce)

Serves 4

Estimated time to complete: 30 minutes

Ingredients	Equipment
2 trout, filleted	Kitchen tweezers
100 grams (7 tablespoons) unsalted butter	Plate
75 grams (about 2 to 3 slices) white bread, cut into 7-millimeter (¼-inch) squares	Plastic film
2 lemons	Medium *sautoir*
Coarse salt and freshly ground pepper to taste	Slotted spatula
150 grams (5¼ ounces) all-purpose flour	Paper towels
50 grams (3 tablespoons plus 1 teaspoon) clarified butter	Chef's knife
40 grams (1½ ounces) capers, drained	Paring knife
10 grams (2 tablespoons) chopped fresh-flat leaf parsley	*Poêle*
	Fish spatula
	Warm serving plate
	Aluminum foil

Prepare your *mise en place.*

Carefully remove the tiny bones from the trout fillets with kitchen tweezers. Place the fish on a plate, cover with plastic film, and refrigerate until ready to use.

Heat 30 grams (2 tablespoons) of the butter in a medium *sautoir* over medium heat. Add the bread cubes and sauté for about 5 minutes or until golden brown. Using a slotted spatula, transfer the croutons to a double layer of paper towels to drain. Set aside.

Using a chef's knife, slice the top and bottom off the lemons. Peel the rind off one of the lemons so that no pith or fiber remains attached to the flesh (*peler à vif*).

Using a paring knife and cutting against the membrane, carefully remove the lemon sections (*suprêmes*) from the peeled lemon. Cut each section into 1.3-centimeter (½-inch) pieces. Set aside.

Using a chef's knife, cut the remaining lemon crosswise into thin slices and then cut the slices in half. Set aside to be used as plate decoration.

Remove the fillets from the refrigerator. Season with salt and pepper to taste and lightly dust with flour, shaking off any excess.

Heat the clarified butter in a *poêle* over high heat. Carefully place the fillets in the hot butter, presentation side down, and cook for about 3 minutes or until golden. Using a fish spatula, carefully turn and cook the remaining side for about 3 minutes or until the fish is cooked through and golden brown.

Transfer the fillets from the pan to a warm serving plate. Lightly tent with aluminum foil to keep warm.

Using paper towels, wipe the *poêle* clean.

Return the *poêle* to medium heat. Add the remaining whole butter and cook for about 5 minutes or

until it reaches the *noisette* stage. Add the capers and
parsley along with the diced lemon and cook to just
barely heat through. Add the croutons and toss to
coat. Immediately spoon the butter mixture over the
fillets. Garnish the plate with the reserved lemon
slices and serve.

Demonstration

Goujonettes de Sole aux Deux Sauces

(Fried Slices of Sole with Two Sauces)

Serves 4
Estimated time to complete: 90 minutes

Ingredients	Equipment

For the fish

One 750-gram (1-pound, 7-ounce) sole
  or flounder, cleaned and filleted

2 large eggs

30 milliliters (2 tablespoons) peanut oil

Coarse salt to taste

150 grams (5¼ ounces) all-purpose flour

250 grams (8¾ ounces) white breadcrumbs

Freshly ground pepper to taste

For the tartar sauce

1 large egg yolk

10 grams (⅓ ounce) Dijon mustard

10 milliliters (2 teaspoons) white wine vinegar

Coarse salt and freshly ground white pepper to taste

150 milliliters (⅔ cup) peanut oil

10 grams (⅓ ounce) chopped *cornichons*

10 grams (⅓ ounce) capers, drained

5 grams (1 tablespoon) fresh chervil, *haché*

5 grams (1 tablespoon) fresh tarragon, *haché*

5 grams (1 tablespoon) fresh flat-leaf parsley, *haché*

For the red pepper sauce

20 milliliters (4 teaspoons) olive oil

300 grams (10½ ounces) red bell peppers, washed,
  seeded, cored, and cut into strips

Equipment:

Chef's knife

3 small shallow bowls

Plate

Sauté pan

Parchment paper

Sautoir or *russe*

Blender or food processor

Chinois

Small bowl

Rubber spatula

Small saucepan

Wooden spoon

Bain-marie

Deep-fat fryer

Instant-read thermometer,
optional

Slotted spatula

Paper towels

4 warm dinner plates

1 clove garlic, peeled and crushed
Coarse salt and freshly ground pepper to taste
125 milliliters (½ cup plus 1 teaspoon) heavy cream

To finish the dish
2 liters (2 quarts, 4 ounces) vegetable oil
Handful fresh curly-leaf parsley sprigs, washed and thoroughly dried
Potato *gaufrettes*, optional (see page 114)
8 lemon wedges
Coarse salt to taste

Note

It is possible to season and flour the *goujonettes* at the last minute. If you do, it will be especially important to shake off the excess flour. A good method is to set the *goujonettes* in a drum sieve on top of a bowl and shake the sieve back and forth. Fry as instructed.

Prepare your *mise en place*.

Using a chef's knife, cut the fillets on the bias to form pieces about 5 centimeters long by 1 centimeter thick (2 inches by ⅜ inch).

Beat the eggs, peanut oil, and salt together in a small shallow bowl. Place the flour in another shallow bowl and the breadcrumbs in a third. Place the bowls in a row with the flour first, followed by the egg mixture, and then the breadcrumbs (see note).

Season the fish with salt and pepper to taste. Roll the *goujonettes* in the flour, lifting them up and shaking off any excess. Dip them into the egg mixture and

then roll them in the breadcrumbs. Shape the coated fillets by rolling them on the work surface. Place the coated fillets on a plate and refrigerate, uncovered, until ready to cook.

To make the tartar sauce (*sauce tartare*), use the egg, mustard, vinegar, salt, white pepper, and oil to make a mayonnaise as directed on page 87. When the mayonnaise has thickened, stir in the *cornichons*, capers, chervil, tarragon, and parsley. Taste, and if necessary, adjust the seasoning. Cover and refrigerate until ready to use.

To make the red pepper sauce (*sauce aux poivrons rouge*), heat the olive oil in a sauté pan over medium heat. Add the bell pepper strips and cook, stirring occasionally, for about 5 minutes or just until the peppers have sweated their liquid. Add the garlic along with salt and pepper to taste and just enough water to moisten the pan (about 3 tablespoons). Cover with a piece of parchment paper that has been cut to

fit the pan and has a small hole cut in the center. This will cause steaming and keep the peppers from browning. Cook, covered, for about 20 minutes or until the peppers are almost mushy. Remove from the heat.

While the peppers are cooking, reduce the heavy cream. Place the cream in a *sautoir* or *russe* over medium heat and bring to a simmer. Lower the heat and cook without stirring, watching carefully to prevent the liquid from boiling over, for about 10 minutes or until reduced by about one half and thickened. Remove from the heat.

Place the peppers in a blender or food processor fitted with the metal blade and process to a smooth purée. Add a touch of water if the peppers are too thick. Transfer to a *chinois* set over a small bowl and, using a rubber spatula, press to strain.

Transfer the pepper purée to a small saucepan over medium-high heat. Bring to a simmer and then lower the heat and cook for about 5 minutes or until slightly thick. Begin adding the reduced cream, a tablespoonful at a time, stirring until saucelike and delicately colored. You may not need all of the cream. Taste, and if necessary, adjust the seasoning with salt and pepper to taste. Transfer to a *bain-marie* to keep warm until service.

Heat the vegetable oil to 180°C-185°C (355°F-365°F) in a deep-fat fryer, using an instant-read thermometer if needed to confirm the temperarture.

Remove the *goujonettes* from the refrigerator. Carefully plunge them into the hot oil and fry for about 3 minutes or until golden brown and crisp. Using a slotted spatula transfer the fish to a double layer of paper towels to drain.

Quickly drop the parsley sprigs into the hot oil; they will crisp and brown immediately. Transfer to a double layer of paper towels to drain.

Sprinkle the fried fish and parsley with salt to taste. Serve hot, with an equal portion of the *goujonettes* placed in a basket made from potato *gaufrettes*, if desired, on each of four warm dinner plates garnished with the red pepper sauce and the tartar sauce. (You can also place the tartar sauce in a radicchio leaf, a hollowed cucumber cup, or a halved tomato.) Put a few fried parsley sprigs on top of the fish and two lemon wedges on each plate and serve.

André Soltner | *Dean of Classic Studies, The French Culinary Institute*

Filet de Poisson Confit à l'Huile d'Olive (Fish Fillet Confit)

Serves 4

This simple dish was extremely popular at my New York City restaurant, Lutèce. *Confit* was a term I used only when cooking duck and pork when I was a young chef, but it is now used to describe slowly cooked fruits and vegetables. The lemon-scented oil can be used to season or sauté vegetables, pork, poultry, and fish.

475 milliliters (2 cups) olive oil
12 large lemon slices
8 large capers, drained
Four 170-gram (6-ounce) fish fillets (such as halibut, bass, or salmon)
Sea salt and freshly ground pepper to taste
30 milliliters (2 tablespoons) white wine vinegar
30 milliliters (2 tablespoons) fresh basil-leaf purée
10 grams (2 tablespoons) fresh flat-leaf parsley, *haché*

Prepare your *mise en place.*

Preheat the oven to 93°C (200°F).

Heat the oil in a heavy-bottomed casserole over low heat to 83°C (205°F) on an instant-read thermometer. Add the lemon slices and capers and cook slowly for about 30 minutes or until the lemons are very tender.

About 10 minutes before the lemons are ready, season the fish with salt and pepper to taste and let stand for 10 minutes.

Remove 60 milliliters (¼ cup) of the oil from the casserole and place it in a small sauté pan. Set aside.

Carefully add the seasoned fish to the casserole. Transfer the pan to the oven and cook the fish for about 15 minutes or until just cooked through.

While the fish is cooking, prepare the sauce. Place the reserved oil over medium heat. When hot, add the vinegar and basil purée. Cook for a minute or two to just heat. Remove from the heat.

Remove the fish from the oven and place one fillet on each of four dinner plates. Spoon some of the lemons and capers over the fish. Sprinkle with parsley and spoon the basil sauce around the plates. Serve immediately.

Wylie Dufresne

Chef-Owner, wd~50, New York City
The French Culinary Institute, Class of January 1993

Halibut, Smoked Mashed Potatoes, Pickled Mushrooms, and Red Pepper Oil

Serves 4

It is said that I push the limits of culinary expression, and I guess that I sometimes do. However, it is my experience at FCI that has allowed me the base from which I can explore new methods and techniques of preparing familiar and not-so-familiar foods. This dish has some simple elements and some exotic ones, but I think that they come together to express classic ideas. (Note: Most of the components require advance preparation.)

Four 200-gram (7-ounce) pieces halibut or other firm, white fish
Coarse salt to taste
Cayenne pepper to taste
45 milliliters (3 tablespoons) clarified butter
Smoked Mashed Potatoes (recipe follows)
Pickled Mushrooms (recipe follows)
Crispy Fish Skin (recipe follows)
5 grams (1 tablespoon) chopped fresh tarragon
Red Pepper Oil (recipe follows)

Prepare your *mise en place.*

Season the halibut with salt and cayenne to taste.

Heat the clarified butter in a large sauté pan over low heat. Add the seasoned fish and cook very slowly, spooning the butter over the top, for about 7 minutes or just until the fish is barely cooked through.

To serve, place an equal portion of the mashed potatoes in the center of each of four dinner plates. Spoon an equal portion of the mushrooms beside the potatoes. Sprinkle the fish skin and tarragon over the mushrooms. Place a piece of fish on top of the potatoes and drizzle the pepper oil all around the plate. Serve immediately.

Smoked Mashed Potatoes

3 large russet potatoes, peeled
3 Yukon Gold potatoes, peeled
57 grams (¼ cup) unsalted butter, softened
237 milliliters (1 cup) hot heavy cream
Coarse salt and freshly ground pepper to taste

Prepare your *mise en place.*

Place all the potatoes in a large saucepan with cold water to cover by 2.5 centimeters (1 inch) over medium-high heat. Bring to a boil, then lower the heat and simmer for about 25 minutes or until the potatoes are tender when pierced with the point of a small, sharp knife. Remove from the heat and drain well.

Prepare a smoker using 1 cup wood chips.

Place the potatoes in the hot smoker and smoke until the chips are burned out.

Remove the potatoes from the smoker. Using a ricer, push the potatoes into a mixing bowl. Add the butter and cream and fold to blend well. Season with salt and pepper to taste and serve hot.

If not serving immediately, place in a *bain marie* and keep warm until ready to serve.

Pickled Mushrooms

113 grams (½ cup) sugar
950 milliliters (4 cups) water
950 milliliters (4 cups) white wine vinegar
14 grams (1 tablespoon) coarse salt
10 grams (1 tablespoon) toasted cumin seeds
10 grams (1 tablespoon) toasted fennel seeds
10 grams (1 tablespoon) toasted coriander seeds
1.5 grams (¼ teaspoon) red pepper flakes
57 grams (½ cup) shiitake mushroom *julienne*
57 grams (½ cup) honshimeji mushrooms
57 grams (½ cup) enoki mushrooms
4 fresh shiso leaves

Prepare your *mise en place.*

Place the sugar in a heavy-bottomed saucepan over medium heat. Cook, stirring frequently, for about 5 minutes or until the sugar has caramelized. Add the water, vinegar, salt, cumin, fennel, coriander, and red pepper flakes. Bring to a boil, then remove from the heat and set aside for 20 minutes.

Place the mushrooms in a nonreactive container. Pour the vinegar mixture through a fine sieve over the mushrooms. Add the shiso leaves, cover, and marinate for at least 24 hours before using. It will keep, covered and refrigerated, for at least one week.

Crispy Fish Skin

1 large piece halibut skin, cleaned of any flesh
    and scales

Prepare your *mise en place*.

Place the fish skin on a wire rack in a cool, dry spot and let stand at least 12 hours or until quite dry.

Preheat the oven to 135°C (275°F).

Place the dried skin between two sheets of Silpat or aluminum foil on a baking sheet. Bake for 1 hour or until very dry and crisp.

Remove from the oven and place on a wire rack to cool.

When cool, cut into small triangles. Use as directed in the recipe.

Red Pepper Oil

4 red bell peppers, well-washed, stemmed, seeded,
    and roughly chopped
About 237 milliliters (1 cup) grapeseed oil

Prepare your *mise en place*.

Place the peppers in an electric dehydrator set at 52°C (125°F) and dry for 3 days or until thoroughly dried.

Place the dried peppers in a spice grinder or blender and process to a fine powder.

Place the powder in a blender and, with the motor running, slowly add the oil until a thick sauce has formed. Transfer the mixture to a *chinois* and, using a spatula, firmly press the mixture through the sieve.

Store in a nonreactive container, covered, until ready to use.

Chef Daniele Kay
Executive Chef, Takashimaya, New York City
The French Culinary Institute, Class of February 1989

Broiled Salmon in "Barbecue" Sauce

Serves 4

This simple dish is made complete by the gentle marination and the beautiful caramelization of the fish, both techniques I remember from my days in the FCI classroom.

   The sauce is a long-time favorite of mine that I learned from a wonderful American chef, the late Patrick Clark. Not only does it work on fish, it is terrific for poultry, pork, mashed potatoes, couscous, and other grains. (This recipe makes a lot of sauce and will keep for weeks in the refrigerator. You need only about a cup for the salmon.)

Four 227-gram (8-ounce) salmon fillets
"Barbecue" Sauce (recipe follows)

Prepare your *mise en place.*

Generously coat both sides of the salmon with the sauce. You will use about 240 milliliters (1 cup). Place on a platter, cover with plastic film, and refrigerate for 1 hour.

Preheat the broiler or oil and preheat a grill.

Remove the fish from the refrigerator, uncover, and let stand for about 10 minutes to come to room temperature.

Place the salmon under the broiler or on the grill and broil or grill, turning once, for about 7 minutes or until the fish is beautifully caramelized and just cooked through.

Place the salmon on a serving platter and drizzle a little additional sauce around the plate.

"Barbecue" Sauce

240 milliliters (1 cup) seasoned rice wine vinegar
120 milliliters (½ cup) low-sodium soy sauce
Juice of 2 limes
1 kilogram (about 2½ cups) honey
280 grams (1 cup) ketchup
3 whole star anise pods
2 cinnamon sticks

Prepare your *mise en place.*

Place the vinegar, soy sauce, and lime juice in a medium nonreactive saucepan. Stir in the honey and ketchup. Add the star anise and cinnamon and place over medium heat. Bring to a boil, stirring frequently. Lower the heat and simmer for about 30 minutes or until slightly reduced and thickened.

Remove from the heat and strain through a *chinois* into a clean, nonreactive container. Cover and refrigerate until ready to use.

Chef Nino Antuzzi

Chef/Owner, Red Restaurant, Huntington, New York
The French Culinary Institute, Class of April 1990

Roasted Codfish with Lemon-Caper Emulsion and Artichoke *Ragoût*

Serves 4

This is an easy but aromatic and satisfying dish, enriched by the simple *beurre blanc* sauce. I find that, although diners often say they don't want to eat butter, they always seem to enjoy this classic French sauce. I have used this traditional sauce with a zesty Italian-seasoned *ragoût*.

227 grams (1 cup) unsalted butter
2 shallots, minced
Juice of 2 lemons
28 grams (2 tablespoons) capers, drained
237 milliliters (1 cup) dry white wine

Coarse salt and freshly ground pepper to taste
Four 170-gram (6-ounce) cod fillets, skin removed
30 milliliters (2 tablespoons) olive oil
Artichoke *Ragoût* (recipe follows)
4 caperberries (see note)

Prepare your *mise en place*.

Preheat the oven to 204°C (400°F).

Melt 28 grams (2 tablespoons) of the butter in a small sauté pan over medium heat. Add the shallots and sauté for about 3 minutes or until translucent. Add the lemon juice and capers, stirring to combine. Add the wine and bring to a simmer. Season with salt and pepper to taste and continue simmering for about 10 minutes or until reduced by half.

Transfer to a blender and, with the motor running, begin adding the remaining butter, a bit at a time. Process until the sauce is smooth and emulsified. Transfer to a *bain marie* to keep warm until ready to serve.

Season the fish with salt and pepper.

Heat the olive oil in a large, ovenproof sauté pan over medium-high heat. When it is very hot but not smoking, add the fish and sear one side for 3 minutes. Carefully turn the fillets and transfer the pan to the oven. Roast for about 6 minutes or until the fish is just set in the center.

To serve, spoon an equal portion of the *ragoût* in the center of each of four serving plates. Place a codfish fillet on top of the *ragoût*. Drizzle about 2 tablespoons of the emulsion over the fish and around the plate. Garnish with a caperberry and serve.

Artichoke *Ragoût*

90 milliliters (6 tablespoons) olive oil
8 baby artichokes, well-washed, outer leaves trimmed, and quartered
1 Italian eggplant, peeled, trimmed, and cut into a small dice
5 Italian plum tomatoes, peeled, cored, seeded, and diced
Coarse salt and freshly ground pepper to taste
2 cloves garlic, minced
15 grams (3 tablespoons) chopped fresh flat-leaf parsley

Prepare your *mise en place*.

Heat 30 milliliters (2 tablespoons) of the olive oil in a medium sauté pan over medium heat. Add the artichokes and sauté for about 7 minutes or until starting to color and soften. Transfer the artichokes to a bowl.

Return the pan to medium heat, adding an additional 30 milliliters (2 tablespoons) of olive oil. Add the eggplant and sauté for about 5 minutes or until tender. Scrape the eggplant into the bowl with the artichokes.

Again, return the pan to medium heat, adding an additional 30 milliliters (2 tablespoons) of olive oil. Add the tomatoes and sauté for about 5 minutes or until very soft. Scrape the tomatoes into the bowl with the other vegetables.

When ready to serve, return the vegetable mixture to the sauté pan over medium heat. Season with salt and pepper to taste. When hot, stir in the garlic and parsley and stir to heat through. Serve immediately.

Note

Imported from Spain, caperberries are left whole, complete with stems, and brined. They are generally used only as a garnish.

Session 16

Working with Shellfish

Theory

General Information About Shellfish (*Les Coquillages*)

One of the most intriguing culinary questions remains "who first had the courage to dine on the hard-shelled and somewhat vicious-looking creatures of the sea?" The answer is probably quite simple — someone who was extremely hungry! Whoever it was, we do know that diets that included shellfish have been with us for centuries. Throughout the development of civilization, shellfish have offered a significant source of nutrition.

The French are particularly adept at preparing shellfish. Paris is known for its *assiette de fruits de mer,* a fabulous tiered presentation of both raw and cooked seafood. The south of France offers the extraordinary fish stew *bouillabaisse,* and Marseilles is famous for its *soupe de poisson de Marseilles.*

Today, shellfish, depending upon their type, are considered both an inexpensive source of protein (mussels) and a luxury food (lobster). The demand is so great that many types are now aqua-farmed to meet consumer needs. Some shellfish, such as shrimp, come to the United States market from all over the world, while others, such as lobster, are sourced primarily from a specific area. Most shellfish are delicately fleshed creatures that can be eaten raw as well as cooked in a wide array of preparations. They are all high in protein, iron, and vitamin B but relatively low in calories and fat.

Because of their delicacy, most shellfish require little cooking. Their connective tissue is fragile and they have little fat to add moisture. When heated, the protein molecules break down and force out moisture, so shellfish should be cooked only until the protein begins to coagulate, which generally happens within a few minutes, at the most. The longer it is cooked, the more rubbery and tough it becomes.

Shellfish can be divided into three distinct categories:

○ **Crustaceans (*crustacés*):** Invertebrate animals with an external skeleton or shell, such as lobster.
○ **Mollusks (*mollusques*):** Mollusks are both univalved and bivalved — that is, having one shell or two. Periwinkles, abalone, and conch are some of the univalved mollusks, and oysters and clams are representative of bivalves.

○ **Cephalopods (*céphalopodes*):** Animals with a reduced internal skeleton, such as squid and octopus. The cuttlefish, a relative of the squid, has a cuttlebone as an internal shell.

A Note About Shellfish Safety

Shellfish can often be tainted by certain bacteria, toxic algae, and chemical contaminants. Because some shellfish, particularly mollusks, are often eaten raw, it is imperative that they be purchased from the most reputable dealers. Although the risk of gastrointestinal illness is slight and the infection is usually more uncomfortable than life-threatening, it can be extremely serious for children, the elderly, or people with compromised immune systems.

All legal mollusks are harvested from licensed and inspected areas, and the harvesters are required to tag their catch with their name as well as the area from which the seafood was taken. Most health departments are quite vigilant about this issue, and if any contamination is found, it is usually quickly dealt with.

Crustaceans

Crustaceans are, for the most part, saltwater animals, with crayfish (*l'écrevisse*) the freshwater exception. In France, the saltwater crayfish is referred to as *langousté*. The crustacean family includes cold-water lobster (*homard*), warm-water spiny lobster (*langouste*), rock lobster (*langouste*), crab (*crabe*), shrimp (*crevette grise*), prawns (*crevettes rose*), and crayfish (*l'écrevisse/langouste*).

Lobster

There are many, many types of lobster in the world, but all of them are divided into two groups — those with claws and those without. In the United States, the best known and most coveted is the Maine lobster, which has claws and is harvested in the wild along the upper Atlantic seacoast. Most cooks feel that lobsters with claws are much superior to those without. However, all lobster meat can be used interchangeably.

Crab

There are also many different species of crab. In the United States, we have just a few, but they all have very sweet, pale white flesh. Among them are blue, king, snow, Dungeness, and stone crab; some are available live only locally, while others are shipped live nationally or sold frozen. Soft-shell crabs are simply blue crabs, usually from the Chesapeake Bay area, that are in the process of growing a new shell, a normal activity of the crab.

Shrimp

Shrimp, also called prawns, are the most popular crustacean worldwide. They are harvested in such huge amounts that shrimp farming is now widely practiced in all parts of the world. In the United States, most of the wild shrimp brought to the commercial market is from the Gulf of Mexico and along the California coast. Wild shrimp is found in many other coastal areas, but it is generally consumed locally. In many places, very small shrimp are called "shrimp," while large ones are called "prawns."

The most commonly available shrimp are:

- Gulf pink or brown: Mostly wild, with pale pink or brown shells. The brown often have a strong iodine flavor that is appreciated by some shrimp lovers.
- Gulf white: Wild and farm raised, with very pale shells. Various sizes but can be exceptionally large, with equally exceptional flavor.
- Ecuadorian (or Mexican) white: Mostly farm raised, with very pale shells. Very similar to Gulf whites.
- Black tiger: Usually farm raised in Asia with pale gray shells and black, yellow, or red feelers. Most widely available throughout the United States. Many cooks find this species to be the least flavorful.

Crayfish

In the United States, crayfish are often called crawfish or crawdaddies and are also known as freshwater shrimp. They look a bit like miniature lobsters. Their only edible meat is in the tail, which is usually snapped off and split open. However, many aficionados feel that the head juices and the fat found between the body and the tail are of equal if not better flavor than the tail meat.

Crustaceans

Type	Market Form	Yield	Cooking Methods
Shrimp	Raw, with or without head; in shell or peeled; frozen, cleaned or not	40+ (cocktail) per pound 35–40 per pound 31–35 per pound 26–30 per pound 21–25 per pound 16–20 per pound Unit 15 per pound Unit 12 per pound	Boil/poach, broil/ grill, bake, sauté, deep-fat fry
Blue crab	Live in shell, cooked, canned, frozen	1–2¼ pounds	Bake, steam, boil, fry
Soft-shell crab	Live in shell, cooked, canned, frozen	⅛ – ⅓pound	Bake, steam, boil, fry
Dungeness crab	Live in shell, cooked, canned, frozen	1¼–2¼ pounds	Bake, steam, boil, sauté
King (Alaska) crab	Live in shell, cooked, canned, frozen	6–20 pounds	Bake, steam, boil, fry
Rock, stone crab	Live in shell, cooked, canned, frozen	⅓ pound	Bake, steam, boil, fry
Lobster	Live in shell, frozen, canned	¾–6 pounds	Bake, steam, boil, broil/grill
Spiny/rock lobster	Live in shell, headless raw, tail only	1–4 pounds	Bake, steam, boil, broil/grill
Crayfish	Live in shell, cooked, frozen	4–7 inches long 28–30 per pound	Bake, steam, boil, broil/grill

Determining the Freshness of Crustaceans

When purchased, crustaceans must be alive and vigorous, with the exception of shrimp, which are almost never alive when brought to market. Lobster and crayfish (either freshwater or salt water) should feel heavy and full, with their claws and feet intact. The tail of a fresh lobster will curl under strongly when the lobster is lifted from the water. If clawed, the freshest crustaceans will probably be angry enough when touched to make a strong effort to pinch their handler.

Since crustaceans begin to atrophy almost immediately upon being removed from their natural environment, they should be purchased as quickly as possible after being caught. Once dead, the flesh of crustaceans begins to break down immediately. In fact, it actually liquefies so that, when the shell is opened, it runs out as a transparent mucous. The longer they are in captivity, even alive, the more muscle tissue they lose. It is for this reason that the meat seems to have shrunk from the shell when the shell is cracked open. All these reasons make it imperative to purchase only the freshest shellfish at all times.

Methods of Cooking Crustaceans

There are a number of classic methods used to prepare shellfish. Among the most frequently used are:

Américaine/Armoricaine

Both of these names refer to the same thing, which can be either a method of preparation or a sauce served to accompany seafood. The only difference lies in the order in which everything is prepared. There is some dispute over the origin of the name *"américaine"*—some attribute it to an American chef who extemporaneously created a seafood dish for late-dining restaurant customers, while others believe that the proper name is *"armoricaine"* derived from Armorica, the ancient Gallic name for Brittany. Either title results in the same method and end result.

To make a *sauce américaine/armoricaine,* the shellfish meat is removed from the shell and prepared separately. The shells are crushed and sautéed, *mirepoix* is added, the preparation is then *flambéed*, moistened with white wine, and simmered with fish stock (*fumet*, see page 54) and tomatoes to make the sauce. The mixture is puréed to extract the full flavor from the shells and then strained for smoothness.

To prepare a *"sauté en sauce"* such as for *homard à l'américaine/armoricaine*, the shellfish is cleaned, sectioned, and sautéed in the shell. The meat is then removed from the shell and *flambéed* and the sauce prepared in the manner outlined above.

Shellfish *bisques* are basically a *sauce américaine* base with the addition of cream. Lobster, spiny lobster, crab, langoustine, and crayfish can all be prepared according to the above method.

Deep-Frying

The same principles and guidelines followed for deep-frying fish, discussed on page272, can be applied to deep-frying lobster, spiny lobster, crab, shrimp, and crayfish.

Court-Bouillon

A *court-bouillon* is used primarily for poaching seafood but can also be used for chicken and other white meats as in a *galantine*. It is a spiced, aromatic liquid that usually has white wine or vinegar added to help infuse flavor into the item being poached.

Mollusks

Bivalve mollusks are saltwater creatures with two shells, such as mussels (*moules*), clams (*palourdes*), oysters (*huîtres*), and scallops (*coquilles Saint-Jacques*). Univalves, which include snails (*escargots*) and winkles (*bigorneaux*), are one-shelled inhabitants of either fresh water, saltwater, or land.

Of all commonly available mollusks, scallops are the only ones always sold shucked. The tiniest available are calico scallops, and the largest are sea scallops. Bay scallops fall somewhere in between. "Day-boat" scallops are now sold across the country, but this term signifies only that they are freshly harvested and brought to market in a day. In the Pacific Northwest, pink scallops are sold live in the shell, but they are not usually shipped outside the area. Occasionally, the finest purveyors now have scallops in the shell along with their roe.

Farmed blue mussels are the most economical and commonly available mussels, although large, green-tinged New Zealand mussels are now a familiar sight in the fish market. Mussels, even those that have been farmed, often carry a whole aquarium on their shells and must be carefully cleaned before being cooked. They are the main ingredient of one of the best-loved French dishes, mussels marinara (*moules marinière*).

There are two types of clams: soft-shell and hard-shell. Soft-shell clams include the common steamer clam as well as geoduck (pronounced gooey-duck) clams, razor clams, mud clams, and jackknife clams. These clams have vitreous shells that are easily cracked and broken. Because they cannot close their shells fully, they are usually very gritty and must be cleaned before cooking.

Hard-shell clams include the familiar littleneck, cherrystone, Manila, and quahog or chowder clams. They range in size from about an inch across to hundreds of pounds. The color and weight may vary, but they all have the recognizable shape.

In the United States, there are five oyster species grown commercially. Two are indigenous: the Eastern oyster, harvested from Nova Scotia to Texas, and the very tiny Olympia oyster from Washington State. The remaining three species are imported from Europe or Asia. However, most oysters are not known by species but by the area from which they were harvested. This is because their growing environment has a great impact on their flavor and texture. Oysters, more than any other mollusks, carry age-old safety warnings — the best known only eat oysters in months that have an *r* in them. (Another such rule is only buy oysters with a harvested tag.) It is true that oysters are more likely to carry bacterial contamination in the summer months because of warmer waters, but it's not only that; they also spawn in the summer, which leaves them chalky and bitter-tasting. Just after spawning, they are flaccid and lacking in flavor. (The one exception to this is the Kumamoto oyster, which does not spawn until fall.) So this is one rule that does make culinary sense.

All mollusks must be extremely fresh for human consumption. Except for scallops, they should be purchased in the shell, which should be tightly closed and free of cracks or breaks. The shells of healthy mussels and clams may gape slightly but will close when tapped. Soft-shell clams and geoduck clams always gape because of their protruding siphons, but the siphon should retract quickly when touched. Clams should feel full when tapped and solid when held. Healthy, live oysters will always be tightly closed.

Mollusks

Type	Market Form	Yield	Cooking Methods
Mussel	Live in shell, canned, smoked	55# Bushel 32–40 per quart	Steam
Hard-shell clam	Live in shell, fresh shucked, frozen in shell	80# Bushel 25–30 per quart	Raw, steam, fry, bake, broil
Soft-shell clam	Live in shell, fresh shucked, frozen in shell	45# Bushel 50–175 per quart	Steam, fry, bake, broil
Eastern oyster	Live in shell, fresh shucked, frozen, canned, smoked	80# Bushel 40–50 per quart	Raw, steam, bake, boil, fry
Pacific oyster	Live in shell, fresh shucked, frozen, canned, smoked	80# Sack 12–60 per quart	Raw, steam, bake, boil, fry
Bay scallop	Shucked, fresh or frozen	62–85 per quart	Fry, broil, bake
Sea scallop	Shucked, fresh or frozen	25–30 per quart	Fry, broil, bake
Snail	Canned, fresh in Asian markets	Fresh by the piece, about 1–1¾ inches	Sauté, broil, bake

Methods of Cleaning and Opening Mollusks

Clams

Do *not* open clams until ready to serve raw or to cook. Soft-shell clams must always be cleaned. Hard-shell clams may be immersed in salt water for at least 20 minutes to eliminate any sand or grit; however, many chefs believe that this soaking results in the loss of flavor. Scrub the shells to clean off any debris that clings to them.

To open, hold the clam in one hand protected with a clean, folded kitchen towel and place the sharp edge of the clam knife into the crack between the shells. Squeeze with the fingers of the hand that is holding the clam and force the knife between the shells. Taking care not to damage the soft muscles against the lower shell, carefully slide the knife against the top shell to cut the adductor muscle to loosen the clam completely. Discard the top shell. If serving raw, keep the clam in the bottom shell. Carefully brush away any loose particles of shell that might be left in the remaining shell.

Oysters

Do *not* open oysters until just before using. Scrub the shells to clean off any debris that clings to them. To open, hold the oyster in one hand protected with a clean, folded kitchen towel or set the oyster on a solid

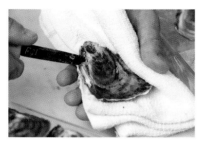

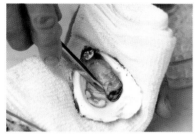

surface and hold it down against the surface with a clean kitchen towel. Either way, be very careful since the knife can easily slip.

Holding an oyster knife in the opposite hand, insert the blade into the crack between the shells near the hinge. Twist the knife to break the hinge, then slide the knife under the flat top shell. Cut through the adductor muscle near the top shell, taking care not to damage the oyster flesh or lose the juices. Remove and discard the top shell. Carefully cut the lower end of the muscle from the bottom shell to loosen the oyster. Carefully brush away any loose particles that might be left in the remaining shell. For traditional service, oysters are served in the bottom shell on a bed of crushed ice with a shallot *vinaigrette* (**sauce mignonette**) and garnished with thin slices of rye bread and lemon wedges.

Mussels

Healthy mussels should be tightly closed and free of cracks or breaks. If any mussels are slightly open, using your thumb and forefinger, push the shells sideways; if the shell closes the mussel is alive and healthy, if not, discard it. Using a small, sharp knife, carefully scrape off any barnacles, grit, or seaweed that cling to the shells. Do not remove the beard (the byssal threads by which the mussel suspends itself in the water) until just before using or the mussels will die and be rendered unusable. If very sandy, mussels may be soaked in cold, salted water for a couple of hours; however, many chefs believe that this soaking results in loss of flavor. If cultivated, the mussels are usually quite clean and the soaking is not necessary. If soaked, drain well and place in a bowl or mesh bag, cover with a damp towel, and refrigerate until ready to use but for no longer than a couple of days.

Scallops

Unlike other mollusks, it is the adductor muscle of the scallop that is eaten. Because they perish so quickly once removed from seawater, scallops are almost always sold shucked. Purchase only those that are creamy in color with a slight pink tint; never pur-

chase scallops that are pure white (they have been bleached or are not scallops at all), brownish, or of a dull sheen. Shucked scallops often still have the tough hinge clinging to them. If so, remove it by hand or with a knife.

If buying scallops in the shell, choose heavy specimens that are firmly closed. Rinse first under cold running water. Then hold the shell in the palm of your hand with the muscle facing away from you. As a safety measure, cover your hand with a thick towel. Carefully insert a rigid blade between the two shells. Cut or scrape off the white muscle from the top side of the shell. When the muscle is cut, the shell will open automatically. Remove the band of nerves surrounding the scallop, as it will retract when cooked. Rinse the scallop under cold running water to eliminate any sand. Cook as quickly as possible after purchasing.

Snails

There are two types of snails that are commonly used: *escargots de Bourgogne* (large, meaty snails from the Burgundy region of France) and *escargots petits gris* (small gray snails). Live snails must be degorged to rid them of impurities and excess juices. To do so, mix them with rock salt and let them rest for at least 3 hours, then rinse them well under cold running water. Bring a large pot of water to a rolling boil, add the snails, and boil for 5 minutes. Drain well but do not refresh. Using a small pick, remove the snails from their shells.

Methods of Cooking Mollusks

In addition to the specific cooking methods that follow, mollusks may also be shelled and served as a garnish for *poisson en sauce* or poached and served with mayonnaise as a cold *hors d'oeuvre*.

Clams

Small hard-shell clams are most often enjoyed raw. To cook, after cleaning, place them in a saucepan over high heat with a small amount of fish stock (*fumet*), *court bouillon*, seawater, or white wine along with some diced shallots and salt and pepper to taste. Cover, bring to a simmer, and steam for about 5 minutes or just until the clams open. Do not overcook or the clams will toughen. Small hard-shell clams may also be sautéed in olive oil and butter or grilled. Soft-shell clams are generally shucked and then cut up for use in chowders and stews.

Oysters

Oysters are most often served raw, on the half shell. For traditional service, they are presented in the bottom shell on a bed of crushed ice with a shallot *vinaigrette* (*sauce mignonette*) and garnished with thin slices of rye bread and lemon wedges. To cook, after opening, the oyster is cut out of the shell, reserving the liquid inside. If not being used in the immediate preparation, the liquor can be reserved—refrigerated for a day, or frozen for longer storage—for another use. Oysters may be cooked in several different ways. They can be just warmed in *fumet*, *court bouillon*, or seawater with the addition of a little white wine and diced shallots. Do not overcook or the oysters will toughen. The resulting liquid can be made into a sauce. Oysters can also be *gratinéed* or used in stews or soups.

Mussels

After cleaning, place the mussels in a saucepan over medium-high heat. Add white wine, diced shallots, a few lumps of butter, and salt and pepper to taste. Cover, bring to a simmer, and steam, uncovering and stirring occasionally, for about 10 minutes or just until the shells open and the meat has firmed slightly. To serve, remove the top half of each shell and place the mussels in their half shell in a large, shallow soup bowl. Return the cooking liquid to high heat and *monter au beurre* (see page 73). Remove from the heat and allow to rest for a couple of minutes so that any sand will settle in the bottom of the pan. Using a ladle, carefully, and without disturbing the bottom of the pan, transfer the hot broth to the mussels and serve. Mussels can also be cooked, shucked, and returned to their shells, placed between two layers of savory stuffing, and served as an appetizer or *hors d'oeuvre*.

Scallops

In classic French cooking, scallops are generally served in one of the following ways:

○ **Poached** — Carefully rinse shucked scallops and pat dry. Heat butter and diced shallot in a *poêle* over medium-high heat. Add white wine, fish stock (*fumet*), and a *bouquet garni* and bring to a simmer. Poach for 2 to 4 minutes, depending upon size. Do not overcook or the scallops will toughen. Scallops may also be poached in heavy cream in the same manner, replacing the wine with heavy cream.

○ **Sautéed** — Season the shucked scallops (and their coral, or roe, if any) with salt and pepper to taste. Lightly dredge in flour, shaking off any excess. Heat an equal portion of vegetable oil and butter in a sauté pan over high heat. Add the scallops, without crowding the pan, and sauté for about 2 to 4 minutes, depending upon size, until golden brown, taking care not to burn the cooking oil. Do not overcook or the scallops will toughen. Variations to the basic sauté are *bordelaise*, sautéed with diced shallots, and *Provençale*, sautéed with a **persillade** (a ground mixture of garlic, shallots, and parsley), and optional breadcrumbs.

○ **Grilled** — The shucked scallops are placed on skewers to make *brochettes*, alternately with other shellfish, if desired. The *brochettes* are marinated in a mixture of vegetable oil, lemon juice, and fresh thyme and grilled.

Snails

Place the snails in a highly aromatic *court bouillon* made with equal parts white wine and water. Depending on their size, snails require from 1½ to 3 hours of simmering to tenderize them. Cool the cooked snails in their liquid and return them to their shells for serving or place them in a small crock with warm garlic butter.

Cephalopods

Squid (*calamar*), octopus (*poulpe*) and cuttlefish (*seiche*) are three shellfish that fall into the category of cephalopods. All have ink sacs that can be used as a cooking medium for the meat and are often used in the preparation of regional Mediterranean dishes. Cephalopods are available fresh or frozen.

Squid

Squid has a wonderful sweet flavor, and when properly cooked, a delicate texture. It must either be cooked very quickly over very high heat or simmered for a long period in an aromatic sauce to achieve its best texture. Large squid always require a long cooking period to be tenderized.

Before using, squid must be cleaned. To do so, pull on the head and innards as gently as possible. If the quill remains, pull it out. Scrape any remaining interior matter out with a small, sharp knife. Cut the tentacles just above the hard ball on the squid's head. Squeeze on the tentacles, pushing until the hard ball, known as the "beak," pops out. Discard everything but the body and the tentacles. Using your fingertips, pull the outer skin (it is usually almost purple) from the body and tentacles. It should come off with a couple of tugs. Rinse the body and tentacles under cold running water and pat dry. Depending upon the size

and the preparation, the body and tentacles can either be sliced crosswise into bite-sized rings or left whole.

Squid can be cooked quickly on a grill, under a broiler, poached, or sautéed. Slow-cooking methods would be in a stew, soup, braising, or poaching. Cuttlefish is dealt with in the same manner.

Octopus

Octopus is usually sold cleaned and most often also frozen. Since octopus shrinks greatly when cooked, large-size specimens are most desirable. Octopus must be precooked by simmering in salted water seasoned with a *bouquet garni* for at least 1 hour (cooking time depends on size and age — it can take up to 3 hours) or until very tender when pierced with the point of a small, sharp knife. Once precooked, octopus can be grilled, sautéed, or stewed.

Demonstration

Moules à la Poulette

(Mussels in Cream Sauce with Parsley and Spinach)

Serves 4

Estimated time to complete: 30 minutes

Ingredients	Equipment
210 milliliters (¾ cup plus 2 tablespoons) heavy cream	2 *sautoirs* or *russes*, 1 with lid
150 milliliters (⅔ cups) dry white wine	Whisk
30 grams (1 ounce) shallots, *ciselé*	Slotted spoon
750 grams (1 pound, 7 ounces) mussels, prepared for cooking (see page 298)	Large bowl
Fresh lemon juice to taste	Measuring cup
Coarse salt and freshly ground pepper to taste	*Chinois*
150 grams (5¼ ounces) fresh spinach leaves,	Medium bowl
cooked *à l'anglaise* and well-drained; or tomatoes, *concassé*; or *duxelles*	Small saucepan
10 grams (2 tablespoons) fresh-flat leaf parsley, *haché*	Baking sheet
	Bain-marie
	Poêle

Prepare your *mise en place*.

Preheat the oven to 121°C (250°F).

Place 125 milliliters (½ cup plus 1 teaspoon) of the cream in a *sautoir* or *russe* over medium-high heat and simmer, whisking from time to time, for about 10 minutes or until reduced by half. Watch carefully, as cream can quickly boil over. Remove from the heat and set aside.

Place the wine and shallots in another *sautoir* or *russe* over medium-high heat and bring to a simmer. Add the mussels, cover, and cook for 2 minutes. Uncover, toss, recover, and cook for another 5 minutes or until the shells have opened and the meat has pulled away from the sides of the shells. Using a slotted spoon, transfer the mussels to a large bowl.

Measure out and set aside 50 milliliters (3½ tablespoons) of the cooking liquid. Leave the remainder in the pan and place over high heat and simmer until

reduced by three-quarters. Remove from the heat and strain through a *chinois* into a clean bowl. Set aside.

Remove the mussels from their shells, pulling off and discarding the foot and any remaining beard filaments. Set the shells aside. Combine the mussels with the reserved cooking liquid in a small saucepan to keep them moist.

Rinse the reserved shells and pat dry. Place them on a baking sheet in the oven and bake for about 5 minutes or until very dry. Remove from the oven and set aside.

Return the reserved reduced cream to low heat. Gradually whisk in the reserved reduced cooking liquid. Season with lemon juice, salt, and pepper to taste. Place in a *bain-marie* to keep warm.

When ready to serve, heat the remaining 85 milliliters (5¾ tablespoons) heavy cream in a *poêle* over medium-high heat. Cook, stirring frequently with a whisk,

Note

Mussels cooked in this manner can also be served on a bed of sea salt or seaweed.

for about 5 minutes or until thick. Add the spinach and toss just until it has absorbed the cream. Season with pepper to taste. Remove from the heat and keep warm.

Place the mussels in the cooking liquid over medium heat and bring to just a simmer.

Place an equal portion of the spinach mixture in the bottom of as many of the reserved shells as you have mussels. Place a mussel on top of each shell and nap each with a bit of the warm cream sauce (see note). Sprinkle with parsley and serve.

Demonstration

Sauce Américaine/Armoricaine

Makes 4 cups
Estimated time to complete: 90 minutes

Ingredients	Equipment
500 grams (1 pound, 1½ ounces) lobster bodies (shells)	Chef's knife
20 milliliters (1 tablespoon plus 1 teaspoon) vegetable oil	2 *sautoirs*
100 grams (3½ ounces) carrots, *mirepoix*	Wooden spoon
100 grams (3½ ounces) onions, *mirepoix*	Skimmer
50 milliliters (3½ tablespoons) cognac	*Chinois*
100 milliliters (7 tablespoons) white wine	Whisk
2 liters (2 quarts, 4 ounces) Fish Stock (see page 54), or half stock, half water	
200 grams (7 ounces) canned tomatoes, drained and chopped	
30 grams (1 ounce) tomato paste	
2 cloves garlic, peeled and crushed	
1 sprig fresh tarragon	
Coarse salt and freshly ground pepper to taste	
75 grams (5 tablespoons) unsalted butter	
30 grams (1 ounce) all-purpose flour	
3 grams (2 teaspoons) fresh chervil, *haché*	
3 grams (2 teaspoons) fresh tarragon, *haché*	
3 grams (2 teaspoons) fresh flat-leaf parsley, *haché*	

Prepare your *mise en place*.

Cut the lobster bodies in half lengthwise. Remove the gills and sac from the head. If the bodies are fresh, reserve the coral (red roe) and the tomalley (liver). If frozen, discard both the roe and liver. Rinse the bodies under cold running water and pat dry. Using a chef's knife, coarsely chop them.

Heat the oil in a large *sautoir* over high heat. Add the chopped lobster bodies and sauté for about 5 minutes or until they turn orange and emit a deep, rich aroma.

Add the carrots and onions to the pan and sauté for 3 minutes or just until slightly soft. Add the cognac and *flambé*. Immediately add the white wine and bring to a simmer. Simmer for about 10 minutes or until the liquid has reduced by half.

Add the fish stock, tomatoes, tomato paste, garlic, and tarragon. Season with salt and pepper to taste. Bring to a simmer and reduce the heat to a bare simmer. Cook, skimming the surface frequently, for about 40 minutes or until a rich stock has formed.

Remove from the heat and strain through a *chinois* into a clean *sautoir*. Return to medium-high heat and bring to a simmer. Simmer, stirring occasionally, for about 15 minutes or until slightly reduced and fully flavored.

Make a *liaison* with 30 grams (2 tablespoons) of the butter and the flour. Whisk it into the sauce and bring to a simmer. Lower the heat and cook, whisking occasionally, for 10 minutes.

Remove from the heat and swirl in the remaining butter. Add the chervil, tarragon, and parsley. Taste, and if necessary, season with salt and pepper.

Traditionally this sauce is served with lobster, but it can also be used with other shellfish.

Demonstration

Coquilles Saint-Jacques

(Scallops in White Wine–Cream Sauce)

Serves 4 as appetizer or luncheon entrée
Estimated time to complete: 40 minutes

Ingredients	Equipment
30 grams (2 tablespoons) unsalted butter	Small bowl
30 grams (1 ounce) all-purpose flour	Whisk
2 large egg yolks, at room temperature	*2 sautoirs*
150 milliliters (⅔ cup) heavy cream	Slotted spoon
200 milliliters (14 tablespoons) white wine	Medium bowl
150 milliliters (⅔ cup) Fish Stock (see page 54)	4 clean *coquilles* (scallop shells)
100 grams (3½ ounces) button mushrooms, *émincé*	
20 grams (¼ ounce) shallots, *ciselé*	
12 medium scallops, trimmed (see page 298)	
Coarse salt and freshly ground white pepper to taste	
Fresh lemon juice to taste	

Note

Coquilles Saint-Jacques may also be served in the shell surrounded by a ring of prebaked *Pommes Duchesse* (see page 124).

Prepare your *mise en place*.

Using 20 grams (4 teaspoons) of the butter plus the flour, prepare a white *roux* (see page 62). Set aside.

Whisk the egg yolks into 25 milliliters (1½ tablespoons) of the heavy cream in a small bowl. Set aside.

Place the remaining 125 milliliters (½ cup plus 1 teaspoon) heavy cream in a *sautoir* over medium heat and bring to a simmer. Remove from the heat and keep warm.

Lightly coat the bottom of a *sautoir* with the remaining butter. Add the wine, fish stock, mushrooms, and shallots and place over medium heat. Bring to a simmer. Add the scallops and poach gently for about 5 minutes or just until set. Do not overcook.

Using a slotted spoon, transfer the scallops to a medium bowl and cover them with just enough of the cooking liquid to keep them moist.

Place the remaining cooking liquid over high heat and bring to a boil. Lower the heat to a simmer and whisk in just enough of the reserved *roux* to slightly thicken the sauce. Whisk in the warm cream, bring to a simmer, and cook, whisking frequently, for 10 minutes. Whisk in the liquid from the scallops and check the consistency. It should be a thin sauce.

Whisk in the reserved egg yolk mixture. Season with salt, white pepper, and lemon juice to taste. Fold the scallops into the sauce.

Place an equal portion of the scallops in the sauce in each of four clean scallop shells (see note). Place under the salamander or a preheated broiler to glaze slightly before serving.

Demonstration

Court-Bouillon

Makes about 4 liters (1 gallon)
Estimated time to complete: 1 hour

Ingredients	Equipment
3 liters (3 quarts, 2 ounces) water	Stockpot
2 liters (2 quarts, 4 ounces) white wine	*Chinois*
675 grams (1½ pounds) onions, *émincé*	
675 grams (1½ pounds) carrots, *émincé*	
60 grams (2 ounces) fresh parsley stems	
6 sprigs fresh thyme	
5 bay leaves	
50 grams (1¾ ounces) coarse salt	
10 peppercorns	

Prepare your *mise en place.*

Combine the water and wine with the onions, carrots, parsley stems, thyme sprigs, and bay leaves along with the salt in a stockpot over medium-high heat. Bring to a boil and then lower the heat to maintain a gentle simmer. Cook for 20 minutes. Add the peppercorns and continue to simmer for another 10 minutes. Remove from the heat and allow to cool. Strain through a *chinois* and use as directed in a specific recipe.

Demonstration

Court-Bouillon Vinaigré (Vinegar Court-Bouillon)

Makes about 3 liters (3 quarts)
Estimated time to complete: 45 minutes to 1 hour

Ingredients	Equipment
3 liters (3 quarts, 2 ounces) water	Stockpot
500 milliliters (2 cups plus 2 tablespoons) white wine vinegar	*Chinois*
250 grams (8¾ pounds) onions, *émincé*	
250 grams (8¾ pounds) carrots, *émincé*	
30 grams (1 ounce) fresh parsley stems	
3 sprigs fresh thyme	
3 bay leaves	
40 grams (1½ ounces) coarse salt	
10 peppercorns	

Prepare your *mise en place.*

Combine the water and vinegar with the onions, carrots, parsley stems, thyme sprigs, and bay leaves in a stockpot over medium-high heat. Add the salt. Bring to a boil and then lower the heat to maintain a gentle simmer. Cook for 20 minutes. Add the peppercorns and continue to simmer for another 10 minutes. Remove from the heat and allow to cool. Strain through a *chinois* and use as directed in a specific recipe.

Chef Laura Pensiero

*Owner, Gigi Trattoria, Rhinebeck, New York
The French Culinary Institute, Class of February 1992*

Shrimp and White Bean *"Cassoulet"*

Serves 4

Cassoulet, the classic casserole dish from southwest France, usually contains a variety of cuts of pork, goose, and duck mixed with white beans and herbs and takes many hours to cook. My very loose interpretation, which is a "healthy" take on the original, keeps the beans but substitutes shrimp for the meats. This dish can land on the table in 30 minutes.

45 milliliters (3 tablespoons) olive oil, plus additional oil or olive oil cooking spray for the dish
2 leeks, white and some green parts, thinly sliced
2 cloves garlic, minced
Pinch dried hot pepper flakes or ½ jalapeño chile, seeded and minced
450 grams (1 pound) medium shrimp, peeled and deveined
20 grams (¾ ounce) chopped fresh flat-leaf parsley
Coarse salt to taste
5 grams (2 teaspoons) all-purpose flour
45 milliliters (3 tablespoons) dry white wine, optional
450 grams (2½ cups) cooked white beans, or two-14.5 ounce cans, drained and rinsed
120 milliliters (½ cup) vegetable or chicken broth
28 grams (¼ cup) breadcrumbs

Prepare your *mise en place.*

Preheat the oven to 191°C (375°F).

Lightly coat the interior of four 227-gram (8-ounce) *soufflé* dishes or a 950 milliliter (1-quart) casserole with olive oil cooking spray or lightly rub with olive oil.

Heat 30 milliliters (2 tablespoons) of the olive oil in a medium nonstick sauté pan over medium heat. Add the leeks, garlic, and red pepper flakes and cook, stirring frequently, for about 3 minutes or until the leeks have softened. Do not brown.

Add the shrimp and 10 grams (2 tablespoons) of the parsley and cook for about 1 minute or just until the shrimp begins to turn pink. Season with salt and sprinkle the flour over the surface. Using a wooden spoon, stir until combined and the flour is no longer visible. Stir in the wine, if using, and cook for a minute just to incorporate. Add the beans along with the broth and cook, stirring constantly, for 1 minute or until slightly thickened. Transfer to the prepared dishes or casserole.

Combine the breadcrumbs and remaining 10 grams (2 tablespoons) of parsley in a small bowl. Add the remaining 15 milliliters (1 tablespoon) of olive oil and stir to blend. Sprinkle the breadcrumb mixture over the top of the dishes or casserole.

Place in the oven and bake for about 15 minutes or until the top is golden and the sides are bubbling.

Remove from the oven and let rest for 5 minutes before serving.

Chef Dan Silverman

Executive Chef, Lever House Restaurant, New York City
The French Culinary Institute, Class of June 1988

Maryland Crab *Gratin* with Green Apple and Cucumber

Serves 4

Gratins are very easy to put together once the components have been prepared — the old "remember to prepare your *mise en place*" learned at FCI. This popular Lever House menu item is based on a classic old New York recipe. The Green Goddess Dressing recipe makes more than you will need, but it is wonderful on salads as well as being an excellent complement to grilled fish.

170 grams (¾ cup) mayonnaise
70 grams (¼ cup) Heinz chili sauce
5 milliliters (1 teaspoon) white wine vinegar
1.5 grams (1 teaspoon) finely chopped fresh tarragon
1 gram (¼ teaspoon) paprika
1 gram (¼ teaspoon) dry mustard
1 milliliter (scant ¼ teaspoon) hot sauce
Scant 1 gram (¼ teaspoon) cayenne pepper
450 grams (1 pound) jumbo lump crabmeat, picked clean of all shell and cartilage
½ lemon
Coarse salt and freshly ground pepper to taste
1 large cucumber, peeled, halved lengthwise, seeded, finely diced, and lightly salted
1 tart green apple, peeled, cored, finely diced, and slightly acidulated
Approximately 150 grams (5¼ ounces) baby lettuce *chiffonade*
Green Goddess Dressing (recipe follows)

Prepare your *mise en place.*

Make the *gratin* mix. Combine the mayonnaise with the chili sauce, vinegar, tarragon, paprika, mustard, hot sauce, and cayenne in a small bowl. Whisk to combine. Cover with plastic film and refrigerate until ready to use.

Set the broiler rack about 10 centimeters (4 inches) away from the heat. Preheat the broiler.

Lightly season the crab with a bit of lemon juice, salt, and pepper.

Place the cucumber, apple, and lettuce in a mixing bowl. Add just enough of the Green Goddess Dressing to very lightly coat the salad mixture.

Place a small flan ring in the center of each of four luncheon plates. Press an equal portion of the salad down into each ring. Carefully remove the rings, keeping the salads in a perfect round.

Quickly rinse the rings and place them on a baking sheet large enough to accommodate them. Place an equal portion of the seasoned crab into each ring, pressing down firmly to make a neat circle. Spoon a thin, even layer of the *gratin* mix over the crab in each flan ring. Place under the preheated broiler and, watching carefully to prevent burning, broil for about 2 minutes or until the *gratins* begin to bubble and brown. Rotate the pan and continue to broil for another 2 minutes or until the *gratins* are golden brown and bubbling.

Remove from the broiler and carefully run a paring knife around the inside of each flan ring to loosen the *gratins.* Using a flat metal spatula and working with one at a time, carefully transfer a *gratin* to the top of each salad. Remove the flan ring and serve immediately.

Green Goddess Dressing   Makes about 2¼ cups

1 shallot, peeled and minced
1 clove garlic, minced
45 milliliters (3 tablespoons) white wine vinegar
Juice of ½ lemon
Juice of ½ lime
2 canned anchovy fillets, drained and finely chopped
½ ripe avocado
180 milliliters (¾ cup) extra virgin olive oil
120 milliliters (½ cup) heavy cream
20 grams (¾ ounces) chopped fresh flat-leaf parsley
15 grams (3 tablespoons) chopped fresh tarragon
10 grams (2 tablespoons) chopped fresh cilantro
5 grams (1 tablespoon) chopped fresh basil
1.5 grams (1 teaspoon) chopped fresh savory
Coarse salt and freshly ground pepper to taste

Prepare your *mise en place*.

Combine the shallot and garlic with the vinegar and lemon and lime juice in a nonreactive mixing bowl. Set aside to macerate for 10 minutes.

Add the anchovy and avocado and, using a fork, mash the ingredients together.

Using a wooden spoon, stir in the olive oil and cream. The mixture should have the consistency of thin mayonnaise. Stir in the parsley, tarragon, cilantro, basil, and savory. Season with salt and pepper to taste. Cover and refrigerate until ready to use or up to 2 days.

Session 17

Braising and Marinades

Theory

The Braising Method of Cooking

Larousse Gastronomique defines braising (***braisé***) as "a method of cooking food in a closed vessel with very little liquid at a low temperature for a very long time." The word *braiser* comes from the French word for "ember," which, in turn, refers to the original open-hearth cooking technique, where the cooking vessel was placed in hot embers in the hearth and then additional hot embers were placed on top of the lid so that the heat came from both the top and bottom. The cooking was often done overnight, at the local bakery after the bread baking was done for the day. During the seventeenth and eighteenth centuries, most serious French dishes were braises. In fact, much of the French reputation for fine cooking was based on these long-simmered dishes. Nowadays, braises are not very popular in the home kitchen, probably because they take a long time to prepare and are somewhat difficult to cook correctly. However, in recent years, they have made a comeback in the restaurant kitchen as chefs look backward for inspiration.

The general braising technique is cooking by wet heat with the food to be cooked partially immersed in liquid. The principle behind braising is exchange: the item being cooked gives off juices to the liquid and, in return, the flavorful liquid infuses it. Although most often used for large pieces of second-category (see page 166) meats, braising can be applied to all types of food.

Food scientist Harold McGee, in his book *On Food and Cooking*, uses the example of the American pot roast in his explanation of the physics of braising. He explains that scientifically, "the braise is characterized by a relatively low maximum temperature, the boiling (simmering) point of water, and a more efficient transfer of energy than is possible in dry heating. In practice, this means that a large piece of meat will reach temperatures near this maximum relatively quickly, and can be kept there for prolonged periods without any danger of the outside burning. Such treatment is exactly what is called for in order to convert collagen to gelatin." (Collagen is part of the composition of the tough connective tissues that hold muscle fibers together in meat.) McGee compares collagen conversion in a rump roast when it is roasted well done, which takes an hour or two, and when it is braised for 30 minutes and for 90 minutes. The roasted sample had 14 percent of its collagen gelatinized, the 30-minute braise 11 percent, and the 90-minute braise 52 percent. The obvious conclusion is that a long, slow braise is the most effective method of tenderizing meat that is tough because of its connective tissue content.

A braise differs from a ***ragoût*** (stew) in that a stew employs more liquid and is usually the cooking method preferred for small pieces of meat. Stews are generally prepared on the stovetop, and braising can be done on the stovetop or in the oven. The oven method provides more even heat and is more in tune with the origins of the technique.

Items to be braised are often marinated before cooking and are often also first sautéed or seared (see concentration, page 168) before cooking. The combination of searing followed by simmering (see extraction, page 168) is the *mixte* method of cooking (see page 182). In fact, most braising recipes call for the item to be browned before being immersed in liquid. The browning causes caramelization, which will add color and flavor to the braise. In addition, when the item is browned, the *sucs* that form on the bottom of the pan, once deglazed, will add more flavor to the sauce. When using white meats, such as veal, the meat is usually seared with little or no coloration, so the sauce is normally quite pale in color. Fish and vegetables are not usually seared prior to braising.

Whatever the initial approach, the item to be cooked is moistened, usually with very little liquid, until it is just partially submerged, covered with a tight-fitting lid, and cooked either on the stovetop or in a preheated oven. It is a particularly effective cooking method for second- and third-category meats that are too tough for other quicker methods of cooking. It can also be applied to vegetables, such as cabbage, endive, artichokes, and lettuce, as well as to large birds and whole, firm-fleshed fish.

In a typical meat braise, the slow interaction of the meat juices, herbs, aromatic vegetables, and liquid (wine, stock, or a combination thereof) is responsible for the complex flavor of the finished dish. As braising advances, the meat begins to relax and absorb the liquid in which it is cooking.

It may seem surprising that chewy, dried-out meat is a common fault in a finished braise. This is because the meat chosen was too lean or too tender to undergo extended cooking, or because the dish was boiled rather than gently simmered — boiling toughens the proteins in the meat. Braising is best applied to gelatinous cuts of meat that will soften during cooking and be less likely to dry out over a long period of cooking.

Another common mistake is to assume that fully covering the meat with liquid will prevent it from drying out when, in fact, the opposite is true. Excessive liquid will dry out meat more rapidly than dry heat. Fat, more than any other element, will ensure that meat stays moist. Therefore, fatty cuts of meat are a good choice for braising, and less fatty cuts can benefit from being larded with fatback.

About Marinades

A marinade (**marinade**) is a scented and flavored liquid in which certain food items, such as meat, poultry, game, and fish, are soaked in order to imbue them with the aromatic qualities of the ingredients that compose the marinade (usually wine or another acidic liquid). Marinating can also help tenderize the fibers of tough meat and is often used for this in braises and stews. The acidic element of the marinade determines the degree of tenderizing, so tougher meats or larger cuts may require a more acidic marinade. The length of marinating time is dependant upon the nature and size of the food item as well as the amount of flavor to be absorbed.

When working with food placed in a marinade, the cook should only place hands covered with new gloves in the liquid, as it is the perfect habitat for bacterial growth. In addition, a marinade that has had raw meat in it can *only* be used as a sauce after it has been boiled; otherwise, there is a risk of contamination of the cooked food through bacteria from the uncooked (raw) marinade. Items that are being marinated must always be refrigerated.

Chef's Tip

"Marinating time should be dependent upon the age and type of bird or meat."
Chef Sixto Alonso

There are an infinite number of marinade possibilities. The following are just a few of the standards:

Cooked Marinade

A cooked marinade is heated and cooled before being used, generally for red meat and game. When marinating poultry and game with a cooked marinade, add juniper berries to the basic recipe; for rabbit, add sage and rosemary. The recipe on page 324 is a classic cooked marinade that makes enough to adequately marinate one large piece of meat or poultry.

Uncooked Marinade

The ingredients of an uncooked marinade are first combined and then the marinade is poured over the items to be marinated. It is used for red meat, poultry, and game. If using as a component of the finished dish, the marinade must be boiled, as for a cooked marinade, after the marinated item is removed. The recipe on page 325 will make enough uncooked marinade to flavor a large piece of meat or poultry.

Instant Marinade

This type of marinade is used just before the item is to be cooked. The food is not soaked in a liquid; it is just lightly moistened with oil and an acidic element, such as lemon or wine, and gently flavored with aromatics. This method is used when you wish the item to be cooked to be lightly flavored.

For fish: Prepare the fish as for cooking and place it in a nonreactive dish. Sprinkle with a bit of oil (vegetable or olive) and fresh thyme to taste, then add lemon slices and a couple of bay leaves.

For shrimp, organ meats, and poultry: Cut the item into small pieces and arrange in a single layer in a nonreactive dish. Sprinkle with a bit of oil (vegetable or olive), lemon juice, chopped parsley, salt, and pepper.

For *terrines, pâtés, and galantines*: Season the item to be marinated. Add cooked *ciseler* shallots and moisten with cognac, Madeira, or port wine. The item to be marinated is turned from time to time. The desired amounts of seasoning will be found in the specific recipe.

Demonstration

Jarret d'Agneau Braisé (Braised Lamb Shanks)

Serves 4

Estimated time to complete: 3 hours

Ingredients	Equipment
2 large (675 grams or 1½ pounds) lamb shanks	Chef's knife
Coarse salt and freshly ground pepper to taste	*Sautoir* with cover
40 milliliters (2 tablespoons plus 2 teaspoons) olive oil	Tongs
4 cloves garlic, peeled and crushed	Ladle
150 grams (5¼ ounces) carrots, large *mirepoix*	Warm plate
150 grams (5¼ ounces) onions, large *mirepoix*	Aluminum foil
100 grams (3¼ ounces) celery, strings removed, cut into 1-inch pieces	
2 sprigs fresh thyme	
2 bay leaves	
1 sprig fresh rosemary	

300 milliliters (1¼ cups) red wine
500 milliliters (2 cups plus 2 tablespoons) Brown Veal Stock (see page 57)
150 grams (5¼ ounces) very ripe tomatoes, *concassé*
Basic Couscous (recipe follows)

Prepare your *mise en place.*

Preheat the oven to 149°C–162°C (300°F–325°F).

Using a chef's knife, trim the lamb shanks of excess fat, leaving a thin layer covering the shank. Season with salt and pepper to taste.

Heat the olive oil in a *sautoir* over medium heat. Add the lamb shanks and sear, turning frequently, until all sides are nicely browned. Using tongs, remove the shanks from the pan and set aside. Leave the pan on the heat.

Add the garlic, carrots, onions, and celery and sauté for about 4 minutes or until the vegetables begin to color. Remove from the heat and carefully drain off the fat.

Return the pan to medium heat and stir in the thyme, bay leaves, and rosemary.

Add the wine and stir to deglaze the *sucs.* Stir in the stock and tomatoes. Season with salt and pepper to

taste and return the reserved shanks to the pan.

Cover, place in the oven, and braise for approximately 2½ hours or until the shanks are very tender but not falling off the bone.

Remove the pan from the oven and uncover. Allow the shanks to rest in the hot liquid for 10 minutes. Using a ladle, carefully skim off and discard the fat that is floating on top of the sauce.

Transfer the shanks to a warm plate. Tent lightly with aluminum foil to keep warm.

Return the pan to medium-high heat and bring to a simmer, continuing to skim off any fat that rises to the surface. Simmer for about 10 minutes or until slightly reduced. Taste, and if necessary, adjust the seasoning with salt and pepper.

Using a chef's knife, cut the meat from the shank and place it into the sauce. Serve hot, with Basic Couscous (recipe follows).

Demonstration
Basic Couscous

Serves 4

Estimated time to complete: 30 minutes

Ingredients

Equipment

185 grams (6½ ounces) couscous
240 milliliters (1 cup) defatted White Chicken
  Stock (see page 53)
20 grams (1 tablespoon plus 1 teaspoon) unsalted butter, melted
Coarse salt and freshly ground pepper to taste

Stainless steel bowl
Small saucepan
Plastic film
Fork

Note

The seasoned couscous can be reheated over steam or in a *sautoir* with a spoonful of water added. If reheated, taste and, if necessary, adjust the seasoning.

Prepare your *mise en place*.

Place the couscous in a stainless steel bowl.

Place the stock in a small saucepan over medium heat and bring to a simmer.

Immediately pour the hot stock over the couscous and cover tightly with plastic film.

Allow the couscous to rest for 20 minutes, then add the melted butter and season with salt and pepper to taste, fluffing the couscous, layer by layer, with a fork (*egrainer*).

Serve warm (see note).

Demonstration

Coq au Vin (Chicken in Red Wine Sauce)

Serves 4
Estimated time to complete: 3 to 8 hours marinating time; 2 hours preparation time

In France, **coq au vin** is a regional stew (*ragoût*) that is, traditionally, made with a rooster, which can withstand a long period of slow cooking. The wine is generally a red wine from Burgundy, but any wine can be used. If not red wine, the name of the dish will often reflect the type of wine used, as in *coq au Riesling*. Nowadays, it is not so easy to find a rooster and we have to content ourselves with a fat hen and a shorter cooking time. *Coq au vin* is traditionally served with fresh noodles (recipe follows).

Ingredients	Equipment
For the marinade	Chef's knife
600 milliliters (2½ cups) red wine	Large nonreactive bowl
80 grams (2¾ ounces) carrots, *mirepoix*	Plastic film
80 grams (2¾ ounces) onions, *mirepoix*	Tongs
40 grams (1½ ounces) celery, *mirepoix*	*Chinois*
8 peppercorns	2 bowls
2 bay leaves	*Sautoir*
1 clove garlic, peeled and crushed	Slotted spoon
1 sprig fresh thyme	Paper towels
	Plate

For the chicken

One 1.5-kilogram (3⅓-pound) chicken
20 milliliters (4 teaspoons) vegetable oil
Course salt and freshly ground pepper to taste
20 grams (¾ ounce) all-purpose flour
15 milliliters (1 tablespoon) cognac
500 milliliters (2 cups plus 2 tablespoons) Brown
  Veal Stock (see page 57)

For the garnish

100 grams (3½ ounces) bacon, cut into *lardons*
180 grams (6⅓ ounces) button mushrooms
30 grams (2 tablespoons) unsalted butter
Coarse salt and freshly ground pepper to taste
180 grams (6⅓ ounces) pearl onions, peeled
21 grams (1 tablespoon) sugar
2 slices white bread
15 grams (1 tablespoon) clarified butter
7 grams (1½ tablespoons) fresh flat-leaf parsley, *haché*
Fresh Noodles (recipe follows)

Metal spoon
Sauté pan
2 small saucepans
Heart-shaped cookie cutter
Small frying pan
Warm plate
Warm serving platter

Prepare your *mise en place*.

Using a chef's knife, cut the chicken into quarters. Rinse well.

Combine the red wine, carrots, onions, celery, peppercorns, bay leaves, garlic, and thyme in a nonreactive bowl large enough to hold the chicken. Add the chicken, cover with plastic film and refrigerate for at least 3 hours but preferably 8 hours.

Remove the chicken from the refrigerator. Using tongs, lift the chicken pieces from the marinade and set them aside. Strain the marinade through a *chinois*, separately reserving the liquid and the aromatic vegetables and herbs.

Preheat the oven to 149°C (300°F).

Heat the oil in a *sautoir* over medium heat. Add the bacon and sauté for about 5 minutes or until it is nicely browned. Using a slotted spoon, transfer the bacon to a double layer of paper towels to drain. Do

not remove the pan from the heat. Set the *lardons* aside for garnish.

Pat the chicken pieces dry with paper towels; then season them well with salt and pepper to taste. Place the chicken in the hot pan and sear, turning frequently, until all sides are golden, about 10 minutes. Using tongs, transfer the chicken to a plate.

Pour any excess fat from the pan. Return the pan to medium heat and add the reserved aromatic vegetables and herbs. Sauté for 10 minutes or until the vegetables begin to color nicely. Stir in the flour and cook, stirring (*singer*), for 2 minutes.

Return the chicken to the pan and *flamber* with the cognac. Add the stock along with the reserved marinade and bring to a boil. Lower the heat and simmer, stirring and skimming off the fat occasionally with a metal spoon, for 10 minutes. Cover and transfer to the oven. Braise for about 30 minutes or until the chicken is very tender.

While the chicken is cooking, prepare the rest of the garnish.

Clean the mushrooms and, if they are large, quarter them.

Heat half of the butter in a sauté pan over medium heat. Add the mushrooms and season with salt and pepper to taste. Sauté for about 12 minutes or until nicely browned. Remove from the heat and set aside.

Place the pearl onions in a small saucepan with a little water, the sugar, and the remaining butter and *glacer à brun*. Set aside.

Using a heart-shaped cookie cutter, cut out four hearts from the bread.

Heat the clarified butter in a small frying pan and place the bread hearts in it. Fry, turning once, for about 4 minutes or until the bread is golden brown. Set aside.

When the chicken is tender, remove the pan from the oven. Using tongs, transfer the chicken to a warm plate. Strain the cooking liquid through a *chinois* into a clean saucepan, discarding the solids. Carefully skim off any fat that rises to the surface.

Place the pan over medium-high heat and bring to a boil. Lower the heat and simmer for about 12 minutes or until a saucelike consistency is reached. Taste, and if necessary, adjust the seasoning with salt and pepper.

Place the chicken on a bed of fresh noodles (recipe follows) placed on a serving platter. Pour the hot sauce over the top. Dip the bottom tip of reserved bread hearts into the sauce and then into the chopped parsley. Place the decorative hearts around the edge of the plate and finish the garnish with the reserved bacon *lardons*, mushrooms, and pearl onions. Serve immediately.

Demonstration

Pâtes à Nouilles Fraîches (Fresh Noodles)

Serves 4

Estimated time to complete: 2 hours

Ingredients	Equipment
200 grams (7 ounces) semolina flour (see note)	Fork
or half semolina and half all-purpose flour, plus more for rolling the dough	Plastic film
2–3 large eggs (see note)	Pasta machine
5 grams (¾ teaspoon) coarse salt, plus more to taste	Clean, damp kitchen towel
10 milliliters (2 teaspoons) olive oil	Rolling pin
Freshly ground pepper to taste	Large pot
Unsalted butter to taste, optional	
6 grams (1 tablespoon plus 1 scant teaspoon) fresh herbs	
such as parsley or chives, *haché* to taste, optional	

Note

Pâtes, or pasta doughs, are traditionally made with semolina flour, a coarse-textured flour that is very high in gluten. When using all semolina flour, less moisture is often required; therefore use 2 eggs instead of 3.

Prepare your *mise en place*.

Place the flour on a clean work surface. If using the half-and-half mixture to make a firmer noodle, mix the flours together. Mound the flour slightly and make a well in the center.

Break the eggs into the well and add the 5 grams (¾ teaspoon) salt. Add the oil and, using a fork, beat the wet ingredients together.

Using your hands, begin working the flour into the liquid, moving from the sides into the center. When the ingredients are well mixed, form the dough into a ball and knead it with your hands for about 10 minutes or until the dough is smooth and feels leathery.

Form the dough into a ball, wrap with plastic film, and refrigerate for at least 1 hour. The longer the dough rests, the easier it will be to roll out.

Set up a pasta machine on its widest opening, usually number 1.

Cut the chilled dough into three equal pieces. Cover two with a clean, damp kitchen towel to keep them from drying out. Flatten the remaining piece with a rolling pin. Feed the dough through the rollers of the pasta machine at least three times, folding it into thirds after each roll to further knead and smooth out the dough. If necessary, dust the dough with a little flour to keep it from sticking. When the dough is smooth and satin like, it has been sufficiently rolled.

Begin to narrow the settings on the pasta machine, running the dough through each progressively smaller opening once until you reach the desired degree of thickness.

Lay the dough out to dry for no more than 30 minutes. The time will depend on the temperature and

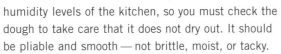

humidity levels of the kitchen, so you must check the dough to take care that it does not dry out. It should be pliable and smooth — not brittle, moist, or tacky.

Cut the dough into the desired shape by hand or machine. For *coq au vin*, standard egg noodles would be the usual shape.

When ready to serve, bring a large pot of salted water to a boil over high heat. Add the pasta and cook until just tender (*al dente*, the Italian phrase meaning "to the tooth" describes pasta that is slightly resistant to the bite). Drain well, season with salt and pepper to taste and, if desired, butter and fresh herbs to taste.

Demonstration

Basic Cooked Marinade

Makes about 1 liter (1 quart)

Estimated time to complete: 45 minutes

Ingredients	Equipment
100 milliliters (7 tablespoons) vegetable oil	Heavy saucepan
60 grams (2 ounces) carrots, *émincé*	Wooden spoon
50 grams (1¾ ounces) onions, *émincé*	
40 grams (1½ ounces) celery, *émincé*	
20 grams (¾ ounce) shallots, *émincé*	
750 milliliters (3¼ cups) red or white wine	
150 milliliters (⅔ cup) red or white wine vinegar	
Bouquet garni	
1 whole clove	
Garlic cloves to taste, peeled and crushed	
Peppercorns to taste	

Prepare your *mise en place.*

Heat the oil in a heavy saucepan over medium heat. Add the carrots, onions, celery, and shallots and, using a wooden spoon, stir to combine. Pour in the wine and vinegar, then add the *bouquet garni*, clove, garlic, and peppercorns and bring to a simmer. Lower the heat and cook at a gentle simmer for 30 minutes. Remove from the heat and set aside to cool completely before using.

Demonstration

Basic Uncooked Marinade

Makes about 1 liter (1 quart)
Estimated time to complete: 30 minutes

Ingredients	Equipment
100 milliliters (7 tablespoons) vegetable oil	Large nonreactive bowl
60 grams (2 ounces) carrots, *émincé*	Wooden spoon
50 grams (1¾ ounces) onions, *émincé*	
40 grams (1½ ounces) celery, *émincé*	
20 grams (¾ ounce) shallots, *émincé*	
750 milliliters (3¼ cups) red or white wine	
150 milliliters (⅔ cup) red or white wine vinegar	
Bouquet garni	
20 parsley stems	
1 whole clove	
Peppercorns to taste	

Prepare your *mise en place*.

Combine the oil with the carrots, onions, celery, and shallots in a large nonreactive bowl. Add the wine and vinegar and then stir in the *bouquet garni*, parsley, clove, and peppercorns. Add the items to be marinated and marinate for the time designated in the specific recipe.

Session 18

Basic Stuffings

Theory
About Stuffing

Stuffing or forcemeat (*farce*) is a flavorful amalgam of raw or cooked ingredients that have been chopped or ground for use as a stuffing for meat, poultry, game, fish, vegetables, eggs, or pastas. Forcemeats are also the base for *pâtés*, *terrines*, *ballottines*, *galantines*, and sausages, as well as used as a topping on *croutons*. The exact composition of a stuffing depends on the food to be filled as well as the texture required.

There are three types of standard stuffing: those made with meat, game, offal, or poultry; those made with vegetables; and those made with seafood. There is a minor fourth category of stuffings based on cooked egg yolk. Many stuffings are bound with cornstarch, gelatin, egg, or a bread-based paste known as a *panade*. In all types, proper seasoning is extremely important, providing both the stuffing and the item stuffed to be with sufficient flavor.

The use of stuffing is a prime example of French economy in the kitchen, as it gives the chef the opportunity to use up the trimmings from meat, poultry, fish, or vegetables in a most delicious way. A simple meat or poultry stuffing can be used to make a quick *hors d'oeuvre* when used as a filling for mushroom caps, or to create a vegetable entrée when used as a filling for hollowed-out squash, eggplant, tomatoes, or onions.

The following chart outlines some basic stuffings and their uses:

Dean's Tip

"A stuffing should complement the basic ingredient and enhance the dish, not just be used as a filler."

Dean Jacques Pépin

Basic Stuffings

Stuffing	Composition	Use
Mushroom stuffing (*duxelles à farcir*)	Mushrooms, shallots, veal stock, tomatoes, fresh bread-crumbs, white wine	To stuff vegetables, especially eggplant, onion, summer squash, artichoke bottoms, and onions
American-style stuffing (*farce américaine*)	Smoked streaky bacon, onion, fresh breadcrumbs	To stuff pigeons and baby chickens

Stuffing	Composition	Use
Fish *mousseline* (see note) (*farce de poisson*)	Pike or whiting, ocean perch, egg white, heavy cream	To stuff fish, *paupiettes* of sole, *terrines*, *ballottines*
Toasted forcemeat (*farce à gratin*)	Pork fat, chicken livers, shallots, cognac	Spread on croutons as a garnish for poultry and some game bird dishes
Veal or chicken *mousseline* (*farce mousseline de veau* or *de volaille*)	Veal or poultry, egg white, heavy cream	To stuff poultry, to make quenelles, *terrines*
Various stuffings (*farces diverses*)	Pork or veal trimmings along with the ingredients that determine the name of the stuffing	*Terrines*, *pâtés*, *galantines*, *ballottines*

Technique
Preparation of Standard Stuffings

The pages that follow contain guidelines for preparing a number of standard stuffings.

Mushroom stuffing for vegetables (*duxelles à farcir*)

1. Finely dice (*ciselé*) the shallots.

2. Sweat the shallots in butter over medium heat.

3. Chop the mushrooms, preferably just the stems and trimmings, reserving the caps either for stuffing or another use.

4. Add the mushrooms to the shallots. Season with salt and pepper to taste. Cook, stirring constantly with a wooden spoon, until all the exuded juices have evaporated.

5. Add white wine and cook, stirring occasionally, until the pan is almost dry.

6. Add some Veal Stock (see page 57) and again cook until the liquid has evaporated.

7. Just before using, stir in just enough finely sifted breadcrumbs to make a thick but moist mixture. Taste, and if necessary, adjust the seasoning.

8. Proceed to use as a stuffing in a specific recipe.

American-style stuffing (*farce américaine*)

1. Finely dice (*ciseler*) onions and dice bacon.

2. Combine the onions and bacon in a large *sautoir* over medium heat. Cook until the bacon renders some fat and cooks slightly.

3. Stir in the breadcrumbs to absorb excess fat.

4. Add chopped fresh thyme and sage.

5. Season with salt and pepper to taste, and if necessary, adjust the seasoning.

6. Proceed to use as a stuffing in a specific recipe.

Fish *mousseline* (*farce de poisson*)

All ingredients and equipment must be cold to begin and kept cold throughout the procedure.

1. Purée the fish in a food processor fitted with the

metal blade or in a meat grinder fitted with the finest disk.

2. To obtain the smoothest texture, push the purée through a very fine wire sieve (*tamis*).

3. Transfer to a clean bowl and refrigerate for at least an hour or until very cold.

4. Place the chilled purée over a bowl filled with ice.

5. Beat in egg whites, one at a time.

6. Gradually begin to add very cold heavy cream, beginning with about 125 milliliters (½ cup plus 1 teaspoon) for every pound of fish purée.

7. Add seasonings.

8. To check for proper consistency and seasoning, bring a small saucepan of water to boil. Shape a small *quenelle* of the mixture and poach it briefly in the boiling water.

9. Drain well and taste. If necessary, continue adding cream until the *mousseline* has a very light, creamy texture. If necessary, adjust the seasonings.

10. If the *mousseline* warms or softens at any point, return it to the refrigerator until well chilled.

11. Proceed to make *quenelles* or use as a stuffing in a specific recipe.

Toasted forcemeat (*farce à gratin*)

1. Finely dice (*ciselé*) the shallots and set them aside.

2. Cut the pork fat into very small cubes.

3. Place the pork cubes in a *sautoir* placed over medium-high heat. Sauté until all the fat has been rendered from the pork. Set aside the pan and the fat.

4. Sear the chicken livers in the pork fat, browning but leaving the livers rare. Season with salt and pepper to taste. Set the livers aside.

5. Add the shallots and thyme to the sauté pan.

6. Add the cognac and *flambé*.

7. Drain off all fat from the pan.

8. Pass the livers, shallots, and thyme through a *tamis* into a clean bowl. Stir until very smooth.

9. Cover with parchment paper until ready to use in a specific recipe.

Veal or chicken *mousseline* (*farce mousseline de veau* or *de volaille*)

1. Trim the veal or chicken to remove the tough nerves and skin.

2. Pass the trimmed meat though a meat grinder fitted with the finest disk. Alternatively, finely mince by hand using a chef's knife.

3. Place the ground meat in a food processor fitted with the metal blade. Add just enough egg white to moisten and process to a smooth purée. To obtain the smoothest texture, push the purée through a *tamis*.

4. Place the purée over a bowl filled with ice.

5. Beat while adding chilled heavy cream, a bit at a time.

6. Season with salt and pepper to taste.

7. To check for proper seasoning, bring a small saucepan of water to boil. Shape a small *quenelle* of the mixture and poach it briefly in the boiling water. Drain well and taste.

8. Proceed to use as directed in a specific recipe.

Various stuffings (*farces diverses*)

There is not one singular recipe for the preparation of these stuffings. They are normally composed of lean and fatty pork and sometimes veal, along with another major ingredient, which determines the name of the stuffing. The amount and ratio of meats, the seasoning, and the texture of each ingredient will vary.

Preparation and Cooking of Stuffed Vegetables

The following instructions lead you through the steps necessary to stuff and cook a variety of vegetables:

Eggplant (*aubergine*)

1. Wash the eggplant well and cut it in half lengthwise.

2. Cut away 2 to 3 millimeters (1/16 inch) of the skin along the side edges.

3. Cut slashes through the flesh but not through the skin. This will facilitate the cooking of the flesh and later removal of the skin.

4. Heat oil to 177°C (350°F) in a deep-fat fryer.

5. Drop the eggplant halves into the hot oil and cook for about 5 minutes or until the skin easily pulls away from the flesh. (Alternatively, the eggplant halves may be brushed with oil and placed, cut side down, in a preheated 177°C (350°F) oven and baked for about 30 minutes or until very soft.)

6. Remove the eggplant from the hot oil and place on a double layer of paper towels to drain.

7. Preheat the oven to 177°C (350°F).

8. Scoop out the interior flesh and set aside the flesh and the skin separately.

9. Chop the eggplant flesh.

10. Finely dice (*ciselé*) the onions.

11. Heat olive oil in a *sautoir* over medium heat.

12. Add the onions and sauté until they have sweated their liquid but not taken on any color. Season to taste with salt and pepper.

13. Add the chopped eggplant and cook, stirring to combine. Return the eggplant mixture to the reserved skins.

14. Place the filled eggplant halves in the oven and bake for 15 minutes or until nicely browned.

15. While the eggplant is baking, cut enough 7 millimeters (1/4 inch) thick tomato slices to cover the top of each eggplant half.

16. Sauté the tomatoes in olive oil for about 3 minutes to just cook slightly.

17. Place the tomato slices on the baked eggplant and serve hot or at room temperature.

Zucchini (*courgette*)

1. Wash the zucchini well and then cut them crosswise into 4-centimeter (1½-inch) lengths.

2. Bring a small saucepan of water to a boil.

3. Add the zucchini pieces and blanch. (Alternatively, the zucchini may be cooked with a small amount of butter, *à l'étuvé*.)

4. Refresh and pat dry.

5. Preheat the oven to 163°C (325°F).

6. Using a melon baller, hollow out the zucchini flesh to make a cup shape.

7. Stuff the cups with tomato *concassé, duxelles*, well-seasoned cooked rice, or chopped, cooked zucchini flesh.

8. Place the stuffed zucchini in a buttered baking dish. Bake for about 20 minutes or until cooked through.

9. Serve hot or at room temperature.

Onions (*oignons*)

1. Peel and blanch whole onions.

2. Pat dry.

3. Preheat the oven to 149°C (300°F) and generously butter a baking pan or sauté pan.

4. Using a chef's knife, carefully cut the top off each onion.

5. Carefully remove the center flesh to leave a hollow cavity.

6. Chop the center flesh and add it to whatever style of stuffing is being used to fill the cavity.

7. Stuff the onions with the *farce*.

8. Place the onions in the prepared pan and cover with a piece of parchment paper cut to fit the top of the pan.

9. Bake, *à l'étuvé*, for about 45 minutes or until, onions are cooked and, stuffing is hot.

10. Serve hot or at room temperature.

Tomatoes (*tomates*)

1. Wash and dry the tomatoes.

2. Using a chef's knife, carefully cut off the stem end to make a neat lid. Set the lids aside.

3. Preheat the oven to 149°C (300°F) and generously butter a baking dish.

4. Using a teaspoon, carefully remove the pulp, seeds, and membrane from the center of the tomatoes.

5. Season the interior with salt and pepper to taste. Fill the hollows with a meat, *duxelles*, or rice stuffing.

6. Place a reserved lid on top of each filled tomato.

7. Place the stuffed tomatoes in the prepared baking dish and cover with a piece of parchment paper cut to fit the top of the dish.

8. Bake for about 30 minutes or until the tomatoes are cooked but still holding their shape.

9. Serve hot or at room temperature.

Mushrooms (*champignons*)

1. Remove the stems from large mushrooms and reserve them to use in the *farce*, if needed.

2. Fill a bowl with cool water with a teaspoon of lemon juice added. Place the mushrooms along with any stems and trimmings into the bowl of lemon water and swish to remove dirt or debris. Drain well and pat dry.

3. Preheat the oven to 149°C (300°F).

4. Heat olive oil (or butter) in an ovenproof *sautoir* over medium heat.

5. Add the mushroom caps, top down. Season with salt and pepper to taste.

6. Transfer the pan to the oven and cook for about 5 minutes or until the excess moisture has been removed.

7. Remove the mushrooms from the oven and, using a slotted spoon, place them on a double layer of paper towels to drain. Do not turn off the oven.

8. Set the *sautoir* aside.

9. When well drained, stuff the mushrooms with whatever filling is specified in the recipe, incorporating the chopped stems and trimmings, if possible.

10. Return the filled mushrooms to the *sautoir* and bake for about 15 minutes or until the filling is hot.

11. Remove from the oven and place under a salamander or broiler to *gratiner*.

12. Serve hot or at room temperature.

Potatoes (*pommes de terre*)

1. Wash large potatoes and dry them well.

2. Preheat the oven to 177°C (350°F).

3. Using a channel knife, cut a rim around the edge of the skin about 1 centimeter (⅓ inch) from the top of each potato.

4. Place a layer of coarse salt in the bottom of a roasting pan and place the potatoes in it.

5. Bake the potatoes for about 50 minutes or until the centers can be easily pierced with the point of a small, sharp knife.

6. Remove from the oven. Do not turn off the oven.

7. Using a chef's knife, cut off and reserve the piece that had been delineated by the channel knife. This will serve as a lid.

8. Using a melon baller, hollow out the flesh from each potato, leaving a "pocket" just thick enough to hold its shape.

9. Prepare whatever stuffing is specified in the recipe, incorporating the potato flesh, if possible.

10. Fill the potatoes with the stuffing.

11. Return the top piece to each potato, pushing down to cover firmly. (If necessary, use a toothpick to hold it in place.)

12. Generously butter a baking dish and place the filled potatoes in it.

13. Bake the potatoes for about 30 minutes or until the interior is very hot.

14. Remove from the oven and serve hot.

Demonstration

Paupiettes de Boeuf (Stuffed Beef Rolls)

Serves 4

Estimated time to complete: 90 minutes

Ingredients	Equipment
For the *duxelles*	Medium *sautoir*
20 grams (1 tablespoon plus 1 teaspoon) unsalted butter	Sharp chef's knife
20 grams (¾ ounce) shallots, *ciselé*	Plastic film
50 grams (1¾ ounces) button mushrooms, *brunoise*	Meat hammer
Coarse salt and freshly ground pepper to taste	Small bowl
10 grams (2 tablespoons) fresh flat-leaf parsley, *haché*	Small nonstick *sautoir*
3 grams (1 teaspoon) fresh tarragon, *haché*	Kitchen string or toothpicks
	Ovenproof *sautoir*
For the beef rolls	Wooden spoon
Four 227-gram (½-pound) pieces beef top round	Slotted spoon
200 grams (7 ounces) ground veal or pork or sausage meat	Warm plate
Coarse salt and freshly ground pepper to taste	Aluminum foil
20 grams (¾ ounce) all-purpose flour	Metal spoon
20 grams (1 tablespoon plus 1 teaspoon) unsalted butter	Serving platter
15 milliliters (1 tablespoon) vegetable oil	
For the garnish	
10 grams (2 teaspoons) unsalted butter	
50 grams (1¾ ounces) onions, *ciselé*	

30 grams (1 ounce) carrots, *brunoise*
100 milliliters (7 tablespoons) red wine
About 150 milliliters (⅔ cup) Brown
   Veal Stock (see page 57)

Prepare your *mise en place*.

To prepare the *duxelles*, heat the butter in a medium *sautoir* over medium heat. Add the shallots and sauté for about 3 minutes or just until the shallots have sweated their liquid. Add the mushrooms and salt and pepper to taste and cook for an additional 5 minutes or until the mushrooms have exuded most of their liquid and the mixture is almost dry. Remove from the heat and stir in the parsley and tarragon. Set the *duxelles* aside to cool.

To prepare the beef rolls, using a sharp chef's knife, cut the beef into thin slices against the grain.

Working with one slice at a time, place the beef between sheets of plastic film and, using a meat hammer, pound into thin, even scallops (*escalopes*). Set aside.

Place the ground meat in a small bowl. Stir in the *duxelles* and season with salt and pepper to taste.

When well combined, form a small portion into a patty and place the patty in a small nonstick *sautoir* over medium heat. Fry until cooked through, then taste and, if necessary, adjust the seasoning before using the mixture as a stuffing for the meat.

Working with one piece of meat at a time, place a quarter of the *duxelles* mixture into the center of each beef scallop. Pull opposite sides up and over to almost meet in the center, then roll up the scallop to form a neat packet. Using kitchen string or toothpicks, secure the *paupiette* so that it will hold its shape during cooking.

Preheat the oven to 149°C (300°F).

Season each *paupiette* with salt and pepper to taste and dust lightly with the flour.

Place an ovenproof *sautoir* over medium-high heat. Add the butter and oil and, when hot, add the seasoned *paupiettes*. Sear, turning frequently, for about 4 minutes or until all sides are nicely browned. Remove the *paupiettes* and set them aside.

To prepare the garnish, pour off the fat from the pan, then return the pan to medium heat. Add the butter for the garnish and, when melted, add the onions and carrots. Cook, stirring with a wooden spoon, for about 5 minutes or just until the vegetables have softened but not taken on any color.

Add the wine and stir, scraping well to dislodge all of the *sucs* and deglaze the pan. Bring to a simmer and cook, stirring frequently, for about 5 minutes or until the liquid has reduced by half.

Return the *paupiettes* to the pan. Add enough stock to come halfway up the sides of the meat. Bring to a simmer, cover, and place in the oven.

Bake, turning at least once and basting frequently, for about 30 minutes or until the meat is well cooked and the filling is hot.

Remove from the oven and, using a slotted spoon, transfer the *paupiettes* to a warm plate. Tent lightly with aluminum foil to keep warm.

Using a metal spoon, remove and discard any fat floating on top of the cooking liquid. Taste for season-ing and consistency. If necessary, season with salt and pepper to taste or return to the stovetop over medium heat to cook until reduced to desired consistency.

Remove and discard the string or toothpicks from the *paupiettes*. Using a chef's knife, cut each one cross-wise into thin slices. Arrange the slices, slightly over-lapping, on a serving platter and nap with the hot sauce. Serve hot.

Demonstration

Lègumes Farcis (Stuffed Vegetables)

Serves 4

Estimated time to complete: 90 minutes

Ingredients	Equipment
One 300-gram (10½-ounce) zucchini, washed and dried	Chef's knife
8 medium to large button mushrooms, cleaned	Melon baller or small spoon
2 large ripe tomatoes, washed and dried	Small bowl
15 milliliters (1 tablespoon) olive oil	*Sautoir*
57 grams (2 ounces) bacon, *macédoine*, blanched	Spatula
30 grams (1 ounce) shallots, *ciselé*	Small heatproof bowl
1 clove garlic, peeled, *haché*	Small *sautoir*
3 grams (2 teaspoons) fresh thyme, *haché*	Slotted spoon
Coarse salt and freshly ground pepper to taste	Paper towel
30 grams (1 ounce) freshly grated Parmesan cheese	Small baking pan
10 grams (2 teaspoons) unsalted butter	
About 180 milliliters (¾ cup) White Chicken Stock (see page 53) or vegetable stock	

Prepare your *mise en place*.

Using a chef's knife, trim off both zucchini ends. Cut the zucchini into four pieces about 5 centimeters (2 inches) long, setting aside any leftover pieces. Using a melon baller or small spoon, scoop out about three-quarters of the interior flesh from each. Chop the flesh along with any leftover pieces of zucchini. Set the zucchini pieces aside and place the chopped flesh in a small bowl.

Remove the stems from the mushrooms and finely chop them. Add the chopped stems to the chopped zucchini. Set the caps aside.

Using a chef's knife, cut the tomatoes in half cross-wise. Using a melon baller or small spoon, scoop out and discard all the seeds and about a third of the pulp. Set the tomato halves aside.

Heat the olive oil in a *sautoir* over medium heat. Add the bacon and fry for about 4 minutes or just until lightly browned. Add the shallots and sauté for 1 minute. Stir in the garlic and sauté for an additional minute. Add the reserved zucchini-mushroom mixture and sauté for about 7 minutes or until all the moisture has evaporated. Add the thyme, season with salt and pepper to taste, and sauté for 1 more minute. Using a spatula, scrape the mixture into a small heat-proof bowl and set aside to cool.

When the stuffing mixture has cooled, stir in about three-quarters of the Parmesan cheese. Set aside.

Cook the reserved zucchini pieces *à l'étuvé*. When cooked, remove from the pan and pat dry. Fill each piece with an equal portion of the stuffing. Set aside.

Heat the butter in a small *sautoir* over medium heat. Add the mushrooms, cap side down, and cook for 2 minutes or until just slightly softened. Season with salt and pepper to taste and, using a slotted spoon, transfer the mushrooms to a double layer of paper towels to drain.

When well drained, fill each cap with an equal portion of stuffing. Set aside.

Season the tomato halves with salt and pepper to taste. Fill each half with an equal portion of the stuffing and set aside.

When ready to serve, preheat the oven to 177°C (350°F).

Sprinkle the tops of the filled vegetables with the remaining Parmesan cheese.

Place a thin layer of stock in the bottom of a small baking pan and place the vegetables in the pan. Bake for about 10 minutes or just until heated through. For additional color, the cooked vegetables may be briefly placed under a salamander or preheated broiler.

Serve hot or at room temperature.

Session 19

Organic Meats: Making *Terrines, Ballottines,* and *Pâtés en Croûte*

Theory

Classification of Organ Meats

Organ meats, or *les abats*, are the main internal organs of an animal. In the United States, they are also called variety meats, nomenclature that incorporates the animal's exterior parts such as ears and feet as well as bony pieces. In ancient times, when the slaughtering of an animal was bathed in ritual, the organ meats, particularly the liver, were the first to be extracted from the animal and the first to be grilled, with their aromas offered to the gods. In contemporary American cooking (restaurant and home), organ meats, with the exception of calf's liver and, occasionally, sweetbreads, are not often found on the menu. Although they are economical to purchase and, when well prepared, extremely tasty, they are so associated with penurious cooking that they hold little appeal to the modern palate.

In classic French cooking, organ meats are classified in two groups, red organs and white organs. Both types can come from mutton, lamb, beef, or veal.

The classifications are as follows:

Red organs (*abats rouge*)

- Heart (*coeur*) — Very little heart is used in current restaurant cooking in the United States.

- Liver (*foie*) — Calf's liver is the most tender and choicest of all, but beef, pork, chicken, goose, duck, and lamb liver may also be used.

- Tongue (*langue*) — Tongue from veal, beef, or mutton is used mainly in cold dishes.

- Kidneys (*rognons*) — Kidneys from veal, beef, or mutton are used in sautés and stews.

White organs (*abats blancs*)

- Bone marrow (*moëlle*) — Beef and veal bone marrow is often used to garnish savory sauces.

- Feet (*pieds*) — Pork and beef feet are used mainly in *charcuterie.*

- Sweetbreads (*ris*) — Sweetbreads are the thymus glands of veal, young beef cattle, lamb, and pork. Sweetbreads from milk-fed veal or young calves are considered to be the choicest and most tender.

- Brains (*cervelles*) — Both veal and lamb brains are used in sautés.

- Head (*tête*) — Head, especially that of the pig, is used in *charcuterie* for *le museau* (head-cheese).

Technique
Preparation of Organ Meats

Although organ meats can be daunting to the cook, they are delicious when properly prepared. Following is information on preparing the various organ meats for cooking, as well as possible uses. Note that when purchasing, it is extremely important to buy only the very freshest and best-quality organ meats to ensure that they come from absolutely clean and healthy animals.

Deans' Tips

"There is mystery and a great complexity to the proper handling of organ meat; the refined palate enjoys it."

Dean Jacques Pépin

"All types of organ meats, which are delicacies in Latin countries, should be thoroughly cooked."

Dean Alain Sailhac

Red Organs

Calf's Liver

To prepare calf's liver, it is necessary to first peel off and discard the outer membrane, the thin, transparent film that covers the liver. The membrane should be removed only from the portion of the liver that is going to be cooked, since it acts as a seal that prevents the liver from oxidizing when stored; any remaining liver will oxidize quickly if peeled. When cutting the liver into individual slices, it should be cut very thin, on the bias.

Large pieces of liver may be roasted or grilled while tender, sliced calf's liver can be grilled or sautéed.

Tongue

Pull or cut off the larynx and degorge the tongue under cold running water. Place the tongue in a saucepan with cold water to cover by at least 1 inch. Bring to a boil over medium-high heat, then lower the heat and simmer for 10 minutes. Drain well and refresh under cold running water. Peel off and discard the tough outer layer of skin.

The cleaned tongue can be braised or poached.

Kidneys

The fat and transparent membrane surrounding the kidney enable it to be stored, refrigerated, for short periods of time. When ready to cook, remove and discard them. As with liver, remove only that portion of the membrane covering the amount being cooked, as any remaining kidney will oxidize quickly if peeled.

Kidneys can be sautéed, grilled, or braised.

White Organs

Marrow

Before being used, marrow must be degorged for anywhere from 2 to 6 hours or until it turns completely white. Once degorged, the marrow is poached in *consommé* (see page 215), but for a few seconds only. If poached for too long, the marrow will melt and be unusable. The marrow is then drained well, thinly sliced, and used as a garnish.

Feet

Before being used, feet must be degorged under cold running water. Once degorged, the feet are placed in a saucepan with cold water to cover by at least 1 inch. Bring to a boil over medium-high heat, then lower the heat and simmer for 10 minutes. Drain well and refresh under cold running water. Feet may or may not be boned before use.

Feet are very high in gelatin and are used to prepare aspics (*gelées*) as well as for rich braised dishes such as *boeuf à la mode* (larded beef braised with carrots in white wine). Feet are usually braised or poached. Split feet are an excellent addition to stocks to which they will add a much-desired gelatinous quality.

Sweetbreads

Before being used, sweetbreads must be degorged under cold running water. Once degorged, the sweetbreads are placed in a saucepan with cold water to cover by at least 1 inch. Bring to a boil over medium-high heat, then lower the heat and simmer for 3 minutes. Drain well and refresh under cold running water. Using your fingers, eliminate any nerves or cartilage.

337

Place the sweetbreads between two clean kitchen towels under a press made from a weighted-down board, taking care not to crush the meat. The weight is necessary to force out any excess water absorbed during the preliminary preparations as well as to shape the sweetbreads into an even form.

Sweetbreads may be braised, grilled, or sautéed.

Brains

Before being used, degorge the brains under cold running water. Using your fingers, carefully remove any traces of blood from the surface.

Once degorged, place the brains in a saucepan with cold, salted water to cover by at least 1 inch, along with a teaspoon of white vinegar and a *bouquet garni*. Bring to a boil over medium-high heat, then lower the heat and simmer for 10 minutes. Remove from the heat and allow the brains to rest in the cooking liquid until ready to prepare.

Brains can be sautéed *meunière*, served with *beurre noisette*, prepared *Grenobloise*, or deep-fat fried as *fritots* or *beignets* (savory fritters).

Veal Head

Using a cleaver, bone the head by cutting an incision down the whole length of the skull from the forehead to the muzzle. Remove the tongue and split the skull in two, carefully removing the brain.

Soak the head (*degorger*) in cold water for 4 hours.

Once degorged, place the head in a saucepan with cold water to cover by at least 1 inch. Bring to a boil over medium-high heat, then lower the heat and simmer for 5 minutes. Drain well and refresh under cold running water.

Rub all surfaces with a cut lemon half before cooking *dans un blanc*.

Dean's Tip

"To have a flavorful, shiny and gelatinous brown sauce, be sure to include a calf's foot in the base preparation."
Dean Alain Sailhac

Theory
General Information About *Pâtés en Croute, Terrines*, and *Ballottines*

Although the terms *pâté* and *terrine* are now used interchangeably, there were, originally, very specific differences. A *pâté* referred to a savory meat mixture wrapped in pastry and baked (*pâtés en croûte*), while a *terrine* was either a savory or sweet-spicy mixture of meats, fish, poultry, vegetables, or fruit cooked in gelatin in a lidded mold also referred to as a *terrine* (*pâté en terrine*) and served cold. In the contemporary kitchen, the terms are somewhat ambiguous, but occasionally a *pâté* will not be made and served in a molded form while a *terrine* is always made in and cut from a mold.

The term *pâté* derives from the word *pâte* (dough), which, in turn, refers to pastry shells containing combinations of meat, vegetables, or fruits. The rough equivalent, in English, would be pie. Both *pâtés* and *terrines* are preparations of forcemeat (see *farce*, page 326), a savory mixture of chopped or minced meat, game, poultry, or fish that is baked, allowed to cool, and served, usually sliced. The ingredients in a forcemeat depend upon the type of dish in which the mixture will be used. It is the combination of different forcemeats with various seasonings, garnishes, and binding elements that gives a specific dish its individual character. Unmolded *pâtés* are generally served cold. *Terrines* may be served warm or cold.

It is important to remember when making a *pâté* or a *terrine*, be it a simple country *pâté* (*pâté de campagne*) or an elaborate wild game *terrine* (*terrine de gibier*), to treat the various components of it differently so that distinct flavors and textures are experienced on the palate. If all the components were to be placed together in a meat grinder, the resulting mixture would create an uninteresting loaf of uniform taste and texture.

Ballottines and *galantines* are very similar in composition to *pâtés* and *terrines*, but are either rolled or stuffed into an enclosure of meat, poultry, game, or seafood. A *ballottine* is poached or braised and can be served either hot or cold. If served cold, it generally has a gelatin coating. A *galantine* is poached, molded in gelatin, and served cold.

All these dishes should be made with ingredients of the highest quality that have been kept well chilled throughout the preparation process. All equipment used should be pristine to guarantee a bacteria-free, impeccably prepared dish.

Pâtés and *Terrines*

Pâtés and *terrines* are composed of diverse forcemeats brought together to create a contrast in texture and flavor. They are usually cooked (baked) in deep, earthenware molds (*terrines*) that have been lined with thin sheets of pork fat or bacon. The dominant element or ingredient determines the name of the dish.

Components of *Pâtés* and *Terrines*

The success of a *pâté* or *terrine* greatly depends upon the quality of the ingredients used, the proportion of meats, the subtle balance of the seasonings, and the attractiveness and propriety of the garnish. There are three components to a well-made mixture for a *pâté* or *terrine*:

○ A fine forcemeat (*farce*) that consists of finely puréed or ground ingredients along with breadcrumbs that act as a binding element.

○ A coarse forcemeat (*farce*) with small bits of minced or chopped marinated meats and fats.

○ The garnish, which might include cubes of meat (such as ham), pistachios, truffles, or other morsels. The garnish provides additional contrast to the forcemeat and adds an attractive look to the finished dish.

When all three components have been combined, a small patty of the mixture should be cooked and tasted for correct seasoning before proceeding further. Most beginning *charcutiers* make the mistake of underseasoning, so this is a very significant step.

The forcemeat for a *pâté* is usually a combination of finely ground and minced or chopped meat (pork, veal, beef, game, or poultry). Pork, both lean and fatty, is essential for a successful dish as it ensures that the end product, once cooked, will be moist and smooth. Usually the fat content is about 20 to 30 percent of the total weight.

All elements of a forcemeat are ground or minced separately and then mixed together. The method of grinding, the degree of coarseness in the grind, the various ingredients used, and the ratio of ingredients vary in each recipe. In general, half of the ingredients of a terrine are used as the main element of the dish and the other half bind everything together. A *pâté* or *terrine* may contain a binder of egg whites, whole eggs, or breadcrumbs. The job of the binding element is to supplement the albumin in the ground meat mixture so that it will coagulate and make a *liaison* once it reaches a certain temperature.

The forcemeat is seasoned with salt, pepper, herbs, and spices and then, typically, marinated in a combination of Madeira, wine, cognac, or other alcohol for anywhere from one hour to an entire day. Any garnish is usually marinated in an alcohol separately.

A forcemeat mixture should always be checked for seasoning before being used. However, since it must never be tasted raw, a small portion should be formed into a patty and fried until cooked through. It is then tasted and any adjustments to seasonings are made.

At this point, the mold is lined with thin sheets of pork fat or bacon, and the properly seasoned forcemeat is packed into it, along with any garnish being used. The top is also covered with pork fat or bacon, often by bringing it up from the sides and enclosing the entire mold. The filled mold is then covered with a lid, placed in a *bain-marie* in a slow oven, and baked

until cooked through. The mold is removed from the oven, uncovered, and allowed to cool on a wire rack. Once cooled, the mold is refrigerated and the *terrine* is allowed to ripen, causing the flavors to deepen, for a couple of days before serving. It can be served immediately after cooking, but the flavors will not have much depth.

Pâtés en Croûte

The method of preparation for *pâtés en croûtes* is the same as that for *pâtés* and *terrines* except that the forcemeat mixture is wrapped in either *pâte feuilletée* (see page 356) or *pâte à pâté* (*pâté brisee* made with lard using less fat). They may be formed in different shaped molds — either round, rectangular, or oval — or freeform. If a mold is used, it is lined with pastry large enough to completely envelope the filling, and the top is also covered with pastry. Round holes (*cheminées*) are cut into the top to allow vapors and steam to escape during baking.

Ballottines and Galantines

Ballottines and galantines are prepared identically, the only difference being that a *ballottine* may be served hot or cold, and a *galantine* is always served cold. Classically they are made with a large spring chicken or duck. The poultry is boned, keeping the skin as intact as possible, and the skin is set aside. The meat is finely ground, seasoned, and placed inside the intact skin and rolled. It is then wrapped in a clean towel or piece of linen, tied securely with kitchen string, and poached in an aromatic white stock. *Ballottines* may also be roasted. The interior design may include small diced pieces (**salpicons**) of poultry and garnishes of pork fat, hazelnuts, pistachios, or other appropriate ingredients.

Technique
Guidelines for Preparation of *Pâtés, Terrines, Ballottines*, and *Galantines*

There are five steps common to the preparation of *pâtés, terrines, ballottines,* and *galantines*:

1. Boning (*désossage*): Completely trimming the meat of all bones.

2. Marinating (*marinade*): Soaking the meat to be used for the forcemeat in alcohol and then seasoning it.

3. Designing (*façonnage*): The shaping and molding of the filling, along with its placement in a lined mold.

4. Cooking (*cuisson*): Baking in a *bain-marie* until the interior reaches a designated temperature on an instant-read thermometer.

5. Preservation (*conservation*): Covering the filling with a layer of pork lard or gelatin.

Cooking times for forcemeat mixtures and molds vary

according to the size of the molded product, the temperature of the forcemeat when placed in the oven, as well as the oven temperature. Each one must be individually tested using one or all of the following methods to determine doneness.

○ Observe the juices coming from the ventilation holes; they should be running clear.

○ Stick a trussing needle all the way to the bottom of the mold. After exactly 12 seconds, pull it out and place it against your bottom lip. It should feel extremely hot at both the tip and the middle.

○ Insert an instant-read thermometer into the center of the mold. After 2 minutes, the thermometer should read 60°C–66°C (140°F–150°F).

Demonstration

Ris de Veau Braisés, Petits Pois Paysanne

(Braised Sweetbreads with Country-Style Peas)

Serves 4

Estimated time to complete: 12 hours

Ingredients	Equipment
For the sweetbreads	Bowl
750 grams (about 1½ pounds) calf's sweetbreads	2 *sautoirs*, 1 with lid
45 grams (3 tablespoons) unsalted butter	2 kitchen towels
25 milliliters (1½ tablespoons) vegetable oil	Weighted board
Coarse salt and freshly ground pepper to taste	Slotted spatula
100 grams (3½ ounces) carrots, *mirepoix*	Paper towels
100 grams (3½ ounces) onions, *mirepoix*	Wooden spoon
85 milliliters (5¾ tablespoons) white wine	2 small saucepans
40 milliliters (2 tablespoons plus 2 teaspoons) port wine	Heatproof platter
or Madeira	Aluminum foil
About 400 milliliters (1⅔ cups) Veal *Demi-glace* (see page 59)	*Chinois*
	Metal spoon
For the garnish	Chef's knife
200 grams (7 ounces) fresh English peas	4 warm dinner plates
20 grams (1 tablespoon plus 1 teaspoon) unsalted butter	
Sugar to glaze	
100 grams (3½ ounces) pearl onions, peeled	
100 grams (3½ ounces) carrots, *bouquetière*	
100 grams (3½ ounces) turnips, *bouquetière*	
1 small head Boston lettuce, well-washed,	
trimmed, and cut into *chiffonade*	
Coarse salt and freshly ground pepper to taste	

Prepare your *mise en place.*

Place the sweetbreads in a bowl with cold water to cover for at least 2 hours and preferably overnight to extract all the blood. Drain well.

Place the soaked sweetbreads in a *sautoir* with cold water to cover. Bring to a simmer over medium-high heat and blanch for 3 minutes. Remove from the heat, drain well, and refresh under cold running water. Pat dry. Rinse the *sautoir.*

Using your fingertips, remove the fatty parts and the membranes.

Place the sweetbreads between two clean kitchen

towels under a press made from a weighted-down board, taking care not to crush the meat. Place in the refrigerator for at least 1 hour or until ready to use.

When ready to cook, preheat the oven to 163°C (325°F).

Heat the *sautoir* over medium heat. Add the butter and oil and when hot, season the sweetbreads with salt and pepper to taste and place them in the hot pan. Sear, turning frequently, for about 3 minutes or until the sweetbreads are nicely browned on all sides.

Using a slotted spatula, transfer the sweetbreads to a double layer of paper towels to drain.

Drain any excess fat from the pan, leaving just enough to sauté the *mirepoix*. Return the pan to medium heat and add the carrots and onions. Sauté for about 5 minutes or until lightly browned.

Add the white wine and, using a wooden spoon, deglaze the *sucs*. Bring the liquid to a simmer and simmer for about 5 minutes or until reduced by half. Add the portwine, return the liquid to a simmer, and reduce by half.

Return the sweetbreads to the pan. Add enough *demi-glace* to come halfway up the sides of the meat. Bring to a simmer, cover, and place in the oven. Cook for 30 minutes or until the sweetbreads are cooked through and well flavored.

While the sweetbreads are cooking, prepare the garnish.

Cook the peas *à l'anglaise*.

Using the butter and sugar, cook the pearl onions, carrots, and turnips *glacer à blanc*.

Bring a small saucepan of water to a boil over high heat. Add the lettuce *chiffonade* and blanch for 15 seconds. Drain well, refresh under cold running water, and pat dry.

When all the vegetables have been cooked as directed and the sweetbreads are about ready, mix the warm vegetables together in a *sautoir*, season with salt and pepper to taste, and set aside on the stovetop to keep warm.

Remove the sweetbreads from the oven, uncover, and transfer to a warm, heatproof platter. Tent lightly with aluminum foil to keep warm.

Strain the cooking liquid through a *chinois* into a clean saucepan. Using a metal spoon, skim off and discard any fat that rises to the surface. Taste, and if necessary, adjust the seasoning with salt and pepper to taste. If the consistency is not smooth and sauce-like, place over medium heat and cook, stirring occasionally, until the proper consistency is reached. Nap the sweetbreads with some of the sauce and briefly place them under the salamander or broiler to glaze.

Using a chef's knife, cut the sweetbreads into neat slices on the bias. Place an equal portion on each of four warm dinner plates. Nap each portion with some of the remaining sauce. Spoon the vegetables over the top or arrange them on the side. Serve immediately.

Chef's Tip

"I add the raw chiffonade of lettuce to the glazed vegetables to avoid the unnecessary step of blanching. Because the lettuce is so tender, it also melds into the mixture very easily."
Chef Sixto Alonso

Demonstration

Foie de Veau à la Lyonnaise (Calf's Liver Lyonnaise)

Serves 4

Estimated time to complete: 45 minutes

Ingredients	Equipment
60 grams (4 tablespoons) unsalted butter	*Sautoir*
400 grams (14 ounces) onions, *émincé*	Shallow bowl
50 grams (1¾ ounces) all-purpose flour	*Poêle*
Four 120-gram (4 ½-ounce) slices calf's liver	Tongs
Coarse salt and freshly ground pepper to taste	Warm serving platter
10 milliliters (2 teaspoons) vegetable oil	Aluminum foil
30 mililters (2 tablespoons) white wine vinegar	Wooden spoon
200 milliliters (14 tablespoons) Veal *Demi-glace* (see page 59)	
5 grams (1 tablespoon) fresh flat-leaf parsley, *haché*	

Prepare your *mise en place.*

Heat a *sautoir* over medium-high heat. Add 10 grams (about 2 teaspoons) of the butter and, when melted, stir in the onions. Lower the heat and cook, stirring frequently, for about 15 minutes or until the onions are soft and translucent.

Place the flour in a shallow bowl.

Season the liver with salt and pepper to taste. Dip both sides of the seasoned liver into the flour, shaking off any excess.

Heat the oil in a *poêle* over medium-high heat. Add 30 grams (2 tablespoons) of the remaining butter. When bubbling, add the liver and fry for about 1 minute or until nicely browned. Using tongs, turn the liver and fry for another couple of minutes or until the outside is nicely browned and the interior remains pink. Transfer the liver to a warm serving platter. Tent lightly with aluminum foil and set aside to rest.

Leaving the *poêle* on medium-high heat, transfer the cooked onions to the pan. Cook, stirring frequently, for about 5 minutes or until caramelized. Add the vinegar and, using a wooden spoon, scrape the *sucs* to deglaze the pan. Cook for 1 minute. Add the *demi-glace*. Taste, and if necessary, adjust the seasoning with salt and pepper. Using the remaining butter, *monter au beurre.*

Pour the sauce over the liver, sprinkle with the parsley, and serve immediately.

Demonstration

Rouelles de Rognons à la Dijonnaise (Kidneys with Mustard Sauce)

Serves 4

Estimated time to complete: 30 minutes

Ingredients	Equipment
680 grams (about 1½ pounds) veal kidneys	Chef's knife
45 grams (3 tablespoons) unsalted butter	*Poêle*
25 milliliters (1½ tablespoons) vegetable oil	Slotted spatula
40 grams (1½ ounces) shallots, *ciselé*	Paper towels
25 milliliters (1½ tablespoons) cognac	Wooden spoon
150 milliliters (⅔ cup) Veal *Demi-glace*	Warm serving platter
(see page 59)	
60 milliliters (¼ cup) heavy cream	
Dijon mustard to taste	
Coarse salt and freshly ground pepper to taste	
5 grams (1 tablespoon) fresh flat-leaf parsley, *haché*	

Prepare your *mise en place*.

Peel the outer skin from the kidneys. Using a chef's knife, cut them in half lengthwise, and remove the center fat. Cut each half into 1-centimeter (⅓ inch)-thick slices.

Heat a *poêle* over high heat and add 30 grams (2 tablespoons) of the butter along with the oil. When hot, add the kidneys in a single layer and sear on both sides until nicely browned on the exterior but still pink inside. Using a slotted spatula, remove the kidneys from the pan and transfer to a double layer of paper towels to drain. (Alternatively, you can place the kidneys on a plate and then lift it up and tilt it slightly to drain off the fat and juices.)

Using a paper towel, wipe out the pan and then return it to medium heat. Add the remaining 5 grams (1 tablespoon) butter and, when hot, add the shallots. Cook, stirring frequently with a wooden spoon, for about 3 minutes or just until soft with no color.

Add the cognac and stir to loosen the *sucs* and deglaze the pan. Add the *demi-glace* and then the cream and cook, stirring occasionally, for about 10 minutes or until reduced to a saucelike consistency.

Remove the pan from the heat and stir in the mustard. Season with salt and pepper to taste. Add the reserved kidneys and return the pan to medium-low heat. Do not allow the sauce to boil or it will break.

Pour the kidneys onto a warm serving platter, sprinkle with the parsley, and serve.

Demonstration

Pâté de Campagne (Country Pâté)

Makes one 33-x-10-centimeter (13-x-4-inch) pâté
Estimated time to complete: 3 hours to prepare and cook; at least 12 hours to rest

Ingredients	Equipment
For the fine forcemeat	Sauté pan
15 milliliters (1 tablespoon) vegetable oil	Wooden spoon
227 grams (½ pound) chicken livers	2 mixing bowls
4 cloves garlic, peeled and worked into a paste	Meat grinder
2 shallots, *ciselé*	Chef's knife
Fresh marjoram, *haché*, to taste	Small nonstick skillet
Fresh thyme leaves, *haché*, to taste	33-x-10-x-9-centimeter
600 grams (1 pound, 3 ounces) pork shoulder, diced	(13-x-4-x-3½-inch) *terrine*
300 grams (10½ ounces) fatback	Large baking pan
250 grams (8¾ ounces) boneless, skinless chicken	Instant-read thermometer
	Wire rack
For the coarse forcemeat	Weight
600 grams (1 pound, 3 ounces) pork shoulder	

For the marinade
90 milliliters (6 tablespoons) cognac
60 milliliters (¼ cup) port or red wine
3 grams (1 scant teaspoon) *sel rose* for every
    kilogram (2¼ pounds) meat (see note) and fat
15 grams (1 tablespoon) coarse salt for
    every kilogram (2¼ pounds) meat and fat
Freshly ground pepper to taste
Fresh flat-leaf parsley, *haché*

For the garnish
150 grams (5¼ ounces) fatback, diced
150 grams (5¼ ounces) lean ham, diced
Approximately 115 grams (4 ounces) shelled pistachios, as needed

To finish
About 150 grams (5¼ ounces) fatback, thinly sliced
Bay leaves for decoration

Note

Sel rose is saltpeter or potassium nitrate. It is used as a preservative and to help the meat retain a nice rosy hue once baked.

349

Prepare your *mise en place.*

First, prepare the fine forcemeat.

Heat the oil in a sauté pan over high heat. Add the livers and fry, turning occasionally, for about 10 minutes or until cooked through. Stir in the garlic, shallots, marjoram, and thyme and sauté for another 3 minutes or just until the aromatics have sweated their liquid. Remove the pan from the heat to cool.

Combine the cooked liver mixture with the pork shoulder, fatback, and chicken in a mixing bowl and then grind the mixture together through the fine disk of a meat grinder into a clean mixing bowl.

Preheat the oven to 163°C (325°F).

Using a chef's knife, coarsely chop the pork shoulder for the coarse forcemeat, noting that the texture must be a strong contrast to the fine forcemeat.

To make the marinade, combine the cognac, port, *sel rose*, salt, pepper to taste and the parsley.

Add the coarse forcemeat to the fine forcemeat mixture. Add the marinade and the garnish ingredients and mix them thoroughly but without mashing them together.

Form a small portion of the mixture into a small patty. Place in a small nonstick skillet over medium heat and fry until cooked through. Remove from the heat and taste. If necessary, adjust the seasonings.

Line a 33-x-10-x-9-centimeter (13-x-4-x-3½-inch) *terrine* with the fatback slices, allowing the fatback to overlap the sides of the mold with enough of an overhang to completely cover the top of the mold.

Transfer the forcemeat mixture to the lined mold, patting down gently.

Arrange the bay leaves on top of the forcemeat in an attractive pattern.

Bring the fatback up and over the filling to completely cover it.

Place the mold in a larger pan filled with hot water to come at least halfway up the sides of the mold. Then place the pans in the oven and bake for about 90 minutes or until the internal temperature of the *pâté* reaches 60°C–66°C (140°F–150°F). Check the oven from time to time; the water must never come to a boil or it will cause the meat to shrink and toughen. If necessary, add a bit of cool water to decrease the heat.

Remove the *pâté* from the oven and transfer to a wire rack to cool. When cool, weight the top and refrigerate for at least 12 hours to allow the flavors to meld.

Serve chilled.

Theory

About Pastry Dough

A *pâte* or pastry dough is a flour-based preparation that, when rolled out into a thin sheet and molded, acts as a container for a filling. (Do not confuse *pâte* with *pâté*, a more recognizable French term for baked ground meat preparations.) All pastry doughs are comprised of four basic ingredients: flour, water, fat, and salt. Occasionally a dough will also call for the addition of either a raw egg or a hard-cooked egg yolk. The proportions of the four basic ingredients and the method by which they are combined will determine the type of dough created. The word *pâte* can also refer to a batter (covered in Session 21), as well as to fresh pasta dough (*pâte fraîches*) and fresh noodle dough (*pâte à nouilles*).

A pastry dough that is rolled out, fitted into a mold, and baked is called a tart or a pie shell. A tart generally refers to the French open-faced shell, whereas a pie usually refers to the traditional English two-crusted (top and bottom) pastry version. The fillings contained in a pastry dough tart or pie are many and varied. Fruit, meat, vegetables, fish, creams, custards, nuts, and chocolate are just some of the possibilities.

Dough gets its strength from the gluten in the flour and its tenderness from the fat. The amount of water added to the basic mixture is crucial, as the water enables the gluten molecules to form when the flour is mixed with the liquid. Too much water and the dough will be hard and dry; with too little water, it will be crumbly and unworkable. In addition, the amount of water needed depends upon external factors such as temperature and humidity as well as the moisture in the flour, the type of fat used, and how the fat and flour have been mixed together. As a general rule, just enough water should be added to allow the flour and fat mixture to hold together when pressed between your fingertips.

There is absolutely no mystery to making perfect pastry, but there is definitely a lot of fear associated with it. In fact, many cooks avoid pastry making. This limits them greaty in the kitchen. The basic pastry doughs are *pâte brisée*, *pâte sucrée*, *pâte sablée*, *pâte feuilletée*, and *pâte à choux*. With the exception of *pâte sablée*, all are covered in this chapter. *Pâte à crêpes* and *pâte à frire* are batters, which are discussed in Session 22. All these doughs are essential, not only to pastry and baking, but to French cuisine in general. Much like the basic skills of *tournage*, pastry making is best mastered through practice. It is, therefore, a good plan to create menus around pastry-based dishes so that you have no waste as you learn.

Pâte brisée is the basic French flaky tart dough created through the mixture of the four basic ingredients of flour, water, fat, and salt. Some recipes for this basic dough may also call for the addition of an egg yolk, either raw or hard-cooked. If sugar is added to the *pâte brisée* (pie pastry), the dough becomes *pâte sucrée* (sweetened pastry). *Pâte sablée* (short pastry) has more fat and less liquid than the other basic doughs, which produces a crumbly texture similar to a shortbread cookie dough.

Pâte feuilletée, or puff pastry, is a classic, delicate, multilayered pastry dough made by encapsulating large amounts of butter in a basic mixture of flour, water, salt, and a small amount of melted butter. The entire package, called a *pâton*, is rolled out and folded (or turned) six times, creating a dough with more than 700 paper-thin layers of flour and butter. When baked, the butter creates steam, which causes the dough to puff up dramatically and separate into hundreds of flaky, crunchy pastry layers. This is the dough used to make *napoleons* and other classic pastries.

Pâte Brisée and *Pâte Sucrée*

The two most basic types of classic pastry dough are *pâte brisée*, which is used for all manner of tarts (both savory and sweet), and its sister, *pâte sucrée*, which, because it contains a substantial amount of sugar, is used solely with sweets. As with all pastry doughs, making either one of these doughs successfully requires the use of specified ingredients, the exact measurement of those ingredients, and careful adherence to the procedure outlined in the recipe. Always follow the directions given with each pastry recipe; never improvise or substitute ingredients until you have completely mastered the recipe.

Because of its versatility, *pâte brisée* is the most frequently made basic dough. A small amount of sugar can be added to it to increase its ability to take on color or to heighten its flavor when used with a sweet filling. When eggs are added to this dough, the result is a firmer, sturdier, and slightly less delicate finished pastry.

The first rule to remember when making *pâte brisée* is to always use an easy hand, working the dough as little as possible to keep from developing the gluten. This occurs when the protein molecules in the flour are moistened with liquid as the ingredients are worked together. A small amount of gluten is necessary so that the dough will hold together, but if the dough is overworked and the gluten is overexpanded, the pastry will be too elastic, shrink, and be hard and tough when baked.

Basic Components of *Pâte Brisée* and *Pâte Sucrée*

The fat used when making pastry dough coats and softens the gluten particles and creates the flakiness in the finished pastry. Although lard and vegetable shortening can be used, butter is almost always the fat of choice in the preparation of classic French pastry doughs. The exception to this is in regional French specialties, where lard or poultry fat or game fat is used to make pastry dough. Whatever fat is used, it must always be well chilled. If it is too soft, it will break down too early and melt into the flour; if it is frozen, it will be too hard to combine easily with the flour.

When adding the liquid ingredients to the flour-and-fat combination, keep in mind that the amount of liquid required varies depending on the moisture content of the flour, the kind of fat used, and the temperature and humidity of the day. The liquid should be ice-cold, which also helps retard the development of the gluten in the flour. A bit of acid, such as lemon juice, sour cream, or vinegar, added to liquid also softens the gluten, resulting in a very flaky crust. The liquid should be added little by little, mixing it in quickly and easily, adding just enough to hold the dough together when pressed lightly into a ball between your fingertips. If the dough is sticky or easily pulls into a mass, too much liquid has been added. A dry dough is difficult to roll and will crack and fall apart, while a wet dough sticks to the work surface, is almost impossible to roll, and shrinks when baked. The addition of the liquid is perhaps the most crucial step in making a light and flaky finished product. Like many other kitchen techniques, it simply requires patience and practice to succeed.

When eggs are added to a pastry dough, they count toward the liquid portion of the basic ingredients. Because of their viscosity, eggs will not combine easily with the flour if not thoroughly beaten before being added. Therefore, eggs should always be well-mixed, either by themselves or with any other liquid ingredients, before being added to the flour-and-fat mixture or the dough will have to be overworked to get them to meld into the flour.

Pâte à Choux

Although *pâte à choux* is made from the basic flour-water-fat combination of other pastry doughs, unlike the other doughs it is leavened through the addition of eggs and cooked before it is shaped. The initial dough is formed by beating flour into a heated mixture of water, butter, sugar, and salt. The heat causes the flour to swell and form a paste. The paste is then cooked on the stovetop, where it is beaten constantly to pull out enough moisture and dry the paste enough to enable it to absorb the eggs. The French term for this process is *dessécher*. The paste is then removed from the heat and beaten to develop the gluten structure and to cool slightly so that the eggs can be added safely. If the eggs are added before the mixture has cooled enough, they will begin to cook and will not blend into the paste.

Because of the extra moisture content — through the addition of eggs and more water than usual — *pâte à choux* behaves very differently than other pastry. When making *choux* pastry the proportion of ingredients will change on any given day. For instance, the number of eggs required will vary according to the size of the eggs, the amount of moisture in the air, and the amount of moisture extracted from the paste during cooking. The finished dough should be very thick and smooth and quite shiny. Again, practice will yield perfect pastry.

When making *choux* pastry, the dough is usually transferred to a pastry bag and piped in a shape designated by the particular recipe onto baking sheets lined with parchment paper. During baking, the excess moisture and the eggs in the dough expand and turn to steam, causing the pastry to puff up and form an internal hollow cavity. If piped into small rounds, the resulting pastry puffs resemble little cabbages from which the pastry gets its name, *choux* being French for cabbage.

After baking, some steam remains inside the pastry. It must be eliminated to keep the pastry puffs crisp. When properly baked, *choux* pastry will feel hollow and almost feather-light. The method for assuring this depends on the type of heat used. If using a conventional oven, the oven temperature is turned down to its lowest setting and the oven door is opened and left ajar for 10 minutes. If using a convection oven, the oven is turned off just when the pastry is golden brown, and the pastry is allowed to sit in the closed oven for an additional 5 to 10 minutes (again, the time depends on the amount of moisture remaining in the dough — a taste test is the best barometer).

Pâte à choux can be deep-fried or poached in liquid. It can be used for savory preparations as well as for desserts. Among its savory uses are for *beignets* (fritters), *gougères* (cheese puffs), *pommes dauphine* (potato croquettes), and *gnocchi parisienne* (dumplings). It is a most versatile pastry dough.

"When making choux paste, keep the paste moving as it dries or it will burn. You know that the paste is dry when it begins to leave a thin film on the bottom of the saucepan."

Dean Jacques Torres

"Pâte à choux is the most versatile dough to be used in savory as well as sweet preparations — from gnocchi to gougères to quenelles to pommes dauphine to Saint-Honoré cake or to a towering croquembouche."

Dean Jacques Pépin

"When making a croquembouche, make sure that the caramel is at the hard crack stage or your guests will have problems with their teeth."

Dean Alain Sailhac

Chef's Tip

"When scaling out liquids in a measuring cup before heating them, measure them and pour them directly into the pot. There is no need to measure them into a bowl and then pour them into the pot."

Chef Susan Lifrieri

Many of the classic French desserts are prepared with *pâte à choux*:

- **Choux à la Crème Chantilly:** Puff pastry rounds filled with sweetened whipped cream (see *Crème Chantilly*, page 376).

- **Profiteroles:** Puff pastry rounds filled with ice cream and served with warm chocolate sauce.

- **Éclairs:** Elongated puff pastries that are, classically, filled with pastry cream (see *crème pâtissière*, page 390) and dipped in ***fondant*** icing (see page 380).

- **Paris Brest:** A classic dessert that consists of a ring of almond-topped *pâte à choux* filled with praline flavored pastry cream.

- **Gâteau Saint-Honoré:** A round of *pâte sucrée* (see page 360) that is encircled by caramel-dipped cream puffs filled with *crème chiboust* (pastry cream lightened with meringue and stabilized with gelatin).

- **Croquembouche:** A pyramid of pastry puffs held together by caramel that is a traditional French centerpiece often featured at celebratory occasions.

Technique
Rolling Out and Baking Dough

Once pastry dough has been mixed, it should be formed into a ball or slightly flattened disk with clean, cool, dry hands. It is then wrapped in plastic film and chilled. Chilling is one of the most important steps in pastry making. It allows the gluten to rest and assists in the creation of a flaky, tender pastry that does not shrink when baked. All pastry dough should be refrigerated for at least 15 minutes after being made. It is even more beneficial to refrigerate a dough for at least 24 hours before it is rolled out. In most cases, the dough should be chilled again after it has been rolled out and shaped. The only exception to the chilling process is when making *pâte à choux* (see page 373).

Rolling out the dough is where many cooks panic. Don't! Just remember the light hand and proceed. All doughs should be rolled out on a clean, cool surface — well-chilled marble is an exceptional anchor. (Some cooks have a piece of marble just for this purpose.) Prepare the rolling surface by lightly coating it with flour. Lightly press the dough onto the floured surface, using the heel of your hand to flatten it slightly. If the dough is too firm, strike it a few times with the rolling pin to make it pliable. Lightly flour the rolling pin and, using quick, firm, consistent strokes, begin rolling the dough from the center outward in every direction. Continue rolling until you have a circle (or other shape specified in a recipe) of the desired diameter and thickness. It is usually recommended that the diameter be about 2 inches greater than the diameter of the pan. For a classic French tart, the dough is rolled into a circle approximately 3 millimeters (⅛ inch) thick.

Once rolled, the pastry circle may be transferred to the pan by gently lifting and folding it in half over the rolling pin and then slipping it, still folded, into the pan. Unfold the circle to cover the bottom of the pan and remove the rolling pin. Take care not to pull or stretch the dough or it will shrink as it bakes. Smooth the pastry into the pan with quick, light, pressing movements, making certain there are no holes from which juices can escape. If using a bottom crust only, as for a tart, make sure that the edges are neat and pressed into the corners of the pan.

When filling a pastry shell with a soft filling such as a custard, the pastry shell must be thoroughly baked beforehand to prevent it from becoming soggy with the addition of the filling. The process is called *cuire à blanc*, or blind baking. The molded pastry shell is first refrigerated for at least 15 minutes; then it is lined with a piece of parchment paper cut to fit the bottom and come up the sides of the pan. The paper-coated pastry is then filled with dried beans or pastry weights (small metal rounds made for this purpose) to weight it down so that it does not form air pockets and will keep its shape during the initial phase of baking. The prepared shell is placed in a preheated oven of fairly high temperature (usually 204°C/400°F) and baked until it looks chalky-white. It is then removed from the oven, the weights and parchment paper are taken out, and the pastry is returned to a moderate (usually 163°C/325°F) oven to be baked until golden and cooked through.

When the filling requires substantial cooking, the pastry shell is still prepared in this fashion, but it is baked just until cooked through without turning color. It is removed from the oven and allowed to cool before filling. Once cooled and filled, the shell is returned to the oven for complete baking.

Theory

Puff Pastry (*Pâte Feuilletée*)

As discussed, puff pastry is a rich, light, and delicious pastry dough that is the base for a wide variety of sweet and savory dishes in the classic French culinary repertoire. Although time-consuming to prepare, contrary to its reputation, puff pastry is not particularly difficult to make. It is used for pies, tarts, *allumettes* (puff pastry strips), and *vols-au-vent* (puff pastry shells), as well as many other dishes (see page 358).

According to the culinarian's bible, *Larousse Gastronomique*, puff pastry was known and made as far back as ancient Greece. In French culinary lore, a mention of puff pastry is found in a fourteenth-century charter drawn up by the Bishop of Amiens. However, it seems that the techniques for its perfection were formalized by two seventeenth-century cooks — a chef named Feuillet, who served as pastry cook to an aristocratic family, and a renowned French landscape painter, Claude Lorrain, who also happened to have served a pastry apprenticeship in his youth. Some historians credit Feuillet as the inventor, some credit Lorrain, but whichever one it was, by the eighteenth-century *pâte feuilletée* was firmly entrenched in the classic French pastry kitchen.

Several specialized terms are associated with the making of puff pastry. The process begins with a simple dough composed of flour, salt, water, and melted butter called a *détrempe* and a block of butter called a *beurrage*. The *détrempe* is folded around the *beurrage* to form a package called a *pâton*. The *pâton* is then folded, turned, rolled, and chilled many times, until a multilayered dough has been created. The more folds, turns, and rolls there are, the more layers in the finished pastry.

This process of folding, rolling, and turning is called *tourage*. Typically, the dough is rolled out at intervals of two turns at a time, followed by a substantial refrigerated resting period, which firms the fat and prevents it from melding into the dough. The classic number of turns is six, but four or five can also be done, depending on the final use of the pastry. The dough will not rise as much when fewer turns are done.

Since puff pastry has no leavening agent such as yeast, eggs, or baking powder, the layers created by *tourage* are necessary to buoy up the dough. Through *tourage*, each layer of fat or dough is rolled thinner than a piece of paper but remains separate and intact. When baked, the moisture in the dough and the melting (or boiling) butter creates steam that pushes the layers, forcing them to rise, one by one, puffing up the pastry and causing it to become flaky and light.

Depending on the use of the finished pastry, the butter can be replaced with other fats, such as lard or goose fat. A less delicate type of puff pastry known as rough puff pastry (*pâte feuilletée rapide*) can be made in a much shorter period of time by eliminating the refrigerated resting period. Leftover puff pastry pieces, called *demi-feuilletage* or *rognures*, can be rolled out and used to make small pastries such as tiny tart shells, or *barquettes* (small boat-shaped pastry shells), or used to make decorative pastry trim.

Dean's Tip

"Here is a trick that I use when I bake a tart shell without filling: Immediately after baking, brush the tart shell with a little bit of corn syrup and dry it in the oven for about 5 minutes. This keeps the shell from becoming soggy."

Dean Jacques Torres

Guidelines for Making Puff Pastry

It is important to keep the following points in mind when making puff pastry:

Keep the work environment cool.

The kitchen should be cool, and there should be a cool surface to work on, preferably marble. Otherwise, puff pastry can be very difficult to manage. It must be rechilled as soon as it starts to soften and before the butter begins to melt or it will be impossible to manipulate.

Do not overdevelop the gluten.

When making the *détrempe*, mix the ingredients as little as possible, just enough to form a rough mass that holds together. Too much mixing will cause excessive development of gluten, which, in turn, will make the dough difficult to turn. The long rest periods between the turns also aids in containing the gluten development by letting the dough relax.

Some pastry chefs use combinations of different types of flour to adjust the gluten strength. For instance, the addition of cake flour to all-purpose flour creates a lower gluten content, which produces a dough that better tolerates the repeated working and rolling of the pastry. The ratio of one flour to the other depends on the individual requirements.

Make sure that the *détrempe* has time to rest before proceeding with the *beurrage*.

Always begin by resting the *détrempe* in the refrigerator before incorporating the butter. Form the *beurrage* just before incorporating it into the *détrempe*.

Carefully control the temperature and consistency of the *détrempe* and the *beurrage*.

The *détrempe* and the *beurrage* should be as similar in consistency as possible so that they will easily roll together. If the *beurrage* is chilled, it will be much harder than the *détrempe*.

When shaping puff pastry, roll it out to the desired thickness and then chill it. This allows the dough to rest; resting prevents shrinkage during the baking period. Once firm, the *pâton* can be removed from the refrigerator or freezer, cut into the desired shapes and then chilled again before baking.

Keep the shape of the dough even during *tourage*

When incorporating the *beurrage*, and when rolling out and turning the *pâton*, keep the dough in an even rectangle of an even thickness as much as possible, continually squaring the sides of the *pâton* with a rolling pin as you work. Even layers result in pastry that rises perfectly when baked.

Make sure that the pastry is cooked completely before removing from the oven.

To be edible, crisp, and delicious, puff pastry must be cooked until it is brown throughout all layers. Unless the pastry is rolled very thin, the oven temperature may have to be lowered to ensure that all layers brown evenly. Unbrowned layers of dough inside the pastry are heavy, somewhat gummy, and unpleasant on the palate.

Puff pastry scraps should never be wasted.

Because it is so time-consuming to produce, even a bit of leftover puff pastry should be put to use. Scraps, also known as *demi-feuilletage* or *rognures*, are suitable for making many types of small pastries, such as cheese straws, tart bottoms, and *palmiers* (strips of puff pastry dough formed into a circular shape, sprinkled with sugar, and baked to golden crispiness). In fact, any pastry item that does not need to rise much can be made with scraps. Never roll the scraps into a circle; they should be kept flat and layered as evenly as possible to avoid destroying the delicate layers, chilled, and then rolled out into the desired shape.

Theory

Classic Sweet and Savory Preparations Based on *Pâte Feuilletée* (Puff Pastry)

Among the wide variety of sweet and savory classic French items based on puff pastry are the following:

Napoleon: Classic French sweet pastry consisting of three paper-thin layers of puff pastry that are weighted down during baking so that they remain very thin and crisp. These crisps are layered with pastry cream and sprinkled with confectioners' sugar or iced with fondant.

Pithivier: A specialty of the French town of the same name, this large, round tart with scalloped edges is made by sandwiching almond cream between two layers of pastry and baking to a golden crispiness.

Palmier: Small, palm leaf–shaped pastry made from sugared, double-rolled puff pastry; often served with tea or as a garnish for cold desserts such as ice cream. *Palmiers* can be made with puff pastry scraps.

Sacristain: A classic pastry, usually made with puff pastry scraps, created by twisting thin strips of pastry together, sprinkling with almonds, and baking.

Tarte tatin: An upside-down apple tart made by caramelizing the apples then topping them with a layer of puff pastry and baking. The tart is inverted when served so that the apples are on top and the crisp pastry is at the bottom.

Chausson: A turnover formed by filling thin circles of puff pastry with a stewed fruit or savory filling and folding the circle over to create a half-moon shape.

Allumette: Rectangular puff pastry strips baked with a savory topping or baked and then covered with a sweet glaze or icing. Sometimes *allumettes* are also made by sandwiching a savory filling between two layers of baked puff pastry strips.

Vol-au-vent: Round puff pastry cup, with or without a lid, used as a container for a savory entrée or *hors d'oeuvre*. The traditional fillings are poultry, fish, or vegetables bound with a creamy sauce.

Dean's Tips

"Demi-feuilletage *is very useful as a wrapping for fish or chicken.*"

"*To make a crispy, tasty* napoleon, *make the* feuilleté *with some sugar on top. The sugar will caramelize and add another dimension to the dessert.*"

"*Baking* pâte feuilletée *at a slightly lower temperature than given in the classic recipe lessens the risk of burning. You must make sure that, when baking* pâte feuilletée, *it achieves a perfectly golden brown color to ensure that it has the required nutty, butter taste.*"

Dean Alain Sailhac

Demonstration

Pâte Brisée ("Broken Dough" Pie Pastry)

Makes pastry for one 20-centimeter (8-inch) tart
Estimated time to complete: 45 minutes

Ingredients

200 grams (7 ounces) all-purpose flour
5 grams (¼ teaspoon) salt
100 grams (7 tablespoons) very cold unsalted
    butter, cut into small pieces
60 milliliters (¼ cup) very cold water,
    or 1 large egg mixed with 5 milliliters
    (1 teaspoon) very cold water plus additional ice
    water, if needed

Equipment

Sifter
Metal or plastic pastry scraper (optional)
Plastic film

Prepare your *mise en place*.

Sift the flour and salt together directly on the work surface.

Add the butter to the sifted flour mixture and either rub it into the flour with your fingertips, working quickly to keep the warmth of your hands from melting the butter, or cut it into the flour with a pastry scraper, working until the mixture becomes sandy in texture. There should be no large butter particles. This procedure is called *sabler* in French.

Form a well in the center of the butter-and-flour mixture and pour the water or the water-and-egg mixture into it. Working quickly and smoothly, incorporate the liquid into the butter-and-flour mixture just until the dough holds together, adding ice water if necessary. Do not add too much liquid or the dough will be sticky and tough. Do not overwork the dough. Crush any lumps against the work surface with the heel of your hand or the pastry scraper, and press them back into the dough to combine. This process is called

fraisage, from the verb *fraiser* (to mill).

Gather the dough together and form it into a disk. Wrap the dough in plastic film and refrigerate it for at least 30 minutes before rolling it out into the shape required.

Demonstration

Pâte Sucrée (Sweetened Pie Pastry)

Makes pastry for one 20-centimeter (8-inch) tart

Estimated time to complete: 45 minutes

Ingredients	Equipment
200 grams (7 ounces) all-purpose flour	Sifter
30 grams (1 ounce) sugar	Metal or plastic pastry scraper (optional)
5 grams (¾ teaspoon) salt	Plastic film
100 grams (7 tablespoons) very cold unsalted butter, cut into small pieces	
1 large egg mixed with 5 milliliters (1 teaspoon) very cold water, plus additional ice water, if needed	

Prepare your *mise en place.*

Sift the flour, sugar, and salt together directly onto the work surface.

Add the butter to the sifted flour mixture and either rub it into the flour with your fingertips, working quickly to keep the warmth of your hands from melting the butter, or cut it into the flour with a bench scraper, working until the mixture becomes sandy in texture. There should be no large butter particles. This procedure is called *sabler* in French.

Form a well in the center of the butter-and-flour mixture and pour the water-and-egg mixture into it. Working quickly and smoothly, work the liquid into the butter-and-flour mixture just until the dough holds together, adding ice water if necessary. Do not add too much liquid or the dough will be sticky and tough. Do not overwork the dough. To ensure that it is smooth, remove any large lumps from it, crush them against the work surface with the heel of your hand or with the pastry scraper, and press them back into the dough to combine. This process is called *fraisage*, from the verb *fraiser* (to mill).

Gather the dough together and form it into a disk. Wrap the dough in plastic film and refrigerate it for at least 30 minutes before rolling it out into the shape required.

Demonstration

Tarte à l'Oignon (Onion Tart)

Makes one 20-centimeter (8-inch) tart
Estimated time to complete: 2 hours

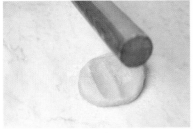

Ingredients

Butter for flan ring and baking sheet
All-purpose flour for dusting
1 recipe *Pâte Brisée* (without egg), chilled (see page 358)
5 milliliters (1 teaspoon) vegetable oil
40 grams (1½ ounces) bacon, cut into *lardons*
20 grams (1 tablespoon plus 1 teaspoon) unsalted butter
400 grams (14 ounces) onions, *émincé*
Coarse salt and freshly ground pepper to taste
1 large egg
1 large egg yolk
125 milliliters (½ cup plus 1 teaspoon) whole milk
125 milliliters (½ cup plus 1 teaspoon) heavy cream
Freshly ground nutmeg to taste

For the egg wash

1 large egg, at room temperature
5 milliliters (1 teaspoon) heavy cream

Equipment

20-centimeter (8-inch) flan ring
Rolling pin
Pastry brush
Black steel baking sheet
Large *sautoir*
Wooden spoon
Slotted spoon
Paper towels
23-centimeter (9-inch) round
piece parchment paper
Pastry weights or dried beans
2 small bowls
Whisk
Wire rack

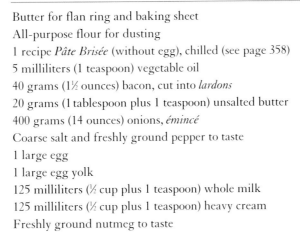

Prepare your *mise en place.* Butter and flour a 20-centimeter (8-inch) flan ring and set it aside.

Lightly dust a clean, flat working surface with flour. Place the chilled *pâte brisée* in the center of the floured surface and lightly dust the top with flour. Bang out and begin rolling the dough, dusting it frequently with flour to keep it from sticking to the rolling pin. Working, from the center outward, roll until the dough is a fairly even 23-centimeter (9-inch) circle. Using a pastry brush, lightly dust off excess flour.

Lightly butter a 20-centimeter (8-inch) circle in the center of a steel baking sheet. Place the prepared flan ring on the circle. Carefully fold the dough in half and transfer it to the prepared ring, snugly fitting it into the sides and bottom. Trim and discard (or save for another use) the excess dough hanging over the edges, leaving an even 7-millimeter (¼-inch) edge. Transfer the pastry to the refrigerator and allow to chill for at least 30 minutes.

Heat the oil in a large *sautoir* over medium-low heat. Add the *lardons* and cook, stirring frequently with a wooden spoon, for about 7 minutes or until golden brown. Using a slotted spoon, transfer the *lardons* to a double layer of paper towels to drain. Do not take the pan off the stove.

Lower the heat under the *sautoir* and add the butter to the bacon fat. When hot, add the onions and cook, stirring frequently with a wooden spoon, for about 30 minutes or until the onions are golden brown, meltingly soft, and caramelized. (If the onions do not exude sufficient liquid to begin the caramelization process, cover them tightly with a lid for about 5 minutes or until their liquid has been expressed, then uncover and continue cooking.) Taste and, if necessary, adjust the seasoning with salt and pepper.

Preheat the oven to 204°C (400°F).

Remove the pastry shell from the refrigerator. Place a 23-centimeter (9-inch) round piece of parchment paper in the bottom of the shell and push it into the sides. The paper should come up against the sides, leaving an edge with which you can lift it out of the shell when needed. Add the pastry weights or dried beans, spreading them out in an even layer over the bottom. Bake for about 10 minutes or until the pastry is dry and chalky-white. Lift out the parchment paper and weights and continue to bake for about 15 minutes or until the pastry is lightly browned and cooked through. This process is referred to as *cuire à blanc*, or blind baking. Remove the pastry shell from the oven and set aside to cool.

Reduce the oven temperature to 163°C (325°F).

Combine the egg and egg yolk in a small bowl, whisking to blend well. Add the milk, cream, and salt, pepper, and nutmeg to taste. Whisk gently, taking care not to create too much air, which will result in excess froth or bubbles.

Make the egg wash by whisking the egg with the cream in a small bowl. Set aside.

Spread the reserved onions and bacon over the bottom of the baked pastry shell. Carefully pour the egg custard over the onions, filling the shell completely

(see note). Transfer the filled tart to the oven. After 20 minutes of baking, carefully remove the flan ring and, using a pastry brush, lightly coat the crust with the reserved egg wash. Return the tart to the oven for about 10 minutes or until the custard is just set. Do not allow the custard to blossom and rise up, as this means that it has baked too long and will begin to dry out.

Remove the tart from the oven and let rest on a wire rack for at least 5 minutes before cutting into wedges and serving. The tart may be served warm or at room temperature.

Note

To avoid spilling as the filled shell is transferred to the oven, the shell can be filled while sitting on the oven rack. Take care not to spill into the hot oven or you will create a strong burning odor as the spillage burns off the oven bottom. This odor will permeate the cooking custard and make it unappetizing.

363

Demonstration

Quiche Lorraine

Makes one 20-centimeter (8-inch) tart
Estimated time to complete: 2 hours

Ingredients	Equipment
Butter for flan ring and baking sheet	One 20-centimeter (8-inch) flan ring
All-purpose flour for dusting	Rolling pin
1 recipe *Pâte Brisée* (with egg), chilled (see page358)	Pastry brush
5 milliliters (1 teaspoon) vegetable oil	Black steel baking sheet
50 grams (1¾ ounces) bacon, cut into *lardons*	Large *sautoir*
50 grams (1¾ ounces) Gruyère cheese, grated	Wooden spoon
1 large egg	Slotted spoon
1 large egg yolk	Paper towels
125 milliliters (½ cup plus 1 teaspoon) whole milk	23-centimeter (9-inch) round
125 milliliters (½ cup plus 1 teaspoon) heavy cream	piece parchment paper
Coarse salt and cayenne pepper to taste	Pastry weights or dried beans
Freshly ground nutmeg to taste	2 small bowls
8 sprigs flat-leaf parsley, washed	Whisk
and dried, optional	Wire rack

For the egg wash
1 large egg, at room temperature
5 milliliters (1 teaspoon) heavy cream

Prepare your *mise en place*. Butter and flour a 20-centimeter (8-inch) flan ring and set it aside.

Lightly dust a clean, flat working surface with flour. Place the chilled *pâte brisée* in the center of the floured surface and lightly dust the top with flour. Begin rolling the dough, dusting it frequently with flour to keep the dough from sticking to the rolling pin. Working from the center outward, roll until the dough is a fairly even 23-centimeter (9-inch) circle. Using a pastry brush, lightly dust off excess flour.

Lightly butter and flour a 20-centimeter (8-inch) circle in the center of a black steel baking sheet. Place the prepared flan ring on the circle. Carefully fold the dough in half and transfer it to the ring, snugly fitting

it into the sides and bottom. Trim and discard (or save for another use) the excess dough hanging over the edges, leaving an even 7-millimeter (¼-inch) edge. Transfer the pastry to the refrigerator and allow to chill for at least 30 minutes.

Heat the oil in a large *sautoir* over medium-low heat. Add the bacon and cook, stirring frequently with a wooden spoon, for about 7 minutes or until golden brown. Using a slotted spoon, transfer the bacon to a double layer of paper towels to drain.

Preheat the oven to 204°C (400°F).

Remove the pastry shell from the refrigerator. Place a 23-centimeter (9-inch) round piece of parchment paper in the bottom of the shell and push it into the sides. The paper should come up against the sides, leaving an edge with which you can lift it out of the shell when needed. Add the pastry weights or dried beans, spreading them out in an even layer over the bottom.

Bake for about 10 minutes or until the pastry is dry and chalky-white. Lift out the parchment paper and weights and continue to bake for about 15 minutes or until the pastry is lightly browned and cooked through. This process is referred to as *cuire à blanc*, or blind baking. Remove the pastry shell from the oven and set aside.

Reduce the oven temperature to 163°C (325°F).

Spread the cheese over the bottom of the baked pastry shell and sprinkle the *lardons* on top of the cheese.

Combine the egg and egg yolk in a small bowl, whisking to blend well. Add the milk, cream, and salt,

cayenne, and nutmeg to taste. Whisk gently, taking care not to create too much air, which will result in excess froth or bubbles. Carefully pour the egg custard over the cheese and bacon, filling the shell completely (see note, page 363).

Make the egg wash by whisking the egg with the cream in a small bowl. Set aside.

Transfer the filled tart to the oven. After 20 minutes of baking, carefully remove the flan ring and, using the pastry brush, lightly coat the crust with the egg wash. Return the tart to the oven and bake for about 10 minutes or until the custard is just set. Do not allow the custard to blossom and rise up, as this means that it has baked too long and the eggs will scramble.

Remove the tart from the oven and let rest on a wire rack for at least 5 minutes before cutting into wedges and serving, garnished with parsley sprigs, if desired. The tart may be served warm or at room temperature.

Demonstration

Tarte aux Pommes (Apple Tart)

Makes one 20-centimeter (8-inch) tart

Estimated time to complete: 2 hours, 30 minutes

Ingredients

Butter for flan ring and baking sheet

Flour for dusting

1 recipe *Pâte Sucrée* (see page 360), chilled

For the apple compote

1 kilogram (2¼ pounds) Golden Delicious apples

½ lemon

50 grams (1¾ ounces) sugar

30 milliliters (2 tablespoons) water

For the garnish

800 grams (1¾ pounds) Golden Delicious apples

½ lemon

50 grams (3 tablespoons plus 1 teaspoon) melted butter

For the glaze

100 grams (3½ ounces) apricot jam, puréed

20 milliliters (1 tablespoon plus 1 teaspoon) water

Equipment

One 20-centimeter (8-inch) flan ring

Rolling pin

Pastry brush

Black steel baking sheet

Vegetable peeler

Paring knife or melon baller

Sautoir or *russe*

20-centimeter (8-inch) round piece parchment paper with a small hole cut in the center

Wooden spoon

Small bowl

Spoon

Wire rack

Small pan

Whisk

Prepare your *mise en place*. Butter and flour a 20-centimeter (8-inch) flan ring and set it aside.

Lightly dust a clean, flat working surface with flour. Place the chilled *pâte sucrée* in the center of the floured surface and lightly dust the top with flour. Begin rolling the dough, dusting frequently with flour to keep it from sticking to the rolling pin. Working from the center outward, roll until the dough is a fairly even 25-centimeter (10-inch) circle about 3 milliimeters (⅛ inch) thick. Using a pastry brush, lightly dust off excess flour.

Lightly butter and flour a 20-centimeter (8-inch) circle in the center of a black steel baking sheet. Place the prepared flan ring on the circle. Carefully fold the

dough in half and transfer it to the ring, snugly fitting it into the sides and bottom. You should have about 1.3 centimeters (½ inch) of dough hanging over the sides of the pan. Using the rolling pin, remove the excess dough around the edges by rolling the pin over the top of the pan. Using your fingertips, shape the edge into a decorative border. Transfer the pastry to the refrigerator and allow to chill for at least 30 minutes.

While the dough is chilling, prepare the apple compote.

Using a vegetable peeler, peel the apples and cut them in half lengthwise. Remove the cores with a paring knife or melon baller. Generously rub the apples with the cut lemon to prevent discoloration. Do not

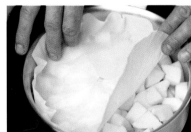

put the apples into acidulated water or the natural juices and sugars will be leached out. Cut the apples into 2.5-centimeter (1-inch) cubes.

Place the sugar and water in a *sautoir* or *russe* over medium heat. Add the apples and cover with the prepared parchment paper. Cook for about 5 minutes or until the apples begin to exude their juices. Remove the parchment paper and continue cooking, stirring frequently with a wooden spoon, for about 15 minutes or until all the moisture has evaporated, taking care that the apples do not disintegrate—you want a chunky mixture. Remove from the heat and set aside to cool.

While the compote is cooling, prepare the garnish.

Peel the apples and cut them in half lengthwise. Remove the core with a paring knife or melon baller. Generously rub the apples with the cut lemon to prevent discoloration. Do not place the apples in acidulated water or the natural juices and sugars will be leached out.

Using a paring knife, cut each apple half into very thin slices, no more than 3 millimeters (⅛ inch) thick. Place the apple slices in a small bowl and, using the lemon half, squeeze lemon juice over the apples. Toss to coat to prevent discoloration.

Preheat the oven to 218°C (425°F).

To assemble the tart, remove the pastry shell from the refrigerator. Spoon the apple compote into the shell,

spreading it out to make an even layer that fills the shell three-quarters full.

Arrange some of the apple slices in two very tight concentric circles around the edge of the shell. Using a pastry brush, lightly coat the apple circles with melted butter.

Arrange the remaining apple slices in a rosette design or in continuing concentric circles, noting that apples shrink as they cook. The top should be generously covered with apple slices so that the decorative pattern remains as it bakes. There should be no compote visible. Using a pastry brush, lightly coat the entire top with melted butter.

Place the tart on the bottom rack of the oven and bake for 10 minutes. Lower the heat to 177°C (350°F) and continue to bake for about one hour or until the apples are soft and lightly browned on the edges and the pastry is golden.

Remove from the oven and place on a wire rack to cool.

To make the glaze, combine the apricot jam and water in a small pan over medium heat. Bring to a simmer and cook, whisking constantly, for about 2 minutes or until hot and well combined. Remove from the heat and, using a pastry brush, lightly coat the entire top of the cooling tart with the glaze. Let stand until completely cool.

Cut into wedges and serve.

Demonstration

Tarte aux Poires à la Frangipane (Pear Tart with Almond Cream)

Makes one 20-centimeter (8-inch) tart
Estimated time to complete: 1 hour, 30 minutes

Ingredients	Equipment
Butter for flan ring and baking sheet	One 20-centimeter (8-inch) flan ring
Flour for dusting	Rolling pin
1 recipe *Pâte Brisée,* (with or without egg), chilled (see page 358)	Pastry brush
	Black steel baking sheet
For the pastry cream	Crimping tool, optional
10 grams (⅓ ounce) all-purpose flour	*Russe*
10 grams (⅓ ounce) cornstarch	2 small bowls
250 milliliters (1 cup plus 1 tablespoon) whole milk	Whisk
¼ vanilla bean, split lengthwise and scraped,	Wooden spoon
or 5 milliliters (1 teaspoon) pure vanilla extract	Stainless steel bowl
2 large egg yolks, at room temperature	Plastic film, optional
40 grams (1½ ounces) sugar	Electric mixer, optional
3 grams (¾ teaspoon) unsalted butter, melted, optional	Bowl
	Cutting board
For the almond cream	Chef's or paring knife
100 grams (7 tablespoons) unsalted butter, at	Pastry spatula
room temperature	Wire rack
100 grams (3½ ounces) sugar	Small pan
100 grams (3½ ounces) almond flour	*Sieve*
2 large eggs, at room temperature	
For the fruit garnish and glaze	
8 poached fresh pear halves or canned pear	
halves, well-drained and patted dry	
100 grams (3½ ounces) commercially prepared	
apricot glaze or apricot jam	
20 milliliters (1 tablespoon plus 1 teaspoon) water	

Prepare your *mise en place.* Butter and flour a 20-centimeter (8-inch) flan ring and set it aside.

Lightly dust a clean, flat working surface with flour. Place the chilled *pâte brisée* in the center of the floured surface and lightly dust the top with flour. Begin rolling the dough, dusting frequently with flour to keep it from sticking to the rolling pin. Working from the center outward, roll until the dough is a fairly even 25-centimeter (10-inch) circle about 3 millimeters (⅛ inch) thick. Using a pastry brush, lightly dust off excess flour.

Lightly butter and flour a 20-centimeter (8-inch) circle in the center of a black steel baking sheet. Place the prepared flan ring on the buttered and floured circle. Carefully fold the dough in half and transfer it to the ring, snugly fitting it into the sides and bottom. You should have about 1.3 centimeters (½ inch) of dough hanging over the sides of the pan. Using the rolling pin, remove the excess dough around the edges by rolling the pin over the top of the pan. Using a crimping tool or your fingertips, shape the edge into a decorative border. Transfer the pastry to the refrigerator and allow to chill for at least 30 minutes.

While the pastry is chilling, prepare the pastry cream.

Sift the flour and cornstarch together. Set aside.

Place the milk and vanilla in a *russe* over medium

heat and bring to a simmer. Remove from the heat and set aside.

Combine the egg yolks and sugar in a small bowl. Using a wooden spoon, work the sugar into the egg yolks (*blanchir*), stirring until the mixture is pale yellow. Whisk the flour-cornstarch mixture into the egg mixture until it is smooth.

Whisking constantly, pour half the hot milk into the egg mixture to temper (see page 386), then return the mixture to the *russe*, whisking it into the milk in the pan.

Return the pan to medium heat and, whisking constantly, bring to a boil, taking care to scrape the bottom and lower inner edges of the pan to prevent sticking and lumps. Lower the heat slightly and cook, whisking constantly, for 3 minutes or until thickened.

Remove the thickened cream from the heat and transfer it to a stainless steel bowl. Cover the top of the cooling cream with either melted butter or plastic film to prevent a layer of "skin" forming over the surface as the cream cools. If covering with butter, using a pastry brush, lightly coat the top of the cream. If using plastic film, place the film directly on top of the cream, pushing down slightly so that the entire surface is covered.

Set aside to cool.

While the pastry cream is cooling, prepare the almond cream.

Note

You will have more pastry and almond cream than required for the recipe. Use the pastry cream to make *éclairs* or use it with the almond cream to line a puff pastry tart shell that can be covered with fresh fruit.

Place the butter in a small bowl and beat with a wooden spoon or electric mixer until light and fluffy. Add the sugar and continue to beat until smooth. Add the almond flour and beat to just combine. Do not overwork or the mixture will be pasty.

Add the eggs, one at a time, beating to incorporate well. Set aside.

Preheat the oven to 177°C (350°F).

To assemble the tart, remove the pastry shell from the refrigerator. Combine the pastry cream with the almond cream in a bowl to make *frangipane*. Use either one part pastry cream to three parts almond cream or one part pastry cream to two parts almond cream, depending on the desired density and amount of almond flavor (see note).

Lay the pear halves cut side down on a cutting board. Using a chef's knife or a paring knife, cut the pear halves crosswise into thin slices.

Using a pastry spatula, spread the *frangipane* in an even layer over the bottom of the pastry shell, filling to one quarter of the depth. Cover the *frangipane* with a thin layer of pears, arranging them in a decorative pattern.

Bake for 20 minutes. Remove the flan ring and continue to bake for an additional 10 minutes or until the center is set. Remove from the oven and place on a wire rack to cool slightly.

To make the glaze, combine the apricot glaze or apricot jam with the water in a small pan over medium heat. Bring to a boil, whisking constantly to remove any lumps. If using apricot jam, you may have to push it through a sieve to remove all lumps. Remove from the heat and, using a pastry brush, lightly coat the surface of the tart with the glaze.

Cut into wedges and serve warm or at room temperature.

Demonstration

Pâte à Choux (Choux Pastry/Cream Puff Pastry)

Makes 24 choux puffs or 12 éclairs
Estimated time to complete: 1 hour, 15 minutes

Ingredients	Equipment
250 milliliters (1 cup plus 1 tablespoon) water	2 baking sheets
113 grams (½ cup) unsalted butter	Parchment paper
Pinch of salt	Stainless steel *russe*
Pinch of sugar	Wooden spoon
140 grams (5 ounces) all-purpose flour	Rubber spatula
4 to 5 large eggs, at room temperature	Medium bowl
	2 small bowls
For the egg wash	Pastry bag fitted with 1.25-centimeter
1 large egg	(½-inch) plain (round) tip
15 milliliters (1 tablespoon) heavy cream or milk	Whisk or fork
Pinch of salt	Pastry brush
	Wire rack

Prepare your *mise en place*.

Preheat the oven to 177°C (350°F) for a convection oven, 204°C (400°F) for a conventional oven.

Line two baking sheets with parchment paper. Set aside.

Combine the water, butter, salt, and sugar in a stainless steel *russe* over medium-high heat and bring to just a boil. Do not allow the water to boil for any length of time or it will begin to evaporate, and the proportion of liquid to dry ingredients will change, compromising the final dough. Once boiling, immediately remove the pan from the heat and using a wooden spoon, quickly beat in the flour.

Return the *russe* to medium heat and continue beating in the flour for 30 seconds. The mixture should begin to thicken, dry out, and form a mass that does not stick to the pan. Lower the heat and continue beating for about a minute or until the mixture is quite dry (*dessécher*).

373

To make the egg wash, combine the egg, cream, and salt in small bowl and, using a wire whisk or fork, beat until well blended. Set aside.

Pipe the dough onto the prepared baking sheets, leaving about 2.5 centimeters (1 inch) between each piece. (The dough is piped according to the size required in a specific recipe. Cream puffs [*choux à la crème Chantilly*, see page 377] and *profiteroles* require that the dough be piped into small rounds, while classic *éclairs* [see page 379] call for an

Remove the pan from the heat and, using a rubber spatula, scrape the dough into a clean bowl. Crack one egg at a time into a small bowl. If the egg is perfect, with an unbroken yolk, transfer it to the dough. Using a wooden spoon, beat each egg into the dough, incorporating very well before making the next addition. Continue beating until the dough is smooth and shiny. The dough is well blended when a spatula or spoon lifted out of the bowl forms a ribbon connecting the utensil to the dough, when a finger run through the batter leaves a channel that slowly fills, or when a bit of batter lifted on a spatula or spoon curls over on itself and forms a hook.

Transfer the dough to a pastry bag fitted with a 1.3-centimeter (½-inch) plain (round) tip.

Dean's Tip

"If the choux *are allowed to dry for 30 minutes or so after being brushed with the egg wash, they will be shinier when cooled."*

Dean Jacques Pépin

Chef's Tip

*"*Choux *paste should be smooth. When baked, it should be brown throughout with a center that is soft and hollow, not wet or gooey."*

Chef Tina Casaceli

elongated shape 10 centimeters [4 inches] long by 2.5 centimeters [1 inch] wide. The dough can also be piped into smaller pieces for individual desserts.)

Using a pastry brush, lightly coat each piece of dough with the egg wash.

Place the baking sheets in the oven and bake for 30 to 40 minutes or until the pastry is golden brown and nicely puffed. If using a convection oven, turn it off and leave the pastry in the oven for an additional 10 minutes to dry out. If using a conventional oven, lower the oven temperature to 149°C (300°F), open the oven door, leave it ajar, and allow the pastry to sit for an additional 10 minutes to dry out.

When the pastry feels dry, light, and hollow, remove the baking sheets from the oven and place them on a wire rack to allow the pastry to cool for 20 minutes. Then proceed with the cutting and filling required for a specific recipe.

Demonstration

Crème Chantilly (Sweetened Whipped Cream)

Makes about 475 milliliters (2 cups)
Estimated time to complete: 7 minutes

Ingredients	Equipment
300 milliliters (1¼ cups) heavy cream	Medium stainless steel bowl
5 milliliters (1 teaspoon) pure vanilla extract	Large stainless steel bowl filled with ice
20 grams (¾ ounce) confectioners' sugar	Whisk

Prepare your *mise en place*.

Place the heavy cream in a medium stainless steel bowl. Whisk in the vanilla.

Set the cream-filled bowl into a large bowl with ice and, using a whisk, beat the cream until it begins to thicken. Add the confectioners' sugar and continue beating until the cream is stiff, taking care not to overbeat, as the cream will turn to butter if you do.

Use as a filling for baked *pâte à choux* or as a garnish for other desserts.

Dean's Tip

"Heavy cream is 36 percent butterfat while crème fraîche, *in France, is about 46 to 48 percent. With less than 30 percent butterfat, cream will not whip properly and the liquid will separate from the foaming part."*

Dean Jacques Pépin

Demonstration

Choux à la Crème Chantilly (Cream Puffs)

Makes 24

Estimated time to complete: 30 minutes

Ingredients	Equipment
1 recipe *Pâte à Choux*, piped into 1.3-centimeter (½-inch) rounds and baked (see page 373) 1 recipe *Crème Chantilly*	Serrated knife Pastry bag fitted with the 1.3-centimeter (½-inch) star tip

Prepare your *mise en place*.

Using a serrated knife, split the pastry rounds cross-wise into two equal parts. Keep each pastry round together so that you have an even fit once filled.

Place the *crème Chantilly* in the pastry bag and pipe enough whipped cream into the bottom of each round to generously fill it. Cover each bottom with its corresponding top. Do not fill too long before service or the pastry will get soggy. Refrigerate until ready to serve.

Demonstration

Éclairs

Makes 12

Estimated time to complete: 2 hours, 30 minutes

Ingredients	Equipment
1 recipe *Pâte à Choux* (see page 373), piped 10 x 2.5 centimeters (4 x 1 inch) long and baked	7-millimeter (¼-inch) round pastry tip
1 recipe Pastry Cream (see page 390)	Pastry bag
1 recipe *Fondant* (see page 380)	Shallow bowl
	Wire rack

Prepare your *mise en place.*

Using the pastry tip, poke small holes at both ends at the top of each pastry.

Fill the pastry bag with the pastry cream. Place the tip in one hole and turn the bag to press the cream into the prepared pastry, taking care not to overfill it, as this will cause the pastry to break. Repeat with the second hole.

When all *éclairs* are filled, place the prepared fondant in a shallow bowl.

Working with one piece at a time, holding the filled pastry upside-down, dip the top, rounded side into the fondant. Carefully lift the pastry from the glaze, allowing the excess to drip off. If necessary, remove excess fondant with your fingers. Return the iced *éclairs* to the wire rack that they cooled on and refrigerate for about 15 minutes to allow the glaze to set.

Serve immediately or the pastry will get soggy.

Demonstration

Fondant

Makes about 340 grams (¾ pound)
Estimated time to complete: 10 minutes

Ingredients	Equipment
60 milliliters (¼ cup) water	Small saucepan
28 grams (1 tablespoon plus 1 teaspoon) sugar	*Bain-marie*
150 grams (5¼ ounces) prepared fondant	Wooden spatula

Notes

Fondant is a glaze prepared by cooking sugar to the soft-ball stage (112°–116°C [234°–240°F]), then working it on a marble surface until opaque. Nowadays, most chefs purchase ready-made fondant at baking supply stores, as do we at The French Culinary Institute—it is very labor-intensive to make. Traditionally, the color of the fondant icing, whether chocolate, coffee, or white (vanilla), designates the flavor of the pastry cream filling.

Simple syrup, also known as sugar syrup, is a basic pantry item used as a sweetener, glaze, poaching or preserving liquid, or as a base for candies, icings, and frostings, as well as many other desserts and drinks. Simple syrup is made in three different thicknesses: thin (3 parts water to 1 part sugar), medium (2 parts water to 1 part sugar), and thick(equal parts water and sugar).

Prepare your *mise en place.*

Make a medium simple syrup (see note) by combining the water and sugar in a small saucepan over low heat. Cook for about 4 minutes or until a clear liquid forms. Raise the heat and boil for 1 minute. Remove from the heat and set aside to cool.

Place the prepared *fondant* in a *bain-marie* over low heat. Cook, stirring frequently with a wooden spatula, until the *fondant* reaches 36°C (97°F).

The temperature is best determined by touching the *fondant* to the lip — it should feel neither hot or cold.

Begin adding the simple syrup to the *fondant* a bit at a time, stirring with the spatula and adding syrup until the *fondant* forms a short ribbon when lifted on the spatula and held over the bowl. If using a flavoring such as vanilla, add it along with the syrup.

Use the *fondant* as directed in a specific recipe.

Demonstration

Pâte Feuilletée (Puff Pastry)

Makes about 340 grams (¾ pound)
Estimated time to complete: 2 hours, 15 minutes

Ingredients	Equipment
For the *détrempe*	Sifter
250 grams (8¾ ounces) all-purpose flour (or a combination of all-purpose and cake flours), plus more for dusting	Pastry or bowl scraper
	Plastic film
3 grams (scant ½ teaspoon) salt	Rolling pin
	Pastry brush
	Freezer paper, optional

150 milliliters (⅔ cup) cool water
50 grams (3 tablespoons plus 1 teaspoon) unsalted
    butter, melted and cooled

For the *beurrage*
175 grams (12 tablespoons) unsalted butter, chilled

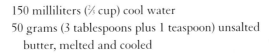

Prepare your *mise en place*.

To make the *détrempe*, sift the flour and salt together onto a clean, cool work surface. Using your fingertips, make a well in the center of the mound of flour. Run a finger through the center of the ring of flour to make a channel in the flour. Pour in the water and using your fingertips, work the water into the first ring of flour to make a paste.

Add the melted butter and, using your fingertips and

then a scraper, work the butter into the paste. When a rough dough has formed (it should be softer than a *pâte brisée*), shape it into a square block.

Using the scraper, cut an X in the top and about halfway down into the block. This will cut the gluten strands and help them to relax more quickly. Wrap the dough in plastic film and refrigerate for at least 30 minutes.

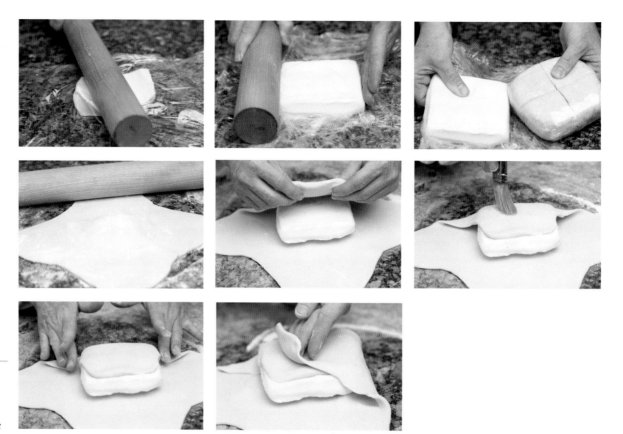

Depending on the requirements of a specific recipe, puff pastry can be turned four, five, or six times. No matter what the number of turns, the dough must be refrigerated to chill thoroughly after every two turns.

To make the *beurrage*, remove the chilled butter from the refrigerator. Place it between two sheets of plastic film and, using a rolling pin, beat on the butter to flatten it. The butter should become pliable without any lumps and should remain very cold. Form the butter into a square block.

Remove the *détrempe* from the refrigerator. Check to make sure that both the *détrempe* and *beurrage* are as near the same consistency as possible. If not, return them both to the refrigerator until equal consistency is reached.

Using a rolling pin, roll out the *détrempe* to form a square just large enough to enclose the *beurrage*.

Lightly flour the work surface and, from this point on, when rolling and turning the dough, make sure that the surface is coated with enough flour to keep the

dough from sticking. The dough must never stick to the surface; if it does, it will not form proper layers.

Place the *beurrage* on top of the *détrempe* so that it looks like a diamond inside of a square. Fold the edges of the *détrempe* over the *beurrage* to enclose it and then pinch the dough together to lightly seal, forming the *pâton*.

Using a rolling pin, press on the *pâton* about four or five times along its length or until it is about 23 centimeters (9 inches) long.

Dust the work surface with flour and roll the dough out to a piece about 56 centimeters (22 inches) long, keeping the sides even and square as you work. Roll only the length of the *pâton*; do not roll the width.

Using a pastry brush, brush off excess flour and fold the dough into thirds. Again roll the dough out to a piece about 56 centimeters (22 inches) long as above. You have rolled two turns. Using your fingertips, make two marks in the dough to indicate the two turns (see note). Wrap the *pâton* in plastic film and refrigerate for 20 to 30 minutes or until very cold.

Remove the dough from the refrigerator, unwrap, and put in two additional turns as directed above. Using your fingertips, make four marks in the dough to indicate four turns. Again, wrap the *pâton* in plastic film and refrigerate for 20 to 30 minutes or until very cold.

Remove the dough from the refrigerator, unwrap, and put in two more turns as above. Then, either rewrap, refrigerate for 30 minutes, and proceed with your recipe, or wrap in freezer paper, date, and freeze until ready to use. Thaw before using.

Chef Melissa Murphy

Pastry Chef / Co-Owner, Sweet Melissa Patisserie, Brooklyn and Manhattan, New York
The French Culinary Institute, Class of October 1995

Caramel-Apple Turnovers with Sweet Ricotta Filling

Makes 4

My love of the art of pastry was sealed during my time at FCI. Having my own "sweet" shop has truly been the icing on the cake. This recipe combines some all-American flavors with many techniques that I first experienced at the school. For this recipe, you can use purchased frozen puff pastry with great results.

106 grams (3½ ounces) fresh ricotta cheese
2 large egg yolks
85 grams (3 ounces) sugar
47 grams (1¾ ounces) all-purpose flour
2.5 milliliters (½ teaspoon) pure vanilla extract
3 grams (½ teaspoon) freshly grated orange zest
50 milligrams (⅛ teaspoon) plus pinch salt
59 milliliters (¼ cup) water

2 Granny Smith apples, peeled, cored, and cut into
   6-millimeter (¼-inch) dice
15 milliliters (1 tablespoon) milk
One 6-millimeter (¼-inch)-thick, 30.5-centimeter (12-inch)-square puff pastry, chilled
14 grams (1 heaping tablespoon) cinnamon sugar

Prepare your *mise en place.*

To prepare the ricotta filling, place the ricotta in a cheesecloth-lined sieve placed over a small bowl and refrigerate for 12 hours or until most of the moisture has drained off.

Combine the drained ricotta with 1 of the egg yolks, 28 grams (2 tablespoons) of the sugar, 9 grams (1 tablespoon) of the flour, the vanilla, orange zest, and 50 milligrams (⅛ teaspoon) of the salt, beating with a wooden spoon until smooth. Cover and refrigerate until ready to use.

To prepare the caramel-apple filling, combine the remaining sugar with 30 milliliters (2 tablespoons) of the water in a heavy-bottomed saucepan over medium heat. Cook, stirring frequently, for about 10 minutes or until the mixture is a deep amber color.

Add the apples, stirring to combine. Lower the heat and cook, stirring frequently, for about 5 minutes or until the apples begin to soften. Add the remaining water and cook, stirring frequently, for about 5 minutes more, or until the apples are cooked to a chunky applesauce consistency. Remove from the heat and set aside to cool. (The apples may be cooked and stored, covered and refrigerated, for up to 3 days before using.)

Combine the remaining egg yolk and the milk in a small bowl, whisking to combine. Set aside.

Using the remaining flour, lightly flour a clean, flat

work surface. Place the chilled puff pastry on the floured surface and cut the pastry into four equal squares. Place an equal portion of the ricotta mixture just off the center of each square. Place an equal portion of the apple mixture on top of the ricotta mixture on each square. Using a pastry brush, lightly coat the edge of each square with a bit of the reserved egg wash. Cover and reserve the remaining egg wash in the refrigerator.

Fold each pastry square in half, corner to corner, to make a neat triangle. Gently press the edges together to make a firm seal. Then gently pat each mound of filling so that it fills the interior of each triangle.

Transfer the pastries to a small baking sheet and refrigerate for about 1 hour or until chilled. (The pastries may be made up to this point and frozen, tightly wrapped, for up to 3 weeks.)

Preheat the oven to 191°C (375°F).

Remove the pastries from the refrigerator. Using a pastry brush, lightly coat the top of each turnover with the reserved egg wash. Sprinkle with cinnamon sugar. Using a small, sharp knife, cut 3 vents in the top of each turnover.

Place in the oven and bake for 45 minutes or until golden brown. If frozen, the pastries may take an additional 10 minutes to bake. Remove from the oven and place on a wire rack to cool slightly before serving.

Session 21

Creams and Custards

Theory

Overview of Creams and Custards (*Crèmes*)

Creams and custards are nothing more than the simple combination of eggs, milk or cream, and sugar. Done well, they are silky smooth, just sweet enough to please, and eminently satisfying. They can be used as dessert, on their own, or, to again quote *Larousse Gastronomique*, "as fillings, toppings, or accompaniments to pastries". Whether custard or cream, they are referred to as **crèmes** in classic French pastry making.

A *crème* can be as straightforward as a simple cup custard or as elegant as a crackling *crème brûlée*. Almost all creams and custards are cooked, although they may be eaten either warm or cold. No matter the type, the technique to master is the heating of the milk and eggs. When the perfect temperature is achieved, the result is a creamy satin like texture. When the mixture becomes too hot, the protein in the eggs turns into lumps and immediately cancels the egg mixture's ability to hold moisture. When the intense heat is prolonged, the lumps become dessicated chunks floating in a watery bath.

This heating process starts before the milk (or cream or other liquid) is added to the eggs (and sugar or other ingredients). In preparation for mixing, the liquid should be heated *just* to the boiling point. The egg mixture should then be tempered with the slow addition of the hot liquid. The heat from the liquid will melt the sugar and diffuse the egg yolks and begin the cooking process. After cooking, the mixture must always be strained through a *chinois* to eliminate the tiny strands of solid egg that are formed by the strong chalazac that hold the yolk in place.

The basic recipes for creams and custards can be divided into three categories:

° starch-bound custards such as pastry cream (*crème pâtissière*)

° stirred custards such as custard cream (*crème anglaise*) and

° baked custards such as *crème caramel*, *pot de crème*, and *crème brûlée*

These creams and custards are all covered in this chapter.

Starch-Bound Custards

These custards are cooked over direct heat and stirred continually to ensure that they remain smooth. They are thickened with cornstarch, flour, or other starches, with or without the addition of eggs. When eggs are a component of a starch-bound custard, they are first beaten together with the starch and sugar before cooking. The starch coats the eggs and prevents curdling when the custard is cooked. As with stirred custards, the cooking time and stirring process is crucial to a perfect ending. Overheating may cause the corners of the pan to burn, and both overheating and

"Crème patissière *should be very smooth with no lumps, dried skin, or burnt eggs and with no starchy taste. It should be very firm when cooled and soften easily when whisked. Although it is generally used on the day it is made, it will keep, covered and refrigerated, for up to 2 days."*

Chef Tina Casaceli

"When boiling milk to make a cream or custard, add a portion of the sugar to the milk to keep it from scorching on the pan bottom."

Chef Sixto Alonso

"When making custards, first begin heating the liquid as you assemble the rest of the ingredients."

Chef Susan Lifrieri

overstirring causes the custard to become runny; undercooking results in a raw starchy flavor. *Crème pâtissière* is the primary starch-bound custard.

Pastry Cream (*Crème Pâtissière*)

Pastry cream is not meant to be served on its own but rather to be used as a filling for cakes or pastries, or as the basis for other dessert preparations. It is more substantial and denser than the other creams or custards and will withstand higher heat and longer cooking times.

The flour and cornstarch contained in pastry cream add stability to the mixture and protect the eggs from breaking or curdling during cooking. Unlike *crème anglaise*, which should never boil, pastry cream must be brought to a boil to eliminate the raw starch taste of the flour or cornstarch and to cause it to thicken to the proper consistency. An all-purpose custard used frequently throughout French pastry making, it can be used as a filling for fruit tarts, *napoleons*, *pâte à choux*, and a variety of other pastries and cakes.

Pastry cream is also used as the basis for numerous other dessert creams such as *crème légère* (pastry cream lightened with whipped cream), *crème chiboust, frangipane* (pastry cream combined with almond cream, or *crème d'amandes.*

Some points to remember about pastry cream are:

- It is very fragile and susceptible to bacterial growth. Extreme caution should be taken to avoid contamination.

- Use only pasteurized milk and bring it to a boil before using.

- Make sure that the eggs are fresh and the eggshells are clean, as residue on the shells can contaminate the eggs when they are cracked open.

- Cook the pastry cream for 3 minutes after it has come to a boil.

- After cooking is completed, cool the cream as quickly as possible by transferring it to a shallow container placed in an ice bath.

- Always refrigerate until needed.

- Classical flavorings for pastry cream include chocolate, rum, coffee, and praline.

Stirred Custards

Stirred and baked custards have the same ingredients, but stirred custards differ in that they are cooked on top of the stove and are stirred constantly, usually with a wooden spoon or heatproof rubber spatula, to keep them from curdling and sticking to the bottom of the pan. The continual stirring keeps the mixture liquid by preventing the bonding of the eggs, which results in a pudding that is poured as a sauce rather than solidified. The stirring should be steady, with regular sweeps over the bottom and sides of the pan to keep the mixture homogenized. It is important that stirred custards not be heated to more than 77°C (170°F) or they will curdle. It is equally important that they be gently stirred, as aggressive stirring upsets the egg bonding and will result in a runny custard. The slower the custard heats and the more gently it is stirred, the creamier it will be.

About Custard Cream (*Crème Anglaise*)

Crème anglaise is an example of a stirred custard and is *the* classic French dessert sauce. It is also used as the base for ice creams, *pots de crème* (see page 397), and Bavarian creams (richly flavored custard with the addition of whipped cream and gelatin).

When making a stirred custard, the objective is to thicken it by gently poaching the egg yolk and sugar mixture in hot milk without allowing it to form a solid mass. To achieve this, during the cooking process the custard must be kept in constant motion by stirring with a wooden spatula in a Z or figure-8 pattern. This ensures that the protein of the yolks coagulates evenly, with no lumps.

Stirred custards are stirred constantly over direct heat until the mixture reaches 74°C (165°F). At this temperature, the custard will be quite thick and will coat the back of the wooden spatula (*nappant*). To sterilize the custard, it is held at 79°C (175°F) for one minute. If the mixture goes above 82°C (180°F), the yolks will hard-cook instead of poach, thereby curdling, and the mixture will turn grainy instead of smooth and creamy.

When making ice cream, basic *crème anglaise* may be flavored with any number of different ingredients and flavorings. To flavor, milk (or cream or a mixture of both) is heated, and the flavoring agent is added and left to infuse for a period of time, often overnight under refrigeration. The infused milk is then strained and the specific ice cream recipe is followed.

Some common flavorings include:

° Citrus: Finely grated orange, lemon, or tangerine zest

° Cinnamon: Either ground (not strained) or whole sticks

° Coffee: Roasted espresso beans

° Nuts: Toasted, ground, or grated almonds, hazelnuts, or other aromatic nuts

° Coconut: Toasted

° Chocolate: Melted bittersweet chocolate added to the infusion (not strained)

° Liqueurs: Added to finished, cool custard (not strained)

° Dried fruits: Poached, pureed, and added to finished, cool custard (not strained)

° Praline: Praline paste added to finished, cool custard or crushed praline folded into finished ice cream

Baked Custards

There are two types of baked custards: those that are served in the molds in which they were baked and those that are served unmolded. A baked custard that is unmolded must be firmer than one that remains in its container. For that reason, an unmolded, baked custard usually contains whole eggs or a combination of whole eggs and egg yolks, as the egg whites stiffen during cooking, helping the custard to retain its shape. As a general rule, a baked custard that will be unmolded requires at least six whole eggs per liter (quart) of milk.

Baked custards can be considered done when a skewer inserted near the middle comes out clean. The very center should still be a little quivery, a bit like set gelatin. As the custard sits, the heat accumulated in the hot custard penetrates to the center and finishes the cooking process. To ensure that a custard is ready, tilt the container to about a 45-degree angle; if the center of the custard stays put, the custard is done. If a custard is overbaked, it will separate or the edges will pull away from the mold. It will also toughen and the surrounding custard will take on an unpleasant, slightly grainy texture.

Most baked custards must be cooked in a *bain-marie* or water bath to keep an even heat around each container—this prevents overcooking. An oven water bath is made by placing the filled custard cups or molds in a hotel pan large enough to hold them without the containers touching each other or the edges of the pan, and then adding boiling water to come halfway up the sides of the containers. The bottom of the pan is usually covered with parchment paper, a wire rack, or a kitchen towel to insulate the custards from direct contact with the hot bottom. The water is most easily added to the pan once it is placed in the oven. This prevents water splashing into the custards when the pan is moved. The classic baked custards are *crème caramel*, *crème brûlée*, and *pot de crème*.

Chefs' Tips

"Crème anglaise can be flavored with many things — chocolate, alcohol, nuts — in fact, anything that can be steeped in hot milk."
Chef Tina Casaceli

"When baking custards in a water bath, place the bain-marie *with the custards in the oven, remove one ramekin from a corner and pour in the water. Then, replace the ramekin. In this way, there is no chance for water to splash into the custards."*
Chef Susan Lifrieri

Crème Caramel

This custard dish is one of the best known and most loved French baked custard preparations. A ramekin or charlotte mold is coated with caramel and then the custard is poured into the mold and baked in a *bain-marie*. Once baked, the custard is chilled until unmolded for service. The caramel is soft and runny and makes a saucelike coating over the custard.

Crème Brûlée

Another classic baked custard that consists of cream, egg yolks, and sugar baked in a *bain-marie* in a shallow dish made specifically for it. After it has been baked and chilled, a thin layer of brown sugar is placed over the top and then burned with a blowtorch or placed under a salamander or broiler to form a warm, brittle, burnt-sugar crust that entirely covers the smooth, satiny cold custard. When a spoon is dipped into the custard, the crust makes a snap and shatters. *Crème brûlée* is always served in the dish in which it was baked.

Pot de Crème

Richer than an American pudding, this dessert is the French version of a basic cup custard. It gets its name from the traditional porcelain lidded dish in which it is prepared. The French word *pot*, in this instance, is pronounced "po."

All types of custards may be infused with any number of different ingredients and flavorings. In some instances, the infusion is made by adding the flavoring agent to the heating milk and then allowing the mixture to steep off the heat until the flavor is well-absorbed into the milk. The flavoring agent, if a solid such as a vanilla bean or citrus peel, is strained out either before the milk is combined with the remaining ingredients or before the custard is baked or chilled. Some of the commonly used flavorings include:

° Citrus: Finely grated orange, lemon, tangerine, or other citrus zest

° Vanilla: Either the whole bean, scraped seeds, or pure vanilla extract

° Cinnamon: Either cinnamon sticks or ground cinnamon

° Coconut: Toasted coconut or coconut milk

° Nuts: Ground or grated, toasted almonds, hazelnuts, or other nuts.

Dean's Tip

"When preparing a custard that will be baked, do not beat the milk into the egg mixture or it will become foamy and the bubbles will break on top of the baking pudding, giving an unattractive appearance to the finished custard."

Dean Alain Sailhac

Demonstration

Crème Pâtissière (Pastry Cream)

Makes about 710 milliliters (3 cups)
Estimated time to complete: 15 minutes

Ingredients	Equipment
20 grams (¾ ounce) all-purpose flour (see note)	Sifter
20 grams (¾ ounce) cornstarch (see note)	3 small bowls
500 milliliters (2 cups plus 2 tablespoons) whole milk	*Russe*
	Small, sharp knife
	Whisk

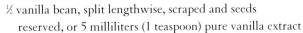

½ vanilla bean, split lengthwise, scraped and seeds
    reserved, or 5 milliliters (1 teaspoon) pure vanilla extract
4 large egg yolks, at room temperature
75 grams (2½ ounces) sugar
3 grams (¾ teaspoon) unsalted butter, melted, optional

Pastry brush, optional
Plastic film, optional

Prepare your *mise en place*.

Sift the flour and cornstarch together into a small bowl. Set aside.

Place the milk in a *russe*. Add the vanilla bean and reserved seeds to the milk and place over medium heat. Bring to a boil, then immediately remove the pan from the heat and allow the milk to cool for 1 minute.

Combine the egg yolks and sugar in a small bowl and whisk until the mixture is pale yellow (*blanchir*). Sift the flour and cornstarch mixture into the egg mixture, whisking until it is smooth.

Whisking constantly, pour half the hot milk into the egg mixture to temper, then return the mixture to the *russe*, whisking it into the milk.

Return the mixture to medium heat and, whisking constantly, bring to a boil, taking care to scrape the bottom and lower inner edges of the pan to prevent sticking and lumps. Lower the heat slightly and cook, whisking constantly, for 3 minutes or until thickened.

Remove the thickened cream from the heat and transfer to a small bowl; remove and discard the vanilla bean.

It is necessary to cover the top of the cooling cream with either melted butter or plastic film to prevent a skin forming over the surface. If using melted butter, use a pastry brush to lightly coat the top of the cream with the butter.

If using plastic film, cover the top of the cream with film, pushing down slightly so that the entire surface is covered.

Set aside to cool slightly before using as a filling. Refrigerate if not using immediately.

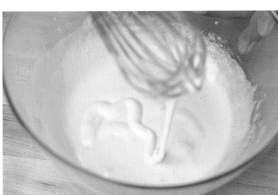

Note

You may also use all flour or all cornstarch. Flour gives a starchy taste; cornstarch will be lighter.

391

Demonstration

Crème Anglaise (Custard Cream)

Makes about 4 cups

Estimated time to complete: 40 minutes

Ingredients	Equipment
500 milliliters (2 cups plus 2 tablespoons) whole milk	*Russe*
½ vanilla bean, split lengthwise, seeds scraped and reserved	2 mixing bowls
5 large egg yolks, at room temperature	Whisk
100 grams (3½ ounces) sugar	Wooden spatula
	Metal spoon
	Candy thermometer
	Chinois
	Ice bath
	Wooden spoon
	Plastic film

Prepare your *mise en place*.

Place the milk in a *russe*. Add the vanilla bean and its seeds to the milk and place over medium heat. Bring to a boil, then immediately remove the pan from the heat and allow the milk to cool for 1 minute.

Combine the egg yolks with the sugar in a mixing bowl, whisking until the mixture is very pale yellow (*blanchir*).

Whisking constantly, pour half the hot milk into the egg mixture to temper, then slowly pour the tempered mixture into the *russe*, whisking. Cook, stirring constantly with a wooden spatula, for about 12 minutes or until the custard coats the back of a spoon (*nappant*) and a finger drawn through it leaves a clean, stable line. While stirring, pay special attention to the bottom corners of the pan, as the egg will tend to coagulate there.

To pasteurize the cream, bring it to 79°C (175°F) on a candy thermometer and hold it, stirring constantly, at that temperature for 5 minutes. Do not exceed 82°C (180°F) or the cream will curdle.

Remove the cream from the heat and pour it through a *chinois* into a mixing bowl set over an ice bath, stirring constantly with a wooden spoon until the mixture stops steaming.

When cool, cover with plastic film and refrigerate until chilled. Use as directed in a specific recipe.

Demonstration
Crème Caramel (Caramel Custard)

Serves 4

Estimated time to complete: 1 hour

Ingredients	Equipment
For the caramel	Kitchen towel
200 grams (7 ounces) sugar	Four 6-ounce ramekins
50 milliliters (3½ tablespoons) water	Hotel pan
	Parchment paper
	Stainless steel saucepan or
For the custard	copper *poêlon*
500 milliliters (2 cups plus 2 tablespoons) whole milk	Pastry brush
½ vanilla bean, split lengthwise, seeds scraped and reserved	Spoon
3 large eggs, at room temperature	Small heatproof plate
75 grams (2½ ounces) sugar	Ice cube
	Medium-sized heavy-bottomed saucepan
	Small bowl
	Whisk
	Chinois
	Medium bowl
	Ladle
	Boiling water
	Ice water bath
	Paring knife
	4 dessert plates

Prepare your *mise en place*.

Preheat the oven to 163°C (325°F).

Using a clean kitchen towel, wipe the ramekins so that they are very clean and dry. Set aside.

Line a hotel pan or other deep baking pan large enough to hold the ramekins with parchment paper. Set aside.

To prepare the caramel, combine the sugar and water in a stainless steel saucepan or a copper *poêlon* over medium heat and bring to a boil.

As the syrup begins to cook, dip a pastry brush in cold water and brush down the sugar crystals that form on the inside of the pan.

When the sugar begins to turn golden, swirl the pot so that it caramelizes evenly. To test for correct color, spoon a bit of the caramel onto a heatproof plate and add an ice cube to stop the cooking. If the color holds at a clear, light brown, remove the saucepan from the heat. If not, continue to cook until the proper color is achieved.

Note

Crème caramel may be served with petits fours secs such as *tuiles* (see page 399) or *cigarettes russes* (crisp tubular biscuits).

Pour a thin layer of the caramel syrup into each of the ramekins. Place the ramekins in the prepared pan and set aside.

To prepare the custard, place the milk in a medium heavy-bottomed saucepan. Add the vanilla bean and its seeds and place over medium heat. Bring to a boil, then immediately remove the pan from the heat and allow the milk to cool for 1 minute.

Combine the eggs with the sugar in a small bowl, whisking until the mixture is very pale yellow (*blanchir*).

Whisking constantly, pour half the hot milk into the egg mixture to temper, then slowly pour the mixture into the *russe*, whisking. When well combined, pour the custard through a *chinois* into a clean medium

bowl. Using a ladle, skim off any foam that forms on the surface.

Pour the custard into the prepared ramekins.

Transfer the hotel pan to the middle rack of the oven. Add enough boiling water to come halfway up the sides of the ramekins. Bake for about 40 minutes or until the custard no longer moves when the edge of a ramekin is tapped.

Remove the pan from the oven and immediately transfer the ramekins to an ice-water bath to chill.

Crème caramel is always served cold. You may serve it as soon as it is chilled or refrigerate until ready for service.

When ready to serve, run a paring knife around the inside of each ramekin and then invert it onto a dessert plate. Carefully lift off the ramekin so that the custard remains intact and the caramel layers the top and gently drizzles down the sides.

Demonstration

Pots de Crème (Individual Baked Custards)

Serves 4

Estimated time to complete: 1 hour

Ingredients	Equipment
400 milliliters (1⅔ cups) whole milk	4 porcelain *pots de crème* dishes, preferably with lids,
½ vanilla bean, split in half lengthwise,	or ceramic ramekins
seeds scraped and reserved	Aluminum foil, optional
50 grams (1¾ ounces) sugar	Hotel pan
4 large egg yolks, at room temperature	Parchment paper
	Medium heavy-bottomed saucepan
	Small bowl
	Whisk
	Chinois
	Medium bowl
	Metal spoon
	Boiling water
	Small tray

Note

Pots de crème may be served with petits fours secs such as *tuiles* (see page 399) or *cigarettes russes* (crisp tubular biscuits).

Prepare your *mise en place*.

Preheat the oven to 163°C (325°F).

If your porcelain *pots de crème* dishes do not have their own lids, or if using ramekins, cut four pieces of aluminum foil large enough to cover them. Set aside.

Line a hotel pan (or other deep baking pan large enough to hold the dishes) with parchment paper. Set aside.

To prepare the custard, place the milk in a medium heavy-bottomed saucepan. Add the vanilla bean and its reserved seeds to the milk and place it over medium heat. Bring to a boil, then immediately remove the pan from the heat and allow the milk to cool for 1 minute.

Combine the egg yolks with the sugar in a small bowl, whisking the yolks and sugar until the mixture turns very pale yellow (*blanchir*).

Whisking constantly, pour half the hot milk into the egg mixture to temper, then return the mixture to the saucepan, whisking it into the remaining milk in the pan. When well combined, pour the mixture through a *chinois* into a clean medium bowl. Using a metal spoon, skim off any foam that forms on the surface.

Pour the custard into the porcelain dishes. Cover each one with its lid or a piece of the aluminum foil and place in the prepared hotel pan.

Transfer the hotel pan to the middle rack of the oven. Add enough boiling water to come halfway up the sides of the porcelain dishes. Bake for about 40 minutes or until the custard no longer moves when the *pots* are moved back and forth. Check the custard about every 10 minutes to make sure that the water does not come to a boil. If the water does begin to boil, lower the oven temperature. If the custard gets too hot, it will pit or curdle, which will make the dessert unpalatable.

Remove the *pots de crème* from the oven and transfer them to a tray. Refrigerate for a couple of hours or until ready to serve, well-chilled.

Demonstration

Tuiles (Tile-shaped Crisp Cookies)

Makes about 50 cookies
Estimated time to complete: 1 hour, 30 minutes

Ingredients	Equipment
100 grams (7 tablespoons) unsalted butter, melted	Sifter
190 grams (6¾ ounces) sugar	Sheet pan
5 large egg whites	Silpat or other reusable pan liner
100 grams (3½ ounces) all-purpose flour, sifted	Wooden spoon
	Medium mixing bowl
	Metal spoon, optional
	Offset spatula, optional
	Stencil, optional
	Thin metal spatula, optional
	Steel or clean pencil or pen
See notes on page 402	Wire rack

Prepare your *mise en place*.

Preheat the oven to 177°C (350°F).

Cover the bottom of a sheet pan with a Silpat sheet or other reusable liner (or lightly butter and dust with pan flour). Set aside.

Using a wooden spoon, combine the melted butter with the sugar in a medium mixing bowl. Add the egg whites, one at a time, stirring well after each addition but taking care not to beat in air. The batter should begin to get creamy after about half the egg whites have been added.

Stir the flour into the batter, mixing until just incorporated.

Cover the batter and refrigerate for at least 1 hour.

Spread the batter onto the prepared pan in one of the following ways:

○ Using the back of a metal spoon or an offset spatula, make neat, even circles.

○ Cut a stencil to the size required and, using an offset spatula, fill in the cut to make a neat, even circle.

Whatever system you use, the edges must be even and all the circles must be of the same thickness and diameter.

Place the pan in the oven and bake, rotating it occasionally so that the *tuiles* brown evenly, for about 15 minutes or until golden brown.

Remove the pan from the oven and, using your fingers or a thin metal spatula, immediately lift the cookies one at a time from the pan and wrap them around the end of a wooden spoon, a steel, or a clean pen or pencil to roll a cigarette shape, taking care that the end is rolled completely under so it looks perfect. The top of the cookie should be the outside of the *tuile*. Finish cooling on a wire rack.

Demonstration

Bande de Tarte aux Fruits (Rectangular Fruit Tart)

Serves 12

Estimated time to complete: 1 hour

Ingredients	Equipment
1 large egg	2 small bowls
500 grams (1 pound, 1½ ounces) Puff Pastry, ready to roll (see page 380)	Whisk
	Rolling pin
All-purpose flour, for dusting	2 sheet pans
57 grams (2 ounces) apricot glaze (see note)	Paring knife
Kirschwasser, Poire William, or other fruit brandy to taste, optional	Roller-docker or dinner fork
	Pastry brush
500 grams (1 pound, 1½ ounces) washed fruit, trimmed, sliced, and, if necessary, poached	Plastic film
	Small saucepan
1 recipe Pastry Cream (see page 390), chilled	*Chinois,* optional
	Rubber spatula
	Pastry spatula

Prepare your *mise en place.*

Place the egg in a small bowl, add about a teaspoon of water, and whisk to combine. Set aside.

Place about 400 grams (14 ounces) of the puff pastry on a lightly floured surface. Using a rolling pin, roll it out to a strip about 20 centimeters (8 inches) wide by 51 centimeters (20 inches) long. Carefully transfer to an upside-down sheet pan or large baking pan.

Using a paring knife, cut a 2.5-centimeter (1-inch)–wide strip from each long side of the pastry rectangle. Set the strips aside.

Using a roller-docker or a dinner fork, dock each side (prick or lightly press down the edges) of the large rectangle to prevent it from rising too much. Using a pastry brush, lightly coat the entire top of the rectangle with some of the reserved egg wash, taking care that the wash does not run down the sides of the dough or the layers will stick together and the dough will not be able to rise properly. Reserve the remaining egg wash for later use.

A Note About the Fruit Tart

When making a fruit tart, it is easier to make the puff pastry the day before requires poaching should be poached in a thick simple syrup (see page 424), which can be flavored with citrus zest or a vanilla bean.

Since this is a rectangular tart rather than a round one, if using more than one type of fruit, make sure that all types are evenly distributed over the length of the tart. This ensures that, when cut for service, each slice will have an equal portion of each fruit.

In this recipe, pastry cream is used as a base for the fruit. It is possible to substitute other lighter creams, such as lemon curd, or to lighten the pastry cream itself by folding in about one quarter of its volume of whipped cream. You can also add beurre noisette *to stiffen the cream, as well as to add a richer, more complex flavor and unctuous texture. Whenever possible, the pastry cream should be spread over the crisp puff pastry just before service to keep the pastry from getting soggy.*

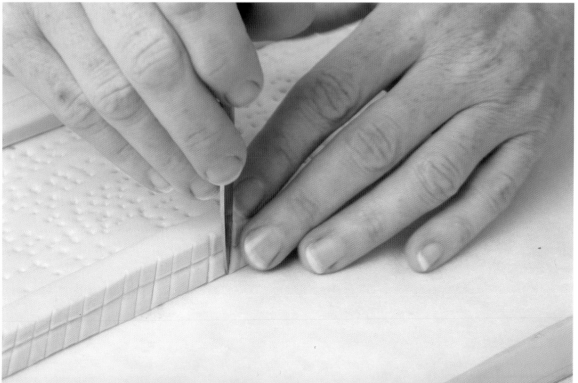

401

Carefully lay a reserved strip of dough on each of the long sides of the rectangle. Press down gently to hold the strips firmly in place. Using the sharp side of a paring knife, cut decorative slits into each strip. Cover lightly with plastic film and refrigerate for about 1 hour or until well chilled.

Preheat the oven to 204°C–218°C (400°F–425°F).

Lightly sprinkle a sheet pan or large baking sheet with cold water. This will prevent the dough from sticking to the pan while baking. Carefully transfer the chilled pastry to the sheet pan.

Using a pastry brush, again lightly coat the pastry with the reserved egg wash.

Place the pastry in the oven, lower the heat to 177°C–191°C (350°F–375°F), and bake for 15 minutes or until golden brown and beginning to rise. (If the pastry browns too quickly, reduce the heat further so it can cook through and rise without burning.) As soon as the pastry turns golden, lower the heat to 163°C–177°C (325°F–350°F) and continue to bake for another 15 minutes or until the pastry has risen and is nicely browned and crisp.

Place the glaze in a small saucepan. Add a bit of water to thin slightly and place over low heat. Cook, stirring constantly, to eliminate lumps. If lumps remain, remove from the heat and push through a *chinois* into a clean bowl. Set aside.

Remove the chilled pastry cream from the refrigerator. Using a rubber spatula, fold in the liqueur, if using.

Using a pastry spatula, evenly spread the cream over the base of the puff pastry, taking care that the cream does not spread onto the decorative sides. Arrange the fruit in a decorative pattern over the cream.

Using a pastry brush, lightly coat the fruit with the apricot glaze. Serve immediately.

Notes for Tuiles

Take great care when measuring the ingredients, as the amounts must be exact or the cookies will not form correctly.

Although you can make these cookies without chilling the batter, it is much easier to work with cold. The batter can be made in advance, covered, and refrigerated for up to five days.

Always place the batter on cool baking pans. If the pan is warm, the batter will spread and the cookies will not form properly.

Session 22

Crêpes, Frying Batter, and Brioche

Theory

About Crêpes

A *crêpe* is a delicate, almost paper-thin pancake made with an eggy batter. In classical French cooking, they can be either sweet or savory and may be fried, sautéed, *flambéed*, stuffed, rolled, folded, *gratinéed* with cheese, or *glacéed* with sugar. In traditional cooking, *crêpes* were served as a hot *hors d'oeuvre* filled with a thick, savory mixture based on a *béchamel* or a *velouté* sauce with mushrooms, ham, cheese, seafood, or other rich ingredients. *Crêpes* are generally prepared in a special shallow-sided skillet about 19 centimeters (7½ inches) in diameter called simply a *crêpe* pan.

When correctly prepared, the *crêpe* has an even, pale golden color and no thick areas. It is not uncommon when cooking *crêpes* to find that the first few will not be acceptable, as it takes time for the pan to reach the correct temperature. And, then, of course, the longer the pan stays on the heat, the hotter it becomes, so it is necessary to adjust the temperature often as you cook. Once the perfect temperature is attained, the *crêpes* can be produced very quickly. In kitchen production, a chef may use more than one pan at a time, filling and swirling, flipping and moving the *crêpe* in each pan in succession. A very impressive feat to watch!

Throughout France, there are many regional variations for the preparation of *crêpes*. They are a specialty of Agen, where they are a part of every celebration. The French writer Anatole France wrote in his book *Les Temps*, "They are so light that after a good dinner, a man from Agen is still willing to sample three or four dozen." Other regional *crêpes* include the *tantimolles* of Picardy, the *sanciaux* of Limousin, the *crespets* of Bèarn, and the most famous of all, the buckwheat *crêpes* of Brittany served with lots of salted butter and, occasionally, a dusting of grated Gruyère cheese.

Some of the most common fillings for savory *crêpes* are ham (*crêpes au jambon*), mushrooms (*crêpes aux champignons*), Roquefort cheese (*crêpes au Roquefort*), seafood (*crêpes aux fruits de mer*), and cheese (*crêpes au fromage*). Although not currently in vogue in contemporary American cooking, savory crêpes are sometimes found on lunch or brunch menus.

Nowadays, *crêpes* are most often prepared as sweet dishes. They are usually served warm, filled with jam, pastry cream or whipped cream, fruits, honey, melted chocolate, or chestnut cream, and dusted with confectioners' sugar. Commonly served sweet *crêpes* include the well-known *crêpes Suzette* (flamed with orange liqueur), *crêpes soufflés* (a soufflé made with *crêpe* batter that puffs up when baked), *crêpes aux fruits* (folded with fresh or cooked fruit), and *crêpes à la confiture* (with jam).

Dean's Tip

"A crêpe *is the pinnacle of French desserts — simple and sophisticated, delicate, light, and seductive —* delicieux!*"*

Dean Jacques Pépin

Crêpe Batter (*Pâte à Crêpes*)

Crêpe batter can be made with white, whole wheat, or buckwheat flour and mixed with water or milk. Occasionally, beer is used, but it causes the batter to rise somewhat and the crêpes will be airier than usual. The proportion of eggs to flour depends on the specific recipe, but the batter will always be egg-rich and easily poured. Some batters also require the addition of a sweetener. *Crêpe* batter is always prepared in advance to allow it to settle.

Crêpe batter is very thin. It is swirled in a hot *crêpe* pan to produce a thin, almost lacy-edged, pancake. To achieve the perfectly smooth consistency required, it is important to mix the batter very carefully.

After the batter is mixed, the gluten in the flour has developed and the batter must be allowed to rest; otherwise, the *crêpes* will be tough and rubbery when cooked. The batter should be covered and refrigerated. After the batter has rested, it must be brought back to room temperature. At this point, melted butter is gently whisked in. The purpose of the butter is to help make the *crêpe* more pliable so that it can be folded or rolled without breaking.

About Frying Batter (*Pâte à Frire*)

Frying batter (*pâte à frire*) is a *crêpe*-like batter that is used to enrobe food that is being deep-fat fried. It must be used the day it is prepared or the yeast in the batter will cause it to ferment. It is most commonly used for vegetables (such as zucchini, onions, eggplant, salsify), fish and crustaceans (fillet of sole, shrimp), certain meats, particularly offal, and for fruits, as for *beignets*. For optimum taste, the batter should be light, creamy, and very smooth. Beer is used most often as the liquid, as its yeast content causes the batter to swell during frying, which makes a very attractive presentation. All items to be battered and fried must be perfectly cleaned, trimmed, and dried before being dipped into the batter, and they must be completely coated. Once fried, the item should be drained on a double layer of paper towels and served immediately, as it will quickly begin to lose its crispness.

About *Brioche* (Egg Bread)

One of France's oldest breads, dating back to the Middle Ages, *brioche* has found its place in history through the oft-quoted "*Qu'ils mangent de la brioche!*" (usually translated as "Let them eat cake!") purportedly uttered by Marie Antoinette during the Paris bread riots of 1789. It is the first bread to which sugar was added, making a cakelike loaf. It is a versatile dough, used for a whole range of breads. The classic loaf, called a *brioche à tête*, is baked in a fluted pan made especially for it. It can be either large or small and it always has a little round topknot as a finish.

Brioche dough can be either sweet or salty, depending on how it is going to be used. Sweetened dough is used for desserts, breakfast breads, and sometimes as a crust for a tart. Salted dough is used as an enclosure for ham, sausage, filet of beef, or as a coating for a mixture of salmon and rice in the traditional Russian dish *coulibiac*.

The recipes for sweet and salty *brioche* doughs are slightly different. Here are two classic recipes for comparison:

Sweet (*Sucré*)	Ingredient	Salty (*Salé*)
500 grams (1 pound, 1½ ounces)	All-purpose flour	500 grams (1 pound, 1½ ounces)
25 grams (scant 1 ounce)	Yeast	25 grams (scant 1 ounce)
20 milliliters (4 teaspoons)	Milk or water	20 milliliters (4 teaspoons)
7	Large eggs	7
10 grams (1½ teaspoons)	Salt	14 grams (2 tablespoons)
50 grams (1¾ ounce)	Sugar	21 grams (1 tablespoon)
300 grams (10½ ounces)	Unsalted butter	250 grams (8¾ ounces)

Just as in other yeast breads, the yeast in *brioche* dough causes fermentation, creating thousands of tiny gas bubbles that make the dough rise and increase in volume. The fermentation period cannot be prolonged or the dough will start to toughen too much. Certain breads, however, do require a long-fermented dough; these breads have a strong taste and dense texture, such as sourdough bread (a bread made with a mixture called a "starter" or fermented yeast dough).

When making a salty *brioche* (or other bread) dough, never put the salt in direct contact with the yeast. Salt destroys the active yeast culture. All yeast-risen doughs are categorized as raised doughs (*pâtes levées*), and because yeast rises best in a warm atmosphere, less yeast is required to raise a dough in warmer climates.

Demonstration

Crêpes Suzette

Serves 4

Estimated time to complete: 2 hours

Ingredients	Equipment
For the batter	2 medium mixing bowls
125 grams (4⅓ ounces) all-purpose flour	3 small bowls
20 grams (¾ ounce) sugar	Whisk
Pinch of salt	Plastic film
2 large eggs	Parchment paper
250 milliliters (8¾ ounces) milk	Rolling pin
	Wooden spoon

For the orange butter

1 large orange, well-washed

50 grams (1¾ ounces) sugar cubes

150 grams (10 tablespoons plus 1 teaspoon)
   unsalted butter, at room temperature

25 milliliters (1½ tablespoon) Grand Marnier liqueur

For the orange garnish

2 large oranges, well washed

10 milliliters (2 teaspoons) grenadine syrup

30 milliliters (2 tablespoons) water

20 milliliters (1 tablespoon plus 1 teaspoon) clarified butter

To finish the crêpes

Oranges

Grenadine

Water

Clarified butter

15 milliliters (1 tablespoon) cognac

Vegetable peeler
Chef's knife
Small saucepan
Slotted spoon
Paper towels
Chinois
Crêpe pan
Pastry brush
Ladle
Spatula, optional
Baking shee
Large *sautoir*
4 warm dessert plates

Prepare your *mise en place.*

To make the batter, place the flour, sugar, and salt in a medium mixing bowl. Form a well in the center.

One at a time, crack the eggs into a small bowl. If the egg is perfect and the yolk unbroken, pour it into the well in flour. Using a whisk, begin mixing the flour mixture into the eggs, adding some of the milk to make a paste. When the mixture is smooth, add the remaining milk and whisk until creamy. Cover with plastic film and refrigerate for at least 1 hour.

While the batter is resting, make the orange butter and orange garnish.

To make the orange butter, working with one sugar cube at a time, rub the sugar cubes firmly on the skin of the orange to extract some of the oil (you want the oil to penetrate and flavor the sugar). Cut the orange in half crosswise, and squeeze the juice into a small bowl. Warm the orange juice slightly. Set aside.

Place the sugar cubes on a piece of parchment paper and cover them with another piece of parchment paper. Using a rolling pin, crush the sugar cubes. Set aside.

Place 130 grams (9 tablespoons) of the butter in a small bowl. Add the crushed sugar cubes and, using a wooden spoon, beat to blend well. Add the Grand

Marnier and reserved warm orange juice a bit at a time, beating until the butter absorbs all the liquid. Set aside.

To make the garnish, zest one of the oranges with a vegetable peeler. Using a chef's knife, *julienne* the zest. Cut the peeled orange and the remaining orange into *suprêmes*. Set the zest and the *suprêmes* aside separately.

Bring a small saucepan of water to a boil over high heat. Add the zest and bring to a simmer. Lower the heat and simmer for 5 minutes or just until the zest is soft. Using a slotted spoon, remove the zest from the water and place on paper towels to drain.

Lay a piece of parchment paper out on a flat surface.

Place the grenadine with the water in a small saucepan over low heat. Add the drained zest and

bring to a bare simmer. Lower the heat and simmer for about 8 minutes, adding water if the liquid evaporates too quickly. Using a slotted spoon, remove the zest from the pan and place it on the parchment paper.

About 1 hour before using, remove the *crêpe* batter from the refrigerator. Uncover and allow to come to room temperature.

When the batter has reached room temperature, melt the remaining butter and whisk it in. When combined, pour the batter through a *chinois* into a clean bowl.

Heat the *crêpe* pan over medium heat. Using a pastry brush, brush with just enough of the clarified butter to lightly coat the bottom of the pan, pouring off any excess.

Ladle 59 milliliters (about ¼ cup) of the batter into the hot pan, lifting the pan from the heat and tilting and rolling it, swirling to coat the entire bottom with an even, thin layer of batter. Cook for about 1 minute or until just set and beginning to color on the bottom. Using a spatula or the tips of your fingers, carefully lift the *crêpe* up and turn it over. Continue to cook just until the remaining side is light brown. Transfer the finished *crêpe* to a piece of parchment paper or

placed over a baking sheet to cool. Continue to butter the pan and make *crêpes* until all the batter has been used, whisking before each one.

Allow the *crêpes* to cool in a single layer placed on parchment paper before stacking because, if stacked while still hot, they will stick together. Even when cooled, it is a good idea to stack them between sheets of parchment or waxed paper to prevent sticking.

When ready to serve, place the orange butter in a large *sautoir* over medium heat. If necessary, add additional reserved orange juice to achieve a saucelike consistency.

Working with one *crêpe* at a time, dip a *crêpe* in the hot orange butter, fold it into quarters, and place it on the side of the pan. Continue dipping and folding until all the *crêpes* are done.

Add the cognac to the pan and *flamber*. Place two *crêpes* on each of four dessert plates, pour some of the orange butter sauce over the top, and garnish with the reserved zests and *suprêmes*. Serve immediately.

Chefs' Tips

"For an even stronger orange flavor, add orange zest to the batter and replace some of the milk with orange juice. Let the batter rest with the zest and then strain it out before cooking."
Chef Tina Casaceli

"When making crêpes *Suzette, be sure to diligently rub the orange peel with the sugar cube to extract maximum flavor. And don't stack the* crêpes *while warm or they will stick together."*
Chef Dominick Cerrone

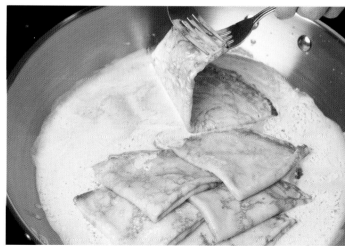

Demonstration

Beignets aux Pommes, Coulis de Fruit (Apple Fritters with Fruit Purée)

Serves 4

Estimated time to complete: 1 hour

Ingredients	Equipment
	Chinois
For the fruit coulis	Spatula
230 grams (8 ounces) fresh or thawed frozen fruit purée	Chef's knife
(such as raspberry or mango)	Large plate
About 60 milliliters (¼ cup) Simple Syrup (see page 424)	Medium mixing bowl
About 2½ milliliters (¼ teaspoon) fresh lemon juice, optional	Small mixing bowl
	Whisk
For the apples	Plastic film
600 grams (1 pound, 3 ounces) apples, peeled and cored with a corer	Electric mixer, optional
30 milliliters (2 tablespoons) Calvados	Deep-fat fryer
Juice of ½ lemon	Instant-read thermometer
40 grams (1½ ounces) sugar	Slotted spatula
Ground cinnamon to taste	Paper towels
	Baking sheet
For the batter	4 warm dessert plates
175 grams (6 ounces) all-purpose flour	
170 milliliters (¾ cup) beer	
1 large egg yolk	
Pinch of sugar	
Pinch of salt	
15 milliliters (1 tablespoon) peanut oil	
2 large egg whites	

To finish the *beignets*

1.5 liters (1⅔ quarts) vegetable oil, for frying

Confectioners' sugar for sprinkling

Prepare your *mise en place*.

To make the *coulis*, place the fruit purée in a *chinois* and, using a spatula, push to strain out all solid matter. Combine the strained fruit purée with just enough syrup to thin and sweeten slightly. If necessary, stir in a bit of lemon juice to wake up the flavor. Set aside.

Using a chef's knife, carefully cut the apples crosswise into 4-millimeter (⅙-inch)–thick slices so that each slice is neat with a perfect hole in the center. Arrange the slices on a plate large enough to hold

them in a single layer and sprinkle with the Calvados and lemon juice and then with the sugar and cinnamon. Set aside to marinate for 30 minutes, turning occasionally, so that all sides of the apples are moistened with the Calvados.

Make the batter while the apples are marinating.

Place the flour in medium mixing bowl and form a well in the center.

411

Combine the beer, egg yolk, sugar, and salt in a small mixing bowl. Using a whisk, beat until smooth. Pour the mixture into the flour well and whisk until smooth. The batter will be quite loose.

Cover the batter with plastic film and set aside in a warm spot (preferably warmer than room temperature) for 30 minutes.

When ready to cook, using an electric mixer or a whisk, beat the egg whites until soft peaks form. Using a spatula, fold the beaten egg whites into the batter.

Heat the vegetable oil in a deep-fat fryer to 177°C (350°F) on an instant-read thermometer over medium-high heat.

Working in small batches, dip the apple rings into the batter and place them in the hot oil. When the apples rise to the surface and are golden brown on the bottom, turn them to brown the remaining side. It should take no more than 5 minutes for both sides to cook.

Using a slotted spatula, transfer the fried apples to a double layer of paper towels to drain. Sprinkle with confectioners' sugar and place on a baking sheet.

When all the apples are fried and sprinkled with sugar, place them under a salamander or broiler to glaze slightly.

Coat the bottom of each of four dessert plates with the reserved fruit *coulis*. Place an equal number of the warm *beignets* on each plate and serve.

Demonstration

Brioche

Makes 1 large loaf or several smaller ones

Estimated time to complete: 15 hours, including rising time

Ingredients	Equipment
25 milliliters (1½ tablespoons) milk	*Russe*
30 grams (1 ounce) sugar	Fork, optional
12 grams (1 tablespoon) fresh yeast, or 6 grams (scant 1 tablespoon) dry yeast	Large bowl
250 grams (8¾ ounces) all-purpose flour, plus more for rolling and shaping	Plastic film
	1 large *brioche à tête* mold
5 grams (¼ teaspoon) salt	or several small ones
3 large eggs, at room temperature, beaten	Whisk
150 grams (10 tablespoons plus 1 teaspoon) unsalted butter, at room temperature, plus more for the mold	Pastry brush
	Small, sharp knife
Vegetable oil for the bowl	Wire rack
1 large egg yolk	
15 milliliters (1 tablespoon) water	

Chef's Tip

"Brioche *dough should be yellow, smooth, and very soft or loose after mixing. The baked bread should be evenly browned and shiny.*"

Chef Tina Casaceli

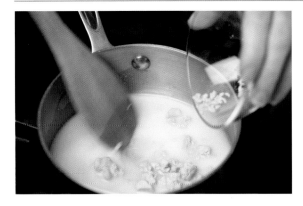

Prepare your *mise en place.*

Warm the milk in a *russe* over low heat until it is about 50°C (120°F), then remove it from the heat. Stir in the sugar and yeast. Allow the yeast to dissolve for 5 minutes.

Combine the flour and salt on a clean work surface. Make a well in the center and add the warm milk mixture and the eggs to it. Using your fingertips or a fork, slowly incorporate the liquid ingredients into the flour. When combined, begin kneading and stretching the dough. Knead for about 15 minutes to develop the gluten. The dough should become elastic and satin smooth, and you should be able to pick it up in one mass.

Using your hands, begin incorporating the butter, bit by bit, squeezing and mixing it into the dough. Work quickly as the butter can melt quickly. When all the

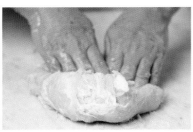

butter has been incorporated, work the dough for a few more minutes to ensure that the whole mixture is perfectly combined.

Lightly oil a large bowl and place the dough in it. Cover with plastic film and set aside to rise at room temperature for about 3 hours or until doubled in bulk.

Punch the dough down, turn it, cover it with plastic film, and refrigerate for 8 hours or overnight. (It can remain in the refrigerator for up to 24 hours.)

When ready to bake, lightly flour a clean work surface and lightly butter the *brioche* mold.

Turn the dough out onto the work surface. The dough must be well-chilled or the butter will soften and leak out and the dough will turn sticky.

Divide the dough into 300-gram (10½-ounce) pieces for a large mold and 35-gram (1¼-ounce) pieces for small molds.

Shape each piece into a round, place it on the floured work surface, cover with plastic film, and let rest. The resting time allows the gluten to relax and depends on the size of the rounds. A large loaf should rest for about 10 minutes; the small ones need no more than 5. The dough should not soften.

Roll each piece into a gourdlike shape, using just enough flour to keep the dough from sticking to your hands or to the work surface. Using the side of your hand, simulate cutting the dough in half from the narrow side of the gourd shape to the base. This will form two balls connected by a narrow strand of dough. The smaller one will be the head (*tête*) of the *brioche*.

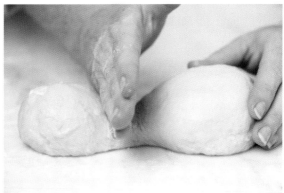

Place the larger, rounded end of the dough in the prepared mold and, with your index fingers, form a well in the center of the dough. The smaller ball will naturally drop into the well. Continue tucking the smaller ball into the well until it is securely set. If you do not tuck it deeply enough, it will rise over the base and possibly roll off during the baking process.

Cover the dough with plastic film and set aside at room temperature for about 1 hour or until doubled in bulk.

Preheat the oven to 177°C (350°F) for a large bread or 204°C (400°F) for small breads.

Using a whisk, beat the egg yolk and water together. Uncover the dough and, using a pastry brush, lightly coat the dough with the egg wash. Do not allow the wash to drip down the side of the mold, as this will cause the bread to stick.

Place the bread in the oven and bake for about 25 minutes or until it is a deep, golden brown and the point of a small, sharp knife inserted into the center comes out clean. Remove from the oven and immediately unmold onto a wire rack to cool. If you leave the bread in the mold, steam will accumulate in the bottom and the *brioche* will get soggy.

Session 23

Génoise

Theory

About *Génoise*

Génoise (sponge cake), the classic layer cake of France, is one of the cakes used most often in French *pâtis-serie*, and is a component of many dessert preparations. It differs from the traditional American sponge cake, as well as the classic French *biscuit*, in that the eggs are heated and beaten whole rather than whipped separately. All sponge cakes rely on eggs for their light texture. No other leavening agent, such as baking soda or baking powder, is used to create the desired airiness. The cake rises as the heat of the oven causes the air in the batter to expand — the air that was trapped in the whipped eggs and the air produced as the water in the butter turns to steam. Although a properly made *génoise* is light and delicious on its own, the ways in which it can be decorated or finished are myriad. It particularly shines when brushed with a flavored syrup and layered with buttercream.

 Génoise batter may be baked in individual round pans or in large sheet pans. If baked in a flat sheet to a thickness of 1.25 centimeters (½ inch), it can be rolled for jellyrolls, used to line a *charlotte* mold, used as a base for a baked Alaska (*omelette Norvégienne*), filled with *crème mousseline* (aka "German buttercream": one part pastry cream to one part soft butter) and strawberries to make a *fraisier*, or sieved through a fine mesh sieve to make crumbs to spread on or around another dessert.

 The technique for making *génoise* is not easy to master. The whole eggs and sugar are heated over a *bain-marie*. If the mixture becomes too hot, the eggs will scramble and be unusable. The gentle heating of the eggs must just partially coagulate the protein and transform them into an elastic mass. The eggs are continually beaten until they, in combination with the sugar, form a thick ribbon when lifted from the bowl. This mass is capable of holding large quantities of air.

 Flour is sifted over the egg mixture and gently folded into it. The folding must be done quickly but very gently. The success of the cake depends on tightly controlling ingredient temperatures and taking care that the eggs are whipped properly and do not deflate when the flour is folded in. The entire operation should be done quickly and sensitively. A properly made *génoise* should be light, buttery, and delicate with a dry crumb.

Dean's Tip

"For génoise, *I like to use a pastry flour that is unbleached and unbromated, such as that made by King Arthur. The bleaching process cooks out the starch and toughens the gluten, which will keep the cake from rising as nicely. Unbromated flour does not contain potassium bromate, a potentially carcino-genic chemical sometimes added to flour to adjust its protein level or encourage it to quickly mature or oxidize."*

Dean Jacques Torres

Guidelines for Preparing *Génoise*

° When making the batter, do not allow the eggs to heat above 49°C–52°C (120°F–125°F), as they will coagulate at higher temperatures.

° The flour should be finely sifted through a fine sieve (usually a drum sieve) onto a piece of parchment paper by shaking the sieve back and forth. (This is to eliminate lumps and impurities.)

° Add the sifted flour slowly and steadily and very gently fold it into the egg mixture with a rubber spatula. The manner in which the flour is incorporated is key to the success of the cake. It is a touch that comes only with practice. If the flour is added too quickly, you will create a lumpy batter.

° Butter and flour the pans and line them with parchment paper to facilitate removing the cake, as well as to keep it from drying out.

° Always preheat the oven to 177°C (350°F).

° Place the filled pans in the center of the oven allowing air space between each pan. Gently close the oven door.

° Maintain an even 177°C (350°F) temperature throughout the baking. Do not open the oven door before the last 5 minutes of baking or the cake might fall.

° The cake is fully baked when no indentation remains after it is lightly touched in the center, it is light gold in color, and it has begun to shrink away from the sides of the pan.

° Remove the cake from the pan while it is still warm. The cake may be cooled upside down to achieve a smooth top layer.

° Do not cut the cake until it is completely cooled.

° Once cooled, the cake can be covered with a slightly damp, clean kitchen towel for about 4 hours to prevent drying out.

Cooking Sugar

In classic French pastry making, there are many, many solutions made by heating sugar and liquid together. The resulting syrups (*sirops*) are used for poaching fruit, moistening cakes, and making icings, buttercreams, meringues, glazes, fondants, caramels, and *pâte à bombe* mixtures. Some are thin syrups that are boiled just briefly to dissolve the sugar. Others are "cooked sugars" that are taken beyond the boiling point in order to evaporate the water content and concentrate the syrup for greater density and flavor.

In this session, a simple syrup (**sirop simple**), made by boiling equal parts of water and sugar together, is prepared and used to moisten *génoise* layers before assembling them into a finished cake. The cooked syrup is generally flavored with liqueur and brushed on cake layers. The syrup compensates for the natural dryness of the cake, and the cake's natural sponginess allows it to absorb large amounts of liquid without becoming soggy.

A "cooked sugar" is also used as part of the preparation of buttercream (*crème au beurre*). To properly cook sugar, a copper *poêlon* (sugar pot) is ideal. If one is not available, a heavy-bottomed, non-reactive saucepan will do. The most important factor is to keep the sides of the pot clean while cooking sugar syrup so that crystals don't form and taint the final mixture. Crystal formation on the sides of the pan will make the final syrup grainy if they come into contact with the syrup. To prevent this, use a pastry brush dipped into cold water to clean the sides of the pan throughout the cooking process. The water in the brush will dissolve any sugar crystals that have formed and push the liquid down into the pan.

When cooking sugar, the use of a sugar or candy thermometer gives regular, precise control of the process. During cooking, sugar goes through several successive stages that are referred to by the way the sugar reacts when dropped into a glass of cold water.

Temperature	Stage	Cold-Water Test
110°C–112°C (230°F–234°F)	Thread	Syrup dropped from a spoon spins a 5-centimeter-long (2-inch) thread; will not form a ball
112°C–116°C (235°F–240°F)	Soft ball	Syrup can be shaped into a ball that flattens when removed from the water
116°C–120°C (244°F–248°F)	Firm ball	Syrup can be shaped into a firm ball that holds its shape when removed from the water
121°C–130°C (250°F–266°F)	Hard ball	Syrup forms a hard but pliable ball
132°C–143°C (270°F–290°F)	Soft crack	Syrup separates into threads that are not brittle
149°C–154°C (300°F–310°F)	Hard crack	Syrup separates into hard, brittle threads
160°C (320°F)	Clear liquid	Hardens and turns light amber in color
170°C (338°F)	Brown liquid	Hardens

About Buttercream (*Crème au Beurre*)

Buttercream is a suitable filling or frosting for *génoise* as well as many other cakes.

There are three types of buttercream:

◦ Classic buttercream (or *pâte à bombe* buttercream): Soft-ball sugar is poured into whipped egg yolks and then combined with a large quantity of unsalted butter.

◦ Italian meringue buttercream: Soft-ball sugar is poured into whipped egg whites and the resulting meringue is combined with a large quantity of unsalted butter.

◦ *Crème mousseline*: Pastry cream (see page 390) is beaten into a large quantity of unsalted butter.

Buttercream can be flavored by a variety of added ingredients, such as melted chocolate, vanilla, coffee, praline or citrus extracts, and all measure of liqueurs. Buttercream is very, very rich and should be used sparingly. Thick layers of buttercream between layers of a delicate cake make the whole quite unpalatable. Because of its high butter content, buttercream should always be served at room temperature so that the butter can soften slightly. Desserts made with buttercream should be removed from refrigeration at least 30 minutes before serving.

Demonstration

La Génoise (Sponge Cake)

Makes one 15-centimeter (6-inch) or one 20-centimeter (8-inch) cake
Estimated time to complete: 1 hour

Ingredients	Equipment
	6- or 8-inch round cake pan
For the small cake	Parchment paper
45 grams (3 tablespoons) unsalted butter, for	Saucepan
the pan	Heatproof bowl
75 grams (2½ ounces) cake flour, plus more for the pan	Whisk
3 large eggs, at room temperature	Sifter
75 grams (2½ ounces) sugar	Rubber spatula
15 grams (1 tablespoon) unsalted butter, melted and cooled,	Wire rack
optional	

For the large cake
45 grams (3 tablespoons) unsalted butter, for
  the pan
125 grams (4⅓ ounces) cake flour, plus more for the pan
5 large eggs, at room temperature
125 grams (4⅓ ounces) sugar
25 grams (1 tablespoon plus 2 teaspoons) unsalted butter, melted and
  cooled, optional

Prepare your *mise en place*.

Preheat the oven to 177°C (350°F).

Lightly butter and flour a cake pan. Place a piece of parchment paper cut to fit the bottom of the pan into it. Refrigerate the pan until ready to use.

Fill a saucepan with about 7.5 centimeters (3 inches) of water. The saucepan must be of a size that will allow your heatproof bowl to fit snugly into it without touching the water. Place the pan over high heat and bring the water to a boil. Immediately remove the pan from the heat.

Combine the eggs and sugar in the bowl. Place the bowl into the pan of hot water and immediately begin

whisking. Continue to whisk until the mixture has doubled in volume and forms a ribbon when lifted from
the bowl. Do not allow the mixture to exceed 49°C
(120°F) or the cake will be dry and tough.

Remove the bowl from the heat and continue to whisk
for 1 minute.

Begin sifting the flour directly into the whipped mixture, folding with a rubber spatula as you sift. Do not
allow the flour to clump.

If using melted butter, which makes the cake moister,
fold it in after all the flour has been incorporated.

Remove the prepared cake pan from the refrigerator
and gently pour the batter into it. Spin the pan

slightly to even out the surface, which will help the
cake rise evenly.

Place the cake into the oven and bake for 25 minutes
or until no indentation remains when the cake is
lightly touched in the center, it is light gold in color,
and has begun to shrink away from the edge of
the pan.

Immediately remove from the oven and invert onto a
wire rack to cool.

When cool, slice into even layers, moisten each with
simple syrup, and fill and decorate with buttercream
or use as directed in a specific recipe.

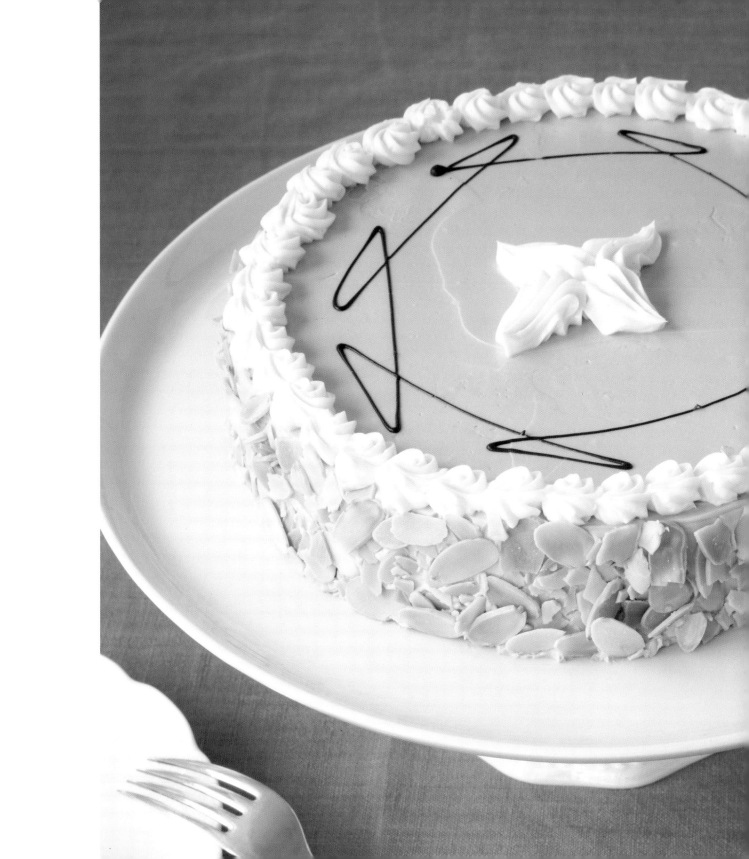

Notes

Simple syrup is most commonly 1:1 ratio (16 oz. sugar: 16 oz. water)

Beurre en pommade refers to butter that has been softened to room temperature without melting or separating and then beaten until light and fluffy.

Dean's Tip

"Granulated sugar is available in about five categories of fineness, but I always use 'regular,' which is fine or extra-fine."
Dean Jacques Torres

Demonstration

Sirop Simple (Simple Syrup)

Makes about 2 liters (2½ quarts)
Estimated time to complete: 30 minutes

Ingredients	Equipment
1 kilogram (2¼ pounds) sugar	*Russe*
1 liter (1 quart) water	*Chinois*
	Heatproof bowl
	Ice bath

Prepare your *mise en place.*

Combine the sugar and water in a russe over medium-high heat. Bring to a boil, stirring frequently. Immediately remove from the heat and strain through a *chinois* into a clean heatproof bowl. Place in an ice bath to cool. Use as directed in a specific recipe Simple syrup can be stored, covered and refrigerated, for up to 1 month.

Demonstration

Crème au Beurre (Buttercream)

Makes enough to fill and cover for two 6-inch cakes
Estimated time to complete: 40 minutes

Ingredients	Equipment
600 grams (1 pound, 3 ounces) unsalted butter, at room temperature	Wooden spoon
	Copper *poêlon* or heavy-bottomed *sautoir* or *russe*
300 grams (10½ ounces) sugar	Candy thermometer
100 milliliters (7 tablespoons) water	Pastry brush
6 large egg yolks, at room temperature	Whisk or electric mixer

Prepare your *mise en place.*

Using a wooden spoon, beat the butter to the *pommade* stage (see note). Set aside.

Place the sugar and water in a copper *poêlon* or heavy-bottomed *sautoir* or *russe* over high heat and bring to a boil. Cook the sugar syrup at a high, steady heat, without shaking the pan, until it reaches the soft-ball stage, 112°C–116°C (234°F–240°F) on a

candy thermometer. Throughout the cooking, use a pastry brush dipped into cold water to brush down the interior walls of the pan to prevent crystallization.

Using a whisk or an electric mixer, beat the egg yolks until very pale yellow. Whisking constantly, slowly add the soft-ball sugar in a slow, steady stream. Do not allow the syrup to splash on the sides of the pot or on the whisk. When all the syrup has been added, beat the mixture for about 10 minutes or until very smooth and cool.

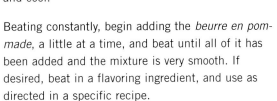

Beating constantly, begin adding the *beurre en pommade*, a little at a time, and beat until all of it has been added and the mixture is very smooth. If desired, beat in a flavoring ingredient, and use as directed in a specific recipe.

Session 24

Frozen Desserts and *Meringues*

Theory

A Brief History of Frozen Desserts

There are several styles of ices and ice creams, and several definitions, some of which overlap slightly, with differences between French, Italian, and American terminology. By general definition, we can say that all ices — milk-, cream-, or water-based — are made up of sugar and one or more of the following liquid ingredients: milk, cream, water, and sometimes whole or separated eggs.

Many myths exist regarding the origins of ices and ice creams. It has been said that Alexander the Great had a penchant for wine-flavored ices, that the Roman Emperor Nero served his guests the first sorbet consisting of fruits crushed with snow and honey, that Marco Polo observed the practice of ice cream making in China and brought the concept home to Europe, that Catherine de Medici brought the fashion of sorbets from Italy to France in 1533, that a servant to Charles the First of England created the first ice cream as we know it today. Interesting as these stories are, scholars cannot confirm that they have any basis in historical fact (see note).

Some historical evidence does exist that tells us that the Chinese were among the first to experiment with refrigeration and, as early as the third century BC, had discovered that blocks of river ice could be stored underground and used in hot weather to cool food and drink. It is also known that the evolution of frozen desserts has been closely related to scientific discoveries of the endothermic effect of salt on ice, the harvesting, preservation, and distribution of natural ice, and finally the development of mechanical refrigeration.

Ices did not arrive in Europe until many centuries later, having first made the trek along the Silk Road to the Middle East. In fact, the words *sorbet* and *sherbet* are derived from the Arabic word *shariba*, cool drink. Water ices first appeared in France, Spain, and Italy in the mid 1600s. In France, the earliest known recipe for a water ice appeared in Nicholas Lemery's *Recueil de Curiositéz Rares et Nouvelles des Plus Admirables Effets de la Nature* (*Book of Rare Curiosities and News of the Most Marvelous Effects of Nature*), published in Paris in 1674. Records also indicate that ices were served in England as early as 1672, and in 1700 in the United States. However, although these recipes existed, the actual serving of ice cream was extremely rare, as it was expensive and time-consuming to make and difficult to keep. It was, consequently, a delicacy for either royalty or the very wealthy.

Early ice creams and ices were literally frozen, iced cream mixed with sugar, flavorings, and fruits. Eggs were added later, making a smoother, richer mixture more like today's frozen custard. French recipes of the early eighteenth century did not call for eggs; when they finally did appear as an ingredient, the resulting frozen desserts were called *fromages glacés*. In 1733, Vincent La Chapelle, a French chef, published *The Modern Cook*, which is significant to the history of ice cream for its description of the elegant uses of ices and decorative molds, as well as for its many ice cream recipes.

The first commercial ice cream factory in America was established in Baltimore, Maryland, in 1851 by Jacob Fussell, Jr., a milk dealer who made ice cream to use his surplus cream. His local venture was successful enough to allow him to expand to other cities and his large-scale manufacturing made commercially produced ice cream available for the first time to the general public at a reasonable cost. By the end of that century, refrigerated rail shipping increased ice cream distribution across the United States, and by the early twentieth century, technology brought refrigeration to the home kitchen. America's devotion to ice cream was set.

In classic French cooking, there are many methods and techniques for making ice cream. A traditional method is to simply put a chilled, classic, milk-based *crème anglaise* mixture (containing no cream) into an ice cream machine and churn it until it freezes. Ice cream made in this manner tastes more like an ice milk and seems light to the American palate. Ice cream made with milk and half-and-half that has been heated to 79°C (175°F) will have a noticeably smoother texture than other ice creams. The vanilla ice cream **(glace à la vanille)** recipe on page 434 in this session uses a rich, cream- and milk-based *crème anglaise*, which makes the rich ice cream familiar to Americans.

The Structure of Ice Cream

Scientifically speaking, ice cream is a foam and an emulsion that has been stabilized by the freezing of much of its liquid. According to food scientist Harold McGee in his book *On Food and Cooking*,

The structure of ice cream, when viewed under a microscope, reveals four phases. Even at freezer temperature, there is some liquid left, containing dissolved salt, sugars and suspended milk proteins. There are tiny ice crystals, composed of pure water, and there are solid globules of milk fat. Finally, there are air cells, which should be very small. Sometimes there is a fifth, undesirable phase, which are crystals of lactose (milk sugar), usually occurring with custards made from whole cream, which give a gritty texture to the final product. Each phase makes its own contribution to the character of the ice cream.

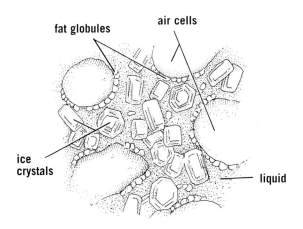

Fruit or Water Ices

Ices fall into two categories; those that are stirred very little (*granités*), and those that are stirred frequently or churned (*sorbets*). An equally important element in an ice mix is the sugar content, because sugar lowers the freezing point of water (without sugar, water molecules would join to form a solid mass of ice). The general ingredients for *granités* and *sorbets* are sugar, water, and lemon juice for acidity (optional)—plus fruit purée, fruit juice, liqueur, wine, spirits, brewed tea, coffee, or an herbal infusion.

A *granité* usually has a lower sugar content than a *sorbet* and is prepared with little stirring during the freezing process, which results in coarse ice crystals. *Granités* are generally mixed and placed in a stainless steel pan, still-frozen in the freezer, and stirred occasionally to prevent separation and to ensure distribution of flavor. They are served by scraping an ice cream scoop or large fork across the frozen surface, thereby shaving off bits of the flavored ice. Occasionally they are completely frozen without stirring and then crushed in an ice crusher for a coarse texture, or processed in a food processor for a finer texture. *Granités* should be served in a well-chilled dish as a dessert or palate cleanser.

The texture of a *sorbet* should be perfectly smooth. In order to obtain this smoothness, it has to be churned very rapidly so that large ice crystals don't have time to form. If *sorbet* is frozen overnight, it has a tendency to crystallize. If so, it can be melted and returned to the ice cream machine to restore the proper texture (this cannot be done with ice cream).

The texture of *sorbet* is totally affected by its sugar content. If it is too low, the *sorbet* will be grainy and hard; if it is too high the *sorbet* will be loose and soupy. Unfortunately, because different types of fruit and other ingredients have differing sugar contents, there is no standard amount of sugar to be added to a *sorbet* mixture. The sugar in the *sorbet* base is adjusted by the addition of either water or simple syrup (see page 424). The sugar content can best be tested using a refractometer. If one is not available, it is often necessary to completely prepare (including freezing) the *sorbet* mixture and then thaw it to adjust the sugar content. If the *sorbet* is the right texture but tastes too sweet, lemon juice can be added to adjust the flavor.

Terminology for Frozen Desserts

There are many types of ice creams, ices, and other frozen desserts, and the subtle differences can be confusing. The following nomenclature is used for frozen desserts.

French-Style or Custard-Based Ice Cream

French-style ice cream is based on an egg custard, usually with a high ratio of cream to milk and eggs. In France, it is referred to as a *glace* and, by definition, has a specific minimum percentage of its components required by the government. Extremely rich, it is based on the same technique as that for *crème anglaise* (see page 392) and, in fact, a classic milk-based *crème anglaise* was, for many years, used as the base for French ice creams.

Fruit-flavored French ice creams have their own specific name — *les glaces aux fruits*. French eggless ice creams, based on a mixture of milk, cream, sugar, and flavoring, are referred to as *les crèmes glacées*. These are either stir-frozen or churned.

In American terminology, *ice cream* generally refers to a rich cream, and egg-based frozen mixture. Commercial ice creams of this type are required by the United States Food and Drug Administration to contain no less than 10 percent butterfat and at least

20 percent milk-solids-no-fat (MSNFs). A good ice cream will have 40 percent solids (fats, sweetener, and MSNFs), and it may also have up to 50 percent overrun. *Overrun* is the extra volume of ice cream produced as air is introduced during the churning process, and is usually expressed by a percentage of the original volume of the base mixture. American ice cream may also contain stabilizers and emulsifiers.

All ice creams are judged or rated on texture and smoothness, mouth feel or body, richness, and flavor.

Philadelphia-Style Ice Cream

Also referred to as American-style ice cream, Philadelphia-style ice cream is milk- or cream-based and frozen in the same manner as a custard-based ice cream. Traditionally uncooked and by strict definition without eggs, it is more sherbetlike in composition, with a grainy texture.

Gelato

Dense, Italian-style ice cream that contains less air than American-style ice cream and may or may not contain eggs.

Sorbet

A true *sorbet* does not contain any dairy product and is produced with only sugar, water, and a flavoring. Although often confused with sherbet, they are two different desserts. A *sorbet* is light and refreshing, while a dairy-based sherbet is a richer, heavier frozen treat. French *sorbets* are based on a mixture of sugar combined with a variety of fruit juices or purées, wines, spirits, or liqueurs. Sorbets may also be based on infusions made from aromatic or fragrant plants such as mint or lemon verbena. Depending upon the degree of sweetness, *sorbet* may be served as dessert or as an intermezzo between courses of a lengthy, elegant meal to cleanse the palate.

Sherbet

Sherbet is generally a fruit-based mixture made with cream or milk and sometimes eggs. It resembles Philadelphia-style ice cream in texture and is, unlike sorbet, always a dessert.

Spoom

Spoom is a sorbet to which 25 to 50 percent Italian meringue has been added, making it light and airy.

Granité (French) or *Granita* (Italian)

Closely resembling sorbet, this is an ice with a low sugar content and a characteristic grainy texture. The name derives from the Italian word, *grana*, meaning grainy—a reference to both the texture and the gran- itelike appearance of the finished dessert. Usually made by combining simple syrup and water with a fruit purée, liqueur, wine, coffee, or tea, *granité* is typically frozen in shallow pans, without churning and with infrequent stirring.

Ice Milk and Frozen Yogurt

Ice milk is a milk-based frozen dessert with a low per- centage of butterfat. Frozen yogurt is a sweetened yogurt-based frozen dessert.

Hygiene in Ice Cream Making

It is especially important that strict rules of sanitation are followed when making ice cream because the dairy products in the mixtures provide the perfect breeding ground for bacteria. And, in those mixtures containing eggs, a high-protein food that is easily contaminated by salmonella, even greater care must be taken.

The following rules should always be maintained when preparing ice cream and ice cream products:

◦ Wash hands thoroughly before beginning preparation.

◦ Use only clean, sanitized bowls, and stainless steel or other noncorrosive utensils and storage containers.

◦ Use only the highest quality pasteurized dairy ingredients.

◦ Submerge small equipment in water with a temperature of 82°C–100°C (180°F–212°F) for at least 10 minutes.

◦ Follow manufacturer's directions for operating and cleaning the machine and, even if not instructed to do so, always clean following these rules of sanitation:

◦ Ice cream machines should be cleaned with a chemical solution that has the proper concentration of an active chemical and sanitizing agent, such as regular laundry bleach. The surface being cleaned should be in contact with a mixture of 15 to 30 milliliters (1 to 2 tablespoons) bleach per 3.8 liters (1 gallon) warm (not above 38°C/ 110°F) water for at least 1 minute.

◦ Do not use kitchen towels to wipe out machinery; they are not sterile. Instead, let the machine air dry.

◦ When breaking open eggs, do not allow the exterior of the eggshell to come in contact with the raw egg.

◦ Heat milk to just below the boiling point before combining with eggs.

◦ Cooked ice cream bases containing milk and eggs should be brought to 77°C–79°C (170°F–175°F) and held there briefly; whole eggs and egg yolks can be pasteurized by heating to 79°C (175°F).

◦ Use a clean spoon to taste mixtures.

◦ Cover any open wounds while handling ingredients and equipment.

◦ Do not blow on hot mixtures to speed cooling.

◦ Chill the finished product quickly in an ice bath and refrigerate immediately until ready to use.

Some Classic Ice Cream Desserts

Ice cream may be served alone, with sauce or fruit, with meringues or in molds, or as a component of other desserts.

Following are some of the classic desserts that contain ice cream:

◦ Goblets (*coupes*): *Coupes de glace* are different types of ice creams, *sorbets*, or fresh fruits (*coupe de fruits*) served frozen in the large *coupe* glasses from which they take their name. They usually also include other ingredients such as fruit or chocolate sauce, chopped toasted nuts, *crème anglaise*, and so forth. In America, a *coupe* might be called a sundae. Auguste Escoffier made this category of dessert famous with his many memorable classics, often named after well-known women, such as peach Melba (*coupe pêche Melba*), a poached peach with vanilla ice cream and raspberry sauce named after Dame Nellie Melba, an opera star, and *coupe poire belle Hélène*, a poached pear with vanilla ice cream and chocolate sauce, named after the heroine of an Offenbach operetta.

◦ Baked Alaska (*omelette Norvégienne*): One or more sorbets encased in *génoise* (see page 421) and baked Italian *meringue*.

- Ice cream–filled meringues (*vacherins glacés*): Shells or rings of *meringue*, filled with sorbets and ice creams and then decorated with piped *crème Chantilly* (see page 376); may be garnished with smaller decorations of candied flowers or fruits and nuts.

- Ice cream–filled cream puffs with chocolate sauce (*Profiteroles glacées au chocolat*): Cream puffs (see page 377) filled with ice cream and kept frozen until served accompanied by hot chocolate sauce.

Other Frozen Desserts

In addition to the classics discussed above, there are a number of other frozen desserts that come from the French kitchen.

Bombe (*Bombe Glacé*)

The word *bombe* is often used loosely, referring to both a dessert and to a frozen dessert base mixture. In more specific and correct terminology, the frozen dessert is a *bombe glacé*, which is traditionally made by lining a chilled half-sphere mold with a firm mixture of ice cream, *sorbet*, or sherbet, sometimes in multiple layers. The shell is allowed to set then filled with a lighter *bombe* mixture, and the entire mold is frozen.

A *bombe* mixture, *appareil à bombe* or *pâte à bombe*, is made primarily from egg yolks and soft-ball sugar. It can be prepared in several ways: by adding sugar cooked to the soft-ball stage to whipped yolks; by cooking the yolks with the sugar syrup in a double boiler over low heat, or by cooking the yolks in sweetened milk, as is often done when making *crème anglaise*. The most common is the first method.

Parfait

In French, the term *parfait* refers to a specific type of frozen cream. It should not be confused with the American parfait, which is a layered sundae served in a tall glass. A French *parfait* is a *bombe* mixture that is prepared using cooked sugar, sugar syrup, or *crème anglaise*. The *bombe* mixture is folded with whipped cream, flavored, and frozen. An additional technique of folding cold, cooked fruit pulp into whipped cream

can also be applied to the preparation of *parfaits* and frozen *soufflés*.

Frozen *Soufflé* (*Soufflé Glacé*)

In French culinary terms, *soufflé glacé* means a smooth, light-textured cream based on a variety of fruits, liqueurs, and natural flavorings. A frozen soufflé is prepared in much the same way as a *parfait*. The only difference is that in the *soufflé glacé*, the basic *bombe* mixture is combined with Italian *meringue* (see page 432) as well as, sometimes, whipped cream, instead of whipped cream alone. The *meringue* lightens the mixture and gives it a stiffer texture, which makes it easier to freeze on its own without the support of an ice cream lining. Another defining difference between a *parfait* and a frozen *soufflé* is that the latter is usually served in a *soufflé* mold with a paper collar extending above the top so that it looks like a hot *soufflé* that has risen (although the two methods of preparation have nothing else in common).

Classic frozen soufflés may be divided into two basic categories:

- Frozen soufflés flavored with natural extracts, liqueurs, or liquor. These mixtures are made of a standard *bombe* base that is folded with Italian *meringue* and whipped cream.

○ Frozen soufflés flavored with fruit. These *soufflés* are based on reduced fruit pulp or purée that is then combined with whipped cream and Italian *meringue* as in the recipe for Frozen Fruit *Soufflé* on page 436.

Frozen Sabayon (*Sabayon Glacé*)

Some frozen *soufflés* are actually *sabayons* (see page 79). French *sabayons* are based on the Italian *zabaglione*, which is a mixture of egg yolks, sugar, and Marsala wine beaten over heat to form a light emulsion. In the French version, the base may be prepared using dry white wine or wines with pronounced character such as Muscat Tokay, Riesling, gerwürtztraminer, sherry, Madeira, port, or champagne, or with liqueurs such as Grand Marnier. The finished *sabayon* sauce is combined with whipped cream before being frozen, usually in an ice cream mold, to serve as the filling for another preparation. It can also be used in *coupes* along with other ices or ice creams. *Sabayon* can be blended with whipped cream or Italian *meringue*, but this must be done very delicately or the mixture will deflate.

Frozen Mousse (*Mousse Glacé*)

This is a light and creamy frozen *mousse*, made using one of two methods:

○ A mixture of egg yolks, milk, sugar, whipped cream, and flavoring.

○ A mixture based on sugar syrup plus puréed fresh fruit and whipped cream called a frozen fruit *mousse* (*mousse glacée aux fruits*).

About *Meringues*

A *meringue* is a composition of egg white and sugar that has been stiffly beaten. According to the *Larousse Gastronomique*, *meringue* may have been invented by a Swiss pastry cook who practiced his art in the small German town Meiringen. Until the early nineteenth century, *meringues* baked in the oven were always shaped with a spoon. It was the famed French chef Antonin Carême who introduced the idea of piping it out of a pastry bag. There are three types of *meringues*:

French *Meringue*

This is the simplest type of *meringue*, made by simply beating egg whites with sugar. It isn't sterilized, so it must always be baked. French *meringue* may be piped into shapes through a pastry bag and then slowly baked until it has a distinctive crunchy texture. It is quite delicate and crumbly and should melt in the mouth. It is also used for shells or rings in a variety of cakes, and as a component of other recipes.

Italian *Meringue*

This *meringue* is made with soft-ball sugar that is poured into firmly whipped egg whites and then beaten into stiff peaks. It is important that the sugar syrup be cooked to the correct stage — the soft-ball stage of 112°C–116°C (234°F–240°F)

The egg whites poach in the hot syrup to sterilize the *meringue* as well as stabilize it. While whipping constantly, the hot syrup must be carefully poured into the whipped egg whites and then the mixture beaten until cool. A well-prepared Italian *meringue* should have a soft, creamy texture and be light and shiny. It is the most difficult *meringue* to make because the whites and the syrup must be ready simultaneously. It is usually necessary to raise and lower the heat and the mixer speed to get the correct mix. Italian *meringue* is very stable and has myriad uses in decorating pastries, icing cakes, and lightening batters.

Swiss *Meringue*

This is similar to French *meringue*, except that the egg whites and sugar are combined and heated over a *bain-marie* until they reach 54°C (130°F) and start to thicken. The mixture is then removed from the heat and beaten until cool. Swiss *meringue* should be light, perfectly smooth, and very firm. The preliminary cooking makes it a stable, sturdy *meringue* that is useful for decorations such as the little mushrooms that decorate a traditional yule log (*bûche de noël*).

Guidelines for Working with *Meringue*

- *Meringues* are very fragile. They should be made right before they are to be used. If allowed to sit for any length of time, they will begin to break down.

- All utensils must be perfectly clean. No residue of fat should remain or the whites will not achieve the necessary volume.

- If using copper, clean the bowl with salt and vinegar and wipe it dry with paper towels before adding the egg whites.

- When separating the eggs, make sure that no yolk contaminates the whites because the fat of the yolk prevents the whites from achieving the desired volume.

- Fresh egg whites are more viscous and produce a more stable *meringue*. On the other hand, older egg whites give more volume to when beaten.

- Adding a pinch of salt to (foamy) egg whites reduces viscosity, which increases the volume. However, the addition of salt lessens stability.

- Egg whites beaten by hand with a balloon whisk usually result in a more even-textured meringue than those beaten with an electric mixer.

- Using room-temperature egg whites also increases the volume. On the other hand, cold egg whites produce a more stable *meringue*.

- When egg whites for a *meringue* are beaten, air is trapped in the form of bubbles, which serves to lighten other mixtures. The *meringue* can be folded into mousses, cake batters, pastry creams, and so forth to add airiness. If the *meringue* is folded into a preparation that is then baked, the air expands in the heat of the oven and causes the preparation to rise, as with a *soufflé*.

- A copper bowl, if available, is a good vessel to use to beat egg whites, as the copper reacts with the proteins in the egg whites, yielding more volume than that produced in a stainless steel bowl. This method produces a great, even consistency.

- If using a copper bowl, never add acid to the mixture or a toxic reaction will occur that will turn the whites green.

- The more sugar called for in the specific recipe, the longer the beating process.

- When making a French or Italian *meringue*, the sugar should always be added after the soft peaks have formed.

- Be gentle when folding *meringues* into other mixtures, as they are easily deflated.

Tips on making a French *meringue* using an electric mixer

- Start at the lowest speed to incorporate air.

- If using cream of tartar, add it just when the whites are frothy.

- Once frothy, turn the speed up (to 6 or 8 on a KitchenAid mixer).

- Add sugar just as the soft peaks form.

° Sear the *meringue* by beating at high speed for a few seconds just at the end of the beating process; this will stabilize it.

° The *meringue* should be smooth and shiny; if it is dry, grainy, or cottony, it has been overbeaten.

° A *meringue* can be started with an electric mixer and finished by hand using a balloon whisk to achieve a very smooth texture.

Demonstration

Glace à la Vanille (Vanilla Ice Cream)

Makes 1.5 liters (1⅔ quarts)

Estimated time to complete: 90 minutes

Ingredients	Equipment
500 milliliters (2 cups plus 2 tablespoons) whole milk	*Russe*
500 milliliters (2 cups plus 2 tablespoons) heavy cream	Small, sharp knife
1 vanilla bean	2 mixing bowls
8 large egg yolks, at room temperature	Whisk
200 grams (7 ounces) sugar	Wooden spatula
	Metal spoon
	Candy thermometer
	Chinois
	Ice bath
	Wooden spoon
	Ice cream machine

Prepare your *mise en place*.

Place the milk and cream in the *russe*. Using a small, sharp knife, split the vanilla bean in half lengthwise and scrape the seeds into the milk and cream. Add the scraped bean to the *russe* as well and place over medium heat. Bring to a boil, then immediately remove the pan from the heat and allow the mixture to cool for 1 minute.

Combine the egg yolks with the sugar in a mixing bowl, whisking until the mixture is very pale yellow (*blanchir*).

Whisking constantly, pour half the hot milk and cream into the egg mixture to temper, then slowly pour the mixture into the *russe*, whisking constantly. Cook, stirring constantly with a wooden spatula, for about 12 minutes or until the mixture coats the back of a spoon (*nappant*) and a finger drawn through it leaves a clean, stable line. While stirring, pay special attention to the bottom corners of the pan, as the egg will tend to coagulate there.

To pasteurize the cream, bring it to 79°C (175°F) on a candy thermometer and hold it at that temperature, stirring constantly, for 5 minutes. Do not exceed 82°C (180°F) or the cream will curdle.

Remove the mixture from the heat and pour it through a *chinois* into a clean mixing bowl set over an ice bath, stirring constantly with a wooden spoon until no steam is forthcoming.

When cool, transfer to an ice cream machine and process according to the manufacturer's directions.

Demonstration

Sorbet aux Framboises (Raspberry *Sorbet*)

Makes 1.5 liters (1⅔ quarts)
Estimated time required to complete: 1 hour

Ingredients	Equipment
250 grams (8¾ ounces) sugar	Medium saucepan
50 grams (1¾ ounces) glucose (see note)	Wooden spoon
100 milliliters (7 tablespoons) water	*Chinois*
600 grams (1 pound, 5 ounces) fresh	Medium mixing bowl
raspberry purée	Ice cream machine
Juice of ½ lemon	

Prepare your *mise en place*.

Combine the sugar and glucose with the water in a medium saucepan over medium heat. Bring to a simmer and cook, stirring occasionally with a wooden spoon, for about 5 minutes or until the sugar has dissolved completely. Remove from the heat and set aside to cool.

Pass the purée through a *chinois* and strain it into a medium mixing bowl.

Slowly pour the cooled syrup into the purée, stirring as you pour. Stop from time to time to check the sweetness and density of the mixture. The sweetness can be to taste, but keep in mind that it will intensify once the mixture is frozen. The mixture should be dense enough that a wooden spoon meets slight resistance when pushed through it. The final flavor of the sorbet will be affected not only by the sugar content, but also by the natural acidity and sweetness of the fruit.

Pour the mixture into an ice cream machine and process according to the manufacturer's directions.

Demonstration

Soufflé Glacé aux Fruits (Frozen Fruit *Soufflé*)

Serves 6

Estimated time to complete: 90 minutes

Ingredients	Equipment
15 grams (1 tablespoon) melted butter	Six 4-ounce *soufflé* molds
100 grams (3½ ounces) sugar	Parchment paper
40 milliliters (2 tablespoons plus 2 teaspoons) water	Pastry brush
2 large egg whites, at room temperature	Sheet pan
250 milliliters (1 cup plus 1 tablespoon) fruit purée	Heavy-bottomed saucepan
250 milliliters (1 cup plus 1 tablespoon) heavy cream	Electric mixer
Confectioners' sugar for sprinkling	Balloon whisk
	Chinois
	Chilled bowl
	Ice bath
	Rubber spatula
	Large pastry spatula

Prepare your *mise en place*.

Prepare the *soufflé* molds by cutting strips of parchment paper large enough to fit around the molds, rising from the bottom to about 1.3 centimeters (½ inch) above the rim (or however high you wish the *soufflé* to be). Using a pastry brush, lightly coat one side of each strip with melted butter and wrap it around a mold, buttered side in. Place the prepared molds on a sheet pan in the freezer until ready to use.

Combine 90 grams (3 ounces) of the sugar with the water in a heavy-bottomed saucepan over high heat. Bring to a boil, then lower the heat to a simmer and cook for about 20 minutes or until the mixture reaches the soft-ball stage (112°C/234°F).

While the sugar is cooking, using an electric mixer beat the egg whites until soft peaks form. Add the remaining 10 grams (½ ounce) sugar and whip until firm and satiny.

Beating constantly with a balloon whisk, add the hot

syrup to the beaten egg whites in a slow, steady steam, taking care that no syrup gets on the whisk or on the sides of the bowl.

When all the syrup has been added, continue beating until the *meringue* is cool.

Strain the fruit purée through a *chinois*. Set aside.

Place the cream in a chilled bowl over an ice bath and whip until soft peaks form. Set aside.

Using a rubber spatula, fold half of the purée into the *meringue*, folding until well blended.

Fold the remaining purée into the whipped cream, folding until well blended. Then fold the whipped cream mixture into the *meringue* mixture until well blended.

Remove the prepared molds from the freezer and spoon equal portions of the *soufflé* mixture into each mold, smoothing the tops with a large pastry spatula.

Place the filled molds in the freezer and freeze for at least 1 hour or up to 2 days.

When ready to serve, remove the molds from the freezer and let stand at room temperature for 15 minutes. Sprinkle the tops with confectioners' sugar, remove the parchment paper collars, and serve. Alternatively, the *soufflés* may be served with a dollop of whipped cream.

Chef's Tip

"Try using different combinations of fruits to make fresh purées—this is a great way to use up fresh fruit that might be getting too ripe."

Chef Tina Casaceli

Demonstration

Petit Vacherin Glacé (Ice Cream Cake)

Serves 4

Estimated time to complete: 2 hours

Ingredients	Equipment
For the *meringues*	Heatproof mixing bowl
4 large egg whites	Whisk
250 grams (8¾ ounces) granulated sugar	Saucepan
	Candy thermometer
For the *crème Chantilly*	Baking sheet
150 milliliters (⅔ cup) heavy cream	Parchment paper
10 grams (⅓ ounce) confectioners' sugar	Pastry bag fitted with a small plain tip
Pure vanilla extract to taste	Wire racks
	Stainless steel mixing bowl
To finish the desert	Ice bath
250 milliliters (1 cup plus 1 tablespoon) vanilla ice cream	Electric mixer, optional
About 120 milliliters (½ cup) chocolate sauce	4 chilled dessert plates

Prepare your *mise en place*.

Preheat the oven to 79°C (175°F). A convection oven is preferred, as the *meringues* will cook more evenly.

Combine the egg whites with the sugar in a clean heatproof mixing bowl. Whisk together to just combine.

Fill a saucepan large enough to hold the bowl with just enough water to create a *bain-marie* without the bottom of the bowl touching the water. Place over high heat and bring to a simmer, whisking constantly. Continue to whisk until the sugar dissolves and the egg whites reach 54°C (130°F) on a candy thermometer. Remove the bowl from the saucepan and continue to whip the *meringue* to firm peaks.

Line a baking sheet with parchment paper.

Place the *meringue* in a pastry bag fitted with the small plain tip and pipe it into at least 12 circles about 5 centimeters (2 inches) in diameter onto the

FROZEN DESSERTS AND *MERINGUES*

prepared baking sheet. (If desired, you can also pipe out mushroom-cap-shaped *meringues* to use as decoration for the top of the final dessert.) You will have more *meringue* than needed for the finished dessert but the extra allows for breakage.

Place the *meringues* in the oven and bake slowly for about 1 hour or until they are very dry. Watch carefully, as you do not want them to color, and the time will vary with the oven.

Remove the *meringues* from the oven and place them on wire racks to cool. During the summer months or on humid days, try to use the *meringues* immediately, as they will absorb moisture and get chewy. To store the extra *meringues* for future use, arrange them in an airtight container in layers separated by parchment paper.

When ready to serve, prepare the *crème Chantilly.*

Place the cream in a chilled stainless steel bowl and then place the bowl in an ice bath.

Using either a whisk or an electric mixer, beat the cream just until it starts to thicken. Add the confectioners' sugar and vanilla and continue beating until stiff peaks form, taking care not to overbeat or the cream will turn to butter.

Transfer the cream to a pastry bag fitted with the small, round tip.

To assemble, place a scoop of vanilla ice cream on top of four of the *meringue* circles placed on chilled dessert plates. Top each one with a second circle or a mushroom cap. Pipe five equal strips of *crème Chantilly*, equidistant from one another, over the ice cream, working from the mushroom cap down. Finish the plates with a drizzle of chocolate sauce or, if desired, a chocolate design.

Session 25

Mousses, Soufflés, Bavarian Creams, and Charlottes

Theory
About Mousses

In French, the word *mousse* simply means froth or foam and includes any dish, sweet or savory, that is light and airy, with a flavored base that has usually been puréed and then folded into beaten egg whites or whipped cream. Sweet *mousses* are made from several different bases, including fruit purée, *pâte à bombe* (see page 431), coffee, liqueur, or chocolate. Savory *mousses* can be made with meat, fish, shellfish, or vegetable purées.

The characteristic *mousse* texture is achieved by folding stiffly beaten egg whites or softly beaten heavy cream into a puréed base. The cream should not be too stiffly beaten or it will begin to have a strong, buttery taste and will produce a heavier *mousse*, which is not desirable. When folding the beaten egg whites or cream into the base, one quarter of the beaten ingredients is first added to lighten the base and then the remaining three quarters are folded in all at once. The air bubbles from the beaten egg whites or cream are trapped in the dessert base and provide the airy, almost spongelike texture.

Gelatin is sometimes added to *mousse* in very specific contexts. For instance, if a fruit purée is too thin, it may require gelatin to bind it and create a dense enough base to balance the addition of the beaten ingredients. Or if a *mousse* is being served to a large number of people and must be held, unrefrigerated, for a period of time, gelatin may be added to ensure stability. However, it is important to note that the addition of gelatin does not enhance the texture or flavor. It should be used sparingly and only when absolutely necessary.

About Soufflés

The word *soufflé* means blown up and refers to airy dishes, either sweet or savory, that have a flavored base that gets lightened by the addition of stiffly beaten egg whites, softly beaten heavy cream, or both. A *soufflé* can be either baked or frozen; if baked, the lightening agent is always egg white. When baked, the air beaten into the egg whites expands and the water in the mixture turns to steam, causing the *soufflé* to rise. It must be served the instant it is taken from the oven because the gas contracts as it cools and the towering, fragile puff deflates rapidly.

Although baked *soufflés* have the reputation of being difficult to make, they are quite easy to put together. It is the timing for service that is tricky. Therefore, in restaurant service, a dessert *soufflé* is often ordered at the beginning of the meal to allow the pastry chef time to execute it properly. In addition, with some *soufflés* the batter can be made in advance and held, refrigerated, until ready to bake. Obviously, frozen *soufflés* are both easy to put together and easy to serve.

Dessert *soufflés* may have as their base a pastry cream (*crème patissière*, see page 390), a *bouillie* (stirred pudding made with a boiled mixture of sugar, flour, milk, and egg yolks), a *blanchir* of egg yolks and sugar with flavorings added (a *minute soufflé*), as well as sweetened fruit purées.

Chocolate *soufflés* (*soufflés au chocolat*) are in a class by themselves. They can be made with a *bouillie* base, by folding egg whites into a *ganache* (a rich icing filling made with chocolate and hot cream), or by combining chocolate with egg yolks and sugar.

When beating egg whites for use in a *soufflé*, take care not to overbeat them because when beaten until dry, they impart a tough and unpalatable texture to the finished *soufflé*. (This is a greater danger when there is no sugar added, as sugar softens the beaten whites.) Do not allow beaten egg whites to sit for any period of time, as they begin deflating right away; they should be immediately folded into the *soufflé* base.

The base should be cool or just warm, never hot, when the beaten ingredients are added. As with *mousses*, when folding the beaten egg whites into the base, add one quarter of the beaten ingredients first to lighten the base and then fold in the remaining three quarters all at once. The *soufflé* is then baked immediately.

If a *soufflé* is very delicate or if it is going to be filled to the top of the mold, a collar is needed to keep an even, straight-sided height. A collar is a buttered strip of parchment paper attached around the top edge of a straight-sided *soufflé* mold that allows the *soufflé* to stand up straight. The mold is first buttered and coated with sugar for a hot dessert *soufflé*, or buttered and coated with fine breadcrumbs or grated cheese for a savory *soufflé*. Collars are often used when making frozen *soufflés* so that an impressive, towering presentation can be made. However, collars are labor-intensive and, in the professional kitchen, the incumbent labor costs should be noted when considering their use.

Most *soufflés* are baked at 204°C (400°F), but a large *soufflé* or one with a heavy base can be baked at 177°C (350°F). If the oven temperature is too low, the *soufflé* will not rise properly and the batter will flatten and spill out of the mold. If it is too high, the *soufflé* will form a hard crust but remain liquid in the center. A properly executed baked *soufflé* should be just slightly underdone so that it has a barely crisp exterior and a creamy interior.

About Bavarian Creams and *Charlottes*

Bavarian cream (**crème bavarois**) is a classic molded dessert based on egg custard or fruit purées and served cold. It consists of a *crème anglaise* (see page 392) or a fruit purée that has been stabilized with gelatin and lightened with whipped cream. A Bavarian cream may be served simply unmolded or it may be encased by *génoise* or *biscuit*, in which case it is known as a *charlotte*.

Charlottes may be hot or cold. Cold *charlottes* normally contain a custard-based Bavarian cream, the classic being *charlotte russe*, invented by the renowned chef Antonin Carême. It is an uncooked Bavarian cream poured into a *charlotte* mold lined with ladyfingers and chilled. Once set, the cold dessert is unmolded and often decorated with whipped cream for service. The key to its success is that the cream be firm enough to withstand being unmolded yet retain its light, airy texture. Hot *charlottes* are usually made with a fruit purée base; the classic being an apple *charlotte* (*charlotte aux pommes*). When making hot *charlottes*, the fruit purée is stewed with sugar and lemon juice, poured into a *charlotte* mold lined with white bread, and baked until the bread is golden brown. It is generally served with an accompanying dessert sauce.

MOUSSES, SOUFFLÉS, BAVARIAN CREAMS, AND CHARLOTTES

444

Demonstration

Mousse aux Deux Chocolats (Two-Chocolate Mousse)

Serves 4

Estimated time to complete: 2 hours

Ingredients	Equipment
For the dark chocolate *mousse*	4 medium stainless steel bowls
150 grams (5¼ ounces) bittersweet chocolate, chopped	*Bain-marie*
400 milliliters (1⅔ cups) heavy cream	Rubber spatula
3 large egg whites (see note)	Wooden spoon
30 grams (1 ounce) sugar	Ice bath
Pure vanilla extract or other flavoring to taste, optional	Whisk or electric mixer
	Plastic film
For the white chocolate *mousse*	2 small stainless steel bowls
200 grams (7 ounces) white chocolate, chopped or pistoles	Small saucepan
300 milliliters (1 ¼ cups) heavy cream	Whisk
2 large egg yolks	*Chinois*
30 grams (1 ounce) sugar	4 small, chilled dessert bowls
Pure vanilla extract or other flavoring to taste, optional	

Prepare your *mise en place.*

To prepare the dark chocolate *mousse*, place the chocolate in a stainless steel bowl set over a *bain-marie* of simmering water over low heat. Heat, stirring constantly with a rubber spatula or wooden spoon, until the chocolate has melted. Turn off the heat but leave the bowl on the *bain-marie*.

Place the cream in a stainless steel bowl in an ice bath and, using a whisk or an electric mixer, beat until soft peaks form. Set aside in the ice bath.

Place the egg whites in a stainless steel bowl and, using a whisk or an electric mixer, beat until soft peaks form. Immediately begin gradually adding the sugar and additional flavoring, if using, beating until the whites form firm but not stiff or dry peaks.

Remove the melted chocolate from the *bain-marie*

and, using a rubber spatula, fold in all the reserved egg whites, scraping up from the bottom of the bowl to blend completely. When all the whites have been blended into the chocolate, fold in the reserved whipped cream. When well blended, cover with plastic film and refrigerate for at least 1 hour or until well chilled and set.

To prepare the white chocolate *mousse*, place the chocolate in a medium stainless steel bowl. Set aside.

Place 100 milliliters (7 tablespoons) of heavy cream in a small saucepan over medium heat and bring to a simmer.

While the cream is heating, whisk the egg yolks and sugar together (*blanchir*) in a small stainless steel bowl. Whisking constantly, add a bit of the hot cream to the egg yolk mixture to temper. Then, whisking

445

Note

With recent concerns expressed relative to the use of raw eggs and salmonella contamination, the dark chocolate *mousse* may be prepared by incorporating some Italian *meringue* (see page 432) in place of the raw egg white and sugar mixture. If so, adjust the level of sugar used.

Chefs' Tips

"For a variation in flavor, try experimenting with different types of chocolate."
Chef Tina Casaceli

"When folding a light ingredient like whipped cream or meringue into a heavy one, if you do it all at once you will get lumps and deflate all the air by the time it is incorporated."
Chef Susan Lifrieri

constantly, pour the tempered mixture into the hot cream. Cook, stirring constantly with a wooden spoon and scraping the bottom of the pan, for about 3 minutes or until the mixture coats the back of a spoon (*nappant*).

Immediately remove the mixture from the heat and pass it through a *chinois* directly into the chopped chocolate. Using a wooden spoon, stir until the chocolate has melted. Allow to cool.

Place the remaining 200 milliliters (14 tablespoons) of the heavy cream in a small bowl and, using a whisk or an electric mixer, beat until fairly stiff peaks form, taking care not to overbeat. Set aside.

Using a rubber spatula, fold the reserved whipped cream into the cooled chocolate mixture. When well blended, cover with plastic film and refrigerate for at least 1 hour or until well chilled and set.

When ready to serve, scoop an equal portion of each *mousse* into small, chilled dessert bowls. If desired, decorate with whipped cream.

Demonstration

Soufflé au Chocolat (Chocolate *Soufflé*)

Serves 4

Estimated time to complete: 45 minutes

Ingredients	Equipment
40 grams (2 tablespoons plus 2 teaspoons) unsalted butter	Four 175-gram (6-ounce) soufflé molds
35 grams (1¼ ounces) sugar	*Russe*
30 grams (1 ounce) all-purpose flour	Whisk
120 milliliters (½ cup) milk	Copper or stainless steel bowl
100 grams (3½ ounces) bittersweet chocolate, chopped	Electric mixer, optional
2 large egg yolks	
10 milliliters (2 teaspoons) dark rum	
Few drops pure vanilla extract	
3 to 4 large egg whites	

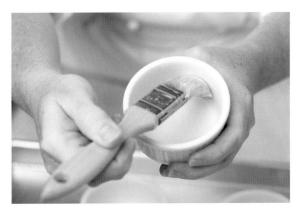

Prepare your *mise en place.*

Preheat the oven to 204°C (400°F).

Using about 10 grams (2 teaspoons) of the butter, lightly coat the interior of the *soufflé* molds. Using about 20 grams (¾ ounce) of the sugar, sprinkle it into the molds and swirl to generously coat the buttered interior, shaking out any excess. Place the molds in the refrigerator until needed.

Make a *beurre manié* (see page 62) with the flour and the remaining 30 grams (2 tablespoons) of butter. Set aside.

Place the milk in a *russe* over medium heat and bring to a boil. Whisking constantly, beat in the *beurre manié* and cook for 3 minutes or until very thick. Remove the mixture from the heat and beat in the chocolate.

When the chocolate has been incorporated, begin beating in the egg yolks, one at a time. When both egg yolks are well incorporated, beat in the rum and vanilla.

Place the egg whites in a copper or stainless steel bowl and, using a whisk or an electric mixer, beat the egg whites until soft peaks form. Gradually add the remaining 15 grams (½ ounce) sugar until firm peaks hold, heeding the guidelines given for beaten egg whites and soufflés on page 443. Fold one quarter of the beaten egg whites into the chocolate base to lighten it and then fold in the remaining three quarters all at once.

Remove the prepared molds from the refrigerator. Spoon an equal portion of the chocolate batter into each mold. Clean the rims of the ramekins, if necessary.

Reduce the oven temperature to 191°C (375°F) and transfer the filled molds to the middle rack. Bake for 8 to 15 minutes, depending upon the size of the molds, or until the soufflés have risen and are just barely set in the center.

Remove from the oven and serve immediately.

Chef's Tip

"If a soufflé rises unevenly, the mold was probably poorly buttered and sugared. A chocolate soufflé should have a strong but not bitter chocolate flavor."
Chef Tina Casaceli

Demonstration

Soufflé à la Liqueur (Liqueur *Soufflé*)

Serves 4

Estimated time to complete: 45 minutes

Ingredients	Equipment
10 grams (2 teaspoons) unsalted butter, softened	Four 6-ounce soufflé molds
135 grams (4¾ ounces) sugar	Pastry brush
250 milliliters (1 cup plus 1 tablespoon) milk	*Russe*
½ vanilla bean	3 stainless steel bowls
3 large egg yolks	Whisk
30 grams (1 ounce) all-purpose flour, sifted	Rubber spatula
20 milliliters (4 teaspoons) Grand Marnier or other liqueur	Copper bowl, optional
4 large egg whites	Electric mixer, optional
10 grams (⅓ ounce) confectioners' sugar, optional	

Prepare your *mise en place*.

Preheat the oven to 204°C (400°F).

Lightly coat the interior of the *soufflé* molds with the butter. Sprinkle about 20 grams (½ ounce) of the sugar into each mold and swirl to generously coat the buttered interior, shaking out any excess. Place the molds in the refrigerator until needed.

Place the milk in a *russe* over medium heat. Scrape the seeds from the vanilla bean into the milk, adding the scraped bean as well. Bring to a boil. Immediately remove from the heat and set aside to steep for 10 minutes.

Blanchir two of the egg yolks with 40 grams (1½ tablespoons) of the remaining sugar in a stainless steel bowl. When well combined, whisk in the flour. Set aside.

Strain the vanilla bean from the milk. Return the milk to medium heat and bring to a simmer. Once the milk returns to a simmer, whisking constantly, pour about half of the hot milk into the egg yolk mixture to temper. Slowly pour the tempered mixture into the pan of hot milk and, whisking constantly, return to a simmer. Simmer for 1 minute.

Using a rubber spatula, scrape the mixture into a clean bowl. Whisk in the liqueur.

Whisking constantly, beat the remaining egg yolk into the milk mixture.

Place the egg whites in a copper or stainless steel bowl and, using a whisk or an electric mixer, beat the egg whites until soft peaks form. Gradually add the remaining 15 grams (½ ounce) sugar until firm peaks hold, heeding the guidelines given for beaten egg whites and *soufflés* on page 443. Fold one quarter of the beaten egg whites into the milk mixture to light at once.

Remove the prepared molds from the refrigerator. Spoon an equal portion of the batter into each mold. Reduce the oven temperature to 191°C (375°F) and transfer the filled molds to the middle rack. Bake for 8 to 15 minutes, depending upon the size of the molds, or until the *soufflés* have risen and are just barely set in the center.

If desired, about 3 minutes before the soufflés are ready, carefully open the oven door and sprinkle the tops with a bit of confectioners' sugar to form a crisp glaze.

Remove from the oven and serve immediately.

Demonstration

Soufflé au Fromage (Cheese Soufflé)

Serves 4

Estimated time to complete: 45 minutes

Ingredients	Equipment
40 grams (2 tablespoons plus 2 teaspoons) unsalted butter	Four 6-ounce soufflé molds
20 grams (¾ ounce) white breadcrumbs	Pastry brush
30 grams (1 ounce) all-purpose flour	*Russe*
120 milliliters (½ cup) milk	Whisk
60 grams (2 ounces) freshly grated cheese, such as cheddar or Gruyère	Copper or stainless steel bowl
2 large egg yolks	Electric mixer, optional
Coarse salt to taste	
Cayenne pepper to taste	
Freshly ground nutmeg to taste	
4 large egg whites	
Paprika for garnish	

Prepare your *mise en place*.

Preheat the oven to 204°C (400°F).

Using 10 grams (2 teaspoons) of the butter, lightly coat the interior of the *soufflé* molds. Sprinkle the breadcrumbs into the buttered molds and swirl to generously coat the interior, shaking out any excess. Place the molds in the refrigerator until needed.

Make a *beurre manié* (see page 62) with the flour and the remaining 30 grams (2 tablespoons) butter. Set aside.

Place the milk in a *russe* over medium heat and bring to a boil. Whisking constantly, beat in the *beurre*

manié and cook for 3 minutes or until very thick. Remove the mixture from the heat and beat in the grated cheese.

When the cheese has melted, using a whisk, beat in the egg yolks one at a time. Season with salt, cayenne pepper, and nutmeg to taste.

Place the egg whites in a copper or stainless steel bowl and, using a whisk or an electric mixer, beat them until firm peaks hold, heeding the guidelines for beaten egg whites and *soufflés* on page 443. Fold one quarter of the beaten egg whites into the batter to lighten it and then fold in the remaining three quarters all at once.

Remove the prepared molds from the refrigerator. Fill each about three quarters full of the cheese batter. Reduce the oven temperature to 191°C (375°F) and transfer the filled molds to the middle rack. Bake for 8 to 15 minutes, or until the *soufflés* have risen and

are just barely set in the center.

Remove from the oven, sprinkle the tops with paprika, and serve immediately.

Dean André Soltner | *Dean of Classic Studies, The French Culinary Institute*

Strawberry Tart with Bavarian Cream

Serves 8

This is a classic French fruit tart that I served for years at Lutèce. It can also be made with fresh kiwis. Whichever fruit you use, the tart will be a beautiful reminder of classic French desserts.

28 grams (1 ounce) all-purpose flour for dusting
1 recipe *Pâte Brisée* (see page 358)
4 large egg yolks, at room temperature
113 grams (4 ounces) sugar
237 milliliters (1 cup) whole milk
1 envelope unflavored gelatin
Juice and grated zest of 1 lemon
237 milliliters (1 cup) heavy cream, whipped
15 large ripe strawberries, washed, dried, and sliced lengthwise
57 grams (2 ounces) strawberry jelly

Prepare your *mise en place*.

Preheat the oven to 191°F (375°F).

Lightly flour a clean, flat work surface. Place the pastry in the center and, using a rolling pin, roll the dough out to a 3-millimeter (⅛-inch)–thick circle about 27.5 centimeters (11 inches) in diameter. Carefully transfer the pastry to a 22.8-centimeter (9- inch) pie or tart pan, firmly pressing the dough down into the pan and crimping the edges to make a neat fit. Cover the pastry with a piece of parchment paper cut to come slightly up the sides. Fill with pastry weights or dried beans and place in the oven. Bake for 20 minutes.

Remove from the oven and carefully remove the paper and weights. Return the pastry to the oven and bake for another 10 minutes or until golden.

Remove from the oven and place on a wire rack to cool.

Place the egg yolks in a mixing bowl. Add 57 grams (¼ cup) of the sugar and, using a whisk, beat until the yolks are thick and fluffy.

Combine the milk with the gelatin and remaining sugar in a small saucepan over medium heat. Cook, stirring constantly, for about 5 minutes or just until the mixture comes to a boil.

Remove from the heat and, whisking rapidly and constantly, slowly pour the milk into the beaten eggs. Return the mixture to the saucepan and place over medium heat. Cook, stirring constantly, for about 4 minutes or until the mixture returns to a boil.

Remove from the heat and strain through a *chinois* into a bowl. Immediately place in an ice bath and chill, stirring from time to time.

When the mixture begins to cool and thicken, stir in the lemon juice and zest.

When thoroughly chilled, fold in the whipped cream.

Spoon the Bavarian cream into the baked pastry shell, smoothing the top with a spatula. Refrigerate for 15 minutes.

Remove from the refrigerator and arrange the sliced strawberries in an attractive pattern on top.

Heat the jelly in a small saucepan over low heat. When melted, use a pastry brush to lightly coat the top of the tart.

Serve immediately.

Dean Jacques Torres

Dean of Pastry Arts, The French Culinary Institute; Chef/Owner, Jacques Torres Chocolate, Brooklyn and Manhattan, New York

Apricot *Charlotte*

Serves 8 to 10

Traditionally, a *charlotte* is a cake with ladyfingers on the outside and Bavarian cream on the inside. There are fancy *charlotte* molds available, but you can use any nice pan as long as it is wider than it is deep. For this recipe, I use a 1.9-liter (2-quart) mold that is 17.5 centimeters (7 inches) wide and 10 centimeters (4 inches) deep. I also created a shortcut by piping the ladyfingers into one long row (like a fence) instead of making individual cookies.

8 fresh apricots, washed, halved, and pitted
4 sheets gelatin, or 1⅓ envelopes unflavored gelatin
393 milliliters (¾ cups plus 1 tablespoon) heavy cream
99 grams (3½ ounces) sugar
1 vanilla bean
15 milliliters (1 tablespoon) Grand Marnier liqueur
1 recipe *Biscuit* Batter (recipe follows)
Flavored Simple Syrup (recipe follows)

Prepare your *mise en place*.

Place the apricots in the bowl of a food processor fitted with the metal blade and process to a smooth purée. Pour the purée into a *chinois* and strain into a small bowl. Measure out 363 grams (12½ ounces) of the purée and place it in a medium mixing bowl. Reserve any remaining purée for another use.

455

Either place the gelatin sheets in a large bowl with about 950 milliliters (1 quart) of cold water or sprinkle the granular gelatin into 59 milliliters (¼ cup) of cold water. Hydrate the sheets for 5 minutes and then remove them from the water and squeeze out all excess moisture or let the granular gelatin sit for about 1 minute or until it has "bloomed" and absorbed all the water.

Combine the hydrated gelatin with one quarter of the apricot purée in a medium, nonreactive saucepan over medium heat. Cook, stirring constantly, until the gelatin has dissolved completely. Whisking constantly, pour the gelatin mixture into the apricot purée.

Place the heavy cream and sugar in the bowl of an electric mixer.

Slice the vanilla bean in half lengthwise. Using a small, sharp knife, gently scrape the seeds from the bean into the cream, reserving the bean for flavoring sugar or another use.

Fit the mixer with the whip and begin beating the cream on medium-high until soft peaks form. Using a rubber spatula, gently fold the apricot purée and Grand Marnier into the whipped cream, taking care not to deflate the mixture.

Line the bottom of your mold with a piece of parchment paper cut to fit. Set aside.

Soak the flat side of the spiral shaped *biscuits* and the ladyfingers with the flavored simple syrup. (Remember to remove the parchment paper backing from the *biscuit* pieces.)

Line the sides of the mold with the soaked ladyfingers. You may have to trim them to fit so that they do not overlap.

Fill the mold about half full with the Bavarian cream. Cover the cream with one soaked biscuit disk. Cover the disk with the remaining Bavarian cream; it should come almost to the top with room for another biscuit disk. Top with the second disk, flat side up, and press down gently. Place in the freezer for about 1 ½ hours or in the refrigerator for 6 hours to set.

Center a serving plate facedown over the mold. In one quick motion, flip both over so the mold is on top. Gently lift the mold from the *charlotte*. Remove and discard the parchment paper lining. Place the decorative wheel of biscuit on the top and lightly press it into the *charlotte*. If possible, serve immediately, but the desert will hold at room temperature for about 2 hours. Cut into serving pieces using a hot serrated knife.

Biscuits (Ladyfingers)

6 large egg whites
149 grams (5¼ ounces) granulated sugar
8 large egg yolks, slightly beaten
147 grams (5¼ ounces) unleavened cake flour
Confectioners' sugar for dusting

Prepare your *mise en place*.

Draw three circles 15.24 centimeters (6 inches) in diameter onto a sheet of parchment paper placed on a baking sheet. Then, draw two 10-centimeter (4-inch) by 25-centimeter (10-inch) rectangles on another sheet of parchment paper placed on a second baking sheet. Turn the paper over to keep the ink from baking into the batter. Set aside.

Preheat the oven to 204°C (400°F).

Place the egg whites in the bowl of an electric mixer fitted with the whip. Beat on medium speed until foamy. Begin adding the granulated sugar, 14 grams (1 tablespoon) at a time, increase the speed to medium-high, and beat for about 7 minutes or until the whites form stiff but not dry peaks. Using a rubber spatula, gently fold in the egg yolks until partially incorporated. Fold in the flour as gently as possible to avoid deflating the batter.

Transfer the batter to a pastry bag fitted with a 19-millimeter (¾-inch) plain tip. Pipe two disks following the lines on the parchment by starting at the center of a circle and using a spiral motion to pipe the batter to the edge of the circle. In the third circle, pipe a pattern that resembles the spokes of a wheel. Pipe each spoke into a teardrop shape that is wider at the edge and ends in a point at the center.

Inside each rectangle on the parchment, pipe evenly shaped ladyfingers, each about 19 millimeters (¾ inch) wide and spaced about 19 millimeters (¾ inch) apart. When baked, they will join together, and the finished piece will resemble a picket fence. Dust the top of all the pieces with confectioners' sugar to give them a nice crust when baked.

Place in the oven and bake for 5 minutes. Remove from the oven and immediately transfer to wire racks to prevent the heat of the pan from continuing to bake the *biscuit*. Break the ladyfingers into individual cookies. Set aside until ready to use.

Flavored Simple Syrup

198 grams (7 ounces) sugar
213 milliliters (¾ cup plus 2 ½ tablespoons) water
15 milliliters (1 tablespoon) Grand Marnier liqueur

Prepare your *mise en place*.

Combine the sugar and water in a medium, heavy-bottomed saucepan over medium heat. Bring to a boil. The sugar should dissolve immediately.

Remove from the heat and pour into a heatproof bowl. Place in an ice bath and chill, stirring occasionally. When chilled, stir in the Grand Marnier. Cover and refrigerate until ready to use.

Previously published in *Dessert Circus: Extraordinary Desserts You Can Make at Home*, by Jacques Torres (Morrow Books, 1998).

Session 26

Introduction to Kitchen Management

Theory
Introduction to Food Control

In the professional kitchen, it is extremely important to understand the cost control of food items, since food and beverage sales are responsible for the largest expense in running a restaurant. The chef is often required to monitor all aspects of food from purchase to production. This session introduces the most common facts and formulas necessary for the informed chef.

The storeroom, or **economat**, is the area where all food is received, checked in, and stored until needed. The tasks of food purchasing, storing, and issuing can be delegated to anyone in the food service operation of the kitchen. However, because of the importance of the task, it should be someone with interest, experience, and skill. It is not uncommon that a chef himself, or a steward (aka a receiver) appointed to manage the task, supervises the provision and distribution of food in a restaurant operation.

Every restaurant has different needs. Specific and standard procedures and techniques to control quality and costs have to be set in each case, with employees in each environment trained to follow the necessary protocol. The quality of purchased food items must conform to the specific needs of the establishment; a cafeteria will not generally have the same needs as a four-star restaurant. A precise checklist of food items that describes the desired quality required by the individual restaurant must be created to meet its specifics. This list, called the Standard Purchases Specifications is used as a reference and guide for ordering, as well as for checking the quality of products entering the operation.

The quantities of food necessary to have in stock for the daily operation are determined by the chef or the steward (receiver) and are subject to change according to the day's needs, including but not limited to special events, menu changes, and seasonality.

Not all food has the same shelf life, and for purchasing purposes, food items are commonly divided into two categories, perishable and nonperishable. Perishables are fresh food such as meat, fish, vegetables, fruits, dairy products, and eggs. Nonperishable food, which generally has a longer shelf life, would include items such as dry goods.

Purchasing

Purchasing rules are generally set by the individual establishment. However, there is some general information that applies to all.

Dean's Tip

"To be a good chef is not enough. To succeed in business, one must know how to buy and how to economize."

Dean Jacques Pépin

458

"Checking the garbage twice a day will give you an idea of how much control the chef has in the kitchen and will potentially save you a lot of money."

"A chef who is wasteful is not a good chef, since the bottom line in the restaurant business is $$$$."

Dean Alain Sailhac

"Being a good chef is a lot more than knowing how to cook. Managing your food costs is equally important."

Chef Candy Argondizza

Perishable Foods

It is not uncommon for a restaurant to use at least three suppliers for each type of perishable food (fish, meat, fresh produce, dairy) in order to assess the best current prices. The steward receives daily market quotations (descriptions of weight, price, quality, etc.) from these suppliers, often via fax or e-mail. This data is entered into a market quotation list or directly on an ordering form. The appropriate vendors are selected depending upon price, quality, and reliability.

Through daily inventories, the steward can determine the food on hand for kitchen use and can order accordingly. The purchasing system should be designed to ensure:

- an adequate supply of ingredients consistent with the required amounts of food for production (the steward must be very careful not to overstock perishable food)

- carefully selected products that conform to the chef's quality specifications

- optimum price

To calculate the amount of nonperishable food needed for a particular time period, the following formula is standard:

Formula		Example
Amount required for upcoming period	**30**	No. 10 cans plum tomatoes
Minus amount presently on hand	**-8**	No. 10 cans plum tomatoes
Plus amount wanted on hand at the end of the period to last until next delivery	**+10**	No. 10 cans plum tomatoes
Amount to Order	**32**	No. 10 cans plum tomatoes

Nonperishable Foods

Nonperishable food orders are usually based on catalogues with preset price lists and weekly or monthly specials, rather than on daily market quotations. This is because nonperishable food tends to have a long shelf life, resulting in less frequent price fluctuations. It can, therefore, be ordered in bulk, and less frequently. Nonperishable food may be ordered biweekly, weekly, or even monthly.

Receiving

A standard procedure for receiving foodstuffs should always be used to verify quality, quantity, and purchase price. The quality delivered should conform to the restaurant's standard purchase specifications. The quality delivered and the price should match those listed on the invoice or bill that accompanies the delivery, the steward's marketing quotation list, and the steward's ordering form.

Storing

Once received, all deliveries should immediately be moved to their respective storage areas to avoid deterioration, contamination, or product loss.

Each item should always be stored in the same designated location. It is the responsibility of the steward and the staff to store new deliveries of an item behind the quantities already on hand to ensure that older items are used first. This is known as FIFO (see page 10). Items should be dated when placed in storage. In some cases a tagging system is set in place where, in addition to the date, the amount and the price are entered on a tag that is attached to or posted next to a particular item. Food should never be stored in such a manner that permits or encourages pilferage. Security should be maintained at all times.

Recommended Temperatures for Cold and Dry Storage

Fresh meats, produce, and dairy products	1°C–2°C (34°F–36°F)
Fresh fish	-1°C–1°C (30°F–34°F)
Frozen food	-12°C–18°C (-10°F–0°F)
Dry storage	18°C–21°C (65°F–70°F)

Issuing Foodstuffs and Supplies

Requisitions and Transfers: A requisition sheet is a form filled in by a member of the kitchen staff that lists the food items along with the quantities required for the day's production. The storeroom staff fulfills the requisition and transfers the requested items from the storeroom to the kitchen.

If the items are not available directly from the storeroom (for example, liquor may be required from the bar), it may be necessary to complete a transfer form. In large restaurant operations, a transfer form may be required to transfer items from one kitchen unit to another.

All paperwork, invoices, bills, requisition sheets, transfers, and so forth have to be accounted for by personnel in any or all divisions, since all records are eventually sent to the accounting department. This is an essential part of good restaurant organization and is crucial to the success of any operation.

Inventory

In all food operations, taking physical inventory is a universally accepted practice. Typically, on the last day of a calendar month, after closing time, the number of units in stock are counted and recorded, along with their value. In addition, daily inventory is very often taken in both the kitchen and storeroom to maintain even tighter inventory control.

Determining Monthly Food Costs

Food cost is the defined expense to an establishment when food is consumed, for any reason, in the course of doing business. Food cost includes the cost of food sold, given away, stolen, or wasted. A basic formula to determine this is:

Formula: Cost of Food Consumed	Example
Opening inventory	$ 3,000.00
Plus purchases for the month	+ $ 8,000.00
Equals total available	= $11,000.00
Minus closing inventory	– $ 2,000.00
Equals cost of food consumed	= $ 9,000.00

Once the actual cost of food consumed and the actual restaurant sales are known, the food cost percent can be determined.

Formula: Food Cost Percent	Example
Cost	$ 9,000.00
Divided by 100 Equals Cost Percent	÷ 100 = 33.3%
Sales	$27,000.00

Stating that the food cost is 33.3% is another way of saying that the food cost is 33.3 cents per dollar of sales. The objective of food cost control is to compare the actual food cost percentage for a certain period of time with the potential food cost. Potential is what the management believes is required to run a profitable operation. It is also of great importance to monitor the eventual fluctuations in food cost percentage and to troubleshoot the possible causes (waste, spoilage, pilferage, etc.).

Food Production Control and Recipe Costing

Control procedures also have to be used to track every food item used in the kitchen for menu production.

Recipes

A standard recipe is a necessary first step for pricing out an item or dish and for effectively controlling the eventual cost to prepare. The standard recipe is a clear and precise list of ingredients and methods required to prepare the dish. Standard recipes are necessary to establish quality, consistency of taste and texture, as well as the final presentation. In some kitchens, recipes are printed on laminated cards and include photographs of the finished dish to maintain this integrity.

Standard Portion Size (Weight, Volume, Count)

The amount of a given portion to be served to each customer must be consistent no matter who executes the dish. This is indispensable for the clear costing of a specific recipe.

Costing Problems

Once a recipe is written and the final portion size determined, it is necessary to determine the purchase price of all the ingredients. For example: One 25-pound bag of flour costs $5.00. That total quantity is then broken down to the most commonly used unit of measurement (pound, ounce, etc.). Assuming that the commonly used unit for flour is 1 pound, its cost would be found using the first following formula below.

If, in a given recipe using flour, two common units (2 pounds) are used, the second following formula below is used.

Formula: Cost Per Unit	**Example**
Purchase cost	$ 5.00
Divided by number of common units	÷ 25
Equals cost per unit	= 20 cents

Formula: Cost of Recipe Ingredient	**Example**
Number of common units times the cost per common unit	2 x 20 cents
Equals the ingredient cost	= 40 cents

These formulas are used for every single ingredient in a recipe. The resulting numbers are then added to establish the total cost of the finished recipe. In general, in the professional kitchen, recipes are costed out for ten portions, but it is possible to find the cost for any number of portions ranging from two on.

Basic ingredients like stocks and sauces are generally costed out only once to establish their unit cost and whenever necessary this basic predetermined cost is computed into the recipe costing procedure. For seasonings such as salt and pepper, a predetermined common cost is entered. For example, 15 cents per ten portions. Since prices do change, this costing has to be updated from time to time.

Formula: Cost Per Portion	**Example**
Total recipe cost	$ 34.00
Divided by number of portions	÷ 10
Equals cost per portion	= $3.40

When costing or ordering, it is important to understand that

Yield = usable portion after cleaning and preparation

For example, if whole fish, unbutchered meats, or fresh vegetables or fruits are used in a recipe, deboning, trimming, and peeling are necessary and affect the cost per unit of those ingredients. Weight loss during cooking also affects the unit cost. For instance, if a fish is purchased whole and needs to be filleted, the price per pound will be higher than the original purchase cost. Or, if carrots are purchased with tops on, once they are peeled and trimmed, the unit cost must take this into consideration and will, of course, be higher than the unit purchase price. Or, if a recipe includes cold, sliced roast beef, weight loss during roasting will need to be accounted for. When ordering food, it is imperative to adjust the actual amount of a specific ingredient needed in a recipe to make up for the weight loss by peeling, trimming, and cooking.

A yield chart or yield test can be done to determine a final yield and a true cost per unit. In this test, the trimmings and peelings are weighed. A cooking test may also be used, in which the product is cooked to determine weight loss and then the true cost per unit is formulated.

Formula: Usable Quantity	**Example**
Purchase quantity	5 pounds carrots with tops
Minus waste	−1 pound trimmings and peelings
Equals usable quantity	=4 pounds usable

Yield percentage is the relation of the usable quantity to the purchase quantity and is easily integrated into food ordering formulas. The formula is:

Formula: Yield Percentage	**Example**
Usable quantity	4 pounds
Divided by purchase quantity	÷ 5 pounds
Times 100	x 100
Equals yield percent	= 80%

For the costing of recipes, it is important to understand the adjustment necessary to the purchase cost by using yield percentage to determine the usable portion cost.

Formula: Usable Portion Cost	**Example**
(Purchase cost) x 100	$ 6.00 x 100
Divided by yield %	÷ 80
Equals usable portion cost	= $ 7.50
Yield percentage	80%

Determining Menu Item Selling Price

Once menu item costs have been calculated, the selling prices can be quickly determined by using a cost multiplication factor (i.e., if a 33 percent food cost is desired, multiply the food cost by 3.3). To obtain the factor, use ths formula:

Formula: Multiplication Factor	**Example**
100 divided by	100
Food cost percentage	3.3
Equals multiplication factor	= 30

The same multiplication factor does not apply to all menu items. There is, in some cases, a wide price gap between the costs of different recipes. The objective is to strike a balance in menu pricing by using a lower multiplication factor for some dishes and a higher one for others. For example, a soufflé may have a low food cost and the multiplication factor (markup) can be made higher to be more in line with the more costly items on the menu.

Another example might be as follows: The food cost for a cheese soufflé might be $1.00. To keep a 33 percent food cost, the factor would be 3.3. Therefore, the selling price would be 3 x $1.00 or $3.30. For this low cost, the multiplication factor can be changed to 6 and the selling price will be made higher, which would keep it in line with other menu items. On the other hand, for a more expensive ingredient such as lamb chops, the factor can be lowered. Doing this, a 33 percent food cost average can still be achieved.

Appendix

Measurements

Throughout this book we have used both Fahrenheit and Celsius, abbreviated to F and C, to measure temperature. The freezing point of Fahrenheit is 32°, 0° for Celsius; the boiling point of water is 212°F and 100°C.

Meter is the unit used to measure length and is divided into increments of centimeters and millimeters.
10 millimeters = 1 centimeter
100 centimeters = 1 meter

Liter is the unit used to measure volume. A liter is divided into deciliters, centiliters, and milliliters.
10 milliliters = 1 centiliter
100 milliliters = 1 deciliter
1000 milliliters = 1 liter

Kilogram is the unit used to measure weight. It is divided into grams.
1 kilogram = 1000 grams

The following approximate equivalents will express the size of various metric units to their American units:
1 kilogram is slightly over 2 pounds
1 liter is just over 1 quart
1 meter is just over 3 feet

Approximate metric measurements used in the recipes are as follows:

Length

1 inch = 25.4 millimeters = 2.54 centimeters
1 centimeter = ⅓ inch

Volume

2 tablespoons = 1 ounce = 30 milliliters
8 ounces (1 cup) = 237 milliliters
1 quart = 950 milliliters

Weight

1 ounce = 28.37 grams
1 pound = 454 grams
1 gram = 0.035 ounce
1 kilogram = 2.2 pounds

Precise Metric Conversions

To convert:

Length

inches to millimeters multiply by	25.4
inches to centimeters multiply by	2.54
centimeters to inches divide by	2.54

Volume

quarts to liters multiply by	0.946
pints to liters multiply by	0.473
milliliters to ounces divide by	29.57
liters to quarts divide by	0.946
liters to cups divide by	0.236

Weight

ounces to grams multiply by	28.35
grams to ounces divide by	28.35
pounds to kilograms multiply by	0.454
kilograms to pounds divide by	0.454

Glossary

A

à blanc: A stage of cooking where the food is cooked or partially cooked, with no coloration.

à la: "In the style of."

à l'anglaise: "In the English style;" vegetables cooked in salted water and then reheated before serving; also vegetables cooked in salted water served with chopped parsley, knobs of butter, melted butter, or herb sauce; also meat or poultry poached, boiled, or cooked in a white stock; also breaded fish cooked in oil.

à l'étuvé: Vegetables slowly cooked in a covered pan with their own juices, a touch of fat (butter or olive oil), salt, and just enough water to allow them to exude their own moisture or cook them through.

à la coque: Served in a shell.

à la croque au sel: "With but a grain of salt;" also a snack sprinkled with salt just before eating.

à la française: "In the French style;" fish breaded on one side of the fillet and then broiled.

à la gelée: "In the style of an aspic;" a product made from various pieces of meat and clarification elements and then chilled.

à la grecque: "In the Greek style;" vegetables cooked in olive oil, onions, and dry white wine and flavored with peppercorns, lemon, salt, coriander seed, and *bouquet garni.*

à la meuniére: "In the style of the miller's wife;" fish seasoned, lightly floured, and fried in clarified butter. A mixture of brown butter, lemon juice, and chopped parsley is spooned over the hot fish just before serving.

à maison: "In the style of the house;" according to the demands of a particular chef or restaurateur.

à point: Medium (for meat).

abats: Organs. Further divided into abats blancs, or white organs (e.g., bone marrow, brains, feet) and *abats rouges,* or red organs (e.g., kidneys, liver, tongue).

aciduler: To make something slightly acidic by adding a little lemon juice, vinegar, or the juice of unripe fruit.

aiguillettes: Thin strips cut lengthwise from any poultry or game bird breast.

aïoli: A cold emulsified sauce made with egg yolk, garlic, and oil; usually served with vegetables and fish.

albumen: The white of an egg.

albumin: Any of several types of protein found in animal substances such as egg whites, meat, and milk; can also be found in some plant matter.

al dente: "To the tooth" (Italian); pasta that is slightly resistant to the bite.

allumettes: A 7-centimeter-x-5-millimeter (2 ¾-x-3/16 inch) cut of potato also called "matchsticks;" also sweet or savory pastry strips.

amandine: With almonds (e.g., cake, crêpes, or sauces).

americaine/armoricaine: A shellfish sauce prepared with crabs and/or lobsters.

andalouse: A garnish of peppers, tomatoes, rice, fried eggplant slices, and, sometimes, chipolata sausages or chorizo; also a sauce.

apparaît: A mixture (e.g., *pâte à bombe*).

appareil à bombe (pâte à bombe): A *bombe* mixture, most commonly made by adding sugar cooked to the soft-ball stage to egg yolks.

Appellation d'Origine Contrôlée (AOC): A label of inspected origin given to guarantee the provenance of an agricultural product.

aspic: Jellied stock.

assiette de crudités: A plate of separately prepared raw, simple salads or vegetables.

aux fines herbes: With a mixture of chopped tender, aromatic herbs such as chervil, chives, parsley, and tarragon.

B

bain-marie: A water bath; made by placing cups or molds filled with the mixture to be cooked in a large pan, then boiling water is poured into the pan halfway up the sides of the molds; used for baking and holding.

ballottines: Meat (usually poultry) that is boned, stuffed, and rolled, then poached and served hot.

bande de tarte aux fruits: A rectangular pastry covered with fruit

banquet chef: The chef responsible for banquets and parties in a large professional establishment.

barquette: A small, boat-shaped pastry shell.

basquaise: "In the Basque style;" with tomatoes, red, peppers, and ham.

baveuse: A method of cooking an omelet so that it remains moist.

béarnaise: A derivative of *sauce hollandaise* which includes a reduction of white wine vinegar, shallots, tarragon, chervil, and a *mignonette* of peppercorns.

béchamel: A white sauce made with butter, flour, milk, and/or onion and flavored with bay leaf, pepper, and nutmeg.

beignet: A fritter.

beurrage: A square block of cold butter used in making puff pastry.

beurre fondue: Melted butter.

beurre manié: "Kneaded butter;" a mixture of soft butter and uncooked flour used to thicken stews and sauces.

beurre nantais: White butter sauce softened with heavy cream.

beurre noisette: "Brown butter;" butter that has been cooked to a light brown color and nutty flavor.

beurre rouge: Cooked butter made with various crustacean shells; used to finish *sauce poisson*; also a sauce made with a red wine reduction.

beurre composée: "Compound butter;" unsalted butter incorporating one or more aromatic ingredients.

bien cuit: Well-done (for meat).

bigorneau: A univalve mollusk (winkle); a one shelled inhabitant of either fresh- or saltwater or land.

bisque: A well-seasoned pureed shellfish soup bound with rice. The shells are used to make the initial broth and then the base is fortified with white wine, cognac, and heavy cream.

blanchir: To quickly bring an item to a boil and then drain; also to whisk together egg yolks and sugar until the mixture turns a pale yellow color and increases in volume.

blanquette: A creamy stew.

bombe: A dessert mixture made from egg yolks and simple syrup.

bombe glacé: Used loosely, a dessert and a frozen dessert base mixture. More specifically, a frozen dessert traditionally made by lining a chilled, half-sphere mold with a firm mixture such as ice cream or *sorbet* (sherbet), sometimes in multiple layers.

bouillie: A stirred pudding made with a boiled mixture of sugar, flour, milk, and egg yolks, or simply flour and water.

bouillon: A plain, unclarified broth obtained by boiling protein and/or vegetables.

bouquet: The aroma produced by the evaporation of the volatile products evident in wine; also aroma in general.

bouquet garni: A sachet of herbs such as thyme, bay leaf, and parsley used to flavor cooking liquids.

bouquetière: Garnished with little bundles of vegetables; also, a 3-centimeter (1 ¼-inch)–square or turned cut of vegetable.

braisè: A stewlike dish with large pieces of meat (such as pot roasts) initially cooked in a small amount of liquid.

braisièr: A brown stock made from veal and beef bones, carrots, onions, and garlic.

bretonne: "In the Brittany style;" with white beans or a white wine sauce made of carrots, leeks, and celery.

bridage: A method of tying a whole bird or large piece of meat with a needle into a compact bundle to facilitate ease of handling while cooking, as well as to hold the legs, wings, and any stuffing in place for neat presentation.

brigade: A roll enriched with butter and eggs; also the kitchen crew.

brine: A liquid solution of water and salt, and occasionally a sweetener or spice, used to preserve or tenderize food.

brioche: A heavily buttered layered dough and one of the oldest French breads, dating back to the Middle Ages; also the first bread to which sugar was added.

brochette: An item skewered for grilling.

brouillés: Scrambled (usually eggs).

brunois: A 1-to-2-millimeter (⅟₃₂-to-⅟₁₆ inch)–square cut of vegetable.

C

cassé: Broken, broken down, or chopped.

Centre de Formation Technologique des Mètiers de l'Alimentation: The official Paris institution for training in the culinary arts.

chalazae: Thick, twisted, ropelike strands of egg white attached to two sides of the yolk that serve to hold in place at the center of the albumen.

Chantilly: Sweetened whipped cream (*crème Chantilly*); also a cold emulsified sauce made with two parts mayonnaise and one part whipped cream (*sauce de chantilly*).

charcuterie: Cured or salted meats, *pâtés*, and other delicatessen-style products.

charlotte: A Bavarian cream served in a *génoise*.

château: An 8-x-4-centimeter (3 ⅛-x-1½-inch) turned cut of potato; also a 7.5-centimeter (2 ¾-inch)–long turned cut of vegetable.

chaud-froid: "Hot-cold;" a cooked dish served cold, usually covered with a cooked cream sauce and then with aspic.

chausson: A turnover formed by filling thin circles of puff pastry with a stewed fruit or savory filling and folding the pastry over the filling in a half-moon shape.

chef de cuisine: An active chef who oversees and supervises the kitchen during preparation and service.

chef de partie: The chef in charge of a specific station, such as *poissioner* or *saucier;* usually accompanied by one or more assistants.

chef pâtissier: The pastry chef, responsible for the preparation and plating of all desserts and pastries.

cheminées: Venting holes cut into pastry to allow steam to escape during cooking.

cheveux: A 7-centimeter-x-.5-millimeter (2 ¾-x-¹⁄₃₂-inch) cut of potato also called "hairs."

chiffonade: A ribbon cut of herbs or greens.

choisy: Any of various preparations or garnishes containing lettuce.

ciseler: To finely dice onions or shallots in a manner that keeps the juices inside the vegetables.

cocotte: A 5-centimeter (2-inch)–long turned cut of vegetable; also a covered casserole.

concasser: To coarsely chop.

confit: A preserve made by cooking meat (usually duck or goose) in its own fat; also fruit in sugar syrup.

conservation: Preservation (in *terrines, pâtès*, etc.) by covering the filling with a layer of gelatin or rendered fat.

consommé: A clarified meat, game, poultry, or fish stock from which all impurities have been removed, leaving an almost-clear broth.

cornichons: Small, sour gherkin pickles.

coupe: A dessert of ice creams, *sorbets*, and fresh fruit served in a glass of the same name. It can also include chocolate sauce, chopped toasted nuts, and *crème anglaise*—in America, a *coupe* might be called a sundae. Also a bowl-shaped container.

court bouillon: "Short broth;" an aromatic liquid used to cook fish for a short time and impart a light flavor. It can be prepared *à la nage, au bleu, au vin blanc, au vin rouge, or au vinaigre*.

crème: For dessert, a custard; also a cream soup finished with heavy cream.

crème anglaise: A stirred custard used as a sauce or base for ice cream.

crème au beurre: Buttercream.

crème Bavarois: Bavarian cream; a classic molded dessert based on egg custard or fruit purée and served cold.

crème béchamel: *Béchamel* sauce with heavy cream and lemon juice.

crème brûlée: A baked custard with a crisped caramel sugar crust or topping.

crème caramel: A baked vanilla custard that, when inverted, has a loose caramel sauce.

crème chantilly: Sweetened whipped cream.

crème chibouste: A pastry cream lightened with Italian *meringue* and stabilized with gelatin.

crème d'amandes: A mixture of sugar, butter, ground almonds, and eggs, sometimes flavored with rum.

crème fraîche: A very heavy cream containing 46–48 percent butterfat.

crème glacée: An eggless ice cream based on a mixture of milk, cream, sugar, and flavoring.

crème légère: A pastry cream lightened with whipped cream.

crème mousseline: A type of buttercream made by beating pastry cream into a large quantity of unsalted butter.

crème pâtissière: Pastry cream.

crêpe: A thin, unleavened pancake.

croquembouche: Cream puffs filled with cream, dipped in caramel, and arranged in a conical tower shape.

croutons: Small pieces of bread that are toasted, lightly browned in butter, fried in oil, or dried in the oven.

cuisson: Cooking, sometimes with wine.

cuisson à blanc: A stage of cooking when the food is partially or fully cooked but not colored; also blind-baking a pastry case.

D

dans un blanc: Cooking easily discolored food (such as freshly cut artichokes) in a mixture of water, flour, lemon, and salt in order to keep them white.

darne: A crosswise slice of a whole roundfish.

déglacer: To deglaze; adding wine, stock, or water to cooking juices and sediment in a pan left after roasting or sautéing to make a sauce or gravy.

dégorger: To soak meat, poultry, fish, or bones in cold water to eliminate impurities and blood; also the process of sprinkling salt on certain vegetables to extract excess water; also the preparing of snails.

dégraisser: To remove excess fat from an ingredient, dish, or cooking vessel.

demi-feuilletage: Puff pastry dough made with less turns than classic puff pastry.

demi-glace: A veal stock that has been reduced by approximately one-half or until very thick, shiny, and full-flavored.

dents de loup: "Wolf's teeth;" cutting a lemon in half in a zigzag manner as a garnish for fish dishes; also triangular croutons arranged around the edge of a dish, pointing outwards, as a garnish.

dessécher: To dry a preparation (such as a dough or starchy vegetable) by slow cooking on the stovetop or in the oven.

dèsossage: Boning.

détrempe: A simple dough composed of flour, salt, water, and butter; a component of puff pastry.

diable: Food that is coated with mustard, dipped in egg, coated in bread crumbs, and then grilled; also an English sauce served with deviled (spicy) foods (*à la diable*).

dry cure: A preservation technique in which all surfaces of the food are rubbed with salt and then the food is left to cure for a designated period of time; also called a salt.

dugléré: A garnish of shallots, onions, chopped fresh tomatoes, and parsley on which fish is cooked and served.

duxelles: Finely chopped shallots or onions and mushrooms cooked in butter until soft (and sometimes dry) and seasoned with lemon juice.

E

eau de vie: Brandy; also other clear spirits distilled from fruits or grains.

éclair: Small, elongated piece of *choux* pastry filled with cream and coated with fondant or icing.

écosser: To shell or hull.

écumer: To skim; also to remove coagulated blood, fat, and other impurities from a stock by skimming.

effiler: To pull off stringy side filaments, as with string beans.

émincer: To slice thinly.

émonder: To peel, prune, or trim.

en cocotte: In a casserole dish.

en crapaudine: A method of preparing poultry in which the bird is split lengthwise and the breast pulled forward. It is then opened, flattened, and secured with a skewer.

en croute: Food that has been wrapped in pastry and then baked.

engrainer: To stir finished rice with a fork in order to separate the grains.

en papillote: Food that has been cooked in a parchment paper bag.

en pommade: Softened butter mixed to a thick, creamy consistency.

entremetier: The chef responsible for vegetable dishes.

épluchage: The process of cleaning, peeling, or unwrapping.

éplucher: To peel a vegetable or fruit by removing the skin or outer layer.

Esaü: A creamy vegetable soup bound by lentils.

escalope: A scallop; also a thin slice of white meat.

executive chef: A chef whose responsibilities include administrating all kitchen-related operations such as menu planning, costing, and scheduling; may also be responsible for running the kitchen.

F

façonnage: The shaping and molding of a filling and its placement in a lined mold for cooking; also designing.

faisander: To tenderize wild game by hanging it in its feathers or skin in a controlled environment for 4 to 5 days.

feuilleté: A piece of baked puff pastry that is split and filled or garnished with cheese, ham, seafood, etc.

financier: A small, almond sponge cake.

fines: Brandies distilled from wine (as opposed from *marc*, which is distilled from the grapes after pressing).

fines herbes: A combination of parsley, chervil, tarragon, and chives.

flageolet: A small, pale green or white French kidney bean.

flamber: To pour spirits over a food and ignite it; also to singe feathers.

flat omelette: An omelet cooked until fairly firm and lightly browned.

foie gras: The fattened liver of a duck or goose.

fond blanc: White stock made from bones, aromatic vegetables, *bouquet garni*, and water.

fond brun: Brown stock made from browned bones, aromatic vegetables, *bouquet garni*, and tomatoes.

fond de braisage: A bed of vegetables on which a food is braised; also the liquid obtained from a *braisage*.

fond de gibier: Game stock made from bones and game such as venison, partridge, pheasant, or hare.

fond de veau: Veal stock.

fond de volaille: Poultry stock.

fondant: Cooked, worked sugar that is flavored and used for icing; also the bitter chocolate high in cocoa butter used for making shiny chocolate; also puréed meat, fish, or vegetables in croquettes; also 8-to-9-centimeter (3 ⅛-3 ½-inch) turned cut of potato.

fonds de cuisine: The stocks of the kitchen; the basic stocks professional chefs use in food preparation.

fondue: A Swiss specialty consisting of one or more cheeses melted in a special pottery dish with white wine and flavoring (can also be melted chocolate or hot oil); also an ingredient, usually an egg, that is slowly cooked down to a soft, concentrated consistency and flavor; also finely chopped vegetables reduced to a pulp by slow cooking.

fraisage: The process of crushing small clumps of dough and fat with the heel of the palm to incorporate thoroughly.

fraiser: To mill.

frangipane: An almond custard filling.

frémir: To simmer.

French *meringue*: The simplest type of *meringue*, made by beating egg whites with sugar.

French-style (or custard-based) ice cream: Ice cream based on an egg custard, usually with a high ratio of cream to milk and eggs.

frites: A 7-centimeter-x-8-millimeter (2 ¾-x-⁵⁄₁₆-inch) cut of potato also called "regular fries."

fritos: A savory fritter similar to a *beignet*.

fromage glaces: The original term for iced cream, sugar, and flavorings with added egg for smoothness and richness.

fumet: Stock made from white fish bones, aromatic vegetables, and sometimes *bouquet garni*.

G

galantine: Poultry that is boned, stuffed, rolled, and then poached; similar to a *ballottine* except that it is served cold.

ganache: A rich mixture made with heavy cream and chocolate.

garde manger: The chef in charge of cold items, hors d'oeuvres, desserts (on occasion), and all decorative work.

garniture: A single item, or combination of items, accompanying a dish; a garnish.

gasconne: "In the Gascon manner"; a garnish that includes *foie gras*.

gastrique: A reduced mixture of acid and a sweetener used in the preparation of hot sauces accompanying dishes made with fruit or requiring a sweet/sour flavor (such as duck).

gaufrette: A small, crisp, light biscuit made from a dough similar to that for waffles but less runny; also a 2-millimeter (¹⁄₁₆-inch), double-waffle cut of potato.

gelato: A dense, Italian-style ice cream that contains less air than American-style ice cream.

gelée: Aspic; a product made from various pieces of meat and clarification elements and chilled.

génoise: A foam cake made with whole eggs.

glace: Ice cream based on egg custard.

glaçage: Intense browning.

glacéed: Melted sugar poured on a food item and then allowed to cool.

glacer: To glaze by cooking food with sugar, butter, and water until a glaze has formed; iced, glazed, or crystallized.

glacer à blond: To glaze until the sugar has begun to lightly caramelize.

glacer à brun: To glaze until the sugar has caramelized to a rich, brown color.

glucose: A liquid sweetener used in desserts that does not readily crystallize.

gougère: A savory *choux* pastry, usually in round or ring shapes, flavored with cheese.

gousse d'ail: A cut of potato the size of a clove of garlic; also a clove of garlic.

grand-mere garniture: A garnish made from potatoes, bacon, and mushrooms.

granité: An ice closely resembling *sorbet*, with a low sugar content and a characteristic grainy texture (Italian *granita*).

gratinéed or *grantiner*: Any item or dish browned on the surface in an oven or salamander.

grenobloise garniture: A garnish of brown butter with capers, finely diced lemon pulp, and croutons.

H

hacher: To mince or finely chop.

hollandaise: A hot emulsified sauce based on egg yolks, lemon juice, and butter.

hors d'oeuvre: A small, savory appetizer served as a snack, usually with cocktails or aperitifs, before a meal.

huile d'olive vierge extra nonfiltrée: Extra-virgin olive oil that has not been filtered and is partially cloudy.

huile extra vierge: Extra-virgin, cold-pressed olive oil, the result of the first pressing of olives with 1% acidity.

I

ice milk: A milk-based frozen dessert with a low percentage of butterfat.

infused oil: A product made by infusing fine quality oil with herbs, spices, or aromatics such as garlic or shallots, ginger, fruit, or fruit peels.

Italian *meringue*: A *meringue* made with cooked sugar syrup that is poured into firmly whipped egg whites and then beaten into stiff peaks.

J

jardinière: A garnish of 5 ¾-centimeter-x-6-millimeter (2 ¼-x-¼-inch) cut root vegetables.

julienne: Meat or vegetables that have been cut into slivers.

jus or *jus de rôti*: The gravy of a roast, made by diluting pan juices with water, clear stock, or any other suitable liquid and boiling it until all the flavor from the pan has been incorporated into the liquid.

L

lardon: A 1.3 centimeter (½ inch)–square cut of salt pork or bacon.

laver: To wash.

liaison: An item that allows ingredients that wouldn't normally mix together to do so; also a mixture of heavy cream and egg yolks.

liard: A 4-centimeter-x-2-millimeter (1 ½-x-¹⁄₁₆-inch) round cut of potato, evenly shaped with a biscuit cutter.

liquid cure: A method of preserving food by the submersion of the food in brine; also called a brine.

lustrer: To brush melted butter on food to enrich it and create a shine.

M

macédoine: A 5 millimeter (³⁄₁₆ inch)–square cut of vegetable based on the *jardinière* cut; also a mixture of diced fruit or vegetables.

mâche: Delicate, tender greens; also known as lamb's lettuce.

maître d'hotel: The head waiter; also a compound butter made with lemon juice and parsley used for grilled meat or fish.

manchonner: A method of preparing an appendage cut of meat for presentation; also to make an incision through the skin and tendons near the knuckle, remove the cartilage, and scrape back the skin.

marinade: A seasoned liquid, cooked or uncooked, in which meat, offal, game, fish, or vegetables are immersed in for varying lengths of time.

marmite: A dish cooked in a small casserole or pot; also the name of the dish itself; also beef stock. A **marmite basse** is a short *marmite*; a **marmite haute**, a tall one.

matignon: Assorted vegetables and ham stewed in butter.

mayonnaise: A cold emulsified sauce consisting of egg yolks and oil blended together and flavored with vinegar, salt, pepper, and mustard.

meringue: A stiffly beaten mixture of egg whites and sugar.

mesclun: A mixture of the young shoots and leaves of wild plants used to make a salad; now the term is commonly used to describe the baby or small leaves of mixed lettuces.

mignonettes: Small cubes of meat (usually beef); also coarsely ground black or white pepper; also a 7-centimeter-x-6-millimeter (2 ¾-x-¼ inch) cut of potato also called "thin fries."

mirepoix: Roughly diced vegetables (usually carrots, celery, and onions) used as aromatics for making stocks, soups, and braises.

miroir: A dish that has a smooth glaze.

mise en place: "Everything put in its place;" having together all ingredients required to prepare and execute a dish.

mixte à blanc: A braise or stew in which the meat is sautéed without allowing any coloring and a white stock is used to complete the cooking.

mixte a brun: A braise or stew in which the meat is sautéed until well colored and a brown stock is used to complete the cooking.

monter au beurre: To add butter to a hot preparation by gradually swirling it in a bit at a time.

mouiller: To moisten; also to add liquid to various food preparations (as water to bones to produce a stock).

mousse: Any dish, sweet or savory, that is light and airy in texture with a flavored base that has been pureed and folded into beaten egg whites or whipped cream.

mousseline: Ingredients that have been lightened with whipped cream, egg whites (*sauce mousseline*), or butter (*brioche mousseline*).

N

Napoleon: A rectangular pastry made with thin layers of crisp puff pastry layered with pastry cream.

nappant: The consistency at which a sauce is thick enough to coat the back of a spoon.

napper: To cover a food item with sauce.

nature: Naturally or simply; also a 6-x-3-centimeter (2 ⅜-x-³⁄₁₆-inch) turned cut of potato.

navarin: A brown stew based on lamb or mutton.

noisette: A hazelnut; also a dessert flavored with hazelnut; also a center cut of lamb chop; also a small, round cut of meat or potato browned in butter.; also a hazelnut-shaped cut of potato.

normande: A vegetable soup similar to *potage cultivateur*, finished with unsalted butter and heavy cream with a garnish of *flageolets*; also a garnish for fillet of sole.

O

oignon brûlée: A burnt onion half, used to add color and flavor to stocks and sauces.

oignon cloûté: An onion with a bay leaf placed inside a cut in the vegetable and skewered with a clove; also a clove.

olive: An olive; also an olive-shaped cut of potato.

omelette norvégienne: Baked Alaska; a sponge cake covered with ice cream and a layer of sweetened, stiffly beaten egg whites and then quickly browned in the oven.

Orléans: A town in the Loire Valley; also an ancient method for making vinegar.

P

paillard: A thin slice of meat (usually pounded lightly for even thickness) and sometimes breaded.

pailles: A 7 centimeter-x-2-millimeter (2¾-x-⅟₁₆-inch) cut of potato also called "straws."

palmier: A small, leaf-shaped pastry made from sugared, double-rolled puff pastry dough.

panade: A basic component of stuffings made with bread, flour, rice, or potatoes.

paner à l'anglaise: A three-step method for breading; the food is first dipped in flour, then egg, and finally in breadcrumbs.

parer: To trim; also to trim *tronçoneed* vegetables to obtain a surface to allow for even cutting.

parfait: A *bombe* mixture prepared with cooked sugar, sugar syrup, or *crème anglaise*.

parisienne: "In the Parisian style;" a vegetable garnish, including potato balls, that has been fried and tossed in a meat sauce; also a small, ball-shaped cut of potato.

Parmentier: A dish with potatoes; also a 1.2-millimeter (½-inch)–square cut of potato.

parties: The stations in a professional kitchen (e.g., *poissonnier*).

passer: To strain or pass a stock or purée through a *chinois* to remove any solids which are then discarded.

pâte: A pastry, dough, or batter.

pâté: Minced meat, game, or fish that is spiced, molded, wrapped in dough, baked, and served either hot or cold.

pâte à bombe (appareil à bombe): A *bombe* mixture, most commonly made by adding sugar cooked to the soft-ball stage to egg yolks.

pâte à choux: A sweet or savory pastry dough that is cooked twice.

pâte brisée: A basic French crumbly tart dough made from flour, water, fat, and salt.

pâté en croûte: A rich meat, game, or fish mixture cooked in a pastry crust and served either hot or cold.

pâté en terrine: A spicy-sweet or savory mixture of meat, fish, poultry, vegetables, or fruit cooked in gelatin in a lidded mold.

pâte feuilletée: Puff pastry dough.

pâte sablée: A sweet pastry dough, similar to shortbread, that is sweeter, richer, and more crumbly than *pâte sucrée* and is sometimes leavened.

paupiette: A thin slice of meat or fish that is stuffed, rolled, and sometimes tied.

paysanne: "In the style of the countryside;" made in a rustic or peasant style, usually including bacon; also a 1–2 millimeter (⅟₃₂–⅟₁₆ inch) cut of vegetable.

peler à vif: To peel citrus fruit with a knife, removing all of the pith.

persillade: A ground mixture of garlic, shallots, parsley, and breadcrumbs (optional).

petits fours secs: Dry *petits fours*; small, delicate cookies served with desserts.

Philadelphia-style ice cream: A milk- or cream-based ice cream that is frozen in the same manner as a custard-based ice cream; also called **American-style ice cream**.

poisson au plat: A method of cooking fish cut into fillets, *darnes,* or *tronçons* in an ovenproof dish it will also be served in.

poisson en sauce: Fish served with a sauce made from the poaching liquid the fish was cooked in.

poissonnier: The chef in charge of the seafood station in large professional establishments.

pommade: Butter that has been softened to room temperature without melting or separating, and then beaten until light and fluffy.

pont-neuf: A thick-cut, French-fried potato; also a small Parisian pastry consisting of a tartlet of puff or short crust pastry filled with *frangipane*; also a mixture of *choux* pastry and confectioner's custard flavored with rum or crushed macaroons.

poste de travail: A kitchen work station.

pot au feu: "Pot on the fire;" a French boiled dinner consisting of beef short ribs and shanks with a variety of root vegetables; also fish poached in fish stock served with vegetables.

potager: The chef in charge of soups, usually found only in very large establishments.

potages taillés: Vegetable soups in which the vegetables are cut and not puréed.

potée: Any dish cooked in a large, earthenware pot; generally applies to a dish made with a mixture of meats (mainly fresh and cured pork) along with vegetables, particularly potatoes and cabbage.

pot de crème: The French version of a basic cup custard, but richer than an American pudding.

poule au pot: A classic, home-style dish originating in Béarn made with a whole chicken poached with aromatics and garnished with root vegetables.

printaniére garniture: A garnish of spring vegetables.

profiteroles: Cream puffs filled with ice cream and served with hot chocolate sauce.

Q

quadrillage: A crisscross marking on an item made using a grill or cut with a knife.

quadriller: To cut an item in a crisscross manner or mark using a grill or knife.

quenelle: A light dumpling made of seasoned minced fish, meat, or vegetables, formed into an oval shape, and poached in stock.

R

réduir: To reduce; to concentrate or thicken a stock or other liquid by boiling, thereby evaporating enough water to reduce the volume.

rémouillage: To remoisten; to add water to cooked bones after making stock to extract the maximum amount of flavor.

rémoulade: A cold sauce made by adding mustard, *cornichons*, capers, and chopped herbs to *mayonnaise*.

ris: Sweetbreads; also the thymus glands of veal, young beef cattle, lamb, pork, or rooster.

rissoler: To brown, either by pan-frying or sautéing.

rognures: Leftover puff pastry scraps.

rôtir: To roast.

rôtisseur: The chef responsible for the spit roast or roasted and broiled meats.

roux: A thickening agent made of equal parts of cooked flour and butter.

roux blanc: A *roux* cooked only long enough for the flour and butter to become cream-colored.

roux blond: A *roux* cooked long enough for the flour and butter to become light golden.

roux brun: A *roux* cooked long enough for the flour and butter to become light brown.

S

sabayon: A sweet preparation of egg yolks, sugar, wine, and flavoring that is whipped while being cooked over a water bath; also the preparation of whipped egg yolks and acid over a water bath for *sauce hollandaise*.

sabler: To cut butter into flour until a sandy texture is achieved.

sacristain: A classic pastry, usually made with puff pastry scraps, created by twisting thin strips of pastry together and sprinkling with almonds before baking.

saignant: Rare or bloody (for meat).

salade digestive: A combination of lettuces, seasoned and tossed with a simple vinaigrette.

salades composées: Salads that feature several ingredients that have been separately seasoned then presented together on a plate, such as the classic *salade niçoise*.

salades mixtes: Salads that are a mixture of several ingredients combined together and seasoned.

salades simples: Salads made with one ingredient, usually a type of lettuce, and seasoned with an appropriate dressing.

salpicons: Small, diced pieces of food.

sauce bordelaise: A brown sauce made with a reduction of red wine, shallots, peppercorns, thyme, and bay leaf combined with a basic brown stock sauce.

sauce charcutière: A sauce made from *sauce Robert* with *cornichon julienne*, sautéed mushrooms, and shallots.

sauces mères: "Mother sauces;" the basic sauces of the French repertoire upon which many derivative sauces are based.

saucier: The chef traditionally responsible for all stocks and sauces; can also work with meat and poultry.

sel rose: A dyed salt mixture containing saltpeter or potassium nitrate, used as a preservative and to help meat retain a rosy hue once it has been cooked.

sherbet: A frozen fruit-based dessert mixture made with milk and sometimes eggs.

singer: To sprinkle ingredients seared or sweated in fat with flour before adding liquid in order to make a sauce; also to burn the pin feathers of poultry.

sirop simple: "Simple syrup;" an item made with granulated sugar and water used as a sweetener, glaze, poaching, or preserving liquid, or as a base for candies, icings, frostings, and other desserts or drinks.

slurry: A thick liquid created by whisking any of several starches into a cold liquid until dissolved and then used to thicken a sauce.

sorbet: A frozen dessert made only with sugar, water, and flavoring; different from sherbet in that it contains no dairy.

soufflé: A dish, either sweet or savory, that is lightened by the addition of either stiffly beaten egg whites (for hot dishes), softly beaten heavy cream (for cold dishes), or both (for cold dishes only).

souffléed: Puffed, as in dough or potatoes.

soufflé glace: A frozen *soufflé*; smooth, light-textured frozen cream flavored with liqueur or natural flavoring.

sous-chef: An assistant chef.

sous-chef pâtisser: An assistant chef responsible for all desserts and pastries.

spoom: A *sorbet* to which contains 25–50% Italian *meringue*, making it light and airy.

sucrés: Sweetened or sugared.

sucs: Caramelized proteins that form on the bottom of a pan as ingredients are browned.

suer: To sweat; to cook ingredients (usually vegetables) on low heat, in a small amount of fat, and often covered with a lid or parchment paper (*à l'étuve*) so that they cook in their own juices without taking on any color.

suprême: A boneless breast of poultry; also a membrane-free segment of citrus fruit.

Swiss *meringue*: A mixture similar to a French *meringue*, except that the egg whites and sugar are whisked constantly while heated over a *bain-marie* until they reach 54ºC (130ºF) and the sugar dissolves.

T

taillage: Methods of cutting.

tamponner: To carefully place flecks of butter on the surface of a hot preparation, such as a sauce or soup, so that as it melts the butter forms a thin film, preventing a skin from forming.

terrine: A ground meat, fish, or vegetable mixture cooked in a mold; also the name of the mold.

tourage: The process of folding, rolling, and turning pastry that results in the hundreds of paper-thin layers of dough and fat characteristic of puff pastry.

tourner: To shape vegetables into a 7-sided oval shape.

tronçonne: A 4–7-centimeter (1 ½–2 ¾-inch)–cut of vegetable.

tronçons: A section cut of round- or flatfish.

V

valois: A garnish for fried or sautéed poultry or small cuts of meat consisting of potatoes Anna and sliced artichoke hearts sautéed in butter.

vanner: To stir a cream, sauce, or other mixture while it is cooking or cooling with a wooden spatula or whisk to keep it smooth, prevent a skin from forming, or cool it more rapidly; also to swirl butter into a brown sauce without stirring it.

vapeur: A 6-centimeter (2 ⅜-inch)–long turned cut of vegetable.

velouté: A sauce made from white stock thickened with a *roux*; also seasoned soups thickened with cream and egg yolks.

vert-pré: A 1.2-centimeter (½-inch) square cut of potato; also grilled meat garnished with straw potatoes and watercress served with *maître d'hôtel* butter; also white meat garnished with a mixture of peas, asparagus tips, and green beans, tossed in butter.

viennoise garniture: A garnish of chopped hard-boiled eggs, parsley, capers. lemon, olives, and anchovy.

vol-au-vent: A round puff pastry cup, with a lid, used as a container for savory entrees or *hors d'oeuvres*; traditional fillings are usually made with poultry, fish, or vegetables bound with a creamy sauce.

Index

Recipe Index

489